The Letters of Sidney and Beatrice Webb
Volume I
Apprenticeships 1873–1892

Sidney Webb at the age of
thirty-two and Beatrice Potter
at the age of twenty-five

The Letters of
Sidney and Beatrice Webb

EDITED BY
NORMAN MACKENZIE

Volume I
Apprenticeships
1873–1892

Cambridge University Press

CAMBRIDGE   LONDON   NEW YORK   MELBOURNE

PUBLISHED IN CO-OPERATION WITH

The London School of Economics
and Political Science

Published by the Syndics of the Cambridge University Press
The Pitt Building, Trumpington Street, Cambridge CB2 IRP
Bentley House, 200 Euston Road, London NWI 2DB
32 East 57th Street, New York, NY 10022, USA
296 Beaconsfield Parade, Middle Park, Melbourne 3206, Australia

First published 1978

Printed in Great Britain
at the University Press, Cambridge

Library of Congress cataloguing in publication data

Passfield, Sidney James Webb, Baron, 1859–1947.
The letters of Sidney and Beatrice Webb.
'Published in co-operation with the London School of
Economics and Political Science.'
Includes index.
CONTENTS: v. 1. Apprenticeships, 1873–1892. – v. 2. Partnership,
1892–1912. – v. 3. Pilgrimage, 1912–1947.
1. Socialists – Great Britain – Correspondence.
I. Webb, Beatrice Potter, 1858–1943, joint author.
II. MacKenzie, Norman Ian. III. London School of
Economics and Political Science. IV. Title.
HX243.P295 1978   335'.14'0922   77-1665
ISBN 0 521 21681 8 Volume I
ISBN 0 521 21682 6 Volume II
ISBN 0 521 21837 3 Volume III
ISBN 0 521 22015 7 Set

Contents

Acknowledgements

The London School of Economics and Political Science has helped in many ways since its Publications Committee launched this project. As the copyright holder of the Webb estate it allowed me unrestricted access to the Webb manuscript holdings, and to other invaluable papers held in the British Library of Political and Economic Science; it also gave me a visiting appointment for the duration of my research which enabled me to use all the facilities of the School. I am deeply grateful to the late Director, Sir Walter Adams, and to his colleagues, especially the Librarian, Derek Clarke, and Geoffry Allen, David Bovey and Angela Raspin, whose knowledge of the Passfield and related collections was a continual support. I also appreciate the help of the Academic Secretary, John Alcock, the Financial Secretary, John Pike, the Publications Officer, Patrick Davis, Jeffrey Weeks, Dr Diana Sanders and other members of the L.S.E. staff. Professor Maurice Cranston, who assumed responsibility for the project, was at all times unfailingly helpful; and both he and Professor W. A. Robson, whose personal knowledge of the Webbs contributed much, were kind enough to read early drafts.

The preparation of this edition was made possible by a grant from the Social Science Research Council, to whom I am much indebted. It appointed a Steering Committee to assist in policy decisions, and I wish to record my thanks to its members: Professor Maurice Cranston (Chairman), L.S.E.; Professor Matthew Anderson, L.S.E.; Professor Samuel H. Beer, Harvard University; Professor David Martin, L.S.E.; Professor T. M. Marshall; Professor B. C. Roberts, L.S.E.; Professor William A. Robson (Emeritus), L.S.E.; Professor John Savile, University of Hull.

My thanks are also due to the University of Sussex, which granted me study leave to complete these volumes, and to its Librarian, Peter Lewis, and his colleagues: apart from the Webb letters held at Sussex, the resources of its Library were an admirable counterpart to those of the British Library of Political and Economic Science.

Many other libraries were of great assistance, either by providing copies of Webb letters or by answering requests for information. I hope those who spent time to assist me will permit me merely to list their libraries without itemising the specific help each gave: my gratitude to them all is substantial, for they greatly reduced the burden of travel and enquiry. They are: Baker Library, Harvard; Bodleian Library; Brighton Public Library;

British Library; Bryn Mawr College Library; the Library of Corpus
Christi College, Oxford; Eawcett Library; General Assembly Library,
New Zealand; House of Lords Library; India House Library; the Library
of King's College, Cambridge; Leeds Central Library; Lewisham Public
Library; Marshall Library, Cambridge; the National Libraries of Ireland,
Scotland and Wales; New York Public Library; the Library of Newnham
College, Cambridge; the Library of Nuffield College, Oxford; Public
Record Office; St Austell Branch Library; Scottish Record Office; Shef-
field City Library; the Sophia Smith Collection, Smith College; Woolwich
Public Library. Much help was also given by the libraries of the following
universities: Aberdeen, British Columbia, Cambridge, Edinburgh, Illinois,
Leeds, Liverpool, McMaster, Manchester, Newcastle, London, Sheffield
and Texas.

All thirty county record offices answered enquiries. Among these I am
particularly grateful to the Greater London Record Office, which dealt
with repeated difficult requests promptly and most effectively and to the
Gloucestershire County Record Office, which also gave much help. I am
also grateful to the fifteen district councils and twelve city archivists who
provided valuable background information.

Letters or important source material were provided by a number of
organisations. I appreciate the assistance given by: the Bishopsgate
Institute; the City Parochial Foundation; Coleg Harlech; the Co-opera-
tive Union; the Fabian Society; the Historical Buildings Record; the
Historical Manuscripts Commission; the Institute of Actuaries; the Labour
Party; Longmans; the Modern Records Centre at the University of
Warwick; the National Union of Teachers; the *New Statesman*; *Punch*;
the Royal Statistical Society; the School of Slavonic Studies; the Trades
Union Congress; the Victoria and Albert Museum; and the Weizmann
Institute.

Many individuals have helped me, some by producing letters, more by
guiding me to sources or by providing information about persons, places
and events. Again I hope I may be forgiven if I thank them by name with-
out itemising their particular contributions. They are: Robin Page Arnot;
Professor A. G. Austin; Olivier and Quentin Bell; the late Mrs Paul
Bland; Professor Lord Briggs; Lord Brockway; Mrs G. H. Brown; Sir
Sydney Caine; Dr Owen Chadwick; Elizabeth Clay; Roger Clements;
Dame Margaret Cole; John Cripps; Jean Darrock; Patrick Dobbs;
Phyllis Dobbs; Professor R. Dore; the late R. Palme Dutt; Professor
George Feaver; H. F. Fells; the Hon. Justice Ferris; Marion Fleischer;
Professor Eduard Goldstucker; Viscount Harcourt; Dr Angela Harris;
Professor J. F. C. Harrison; Professor Royden Harrison; Professor
Gertrude Himmelfarb; Richard Hoggart; Michael Holroyd; Anne D.
Holt; Anthony Howard; Rt Hon. Roy Jenkins; P. W. Jones; Anthony
Lloyd; Professor A. M. McBriar; Ian McDougall; David Marquand,

M.P.; Dr Keith Middlemas; Malcolm and Kitty Muggeridge; Dr Henrietta Noufflard; Dr H. O. Pappe; John Parker, M.P.; Nicholas Pease; Hilary Peek; E. N. Peers; Professor Stanley Pierson; Tom Ponsonby; Chaim Raphael; Dr Benedict Richards; Dr John Rosselli; Sir Stephen Runciman; Professor David Shannon; A. Llewellyn Smith; R. H. Snell; George Spater; R. A. Storey; Professor Barry Supple; Dr Paul Thompson; the late May Wallas; Dr Peter Weiler; Lady Eirene White; Professor Thomas Wilson; Professor Donald Winch; Professor Willard Wolfe.

My debt to Margaret Ralph is great: with assistance from Janet Anthony, Patsy Carle, Jenny Mathias, June Walker, Jackie Watts, Sue Newman and Susannah Pyper she typed several thousand letters, as well as the manuscript of these three volumes; kept track of a complex filing system and much correspondence; and not least became one of the small group of persons who can read Beatrice Webb's handwriting at sight. Julia MacKenzie and Pauline Tear were largely responsible for the indexes, and I am grateful to them both. I thank Jeanne MacKenzie for contributing her own detailed knowledge of the Webbs, her advice on a number of editorial problems, and her ability to decipher the more obscure passages in Beatrice's letters. The staff of the Cambridge University Press who have greatly helped the whole project wish to remain professionally anonymous, but I take this opportunity of thanking them collectively for the contribution they have made.

I would finally like to record my warm appreciation of the many kinds of help, including a most helpful reading of the proofs, by Professor Matthew Anderson since he became Chairman of the Publications Committee of the London School of Economics.

For
HELLMUT AND VERA PAPPE
With affection and regard

Introduction

The lives of Sidney and Beatrice Webb span the ninety years between the publication of Darwin's *Origin of Species* and the dropping of the atomic bomb at Hiroshima. Their working partnership and their marriage lasted for more than fifty of those years. They grew up through the crisis of faith which followed the collapse of revealed religion before the impact of the new biology, geology and cosmology. They came together in the movement for social reform – the fusion between what was then called the 'compunction' of the prosperous and the organisation of the poor – which emerged at the end of the nineteenth century. They played a significant role in Labour and socialist politics. And in the last years of their lives they turned to a new faith in Soviet Communism. They were both professional reformers. They were also pioneers of sociology and social history, skilful organisers and propagandists, and enthusiasts for education. They believed profoundly in the power of the word – that reason and factual knowledge were the levers which could move society. They were not only the dominant figures, together with Bernard Shaw, in the Fabian Society. They also founded the London School of Economics and Political Science in 1895; and in 1913 they launched the *New Statesman*.

The Webbs were gluttons for work and immensely productive. A bibliography prepared in 1973 contains almost five hundred entries but it is far from complete; no one, for instance, has itemised or collected Sidney's ephemeral journalism. Whatever else engaged their efforts they maintained their research, delivered lectures and wrote regularly. Apart from their substantial books, they produced pamphlets and memoranda. Beatrice, moreover, maintained her diary from adolescence to her death: a small proportion of that vast manuscript was used by Beatrice herself in *My Apprenticeship* and *Our Partnership*, which were supplemented by two volumes of extracts edited by Dame Margaret Cole. This huge output has not yet been adequately assessed. A number of books have been written about the Webbs, and more discuss them in passing, but Professor Royden Harrison's authorised biography is the first comprehensive study based upon both published and private material. Until now, moreover, the letters written by both the Webbs have been inaccessible save to researchers. As part of a programme which includes republication of Webb books now out of print and the production of a complete microfiche version of

xi

Beatrice's diary, the London School of Economics decided to commission a three-volume selection from that correspondence.

Almost all the letters published in these volumes appear for the first time. I shall not anticipate their content in this introduction except to say that they reveal much about the personalities of both Sidney and Beatrice that is markedly different from the received image of them. In that, as well as in the comments on contemporary persons and events, lies their interest. As letter-writers they were not in the same class as Shaw. One must turn to Beatrice's diary for material to compare with the informative brilliance of Shaw's correspondence. Yet, especially during the two years of their stressful courtship, they both wrote letters of quality and significance.

The majority of these letters are held in the Passfield Papers in the British Library of Political and Economic Science (BLPES). In addition to the letters exchanged between Sidney and Beatrice and retained by them for eventual deposit, the collection includes letters to relatives and associates acquired by the BLPES over the years, and a considerable number of letters received by the Webbs. Deposit and purchase apart, there were two published appeals for letters. I made a third appeal when these volumes were planned, and located more letters held by the libraries, organisations and individuals thanked in the acknowledgements. With the publication of these volumes my working papers have been deposited in the British Library of Political and Economic Science; all enquiries about these papers and about letters collected but not published should be addressed to its Librarian.

Though several thousand letters have been transcribed and considered in the process of preparing this edition the total collection is inevitably uneven. I cannot estimate how many letters the Webbs wrote. Some were not kept. Some were lost. Some were destroyed by bombing and other accidents. Of those that do survive a number are clearly incomplete. There are, besides, three obvious and important gaps. In December 1890, when he was ill and depressed, Sidney burned a number of letters from Beatrice; and he confessed that on leaving the Colonial Office in the spring of 1892 he made 'a holocaust' of his correspondence. There is also a notable but unexplained lack of letters from Beatrice to Sidney during their courtship in the early months of 1891, when her attitude towards him changed decisively. Though there is no reason elsewhere to suppose that Beatrice suppressed intimate material (surviving letters are as uninhibited as the diary she carefully preserved) it is possible that she did set aside and lost, or even destroyed, her letters for that crucial period in her life. Despite such gaps, however, there are enough letters from all the years of the partnership to make a coherent record. Sidney tried to write a daily letter when they were apart and Beatrice replied fairly regularly. The main deficiency in them arises from the fact that the Webbs were a partnership, together for most of the time, writing only when apart. Many of the most important aspects of their lives, when they were working together, are thus not directly mentioned in their own correspondence: for such purposes Beatrice's diary is the main source for their opinions and activities.

The letters of the Webbs to relatives and friends are an invaluable complement to the diary. Some of Beatrice's letters are almost duplicates of diary entries. Sidney's letters are a different matter. He was not an outgoing man and contemporaries have left little record of him beyond general impressions. He kept no diary and his letters are the only extensive source for his opinions and relationships.

Fewer letters from the Webbs to friends and associates seem to have survived than might have been expected. Those who received letters from Shaw, even when he was young and unsuccessful, apparently recognised a special talent. By 1890 he knew his letters were kept and began to write for posterity as well as the addressee. Though the Webbs were well known by the end of the century and public figures for the rest of their lives, their correspondents were less inclined to retain their letters. Some, such as Arthur Henderson, regrettably did not keep letters from anyone – a serious loss, when one considers the politically important association between Henderson and Webb after 1916. Some, such as Beatrice's sisters, kept only a few of the many letters they received. The same is true of Ramsay MacDonald, William Beveridge, Herbert Samuel, Graham Wallas, R. B. Haldane and even Bernard Shaw. More letters were preserved where, for business reasons, Sidney's correspondence was filed. His notes to Edward Pease, secretary of the Fabian Society for thirty years, are a significant component of the Fabian Papers at Nuffield College, Oxford. There are many routine communications to J. D. McKillop, the secretary of the London School of Fconomics, and to its librarian B. M. Headicar. Yet nothing can be found of any correspondence with the *New Statesman*; there is a dearth of official letters written when he was President of the Board of Trade and Secretary of State for the Colonies; and, unfortunately, I. M. Maisky, the former Soviet ambassador in London, died before he was able to carry out his promise to produce copies of the many letters he had received from the Webbs. I hope that the publication of these volumes may encourage the discovery of additional letters – in particular some dealing with the researches into trade unionism and local government, with the Royal Commission on the Poor Law and the National Committee for the Prevention of Destitution, with Sidney's work as an M.P. (not a single letter to a constituent has turned up) and his other activities in the Labour Party.

Though enough letters have survived to present problems of selection, I am sure that the decision to confine this edition to three volumes was correct, on grounds of both cost and relevance. Nevertheless it led to the omission of a good many letters which are really technical rather than

substantive, dealing with travel arrangements, appointments for inter-
views, dinner and lunch invitations and domestic trivia of various kinds.
Most of these letters are more useful to the researcher than interesting to
the general reader. I have included a few to convey the sense of the life-
style of the Webbs. There is a second group of letters, of which those to
B. M. Headicar about L.S.E. library business are the best example, which
contain book-lists, or discuss business details about Fabian tracts and the
publishing of the Webb books. Here again characteristic examples have
been chosen. A third category of omissions includes some of the very long
letters written by the Webbs during their long overseas journeys in 1899
and 1911. There is much commonplace tourist reporting in these. In the
case of the visit to the United States, New Zealand and Australia in 1899
they largely duplicate the accounts given in the three separately published
sections of Beatrice's diary, though a few of these letters have been included. There is a similar overlap between the letters written from Canada,
Japan and India in 1911–12 and the half-million words of diary which
cover the same journey. This part of the diary, however, remains unpublished. A representative but not comprehensive selection has been
made from these very long travelogues.

In choosing letters from the remainder of the correspondence I have
been guided by four main criteria. First, I have considered whether a
letter casts light on the character, intellectual development, attitudes and
relationships of either Beatrice or Sidney. In marginal cases I have excluded letters which are essentially repetitious. Secondly, I have chosen
letters which contain significant comments on other individuals, especially
those in public life, or add useful information about the Fabian Society,
contemporary politics, the founding of L.S.E., the launching of the
New Statesman and other ventures in which the Webbs were engaged.
Thirdly, I have sought to maintain some continuity of themes, both private
and public, which run through the seventy years of correspondence. There
are, unavoidably, some letters whose exclusion has been a matter of regret
– sometimes merely for a pithy sentence or an intriguing paragraph. In
such cases I have sought to retain the essence of the letter by quotation
in an introductory note. I made an early decision to print all the selected
letters in full and not to adopt the alternative course of printing extracts
from a larger proportion of the total.

When this edition was planned it was decided from the outset that it
would not include letters received by the Webbs and that incoming letters
would be mentioned only where necessary to the sense of the outgoing
letter. Much of the incoming correspondence is fascinating and should be
published. But it does not usefully match what survives of the outgoing
letters: there are few coherent exchanges. There are, moreover, so many
incoming letters that it would have been impossible to include a fair selection of them without extending this edition by at least two volumes: much

quotation from them would have made it more difficult for a subsequent editor to prepare a balanced collection of them.

Although the pressure of space was the primary editorial constraint, another was my desire to avoid unnecessary overlap with Professor Harrison's biography. If this work had not been in hand I should have been tempted to extend both biographical and critical comment, for these letters contain much that suggests a new view of the Webbs as individuals and of their role in public affairs. I believe, however, that it is preferable for both the biographer and the reader to be left free to interpret this material without editorial nudges. For this reason (and also because additional editorial matter could only be inserted at the expense of the letters themselves) I have confined myself to three types of information. There are short introductions to each of the sections into which these volumes are divided, each relating to a distinct phase in the lives of the Webbs. There are headnotes to the majority of the letters which draw upon Beatrice's diary and other sources to maintain a continuity of narrative and provide the context of individual letters. And within each note there is biographical material to identify the persons mentioned. I have kept this to the minimum for all individuals who appear in standard reference books.

There were other editorial problems. One was a matter of transcription. Sidney's handwriting remained consistently round and clear. Beatrice's was notoriously illegible throughout her life. She scrawled, she used a mixture of abbreviations and glyphs which approach a personal shorthand, she often wrote afterthoughts at right-angles across the text, and a number of her letters are in pencil or on faded and cracked paper. At the outset I feared that many words, perhaps whole phrases, would have to be omitted. In the event very little proved undecipherable, though the translation was tedious and time-consuming; I do not think that any of the failures or uncertainties noted in the text relate to a point of substance. Her punctuation, moreover, was a matter of art rather than grammar. Dashes scatter the page where her pen paused. Capitals, used erratically, are not a reliable guide to the beginning of sentences, to proper nouns or emphasis. To save her prose from reading like Mr Jingle's telegraphic ejaculations it was often necessary to substitute conventional semi-colons and full stops for diagonal lines of uneven length. Her careless habits created a further difficulty. Ultimately it was possible to reassemble her unnumbered folios in proper order; it was not possible always to be sure of the dates of her letters. She seldom dated them. Occasionally she put the wrong date, or added the wrong day. By use of internal evidence and other sources, especially her diary, I have managed to provide accurate dates for the majority of letters and reasonable suggestions for the remainder. The Webbs were also careless about addresses. Beatrice, especially, seldom put addresses at the head of her letters; and rarely crossed out what was printed even if she was in a very different place. She also used other people's notepaper, sometimes months after she had visited a house. I have removed printed addresses that were clearly irrelevant, and indicated the presumed place of origin. A final problem was the use, both by Sidney and Beatrice, of many contractions and initials. They were not consistent in this respect, even within a single letter. When Beatrice used letters or extracts from her diary in published form she often silently expanded abbreviations in the original text. I have followed the same course, being guided by common sense. The multitude of ampersands have been written out. In the interest of clarity such words as 'Socy' and 'parlty' for example, have been extended into 'Society' and 'parliamentary'. Initials have been converted into their full names except where they are obvious, familiar or used so frequently that the meaning is unambiguous. In some instances the initials are retained and the meaning inserted in square brackets. Where place names have been changed in the intervening years the original version in the text has been retained.

The use of square brackets is reserved throughout for editorial interpolations. Addresses and dates which have been attributed are thus bracketed, prefaced by a query in cases of doubt. Where a word or phrase cannot be transcribed this is indicated by the word *illegible* in brackets; where the transcription is doubtful a suggested reading is given in brackets with a preceding query. Occasionally individuals mentioned are given a surname or other identification in brackets following the given name, or a word carelessly omitted has been inserted. In a few unsigned letters the signature has been similarly indicated. The rules followed are so simple that these practices should in any case be self-evident to the reader.

All letters are numbered in a running sequence which continues through to three volumes, though each volume is separately paginated. The sequence begins with letters written by Beatrice before she met Sidney, and the letters written by Sidney before his meeting with Beatrice Potter. Thereafter the letters continue in chronological order irrespective of author.

The title of each letter also contains a coded reference to its location (the code for these sources is given below), the name of the author and the name of the recipient. 1 have used the designation which applies at the time the letter was written, except in the cases of Beatrice and Sidney themselves. In their cases the first letters from Beatrice are attributed to Beatrice Potter, those after her marriage to Beatrice Webb, and with respect to her own wishes she remains Beatrice Webb after Sidney's elevation to the peerage; while for consistency he remains Sidney Webb throughout. Other recipients are described by their new titles as they acquire them: William Beveridge, for instance, becomes Sir William Beveridge. In the index individuals have been listed in the name or style obtaining at the time of the reference; and in a very few cases the better-known name or title has been given as well.

So much for mechanics. I hope these volumes will prove as fascinating and informative to the reader as their preparation has proved for me; the letters have enhanced my appreciation of Sidney and Beatrice Webb, both as individuals and as public figures. Like other students of the London School of Economics I owe much to them and I can think of no better way of acknowledging that debt than to help them speak for themselves across the years.

NORMAN MACKENZIE

University of Sussex

A brief chronology

A fuller but far from complete bibliography is available in *Publications of Sidney and Beatrice Webb: An Interim Check List* (British Library of Political and Economic Science, 1973).

1858　Beatrice Potter born 2 January at Standish, Gloucestershire.

1859　Sidney Webb born 13 July in London.

1873　Beatrice begins to keep regular diary which she maintains until her death. In autumn, she visits United States and Canada.

1879　Sidney joins Zetetical Society, meets Bernard Shaw.

1881　Sidney appointed clerk in Inland Revenue. Elected to Committee of Zetetical Society.

1883　Sidney appointed to Colonial Office, meets Sydney Olivier and Graham Wallas. Begins lectures on political economy at Working Men's College. In August joins Land Reform Union. In April Beatrice joins Charity Organisation Society: holiday with father and Herbert Spencer in Germany and Switzerland. Meets Joseph Chamberlain in summer. Visits humble relatives in Bacup.

1884　In the autumn Sidney attends first meeting of 'Karl Marx Club', later Hampstead Historic Society. Beatrice acts as father's hostess in London and at country houses. In August Beatrice makes long visit to Bavaria and Austria; in late autumn replaces sister Catherine Courtney as volunteer rent collector in Katherine Buildings.

1885　Sidney joins Fabian Society on 1 May.

1886　Beatrice has first article published in *Pall Mall Gazette*, 18 February. In March she joins Charles Booth's investigations into London labour conditions. In October she makes a second visit to Bacup.

1887　Sidney writes the 'Basis' of Fabian Society. Sidney Webb: Fabian Tract 5, *Facts for Socialists*. Publishes 'Dock Life in the East End of London' in October issue of *Nineteenth Century*.

1888　In September Sidney visits the United States with Edward Pease. Beatrice gives evidence to House of Lords Committee on Sweating. Decides to make study of Co-operative movement. Beatrice Potter: 'East End Labour' (August) and 'Pages from a Work-Girl's Diary' (September) in *Nineteenth Century*; contributes to Volume 1 of Charles Booth's *Life and Labour of the People of London*.

1889　In August, London dock strike. Sidney Webb: Fabian Tracts 8, *Facts for Londoners*; 9, *An Eight Hour Bill* and 10, *Figures for Londoners*. Also *Socialism in England*.

1890　January, Sidney and Beatrice meet. In May Beatrice and Sidney attend Co-operative Congress, Glasgow and form a 'Working Compact'. Beatrice Potter: 'The Lords Committee on the Sweating System' in the

June *Nineteenth Century*. Sidney Webb: 'The Reform of the Poor Law' in July *Contemporary Review*. And Fabian Tracts 11, *The Workers' Political Programme*; 12, *Practical Land Nationalisation*; 15, *English Progress Towards Social Democracy*; 16, *A Plea for an Eight Hours Bill*; 17, *Reform of the Poor Law*; 19, *What the Farm Labourer Wants*; 22, *The Truth about Leasehold Enfranchisement*.

1891 Beatrice joins Fabian Society. Sidney considers candidature for Parliament and/or London County Council. In May Beatrice and Sidney become secretly engaged at Co-operative Congress at Lincoln. In June they go on holiday in Norway with Wallas. In September Beatrice attends Trades Union Congress. Sidney attends National Liberal Federation meeting in Newcastle in October. On 16 December Sidney adopted as Progressive candidate for L.C.C. in Deptford. Sidney Webb: Fabian Tracts 23, *The Case for an Eight Hours Bill*; 24, *Question for Parliamentary Candidates*; 25, *Question for School Board Candidates*; 26, *Question for London County Councillors*; 30, *The Unearned Movement*; 31, *London's Heritage in the City Guilds*; 32, *The Municipalization of the Gas Supply*; 33, *Municipal Tramways*; 34, *London's Water Tribute*; 35, *The Municipalization of the London Docks*; 36, *The Scandal of London's Markets*; 37, *A Labour Policy for Public Authorities*. Also *The London Programme*. With Harold Cox, *The Eight Hours Day*. Beatrice Potter: *The Co-operative Movement in Great Britain*.

1892 Richard Potter dies on 1 January. Sidney elected to L.C.C. in Deptford on 5 March, and becomes Chairman of Technical Education Board. On 23 July Sidney and Beatrice are married in St Pancras. Later in the year they draft minority report for trade union members for Royal Commission on Labour.

Location codes

The following abbreviations are used in this volume to identify the location of letters.

BL	The British Library
BLPES	The British Library of Political and Economic Science
BUL	Birmingham University Library
BWD	Beatrice Webb's Diary (BLPES)
FP	Fabian Papers, Nuffield College Library, Oxford
HL	House of Lords Library
HRCUT	Humanities Research Center, The University of Texas at Austin
KCC	The Library of Kings College, Cambridge
MA	*My Apprenticeship* (Beatrice Webb)
NYPL	New York Public Library
NLS	National Library of Scotland
PP	Passfield Papers (BLPES)
PFP	Pease Family Papers
PRO	Public Record Office, London
SCL	Shaw: *Collected Letters* (ed: Dan Laurence)
SU	Sussex University Library
UL	University of London Library
WMC	The Working Men's College, London

1. Beatrice Potter

January 1858 – December 1889

Beatrice Potter was born on 2 January 1858 at Standish, a large country house beneath the Cotswold escarpment which her prosperous father, Richard Potter, had leased as the main home for his large family. Close to Stonehouse station on the Great Western Railway, of which he was for many years a director and for a time chairman, and to Gloucester, where he had originally made his fortune in the timber business, it was a substantial but plain Georgian mansion, which Beatrice later described as more like an institution than a home. Even today, as part of a hospital, the grand public rooms contrast with the warren of the rear quarters where the servants and the younger children lived. When Beatrice was still a girl the Potters had other houses – at Rusland Hall in Cumberland, near to another of her father's enterprises at Barrow-in-Furness, in London, and at The Argoed, an enlarged Jacobean farmhouse at Penalt in the Wye Valley which was bought originally as a place for holidays and Richard Potter's retirement. Yet it was Standish which was Beatrice's real home; and the busy crowded family life there shaped her personality.

Her parents were a remarkable couple. Both of them were only one generation removed from humble origins, and both had managed the transition into wealth, status and intellectual company without the awkwardness which characterised many of the newly-rich Victorians. Richard Potter's father had been a small farmer and shopkeeper in Tadcaster who made his money in Manchester cotton and became a Radical M.P. after the Reform Act of 1832. Richard Potter himself, educated at the newly-founded University of London, lost his inheritance in the financial crisis of 1848, started again in the railway boom and laid the foundation of his fortune by supplying huts to the British and French armies in the Crimea. By the time Beatrice was born he had branched out into investments in Canada, Holland and Turkey and had even toyed with a scheme to cut a competitor to the Suez Canal. He was a natural promoter, sometimes winning in some large speculation and sometimes losing heavily. Born a Nonconformist and brought up a Liberal he had become an easy-going Anglican Tory by middle age. He was, nonetheless, liberal-minded, open to new ideas, keen on the cut-and-thrust of intellectual argument and a warm and generous friend.

Richard Potter met Lawrencina Heyworth in Rome, when he was making the grand tour as a young man, and they were married before his financial setback in 1848. He was helped to his new start by her father, Lawrence Heyworth, who had risen in the world in much the same way as Richard Potter's own father. Born into a family of small weavers in Rossendale, he became a rich merchant in Liverpool and M.P. for Derby in 1847. He spoilt his daughter; he also ensured that she was well-educated – an endowment that was a lifelong cause of frustration when, instead of the intellectual life for which she yearned, marriage to Richard Potter trapped her in the unending cycle of childbearing. She was, moreover, a strict utilitarian, believing firmly in beneficent self-interest and, to a degree that made all her daughters parsimonious to the point of public comment, in the virtue of eschewing all forms of extravagance and self-indulgence. She clearly found it difficult to relate warmly to her children or to evoke their affections as easily as her more outgoing husband.

Beatrice was the eighth of her nine daughters. The one son, Richard or 'little Dicky', lived for only two years and died shortly before the birth of the youngest girl, Rosalind, in 1865. The house was full of girls, with their attendant friends and suitors, governesses, tutors and nurses, as well as the staff of indoor and outdoor servants needed to keep up a proper style for a great entrepreneur's household and entertain the stream of businessmen, railway promoters and advanced intellectuals who came to visit Richard Potter. It was a stimulating context for a childhood but, as Beatrice recalled it in *My Apprenticeship*, it was also confusing and even crushing: there was much loneliness in such a crowd, especially for an introverted and often sickly small girl, who found much of the affection she craved in the company of the servants, above all in the motherly figure of her family nurse Martha Jackson, the beloved 'Dada' of whom Beatrice later remarked that she was 'the one and only saint I ever knew'. In the backstairs life, in kitchen, stables, hayloft and garden, she learned a sympathy which struck deep, bridging the Victorian chasm between the governing classes and the governed. From an early age, growing up in a domestic system which was a microcosm of the wider society, she felt an ambivalence of emotional loyalties – to the class into which she was born, where 'the possession of some form of power over other people' was taken for granted, and to those whose labours sustained its life of comfortable leisure. From that conflict stemmed a sense of social guilt, what she herself called the 'self-consciousness of sin', which she and a good many of her contemporaries converted into a public obligation to good works.

This sense of social guilt, which always made her feel something of an outsider even in her own home, reflected deep personal anxieties. Her mother, Lawrencina Potter, despised her feminine role and also depreciated her succession of daughters; she longed for a son on whom she could project her ambitions. When little Dicky was born Beatrice was in effect rejected and she was only making her way towards an emotional understanding with her mother when Lawrencina died: the neglect and even disparagement she endured in her early years led, as she confessed, to a morbid, unhappy and at times near-suicidal childhood. She remembered several occasions when she toyed with a bottle of chloroform, and in after years attacks of depression led again to fantasies of ending her misery with laudanum. Beatrice was not the only sufferer from Lawrencina's collapse when the treasured Dicky died prematurely. Rosy, the youngest of the sisters, was seriously disturbed and much of Beatrice's energy as a young woman was taken up by a well-meant but largely unavailing attempt to cope with Rosy's psychic troubles. Beatrice herself, 'creeping up in the shadow of my baby brother's birth and death', was afflicted by chronic psychosomatic illness, which broke out again in later life whenever she was stressed by overwork or struck by remorse. She had bouts of neuralgia, bronchitic attacks, spasms of indigestion and periods of insomnia: her indispositions, indeed, were so frequent that she had no regular education and her only spell of formal schooling came at the end of her adolescence when she spent a few uncomfortable months at a fashionable school for girls in Bournemouth.

There were, nevertheless, unusual compensations in the Potter household, for

2

Richard Potter was very different from the stereotype of the Victorian pater-familias. 'He admired and loved his daughters', Beatrice recalled in her auto-biography: 'he was the only man I ever knew who genuinely believed that women were superior to men, and acted as if he did'. He was himself a culti-vated man, as well as a successful captain of industry, and he opened the world of intellect as well as business to his children, encouraging them to read widely, to discuss any subject frankly, to understand his ramified commercial interests, to meet him and his notable associates on equal terms. Though Beatrice lacked a formal education she was incomparably advantaged by comparison with most girls of her generation. Both her parents valued things of the mind. She had access for her precocious talents to anything she cared to read, turning from literature to philosophy, from the classics to French, German and Italian, to mathematics and science, getting guidance when she needed it from one or other of the governesses and stimulation from the conversation of her father's friends.

It was from one of these that she learned most. In her autobiography she paid a heartfelt tribute to the kindness and help of Herbert Spencer, whose affection-ate coaching on his frequent visits to Standish made her his intellectual appren-tice. Painfully shy in the presence of adults, self-centred to the point of hypo-chondriacal eccentricity, Spencer could unbend and give real companonship to the young girl who found in him the ideal peripatetic teacher. His encourage-ment was vital to her intellectual growth; his sympathy was an unfailing source of strength; and what Beatrice considered his 'heroic disregard to material prosperity and physical comfort' in his efforts to further human progress served as a model for her own dedication to social enquiry. Even when she grew beyond the ideas of his *Synthetic Philosophy* she retained his faith 'in the application of the scientific method to human nature'. All through her adolescence, as she wrestled with problems of faith that remained tantalisingly unresolved in her long life, Spencer remained the touchstone of intellectual honesty. She was, Spencer once said, 'a born metaphysician', reminding him of George Eliot, the one woman who might have married him. And before she was an adult Beatrice had passed from conventional Christianity, through oriental and occult religious creeds, through the rationalism of the Religion of Science – her father's friends included John Tyndall, Thomas Henry Huxley, Sir William Hooker and Francis Galton – to Auguste Comte's Religion of Humanity. Few young women of her age in England were so affected by the current contemporary thought which was eroding revealed religion and shifting the Evangelical impulse from the service of God to the service of Man.

Yet Beatrice was not simply the earnest bluestocking that such high-minded pursuits might suggest. The earliest entries in the diary that she began to keep regularly from 1873 reveal strong feelings which she thought unworthy: she primly reproved herself for vanity and idleness, for the temptations of the flesh and the pleasure she found in the gay life of the London Season, when she went up to town with her sisters for the round of balls, parties and picnics which form-ed the 'whirlpool' of the fashionable world. Strikingly handsome, she enjoyed being admired and courted – and felt remorseful afterwards. An heiress to what would be a substantial fortune even when divided among nine children, her life was cushioned by creature comforts and servants, and she could expect to marry as well as the older sisters who had found husbands of promise and standing. And she was free of many of the burdensome constraints which convention imposed on most young women of her station: Lawrencina Potter cared little for the world of fashion and stayed away from the Season when she could, while Richard Potter never imposed stuffy rules upon his daughters for the sake of appearances. Beatrice, from the earliest years of adult life, was able to make her own pattern of thought and behaviour, moving about freely and unchaperoned, choosing her friends and interests without fighting the all-too-common campaign of rebellion against parental restrictions. Left much alone in the crucial years of infancy she felt neglected, but she gained her independence at an unusually early age. Her odd upbringing, she said, left her with 'a tireless curiosity together with a double dose of will-power'.

It also left her, as she was well aware, with deep inner conflicts between emotion and intellect, between her feelings as a woman and her ambitions to succeed like a man, and on the same terms. In this respect, as she came to recognise in later years, she was much like her mother who 'was cursed with a divided personality: she was not at peace in herself . . . her soul longed for the mystical consolations and moral discipline of religious orthodoxy' but she occupied her time reading economics, teaching herself foreign languages by an eccentric auto-didactic method, and dolefully wishing that she could have made a career of her own and shone in her own right, not as the wife of Richard Potter.

Such conflicts made it impossible for Beatrice to follow her sisters into marriage and motherhood, though she did not lack suitors. She needed a creed; and she desired a craft. The search for a way of life which could combine both became the driving purpose of her life, demanding all the will-power she could summon and focusing her astonishing abilities upon her work – the work which became the anodyne for emotional pain, the means of expiating guilt, and the outlet for her missionary zeal to do good unto others.

A note on the Potter children

It may be helpful to list here the Potter children. A copy of the family tree is in the Passfield Papers.

Laurencina ('Lallie')	1845–1929	m. 1867	Robert Durning Holt shipowner 5 sons 3 daughters	1832–1908
Catherine ('Kate')	1847–1929	m. 1883	Leonard Henry Courtney politician	1832–1918
Mary Elizabeth	1848–1923	m. 1870	Arthur Twisden Playne millowner 1 son	d. 1923
Georgina '(Georgie')	1850–1914	m. 1873	Daniel Meinertzhagen VI banker 4 sons 3 daughters	1842–1910
Blanche	1851–1905	m. 1877	William Harrison Cripps physician 4 sons 2 daughters	1850–1923

Theresa	1852–1883	m. 1881	Charles Alfred Cripps barrister and politician 4 sons 1 daughter	1852–1941
Margaret ('Maggie')	1854–1921	m. 1880	Henry Hobhouse politician 4 sons 3 daughters	1854–1937
Beatrice ('Bo')	1858–1943	m. 1892	Sidney James Webb politician and author	1859–1947
Richard ('Dickie')	1862–1864			
Rosalind ('Rosy' or 'Rosebud')	1865–1949	m. 1888	Arthur Dyson Williams barrister 1 son	1859–1896
		m. 1898	George Dobbs travel courier 4 sons 1 daughter	1869–1946

1 PP   BEATRICE POTTER TO CATHERINE POTTER

Several childhood letters from Beatrice survive: those omitted are similar in character to the examples printed. The spelling and punctuation are as in the original.

> Standish House
> May 10th 1862

Dear Katie

Papa has bought or is going to buy Blanche and Theresa a pony which is coming tomorrow for him to see it is not nearly as tall as Robin was, it has been accostomed to hunt it is the colour of Martin which is if you remember a dark brown Papa has also bought two Californian partridges The old hen has laid eight eggs which Papa is going to give to sisters for their collection Mamma has bought me a nice new book Do you know that Dicky has got six teeth Dear Kate do you know that poor Miss Macmichael is very ill for she has had a paraletic stroke and I am afraid she is not expected to recover is it not a great pity for she was such a nice person Now my dear Kate I must really finish as I have written a nice little letter so with best love from all I remain your *very* affectionate sister

> Beatrice

Beatrice assigned the date in *My Apprenticeship*.

[?Standish House]
[?1868]

My dear Mama

Thank you for your kind letter I hope you and Lallie are quite well and Grandpapa and cousins. The two Conservetive Candidates were here yesterday one of them is very short and very finely dressed he had his top coat trimed with sealskin he had also silver buckles on his boots and his hands were covered with rings with a very stylish blue tye which covered his waistcoat; he also saied he spoke Italian and french perfectly he played on the piano and sung he seemed not to know what many words ment for he asked Papa what was the meaning of Demonstration, and Major Lees asked the meaning of Hustings and Nomination. Major Lees is very tall and very fat with a great beard mustache and whiskers with an eye glass which he satisfied his curiosity in staring at everybody I must now say goodbye dear mama I remain your dutiful child

Beatrice Potter

Please give my love to Kate Lallie and Robert and Margareta

This letter was presumably written soon after the outbreak of the Franco-Prussian war. The reference is to the *mitrailleuse*, the secret automatic weapon used for the first time by the French.

Standish House
Sunday [?mid-July 1870]

Dear Mother

Thanks so much for your letter.

Mrs Marshall has been extremely kind to me this last week, and we have been a very happy little party. Mary and Arthur were here yesterday they went with Kate, Blanche, and Papa to the [?Curtys Heyward] ball. Mary's sister-in-law is coming over from Germany here in consequence of the war, her husband will be enlisted.

The war on the side of the French has evidently been premeditated, I am afraid they will succeed, they seem to have arranged every-thing beforehand. It is said that they have a gun invented that will mow down 200 at a time. I hope Theresa is improving we were all glad to hear that she was rather better. Papa told us that neither Georgie or I would be able to go on the trip because the hotels will be so full do you think it will be so.

I have bought some bantams for Rosy from the [*illegible*] at 5/- the pair they are quite white and are coming tomorrow. I have made the coops for them just near the door going into the stables so they can get the sun. Rosy came back on Friday she is looking very well. Blanche and Maggie came back also on Friday from the Argoed they seem to have enjoyed themselves very much. Mr Spenser is going to some friends in Wales. I have told Copner to put the corn for Rosy bantams down to you. Now dear mother goodbye with love to sisters and dear old Dar

I remain

your affectionate child

Beatrice Potter

4 PP BEATRICE POTTER TO FANNY

Fanny was probably a nursemaid: Beatrice wrote to her after she went to the United States in terms that suggest she greatly missed her.

It was Richard Potter's habit when in London to take his daughters on Sundays 'to discover the most exciting speaker on religious or metaphysical issues' (MA). Except for this eclectic enjoyment of varieties of spiritual experience, Beatrice recalled, 'the atmosphere of the home was exceptionally free-thinking ... Any question which turned up in classical or modern literature, in law reports or technical journals, from the origin of species to the latest diplomatic despatch, from sexual perversion to the rate of exchange, would be freely and frankly discussed within the family circle'.

Charles Haddon Spurgeon (1839–92) was the famous Baptist preacher at the Metropolitan Tabernacle. Monsignor Thomas Capel (1836–1911), a prominent Catholic proselytiser in fashionable London, was the original of Monsignor Catesby in Disraeli's *Lothair*.

[?47 Princes Gate, S.W.]

[?1872]

My dear Fanny

I am getting so awfully tired of London, I often wish to be in my grotto again. I think we are going [to] [?Kyly, ?Filey] after we have stayed a fortnight at Standish. It is a Yorkshire sea-side place. Papa and the two of sisters have decided to go [to] America, Blanche is to go [to] Scotland to Mrs Menzies place, and Kate is going to Liverpool. I hope my hens are allright, I shall sell or kill nearly all of them when I get to Standish. I think I shall keep the gray cocks and hen with the white hens and few of the best golden [?Hamburg] hens. Are there any chickens and how [is] my grotto looking please send me word by the next post-card.

I went to hear Spurgeon the other day, and – nothing on the earth will ever persuade me to go again! We went to hear Mon Seigneur Capell [Monsignor Capel] a famous Roman Catholic preacher he preached *so* beautifully all against the – Who do [you] think? against the Protestants, no! Against those dishonest people who pretend that they belong to the English Church, when they really are Roman Catholics, the High Church young ladies with long tails, and chignons nearly twice as big as their heads who go poking about the church. I heartily agreed with him, but you know the High Church party is in such a rage, at being shown up like this.

Goodbye dear Fanny
Believe me
Beatrice Potter

5 PP BEATRICE POTTER TO LAWRENCINA POTTER

Richard Potter's interests included the presidency of the Grand Trunk Railway of Canada. It was his practice to take two of his daughters on his visits to North America, where they travelled in great style in his private car. The party that sailed from Liverpool on one of the Holt ships on 13 September 1873 included Arthur Playne, Kate Potter and Beatrice. She was impressed by the 'cleanliness and elegance' of New York (BWD 25 September 73), Niagara Falls and Chicago, where she visited a school and found it 'funny to see a common little Negro girl sitting between two well-dressed banker's daughters, and learning the same thing!' (BWD 7 October 73) Playne and the girls, accompanied by Mr Knowles (apparently a mining engineer and possibly a business associate of Richard Potter) went on without Potter to the Pacific coast, returning by way of Salt Lake City. When they reached Chicago Beatrice was seriously ill with scarlet fever, measles and rheumatism. It was on this journey that she began systematically to keep the diary which she maintained to the end of her life.

San Francisco
Saturday October 25 [1873]

Dearest Mother

We got all your dear letters from home today; the first news we have had since we left Niagara, now nearly three weeks. I think Kitty told you that we left San Francisco for the Yosemite on Wednesday 15 Oct.

We got up very early, and travelled by the cars for 6 hours to Milton, where we met our 'private conveyance' which carried us over the greatest part of our journey. It was a queer sort of carriage, very much like a butcher's cart in appearance, and drawn by four bright little horses, who seemed never to be tired, though our average drives a day, were from 20 to 30 miles. The same day we went on to Murphy's (by carriage) over a fearfully rough road, and through rather uninteresting country. We felt the jolting dreadfully at first, before we got accustomed to it, and before we found out a way of making our legs serve us as springs, by cocking them in a peculiar way under the seat. We arrived at Murphy's later in the evening, and started the next morning at seven o'clock for the big trees. We

8

were very delighted and agreeably surprised with them. They seemed somehow to belong to a different world, and reminded me so much of the descriptions of the plants and trees in Gulliver's Travels when he is with the giants. We brought home some pieces of the wood and some cones, though I don't fancy they will improve our dresses and clothes. The drive there was very pleasant, (if it had not been quite so dusty), through a very fine pine forest, such splendid trees, of all varieties. It would have delighted yours and Father's eyes to have seen all those Wellingtonias, sugar pines, silver firs and cypresses of all sizes and descriptions. The next day we started for the valley, and drove for about 40 miles through the gold mining district. There are three different kinds of mining used there, the 'Stamping', the 'Placer' and the 'Hydraulich'. The Stamping is only used where they find the gold in quartz or stone, and is the least risky and the most expensive. The 'Placer' is the washing system, they can only carry it on, in most places in the wet season, as there is a great scarcity of water in California, in the dry season. The hydraulich is another system of washing, only more complicated.

We were delighted to get to 'Priest's' a very comfortable little inn (on top of a mountain about 5000 ft high) after our long dusty drive. Mrs Priest, (a jolly Scotch woman) gave us a hearty welcome, a capital supper, and beautifully clean little bedrooms.

We had very different accommodation the next night in the midst of the forest at Hogton's, a small farm or ranch (as they call it over here). There was neither milk, nor bread fit to be eaten, in fact our bill of fare consisted of a cup of black coffee and a slice of pork. As for our dormitory, we were shown into a barn, partitioned off, by low wooden screens, into little square places, very much like the loose stalls for horses, and as you can imagine, fearfully draughty and cold.

The next morning we started at seven, half-frozen and very hungry, and arrived at Gentries at the head of the valley about eleven in the morning. There we took horses and descended into the valley. It is impossible to describe the beauty of the scene, as one splendid rock after another burst upon our view, with a beautiful range of blue wooded hills just capped with snow, rising above the dry rocks. The day after we came into the valley, Arthur, Mr Knowles and Kate went [on] an excursion to Mirror Lake and to the different falls, (which by the way nearly all dried up) and I staid at the Hotel to rest, having, with my usual luck a bad cold in the head. On Monday we all went to Glacier Point, from where you can see the whole stretch of the valley. It is almost 8 miles long, and varying from 1 to 2 miles in breadth, surrounded by splendid rocks, of all imaginable shapes. The highest of them is 5300 ft above the valley and perfectly perpendicular on one side and shaped like a dome on the other.

Tuesday we started on our way homeward, and arrived here yesterday, thoroughly tired and dirty and delighted to get a long night's rest. We

9

start for the guisers (hot springs) tomorrow morning early, and we hope to be back on Monday evening. On Tuesday we go to stay at Mr Latham's, and return the next day. I have no more time to write indeed I think I must have rather tried your patience already, so I will leave San Francisco and the Pacific to tomorrow's letter. With love to all the dear girls, fräulein and Miss [?Mitchell.]

Believe me

Yr loving child

Beatrice

6 PP BEATRICE POTTER TO RICHARD POTTER

Beatrice remained at home after her return from America, reading widely despite what she considered a discreditable tendency to indolence. 'I have been extremely irregular in all my duties', she noted on 25 January 1874. 'I have been lazy in getting up; altogether I have been devoid of any method.' The general election that year made her reflect on politics. She felt that she was in 'a complete muddle', confessing that 'I can't help having a sort of sympathy with the Radicals, they are so enthusiastic, but I don't think that their time is come yet – they require a much more perfect state of society than at present'. At the age of sixteen she was more concerned with her religious doubts and the fact that she was 'getting into a nasty and what I should call indecent way of thinking about men, and love'. She felt that she was in danger of becoming 'a silly vain self-conscious little goose'.

In April 1874 she had recovered sufficiently to go up to London for the Season. 'I enjoyed it immensely. It is seldom I have had so much pleasure in so small a space of time.' She took part in amateur theatricals and her first ball: 'how I did enjoy that . . . . I felt considerably satisfied with myself, as I had two or three partners for each dance. Ah, vanity! vanity! Unfortunately for me, my ruling passion'. (BWD 3 August 74).

Despite her religious uncertainties – she felt that she did not have 'enough of that Christian humility which is at the root of all virtue' – she decided that the only means of curing her inflated self-esteem was 'to go heart and soul into religion . . . since I cannot accept the belief of my church without inward questioning let me try and found a firm belief of my own, and let me act up to it'. (BWD 23 September 74) Nevertheless, despite her rejection of the doctrine of the Atonement, she took the Sacrament at Easter 1875.

At seventeen Beatrice was still not old enough to 'come out' like her sisters and she was sent for a short time to Stirling House, a smart finishing school at Bournemouth. She disliked her stay there, feeling superior and intellectually snobbish about her schoolmates. At this school she formed a close friendship with a second cousin, Margaret Harkness, who was already in rebellion against an oppressive clerical home. After training as a nurse–dispenser, she became a radical journalist and wrote a few novels on social themes.

That winter Beatrice became interested in spiritualism: she recalled table-rapping with her sisters, and discussing the problem of faith with Herbert Spencer. In the summer of 1876 she 'came out', going through the exhausting whirl of dances, visits, horse-riding in the Park and picnics at Hurlingham.

In these years of 'irresponsible girlhood' she spent much of her time reading – classical history, sociology and science – but she suffered fits of depression at the apparently aimless drift of her life. In 1878 she made a tour of Austria and Germany with the Playnes, but was bored. When her sister Maggie was married to Henry Hobhouse and they proposed to visit Italy for part of their honeymoon, Beatrice decided to take a long Italian holiday, some of it with her sister Theresa, some with the Hobhouses, and to join her parents in the early Spring of 1881 on the Italian Riviera. She began the visit in company with a Mr and Mrs Cobb and a Mr Watson. Her letters were for the most part descriptions of tourist sights.

Perugia
November 3 [1880]

Dearest Father

In our short stay in Florence I saw sufficient to make me long to return. We only had three days there, so that we had but a glimpse of it.

Sunday morning I spent with Mr and Mrs Cobb making enquiries concerning two pensions. 1 found that Mme Brunold who had been so strongly recommended to me was a such charming and cultivated woman, but her house was stuffy, and the situation doubtful – next to a hospital in a very crowded and smelly part of the town.

The other pension was kept by two Italian decayed gentlewomen. It was recommended to the Cobbs by a spinster friend of theirs, (one of the Norwich Taylors) who would be there herself the end of November. It was the top floor of one of the large homes looking over the gardens of Florence and the river with a magnificent view of the Appennines. There were only 3 other ladies – and it looked beautifully clean and airy. The terms were 7 francs per person, for sitting-room and bedroom. The situation was exceedingly healthy. The Cobbs strongly recommended me to settle in it; so that I shall engage a room from the 20th. If Theresa can join us in Rome we shall all go to Siena, which I believe is a most interesting place, and Theresa and I will break off to Florence, only a couple of hours journey. If you should object to this plan, please telegraph.

I thought it better to decide to go to Florence, as it seems that the climate is so very healthy before Xmas and Mr Cobb strongly recommended me to do so. He and I are great friends and companions.

I like Mrs Cobb too, she is so kind and motherly, but somewhat heavy.

We came here yesterday. The town is quite unique, an old fortified Etruscan city, with wonderfully strong walls and towers. It is quite as it was in the days of Perugino – and the inhabitants have kept their old costumes.

It is today the great fair of the year, and the streets are thronged by a most picturesque multitude of cattle and human beings. There is a most intoxicating view of the Appennines from the Convent tower – Mrs Cobb and I were there this morning at sunrise: it was simply glorious. We afterwards spent ½ hour in the Cathedral, watching the peasants at their devotions, on this great saint's day. It was very touching to see their simple piety. After breakfast, we devoted to seeing Perugino's works. I do not know whether you have seen them – but his frescoe of the Transfiguration, I admire immensely. Perhaps, one ought hardly to take on oneself to criticise, but his conception of human nature seems to me rather narrow and the type of his ideal wanting in largeness of heart and mind. I cannot tell you, Dear Father, how thankful I am to you and Mother for giving me this great treat.

Beautiful memories are a great possession – if in after years one's life should be work-a-day, and filled with the cares of the world. All that I see, seems to be one long dream – and I *feel* too much, to have much energy left for the retailing of my impressions, so you must excuse the uninterestingness of my letters.

When Theresa comes over, it will be delightful. Tell her to bring Murray's *Rome*, Badeker's *Central Italy* – and any other books she is recommended. I have Hughes's *Handbook of Modern Art*. She must bring warm clothing, and have *a fur* on the journey.

We go to Rome tomorrow, where I expect a budget of letters.

With love to all,
Yr loving child
Beatrice Potter

7 PP   BEATRICE POTTER TO RICHARD POTTER

Beatrice had a long attack of lung congestion in Rome and was confined to her room for almost a month. The doctor advised against an early return to England. She met her parents in San Remo at the end of the winter. After her return to England Beatrice continued with her 'wanderings through the intricate labyrinth of theology and metaphysics', but she was aware of the deficiencies in her education: she had little practical knowledge, nor did she care for sports and games. 'One was so early imbued with utilitarianism of the more short-sighted kind that one never had the heart to employ oneself in any way which did not seem productive of some immediate benefit either to oneself or to others.' (MA)

Rome
January [1881]

Dearest Father

We are so distressed to hear that mother is not well. If she really feels our absence she must let me come home and leave Theresa with Miss Gromhead. I could do that as the Ottleys are probably returning to England on Monday week.

I am alright now, but I am obliged to stay in on cold days, so that I cannot do much sightseeing and have to give up the galleries altogether. They say we shall have some warm weather in February, if so it will be delightful to spend our days on the Campagna.

The scenery there grows upon you. I think it is more fascinating in its way than anything I have ever seen. It is such a wonderfully happy country, such a contrast to this dismal old city with all its hideous associations of a debased Empire and a corrupt church. It is a most depressing sight, all those vast ruins and palaces, baths, etc., all built for man's material comfort and for the gratification of all his lowest faculties! Don't you think so yourself?

As for the Church, if you wish to hold it in reverence as a Grand Idea, beware of Rome, where the little glimpses into its inner life through Protestant gossip and observation are quite sufficiently revolting to destroy one's illusions for ever.

But Rome is an experience that I suppose it would be impossible to repeat in any other spot of the universe. There is an uncanny feeling that it is a sort of dead heart to a body that is still living a sort of concentrated essence of historical association, before which one feels rather hopeless, without knowledge as a dissolvent.

To really enjoy it, you ought to have spent years in preparation, otherwise the consciousness of an absolute vacuum within your brain and the crowd of ideas without it is painful.

What is truly enjoyable, are the statuary and some of the frescoes – I have seen so little of the former but I hope to make up for lost time when it is warmer.

We were both so delighted with Raphael's Sybiles. It is quite the most beautiful of his works, to my thinking, in Rome.

Why does not mother come and spend a couple of months in the Riviera, where she could be perfectly comfortable and escape those bitter cold winds in February and March? I do not like the idea of her being seedy without one of us to look after her. It would be a pity for Theresa to leave Rome, she seems to be enjoying herself most thoroughly, and I do not think that the extra cold of the English climate would do me really any harm. But if we could all meet in the Riviera, it would be delightful. We hear that it is such a delicious climate, and if I should have another attack of congestion, we seriously think that we shall ask your permission to move.

Do write and tell us what is going to happen in Parliament.

Tell Rosy to write and tell us all the home news – how mother is and whether the new housekeeper is a success.

With best love, dearest Father to you and mother and Rosebud.

Ever your devoted child
Beatrice Potter

In February 1882 Beatrice stayed with Mary and Charles Booth. Mary was the daughter of Richard Potter's sister and the younger brother of the historian Thomas Babington Macaulay (1800–59). Charles Booth (1840–1916) was a Liverpool shipowner who abandoned his business career to become a notable investigator of social problems. Beatrice was very fond of Mary Booth and thought her husband charming and loveable. This connection was most important in settling her mind towards a career in social work. In April 1883 Beatrice joined the Charity Organisation Society, an influential body which recruited fashionable young ladies as voluntary social workers, 'East-Ending' being much in vogue. Her sister Kate was already active in the C.O.S. and had introduced her that spring to Octavia Hill (1838–1912), a pioneer of housing reform and a notable exponent of philanthropic morality. On 18 May Beatrice reflected that 'it is distinctly *advantageous to us* to go among the poor . . . the study of their lives and surroundings gives us the facts wherewith we attempt to solve the social problems'. (BWD)

In the same month she was at Standish when Lawrencina Potter collapsed and died. This tragedy, which came at a moment when Beatrice felt that after years of difficulty with her mother they were 'on the verge of a true and complete intimacy', left her with 'a new and wondrous faith . . . in goodness – in God' which made her feel 'more able to put aside all compromise with worldliness and to devote myself with single-heartedness to my duty'. (BWD 23 April 83) That duty, immediately, meant her responsibilities to her father and young Rosy, whose neurotic personality was a continuing concern. Beatrice was no longer a subordinate in the household, but its domestic principal, managing its complex affairs, acting as her father's hostess and increasingly becoming his business confidante. Despite her mother's death Beatrice now led an active social life, entertaining at the town house Richard Potter had taken at Prince's Gate, Knightsbridge, and meeting many eminent people at his dinner parties.

That summer she, Richard Potter, Rosy and Herbert Spencer took a long holiday in Germany and the Bernese Oberland. Here Beatrice met in July a 'promising' young teacher of mathematics from London, named John Frederick Main, and enjoyed 'the companionship of a refined and sympathetic mind, deeply appreciative of nature and yet steadfast in devotion to work and duty'. (BWD 24 July 83) A letter from him written at the time (PP 23 July 83) and an entry in her diary by Beatrice (BWD 11 March 85) on hearing he was seriously ill with tuberculosis show that they came close to an understanding. She wrote that they were 'on the threshold of life and on the verge of an ever-uniting love'.

Rosy had returned from an unhappy stay at a boarding school at Fontainebleau. It is not clear whether the G. Smith is George Smith, publisher and founder of the *Dictionary of National Biography* (1824–1901) or George Smith (1841–1909), a Liberal journalist and author. Horace Davey (1833–1907) became Baron Davey in 1894. He was a lawyer and Liberal M.P. who became an eminent judge. James Russell Lowell (1819–91), the American poet and diplomat, was Minister to the Court of St James's from 1880 to 1885. Charles Synge Christopher Bowen (1835–94), who had been junior counsel in the celebrated case of the Tichborne Claimant in 1871–74, had just been raised to the peerage as Baron Bowen on becoming lord of appeal in ordinary. Polly was the Playnes' relative Mary, brought up as an adopted daughter. Sir John Lubbock (1834–

1913), later Lord Avebury, was Liberal M.P. for London University, sponsor of the Bank Holidays Act of 1871, a banker, entomologist and author. Olga de Novikoff (b. 1841) had worked for understanding between Russia and Britain: her letters to Gladstone led to his denunciation of Turkish atrocities in Bulgaria. Living in London for much of the time, she was regarded as an agent of the Tsarist government.

The relationship with Joseph Chamberlain (1836–1914) which began in the summer of 1883 became an emotional obsession for Beatrice for six agonising years. He was then President of the Board of Trade, after making a reputation in Birmingham municipal politics and emerging as the leader of the Radical wing of the Liberal Party. When Beatrice met him his second wife had been dead for eight years and his household consisted of his sister Clara (Mrs Ryland) and his daughter Beatrice Chamberlain. The first impression he made was ambiguous, but after a long talk at Herbert Spencer's annual picnic Beatrice noted that 'his personality interested me'. (BWD 27 June 83) He was soon invited to dine at the Potter home.

Carrie Darling was a member of the Potter household who had come as a governess and stayed after Mrs Potter died as a companion/secretary. She married unwisely, went to Australia and returned after some unhappy years.

47 Princes Gate, S.W.
[July 1883]

Dearest Mary

Very many thanks for your letter and all its news.

I hope you will come once to Standish Sunday, 29th and see us especially as I shall probably return to London during the following week.

Rosy came back Monday. She looks very delicate, and I am not altogether satisfied about her health. She is certainly very undeveloped in every way and quite unfit for much society or responsibility. I shall take her again to Dr Gee before we leave London.

I am quite looking forward to staying with you, so as to get free of 'arrangements' and out of my own home life for a while, in spite of all the attractions.

I had a delightful dinner with Mr G. Smith. Sat between Horace Davey and Lowell (American Minister) with both of whom I got on swimmingly. After dinner I had a long talk with Lord Justice Bowen, and promised to take the [illegible] to lunch with him tomorrow at the new Law Courts.

Tell Polly that I have had another ride with Sir John Lubbock and he has sent me his last book, and asked me to tea with him any day I like to have on the terrace at Westminster – if I had only another dinner to ask him to, I should win my bet!

But the most interesting acquaintance I have made lately is [illegible]'s dear friend, supposed to be a Russian spy – at any rate a most amusing woman.

She is coming in after dinner on Wednesday to meet Chamberlain and the Leonard Courtneys.

And so ends the London Season! and I shall return with clear 'social' conscience to my dowdy dress (black lace and all!) early hours, and dear books.

We must pull the purse strings rather tighter and economise for the rest of the year. I shan't attempt to have any parties at Standish – but shall hope to see a great deal of you and Arthur. I am not quite happy about Carrie Darling tho' I think there is hardly evidence that she is in love with Mr Murdoch.

Ever yours

B.P.

9 PP   BEATRICE POTTER TO MARY PLAYNE

In the early autumn Beatrice was invited to spend a week at the Chamberlain's London house as his daughter Beatrice's guest: during the visit she became increasingly attracted to him though she sensed that his dominating personality might lead to a clash of wills between them. Though both Richard Potter and Herbert Spencer objected to Chamberlain, Beatrice invited him and two of his children to visit The Argoed at the New Year.

Martha Jackson ('Dada') was the old nurse of the Potter children who had married the butler and now lived in a cottage on the Argoed estate.

[The Argoed]
[October 1883]

Dearest Mary

I enclose you a letter from Theresa which may interest you. She refers to a most kind letter from Herbert Spencer advising me to take up 'some definite line of study and research' and offering to overlook my work. I am afraid I am a humbug! as regards my powers tho' not in my intentions.

We are so comfortable here and thoroughly enjoying the change from Standish. We have sent for Rosy's horse and I think shall stay a good three weeks or month.

I think it will do both of us good and if Father gets away for a week it will be a change for him too. I wonder whether Arthur would come next week and bring Henry Cox. Father's room will be vacant and we would try and make him comfortable. I should so like to get some idea about the garden etc., before Father settles it with Driver the week after. He is really completely at sea about a plan for it and of course it is rather important it should be well and economically finished.

I do not know anything about such things and should be so much obliged for advice, before I advise Father. It would be a good opportunity while he is away.

Could not Polly come and stay at Dada's if we do not come back to

16

Standish before you leave for the north? She would find the bracing air and riding good for her – and it would be so pleasant for both of us. What a queer child Rosy is; I must say I am not very happy when I look forward to the next three or four years of her life. It will be some time before she starts fair either physically or mentally. What a wretched thing that education was!

Ever yours affectionately
Beatrice Potter

Send me back Theresa's latter; I think I must keep all this good advice. If as Miss C. [Chamberlain] says – the Right Honourable gentleman takes 'a very conventional view of women', I may be saved all temptation by my unconventionality. I certainly shall not hide it. He would soon see that I was not the woman to 'forward' his most ambitious views.

IO PP BEATRICE POTTER TO RICHARD POTTER

By the end of 1883 Beatrice was settling on a career. What she had learned from Spencer about sociology, especially his emphasis on facts, blended with the Positivist theories of Auguste Comte and her disposition towards charitable work with the poor. 'From the flight of emotion away from the service of God to the service of Man, and from the current faith in the scientific method', she wrote in her autobiography, 'I drew the inference that the most hopeful form of social service was the craft of a social investigator.' (MA)

The decision to make a pilgrimage to Bacup in Lancashire, where her mother's poorer relations still lived, had symbolic and practical value: Beatrice was deliberately crossing the Victorian class barrier. She had only just discovered that Martha Jackson was in fact a poor Lancashire relative who had been with Lawrencina Potter from her marriage to her death. 'Dada' was her guide; Beatrice to avoid embarrassment disguised her true identity and passed herself off as Miss Jones, the daughter of a Welsh farmer.

The first of three letters described her warm reception; the second concerned a detailed account of the habits and attitudes of the mill-hands; the third printed below, enclosed several pages of almost illegible and scarcely comprehensible working notes on her observations. These have been omitted.

Mrs Ashworth was a miserly Heyworth relative whose intestate death in 1892 caused extraordinary family complications.

Arthur Pelham was the younger son of the Earl of Chichester; he and his wife Evelyne had recently settled at Moorcroft, a neighbouring property to The Argoed.

Bacup
Nov. 9th 1883

Dearest Father

I have just received your letter. I will certainly meet you at Manchester Monday, but don't on any account come here; Da says they would never forgive her if they found it out!

The dear people have accepted me so heartily and entertained me so hospitably as one of themselves that it would be cruel to undeceive them.

We dined this morning in a most comfortable cottage, owned by a mill-hand with three young mill hands. Afternoon, I spent in going over two or three mills, introduced by my friends to their managers and finished up by going through the Co-op stores with the managers.

I told him I had been sent by my Father to enquire into the management of Co-ops. as you wanted to start one; and he took me into his counting house, showed me his books and explained the whole thing. It is entirely owned and managed by working men. Membership entails spending a certain amount there; and the dividend is payed according to the amount spent per quarter, tho' it is not payed *out* until the share is payed up through accumulation. In this way there is a double check on the management; the shareholder requiring his dividend, and the consumer requiring cheap and good articles and as the manager remarked 'the females look pretty sharp arter that'.

It has been established 20 years or more and has never payed less than 12½ per cent. The working expenses only come to 5 per cent in capital turned over. No member can have more than £300 in the stock, and anyone can become a member on the payment of 3 per cent entrance fee and on the original terms. The manager gave me a graphic account of his trouble with the committee of working men; and interested me by explaining the reasons of the failure of most of the Co-op mills, all of which I will tell you over one cigarette.

We went to tea in another cottage and have just been listening to a somewhat dreary 'spiritual oration' from our religiously-minded host.

A miner by profession, he finished up by saying that 'God Almighty did all things right, that 'e'ed bouried the coal so deep, 'cause if it 'ud ben o'the top the women would 'ave taken all the cobs and left all the small.' You would be amused at my piety, dear Father; yesterday in one of the Sunday schools, I came to the rescue of a meek elderly teacher who was being pertly questioned by a forward-going woman as to Adam's responsibility for our sin. I asked her whether she did not 'favour' her parents and made her draw the rather far-fetched inference. The meek elderly man shook me warmly by the hand as we left and enquired if 'he could do ought for me while I was in Bacup'. But the only way to understand these people is, for the time, to adopt their faith and look at things in their light. Then one gets a clear picture (undisturbed by any critically antagonistic spirit) of their life both material and mental.

And to me, there is a certain charm and restfulness in their simple piety and absolute ignorance of the world.

As regards their 'material life' I am sometimes rather hard up for meat and my diet is principally nut cake and cheese with the butter which we brought with us. Every evening I have my cigarettes in a rocking chair by the kitchen fire, having persuaded my friends that all Welsh women smoke.

My host accepted a cigarette the first night saying 'I maun 'ave a bit, but a little 'ull go a lung way', so after puffing once or twice he snuffs it out and puts it carefully on the corner of the mantel-piece for the next night: 'One musna tak too mich o' a gude thing, fur mooney is a slattering thing' (easily spent). Their income is only £1 a week so that without the hospitality of our neighbours we should not have much to live on.

We go to Mrs Ashworth's tomorrow: she is universally disliked, being very rich and very close-fisted; and nobody receiving aught from her now or knowing where it will go to at her death. In order to avoid paying the tax on her carriage, she has taken it off the wheels and has some arrangement by which it is mounted when wanted (so say her cousins). I expect a good deal of condescension from her, as when we met her the other day in the butcher's shop, where we were paying a friendly visit, she gave me the slightest nod and did not shake hands. I have made friends with the Howarths the drapers, and if I were staying longer should go with Miss Howarth to Manchester and see her buy her goods from the warehouse-men.

Sunday

I kept my letter back so that you should get it at The Argoed and not be tempted to show it to the sisters.

I like you and Rosebud to know all about my doings, but 'discretion is the better part of valour' as regards one's reputation.

I have spent the day in the chapels and schools. After dinner a dissenting minister dropped in and I had a long talk with him; and he is coming for a cigarette this evening after chapel. He told me that in all the chapels there was a growing desire amongst the congregation to have political and social subjects treated in the pulpit and that it was very difficult for a minister, now, to please. He also remarked that in districts where Co-operation amongst the workmen (in industrial enterprises) existed they were a much more independent and free-thinking set. (There is an immense amount of Co-operation in the whole of his district, the *stores* seem to succeed well, both as regards supplying the people with cheap articles and as savings banks paying good interest.)

Of course I am just in the centre of the dissenting organisation and as our host is the chapel keeper and entertains all the ministers who come here, I hear all about the internal management. Each chapel, even if the same denomination, manages its own affairs, and there are monthly meetings of all the members (male and female) to discuss question of expenditure etc. In fact each chapel is a self-governing community, regulating not only chapel matters but overlooking the private life of its members. One cannot help feeling what an excellent thing these dissenting organisations have been for educating this class for self-government.

19

I can't help thinking too, that one of the best preventions against the socialistic tendency of the coming democracy would lie in weak government, which would force the respectable working man to consider political questions as they came up in local questions. Parliament is such a far-off thing, that the more practical and industrious would say that it is 'gormless meddling with it' (useless) and leave it to the 'gabblers', But they are keen enough on any local question which comes within *their* practical politics and would bring plenty of shrewd sound sense to bear on the actual management of things.

Certainly the earnest successful working man is essentially conservative as regards the rights of property and the non-interference of the Central Government and tho' religious feeling still has an immense hold in this class and forms a real basis for many lives; the most religious of them argue that the younger generation are looking elsewhere for subjects of thought and feeling.

It seems to me of great importance that the political thought should take a *practical* instead of a theoretical line; that each section of a community should try refinements on a small scale and that the *proposers* should see and reap the difficulties and disadvantages in the execution. There is an immense amount of spare energy in this class, now that it is educated, which is by no means used up in their mechanical occupation. When the religious channel is closed up it must go somewhere. It can be employed either in the *practical* dealing of social and economic question or in the purely intellectual exercise of political theorising and political discussion about problems considered in the abstract.

Forgive all these crudely expressed ideas. I have jotted them down just as they have crossed my mind.

I am immensely interested in what I hear and see, but it is a daring thing in a young woman to drop 'Caste' and that is why I am anxious it should not be talked about.

I have sufficient knowledge of men to make them be to me as *I* choose, but not everyone would [not] understand that one had that power, and without it, it would not be a profitful or wise adventure.

I have seen two more Aked brothers. They are all delicate featured melancholy men with beautiful *hands*.

There is a universal interest in our family. I think they would be somewhat horrified if they knew that this 'stirring lass who is up in everything' was one of 'the fashionable Miss Potters who live in grand houses and beautiful gardens and marry enormously wealthy men'.

But they evidently feel that there is something very strange about me. Their generalisations about 'Welsh women' will be rather quaint by the time I go!

Ever yours,

Beatrice Potter

20

Don't speak to the Pelhams about me. I shall be back on Monday. I shan't go to Liverpool. You will of course *not* send this letter to anyone.

II PP BEATRICE POTTER TO ANNA SWANWICK

Anna Swanwick (1813–99) was a pioneer in women's education, being one of the founders of Girton College, Cambridge: she was noted for her translations of Greek and German plays, especially her version of Goethe's *Faust* (1850–78). She published *A Utopian Dream* in 1888. This letter was drafted but not despatched, Beatrice later recalling that she lacked the courage to send this 'priggish pronouncement'. It is printed because she attached considerable importance to it in after years as 'demonstrating the anti-democratic and anti-collectivist bias with which I started out to investigate the working of social institutions'. (MA) She thought it exemplified the dialectical duel between the philosophic Radical and the socialistically-minded politician.
Herbert Spencer's *Man versus the State* was published in 1884.

York House, Kensington, W.
[1884]

Dear Miss Swanwick

I send you *Man and State*.

I feel very penitent for talking to you on social subjects, which I do not, and never hope to, understand!

Nevertheless it is very distressing to be reduced to a state of absolute agnosticism on all questions, divine and human: and that state appears to me now-a-days, the fate of the ordinary mortal, born without an intellectual tendency?

Social questions would seem to me to require for their solution greater intellectual power and more freedom from bias than the problems of other sciences – and I do not quite understand the democratic theory that by multiplying ignorant opinions indefinitely you produce wisdom? I know the democrat would answer: 'The political instincts of the masses are truer than the political theories of the wise men'. But if we approach this great idol 'The majority' and examine the minds of those individuals of it – who are within our reach, we find them roughly divided into three classes: those who are indifferent – whose nervous energy is absorbed in the struggle for existence and well-being: those who accept political opinions as a party faith without really understanding the words they use; and lastly that more promising material, politically considered, that large section of the working-classes who are passionately discontented with things as they are and desirous to obtain what they would consider a *fairer* state of the good things of this world. But we all agree that there are laws governing distribution, though we may differ as to their nature.

Are these discontented men anxious for immediate relief *likely* to arrive at the truth about these laws? Would desperate anxiety to relieve pain teach the patient or his friend the medicine likely to effect it – if they had no knowledge of medicine.

Certainly if one judges the political intelligence of the masses by the speeches addressed to it by party speakers, especially the speeches of those most successful in pleasing it – one cannot estimate it very highly.

What body of scientific men, or even of ordinary shrewd business men, spoken to on the subject that interested them most, whether intellectually or materially, would *tolerate* that extraordinary mixture of personalities, dogmatic assertions as to face and principle, metaphysical theories, grand and vague moral sentiments, affects and personal devotion on the one hand, and self-interest on the other, their extraordinary medley of sentiment, passion and expediency which makes up the argument of the politician.

And then if we turn from the practical man to the theorist, I do not know that one finds much rest there.

Herbert Spencer seems to me to be guilty of what Comte defines as materialism: he applies the laws of a lower to the subject-matter of a higher science – his social theories are biological laws illustrated by social facts.

He bases sociological laws in the analogy of the organism, and this analogy – insofar as it deals with the identity of the functions of the 'being' called society with the functions of the 'being' called the individual – seems to me pure hypothesis.

One might as well attempt to describe the nature of organic life by the laws which govern inorganic existence. Then this analogy of the organism cuts both ways.

Herbert Spencer maintains that because Society is in a natural growth it should not be interfered with. But it is quite possible to argue that the government is a 'naturally differentiated organ' (as he would express it) developed by the organism to gratify its own sensations. This might lead straight to state socialism – logically it leads to pure necessarianism – since whatever happens is natural, even the death of the organism?

So I think, if I were a man, and had an intellect, I would leave political action and political theorizing to those with faith, and examine and try to describe correctly and proportionately what actually haapened in the different states of society; more especially the spontaneous growth of organisation – to try and discover the laws governing its birth, life and death.

I do not believe we can deduce social laws from the laws of another science – nor do I believe that there is an intuitive perception of them in the majority of men's minds – I believe they will only be discovered by great minds working on carefully prepared data – and for the most part this data is yet to be collected and classified.

In the meantime, as a citizen, working for the material and spiritual welfare of my descendants, I object to those gigantic experiments, state education and state intervention in the matters which are now being inaugurated and which flavor of inadequate thought-out theories – the most dangerous of all social poisons. [*Phrase deleted*]

[. . . . *deleted*] Neither do they seem to me to be the result of the spontaneously expressed needs of the people, but rather the crude prescriptions of social quacks for the vague feelings of pain and discomfort experienced by the masses.

[*not signed*]

[*Note added by B.P.*] Not sent. Thought afterwards I would turn it into a letter from intelligent [?person] to Editor of *Pall Mall* [*Gazette*].

12 PP   BEATRICE POTTER TO RICHARD POTTER

In 1884 Richard Potter gave up Standish. He also moved his London home from Prince's Gate to York House, a spacious and fashionable residence in Kensington Palace Gardens. Beatrice was now living a double life – one in what she called the 'whirlpool' of smart society, the other in her growing involvement with social problems. On New Year's Eve 1883 Beatrice noted with dismay 'the horrible dilemma' of feeling and reason.

This conflict, which she had already seen was dramatised in the contrast between York House and the East End, came out clearly in her attitude to Chamberlain. When he arrived at The Argoed for New Year celebrations Beatrice noted that she felt 'as if I were dancing in a dream towards some precipice'. (BWD 12 January 84) She had long and intimate talks with the great man in which physical attraction struggled with her realisation that he was cold and intolerant. 'It pains me', he told her, 'to hear my views controverted', especially by women. At the end of his visit she had a 'stunned feeling' of rejection. She was, however, as unable to terminate the relationship as she was unwilling to submit. She went to stay at Highbury, his Birmingham home, the end of January, attending a political rally where she was fascinated by the manner in which he seduced his audience. She realised that she was in love with him. She had had 'small affairs of the heart' but they had bored her. Now she was caught by a barely-governable passion. 'I don't know how it will all end', she noted on 16 March: 'Certainly not in *my happiness* . . . if the fates should unite us (against *my will*) all joy and light-heartedness will go from me. I shall be absorbed into the life of a man whose aims are not my aims; who will refuse me all freedom of thought in my intercourse with him; to whose career I shall have to subordinate all my life, mental and physical . . . If I married him I should become a cynic as regards my own mental life . . . I should become *par excellence* the mother and the woman of the world intent only on fulfilling practical duties and gaining practical ends.'

Her inner struggle continued. Though she found Chamberlain's temperament and character 'intensely attractive' and believed that she could play a bigger role as his wife than as a spinster, she still wondered whether she would be selling her soul in marriage. The craving for power would be greater than the craving for truth and independence of mind. (BWD 22 April 84) She then made the first of several ineffectual decisions 'to cut the knot', deciding that 'I have loved and lost'. (BWD 9 May 84) She would devote herself to her father and to Rosy: 'I clutch desperately at *my duty* to those around me: that last hope for the soul despairing of its own happiness'. She toyed with the idea of suicide and made her will.

In an effort to raise her spirits by a change of scene she went for a long holiday to Bavaria with Maggie Harkness, now living on the fringe of London's literary and political bohemia.

Richard Potter had a business at Grimsby. Beatrice's reference to his commercial activities show the extent to which she had become something like a consultant in his affairs. Five letters apart from the two printed are largely concerned with tourist descriptions.

Parten Kirchen (Bavaria)

[?Friday, 15 August]

Dearest Father

From your letter of the 8th I gather that you will be at Grimsby by the time this letter reaches its destination. I shall be most anxious to hear the results of the meeting and how it will affect your autumn plans. Also you will probably have been to Newport: I don't feel quite happy about that S.W. Colliery Co. with an incompetent manager like Mick Lawrence or your having the practical responsibility without being on the spot or devoting much time to it. Do let me hear about the French affair. If you spend a day, darling Father, in picturing Maggie and me on the Bavarian mountains, I spend many an hour in thinking of you and Rusebud and the Summerhill party. Especially now that you are alone do I think constantly of you, and wish it were in my nature to give you a more complete sympathy and make up by devotion what want of experience makes me lack as a companion to you. Then I console myself with the thought that you still have by your side a companion whom none of us could supplant, in mother's spirit, with whom I know you to be in constant communion.

Certainly her influence over me, and I believe over many of her daughters, has been strengthened not lessened by death: one realises every day what she did directly and indirectly to give one a love of truth and purity and simplemindedness of aim – now that the friction rising from differences of temperament is gone. Whatever we may think about immortality, it is a strange truth that those who have ceased to be *materially*, should *do* more in directing action than those who are still with us? Death seems to take from them that which prevented us from knowing them; if Death should do the same by us and if there be a future life, we may have a perfect spiritual union.

We had a lovely drive yesterday: starting at 8 o'clock we crawled along a narrow winding lane by a mountain torrent; passed through mountain villages and at last came upon an emerald-green lake in the midst of a pine wood; then resting there for one hour we climbed further up the mountain to the Eibsee, a large tarn surrounded by the bare rocks of the limestone alps.

These are *not* beautiful on a clear day: they are colourless and naked; but when mists wreath round them and sunlight and cloud lighten and darken them they have a weird beauty of their own, reminding one of the old German legands of cloud and forest spirits. There the peasants with their picturesque dresses, and refined features, seem to be part of the land – they own it, and unlike we English, they rest easily and contentedly upon it and wish for nought else. It is curious to think of these generations of simple-minded men and women who live and die among these hills, understanding life better than we do, of worship of God, love and kindliness towards their fellow-creatures, (men and animals) and enjoyment of their own life, be its aim; and who yet achieve so little and have scarcely a perceptible influence on the world's progress towards good or bad – except it be in providing a morally pure atmosphere wherein the beer-drinking bad-tobacco-smoking German student, or greasy unwieldy-figured harsh-voiced German tradesmen may take their yearly holiday.

Certainly one's fellow travellers do not add to the beauty of the scene: they also enjoy life – and look benevolently disposed towards their fellows; but it is the benevolence of a presently full stomach enjoying its own fullness. Wherever and whenever one comes across them, they are sitting stolidly in front of their mug of beer which flattens and stupifies but does not intoxicate. No fear that divine discontent will transform society, while their beer flows freely and the German constitution keeps its capability of unlimited absorption.

If national education destroys this capability, as it promises to do, (if one judges from the spotty faces and dyspeptic expressions of the German youth who are more and more replacing the mug of beer by the pipe) then indeed may Bismarck or his successor tremble, even tho' he be surrounded by military caste or hedged round by state socialism!

Today we thought of leaving for Mittenwald, but it poured in the early morning and we gave up the idea. Instead I went to Church, it being the high-festival of the inhabitants of these parts. The church was crowded with villagers – and the service of the Mass curiously mixed up with certain native customs, the people themselves taking much more active part than in other Catholic countries. The music too was native – every imaginable instrument: guitar, zither, horn and flute, besides the violin and organ.

The voices were some of them unusually sweet and powerful but untrained – and the whole effect was [rather] of the Hungarian than the Italian or German music.

Ever your devoted

Beatrice Potter

From Mittenwald Beatrice went on to Zell, Salzburg and Munich. Reflecting on her impressions she wrote to Richard Potter on 21 August from Innsbruck. 'I am beginning to feel that my small attempts at self-culture have been rather *mis*-directed and that analysis and criticism are rather poor stuff to live on. It is late in the day to find it out! now that one ought to be going in for practical work if one is ever to do anything for one's fellow-mortals – it seems a pity that there is no way of teaching mortals *humility* early in life; it would save them from much pain and trouble. And this worship of intellectualism seems to me all in the wrong direction; corrupting those classes which were before free from a belief and pride in what is worthless.' The distress of her feeling for Chamberlain was not relieved by her holiday. After her return home she noted that 'day and night I cried secretly over the past . . . I can once again go on my way, if I knew only which way to turn'. (BWD 15 October 84).

Mittenwald
Tuesday [19 August 1884]

Dearest Father

We have had three most delightful days since I wrote from Parten Kirchen; and as I know you 'live in the happiness of your children', you will not be bored by a full description of them.

We were glad to leave Parten Kirchen: the hotel was very noisy and my room not very sweet-scented – it rained, and we were neither of us fit for much walking; but as usual we were sorry to leave our hostesses, for in this country the innkeepers (women for the most part) and all attendants – look upon you as real guests and do their best to make you feel at home and don't attempt to *do* you (our board and lodging came to about 6/ each per day including everything, carriages are our extravagance.)

We started in a carriage and pair on Saturday morning 7.30 and drove through high pastures and pine woods: the air was deliciously fresh and we felt delightfully exhilirated with the morning freshness and the sense of our own independence.

Certainly travelling in this way, with a companion of one's own age and tastes, quite out of the track of other English (which gives one a freedom from all convention) has a peculiar charm; and if you know a little of the language and can mix with the people and more or less adopt their habits and realise their love of thought and feeling – it is peculiarly restful for an overstrained mind like Maggie's or for a mental malady brought on by the over-luxury and under-work of a London season, like mine!

Maggie says that for the first time in her life, she feels *at one* with the world and that really there seems no argument against existence, when men and animals slip through it with so little friction or effort and so much unselfconscious enjoyment.

About 11 o'clock we came to Walchensee, the largest of the Bavarian lakes (5 miles long only!) and put up at a rough sort of farmhouse for the middle of the day.

Then while we waited for our midday meal and the arrival of the boat from the market town, we wandered into the pine forest, covering the hills for miles around. This belongs to the King and is left uncared for by him, except as a home for the deer and the chamois. Trees have fallen in all directions and are covered with lichen, fern, moss and in their decayed stumps grow the most delicate leaf and flower plants. This luxuriant undergrowth is the great beauty of the Bavarian forest.

Another beauty, from which the former springs, are the clear limpid streams running over beds of limestone shingle of soft dove colour and yellow – and the clearness of this water and light-brightness of the stone bottom give the lakes those wonderful tones of pink, emerald-green and blue.

Except for their colouring, these lakes would be insignificant; some of them are ludicrously small, more ponds than lakes, and their immediate surroundings are pretty wooded hills; no grandeur; even the limestone mountains, rising in the distance with their beauty of outline and feeling of inaccessibility still remind one of time and not of eternity.

After our excellent lunch of lake trout and German beer we confided ourselves to a rickety boat and a very underdressed oarsman – who rowed us, with much kindly grimacing and attempts to entertain us in his not-to-be-understood dialect to the other end of the lake. Coming back, the waves were so high, that we thought we should in reality slip out of existence without much effort with our Bavarian guide: but we were spared to enjoy some most excellent coffee and cakes and a chat with our hostess. She asked us whether England were not further than Munich and why we travelled: and when I told her I was going to America she threw up her hands with horror and exclaimed 'That such good-looking wenches could surely find husbands at home'. On parting she begged to be allowed to touch my dress (a stout cotton) to see what it was made of.

After six o'clock we arrived here after the most lovely drive along the banks of the Isar which runs immediately beneath the crags of the limestone rock-mountains. You must not tire of my mentioning these; for they have become part of our existence here, are the great personalities of the landscape, the different individuals which we recognise at each new place, and quarrel over the comparative beauties of our special favorites.

This small mountain town was the halting place of merchants on their way to Augsburg: it consists of one or two streets of substantially-built mediaeval houses with their vaulted passages and central halls and of outlying wooden chalets. The houses are wonderfully and curiously painted with frescoes, half-religious and half-comic, by native artists with native rhymes in native dialect explaining them.

To study them would teach you much of the past customs of the people which seem little altered by centuries.

27

We spent the evening sitting out with various attractive looking peasants on the wooden benches by their house-doors, watching the cows with their musical bells returning from the woods and the valleys. They are not *driven*, they come of their own free-will when the vesper bell is rung at the big church and the small chapels by the riverside. One woman amused us much with a tirade against the uselessness of state education.

The children have long school hours up to 13: but it seems that the learning slips off them easily and leaves them much as they were before – the people are free but they *do* very little and look healthy and happy.

Sunday, we spent the whole morning in devotion – early mass in the church and then a procession through the town – stopping at various altars – in honour of the virginity of Mary: virgins old and young wearing artificial orange blossom wreathes.

The great nobleman of the place, Count Pappenheim, came in his German coach-and-four with two sons and three daughters and joined in the procession.

If everyone were wavering on the brink of Catholicism, this would be a more dangerous place than Rome: for here the religion seems to satisfy all the needs of human nature and idealise all the relationships of life. In the little churchyard under the shadow of the church there is a beautiful stone figure of a weeping woman and underneath is written 'Here lie fathers and forefathers. Remember them in thy prayers and honour them and live up to their memory.' (The corpses are carried far out of the town where they injure no one.) Round the churchyard are the 14 stations of the cross describing the death of Jesus and his mother's agony, and appealing to the gratitude and pity of Christians not to fear their superstitious belief in the blood of Christ. Here the peasants will come and pray when the spirit moves them to commune with God and with their dead. It was here that I sat Sunday afternoon and listened to the weird music of the village choir, and read Comte's catechism of Positive religion! and thought it was much like the skulls in the frescoe on the church wall in front of me, over which the risen spirit was hovering, soon to disappear.

Still I am immensely interested in the Positive philosophy and shall make you read some of it when I return: there is a great deal in it which you would thoroughly agree with.

Monday: we got up at 5.30 and started off for one of the mountain tops and when we returned we found a large family of English women established in the hotel, (the first English we have met). However they were so disgusted at the absence of tea and mutton and the impossibility of making their wants understood that they promptly fled in the course of the afternoon. Now, Father, this is for you and Rosy: don't inflict on anyone else: give my very best love to the Cripps and believe me

Ever your devoted child

Beatrice Potter

Laurencina Holt's domestic life was not easy and her relationship with her children was a source of distress in later years. Mary, the adopted daughter of the Playnes, had just married a barrister named Erskine Pollock. Sir William Anson (1843–1914) was the first lay warden of All Souls College, Oxford, and the author of *The Law and Custom of the Constitution* (1886 and 1892). William Wickham (1831–97) was a barrister and chairman of Hampshire County Council.

Leonard Courtney resigned as Secretary of the Treasury in the Gladstone government in 1884: one of his differences was on the matter of proportional representation, of which he was a fervent advocate.

Summerhill
Nov. 84

Dearest Mary

Please let me know what I owe you: then I must make a rough calculation and send it you.

I had a delightful day after you left with Lallie and a company of boys: she is very admiring of Bill and talks rather wistfully of his taking so well to Public School life. Nevertheless she also is a proud mother and believes that Dick will someday be distinguished.

We had a most amusing journey up with an engineer officer (head inspector of the Board of Trade) whom she somewhat astounded by her views, social and political.

She got out at Woking; and I continued a hot religious argument with the said individual and we both nearly missed Vauxhall. As he handed me into a hansom he remarked, 'I *should* like to know my fellow traveller's name – you and that other lady are quite a revelation to me!'

I found out afterwards that he was a certain Colonel Holland, a hot Tory of the old school; but I left him discreetly in ignorance of my name. In fact he had lavished so much abuse on his superiors at the Board of Trade, Chamberlain and Farrer, that I thought it would be awkward if he found out our slight acquaintanceship.

In London, I called on Mary and found her and Erskine at home. The latter was *most* affectionate insisted on walking home with me: dilating on Mary's great conquest at [?Alton], where Lord Douglas was always looking round the corner at her, and Billy Wickham *would* have flirted with her if he had not feared a certain lecture from Lady Ethel. It was rather touching to see his fond admiration of her charms. He also entertained me with the charms of Sir William Anson 'who ought to marry'. Perhaps he thinks he will do me a good turn and give me a chance of marrying a 'gentleman'. He spoke very affectionately of you and Arthur and wished you could stay with them.

He seems rapidly taking a recognised position in the RP [Richard Potter] family as a good-natured, common, clever, uninteresting goose!

29

Clever in his means but 'goose'ish in his ends. Kate's party was a failure from a political point of view: *no* cabinet ministers! and a marked abstention of leading Radicals.

Leonard was down on his luck; evidently feels a cold shoulder from the ministerial party. I can't help admiring the man and his pluck; but I fear he is on the losing side.

I have had a most interesting visit from Clara Chamberlain who came on Monday and left yesterday. She is much happier than she was last year and very full of the trials and glories of her 'great brother'. Evidently the effect of my very temporary connection with him has been of a cementing and settling sort and he has settled down to the companionship of his sister and daughter. 'It's an ill wind which blows no man any good' and it is a comfort to have come out of a painful affair with the respect and affection of his family and to have done no harm anyway. She interested me much by telling me the family history and stories of 'little Jo' in the nursery and schoolroom.

Once when an adoring sister had offended him and implored forgiveness on any terms he insisted on her walking six times round the room with her hands clasped saying 'Please, Pray', 'Please, Pray.'

But the world won't always say that, as he seems *now* to be finding out.

She said her brother 'had a warm personal feeling for Mr Courtney and wished it were *possible* to work with him; but that evidently Mr Courtney was *really* a conservative.'

She talked a great deal about the 'real issues' between them and enquired anxiously whether Leonard intended to hold by minority representation.

I don't know whether I was meant to repeat it to Leonard? or whether it would do much good if I did? It seems to me practically impossible for those two men to work together; they differ really both as to means and ends.

His only chance is his 'crossing the floor of the house' if there should be a reformation of parties on the Radical and Whig lines.

I so enjoyed my short time with you and Arthur and the glimpse into Billie's school life. Your letter was *most* welcome [*five words illegible*].

Ever yours

Beatrice Potter

15 PP BEATRICE POTTER TO MARY PLAYNE

Arthur James Balfour (1848–1930), became the Tory Prime Minister in 1902: he was associated with Lord Randolph Churchill (1848–94) in his abortive 'Fourth Party' of Tory Democracy. Sir George Young (1837–1930), administrator and author, was interested in Irish and educational problems [*name not definitely legible*].

Henry Goschen was probably the nephew of George Joachim Goschen (1857–1907) the conservative statesman.

Before her marriage to Leonard Courtney, Beatrice's sister had worked as a volunteer rent-collector in one of Octavia Hill's housing schemes near Tower Bridge. Beatrice now proposed to take over this work, in which the collector also acted as a social worker. The block, Katherine Buildings, was a new one, five stories high, tenanted by families cleared from near-by slums.

York House, Kensington, W.
[?December 1884]

Dearest Mary

Thanks for your kind and very interesting letter. If you do come up to London, why not come here?

I could no doubt get you information about the cheap dining places if you really think of coming.

Of course the great excitement to the family is Leonard's resignation. All his friends have tried hard to dissuade him. I dined there Wednesday, met [?]G. Smiths, G. Young and Mr Balfour (fourth party) and another political couple.

There was a general gloom over the party. Leonard has lost his official manner and is much more conciliatory and humble. As far as *my* humble opinion goes, I believe that, *given* the man's hopeless hostility to the extreme left and his incapability of subordinating himself to their ways, he has done wisely to retire quixotically rather than be gradually shelved *after* he had lost his prestige as an independent and vigorous political actor. Now, at least, he has a *chance* of a position among that body of men who are discontented with the 'organisation leaders' of either side.

Englishmen like fighting men. If his nature will not allow him to work with, and propitiate a coming force, I think it is better to dare it and defy it openly – at any rate he gets the advantage of the antagonism which must be roused by any power? Don't you admire his speech? There is the eloquence of perfect integrity and simple-minded devotion to principle even if the principle be 'donkey's bridge' [*pons asinorum*] to most of us. And certainly the *critical* part of it is strong – if the scheme itself can be made acceptable to the vulgar mind.

He is evidently going to work hard in the vacation – I suppose now that he is in opposition the more formidable he can make himself the better – even if he does not succeed in carrying his object. He will never get back into a Radical government again unless they find him *too* unpleasant outside?

I went to breakfast there this morning. They were both in good spirits and full of fight; Leonard ever so much happier than before he made his speech.

Evidently it created a sensation in the House, and the marks of esteem

31

and admiration and regret from many influencial members had been very sweet listening to Kate.

I lunched with Miss Swanwick (Greek scholar) yesterday. Seventeen distinguished spectacled women, and two men – one already distinguished and young good-looking (Miss S.'s nephew).

The ladies went arm-in-arm downstairs and somewhat to my astonishment I found myself at the head of the table with the young man. Evidently he had bargained for a young and undistinguished female.

Afterwards I stayed on and had a long and interesting talk to the dear old lady by the firelight and she told me a great deal about her past life and literary labours and begged me to come and see her again. I go down tomorrow to stay with the Henry Goschens and meet the Meinertzhagens there.

On Tuesday I intend beginning my calls so as to get them over and settle down to some work.

Kate has some building she is taking over in the City, perhaps I shall take to that.

Certainly as a 'leisure person' one sometimes wishes that the state did organize labour and that one was stuck in somewhere and *had* to stick to it.

Your undertakings sound most promising. I hear that Polly is dining out every night at all sorts of fine places. None of the family see much of her – I think there is almost an unkind indifference to what is happening to her. She is looking sweetly pretty and very happy.

Ever yours affectionately

Beatrice Potter

16 PP BEATRICE POTTER TO RICHARD POTTER

At a public meeting in support of proportional representation Leonard Courtney was supported by the veteran Radical and freethinker Charles Bradlaugh (1833–91) who was at this time still engaged in his struggle to be seated in Parliament without taking the oath. His third election and exclusion occurred in 1894 and 1895.

Viscount Folkestone had been Conservative M.P. for Enfield 1885–86.

York House, Kensington, W.

[?1885]

Dearest Father

I know you will be anxious to hear about the meeting.

The hall was fairly well filled: the reserved seats with intelligent looking men of the professional classes, chiefly I should say members of the society; and the back part with cadaverous-looking mortals. The regular London, go-to-meeting, radical, odds-and-ends men.

Leonard's speech was debated with great impressiveness and enthusiasm – his personality as a speaker is wanting in 'personal magnetism'. It is not *synpathetic*. But it is *forcible*; it forces your admiration and attention, as the utterance of a strong and absolutely upright man. One feels, however slight his influence may be on the political life of his country – however complete his failure may be as a practical politician – still when he leaves this world, he can leave it with the consciousness that his influence has been entirely towards good in the way of *tone*. *That* after all is something in this life; to some natures the presence of this consciousness is more important to real happiness than mere worldly success and I believe Leonard's is one of these rather exceptional natures.

The meeting was disturbed by a wandering and rabid speech from the body of the hall, much applauded by the back section (of course against the resolution) and the bad effect of this was increased by a ridiculous rigmarole from Lord Folkestone. (A twaddling speaker is a dangerous friend to them – the subject does not admit of any but the clearest and most concise treatment.)

Bradlaugh then came forward and was received with great enthusiasm. *He* really carried the meeting. A powerful and direct speaker – speaks with the authority of an acknowledged leader to the men of his own class.

Just before the close of the whole thing a tall haggard, tragic-looking woman with a powerful and desperately miserable face got up and delivered a tirade against the grinding oppression of the London employer – and the cruel injustice of the non-representation of the most suffering portion of the community.

Thinking over the meeting as a whole – it was *grotesque*. There was no real unity of feeling or thought on the platform or in the hall.

Those in the reserved seats gave the subject a friendly and painstaking consideration from a theoretical point of view. They might have been listening to a new demonstration of a proposition to Euclid: the odds-and-end radical lot at the back were excited by any stray sentiment of independence or antagonism of anything and to anything and it did not much matter whether it was against the government or the platform. The mere *assertion* of Bradlaugh that he believed in it was sufficient to decide them; he would have had their support either way. The subject I fear, is at present a dead one: the educated classes are too cynical as to the possibility of foretelling the result of any scheme to take much interest in this one; the uneducated classes struggling for their bare existence, do not see in it any help towards solving that great problem – how to get more from those who have. That will be the practical question of the future – and success in politics will simply mean success in answering it or evading it to present satistfaction of the 'Have Nots'.

Let us hope, Father, that you and I take a cynical unjust view of the future, but just now it seems very dark to me – full of chaotic sadness.

Perhaps real work will bring about a healthier tone of thought and feeling. It is curious what an ominous feeling I have had lately – as if something terrible were about to happen – publicly or privately – though as far as we are concerned except for the Courtneys' ill success and Theresa's delicacy, things seem bright enough.

Certainly we are wanted here – to keep the family united and strong – if it were not for your inflence there would be a great deal of flying apart and consequent bitterness.

But this life has always seemed to me a painful struggle with one's own nature and outward circumstances. The inner and the outer friction varying inversely. Those with easy circumstances have more difficulty to control themselves, those with self-control have more to conquer in the world. Altogether it is a ghastly tragedy if all the pain ends in nothing!

Ever your devoted child

Beatrice Potter

17 PP   BEATRICE POTTER TO MARY PLAYNE [*incomplete*]

Beatrice's sister Mary was interested in the teaching of household skills to girls: Miss Cook seems to have been one of the instructors with whom she was asssociated.

In her autobiography Beatrice gave a long account of her relationship with the Barnetts. Samuel Augustus Barnett (1844–1913) was the rector of St Jude's, Whitechapel, and the first Warden of the East-End settlement, Toynbee Hall. He was much interested in housing and social reform. His wife Henrietta (1851–1936) was one of the founders of Hampstead Garden Suburb.

Among the fellow-workers to whom Beatrice refers was Ella Pycroft, with whom she came to share the management of Katherine Buildings. Ella Pycroft eventually became responsible for the teaching of Domestic Economy under the London County Council.

Beatrice was referring to the biography of George Eliot by John Cross.

York House, Kensington, W.
Friday [?summer 1885]

Dearest Mary

Thanks for your long interesting letter; I shall certainly take advantage of Miss Cook's instruction if you invite me in July. I see that want of practical knowledge will be my great failing in my own work; it is what curiously enough considering the 'long necessity', the poor themselves are extra ordinary deficient in, but we have an immense pull over them in knowing what to aim at and where to go for our information. I think it is this superior power of organising our time and our means which is about all we can teach them. They seem to me superior in other qualities which go to make up 'savoir-vivre': they enjoy their pleasures, and bear their pains, better than we do.

34

I have made great friends with Mr Barnett and am doing some visiting work for him which fits in with the looking up of tenants and their references. In that way I get to know all about the local authorities and local charities and am beginning to find my way easily in the East End. My fellow workers I thoroughly like . . . I suppose we shall want others eventually if we are to do more work amongst the people than mere rent-collecting.

The last two days I have been much pre-occupied with Rosy who is very poorly with a sort of gastric attack, I think a collapse after her dancing and rather unwholesome food.

I have asked the little doctor who attends her to call in Dr Gee to-morrow – I should like him to see her now she is ill, especially as Dr Tyrrel talks of a *possibility* of chronic kidney complaint. I almost fear she will not be able to come down for the dance – or at any rate for a very short time. Poor child, I fear she won't have a very merry life of it, with her constitution, physical and mental – and will always want looking after by someone.

Theresa is in a wretchedly 'poorly' condition – with a sort of chronic cold; otherwise the family are flourishing enough. Herbert Spencer is deliciously conscious about the 'Miss Evans episode' in G.E.'s life, now the rage of the reading world. Her letters are to my mind horribly dull and sanctimonious. One letter of Mr Carlyle's which appears in the book is like a delightfully fresh breeze and makes one feel the difference between the *true letter* and the unfinished, disjointed, but elaborately expressed essay cut into little notes.

H.S. says she was troubled with 'double consciousness' (which I suppose is a polite name for self-consciousness) and that that accounts for the lack of spontaneity and studied affect of her letters.

18 PP   BEATRICE POTTER TO RICHARD POTTER [*incomplete*]

Beatrice was always meticulous about money matters: at this time she was disbursing substantial sums to charity on behalf of her father.

York House, Kensington, W.
[?summer 1885]

Private

Would you make up my account with you and deduct the £50 sent towards L.C. [Leonard Courtney] expenses and invest the rest in Northern Pacific; if you think them safe.

I would rather the £50 were deducted straight off – and then I shall not touch the interest until it is paid up.

I intend to keep the interest of that £600 to give in lump sums as I did to Carrie Darling.

It is difficult for me to keep a definite account of my personal expenditure except my dress which comes to about £120.

But there are various items such as presents to my own servants, and other people's, travelling expenses and subscription to charities which I cannot clarify. Either they are for my own gratification or given in my position as head of your house. Up to now I have gone on the principle of saving nothing out of my allowance and giving all big presents out of my Capital account and keeping no very definite accounts. But now that I have taken to philanthropy as a pursuit and profession – you might let me know how much you will entrust me to spend for you. We might talk about it when I come to Stoke Nash. There are so many things connected with my work, like the Society for Befriending Young Servants, to which I ought to subscribe on account of the work they do for me – and certain others, as residents in London. My subscriptions for you this year will come to about £20, including your sub. to the reading room.

19 PP   BEATRICE POTTER TO MARY PLAYNE

This is one of the few surviving letters in which Beatrice referred to her ambivalent feelings for Chamberlain. She maintained friendly relations with his sister, Clara Ryland, as a means of indirect contact with him. Emma Lawrence had recently married Francis Buxton (1847–1911), Public Works Loan Commissioner and a member of the London School Board 1899–1904.

York House, Kensington, W.
[?late July 1885]

Dearest Mary

I suppose you will want a 'notice' of our last entertainment – tho' Kate no doubt will have written to you an account which will be better than mine – as my general impression coming home was a hopeless confusion – leading decidedly towards the negative.

The great man and I are painfully shy when we are alone and very anxious that nothing shall be noticed when others are there – a state of affairs which seems destined to lead to endless misunderstandings.

It certainly brings a good deal of unhappiness to me – and I can't imagine *he* finds much amusement in it – I should think one or the other of us would break off this enigmatical relationship this autumn, by refusing to see more of each other.

I shall let the matter end now and try and turn my thoughts to other things perhaps he will do so too, then the relationship will die from inanition. Rosie has come back not much the better for her stay at [*illegible*]. I am going to try rubbing her and generally study her the next fortnight so as to put Miss Darling into a good way. I don't think I could stand more than a fortnight's idleness and ease at present and shall really be glad to get back to hard work when I have got up my strength which has rather run down.

The Hobhouses are very happy and most agreeable. Henry always *is* so nice in the country.

Leonard Courtney's position now, I think is very pathetic. I never feel quite certain whether he is not right all the way round, except in his original belief in Democracy – but I am pretty sure he will be an absolute failure as far as success is concerned – and that will be a sad business, with their want of means.

If I have a spare Sunday in August and can get away on a Friday night shall I come and see you? Could I go back Sunday evening?

Monday and Tuesday will be such dreadful hard days when I have all the collecting to do. I made great friends with Mrs Francis Buxton (Miss Lawrence) on Wednesday and have promised to stay one Sunday with them, and am engaged to the Booths and Charles Rose for another.

I shall be curious to see when Clara Ryland asks me – that will tell me something.

Ever your affectionate

Beatrice Potter

I should very much like to know Kate's version, given to a 3rd person.

20 PP BEATRICE POTTER TO MARY PLAYNE

Lord Dalhousie (1847–87) was secretary of state for Scotland. Sir Charles Dilke (1843–1911) was a Radical politician of great promise and influence, who sat for Chelsea. His career was blighted by a sensational divorce in 1886 in which he was cited as co-respondent. His first wife had died; his marriage to Emilia Pattison took place under the shadow of the allegations made against him by Mrs Virginia Crawford, who claimed Dilke had 'ruined' her. Mrs Crawford was one of seven daughters of Eustace Smith, a wealthy ship-repairer. She was married to the middle-aged Liberal M.P. for Lanark, Donald Crawford. Another of his daughters was married to Dilke's younger brother, Ashton Dilke, a prosperous newspaper proprietor. The matter was complicated by the fact that Virginia Crawford's mother, Mrs Eustace Smith, had previously and briefly been Dilke's mistress – though this was not publicly known at the time. After two divorce actions, which revealed much sexual scandal, Mrs Crawford's allegations were upheld – though her lover, whose name she sought to protect, was in fact a Captain Forster. She and at least two of her sisters, including Mrs Ashton Dilke, were also involved in other clandestine liaisons. Dilke protested his innocence and claimed that he was the victim of a conspiracy, devoting much of the following years to an attempt to reveal the true facts and to rehabilitate himself politically. From the evidence now available it seems probable that Mrs Crawford was a perjurer, weaving a tangle of circumstantial evidence against Dilke. It has also been suggested that there was a conspiracy against Dilke, begun for obscure personal motives but abetted by a political rival. Joseph Chamberlain, much involved in the case, strongly asserted that there was 'an odious conspiracy' against his close friend and political ally. Though London was ripe with gossip against Dilke many of the facts were only unravelled years afterwards by investigators working on behalf of a committee which sought to clear Dilke's name. He subsequently returned to Parliament, becoming a strong champion of organised labour and a spokesman for advanced politics, but he never regained his former standing in public life.

York House, Kensington, W.

[?9 April 1885]

Dearest Mary

You see there is some truth in it. Your prophecy last year of that little woman has come true. Kate has been here and says everyone believes it to be true tho' not so gross a case as is made out by club gossip – which is too insulting in its details.

Lord Dalhousie told Leonard that 'Crawford could not have let it drop or condoned it.'

It is terribly sad – both for the men and the better members of Eustace Smith family. Poor Mrs Ashton Dilke, I believe she is dreadfully upset and has taken her sister away into the country. Sir C. Dilke funked it at first: gave up all his political engagements and attendance at the 'House' – but now he has written a letter to the association denying the charge and is going to have it out.

It is very disgusting. I am so glad to get back to my work and feel thoroughly rested.

It will be hard pull to make those Buildings successful – and one is badly handicapped from want of sufficient experience and power of disciplined work. I think I left Rosy in a satisfactory state and Miss Darling is going to continue the rubbing. If Father will only persistently make her feel that want of health is *not attractive* and *not* deserving of tenderness he will do her an immeasurable kindness.

But she will be slow in her improvement – because he will not really set his mind to take that line. I think her better disposition the last fortnight is a good deal due to the Hobhouses and Mr Spencer showing an evident dislike for her thinness and delicacy.

From the little things she has admitted I am more thoroughly convinced than before that she has for the last two years played the game of delicacy, only poor child, she has carried it too far and now genuinely regrets the extent of it. But she will always be tempted to fall back on the false ideal and may permanently ruin her life by it. It *is* very serious at her age and if it were to continue long, likely to embitter her. Father practically has that girl's fate in his hands, if he can be made to feel the cruelty of any other attitude but that of positive *dislike* to delicacy, contempt for it.

I think it is a good thing for her to have the position of hostess – for six weeks or so. It will give her some chance of rising out of herself.

I do so enjoy your letters and the glimpses they give me of a happy energetic life.

If I am able to come to you it will be for the 30th; as the other Sunday (23rd) you could not have me?

Next Sunday I go to the Booths. The 4th of September I go to the C. Roses. I have promised to go to the Francis Buxtons for the 2nd if they renew their invitation. I shall be anxious to accept it after that picnic.

So it is possible I may not see you. I think on the whole it is better for me to stick to my work and try to forget the past, and the sympathy of sympathetic sisters tends to keep useless feeling alive. During my fortnight's holiday I have thought very seriously about my own future, especially about my relationship to Mr Chamberlain and I think I have arrived at definite conclusions. I certainly do not intend to be forlorn.

Heaven knows there is enough work to be done, with one's thought and one's feeling to make life worth living even without personal happiness and who knows either how personal happiness comes to us. What are the conditions which bring it or destroy it?

One better be guided by a sort of sobered instinct.

I go to Kate early tomorrow and she leaves for Cornwall.

Ever yours affectionately

Beatrice Potter

21 PP   BEATRICE POTTER TO RICHARD POTTER

Leonard Courtney won Bodmin as a Liberal-Unionist candidate. Beatrice stayed at the Courtney house in Cheyne Walk, Chelsea, during their absence.

Beatrice, settling into her work at Katherine Buildings, found 'the pressure of work is rather too much for physical enjoyment'. The dirt, 'collective brutality' and moral squalor depressed her. But she found her new environment interesting and suggestive of 'many lines of enquiry'. (To Richard Potter n.d. ?August 1885) This subsequent letter is supported by an entry in her diary for 22 August 1885 in which she writes of paying a 'typical Jew' four shillings for three warning visits: 'If he gets the disreputable women out without further charge I shall have made a good bargain'. Colonel Henderson (1821–96) was in charge of the Metropolitan Police and a friend of the Potters.

The reference is to Daniel and Georgina Meinertzhagen and their son Daniel.

Not to be read publicly

Katherine Buildings
[?August 1885]

Dearest Father

I was much interested in reading your letter about Leonard. It seems certainly a pity he should not get the safe seat, but I suppose his fight in

Cornwall has gone rather far to withdraw. But Leonard is not an 'opportunist' in the best or the worst sense of the word.

I am here every day but Saturday and Sunday; and sleep here on Monday – I think it would really pay to sleep here oftener as it gives me a better chance of watching the tenants and finding out the bad ones. Our caretaker is a good man – *if* he does not drink – of that I have a slight suspicion. I mean to keep a steady look out.

Drink and immorality I have to wage an incessant war against – not always a pleasant occupation.

I have turned out two women this week for leading bad lives – and I am quite aware there are $\frac{1}{2}$ dozen more – I am not certain of one of my most attractive tenants. A young married woman, whose husband is a sailor and away, I found out is a well-known character among the sailors – and also a favourite with the inspectors at Leman Street Police Station.

The constable on duty watched 3 of his inspectors go upstairs. (This was confidentially told me by our policeman's wife).

The woman is leaving. I am afraid the police down here are far from immaculate – not better than the average East-Ender – in spite of the ultra-respectability of their uniform – and take advantage of their position of authority. I suppose most men do. Our reading room is a fair success – and we are starting refreshments supplied by the caretaker's wife.

I have written to Mary for information. There is any amount of work to do, if one had the strength and ability to do it. I soon get absorbed in a big interest like this. It is a wonder to me how Kate kept so clear of excitement and excited work – and felt content to stick to her own little bit without an attempt to master the whole question of artisan dwellings. No doubt she did her own little bit all the better for her quiet devotion to it – and one thing one admires immensely is the modest way she always kept in the background and refused to become an authority. Clever women who take up work so often like to be *en evidence*.

Please do not show my letters to *anyone* staying in the house – or mention anything I tell you – if I find out you do, I shall keep my experiences to myself!!! and don't for heaven's sake repeat about the policemen to Col. Henderson – or his family. I might get into an awful mess. I wish you would talk about *all* your daughters *except* me. If I am going to lead a working life by your side, it would be such a comfort to think of you as a deep well, in whose sympathetic interest one would rejoice – without trembling for one's reputation as a pleasant ordinary woman. An interested hard-working life, with *just a touch* of adventure! is so delightful, so long as one does not get stamped with that most damaging stamp 'Eccentricity'.

So my darling old Father, you must wipe me clean out of your conversation and then if Rosebud will only get strong and blooming and be prepared to take many of my duties in home and society life – I shall feel myself free to devote a good portion of time and energy to the 'question of the day' with what results time will show.

It is very pleasant having Maggie Harkness at Cheyne Walk. Our friendship has been a long-standing one and in spite of manifold failings on both sides it has never shown any tendency to break or even lessen.

I have just distributed the bunches of flowers to the children. Would you ask Miss D. [Darling] to write and tell the Co. [Company] to call for the two hampers. The flowers are immensely appreciated.

Dee and Georgie and Dan dined with me yesterday. They were very well and jolly. Dan has become the most model of school-boys. Have you heard any more about the Philosopher? [Herbert Spencer] I am glad the Lowick affair is clearing up. I don't feel quite comfortable about money matters with all those speculative investments. I can't help wishing you could see your way to fulfilling your promise of making up the married sister's portions and Kate's. They are all getting on in life and would be glad of the extra income – and their husbands are for the most part men of judgement who would be none the worse for a slight accession of responsibility in investing a small portion of what will be theirs eventually.

I think mother would have thought it a wise and right step to take – now that you are getting on in life.

What do you think? I suggest in a spirit of humility – as one who is more or less a spectator and uninterested. Of one thing I am quite certain: it is wisest to make up your mind what you *really intend to do* – assert it – and *stick to it*. More or less vague promises lead to mischief. Here I speak as an actual observer! You see, dearest Father – tho' I have taken to work, I do not intend to give up that position most prized by the genuine R.P. of giving advice to those I'm living with, more especially if they happen to be my superiors – and the 'Great Superior' of the R.P. family is doomed to get advice from all his children who have inherited his faculty of managing other people's business – one of his most useful functions in life!

By the way, how about [*three words illegible*].

Any branch of R.P. affairs interest me.

Ever your devoted

Beatrice Potter

22 PP BEATRICE POTTER TO RICHARD POTTER

York House, Kensington, W.

[early September 1885]

Dearest Father

My 'threat' as you call it was only a little joke. Do you seriously think that any one of your daughters *could* keep anything from you, even if she made up her mind to it! We have such an inborn love of retailing our experiences, nicely touched-up and finished off, in a way they seldom actually appear in this prosaic world, that we could not deny ourselves the practice of this our only accomplishment, especially to such a highly appreciative audience as our darling old Father! whose assumed clappings or sympathetic groans are heard (in our imagination) through miles of space. But like most mortals we want to eat our cake and have it – enjoy the chewing or our experience which results from the attempt to express them – and have them safely in our own possession untouched and undivided.

There is one experience I wish I could idealize like Mrs Carlyle and rid myself, even for one brief moment of the consciousness, through the dramatising of it – and that is the Presence of Insects. In a picture of the Lady Collector – this Presence should be given – for this continual physical discomfort and disgust is an important factor in her life – and is vicarious suffering of no mean importance.

I slept down there last night and am going down there again tonight as I find my presence has a marked effect in the comparative absence of noise.

The Buildings are undoubtedly healthy, but the facts of structure are against decent and orderly behaviour and must be counteracted by an amount of moral force no Company should count on getting in management and superintendence. It remains to be seen whether Miss Pycroft and I with the help we are able to attract are equal to giving it.

Then the Directors are not aware that the class *willing* and *fit* to live in dwellings where all the arrangements are so wanting in charm and privacy are much more limited than they suppose. There are a large number of applicants who refuse when they see on the one hand, and others whom *we* refuse (or regret it if we don't) when we see. Some of the best who come, 'go' and the worst we turn out, and this constant change means continual loss in bad debts and dirty rooms to the landlord.

But with the help of the reading room and work that is not paid for I hope we shall get a nucleus of steady-going tenants.

There is a decided tendency in the men attending the reading room to develop into a club and take the management and expense of it into their own hands – this body if it became strong and representative of the tenants would be a great help in forming public opinion.

In a tentative sort of way I don't see why one should not gradually use it as a council to consider questions of management and superintendence and any problems for the improvement of the society as a whole.

In these great blocks of working-class dwellings why should not one introduce quietly and carefully the principle of representative government through an [?autocracy] *tempered* by advice from a representative body.

42

All this may seem very theoretical but it is a very humble step in the direction of Corporation Housing. Until you get some corporate *feeling*, like there is in north-country working-class communities, you cannot introduce corporate ownership.

They must learn the difficulties of management, the problems they will have to solve, before they can be expected to manage and solve. Above all they must learn the absolute necessity of *strictness* of dealing of self-control and of patient temper – all qualities they are deficient in, are hardly sufficiently experienced in the art of management to realize that they *must* exist to a great extent in all successful men or bodies of men. On the other hand, they can help enormously by their knowledge of the facts of disorganised life, and the shrewder among them, by a sort of instinctive feeling as to the most natural way in which organisation may be developed; for they after all are not the *root* of the matter – are growing upwards – while we look down from a social plane of complicated structure, and are troubled with over-ingenuity.

This is the sort of 'idealism' with which I interest myself and keep enthusiasm alight, while I am battling with my own deficiency in strength and business capacity. But an 'idea' is often useful as a stimulus towards a much humbler aim than the one it implements: indeed with some natures it is almost impossible to do good work without it – even when it seems to the hardworking and practically successful onlooker a useless and pre-tentious waste of energy. Perhaps the most valuable workers fail to inspire others from the lack of it?

I have one of these useful persons dining with me next week. Miss Rosalind Townsend, the secretary of the Girls' Friendly [Society] in Whitechapel.

She is a philanthropic drudge and does excellently her own work.

She has found places for 10 of my girls. Indeed since their visit to York House there is a [?fine ardour] for domestic service [?raging] in the Buildings.

If it develops into a steady flame, it will [be] a first-rate thing for the individual girls who would otherwise go into low trades, and a good thing for the Buildings – as it connects the females with respectable and well-to-do life.

I am looking forward to my month's holiday – but of course my leaving you again before you return to London will all depend on you and Rosy.

Mrs Pelham has written to ask me when they can come. I have said the 26th Sept.

By that time the Playnes will be away? I wonder how you are all getting on?

Thank Alfred Cripps for his letter – I enclose his [*illegible*].

I would rather wait until October. I shall have more time to follow up the introduction.

If the Cripps care to read this letter they are welcome to.

Give them all my love.

I am so glad to know Theresa and her infants are well and happy.

Ever your affectionate daughter
Beatrice Potter

23 PP BEATRICE POTTER TO RICHARD POTTER

Returning from a visit to Rusland, where she had been engaged in a cultural stocktaking on aesthetics, philosophy and history, Beatrice was working on a report to the trust which owned Katherine Buildings: she was also beginning to keep systematic data on the tenants, summarising their domestic and working conditions.

While she was away she received a consoling letter from Mary Booth (PP) about her resolve to break with Chamberlain: 'the more I hear and read about that man, the more satisfied I am of the rightness of your decision . . . the pain of it is as nothing compared to what it would be if you had decided the other way'. Though Beatrice was convinced throughout this period that she could marry Chamberlain if she wished there is no evidence of any formal proposal from him. She seems to have been cool and discouraging when they met, more ardent and tormented when they were apart.

Gorman was the groom at The Argoed.

[?York House, Kensington, W.]
[? late October 1885]

Dearest Father

I was delighted to get your letter especially as I am in bed, rather knocked up with the mixture of pleasure and work. I went straight from the Lakes to Whitechapel and worked from 11 a.m. to 9 o'clock in the evening except for getting a hardly-cooked meal at a restaurant, slept there, and worked again from 9 to 1 o'clock and yesterday afternoon came back quite exhausted. But I am taking a quiet day and hope to be strong again to finish up the week's work and write a carefully-worded report to the Directors. As they are building another block, it is just as well they should have the benefit of our experience in working this one.

Miss Pycroft comes home on Saturday. We shall want 3 days together and I hope to come up on Thursday of next week by the 11 o'clock train.

I am so glad you have sent the married sisters £500 each. It is just now that an additional income will be of most use to them, with the strain of educating their families – in some cases – and the important crises in the lives of their husbands in others.

But I am quite clear now that I have thought over it (I had not before) that Rosy and I have no right to it – and, I should not think of accepting it

– trusting that my £500 will go to increasing the amount distributed *this year*. If Rosy is of the same mind that will make £250 more for each daughter. But of course, dearest Father it is yours not ours to dispose of.

We really have no more right to it than we have to the original £5000 settled on the girls. We both of us enjoy the luxury of your home and are liberally provided with everything we require; handsome allowances for our dress – Rosy has her horse and I give from out of your pocket to my charities (as your representative in the charitable world).

It would be ridiculous for us to be using the interest of money on the one hand and hoarding it up on the other. Of course when we marry, we shall be given the same amount as the others possess at that time.

I have not spoken to any of the sisters about it – so do not know their view of it – daresay they have none – as they would naturally think it was Rosy's and my business to think out the justness of it before we accepted it.

The only way, in a big family like ours to keep a thoroughly nice feeling about money matters – is for every member to be generously indifferent how much others get, and scrupulously fair how much they receive themselves.

I am not one of those who think parents should be tied down [not] to give where there is a want – without giving to all the others the same amount – a rigid view of *gifts* spoils their charm (if ever I marry a poor man and want £200 to get over some crisis – I shall accept it with gratitude).

I don't see why a Father should be denied the pleasure any more than any other friend or relation of giving in a spontaneous way to meet a special need. But with settlements, or any form of regular distribution of money, I think there should be care on the part of those who receive not to take more than is their right unless there is a special sanction of it (as there was in the case of Kate and Blanche) by the family at large.

Them's my sentiments! Lying in bed and formulating sentiments is a most agreeable occupation and I daresay I could cover another page if I did not fear to bore you.

Would you ask Miss D. [Darling] to let me know by return where Gorman bought those lamps for the stables and what they are called. I want to order two for the boys' club we are getting up. I fancy they were about 2/ each?

Also please ask her to send me a bit of my *terracotta* evening dress – to match. I send back Miss Cook's letter to Mary. Please thank the latter immensely for her.

I shall not start any refreshments until after I return. I should be glad of any letter you care to send.

Ever yours affectionately
Beatrice Potter

In her diary for 8 November Beatrice noted that the idea of forming an association for all agencies housing the poor was her own, though she seems to attribute
it to Barnett in this letter. She remarks that when she put it to Barnett she 'was
rather astounded at the way he took it up and wanted me to elaborate a plan
and to become the moving spirit'. She felt that each agency should collect
detailed statistics on its tenants and that a central office should organise care-
takers, superintendents and lady collectors.

Major Sharp was an officer in the Black Watch who had been stationed at
Kensington Barracks near York House: on one occasion he sent his pipers to
play at a garden-party for East-Enders given by Beatrice. Sharp, giving some
help with rent-collection, was so distressed at the condition of some tenants
that he offered to pay their arrears himself.

Professor Newton: probably Sir Charles Newton (1816–94), Keeper of Greek
and Roman Antiquities at the British Museum and professor of classical archae-
ology at University College, London. Edward Bond (1844–1920) was a wealthy
leader of the Charity Organisation Society and much interested in housing provision for the poor. He is said to have been the object of hopeless love by Octavia Hill and the model for George Eliot's Daniel Deronda. Professor Hill:
probably Alfred Bostock Hill (1854–1932) a pioneer in public health, later professor of hygiene at Birmingham.

Maurice Eden Paul, the son of the publisher Charles Kegan Paul, was a
medical student who worked with Beatrice – who thought him 'a queer youth'
(BWD 12 April 86) – and Ella Pycroft, with whom he had a dismal love affair
which ended when he broke it off just before their planned marriage. He later
became known as a Marxist writer and translator.

York House, Kensington, W.
[early November 1885]

Dearest Father

I sent your coat off immediately and trust you received it safely.

On Sunday we had the A. Cripps and Playnes to lunch – the Playnes
of course were very full of the Pollocks – and Mary delighted to get away
from the home. I think the feeling is not so bitter, but more contemptuous
– and the breach betwen them complete. According to Mary, Polly is
cram full of her parties and dinners she is going to give, etc. In the afternoon I had 4 men stayed from 3 to 7 o'clock. First a young Simpson, a
meek and mild pretty-looking young man, whom I had always put down
as a dancing idiot – but remembering Mr Barnett's admonition I plunged
into philanthropy and found out that he was a hard working 'Co-operator'
and he gave us a most interesting account of the progress of the Co-
operative movement in London.

He has half-promised to help me with the boy's club.

It is extraordinary how much earnestness there is in the air and how shy
everyone is of owning to it. Then entered the great Major Sharp! who is
now quartered at (I can't remember the name, I am so stupid today)

who was most good-natured and tried valiantly to enter into our conversation; and enquired particularly after a very 'great man' whom he had had 'the honour of meeting', whether I had heard from him lately, etc.

Professor Newton and Mr Bond (who had come to talk business) completed our party and we had a lengthy discussion on state education etc. Mr Bond stayed afterwards. He said he regretted he had shown my letter to the board as it had created a commotion, and delayed the final issue of their plans. They are not going to decide until Monday next, when they meet again. They have given way to us about some minor points on our own buildings.

Anyway one will have done one's duty and given them a fair hearing. I am working hard now at a book of all the tenants, past and present: with description of occupation, family etc., and statement of income and previous history – cause of leaving or ejectment.

I have undertaken to do the whole of it: and Miss Pycroft to give me particulars about her tenants. She and I are cut out to work with each other, as she has the practical ability and power to carry things through with steady work and I have more initiative and power of expression.

What I lack is method and strength – both fail me in critical times. I have a much greater *show* of ability than reality – arising from my audacity of mind and plausible way of putting things.

My dear old Father, I am a sort of weak edition of you! There is no doubt about it.

I enjoy the *planting* but don't care for the *tending*.

On Monday I went to bed directly I came from Whitechapel; Mary and Arthur dined with [*illegible*] and met the Alfred Cripps and Arthur.

They were particularly charmed with the latter: wished that *he* had only been their son-in-law.

Yesterday I again went to Whitechapel – and dropped in to the Barnetts to lunch.

Mr Barnett is very full of the idea of a conference which would result in an association of the agencies for Housing the Poor. About 160,000 persons live under the superintendence of these bodies: it seems a pity there should not be some inter-communication and exchange of memorable experiences and a sifting of it for public purposes. But the whole thing wants thinking out. Prof. Hill was dining there that night to discuss it. Mr Barnett thought they would be adverse to it. But it seems that the lady-collectors are deteriorating as a body – and that some stimulus is wanted to attract stronger and finer women into the profession – and Mr Barnett evidently grasps at any plan likely to furnish this.

I believe in the attraction of belonging to a *body* who have a definite mission and a definite expression, and where the stronger and more ambitious natures rise and lead. I admire and reverence women most who are content to be among the 'unknown saints' – but it is no use shut-

47

ting one's eyes to the fact that there is an increasing number of women to whom the matrimonial career is shut and who seek a masculine reward for masculine qualities. There is in these women something exceedingly pathetic and I would do anything to open careers to them in which their somewhat abnormal but useful qualities would get their own reward.

They are a product of civilisation – and civilisation should use them for what they fit and be thankful. At the best – their lives are sad and without joy or light-heartedness – they are now beginning to be deeply interested and warmed with enthusiasm.

I think these strong women have a great future before them – in the solution of social questions. They *are not* just inferior men. They may have masculine faculty but they have the *woman's temperament* – and the stronger they are the more distinctively *feminine* they are in this.

I only hope that instead of trying to ape men and take up men's pursuits, they will carve out their own careers – and not be satisfied until they have found the careers in which their particular form of power will achieve most. Mr Barnett is anxious if the idea bears fruit that I should be the secretary – with Miss Darling's help no doubt I could manage it. I have put in an advertisement for a man [as Richard Potter's valet] and shall hope to choose one whom Rosy will be able to *use* to get strength and beauty and charm of personal appearance etc.

My only desire is to make her independent of me and everyone else – with a sphere of real usefulness and power to influence for good. Certainly, health is the first requisite – charm of appearance, the most powerful of feminine instruments. And both are to be achieved by her with patience and determination and faith. It is a wretched day – and I am resting after the theatre yesterday.

Miss Pycroft, Mr Paul and I are going to a big place of entertainment for the working classes on Friday night in Lambeth.

Ever yours affectionately

Beatrice Potter

25 PP   BEATRICE POTTER TO MARY PLAYNE

Beatrice, distressed by Rosy's physical and psychological condition, had made up her mind at the end of 1885 to take her sister away for six months: her motive may in part have been an attempt to escape her own emotional problems. On Wednesday 25 November Richard Potter and Rosy returned from a month-long visit to Tadcaster relations. The next day, going out to vote in the general election, he was afflicted by a paralytic stroke. In these 'terrible days', Beatrice noted on 19 December 'the future does look gloomy indeed. Companioning a failing mind – a life without physical or mental activity – no work. Good God, how awful!'

Sir Andrew Clark, F.R.S. (1826–93), a fashionable and eminent doctor, was Chief Physician to London Hospital and a friend of Richard Potter. Mrs

Thompson became Mr Potter's steadfast nurse throughout his long illness. Longfords, near Minchinhampton in Gloucestershire, was the home of the Playnes.

Frederic Harrison (1831–1923), the Positivist author and reformer, had been a family friend of the Potters for many years.

York House, Kensington, W.
[?early December 1885]

Dearest Mary

Sir Andrew Clark was here yesterday. He advises us to move Father as soon as convenient and Father himself wishes to go and is becoming restless. He is quite bent on Longfords – and after that perhaps Penzance.

I am afraid it would mean bringing his new man who comes here tomorrow and I think Mrs Thompson – if he remains in the state he is he wants no persons unless your own servants would give their help which perhaps would not be satisfactory.

I should suggest his man slept by him and looked after him in the night – and that Mrs Thompson helped us in the day until he became more independent from them. A. Clark thinks Dr Tyrrel ought travel down with us and see him safely settled. He was up today and walking about but has gone to bed rather tired before tea.

I have written to the G.W. [Great Western] to ask for an invalid carriage, also whether Saturday is a bad day for travelling. Could you receive us then? Or would it be more convenient for us to wait until Tuesday? I think it very likely he will like to go on to a warmer climate and spend the next three months away from London. I thought that I would take a week's holiday while he was at Longfords if you could manage with him. No doubt Georgie would come down for part of the time.

I have had quite a number of callers this afternoon – H. Spencer and the Frederic Harrisons among others but they did not meet happily.

Ever your affectionate

Beatrice Potter

26 PP TESTAMENTARY LETTER

This note, written by Beatrice in despair at the collapse of her career, her frustrated passion for Chamberlain and her father's illness, was the second of its kind within a year.

As soon as Richard Potter was convalescent Beatrice took him to Bournemouth, where they were joined by a depressed Herbert Spencer. Taking her father to London for further medical attention after a relapse, Beatrice realised that their old style of life would have to be abandoned. He had been speculating heavily; though still very wealthy he had lost heavily and there was a need to economise. In the course of 1886 Beatrice had to tidy up his affairs; there was some strain with her brothers-in-law who felt that Beatrice, who had been acting in effect as her father's business associate, was in part responsible for the losses. One necessary economy was the giving up of York House in 1887. During these months, when she could see no prospect of continuing her career, Beatrice distracted herself by reading English mediaeval history.

> Longfords, Minchinhampton, Glos.
> Jan 1st 1886

In case I should not outlive the year – I will that the £600 odd in Father's and his executors' hands should be given to Leonard Courtney towards the expense of his political career. That the diamond brooch should be given to Margaret Hobhouse to whom mother really left it. The rest of my properties may be distributed, every member of the family taking that which they care for most in the following order: Mary, Kate, Georgie, Theresa, Blanche, Margaret, Rosy (I don't suppose Lallie would wish for anything). To Margaret Harkness I leave any books that belong to me and any of the pictures in my room she cares for.

In case my diary books and letters are not destroyed I earnestly beg they may be destroyed immediately on the reading of this – and I should prefer that no one had looked into them.

I am grateful to all those who have shown me love and interest.

If Death comes it will be welcome – for life has always been distasteful to me.

If Father be still alive I should earnestly advise him to beg the Courtneys or some other couple to have him – and if Rosy is wise she will press for this. The position of an unmarried daughter at home is an unhappy one even for a strong woman: it is an impossible one for a weak one.

> Beatrice Potter

27 BUL   BEATRICE POTTER TO JOSEPH CHAMBERLAIN

A trade depression had created serious unemployment in London. Evident distress and the street demonstrations promoted by the Social Democratic Federation led to the establishment of a Lord Mayor's Fund for relief. Beatrice sent a short article to the *Pall Mall Gazette* (18 February 86) on 'A Lady's View of the Unemployed'. On the editor's letter of acceptance she scribbled: 'a turning point in my life'. Chamberlain noticed her comments, based upon her East-End experience, and wrote a letter suggesting a meeting to discuss the problem. This initiative came after some months in which they had not met. The Courtneys had arranged a country picnic in July 1885 to bring Beatrice and Chamberlain together and it had been a failure. He had behaved so arrogantly that, recalling the occasion on 12 May 1887, Beatrice remarked that the day would 'always remain engraved on my memory as the most painful one of my life'.

Kildare, Bournemouth
February 29th [1886]

Dear Mr Chamberlain

I am very sorry that I am out of London and unable to benefit by your kindness in wishing to see me. I fear you would find my experience of East End life superficial and wanting in a thorough knowledge of detail, even of that district in which I have been interested.

The Local Government Board must be in possession of a mass of information; I wonder whether you are satisfied with it and think it in any way conclusive?

If it is like in character to the evidence taken by the Mansion House Committee on the 'Unemployed', it will be a hopeless mess of general impressions and biased collections of facts.

We practical workers have one great desire, perhaps because we are too ignorant to appreciate the difficulties of the undertaking, and wish that there should be some systematic investigation of employment on the one hand, and of labour on the other.

I suppose the former would be comparatively easy: and we think that the large and impartial body of schoolboard visitors might be used, with very little extra expense, to work out a map of labour in all districts of London which could be constantly under revision. It is the only organisation I know of, which grasps the whole of London, and the individuals forming it would [not] be influenced by professional bias or by any form of personal interest.

Otherwise, if we are left in the dark as to facts, I do not see how we are to prevent huge iniquities like the Mansion House Fund, which do an incalculable amount of mischief and throw back work for years. The public will not be convinced without an authoritative statement of facts.

Neither do I see how the question of the housing of the poor is to be dealt with without an official knowledge in each district of the amount and character of employment, and the number of persons within the district who seek it.

The present legal provision to rehouse $\frac{1}{2}$ the population displaced is curiously arbitrary; and in wading through the Blue Books, I did not see why they chose *that* fraction in preference to any other fraction of the whole. Practical workers would say, it should vary according to the neighbourhood.

I fear I have taken your expressed wish to know more of my experience too seriously. I am glad to say my Father is better tho' still in a delicate and dependent state.

[?Believe me]
Yours very sincerely
Beatrice Potter

51

The reply from Chamberlain on 28 February was dignified and friendly. (PP) He assured Beatrice that he valued her opinions and repeated his well-known doctrine of 'Ransom', insisting that 'the rich must pay to keep the poor alive' and proposing a 'rather crude' scheme of public works to provide manual employment.

Beatrice responded with the letter printed below. On 5 March (PP) Chamberlain again tried to reason with her: 'I thought we understood each other pretty well. I fear I was mistaken'. Beatrice, he urged, was 'quite wrong in supposing that I under-value the opinions of an intelligent woman . . . Neither do I dislike independence of thought'. On the point of substance he declined to accept her 'discouraging' objection to public works. 'If men will starve rather than dig for 2s. od. a day, I cannot help them, and I cannot greatly pity them.' His touchy assurance that no further answer was needed stung Beatrice to yet another of her 'final' notes on the relationship: 'And so the agony of two years ends'. (BWD 6 March 86) To Chamberlain she sent a short answer in a letter which he destroyed; this extract comes from a copy in her diary. 'Now I see that I was right not to deceive you. I could not lie to the man I loved. But why have you worded it so cruelly, why give unnecessary pain? Surely we suffer sufficiently. Thank God! – that when our own happiness is destroyed there are others to live for. Do not think that I do not consider your decision as *final*, and destroy this.' She had inferred from the correspondence that Chamberlain had not genuinely sought information but had sought deviously to discover whether her opinions would suit him. Once again Mary Booth consoled her (13 March 86 PP), saying that 'a man so dependent on flattery, so impatient of contradiction; so sensitive with regard to his own feelings; and so indifferent to those of others must be at bottom a very poor and shallow creature. You are well rid of him'.

Beatrice's agony, however, was far from over. She continued to follow Chamberlain's chequered career closely. In April 1886 she was in the gallery of the House of Commons to hear his speech of resignation from the Liberal government – which was soon followed by the Liberal Unionist breakaway from Gladstone on the issue of Home Rule for Ireland. She also kept in touch indirectly through her friendship with Clara Ryland and his daughter Beatrice. She went up again to hear him speak in Birmingham in June 1887. She still felt sufficiently 'weak and romantic' to invite him for a visit to The Argoed on 30 July 1887. When he arrived she burst out with a breathless declaration of love which left her feeling humiliated. He wrote to her afterwards, on 3 August, saying that he had no desire to 'surrender a friendship which ought to be good for both of us'. (PP) He admitted that he was 'solitary and reserved' but he wished for her 'regard and sympathy': there was 'no reason why you should be ashamed of feelings which are purely womanly and for which I have nothing but gratitude and respect'. His formal manner infuriated Beatrice who scrawled across his note 'This letter, after I had, in another moment of suicidal misery, told him that I cared for him passionately'.

From this time she slowly came to terms with her feelings but though the wound healed the scar remained.

Kildare, Bournemouth
Wednesday morning [early March 1886]

Dear Mr Chamberlain

You take me out of my depth! When I leave London, and the peculiar conditions surrounding the working-class there, I am lost in a sea of general principles and crotchets.

As I read your letter, a suspicion flashed across me, that you wished for some further proof of the incapacity of a woman's intellect to deal with such large matters – and if it will in any way serve you, I willingly offer up my thoughts and give that which is needful!

I agree, that 'the rich *must* keep the poor alive': always supposing that the continued existence of that section of the poor, with liberty to increase, is *not* injurious to the community at large. And this depends primarily on fact, of which *I* have no knowledge. You say, that distress is 'universal and increasing': is it permanent? If the depression be due to a permanent relapse from the abnormal activity produced by the extension of railways etc., depopulation is to some extent a necessity?

But if the lack of employment be temporary, then the question resolves itself into the easier one: will the public works you propose, (1) attract the labourer out of employment, (2) and will they keep the labourer in good, or even in fair, working condition, so that he will be available for true productive service after the bad time has passed?

My objection to public works within the Metropolis was not based on this larger question, upon which I have no right to an opinion, but simply on the conviction that the conditions to which the state laborer would be subjected within the Metropolis, would be hopelessly demoralising. And I feel very strongly about this.

Then as to the nature of the work offered. I think there would be two practical drawbacks – and I will illustrate one by a curious Whitechapel fact. 135 men applied to the Relief committee. They were offered street sweeping at 2/- a day, 3d extra for each child. Only 15 accepted, 11 of them went to the work and 4 staid.

We were much disgusted, and thought this an additional proof of the demoralisation of the East End 'out-of-works'. But in discussing the matter quietly with the men attending the reading-room of Katherine Bldgs, we found that there was a strong feeling among the better class that unless they were prepared to sink permanently into the ranks of unskilled labour, acceptance of this work would injure their chance (some said irretrievably) of gaining employment in their own trade.

I confess, I do not attach much importance to this objection: still it was urged by men who were themselves in work.

To my mind the grand difficulty would be enforcing good quality and sufficient quantity of work. It would seem to me to require almost a slave-driving body of overseers.

53

And my impression is – I admit it is not founded on experience – that if the work were sufficiently unskilled *not* to enter into competition with other employment, it *would* be degrading in its nature, likely to become a sham test, and by the subsistence it afforded would increase a parasitic class injurious to the community.

I fail to grasp the principle 'something must be done'.

It is terribly sad that 100 men should die of semi-starvation, should prefer that slow death to this almost penal servitude offered them by the workhouse. But quite apart from the community's point of view – if by relieving these 100 men you practically create 500 more – surely the unsatisfactory nature of these men's lives outweighs in misery the death of the smaller number (and this statement overlooks the possibility of emigration).

Death after all is a slight evil compared to life under many conditions?

We hear the death-groans of the 100, we do not hear the life-groans of the 500, until it is too late!

If I am wrong, it is not from shallow hard-heartedness, but because I have not sufficient intelligence to see how the measure you propose would work towards the good of the community or even towards the happiness of the class you would relieve.

I must have expressed myself badly in my last letter. I did not mean, the thorough investigation of low-class society in London to affect immediately the present question of want of employment – but – I think I won't explain myself – you will say it is a crotchet!

I have no proposal to make: except sternness from the state, and love and self-devotion from individuals, a very old and self-evident remedy.

But is it not rather unkind of you to ask me to tell you what I think? I have tried to be perfectly truthful. Still it *is* a ludicrous idea that an ordinary woman should be called upon to review the suggestion of Her Majesty's ablest minister! especially when I know that he has a slight opinion of even a superior woman's intelligence in these matters (I agree with him) and a dislike to any independence of thought.

I have long ceased to believe in free-will in ideas. We may sacrifice our thought, as we may sacrifice our life, but so long as we live and so long as we think, we must live and think according to our own natures? – even tho' *we* may be the first to admit that our constitution is diseased and our thought wrong. You will say, this is not relevant to 'Public Works for the Unemployed'. It is only a feeble excuse for daring to obey you – in the spirit as well as in the letter!

Believe me

Yours very sincerely

Beatrice Potter

These two letters were undated but there were probably written in early March, while Beatrice was still at Bournemouth with her father. It is not clear which is the first and which is the second. They refer to the preparations for the survey that Charles Booth proposed to make of labour conditions and poverty in East London. It has been asserted, though there is no evidence, that Booth originally planned his work to refute an allegation made by Henry Myers Hyndman (1842–1921), the leader of the Social Democratic Federation, that one quarter of all Londoners earned too little to keep themselves in proper physical health. Booth's study – which eventually appeared as 17 volumes on *The Life of the People in London* – concluded that over 30 per cent were 'in poverty or in want', though only 8 percent were 'in chronic want'.

Beatrice was asked to join Booth's Board of Statistical Research and attended the first meeting, noting in her diary for 17 April 1886 that 'it is just the sort of work I should like to undertake, if I were free'. Though she was committed to caring for her father, in the course of 1886 an arrangement was made for her married sisters to relieve her for about four months in the year for work and holidays.

The 'papers' sent by Booth may have been the preliminary analysis of occupations published in *Journal of Royal Statistical Society* 49. 314–444, 1886. There is an extended account of Beatrice's involvement in the survey in *My Apprenticeship*.

Kildare [Bournemouth]
[?March 1886]

Dearest Mary,

Thanks for your sweet letter. I return the papers sent me by Charlie. I have read them through carefully and *no* criticism to make that is unfavourable! I think that in actual inquiry many of the lines marked out in the classification of the lower classes will be rubbed out and others traced – but they will serve as well as any others to begin with.

In my humble opinion the scheme is very ably worked out in theory – it remains to be seen how far it can be carried out in practice.

I should almost divide instructions for the Board, describing in detail the methods and aims of the inquiry, from a general description of the work which would serve as a credential for inquirers, to give employers and other authorities as an outline of the undertaking.

Of course it is a huge business – but if one or two districts or trades could be *thoroughly* worked out, I think the results would be sufficiently valuable and interesting to attract into its service some of the organisations that grasp London as a whole, and make as complete a *contemporary* record possible. *That* I think would be the great difficulty with a body of individual inquirers to keep the various sections *contemporary*?

In any case even if the end be not arrived at, the work will be interesting and *educating*, and give the workers some idea of the scope and direction of an inquiry which might be undertaken by a more powerful body or even by the government.

Beatrice and Mary Booth described Chamberlain as the 'Great Cham'. The barely legible initials G.Cm may be an abbreviation for this nickname, or may simply be 'J.Cm'.

York House, Kensington, W.

[?early March]

I think I shall have some time in London and should be glad to undertake my own school board district and the London and St Kath. [Katherine's] Docks with the Royal Albert further down [?to run under the same Cd].

That will be in Tower Hamlets? at least St Kath. Docks not the Royal Albert.

It would certainly be an advantage to have a short resume of the objects of the work without specifying details of classification?

How I shall enjoy a talk with you – for I feel lost in an ocean of ignorance – and you no doubt could show me the mainland!

Kate is here full of political gossip and very eager. She and Father talk politics, all day long. What a nightmare the whole thing is!

I read with some satisfaction the debate on Public Works; I was amused to see that [?the G.Cm] made use of *my* 'instructive little anecdote' as *The Times* calls it – and he took exactly the same line that I did in my letter. His anger is still, to me, quite incomprehensible.

I fear I shall never think of him as you do. I shall always be ready to help him even if I *do* get a slash in the face in return. I have no proper pride!

I am enjoying my reading – am at present fascinated by 'Piers Ploughman' – how delightful that early allegory of a young nation, relieved with biting satire on the manners and morals of his kin! But Father is talking on and on about the personalities of politics – and my head whirls with the supposed grumps and capers of the political personages – I hardly know what I am writing, except that I am writing to someone I love very much and would like to give a good kiss.

My love to Charlie. I suppose when the scheme is sanctioned by the Board we shall have it in typewriting. It would be useful, for each inquirer, to have the proposed classification for their own identification.

Ever yours affectionately

Beatrice Potter

31 PP BEATRICE POTTER TO RICHARD POTTER

Sir John Hibbert (1824–1908) was Liberal M.P. for Oldham and held minor office under Gladstone: he was interested in Poor Law problems. Sir Bernhard Samuelson (1820–1905) was an ironmaster who was Liberal M.P. for North Oxfordshire at this time. He was a pioneer of scientific education. William

Stebbing was Leonard Courtney's oldest friend. They had been called to the Bar together in 1858; Stebbing was assistant editor of *The Times* in 1870 when Courtney was writing editorials for the paper. He died in 1925.

Maye Dilke was the widow of Ashton Dilke and Virginia Crawford's sister. Mrs Robert Harrison was another of the Smith sisters, married to the brother of Frederic Harrison. Captain Forster was the officer with whom Virginia Crawford had a clandestine relationship.

The 'little thing' to which Beatrice refers was a planned essay on Social Diagnosis. Two long studies drafted in the autumn and winter of 1886 on 'The History of English Economics' and 'The Economics of Karl Marx' were circulated to relatives and friends for comment but neither was presented for publication.

York House, Kensington, W.
[?early summer 1886]

Dearest Father

So you have not missed me you naughty man! I, who left quietly in the train, hoped that you would immediately telegraph for me back again.

Still there are advantages in not being actually indispensable and I confess to enjoying myself in this wicked Babylon. Yesterday I dined with the Courtneys with Mr Hibbert, Mr Stebbing and an old member, Sir Bernhard Samuelson.

There was no news, except a little scandal about the Dilke and Crawford case, which is coming on the end of this month. It is rumoured that unless there is some arrangement by which Mr Crawford will get his divorce quietly there will come out some very unpleasant stories about Sir Charles Dilke and also about the Eustace Smith family. It is also said that Mrs Robert Harrison and a Captain Forster are dragged in but that her husband is standing by her. I wonder whether it was the man she met at our house.

I saw the wretched little Mrs Crawford yesterday – she is still staying with Mrs [Ashton] Dilke.

There is no political gossip except that all the leaders of the Liberal party are disgusted with the state of affairs except Mr Gladstone who seems to be in fine spirits. Mr Hibbert is decidedly in favour of Home Rule – also he seems to me to be in favour of everything the Birmingham school proposes – only he dislikes the tone! What a convenient word tone is for *tacking* purposes.

Leonard is very staunch to his principles – I am not quite sure that his time may not come – if he were only 10 years younger.

Evidently the extreme radicals are looking to the disendowment of the Church as their next great cry – the parson's wives have enraged them with their attempt to use church doles as bribes – and they intend to turn the tables by offering the whole property as a right instead of a small part as a charity. There seems to be a general feeling that someday or other the great man of Birmingham will settle the Irish question backed by a fierce Democracy – and that he will turn out to be a second Cromwell when Irish despotism in English affairs can no longer be tolerated.

I am taking my first Italian lesson today. I am also trying to make some arrangement by which I can go in for a course of reading which will bear on my work, under proper supervision. In the quiet time I shall have while you are regaining your strength I should like to learn how to write English! It would be useful to me when I wished to describe my small objections to more state interference in my own little province.

[?K. Cron] and Mrs Dilke are coming to tea today.

Please tell Arthur [Playne] that the Hobhouses are very anxious he and I should go to dine with them on Thursday and I have accepted. On Friday I dine quietly with the Farrers; on Saturday we have a family party – on Monday I go to Bournemouth – I hear from Miss E. [Emily] Hobhouse there are some very good houses to let. I am quite looking forward to my turn with you there – scampering about the country and fire-light pondering over the divine Dante – and a 'poor little work of my own' which Mary will despise and see reflected in my complexion.

Now darling Father, goodbye and believe me to be (will Mary let me say!) your devoted child.

Beatrice Potter

32 PP BEATRICE POTTER TO RICHARD POTTER

Marie Souvestre (d. 1905) was headmistress of a fashionable school at Fontainbleau, to which Rosy had been briefly sent, and then of a similar establishment at Wimbledon. She was a member of the Positivist, Freethinking and Radical sets in London. Beatrice thought highly of this 'brilliant and irreligious Frenchwoman', who seemed in some ways a model for herself. On 14 September Beatrice noted that she was now 'a working woman, who has lived through passion and pain – and come out of it with only a kind of hopeless faith'. Yet she still felt (BWD 28 September 86) 'the old craving for love and devotion', although the decision to renounce Chamberlain had resolved her dilemma 'between the life of individual work and the life of womanly love'. (BWD 9 October 86) Edward Lott was Herbert Spencer's closest and lifelong friend.

Beatrice Henderson was the daughter of the chief commissioner of the Metropolitan Police.

York House, Kensington, W.
[?October 1886]

Dearest Father

Thanks for your sweet letter. I am so glad you are so happy and well and that everything is going on as usual.

I have been busy seeing all my friends and hearing about the old work.

I found Ella Pycroft very much overdone and worried so I thought the least I could do would be to offer to take her work for a fortnight and let her go home. So I shall return from Bacup about the 7th of November and plunge into the East End which will be interesting as a contrast. On Friday I ran down to Birmingham to see Clara Ryland who is taking charge of Highbury and the children while the great man and his daughter are away: I thought it would be a good opportunity. She is very happy in her married life, but is very indignant with the physical ills of matrimony and is coming round to the conclusion that women are not *all* made for marriage!

The three little girls are delightful children: the eldest is fast growing up into a pretty young woman with a quiet shy disposition.

Clara and the baby are coming to stay with us the end of January. On Saturday I dined with the Booths and Rosy can imagine how we talked, until 12 o'clock, I think. Sunday morning, Maurice Paul came to see me and unburdened his sorrows, poor boy. I think he is really devoted to Ella and may possibly win her in the end.

In the afternoon that clever French woman, Mrs Souvestre came, and stayed for 3 hours. She says that the most striking thing in English society compared with French is the number of distinguished unmarried women – that they form a distinct class.

Of course as she implied that your charming daughter was included among them, I swallowed the bait and thought her a true observer! She is a very strange person and I am interested in her. The evening I again spent with the Booths.

Yesterday I journeyed down to Brighton to see the philosopher. I found him much better than when I saw him in London. He seemed fairly happy tho' terribly oppressed with the irregular beats of his pulse. He and his London landlady have taken a house at Brighton – so he will not come to live with us at Bournemouth but only to stay probably for Xmas.

He is writing his autobiography and has left his other work.

He was delighted to see me and gave me a most affectionate welcome and enquired with much interest about you and Rosy.

His friend Mr Lott died in September, leaving his affairs in great disorder. He speculated in American railways and now his property is realised there, [it] is hardly sufficient to keep his daughters. It seems a strange fatality that induces men of a certain age to prefer investments which everyone but themselves recognises to be dangerous and to persist in them inspite of repeated warnings.

I saw a letter from Mr Lott's partner, saying that some years ago he had noticed that Mr Lott's judgement was failing and that he had implored him to put his money at once into safe gov. securities – but of course Mr Lott thought himself the exception that proves the rule; and his poor daughters must suffer for it.

Tell Rosy that I met Mary [*illegible*] and Beatrice Henderson at the Barnetts. Mary was looking very ill; Beatrice very blooming; she said she was going to write to Rosy, and would come and stay with us in the Spring at The Argoed. She could not get away for the winter. I met Maye Dilke the other day. Mrs Crawford is staying with her and is then going to Munich to live with Louise Gugenberger (née Bevington) I am sorry, because the latter is a nasty-minded woman; but I fear Mdm [*illegible*] does not intend to do the real penitent.

Ever yours affectionately
Beatrice Potter

33 PP BEATRICE POTTER TO RICHARD POTTER

'Miss Jones' returned to Bacup for a brief visit, staying again with the Aked family, to whom she revealed her real identity at the end of the visit and was delighted that she had given no offence by her previous reticence. In a second letter, printed in *My Apprenticeship*, Beatrice reported to her father that living with these humble people 'Has given me an insight, that it is difficult to express in words, into higher working-class life – with all its charm of direct thinking, honest work and warm feeling; and above all, taught me the real part played by religion in making the English people, of Dissent teaching them the art of self-government, or rather serving as a means to develop their capacity for it!'

Henry du Pré Labouchere (1831–1912) was a journalist who founded *Truth* and, next to Chamberlain and Dilke, the outstanding Radical in the Liberal Party, sitting for Peterborough from 1880 to 1906.

[Bacup]
Monday [October 1886]

Dearest Father

I should have written to you before but I have had a wretched cold in my head which has made me feel stupid. I nearly always have a cold once a year and generally about this time – but it is unfortunate that it should come in this visit.

Still it has not been bad enough to prevent me from going out among the people. Mrs Aked with whom I am staying, is a jolly little Yorkshire widow delighted with an excuse for going again into 'company', so we spend most of our time in and out of the neighbour's cottages and my old friends insist on entertaining me. I can assure you 'Miss Jones' is a very popular person, and her London experiences draw quite an audience in the cottages in which she takes her 'tiffin'. I am more and more charmed with the life of these people: with their warm-hearted integrity and power to act together.

I suppose they are more or less a picked people from among the working-class – if not this section of the working-class are more refined in their motives and feelings than the majority of the money-getting or money-inheriting class. There is a total absence of *vulgarity* – no attempt to *seem* what they are not, or to struggle and strive to be better off than their neighbours.

Then it is the only society I have ever lived in, in which religious faith really guides thought and action and forms the basis to the whole life of the individual and the community.

The religious socialism of the dissenting communities is very remarkable – each circle forming a 'law unto itself' to which the individual must submit or be an outcast. And so all the denominations work heartily together (except the Church which has here, on account of an ill conducted parson, a contemptible position) the censorship on private morality is very severe and a man or a woman cannot well escape it without leaving Bacup.

One sees here the other side of the process, though, which bad workmen and bad characters were attracted to the large towns.

In East End life one notices this attraction, here one can watch the out-casting force. In the first place there are no odd jobs in a community which depends on *Production* industries. Unless a man can work regularly he can't work at all. Then a bad character is socially an outcast, the whole social life depending on the chapel and the 'Co-op'.

The 'Co-op' furnishes amusement and interest, free of expense to all members, and through the system of deposit account, a mutual insurance company. Trades unions are not strong here – class spirit hardly exists because there is no capitalist class, those mills which are not companies, being owned by quite small men of working-class origin and connected with working people.

Then, as a great many working people have shares in the Co-operative mills, there is a recognised desire to keep down wages which reacts on the public opinion and makes even the non-owning men take a fairer view of the employer's position.

Three or four mill hands were smoking here yesterday (my cigarettes!) and they were saying that the workers were getting the best of the bargain just at present. There is no bitter, uneasy feeling among the inhabitants of Bacup, for there is practically social equality; perhaps this accounts for the total absence of vulgarity.

But one wonders what will happen, when the religious feeling of the people is undermined by advancing scientific culture – for tho' the 'Co-op' and the chapel at present work together – the secularism of the 'Co-op' is half-unconsciously recognised by earnest chapel-goers as a rival attraction to the prayer-meeting and the bible-class.

One wonders where all this *feeling* will go and all the capacity for *moral* self-government.

I think the safeguard will be in a strong local government with considerable power to check individual action; and of a sufficiently small area to allow of the working people taking a real every-day part, and not only at election times.

For the active regulation of their own and their neighbour's lives will be far less dangerous than theorising and talking about things of which they have no knowledge. They have been trained to *act* but not to *think* – and in talking over 'imperial politics' they do not show much intelligence – for their one leading idea seems to be to cut down salaries!

Labouchere seems the principal favorite – a man they would not tolerate as a 'Co-op' or 'chapel' leader.

I am glad to say the better class stick to Mr Chamberlain! the G.O.M. [Gladstone] has sadly gone down since I was last there – some good Liberals saying openly that he is on his dotage.

Tomorrow, if my cold is well enough, I am going to Manchester with the draper's daughter to buy goods from the Manchester warehouseman. Ask Mary to let me know how you got over your journey; my address is Miss Jones, 5 Angel Street, Tony Lane, Bacup.

Ever your affectionate child
Beatrice Potter

Will you send this letter on to Mary Booth?

B.

34 PP BEATRICE POTTER TO MARY PLAYNE

Despite a gap in her letters until the Spring of 1888 the course of Beatrice's life is well-documented in her diary and her autobiography. She was still under great emotional strain, writing of her 'duplex personality'. (BWD 10 December 86) Within her, she felt, there was a 'nether being . . . despondent, vain, grasping, gloomily religious' whose 'natural vocation and destiny was the convent' – a description which closely paralleled her judgement on her mother's character. The other personality was 'an enthusiast for Truth'; this intellectual trait 'has its life and origin in my sensual nature'. Beatrice feared that an attempt to satisfy her physical instincts would lead to the destruction of her intellectual independence. The conflict, she wrote, 'was long and terrible because my *Will* was unresolved which side to elect'. At last 'womanly dignity and reserve side with Fate and forbid the inroads of Passion'.

When she was at home with her father she worked at her reading and writing. When she could get away to London she worked hard at her researches in London's dockland, diverting herself with dinners given by family and friends where she kept up her connections with political and social notabilities.

In April her old friend Herbert Spencer named her as his literary executor: 'he can think of me as the child whom he has trained', Beatrice noted, 'and also as the woman he would have loved had circumstances differed'.

In the summer of 1887 she wrote an article summarising her work with Booth, which appeared as 'Dock Life in the East End of London' in the *Nineteenth Century* for October 1887. This 'promising beginning' was 'work I have always longed to do, the realisation of my youthful amibtion'. (BWD 30 October 87) She had now decided to investigate sweating in the tailoring trade and Sir James Knowles (1831–1908), the editor of the *Nineteenth Century*, encouraged her to prepare two more articles, one on Sweating and the other on Co-operation.

Beatrice was thinking much about her chosen role of working spinsterhood in the course of the year. When she met the secularist and socialist orator Annie Besant (1847–1943) who had just joined the infant Fabian Society she reflected that 'it is not womanly to throw yourself before the world. A woman in all the relations of life should be sought. It is only on great occasions, when religious feeling or morality demand it, that a woman has the right to lift up her voice and call aloud to her fellow mortals'. (BWD 27 November 87) At this time Beatrice was opposed to the growing feminist movement and to demands for female suffrage.

Beatrice thought Arthur Dyson Williams, the barrister whom Rosy married, a sickly, depressed and purposeless man. It was at the house of his wealthy relative, Mrs Williams, that Beatrice first met Joseph Chamberlain at dinner. Hadspen, near Castle Cary, was the Hobhouse home; Parmoor, near Henley-on-Thames, was the home of Alfred and Theresa Cripps.

[?Devonshire House Hotel, Bishopsgate Street, E.C.]
[?9 April 1888]

Dearest Mary

Rosie is engaged to Mr Williams. She was so wretched that at last she decided to write to him which she did of her own accord from Hadspen without telling anyone. Of course he responded and on Saturday she came up to Kate's and saw him. I saw them both yesterday and Rosie looked very handsome and happy. (By the way, she has come [?all right] on Saturday!)

She is still in a state of doubt as to whether the family will think him good enough. He is very much in love, and is a good respectable young man. God preserve him! I am glad of it; as I think the risk of Rosie remaining unmarried, or marrying some undesirable character was terrible to think of. We think it better not to write to Father until the journey to Parmoor is over. There Rosie and Mr. W. will write, and Kate.

It is of course not a brilliant affair; but knowing Rosie, I must say I think it is suitable. Her happiness will always be doubtful – her nature is so thoroughly emotional.

So all in all I am to be the old maid of the family! Never mind. I intend to be a credit to you, notwithstanding.

Ever yours affectionately
Beatrice Potter

35 PP BEATRICE POTTER TO MARY PLAYNE

Lady Cavendish was married to the younger brother of the Duke of Devonshire; another brother, Lord Frederic Cavendish (1836–82) was the Chief Secretary for Ireland, murdered by Fenians in Dublin. Four days previously Beatrice had dined with the Chief Rabbi and other leading members of the Jewish community to discuss her impressions of the garment trades: to pursue her research she had disguised herself and secured a temporary job as a trouser-hand. She described this experience in two articles appearing in the *Nineteenth Century* in September and October 1888. Her unexpected conclusion was that sweaters were more the victim of the commercial system than exploiters who caused its miseries. The articles made her much sought after as a social lioness: 'if notoriety be desirable as a step in a literary career, you have achieved it'. (BWD 29 December 88)

Joseph Chamberlain had gone to the United States for a long visit, there becoming engaged to the daughter of the U.S. Secretary for War. 'It is good for me', Beatrice noted. 'A gasp – as if one had been stabbed – and then it is over . . . it comes now that I am happy and settled in my own working life.' (BWD 26 April 88)

Beatrice used the Quaker-run Devonshire House Hotel, near Liverpool Street Station, as her London *pied-à-terre* after York House was given up. The Playnes had gone on a long European tour.

Devonshire House Hotel, Bishopsgate Street, E.C.
April 30 '88

Dearest Mary

I wonder how you and Arthur are getting on and whether Arthur is finding it *tolerable* and you enjoyable?

It will be very interesting to get your first letters.

Rosie is getting on alright with her young man and has settled down to a comfortable state. I don't think they will be married this year; and probably he will settle at Cardiff to try and get work there; as he has many connections. Of course it is not a brilliant marriage and one will be anxious, until he has got a little business. The life with Rosie will not be invigorating.

My time here is drawing to a close – I leave on the 12.17; and I think I am quite satisfied with the little bit of work I have done. Anyway I have now got material to work on and shall settle down to an existence of writing and reading which I always enjoy. I went to tea the other day at *The* Devonshire House. The Cavendishes certainly are the most simple of aristocrats. Lord Edward has a sort of working-class gentleness about him; but he is just the sort of man that gets on with us – and his wife is a jolly good-tempered woman with a reverential admiration for middle-class philanthropists! She is bringing Lady Frederic down here to tea someday and is evidently quite prepared to be very friendly if one had time for it.

The society I have been seeing most of is Jewish of all classes – and on the whole I like and respect them – I almost think I have a *true* feeling for them.

Chamberlain's marriage was placarded all over the city on Friday and an account of it was inserted in all the morning papers. No one knows what to make of it; as he has not contradicted it; but the mother of the young lady indignantly denies it. Anyway he seems to have a knack of publishing his affairs to the outer world – of behaving in such a way hat reports get about.

I saw Lallie at Cheyne Walk last week. She summoned me to talk over Father's affairs, but tho' I tried to lead her on she could only say she thought everything that I did was 'muddled'. Apparently she and Maggie [Hobhouse] have been talking over the family expenditure and as Kate implied they think it ought to be controlled. Hitherto Daniel [Meinertzhagen] has told me we might spend £4,000, which would leave a balance of some £500 of interest from capital. I spent £3,700 last year. Naturally it is a very delicate matter for me, if there is really some feeling in the family that I am not to be relied on. So I wrote a very careful letter to Lallie as eldest sister offering either to reduce the expenditure to what Daniel thought fit; or to have the accounts audited by one of the sisters every six months, or to fall in with any plan proposed. When you return to Liverpool, you can talk it over with her. *She* would make a very good auditor if she would not mind the trouble; and as far as I am concerned I should be delighted to do anything that would set the family mind at rest – for any suspicion about money-matters is hateful and really I think that I have been very careful not to spend an undue amount on my pleasures or interests, considering that I *have* had complete control.

But anything for a quiet life!

It is very hot and I am very tired and longing for the country. Life to me is becoming everyday more interesting and more impersonal – but at times one feels weary and lonely. I suppose one must pay one's penny and take one's choice – and on the whole, so long as I can get 4 months freedom for observation, I am satisfied with my existence – as satisfied I think, as most married women. Write to me at The Argoed.

Ever yours affectionately

Beatrice Potter

36 BUL   BEATRICE POTTER TO BEATRICE CHAMBERLAIN

In the summer of 1888 Beatrice had bouts of suicidal depression. She was afflicted by guilt and remorse after she had inadvertently exaggerated her 'trouser-hand' experience in her evidence to the House of Lords Committee on Sweating. The impression she gave was that she worked twelve hours a day for three weeks. In fact she only worked two full days in one sweater's shop and odd hours in others. An explanatory letter to the press, drafted but withheld on the advice of Charles Booth, is included in her diary.

On 28 August she noted that 'the consciousness of a special mission – of duty to society at large rather than to individuals is constantly present with me in my better moments – ceasing only when I am a prey to passion, self-consciousness or egotism'. In December 1887 she returned to the same thought: 'Every woman has a mission to other women – more especially to the women of her own class and circumstances' whether they were struggling young girls, hard-pressed married women or disappointed spinsters. Yet she resisted Booth's suggestion that she should go on to do a special study of women's work. She had already set her mind on studying the Co-operative movement.

On 7 November when the news of Chamberlain's marriage was made public Beatrice noted: 'The blow has come. I thought the nerve was killed'. Four days later Beatrice Chamberlain sent a friendly letter saying that 'I have been so oppressed by secret-keeping, which is hateful to me, as to be quite unsociable'. By the end of the year Beatrice was calmer, noted in her customary review of the year on 29 December that the 'black cloud' had at last rolled away, having burst 'with a terrific flash and peal of thunder'. She felt that she could face the new year 'with courage and hopefulness'.

Richard Potter had now moved to his new and last home at Box, Minchinhampton, only a few minutes walk away from the Playne's house at Longfords.

[?Box House, Minchinhampton]
[?summer 1889]

My dear Beatrice,

I am so sorry that I shall not be here next week: so that I fear that I shall miss seeing you. I must hope for some other time and opportunity.

You will thoroughly enjoy a good holiday: one almost needs time of freedom from responsibility between the intervals of duty and work of one kind or another – to take stock of oneself and the world.

If you should ever think of joining the working sisterhood (I mean work in its narrow sense) remember that you have an elder sister already established in a flourishing business. In my heart of hearts, I wish you a different fate: but a working life has its attractions: it is full of interest and sympathy – and has its own peculiar charm of an impersonal view of life – anyway it has the element of growth – one is always growing in a working life. Remember, *that if ever you need it*, it is one of the keenest pleasures of life to help those who are beginning the same life-journey as oneself: but you have so many near friends and relations that you will be independent of your faithful old maid friend.

Beatrice Potter

37 PP   BEATRICE POTTER TO FREDERIC HARRISON

In the Spring of 1889 Beatrice took what she afterwards decided was the unwise step of signing an anti-suffrage manifesto drafted by Mrs Humphry Ward (1851–1920), novelist and social worker. When the energetic suffragist Millicent Fawcett (1847–1929) attacked the manifesto Beatrice was asked by Frederic Harrison and James Knowles, 'as the woman most fitted', to reply. 'It is criminal', Harrison wrote on 7 July, 'to bury your talent in a napkin in Monmouthshire.' (PP) On the same day Beatrice noted in her diary that she had insufficient standing to enter the controversy and that she was not sure of her ground: 'I am not certain whether the strong prejudice I have against political life and political methods does not influence my judgement on the question of enfranchising women'.

Mrs Creighton was the wife of Mandell Creighton (1843–1901), then professor of ecclesiastical history at Cambridge and later Bishop of London. Beatrice became a close friend of the Creightons: she thought him 'the most elusive intellect, as well as one of the most lovable characters I have ever come across'. (MA)

[Box House, Minchinhampton]

[9 July 1889]

Dear Mr Harrison

I fully appreciate your most kind estimate of my ability to answer Mrs Fawcett but I cannot agree with it – either on public or personal grounds. From a public point of view I feel that the insignificance of the work I have done does not justify me in entering the lists as a leader against a woman of Mrs Fawcett's standing; I am also a little sceptical of the value of purely controversial writing – more especially when the question is not a pressing one. Personally, I am anxious to keep my hands free, for I think it will enable me to do better work in the future. One dislikes to talk about future plans that may never be fulfilled: but I can tell you, in confidence, that I look upon all my present study of labour and trade questions as leading up to an investigation of the industrial and social position of women in England which I hope to begin some 8 years hence(!) when I am sufficiently educated to undertake it. If I emphasise my hostility to the suffrage movement by controversial writing I shall injure my chances of getting information and I shall also detract from the value of my conclusions. I felt this when I signed the Appeal; and I am not sure that, from the point of view of personal usefulness I was wise in doing it.

Pray forgive this 'personal explanation'; which would be out of place if I did not venture to regard you as a friend.

Surely Mrs Ward and Mrs Creighton – the writers of the original appeal – ought to answer the objections. Mrs Fawcett's reply is easily answered from a controversial point of view and her melodramatic illustration of our wickedness turned against herself – since she refuses the suffrage to married women – exactly the class of women who suffer from the injustice of the Divorce, Guardianship and Probate laws. But the much deeper and wider question of the relation between the sexes, which is involved in the exclusion of the suffrage to married women is one which needs very serious consideration: and I should hardly like to see it treated in a purely political and controversial way.

Yours truly

Beatrice Potter

38 HRCUT BEATRICE POTTER TO RICHARD GARNETT

Richard Garnett (1835–1906), Keeper of Printed Books at the British Museum, proposed to cast Beatrice's horoscope. In a subsequent letter acknowledging a book on astrology, Beatrice confessed herself glad that she could not understand the astronomical symbols: 'I should spend the rest of my life brooding in the labyrinth of occult information'. She reported that she was born between 3 and 5 o'clock in the morning of 22 January 1858. 'Can you make me into a satisfactory existence through these facts?', she asked Garnett. 'If so I should be eternally grateful, for I have spent 31 years in trying to be one and have failed. Some very perverse and contradictory influences must have presided over my nativity!' Sir Spencer Walpole (1839–1907) was a civil servant and historian; Justin McCarthy (1830–1912) was an Irish politician, novelist and historian.

The Argoed
Monmouth
[?1889]

Dear Mr Garnett

I will reveal, with pleasure, my age for the sake of gratifying my egotistical curiosity and satisfying my innate belief in the marvellous: only the exact time of my birth is a matter of delicate research, and I have not yet found the proper sources of information.

I am in search of books which treat of the social and industrial conditions of this country. Are there any historians of this century besides Spencer Walpole and Justin McCarthy? My object is to read up general trade and Labour facts sufficiently to give me a setting to the study of the Co-operative Movement. If you can think of any such books I should be most grateful for a list.

Miss Harkness is at present in Manchester but is returning to London very soon. I believe the 'bottomless pit' has been filled up or safely bridged.

I am glad you have been the one person to get 'something' out of a Liberal Unionist meeting – I have never been so fortunate – except a weary burden of oft-repeated platitudes.

Yours very sincerely
Beatrice Potter

39 PP BEATRICE POTTER TO CATHERINE COURTNEY [incomplete]

In the course of 1889 Beatrice became more interested in the working-class movement, beginning with her belief that the Co-operatives might provide an alternative to the 'catastrophic overturning of the existing order' preached by the Social Democratic Federation members she met working among the unemployed in the East End. She travelled unchaperoned and she mixed freely with workingmen. Among those who helped her particularly were John Burnett (1842–1914), former general secretary of the Amalgamated Society of Engineers and after 1886 the Labour Correspondent to the Board of Trade; Benjamin Jones (1847–1941), manager of the Co-operative Wholesale Society in London and a friend for many years who also assisted in the Booth enquiry; and J. J. Dent (b. 1856), a former bricklayer who was secretary of the Working Men's Club and Institute Union and, in 1893, became Co-operative Correspondent to the Board of Trade. The introductions and encouragement provided by these three men served to ease the path of Beatrice into archives and meetings.

In March 1889 she visited the Creightons at Cambridge and there had a long talk with Alfred Marshall (1842–1924), the professor of political economy who was emerging as the outstanding economist of the day. Marshall supported Booth's suggestion that she should concentrate on women's problems and insisted that she was not qualified to write on Co-operation, on which he considered himself something of an expert. Beatrice amusingly described the discussion in her autobiography. In mid-June she attended the Co-operative Congress at Ipswich, at which Marshall spoke, but she realised that she was being led on to consider trade union questions. The idea of democracies of consumers had to be complemented by democracies of workers, which could enforce standard rates of pay and reasonable hours. She was slowly moving towards a socialist position, believing that society might be reorganised by the application of the scientific method animated by a religious spirit.

Beatrice was sensing the new mood of militancy which found expression in the London dock strike in August, led by Ben Tillett (1860–1943) and John Burns (1858–1943), a former engineer and leading member of the S.D.F. who became the outstanding leader of the 'New Unionism' which organised the unskilled trades. On 29 August, noting the 'solidarity of labour' in this decisive strike, she remarked that the East End had 'roused itself to struggle against the evil growing in its midst'. This 'revelation', she confessed, had 'shown me that in my desire to master commercial and financial facts as the only key to the labour problem I was guided by a true instinct: that in my capacity to master these facts will rest my power to influence for good the condition of my people'. It was with this insight that she went to Dundee where, at the Trades Union Congress, the new militants were beginning their effort to throw over the dominant craft union leadership and to commit the trade unions to independent political action in place of the tacit alliance with the Liberals through the Parliamentary Committee of the T.U.C. She was, however, still more sympathetic to the 'veterans' than to the rebels, who were on this occasion outvoted 177–11. She objected to 'the filthy personalities . . . envy and malice' of the socialist speakers – 'a crew of wretched reputation . . . beardless enthusiasts and dreamers of all ages'.

Henry Broadhurst (1840–1911), a former stonemason, was the dominant figure on the parliamentary committee of the T.U.C., a Liberal M.P. and holder of a minor government post in 1886. Robert Bontine Cunninghame-Graham (1852–1936) was a colourful and eccentric figure. Though elected as a Liberal M.P. in 1886 he was a convinced socialist. He was a famous traveller and author. Beatrice described him as 'a cross between an aristocrat and a barber's block . . . a poseur but also an enthusiast, above all an unmitigated fool'.

In the latter part of 1889 Beatrice felt frustrated by the need to spend so much time with her father. When she was unable to make progress with her Co-operative research she toyed with the idea of writing a novel, as some 'more dramatic representation of facts than can be given in statistical tables – some way of bringing home to the hearts of the people, rich and poor, those truths about social organisation that I may discover'. (BWD 30 September 89) At the end of January 1890 she found herself 'helpless before this ever-accumulating mass of facts which must be carved into some intelligible shape – exiled from the world of the thought and action of other men and women. London is in a ferment: strikes are the order of the day, the new trade unionism with its magnificent conquest of the Docks is striding along with an arrogance arousing employers to a keen sense of danger . . . The socialists, led by a small band of able young men (Fabian Society) are manipulating London Radicals . . . I, from the peculiarity of my social position, should be in the midst of all parties –

sympathetic with all, allied to none – in a true vantage ground for impartial observation of the forces at work . . . I dimly see the tendency towards a socialist community in which there will be individual freedom and public property instead of class slavery and the private possession of the means of subsistence of the whole people. At last I am a *Socialist!*'

In October 1889 Beatrice had read the recently published *Fabian Essays in Socialism*, telling her Co-operative acquaintance J. C. Gray (1854–1912) that 'by far the most significant and interesting essay is the one by Sidney Webb: he has the historic sense'.

The Argoed, Monmouth
[September 1889]

My dear Kate

I had a most interesting but a very exhausting time at Dundee. I stayed in the same hotel as Burnett, Broadhurst, Shipton, Crawford and the other leaders and was admitted under Broadhurst's wing into their private smoking-room, so I saw a good deal of the green room preparations for the Congress platform. The feeling of antagonism to almost hatred of the socialists among the leaders is very apparent: and they are, I think trying to tighten the trade union organisation so as to keep out 'wolves in sheeps clothing'. I doubt the wisdom of this policy of exclusiveness; it is better to let the enemy in and fight him. Owing to this hatred of the socialist leaders the feeling was for the Dock Co.s [Companies] against the men (among the leaders) tho' of course they do not say so. Burnett was rather contemptuous at this want of patriotism; and also at the 'lobbying' that went on to secure the return of the old Parliamentary Committee.

Broadhurst is a regular middle-class philistine; but he knows his men and is delightfully self-complacent at this success in dealing with them. Cunninghame-Graham was there buzzing about like a stingless wasp.

One amusing scene: breakfast table; Broadhurst on my right beaming over ham and eggs and the memories of yesterday's victories; Cunninghame-Graham on my left, poring over the proofs of the *Labour Elector*.

Broadhurst to me: 'Yes, we are now going to take our stand against the intrusion of amateur revolutionists. They blame me for being exclusive; they have made us ten times more exclusive. We have cleared the platform of them: next year we will clear the press-table of intriguers' (all this loud enough for C-G. to hear).

Cunninghame-Graham to me: 'Burns is a grand fellow, different from these slaves in broad-cloth who call themselves trade unionists'. This is said with a wave of the hand towards Broadhurst – wave of the hand which gradually settles down on a loaf of brown bread which C.G. supposes to be common property but which unfortunately happens to be specially prepared by Mrs Broadhurst for her great man's over-taxed digestion. The 'slave in broadcloth' watches with indignation the delicately tapering fingers of the anarchist clutch hold of his personal property and with the large perspiring palm of an outstretched hand Broadhurst grasps the whole thing – loaf and fingers.

'No, Sir, not that', he roars, 'that's my *own* bread, made by my *own* wife, in my *own* house and brought here in my *own* portmanteau, *that* you cannot have.'

C-G withdraws his hand with the apologies of a gentleman; looks unutterably disgusted in this contact with the perspiring palm of the Bourgeois slave and wipes his aristocratic fingers tenderly on fine cambric.

'Not my bread; I would rather he took my reputation than my bread', mutters the dyspeptic but somewhat gluttonous Broadhurst.

2. Sidney James Webb

July 1859 – November 1889

The family into which Sidney Webb was born on 13 July 1859 plainly belonged to the anonymous lower middle class, living in genteel but cramped and ugly style, never in danger of sinking into the dreadful abyss of London poverty but expecting little from life beyond domestic security. It was not the kind of family which kept papers or made social contacts by whom it was afterwards remembered. The Webbs kept themselves to themselves and even in later life the children were discreet about their childhood. That was in part, perhaps, typical of their class. In part it was certainly a matter of temperament. Sidney's brother Charles, a year and a half older, and his sister Ada who was born in 1865, were as reticent as Sidney about personal affairs – to a degree which in all three cases suggests some repression of memories as well as a strong sense of privacy. It is also possible that there was un unrecorded crisis in the family which prompted discretion.*

There is thus no picture of the Webb home in any way comparable to the vivid account Beatrice left of her childhood experience and feelings: the only coherent account of Sidney's background and early years, indeed, was written by Beatrice herself in 1926 and included in the introduction to the second volume of her autobiography, *Our Partnership*. Even this honest but sympathetic description of his humble origins passed over many questions that the biographer is bound to ask. It said almost nothing about the relations between his parents or between them and their children, except to stress that these 'little folk' were modest, honest, personally kind and full of public spirit, 'the last word in respectability'. Both Edward Pease and Bernard Shaw, who met the elder Webbs, made similar comments on their characters, and there is no doubt that Sidney was in all respects a dutiful and affectionate son. Beatrice's account is equally vague on another issue that was important in the raising of any child in the second half of Victoria's reign – the religious climate of the Webb household. Almost all Sidney's close associates in the early years of the Fabian Society were

---

* There is a suggestion that there was a 'missing' elder sister. According to Ada Webb this first-born child was called Minnie and she died young of scarlet fever. Against this must be put the claim of the Canadian descendants of a Mary Elizabeth Webb that she was the sister of Sidney Webb, though no documentation has yet been found to support this assertion or the implication that she was separated from her family as a result of a domestic scandal. There are some fragments of evidence which make it impossible to dismiss the claim out of hand, although they are not sufficient to permit anything more than speculation. The relevance of the issue is twofold. First, it might help to explain the reluctance of Sidney Webb to discuss his childhood and his apparent destruction of some family letters. Secondly, a likely date for a domestic upheaval coincides with the period in which Charles and Sidney were sent abroad for two years and Ada was away at a boarding school – a most unusual action for a family of this relatively low social status. A note of all information on this matter has been deposited in the Passfield Papers.

72

young men who had passed through a searing crisis of faith, struggling to free themselves from the pressure of strict Evangelical parents yet retaining the impress and impulse of Evangelicalism even as they secularised it into political forms. All that is known of Sidney's childhood is that his mother had a 'broad Evangelical feeling' and that she took the children from one church to another to find a preacher 'free from sacerdotalism'; that Sidney once spoke of knowing the terrors of Hell as a child; and that by the time he was twenty he had become an agnostic. Similarly, his father is reported to have been a political Radical, who worked for John Stuart Mill in the Westminster election of 1865 and was a great reader of political pamphlets and newspaper, and to have sat both upon the local Board of Guardians administering the Poor Law and upon the local vestry, or municipal authority. Neither Beatrice nor Sidney made any comment on what may have been a significant and early patterning of his political ideas: there are simply two hints – one in a letter by Sidney and another in his sister's recollections – that there may have been a good deal of argument in the Webb household. Even its financial affairs seem somewhat obscure. Beatrice spoke of a family income of between three and five hundred pounds a year, which was a reasonable competence by the standards of the day, but his father left several thousand pounds when he died in 1892 and Sidney himself had managed to accumulate substantial savings by that time, after only ten years in the civil service. The Webbs may not, as Beatrice put it, have had 'any desire to climb up the social ladder, or to enjoy luxury', but they lived as well as they wished and seem merely to have had a puritanical disinterest in creature comforts.

It is against this obscure background that the few known facts must be set. Sidney's mother, Elizabeth Mary Stacey, married fairly late, probably in her middle thirties. Her father was a ne'er-do-well from a moderately prosperous Essex family of farmers and ship's captains, who was sent to Australia as a remittance-man. Once there he died. His four children were shipped home and distributed among relatives. In 1848 one of Elizabeth's brothers-in-law (probably the husband of her sister Fanny, who kept in close touch with the family and had the Webb children down for holidays at Long Melford in Suffolk) advanced the money on which she opened a millinery and hairdressing shop at 44 Cranbourn Street near Leicester Square. Sidney's father may have come to the shop originally as an assistant, marrying the somewhat older proprietor in 1854. He was undoubtedly the frailer partner, overshadowed by his vigorous wife. The son of a reputedly prosperous innkeeper at Petham in Kent, his occupation has been variously reported as hairdresser, shopkeeper, tax-collector and public accountant. In fact, marrying into the business, he seems to have looked after its books, then to have helped out his neighbours with their accounts and picked up commissions by collecting debts. The main source of income was the shop: its profits were plainly enough to allow Sidney's father to indulge his interests in unpaid public work and his enthusastic membership of the Volunteers.

Mrs Webb brought up her children with sensible if frugal habits and good manners. Sidney was always considerate and polite, though he had no graces of speech or movement. He had the nasal *h*-dropping voice of an inner-Londoner and a tubby frame with short arms and legs: he was, Beatrice frankly admitted, 'homely and plain' and almost ugly. Such shortcomings of appearance were offset, however, by an unusual tolerance which eased his personal relationships and by an extraordinary stock of abilities. He and his brother were sent for a time to a decent middle-class school kept by a Mr Pincher round the corner in

St Martin's Lane. In 1872, supposedly advised by one of her customers, Mrs Webb despatched Charles and Sidney to Neuvéville, near Neuchatel, to learn French: her expectation, justified in the case of the older boy, was that this would fit them for careers as corresponding clerks in a business house. The boys then went on to Wismar, on the Baltic near Rostock, where they spent almost two years in the home of a Lutheran pastor learning German.

Returning home in 1875 Sidney took a clerical job in a colonial broker's in Water Lane in the City where he stayed until he was nearly twenty-one. He was clearly bent on bettering himself and well aware of his talents, for he spent almost all his leisure attending evening classes to such effect that he became a notable prizewinner. At the City of London College between 1876 and 1880 he scored first-classes in French, German, Arithmetic and Bookkeeping, and characteristically won the Medhurst Prize for Proficiency, Punctuality and Regularity. The same kind of record marked his efforts in the examinations of the Society for the Encouragement of Arts, Manufactures and Commerce, where he carried off the first of a series of money prizes which amounted to more than £450 by the mid eighties. At the Birkbeck Literary and Scientific Institute, which he attended in 1879 and 1880, the story was again the same, as he widened his interests to economics, history and geology.

In 1881, anxious to leave the uncongenial world of commerce, Sidney sat the civil service entrance and came second in the Lower Division, securing his first appointment as a clerk in the Inland Revenue. A year later, sitting for the much more difficult Upper Division, he came second again; disliking the post he was offered in the War Office he declined it and repeated the examination in 1882. Again he came second, this time to an Oxford graduate named Sydney Haldane Olivier (1859–1943) who became his colleague when they were appointed to the Colonial Office. His thirst for self-improvement was not slaked by such successes. The Colonial Office work was not overly demanding and he had ample time to read. He turned to legal studies when, having been offered the Whewell Scholarship in International Law, he had to refuse because the Colonial Office would not give him leave to go to Cambridge. Instead he set about a succession of external London University examinations which resulted in his being called to the Bar in Gray's Inn and to a law degree in 1886.

At a time when a public career was only just becoming open to the talents Sidney had proved the epitome of the scholarship boy, rising by a combination of capacity and industry to a responsible position – an experience which decisively shaped his own conception of the ladder of opportunity when he came to play an influential role in shaping educational policy. He had remarkable powers of application, even for the dullest of subjects, the knack of rapid reading and clear exposition, and above all an astonishing memory for detail. His earliest surviving essay, included in the circulating record of the Pro and Con Club (a corresponding literary society he formed with a few friends), was written when he was eighteen; it was on the work and prospects of the London School Board.

Through the years when Sidney was finding his way to a career his opinions were also maturing. He joined a number of the literary clubs and debating societies which catered to the aspiring intellectual proletarians of London, providing improving talk for little or no expense. In 1879 be became an active member of the Zetetical Society, where he first met Bernard Shaw, and begun to display his skill at marshalling arguments. At this point in his life he seems to have been a conventional Radical in politics, a freethinker in religious matters, a follower of Herbert Spencer in sociology and of T. H. Huxley in science. His political economy was fairly conventional, based on the neo-classical school. He does not seem to have been directly affected by the revival of the socialist movement which began after 1880 and was linked to agitation about Ireland and the land reform theories of Henry George: his progression to socialist convictions was slower and more cautious than that of the group of young men who formed the Fabian Society in January 1884.

The first important shift in his ideas came in 1883 from discussions with his friend Sydney Olivier: in the long hours they spent together as resident clerks in Downing Street they played chess and talked. Olivier, who spent some time tutoring the son of the Positivist Henry Crompton, was strongly influenced by the ideas of Auguste Comte. His arguments with Sidney Webb were soon reflected in Webb's lectures. Almost all those which survive from the period 1883 to 1886 are coloured by the Positivist concept of a well-regulated social system governed by an enlightened elite. As late as January 1886, seven months after he joined the Fabian Society, Webb lectured to its members on 'The Economics of a Positivist Community', suggesting that Positivism, Collectivism and Anarchism were all possibly forms of socialism and that it was 'an open question' for socialists whether to opt for the expropriation of capital or the moralisation of the capitalists. It was, moreover, through Olivier that Webb became personally involved with some of the first Fabians, and through Olivier, too, that he met Olivier's college friend Graham Wallas – thus forming the triumvirate which soon became known to Fabians as the 'Three Musketeers'.

When Sidney joined the Fabian Society on 1 May 1885 he considered himself a socialist, though his orderly mind and his penchant for constitutional procedures were in marked contrast to the bohemian and almost insurrectionary disposition of the socialist sects then attracting attention in London. Sidney liked persuasion rather than rhetoric, facts rather than fancies. He saw in the Fabian Society a possible instrument for achieving, as its founders declared, a new moral order as well as an improved social system. In the final stages of his apprenticeship, between 1886 and 1891, he slowly imposed his model of research and propaganda upon a sometimes recalcitrant and suspicious band of Fabians. With Shaw as his powerful ally and Olivier and Wallas as his lieutenants he had converted a small discussion group of doubtful quality and ambiguous purpose into a force which might move the world.

40 PP SIDNEY WEBB TO J. M. FELLS

In 1879 Sidney joined the Zetetical Society, a small discussion society influenced by the ideas of John Stuart Mill, which met at 9 Conduit Street on alternate Wednesdays. Its aim was to discuss 'all matters affecting the interests of the human race; hence no topic, theological or otherwise, discussed with decorum, is excluded from its programme'. Among the active members of the society were George Bernard Shaw (1856–1950), the Reverend Stewart Headlam (1847–1924), an eccentric curate of Radical views; Helen Taylor (1831–1907), the step-daughter of John Stuart Mill, who was active in many advanced causes; John G. Godard, a solicitor who for many years looked after the affairs of Sidney Webb and Bernard Shaw; Dr C. R. Drysdale, active in the birth-control movement; and John Manger Fells (1858–1925), an accountant who wrote books on financial management. He was Hon. Secretary of the Society. Webb and Shaw were committee members in 1880–81.

Shaw met Webb for the first time at the Zetetical in October 1880 and later recalled his first impression of 'a young man of about twenty-one, rather below middle height, with small hands and feet, and a profile that suggested an improvement on Napoleon the Third'. He was struck by Webb's mastery of his material. 'He knew all about the subject of debate; knew more than anybody present; had read everything that had been written on the subject; and remembered all the facts that bore upon it. He used notes, ticked them off one by one, threw them away, and finished with a coolness and clearness that, to me in my then trembling state, seemed miraculous. This young man was the ablest man in England.' (*Sixteen Self-Sketches* London 1949)

The members mentioned have not been further identified.

115 Cranbourne St, London W.C.

28/2/81

Dear Fells,

Our defeat once more makes it I think imperative for us to take a survey of our position. It is not the fact of defeat which is crushing, but it is the fact that in a crusade of over two active years we have made no progress. We have made no converts among the indifferents. We number now, as then, 35 to 45 combatants, with a few – a very few, stray votes. Join to this, that we are confronted by a phalanx at least double our strength, who act at command (e.g. *Eight* Ravenscrofts, and x bank-clerks) and who can if desired, obtain *many* stray votes; who have the advantage of office, and to whom any sense of decency in the use of this advantage is utterly foreign; and I think you will see that the struggle is, for some years, hopeless.

Of course, as individuals nothing need be altered. But it *does* seem to me that it is not worth anybody's while to undertake the work, anxiety and odium of secretarial duties, or to work the agitation with an organisation. At any rate, I cannot continue to do my share.

At the same time, the two years labor has not been fruitless; our principles have borne fruit in the reinforcement of the Committee by such men as Connolly and Richardson; (tho' this had already begun in Carter and H. J. Webb) and in other ways.

There seems to have been a fatality over the agitation; we have been distinguished by a continual swopping of horses when crossing our streams; changes of candidate, changes of secretary; doubtless all necessary, but nevertheless all detrimental. But this is not needed to account for our failure.

You will gather here from that I am for letting the organisation (and the agitation) drop quietly. It has needed indeed, great endeavours, as you well know, to keep it up till now. With Wright, Descours, Denton etc., dropping off, and many others (e.g. Dumsday, H. J. Webb, myself) indicating an opinion that the affair should drop; together with a general lukewarmness and halfheartedness; I do not indeed see how the organisation *can* go on.

I am writing you this lugubrious epistle in order to prepare the ground for a talk I want to have before the Zet. meeting on Thursday next. Be there early if you can; as I intend to be, as I very much want to chat with you. If you think it worthwhile, send a card to one or two more, as the matter is rather serious. Or if you prefer, let us two discuss the matter first.

Excuse ink, paper etc. I am seizing an odd moment to write this in a hurry.

Yours sincerely,

Sidney Webb

41 PP SIDNEY WEBB TO E. GARCKE

Garcke was the Hon. Treasurer of the Zetetical Society, which had been struggling on through the autumn of 1881. Webb had lectured on Heredity and Shaw on Vaccination. Webb wrote to Fells on 14 February 1882 (PP) arguing against an attempt to transfer the members to the Dialectical Society or to the South Place Chapel, another meeting place for high-minded radicals, where Shaw delivered a lecture on Capital Punishment on 8 February. He favoured an attempt to create 'out of the ashes' a private society by invitation only. On the day after this letter to Garcke another letter from Webb to Fells (PP) agreed with the suggestion that the proposed new society should be devoted to 'sociology'. Almost nothing is known about the last stages of the Zetetical nor did any new society of any significance arise from this proposal.

Emma Phipson was a member of the Zetetical committee who gave a talk entitled 'Was Shakespere a Democrat?'

[115 Cranbourne Street, W.C.]
20.2.82

Dear Garcke

I agree with you that we may as well begin at once to discuss what form the society to be founded on the ruins of the Zet. shall take.

I am quite persuaded that too wide a scope will be injurious. You suggest 'sociology', but that means so much that even that seems too wide. In default however of anything better I think it perhaps the best, but I should be inclined to lay especial stress on Pol. Econ., and social *institutions* as they are and should be.

I think the Society should be formed by *invitation*: the nucleus (say six) to be selected by (say) Fells, Miss Phipson, myself and yourself, and the remainder (making say twenty in all) *by* the nucleus. Of course the numbers are suggestions only: I think some such plan of beginning will be the best. Then and afterwards no member to be invited until name passed by majority of present members. A *private* society only.

77

I decidedly think ladies should not be excluded.

I think we should and could manage weekly meetings, as presumably only those would be invited who would be real members. Weekly meetings (allowing for blank dates) should give in a society of 20, 2 openings a year. (You say *fortnightly*, but that would only give *one* each).

We must hire a room somewhere. I think coffee is desirable.

Your idea as to rotation of chairmen is good, I am not quite sure as to the 'current events business'. Some chairmen would make a hash of this. It might however be tried avowedly as an experiment only.

Discussion should not be by formal speeches, I think.

I doubt whether many would like Saturday. If we hire a room, as I think we must, it will cost I suppose £10 a year, and we must therefore subscribe at least 10/- each. This must be borne in mind. We must talk all these things over with Fells. There is, however, considerable agreement so far.

Yours truly,

Sidney Webb

42 WCM   SIDNEY WEBB TO H. R. JENNINGS

H. R. Jennings was the secretary of the Working Men's College founded in 1854 by the Christian Socialist, Frederick Denison Maurice (1805–72) after losing his professorship at King's College, London, for heterodox views. For many years its premises were in Great Ormond Street; it moved to its present site in Camden Town in 1905. Webb gave political economy classes at the College for several years and also served on its governing body. Several other letters to Jennings have been omitted since they deal repetitiously with teaching arrangements.

Colonial Office, London S.W.

3 June /83

Dear Sir,

In reply to your letter of the 22nd as to my taking a class in Political Economy during the October term, I request that you will be good enough to inform the Executive Committee of the Working Men's College, that I shall be very pleased to do so, if they are willing to try the experiment. I will do all in my power to make it a success, but it should be understood it will be my first experience of such work. I may say that I am quite unfettered to dates in October.

I may say I am, dear sir, yours very truly

Sidney Webb

Shaw had been living in London since 1876, doing odd jobs and drifting in London's intellectual bohemia. At the time he met Webb he was at work on *Immaturity*, the first of the five novels with which he began his literary career. In 1882 Shaw was drawn into the land nationalisation movement, which was given fresh impetus by the speaking tour of the American journalist Henry George (1839–97) and the publication of his best-selling *Progress and Poverty*. Like all Radicals he was much affected by the suppression of unrest in Ireland, then in a virtual state of siege. Shaw was one of the group of politically-minded young men who, in April 1883, set up the Land Reform Union and published its struggling journal, the *Christian Socialist*. Its secretary was Henry Hyde Champion (1859–1958), who had resigned an army commission to devote himself to agitation and socialist publishing, becoming the secretary of the Social Democratic Federation. Its other members included James L. Joynes (1853–93), an Eton master who had to give up his post because of his assocation with George and became an active socialist; Sydney Olivier; Hubert Bland (1856–1914), a journalist married to Edith Nesbit (1858–1924) who became a well-known author of books for children, and Stewart Headlam. Headlam was an eccentric figure, whose clerical career was frustrated by his interest in radical politics, his enthusiasm for the stage and his advocacy of unpopular causes. He befriended Oscar Wilde on his release from prison. He was a long-serving member of the Fabian executive and an energetic educational reformer on the London School Board and the London County Council. All this group were involved in the establishment of the Fabian Society in 1884, or joined soon after: they remained close associates. Though Webb joined the L.R.U. he did not play any significant role in it.

The Lambeth 'Parliament' was one of several such 'mock' assemblies which served as political debating clubs.

Colonial Office, Downing St

11/8/83

Dear Shaw,

I don't know how to answer your humorous letter rightly. Let me try seriousness.

I was doubtful about joining the Land Reform Union. I am, I think, an enthusiastic land law reformer, and I brought in a mild Bill last session in the Lambeth Parliament (which was rejected – Mr Winks will tell you why). And an integral part of that scheme was a revision of the Land Tax, though this could not appear in the Bill.

But although I am entirely in favor of the restitution of the land to the people – if it could be done – I am at present not a Land Nationaliser. Even if I were I should not see in this any wonderful panacea. It would enable us to abolish all indirect taxation, which might be a good thing, but I am not enthusiastic at the prospect of cheap gin. It is certainly not worth a revolution: and even the revolution would not abolish rent, that presumed 'destroyer of wages'.

I enclose 2/6 and should like to be a member of your society, if Nationalisation is not an article of faith. I do this because I see it is not mentioned in the prospectus; the 'special methods' which *are* mentioned I do agree with. But if the Committee should not care about such a cold-blooded member, please retain the 2/6 until we meet again, which I hope may be soon. I do not leave town until about the 24th inst. and shall be glad to see you here one night. I am still in on Mondays.

Yours

Sidney Webb

44 BL SIDNEY WEBB TO GEORGE BERNARD SHAW

In the autumn of 1884 the first meetings of what was variously known as the Karl Marx Club and the Hampstead Historic Society were held at Wyldes Farm, Hampstead, which was the semi-rural home of Charlotte Wilson (1854–1944), one of the first students at Newnham College, Cambridge. Married to a stockbroker, Arthur Wilson, she was a prominent member of the Fabian Society for many years, and also edited the anarchist journal *Freedom*.

The meetings continued for a number of years. No adequate record of them or of the membership survives; in the early years the group was heterogeneous including Marxists, anarchists, moral improvers and reformist economists. By 1886 it was largely confined to the inner group of Fabians and became in effect a fortnightly seminar at which they discussed socialist history and theory. These discussions led to the emergence of the distinctively Fabian view of economics which, after close reading and debate of Marx's *Capital* (in both French and German), led Shaw and Webb to combine the theory of rent of David Ricardo (1772–1823), one of the founders of classical political economy, with the newer concepts of marginal utility. The first English edition of Volume I of *Capital* did not appear until 1887, when it was reviewed by Shaw in the *National Reformer* (7, 14 and 21 August 1887), though Shaw had earlier debated the [?] French version with Philip Wicksteed in *To-Day* in October 1884 and January and April 1885.

Both Shaw and Webb were, at the same time, members of another discussion group which included F. Y. Edgeworth (1845–1926), professor of political economy at King's College, London, and Philip H. Wicksteed (1844–1927), a writer on economics who also did much to introduce Ibsen to English readers. This group met at the house of another stockbroker, Henry R. Beeston, and eventually became the British Economic Society. It was particularly concerned with the ideas of the economist William Stanley Jevons (1835–82).

Dr Burns Gibson, a member of several advanced societies with libertarian opinions, was one of the small group which had met in the autumn of 1883 for the discussions which led to the foundation of the Fabian Society on 4 January 1884 and he became one of the original nine members.

The Hunter to whom Webb refers was probably William Alexander Hunter (1844–98), formerly professor of jurisprudence at University College, London, and then Liberal M.P. for North Aberdeen.

Dear Shaw

You were missing, and missed, at Mrs Wilson's economic tea party last Wednesday. We were 11, and you were the faithless Apostle. Mrs Wilson – who appeared to my astonished gaze as a 'Rossetti young woman' with dense hair – read a most elaborate analysis of Ch. 1 of Marx, in English, over which she must have spent weeks. F. Y. Edgeworth, who was in the Chair, then opened the proceedings by expressing his intense contempt for Karl and all his works, and snorted generally on the subject, as Ricardo might have done to an errant economist of the period. The company, most of whom were apparently under the impression that we were assembled for the purpose of reverently drinking in the wisdom of some great seer – were speechless with amazement: and Edgeworth's voice was followed by a silence which was thick enough to have been cut with a knife. In despair, he appealed to me. I rushed in, and the rest of the evening was a kind of Scotch reel *à deux*, Edgeworth and I gaily dancing on the unfortunate K.M., trampling him remorselessly under foot, amid occasional feeble protests and enquiries from Mrs Wilson (who had thrown away her young love upon him), Dr Burns Gibson (who had apparently been impressed by him) and a beaming young Socialist, *inconnu de moi*, (who was without the guile of Pol. Econ. and consequently revered him). There was also a silent 'chorus' of two or three more, Rev. Macdonald keeping still as death, and Mrs M. also, the latter being perhaps under discipline on this subject now.

Now this sort of thing is demoralising – I mean to me. Of course you will already have noted how demoralising it must have been to the others. But unless some utterly unscrupulous socialistic dialectician like yourself turns up there, we shall have discarded *Le Capital* within a month, and be found studying the gospel of Ricardo! Please therefore appear there next meeting, Wednesday, 12th; in great force to defend Ch. 2 and 3, on money. I am going to bring up Olivier to assist you, if possible: but he alone would not be sufficiently 'brazen' in argument on the subject.

I will send you my draft legislative solution of the present Lords difficulty in a few days, which may amuse your conservative mind. I shall try and hear Hunter on the subject tomorrow tho' I have been fearfully busy for weeks one way or another; and tonight am off to explain to my confiding pupils how and why feudalism broke up – a matter which I have utterly failed to understand myself.

Yours

Sidney Webb

Webb had just taken the annual examination in the penultimate year of his studies for the external Ll.B. at London University. Graham Wallas (1858–1932) was the son of an Anglican clergyman; a fellow-student of Sydney Olivier at Oxford, he met Webb when Webb and Olivier became resident clerks in the Colonial Office. After a shaky start in schoolmastering he became a university extension lecturer. Appointed to the staff of the London School of Economics in 1895, he became professor of political science there in 1914. He was a member of the Karl Marx Club and in the previous autumn had started as a classics master at Highgate School. A man of strong principle who had reacted to his Evangelical upbringing with an abiding distaste for all organised religion, he was soon obliged to resign his post for refusing to take part in communion service in the school chapel.

Colonial Office, Downing Street
25/5/85

Dear Wallas,

Although Olivier has unkindly deserted us, I hope you will allow me to continue to see something of you. I am just now very much cast down, partly at being left alone, and partly I suppose by the reaction from the excitement of my last week's examination. I don't like to ask you exactly to come down to see me, as there would be nothing for you to do and you would be bored. But when you do have a blank evening you might come, sending me a prior card if possible.

I am going to call up at Hampstead on Sunday next, and I could, if you should happen to be disengaged, look you up then, or meet you for a walk. But I count on rather more than conventional frankness from you, as to telling me quite straight, if I am for any reason unwelcome.

I find that my leave seasons this year can only be July, and *after* 15th September. Will not either of these be too early or too late for your German trip? I should much like to take advantage of your offer to join you, if you contemplated anything so late as September.

I am absolutely 'flabby' now as to capacity for reading, and am half inclined to the idea that a long walk occasionally would do me good. If you ever waste your expensive tissue in lieu of common steamcoals in this manner, compel me to join you for my health's sake.

Yours sincerely,

Sidney Webb

46 PP SIDNEY WEBB TO GRAHAM WALLAS

Webb was much taken by an historical romance by Arthur Sherburne Hardy, a mathematician who wrote a number of novels: *But Yet a Woman*, first published in 1882, ran through several editions.

Dear Wallas

On arriving last night I found – amid sundry telegrams which I ought to have attended to – a letter from a friend claiming my presence next Saturday evening on an old promise. So don't come then please.

Your conversation was so exciting apparently, that notwithstanding the soporific influence of the beer and the bus and the bed, I had one of my occasional sleepless nights, and 'arranged the affairs of the nation' until about 6 this morning. But this lying in a dreamy state, with will and judgment suspended, consciousness languidly following out its aimless thread, has become not unpleasant to me. Still – I don't mind confessing to a sense of muscular languor today. I don't believe you have been let in for such a walk for a long time, although it was not a bit too far.

Do you feel inclined to take your chance of a seat in the Lyceum pit one night, to see *Olivia*, said to be very fine? I shall probably want to go – but it must be one day between 7–16 June. I have a rush of engagements which is filling up all my evenings.

I am sending you *But Yet A Woman*: please enjoy and appreciate it.

The 'Dialectical' meetings – the last until October – will be 3rd and 17th June, at Anderton's Hotel, Fleet Street, at 8 p.m. I don't yet know subjects.

Yours

Sidney Webb

Your cane shall be carefully preserved: I feel 'debauched' by it.

47 PP SIDNEY WEBB TO GRAHAM WALLAS

De Marsac was a royalist journalist in *But Yet a Woman*, set in France at the time of an Orleanist conspiracy, who was driven to disaster by a hopeless passion. Roger Lande was the hero of the novel, a young doctor whose desire to 'conquer success' led him to suppress 'the instincts of the heart'.

Mark Pattison (1813–84) was Rector of Lincoln College, Oxford, and a follower of Newman and Pusey. He was the author of a notable *Life* of Isaac Casaubon, the 17th-century classical scholar, and his *Memoirs* were thought to be comparable to the *Confessions* of Rousseau. His widow, Emilia, became the second Lady Dilke. The comment to which Webb refers was probably by Lionel Arthur Tollemache (1838–1918), author and essayist.

Colonial Office
8/6/85

Thanks – but don't conclude that I like *But Yet A Woman* by identifying myself with it. I am at best only a combination of De Marsac and Roger

83

Lande, and I frequently fear the former predominates. But I *do* see much of myself in Pattison. I have read all Sophocles again in another translation and adhere to my opinions. [*Written as postscript on first page*]

Dear Wallas

There are, as you will be well aware, advantages in not prolonging your stay at Highgate. I don't say they fully compensate – but at any rate the early termination of your anomalous position is in itself a great gain.

Of course I will not fail to let you know if I hear of anything to suit you, but I am not likely to. I would suggest that, if possible, you should not mind waiting a little while to get what will suit you. At any rate it would be wise not to let it spoil the enjoyment of your holiday. This is a difficult task, but it is one worth attempting. After all – there is nothing lost yet: and you personally will have gained much, and in a form so that it can never be taken away from you. Character is always the safest investment – of good or of evil. There alone are we quite sure to find the bread after many days. And if Sophocles regarded too exclusively the non-human element in the production of events – we are a little apt to go to the other extreme and think that we are entirely 'the master of things'. Providence – a blind and unconscious and therefore *not* a malignant Providence – still has the greatest share in running the concern: and I am (partly and occasionally at any rate) a disciple of Mr Micawber, with a faith in things unseen but about to turn up. At any rate much more comes to us than we have worked for, and of this not much more than half is evil. Let us therefore not exclude Dame Fortune from calculation.

I shall be at home tomorrow from about 8 p.m. – afterwards this week I am afraid I shall be always out. I mention my movements in case you are this way. I find I am very busy doing things before going on leave (about 20th June).

Olivier writes he leaves Paris tonorrow, stays at Rouen, and then at his home, then at Tonbridge, arriving here *alone* on 15th. Great Marx festival on 16th.

I send you Tollemache on Pattison as soon as I have read it again. *Please return it* as I am going to study it. The *P.M.G.* [*Pall Mall Gazette*] quoted the *worst* parts of it.

Yours

Sidney Webb

48 PP SIDNEY WEBB TO GRAHAM WALLAS

Webb felt depressed and at a loose end in the summer of 1885. Sydney Olivier's marriage to Margaret Cox, the sister of his school friend Harold Cox (1859–1936), a Liberal journalist and later an M.P. and editor of the *Edinburgh Review*, had made Webb aware of his own emotional frustrations. He had a number of passing infatuations.

Die verlorene Handschrift was the novel by Gustav Freytag (1816–95), published in 1864.

Ostend
28/6/85

Dear Wallas

We have now been here a week, and I have not found an opportunity of writing to you, as you suggested. But this place does not favor correspondence. It has been windy and chilly, tho' fine, so it is not yet crowded altho' the King and family are here. But it is a splendid place, as regards seafront. The country is dull enough: we have however been all round. The last of the party leave tomorrow (we have been six), and I shall then go to Brussels, until the end of the week alone. Unfortunately a planned tour down the Moselle has fallen through or is at least postponed. I shall therefore be in London again after Monday week for a few days. Then perhaps I shall go to Devonshire, tho' I don't know with what purpose.

I want to say, before I forget it, that what I said at Hampstead about your not hurrying too much to get a place, if delay was any use – about the money, in fact – was fully meant, and you can rely on it. I hope you will not take anything unsuitable or unpromising.

You will have been made free of Olivier's house. I am sorry to be away at his moving in, and shall look forward to seeing him *en famille* quite as if it had always been.

My Brussels address will be

Hotel de Vienne
Rue de la Fourche
Brussels

and as I shall be alone letters (and *P.M. Gazettes*!) will be very welcome.

I have been doing absolutely no reading or work of any kind, and have only managed to get through three-quarters of a volume of *Die verlorene Handschrift*. Had you any purpose in inciting me to read this? I like the quiet way – *ohne Hast ohne Rast* – in which the thing goes on – as if there were unending time.

I dutifully accompanied my mother to church last Sunday – for the first time for years – and had as reward a very dull sermon about God hardening himself to the proud etc. which I took to myself.

I hope your German visit still holds good, and covers the second half of September.

Yours

Sidney Webb

Can I do anything for you in Brussels?

The annual Oxford–Cambridge cricket match at Lords was treated as a holiday in many public schools. 'St Lubbock's Day' was a popular phrase for the Bank Holiday introduced by Sir John Lubbock.

Webb was impressed by the novel *Dr Heidenhoff's Process* (New York 1880 and Edinburgh 1884) by the American utopian socialist Edward Bellamy (1850–98), which described an elementary form of psychic therapy: he felt it offered a way in which will-power might overcome depression.

He was much attached to a young woman who, he implied, had virtually jilted him to marry a young barrister named Corrie Grant-Woodstock (1850–1924) who became a Liberal M.P. Their daughter subsequently married Henry Hermann Schloesser (b. 1883) who was an active Fabian; he changed his name to Slesser in the First World War, and held legal office under Labour, becoming a lord justice of appeal. In a letter Wallas on 26 July 1885 Webb wrote miserably: 'I want you to bear with me whatever I may do as I feel very desolate indeed. Why *did* God put such a thing into life?' In a postscript he added: 'I don't think I told you yet that she is engaged to Corrie Grant-Woodstock'. The Webb family had moved to Keppel Street where Sidney lived at home; they later moved to 4 Park Village East, on the Camden Town edge of Regent's Park.

> until Saturday morning 11th Hotel de Vienne
> Brussels
> until Monday morning 6th Hotel Cour d'Angleterre
> Ostend
> thenceforth 27 Keppel St, Russell Square
> 2/7/85

My dear Wallas

I was glad to get your letter – this is no compliment because I am just now in the state of mind when *any* friendly letter is very welcome. Still, yours was exceptionally so.

I, out of the world, had forgotten that there was such a thing as the Varsity Match, or that it was just on. Never mind, *à quelque chose* even Varsity matches are *bon*, for they got you and some hundreds more a holiday. I shall henceforth think of them with a respect heretofore accorded only to Royal Birthdays and Marriages and St Lubbock.

You are only in fashion in being in low spirits. It seems to me that my acquaintances all round are in trouble. (Only Olivier excepted – he is most unreasonably and unhumanely happy, I know.) Some who have money are sick about other things. Some are sick about money. Those whose external circumstances are darkest are not the most unhappy. And I, whom they nearly all envy, and whom they all persist in regarding as filled with every joy, now pass my life in endeavouring to persuade them that I am a hopeless fraud and entitled to a commiseration which their hard hearts deny. All this means (beyond dull rainy weather) that in my opinion individual happiness is (1) not attainable at all, (2) a fixed quantum in each personality, irrespective of events and circumstances, (3) nearly the same in each one, and (4) not worth consideration so far as, with the help of Dr Heidenhoff, we can avoid so doing. (I am afraid a logical deduction would be (1) Alcohol, (2) Opium, (3) Suicide, but I can't pursue the argument now.)

If you get nothing *at all* until Xmas, it will be only 3 months lost: and much more than that gained, if the delay is worth anything at all. Don't be like me, wanting at each step to see my whole life in advance (this has landed me in the *Impasse du bureau des Colonies* instead of on the *Avenue directe à Mondesir* to use a directory-al metaphor. If you can only bring yourself to wait calmly, and utilise the time just as though your future were secure, there can be little doubt that it would pay you. So much easier is it to preach than to practise.

Thanks for the *P.M. Budget* which was very welcome. But I did not mean to ask you to take that trouble.

What I meant about *Die verlorene Handschrift* was that there is *very much* in it of what I have been talking about lately with you and others and though I agree with the Professor nearly always, I disagree on one point at least – I am not yet convinced that a non-theistic man ought to marry a theistic woman. Whereof more anon as to Ilse, she is very well, but I am not in love with her, and leaving out of account this inexplicable emotion which 'bloweth where it listeth', beyond all ken or reason, I don't think I should have married her. She was not reasonable enough. The Doctor (as Freytag meant) was quite right in objecting that from *das Leben des Geistes die ist so weit entfernt wie die heilige Elisabeth.* Much of what followed arose simply from her not possessing enough of the calm reason of her husband. I am still convinced that this calm reason, unbiassed by any prejudice, instinct or emotion, is the highest and best in the world – that it leads only to unhappiness is only of a piece with the rest. I, at least, am not bound to prove everything to be good, just when I feel that nearly everything is for the bad.

Therefore, since we are both unhappy – or at least *not* happy – (and both without any *really* striking reason [*illegible*]) let us frankly admire and pity ourselves. *Quant à moi*, for a miserable man I am still capable of much enjoyment. (Olivier however says my happiness is largely due to an ascetic avoidance of enjoyments. *Ce n'est pas vrai* – it is only indolence.) The best enjoyment is in friendly intercourse. When I get back I mean to throw myself metaphorically at the feet of Mrs Olivier (as I have already done in 2 or 3 other households) confess my unhealthy state of mind, and request her to allow me to come occasionally, like Saul, to be comforted by David. Please aid me.

The color of the wallpaper, opposite which I write this, is not unpleasing. There are perhaps other circumstances which adequately account for my being today more than usually discontented with myself (i.e. with the world at large et *le bon Dieu*). It is odd that after having been pessimist by profession for at least 7 years, I should not yet have exhausted all the shock of every new surprise and disappointment at finding the world an uncomfortable one. The momentum of existence – the flywheel which alone carries out lives over the 'dead spot' in the revolution – is certainly the most strongly optimistic ally possible. As it indeed should be, being only the instinct of self-preservation evolved in the race by many aeons struggle. (Hence by the way, the Buddhist Nirvana is wrong – evolutionarily false. Query also George Eliotism).

This is a strange letter. You may find it interesting even amusing. Hence I send it, I think it is really from

Yours sincerely

Sidney Webb

50 PP SIDNEY WEBB TO SYDNEY OLIVIER

As a civil servant Webb had more leave than he could use: after he returned from Belgium he took a short holiday in South-West England. The 'bitter cry of outcast Salisbury' was a gloss on *The Bitter Cry of Outcast London,* a pamphlet describing the miseries of London's lower depths which made a powerful impact on middle-class opinion when it was published in 1883. In Richard Sheridan's play *The Critic* Lord Burleigh was a character given to portentous shakes of the head. Sir Edmond Antrobus (1818–99) was a large landowner in Wiltshire, Stonehenge fell within his estate of Amesbury Abbey.

Rougemont Hotel, Exeter
7 July 1885

Dear Olivier

Having got so far I report progress. I left London 11 o'clock Wednesday morning for Salisbury, 1 o'clock. I travelled with a family, eldest a young Backfisch at the most awkward age. *I* was reading a railway novel. The mother, with usual maternal beatific duck-like face, was reading *The Electrician* and an electrical book with diagrams! However, they got out at Andover, so I recovered my rebuked spirits.

Salisbury interested me, as an old town, say, like Courtrai. But race is a mysterious thing, and it remains astonishing that 20 miles of sea should make such a difference. I was amused in picking out the likeness and unlikenesses.

The town is chiefly remarkable for Almshouses. Of these I counted at least *six*, without looking for them: you may judge from this, by the way, that I explored pretty throughly. I think I remember that (Trollope's) Hirams Hospital was here.

The Cathedralosity impressed me, not the thing itself, for that is swept and garnished like a modern workhouse, smells of the builder, all fire-new, in the worst 19th century style. I don't deny that there may be fragments of the old surviving, but the trail of the restoring serpent is over them all and the general impression is of newness. Why, they have actually *polished* the nave pillars, until you can trace each shining Paludina (it is freshwater limestone 'Purbeck marble') across the Church. On the roof there are hideous paintings. I fell into the hands of a specially fatuous verger, who recited his mechanical tale into my ear. 'On removing the yellow wash they discovered sufficient of the old painting to enable the interior to be restored'. Why, I exclaimed, 'you don't mean to say it is thought the ancients painted like that?' He looked at me for a moment, more in pitying sorrow at my stupidity than in anger, and then began again, 'On removing the yellow wash etc.' And then, most unkindest cut of all, I contributed 6d towards completing the vandalism!

But the Close impressed me, and I went there a good deal. The quiet peace of the houses, the easy comfort of the households, the still abstracted life, was very tempting. I remember Ruskin's account of the chief blessing of his boylife, that it taught him peace. I don't think I ever told you much about my own boyhood, but (tho' a *happy* family) we have always been in the thick of the fight, and I feel now that one of the great influences I have missed is this peace, which I have never known.

But some of the courts and alleys restored me, the bitter cry of outcast Salisbury. I remembered in time whence came the Close revenues, and my radicalism revived. If I had grown up there, I should doubtless have been a Conservative, or at least a Tory Democrat, with a High Church, porty, Tory father. No, better fifty years of London than a cycle of decay.

I stayed at the White Hart. How miserably our feeding arrangements fall short of those of the French. The ideas of a dinner never rose beyond a chop or a steak, though the price was high enough. I sighed for the fleshpots of Belgium, e.g. a *3* francs *table d'hote*!

Thursday I went to Stonehenge. You prophesied I should drive, but base is the slave that pays. Besides it isn't Socialistic to monopolise a man and a horse for oneself. So I set out to walk. Before I had got two miles a hare ran across the road, then sat up, and nodded a nod as pregnant of meaning as Lord Burleigh's. I took no notice, so he ran on ahead, and again nodded to me.

What an ugly beast a hare is. It must have been an early aesthetic feeling which led to his form being disguised in the 'jug'.

Such is my irreligious condition that it did not even occur to me that this was an omen, a warning, until a magpie flew up on my left, then two more. (At least the great black and white bird that my Cockneyism thus identifies.) *Then* it did occur to me, but I was infidel, and defied the lightening. (Yet I am not without faith, for I picked up and carried 15 miles two fearfully ugly masses of flint in which imagination fondly fancies palaeolithic implements.)

I duly turned on to the down and saw 'the stones' ahead. Then a ridiculous thing happened. I got so interested in the barrows and the invisible flint implements that I actually lost my way in the undulating sea. However by climbing sundry barrows I again sighted 'the stones' to my left rear, and steered for them.

I was not disappointed at the external view: they look very well (the best approach is however from the Amesbury side). But inside, the circle appears very small. The place was defiled by the presence of a travelling photographer, so I adjourned my meditations among the tombs and pressed on to Amesbury.

I may say at once that nothing more unfortunate came of the hare and the magpies than my finding the photographer and my *not* finding any cider at Amesbury, so I had to have beer, which always gets into my head.

Sir E. Antrobus warns you off the camp, so I started home.

I think it's good to be alone sometimes. I felt almost happy in my thoughts on the way home and built all sorts of castles. (N.B. I notice now this was *after* the beer.) I came to Old Sarum and had a great ramble all over and round it. This is the biggest and finest old camp I have seen.

I got home in time to have another walk round the town and to catch the 7.15 train, which brought me here.

Today I went down the Dart and home by rail from Dartmouth – another bit of England used up. It is very fine: but I felt ill at Dartmouth when they told me they were going to restore the as yet virgin church. True, it is very ugly: but let us keep our ancient monuments.

This 'metropolis of the West' doesn't much please me. It is neither London nor country, and combines the evils of both. The Cathedral is not first rate, and generally I am ill humoured.

You had better send me anything to the Poste Restante *Plymouth*, as I shall get there tomorrow or Sunday.

Please send this on to Wallas, as I said I'd write and can't do anymore tonight. Besides, it occurs to me that this is rather a good letter for me, altho' I did not deliberately so intend it. With salutations to Mrs Olivier, believe me,

Yours

Sidney Webb

If you can put off your water party until August, I shall be able to join. I don't think I *can* be back by the 26th.

51 BL SIDNEY WEBB TO GEORGE BERNARD SHAW

The 'confessions' to which Shaw might have been tempted related to his philandering relationships with women, especially Mrs Jane ('Jenny') Patterson (1839–1924), a widow who was a friend and pupil of Shaw's mother. Less than two weeks previously, on Shaw's 29th birthday on 26 July, Shaw noted his intimacy with Mrs Patterson, saying that this 'was my first connection of the kind. I was an absolute novice'. (Shaw Diary, BLPES)

Olivier was getting up a river party to start from Walton-on-Thames.

Downing St
5/8/85

Dear Shaw

I have bought Vol. 2 of Marx – I fear a very bad investment. Still, it is worth something to be relieved of the sense of privation. (Without having read the book) I am prepared to assert that it is worth little. Everything is still put off – this time until the *3rd* vol.

We shall find it very dull – in fact, I fear, quite unendurable. But we may as well begin it together, if you are in earnest about learning German. My ambition at present is only to see you able to *read* German. You need not trouble to learn to write it correctly: and the speaking will easily come afterwards.

Therefore it is mainly a matter of vocabulary. This means, say, to learn the English equivalents of ten thousand words. The task is rendered easier by the similarity of roots.

You had better give me one evening a week, and we will do at least 2 hours of it. During the week you must learn a short vocabulary, which I will draw up weekly – being key-words, so far as possible, to many others. Before a year you will read German with comparative ease.

Having experimented on you, I shall, if successful apply the method to myself, and polish off Dutch and Italian.

Let me know what evening will suit you best (we can of course change afterwards when required), and come here next week on that evening at 8 sharp. At present I am quite free.

I am conscious of having monopolised you cruelly with my woes on Monday. How like I am to everybody else – a reflection which has come home to me a good deal lately. My consolation is that I was furnishing you with heaps of material, and perhaps even preventing *you* from making confessions to me. But a better excuse is the very bitter and overwhelming reality of the matter to me – the extent of which I shall fail to make you realise, I am really very sick – however absurd it may be.

Yours

Sidney Webb

As to Sunday next, some half dozen of us will go, *if fine*. Leave Liverpool St at 9 a.m. for Walton. price 4/- come if you can.

Wallas had gone for a long stay in Germany to learn the language, and Webb proposed to join him for a holiday, staying in Weimar with a family named Sonntag who were friends of Olivier's. Hubert Campion had been at Tonbridge school with Olivier and at Oxford with Olivier and Wallas.

Wednesday's child was 'full of woe'.

Downing St London

17 Aug/85

Dear Wallas

I have been wanting to talk to you, but have put off day by day, thinking your letter would come. There was no reason why you *ought* to write, only you twice sent out *avant couriers* in the shape of postcards announcing the letter which was to follow.

You will be leading a simple and healthy life – if not dull, the best 'recreation'. You have leisure to think, and so it is the more noteworthy and valuable to have recovered your own soul again. I fancy there is something soporific or at least restful in being so far from the sea. I remember feeling it in Switzerland. Something like the Hamelin children getting into the heart of the mountain. The Continent is gross and dense, and one buries onesself right in, away from the great channel of communication. I have often thought on the shore, that this water touches America and the Coral Islands etc. and been interested and impressed. I suppose the English are Greek in this. I like the great current of the world's life, but it has its bad effects on character. I have no repose of mind, but a self-devouring activity, which is very restless and impatient. Therefore perhaps Weimar will do me good.

I propose to join you, if not prevented, and so far as I can see now, I shall not be. But I shall only be able to stop away three weeks. I have promised to give a lecture at a Fabian Society open meeting on 18th September, that being the only date they could fix (and as I could not in any case have left London before that week). I could start on Saturday, 19th September, and reach Weimar when God pleases, by direct journey.

I must say that all this is D.V. [*Deo volente*] – I see no reason why it should not come off, but everything, great and small, has gone wrong with me this year, down to my losing 5/- at cards the other night – quite unusual for me. It is my *Pechjahr*. My star has gone out, and from being a child of fortune, I am reduced to an ordinary mortal. This is bad, because although I don't believe in luck, I believe very much in the *belief* in luck. However it remains still that I was born on a Wednesday.

When I arrive you may deal with me as you will. Only, I *may* feel inclined to take long walks. And down at the bottom of my heart I secretly cherish a belief that Dresden is close to Weimar. I haven't looked at the map because I don't want to be undeceived. I have an illusion to destroy, and as they are getting scarcer, it is not to be foregone. The San Sisto Madonna is the only ancient picture which really touches me – and that I have never seen. Perhaps I could manage a day there.

I have begun to teach German to G. B. Shaw, the embryo-novelist. He knows 'and' and 'the' only. We began Marx, *Kapital*, vol. 2 – not the easiest of books. We read 2 pages in 2 hours, accompanying each word with a philological dissertation. It was really very *interessant* to me. But when I arrive my speaking will be found to be *ganz schauderhaft* and you will at last believe how little I really know now of it.

Now as to my convalescence. I used to feel myself all over everyday, to see how much I was hurt, and as it were take the temperature and pulse. My deepest depth lasted about 17–18 days, which seems very short. About the 18th day, it occurred to me that after all yesterday wasn't so bad, and had really gone off with comfort. I had been moved into a milder compartment, with less flame.

There I have been ever since. It is compatible with occasional enjoyment and general absence of acute pain. But periodically I go down into Hell again, no doubt when 'my light is low' and 'all the wheels of being slack'. But the more usual feeling is one of dullness and blankness of things, not acute but massive.

I don't think the experience is good for character. I noticed (confirmatory of *But Yet A Woman* and *Through One Administration*) that, a little while, I was distinctly more moral than usual. I did one or two unselfish things which I should not have done usually. But that is evanescent. There is an additional cynicism and 'hardness'. I can't charge it with my pessimism, because that was real, sincere and thorough 5 years ago, but it is now realler, sincerer and thorougher. I have had no *impulse* to suicide, tho' the thought has never been totally absent from my mind for years. That shows the benefit of 'settling' such questions and also, I think, is a consequence of more robust health.

It is interesting to notice how man is still 9/10th an irrational animal – how little influence the intellect has, compared with that exercised by the emotions. It has been a lesson to me. One sees how explanations may seem complete, and yet how very far they are from taking account of everything.

I think Dr Heidenhoff is so much needed that he *must* exist somewhere. What a sale Lethe-water would have done up like Apollinaris, and sent all over the world by a Limited Liability Company. Can't you discover such a spring, somewhere near Weimar?

One more reflection – as has been said often, it is faith-destroying. I am distinctly *more* atheistic than before, and I am afraid also more unsettled as to the Ethical Standard and its application.

I have fallen back into my old life here, reading and loafing, and playing cards. But *I think* I shall probably give up residence here by the time I start, or before.

Will you please explain to Miss Sonntag that I would propose to come from about 20th September to the 11th October? I have no doubt that I can come, but must write again later, positively, as I move in the world now with fear and trembling, in expectation of something uncomfortable turning up. But office arrangements at present indicate that I shall be free.

I suppose, as you say nothing, you have heard nothing of any vacancy for October. You will probably find that 3 months not unuseful to you. I beg to be remembered to Campion – I hope he will survive until I come.

Yours

Sidney Webb

53 PP SIDNEY WEBB TO GRAHAM WALLAS

Wallas had taken a tutoring post in Heidelberg. Webb's estimate, based on half the results, was fairly close to the final figures for the general election of 1885. In this first poll after the Reform Act of 1884 began to create a mass male electorate the ageing William Ewart Gladstone (1809–98) plumped for Irish Home Rule to win the support of Charles Stewart Parnell (1846–91) and his Nationalist supporters. The Liberals finally won 335 seats; Lord Salisbury (1830–1903) came back at the head of 249 Tories, thus leaving Parnell's 86 Irish votes to produce a dead heat – a situation which confirmed Gladstone's tactical support for Home Rule and led to the defection of Chamberlain and the Liberal-Unionists. At the subsequent election in 1886 Salisbury and Chamberlain had a majority of 118 over Gladstone and Parnell, gaining office for most of the next twenty years.

The theories of Pierre-Joseph Proudhon (1809–65), the French anarchist, influenced Shaw at this time: they were discussed at the Hampstead meetings.

27 Keppel Street, Russell Square, London
30/11/85

Dear Wallas

Why have you not written to Olivier or myself? We haven't your address, nor has either of us had the energy to go to Askin's for it, (tho' I did once start to do so) and consequently are excused from writing until you do.

I would have sent you some newspapers, but feared you would not get them, and expected daily to hear from you.

You probably know all about the elections. We have gone a tremendous crash in the towns, causes, (1) 'Fair Trade' (2) the Church (3) The Primrose League (4) Unsuccessful Foreign Policy (5) 'Chamberlainism' (6) The Irish defection. (7) The Atheist taint, which is beginning to be perceived by the religious (made apparent by 'Free Schools').

We stand this afternoon about 170 Liberal, 160 Conservative, 25 Irish. 70 to come: certain, 60 more Irish and 50 more Scotch and Welsh Liberals and 15 Irish Conservatives – uncertain 190 English county seats. Formerly these latter have been 120 to 50 Tory – up to date they are coming in about 20 to 20. If this goes on, we shall be 315 Liberal, 270 Conservative, 85 Parnell. The result will not probably vary more than from 290 to 350 Lib: 295 to 235 Conservatives. Forecast, therefore. It is very probable – unless we do astonishingly well – that Lord Salisbury will remain in *office* – but not in *power*. The Irish problem is the great difficulty. Parnell is the only man who has won, and Home Rule is within a measurable distance. It is more than likely that the Conservs. may do it; perhaps cutting off Scotland too, and including all in some big scheme of Federation of the Empire. The Church and the City and the Land are safe for another two years. Before then we shall have a dissolution, with Disestablishment as a plank. The Church has ruined itself by throwing itself into the hands of one party. All Liberals are full of bitterness against it just now.

I have been able to do or think of nothing else but elections. How are you getting on? We have had fearful weather here, and I have settled down to a very dead level of life – 'no hope no fear' sort of existence, which is however, not incompatible with comfort, altho' it is with reading or working much. I think my special disturbing influence has passed off – that is, so far as its own form is concerned – and I am much as I was 18 months ago, plus experience and several memories, and a certain unrest, and minus some of my youth and hope.

Tell me all about Heidelberg and your surroundings. We have had two evenings of Proudhon, not very satisfactory. I have translated two *Gedichte* in Prose for the *Anarchist*. Olivier has heard from the Sonntags but I not – they were at Hanover and well.

Yours

Sidney Webb

54 PP SIDNEY WEBB TO GRAHAM WALLAS

Webb's sister Ada sat for the Newnham College entrance: she passed but remained at home to care for her parents.

27 Keppel Street, Russell Square, London, s.w.

8/12/85

Dear Wallas

Thanks for your letter. I am glad you have fallen into pleasant places, but I rather grudge your stopping at Heidelberg. One ought not altogether sacrifice the future for the present, and I think you should aim at an endowed Headship – small, perhaps to begin with, but one which would afford a point from which to step on to another. (That is, unless you see your way to a 'private adventure' school, where you could experiment.)

Now the Heidelberg place is, I should think, very little recommendation towards a Headship – whereas a place at Dulwich [College] etc. would be. However, you will know best.

Doubtless I am biased by not wishing you to stop away – tho', as you say, it is a nice place to visit you at. Let me know if you intend coming home at Xmas.

As to your model boy, Olivier suggests he will be too old for ordinary public school scholarships. I should say his best course would be to prepare elsewhere for univ. scholarships – not necessarily in Classics – say either at University College, London (if he has friends here) or at some German university. The former would be best, except for the danger of turning a boy of 17 loose into this great city. There is money to be won at Univ. College, and excellent advanced tuition.

You need not be discouraged at not knowing what to advise him to do for a living. Your ideal education is one of general culture. You don't mean it to earn money. *That* is the function of technical education, which should come later. I don't see why a man should expect to make money out of his general education – nor could he even when this is (as it should be) common to all. He should now consider *what* technical education he will acquire. The careers are mainly

1. The City
2. ,, Bar
3. ,, Pillbox
4. ,, Sacrament
5. ,, Sabretask
6. ,, Pen
7. ,, Hand

7. Manual Labor will not produce more than £100 a year at best.
6. Literature is too uncertain and difficult. 5. Army is not for a poor man.
4. Church or Dissent requires some taste for it, and a grain at least of belief.

I think the choice is between the City at once, or Oxford and then the Bar, or the Ministry, or Cambridge/Aberdeen/Edinburgh and Medicine. The first if there is *no* money: the second or third if there is some and a liking for them. As to teaching, you know best.

I have not had time, what with Virgil and Horace with my sister, and other things, to do much reading, even for my LL.B examination which I may attempt in January, tho' if I do, it will be 'just as I am', without any cram. But I have read through Lucian, which happened to come in my way. I don't think much of it would be accepted by a publisher nowadays. The fact that it, by lucky accident, happens to have survived unburnt for 2000 years does not of course make it any better or worse – only remarkable. I have naturally read and heard much *about* the *Eumenides*, just

96

given at Cambridge – and I must express my candid opinion that neither it nor any of Sophocles is, *as drama* is, anything like as good as Scribe or Daudet, not to say Shakespere. This you will say is a backsliding. But however important the Greeks, like the Celts, have been to our development we are not bound to find either their drama or their stone axes as good as ours.

> 'John P.
> Robinson he
> said they didn't know everything
> Down in Judee!'

Yours

Sidney Webb

There!

55 PP SIDNEY WEBB TO GRAHAM WALLAS

Wallas was hard up: in the course of the summer he had borrowed small sums from Webb, who now redeemed and returned his pawned watch. W. P. Johnson was a fellow-clerk in the Colonial Office.

Webb's brother Charles was married twice. He rose from humble clerical work to become a partner in a relatively prosperous firm making rubber stamps; having modest ambitions he retired early.

27 Keppel Street, Russell Square

24/12/85

Dear Wallas

Herewith the insulted timekeeper. You owe me

	s	d	
	12.	0	Loan
		3	Interest
		8	Packing (too much!)
		3	Postage

13. 2 = being a social waste of 1s/2d, as you could have come here and borrowed the amount from one of us. I hope the parcel will arrive safe.

I played chess with Johnson last night, losing 3 games right off, but then recuperated by going to a whist party and winning, next, about 22 points. And so to bed, about 3 a.m. – not a moment's sleep. This morning at 9.30, 'best man' to my brother's wedding – a most lugubrious and disgraceful remnant of superstition. The mild officiating curate gave us the entire animal, concluding with 'two short rules for happiness in the new state', evidently distributed by some Church organ. These were – gracious

97

heavens, the whole duty of married men – first, to join together in morning prayer, second, to attend church.

And this is the institution which is in touch with the national life.

Yours disgustedly

Sidney Webb

I forgot exactly how we stand on the Dresden hotel business. My impression is that

$$33 \text{ marks} + £1 = \frac{\text{Joint Hotel Bill}}{\text{GW} + \text{SW}} + 25/\text{-}$$

If this is not near about, make it right on the 13s/2d for the watch.

Don't forget to finish the Education Article.

With many wishes

S.W.

56 PP SIDNEY WEBB TO GRAHAM WALLAS

On his way to a summer holiday in Norway Webb stopped at Newcastle-on-Tyne to visit his friend and fellow-Fabian, Edward Reynolds Pease (1857–1955). Pease came from a large and well-connected Quaker family. He gave up his early career as a stockbroker in disgust at the commercial values of the City; he became interested in psychic research, being one of the founders of the Society for Psychical Research in 1882, and in social reform, inspired by a desire for moral improvement. The group which formed the Fabian Society held its early meetings in his apartments in late 1883. Carpentry having been his hobby since childhood Pease decided to look for a suitable opening in the trade 'to identify myself for a time at any rate, with the manual labour class'. ('Recollections for My Sons', MS in Pease family papers.) This search for the Simple Life led him to join a Co-operative furniture workshop in Newcastle in 1886, where he worked as a cabinet-maker and to some extent kept the enterprise going by subsidies from his own savings. He took an active part in local labour politics and trade unionism, serving as secretary to the short-lived National Federation of Labour, which sought to combine socialism and trade unionism by enrolling individual members rather than affiliating organisations. He had become the honorary secretary of the Fabian Society before he went north in 1886; he was temporarily replaced by Sydney Olivier, but after his return to London he resumed the secretaryship which he held until his retirement at the outbreak of the First World War. From 28 March 1890, at a salary of £50 a year, he was the Society's first paid employee. He eventually inherited a substantial sum as part of the Fry chocolate fortune.

William Stubbs (1825–1901) was regius professor of history at Oxford 1866–84; Edward Augustus Freeman (1823–92) succeeded Stubbs as regius professor. Both were specialists on early English History.

Dear Wallas

You see I am at any rate well enough to write. It is a magnificent day, sea almost without a white crest anywhere and I have nothing more serious the matter with me than my usual vibrational headache. We expect to reach Xtiania sometime Sunday night, when I shall post this – unless we put in at Christiansund.

I have had a very good week indeed in Northumberland – splendid weather commenced by an 18-mile walk with Pease over the moors on Sunday, between Hexham, Blanchland and Consett, and discussed everything with him. He seems to be getting on well, but contemplates moving around a bit – perhaps to United States, before settling in London. On Monday we went down the Walker Colliery, and realised some of *Germinal* – but our particular conductor was a most prosperous man, house full of furniture, and a Conservative! He was a 'viewer' however, a sort of foreman. The afternoon and Tuesday we explored the Lower Tyne, and the coast N. and S. of the mouth. Wednesday morning we left for the Roman Wall, traced it five or six miles and investigated several stations and camps, and a huge Roman bridge abutment or quay on the Tyne, getting in to dinner at 10 p.m. to Hexham at a hydropathic establishment. We left there 6.30 Thursday morning, by train, then walked and drove 20 miles to Rothbury, exploring by the way. There I left the party early Friday morning, and came south, stopping 4 hours at York and meeting my Norway friends at Hull.

York seems mainly inhabited by people stopping a few hours between trains. I doubt whether it has any sleeping population at all. The Dean has put up a most Romanish reredos, in the shape of a gilt tryptich by Tinworth of the Crucifixion.

Hull has the worst statues I ever saw. There is one of William the Third on horseback, William dressed like Julius Caesar, with bare head and palm leaves round it, horse and figure both completely gilt!

The Roman Wall lowered my already low opinion of the Romans. No doubt it was a *large* order, but mere size is not impressive – besides the Chinese take the cake there. The wall is carried along steep precipices, where no wall was needed. It is built with childish and idiotic regularity, without regard for local conditions. In order that the stones might be regularly 'squared', (a merely pedantic requirement) they have ignored the hard local stone, and laboriously conveyed softer material from a great distance. It seems indeed just such a red-tape undertaking as might have been expected from a Roman Govt. dept. For *them*, and *for that time*, it was perhaps a creditable work, but absolutely it is a merely contemptible production not worth mentioning in the same breath as the Underground Railway.

We went over one big station, with a forum, and hypocausts. We also found a 'Mote Hill', so-named locally, which the local antiquary persisted in taking for a British camp, never having heard apparently of Stubbs, or Freeman. We chawed him up politely and went on our way triumphant. They are no doubt speaking of me as a disputatious youth today, for I held long arguments with all comers on the Depression of Trade – some metaphysics. Altogether I had a good time, perhaps because there were 3 or 4 clever girls in the party. Pease however scoffed at our zeal, and said we were very comic.

What do you think of running a series of lectures in the Fabian this winter on 'The Mistakes of Socialists'? Just like the Fabian they would say. But we must have some new thing. The only other wild suggestion I have is to run a series of lectures *to* different classes. Address the Aristocratic [*3 words illegible*]. Reproof in Reprobates, Problems for Politicians and so on. If we could only dare to have an address 'To men only' our fortune would be made. I am afraid one 'to Women only', say by Mrs B. [Besant] would not draw!

You have backslided no doubt, and succumbed to your sisters in the way of beard, and are now to be found clothed and in your right mind at lawn tennis – that is, living the typical life of the modern barbarian. Atavism works very quickly once outside London.

Yours

Sidney Webb

57 HRCUT SIDNEY WEBB TO EDWARD PEASE

The Fabian Society was still small, its nominal membership being less than one hundred and the active members amounting to about one dozen: its income in 1885–86 was £35.19.0. It was isolated from practical politics and had little sense of direction, its members mainly contenting themselves with delivering lectures to each other. Shaw was the only member systematically addressing outdoor meetings, which he did for the most part under the auspices of the Social Democratic Federation.

There was no agreement among the Fabians on what they meant by socialism, on the means whereby capitalism should be overthrown or on the kind of society that might replace it. They also were divided on the merits of political action. Charlotte Wilson's anarchist opinions were supported by sympathisers with William Morris (1834–96), the socialist poet and designer, who opposed parliamentary contests; other Fabians were affected by the insurrectionism of Hyndman and the S.D.F.; others, such as Hubert Bland, agreed with the S.D.F. policy but disliked its involvement in street rioting. Webb and Wallas, as active Radicals, wished to preserve the independence of the Society though they themselves were involved in Radical politics.

The issue was complicated by the scandal of 'Tory Gold', when two S.D.F. candidates contested London constituencies in the 1885 election and secured derisory votes of 32 and 27 – an action which helped to discredit the idea of running socialist candidates.

On the initiative of Annie Besant and Hubert Bland a meeting was held in Anderton's Hotel in the Strand on 17 September to discuss a proposal that socialists should organise themselves into a distinct political party. All the socialist groups were invited and the majority of Fabians allied themselves with the S.D.F. members present to defeat an anti-parliamentary amendment moved by William Morris, who argued that the people must first be educated to socialist consciousness. Webb was concerned at the result. He did not support Besant and Bland; he also feared that Mrs Wilson and the anarchists would force a split in the Society. He took the initiative at the meeting of the Fabian Executive, to which he and Wallas had been elected in April, on 5 November to propose a compromise. It was agreed that a separate body, called the Fabian Parliamentary League, should be formed. Wallas became secretary of the F.P.L. in the summer of 1887. It made little political impact: after it had served its tactical purpose and the anarchist challenge died away the parent Society allowed it to fade away.

27 Keppel St, Russell Square.

24/10/86

My dear Pease

I was pleased to have the account of your lecture, and also the report of your 'interview', both of which were excellent. It is curious to think how little Socialism has spread when you are probably the only Socialist on the Tyne.

I do not quite agree with your letters to the Executive about political action. I do not think we, as a Society, are by any means ready to propose a programme. I am quite sure any such action would cause a secession. As it is, it is only with great difficulty that we have been able to hit on a *modus vivendi* which enables Mrs Wilson to remain. Now I don't want a secession. I think we are doing good work in talking over these things by ourselves, and in attracting one bourgeois after another. Nothing in England is done without the consent of a small intellectual yet practical class in London not 2000 in number. We alone could get at that class, and we shall give up that work if we compete with the S.D.F. The two things are incompatible.

You have got strengthened in your faith by residence *in partibus infidelium*, and you have lost touch of our differences. It may be that the extreme State-Actionists are right, but half the Executive doubt the wisdom of precipitate Govt. extension, and I suppose some others in the Society agree with them. I doubt if we could agree on much more than an extreme Radical programme (e.g. free education, revision of land tax, graduated income tax, state railways) for actual work in the next few sessions. I am not prepared to oppose peasant proprietorship in Ireland, though I would in England.

Further, I doubt the wisdom of a separate Socialist party in Parliament except as a means of propaganda. We, like the homeopathists and the old Radicals, shall win without being acknowledged victors, by permeation of the others.

However, Mrs Besant and Bland are forcing the pace, and they no doubt would have a majority on a division. I don't want such a division to take place, as it will range us in two camps and hurry on the split. So we have arranged a compromise for Nov. 5, which no one on the Executive will oppose.

Evidently I am not a man of action. I am surprised to find how few of you agree with me in regarding Collectivist Socialism (as apart from mere socialistic radicalism), as a mere academic ideal like Plato's republic, which wants a lot of thinking about before one could vote for its adoption *en bloc*. I like it better than the present state of things, and work consequently towards its adoption, knowing that no such change can come for many centuries. But how it will work when it does come, I don't feel certain, and I expect that I should even then be a reformer, wanting a better ideal education and this probably makes me rather pessimistic.

I believe you will agree with this, or most of it, and therefore I hardly understand your so heartily supporting the party of action rather than education. I don't believe ten per cent of us are fit for a socialistic state yet. Someone has said that every people has as good a Govt. as it deserves and can live up to; that is very nearly true of industrial systems also.

Now I must close this lecture. I wish we could talk it over. When are you coming up?

Yours

[*no signature*]

58 WMC   SIDNEY WEBB TO GEORGE TANSLEY

One of the most influential figures in the history of the Working Men's College, George Tansley (1836–1904) was first a student, then a teacher and, in later years, responsible for promoting its extension work. Webb took extension classes for a time in Bermondsey and helped generally with promoting such classes.

27 Keppel St, Russell Sq.
7/2/87

Dear Mr Tansley

I find I cannot possibly attend the Executive meetings at the W.M. College. So that you really ought to omit my name. As I cannot come in person I send a few stray suggestions that have occurred to me on the Extension classes.

1) The proposed common tea gathering would be of great use. I hope you will bring this off. I will subscribe £1 towards expenses, if it is done by subscription.

2) Would it not be well to print a general list of the Extension classes that are in existence, giving place, address, subject, teacher, day and hour and fee, with some little par. about the College itself at top? I find an

account of what other clubs *are actually doing*, secures more attention than anything else. I would print the list at once, making it as big as possible; and then use it as such. To any appeals you make in preparation for new classes in October.

3) I think change of teachers is good. After the end of my present course at Bermondsey there had better be a shift. I will see what subjects they favour, and try to arrange a class, but another man had better take it. I will go elsewhere.

4) You will send out a flood of circulars again in the Summer I suppose. I would include

Young men's mutual improvement and other chapel societies
Branches of the National Secular Society, the Social Democratic Federation, and the Socialist League.

With best wishes, yours sincerely,
Sidney Webb

Don't trouble to answer this.

59 WMC SIDNEY WEBB TO H. R. JENNINGS

Webb wrote several letters to Jennings about ways of attracting new students to the Working Men's College.

27 Keppel St, Russell Square
15/5/87

Dear Mr Jennings

I am sorry to say I know of no list of Y.M.C.A. and other similar associations. But I suggest the following attempts to get such a list.

1) The Y.M.C.A., Exeter Hall, would probably supply a list of branch associations in answer to a simple letter of request (not stating object).

2) There *was* a calendar 'annual' *containing a complete list of all these institutions*, but the last was published in 1882 or 1883 I think. I have ransacked my lumber stores but cannot find a copy. I send the *Young Men's Magazine* which refers to it. I don't know whether it would be possible to get a copy (try Elliot Stock, 62 Paternoster Row, the publisher) of the last edition.

3) Otherwise I can only suggest the *gradual* formation of a list by individual help. I offer a small contribution

Bloomsbury Young Men's Club, 103 Gt Russell St
Westminster Chapel Mutual Improvement Society
(J. Nicholls), James Street, Buckingham Gate

4) This would be helped if you had local assistance. What you want is to map out London into ten districts, with one active man and a small Committee for each.

5) Buy a copy of *Justice* (1d) and the *Commonweal* (1d) – these give

long lists of branches of the Social Democratic Federation and the Socialist League.

6) There are 10 or 12 free libraries in London. They *ought* to have
lectures and might, as they can do it for nothing. Why not write to each
offering a literary course?

Yours

Sidney Webb

60 PP SIDNEY WEBB TO GRAHAM WALLAS

In the summer of 1887 several of the leading Fabians had play-acted at getting
into power. In the mock Charing Cross Parliament Webb had become Chancellor of the Exchequer, Annie Besant was Home Secretary, Hubert Bland was
Foreign Secretary, Graham Wallas was President of the Board of Trade, Bernard Shaw was President of the Local Government Board and Sydney Olivier
the Colonial Secretary. They presented draft legislation embodying their ideas.

Webb's mother had had a bad fall. She was in poor health thereafter and
became virtually housebound.

[?27 Keppel Street]
14/6/87

Dear Wallas

I leave in half an hour. But having a few minutes to spare, I write to
impress on you the desirability of your getting called to the Bar, if you
give up schoolmastering.

1) It would interfere very little with going to Germany – you only have
to dine 3 days, 4 times a year, all within 7 months.

2) It would cost, at most £130 and might cost nothing. As you know,
I won £450 during that time, and you could get something with certainty.

3) It gives you two new chances of picking up guineas.

a) You would clearly earn a few pounds at the bar, at the very worst –
you know several solicitors – you would go the Western Circuit – your
father knows Judges etc. Why not keep open this avenue?

b) If you take to coaching it opens up several avenues, bar exams,
London Ll.B. exams, solicitors exams, Oxford Law Pass exams. You
could count on picking up a good pupil or two in Grays Inn alone. I
could have had several. You can't get law coaching without it.

4) It qualifies you, for several things which might come your way in
afterlife, when *we* all get into power!

5) If you are going to spend £200 over your improvement, why not
£320, with foregoing advantages.

I don't know what to advise you to do. But if you cast yourself adrift
at all, I strongly recommend the Bar as an adjunct, and possible way to
success.

Some magnificent roses have just come from Crediton, for which we are all much obliged. My mother is progressing splendidly – sits up daily.

Yours

Sidney Webb

61 PP SIDNEY WEBB TO GRAHAM WALLAS

Queen Victoria's Golden Jubilee fell on 20 June 1887 while Webb was on holiday with the Wilsons. The fourth member of the party may have been H. W. Carr (d. 1931) who became secretary of the Aristotelian Society in 1890 and married the Fabian Geraldine Spooner.

Earlier in the year, at Shaw's suggestion, Webb had produced the first edition of his penny leaflet, *Facts for Socialists,* which in subsequent revisions became one of the Fabian Society's bestsellers. The Society was still in the doldrums and on Webb's initiative a committee drafted a new 'Basis' or statement of principles which was used for the next three decades as the test for admission of the Society. It defined socialism and the Society's role in such general terms – 'the general dissemination of knowledge as to the relation between the individual and society in its economic, ethical and political aspects' – that there was in fact no orthodoxy to which members had to subscribe. This device protected the Fabians from the doctrinal disputes which disrupted other socialist groups. It also emphasised the importance of research and propaganda rather than political action.

Falcide, Nordfjord, Norway
23/6/87

My dear Wallas

We are resting for a day in a place which would be thought of exquisite beauty anywhere else, but which is much excelled by others here. Imagine a winding arm of sea, $\frac{1}{2}$ mile across, between hills 5000 ft high, (the snow-line being 4000), green at foot, the water a dark blue, above the sun shining with fierce brilliancy out of a blue sky, gradually eating up the morning mists.

Yesterday we grilled for 9 hours in 4 stretches, on the boards of open boats, doing, in between, about 4 hours very rough walking, and returning 10 miles over the fjord in a sudden storm which made us ship seas in an uncomfortable manner. Reward, a most lovely lake, bounded by sheer precipices 4000 ft high, capped all round by edges of glaciers, whence *we saw* ice avalanches drop 1000 ft sheer at a time. We attained one of these glaciers up a magnificent gorge, and climbed up its foot.

Thus far we have had a splendid time: the party most *gemütlich*. Mrs W. is piquante as ever, and Mr W. most philosophically tolerant. We pass the most delightful days, with more laughter than I had thought it possible for any of the party to contribute. Carr, our fourth, is a mild stockbroker, unmarried, a metaphysical Pyrrhonist, a Hegelian, and by way of being an admirer of the ancients. He was quite unknown to Mrs W. as to me, and only known to Mr W. commercially. As you may imagine, we are interesting phenomena to him, tho' he is less so to us. We have steered clear of Anarchism fairly well, tho' it has given us one long discussion, and a steady undercurrent to the whole conversation.

We have come through from Bergen by stages of 30–50 miles a day – steamer, carriage and rowboat alternately. The oddest part of the business is that there is no night at all. The sun goes down in fiery splendour about 9 p.m. but it remains just as light as ever. We can read in bed all night without artificial light. The effect is that at 11 p.m. it is impossible to believe that it is more than 6 p.m., and difficult to go to bed.

Mrs W. startled us all on the Jubilee day by saying quite calmly that she hoped the Queen would only get well shaken and not killed! I am waiting impatiently to see whether anything has happened – we have had no word of news since we started which seems ages ago.

I am acting as courier for the party, hitherto with great success but so many people speak a little English that I learn little Norwegian. We have seen two weddings (we made a wedding present of a six-shilling banknote to one bride, which we were told, was ducal munificence.)

I am more and more charmed with this country, and with June in it. This is probably due in great part to the subtle and (what ought to be) the unconscious influence of the composition of the party, which certainly makes it the most charming holiday I have ever had. I have had one laconic telegram from home, indicating that my mother is going on well and I hope to get another in a day or two.

I hope your own affairs are clearing themselves up in your own mind. I don't know what to advise, except the Bar.

Yours

Sidney Webb

62 WMC SIDNEY WEBB TO H. R. JENNINGS

Edward Bibbins Aveling (1851–98), the common-law husband of Karl Marx's daughter Eleanor, had lost his academic post as a science teacher on account of his socialist and secularist views. He was disreputable in both financial and moral matters; his conduct led eventually to Eleanor Marx's suicide in April 1898.

27 Keppel St, Russell Square
17 Sept. 87

Dear Mr Jennings

I fear you have a big job, in the absence from town of so many of your helpers, in starting the classes. I will try to come to the Executive on Tuesday to do what I can in Council.

1) Plumstead Radical Club. Please don't give my name for casual

lecturing. Tell them of the S.P.E.L. [Society for the Promotion of Extension Lectures] (W. T. Sutton, 19 Ludgate Hill is now Secretary) and send them the enclosed Fabian lecture list.

2) I suppose your German class at Old Kent Road would be paid for, and ?also the Bookeeping and at the West Marylebone Club.

If so, you might ask my friend Graham Wallas (note his permanent address 92 Cheyne Walk, Chelsea) to take the German, which he could do well. Would not Descours, 3 Saxby Terrace, Jennings Road, Lordship Lane, S.E., take the Bookeeping? I fear that you will not get teachers in these unless we can pay the 4/- or 5/- a night, and of course, this was contemplated as regards languages at any rate. If you pay for Bookeeping, let me know, as I might find another man to fall back on. Descours, is, of course, the best possible man for French, and he could also take German but Wallas is better.

For your *advanced* Algebra you should use Anderson of the C.O. [Colonial Office] as he is a better mathematician than most – it is much easier to fill up Elementary Algebra, which I think he agreed to take at the college.

Pol. Econ. Olivier, 180 Portsdown Road N10, is willing to take a class in his own neighbourhood. Why not fix him for North Kensington at once? Modern History you ought to manage to fill from the staff. Mr Dodds disposed of?

Aveling I think you know all about. As the grant would not be paid unless and until earned, there is not much risk – except of some scandal. He is a magnificent teacher, and if he can get up a class anywhere I am personally inclined to shut eyes to the past, and chance the future, for the sake of his teaching power.

Yours truly

Sidney Webb

63 HRCUT SIDNEY WEBB TO EDWARD PEASE

Webb had joined the National Liberal Club at least a year before.

While the Fabians debated, the unemployed, urged on by the S.D.F., staged repeated demonstrations in the streets which culminated in the dramatic riot in Trafalgar Square on 'Bloody Sunday', 13 November.

A number of Fabians were involved in this affair, Annie Besant and Bernard Shaw leading one of the columns marching in from East London. Webb's letter is remarkable because it makes no reference to the most sensational political event of the year, but concentrates on the tactics of permeating the Liberal Party. The more moderate Fabians were anxious to avoid being identified with violence, preferring to cultivate middle-class reformers through salon politics and public lectures. From the end of 1887 Webb was very active in promoting advanced resolutions through Radical associations in London as a means of influencing Liberal policy.

John Morley (1838–1923), later Viscount Morley, was a Liberal politician, edited the *Fortnightly Review* and the *Pall Mall Gazette*. He was for years a publisher's reader and journalist and author, publishing a famous *Life of Gladstone* (1903). He was a prominent leader of the Radical wing of the Liberal Party, well known for his agnostic beliefs and a strong individualism which made him an opponent of socialism though an advocate of political reform. He was one of the two M.P.s for Newcastle from 1883–95.

[?27 Keppel Street]
16.11.87

Dear Pease

This is a busy winter for me: hence my not writing to you. But I still grudge your absence from town.

The immediate purpose and spur for this letter is to get you to sign the enclosed. The N.L.C. [National Liberal Club] is doing absolutely nothing, strangled by a few rich Unionists. The Requisition has already been laid before the Committee but we want as many signatures as possible. Don't keep the paper above 2 days, but should you be able to get others in that time, pray do so.

The Fabian still goes on. We are gradually 'living down' the sectarian opposition to us: the S.L. [Socialist League] are quite friendly now, and the S.D.F. branches somewhat mollified, tho' the top is still poisoned. We don't get any funds, however, and are much hampered by debt. It is absurd that a Society of 88 members should not raise more than £30 a year. I wish you would write to Bland (not mentioning me) urging more activity and especially another tract. I am sure we ought to be doing more. The difficulty is that only about 10 members do any work to speak of, *in connection with the Society*, and not more than 20 help us at all. The S.D.F. puts us to shame in this respect.

Our 'Local' meetings are somewhat of a success. A series of drawing room meetings is to grow out of the Hampstead one, which has made some stir. Please try to influence your Hampstead brother to come to some.

Union in the party seems as far off as ever, unless it grows out of the next School Board election, which I want to get taken up by all sections. Please do what you can to disseminate the idea that we ought to run candidates in every division, some from each party, and then all work for each: with a joint central committee.

In preparation for this, or for any general convention of Socialists, we are compiling a general 'Directory' of all who call themselves Socialists. Please send to G. Wallas, 92 Cheyne Walk (Secretary of Fabian Parliamentary League) the names and addresses of *any* non-Fabian Socialists you know of *anywhere*, for absorption into this (private) list. Don't count on their being in already, as it is meagre.

I have got a tract on Taxation of Ground Rents accepted by the respectable Committee working that movement. As it is practically a plea for

Land Nationalisation, I thought it worth doing, to keep them straight on the question, and to have a useful statement of the facts of rent to give away.

Did I tell you, also, that I have got the Sunday Lecture Society (St George's Hall) to put me down on their January programme for a lecture on Socialism? This will be useful propaganda, as those lectures have a special and peculiar audience, and are much advertised.

I am glad to hear you are busy lecturing. The movement is too much centred in London and a few towns. We ought to be able, like the Anti-Corn Law League, to send out a flood of subsidised lecturers to go from town to town.

I believe very much in getting hold of the Liberal caucuses. They are just on the turn, without knowing it, and a little push from inside does much to send them in our direction. I hope you take part in the Newcastle one. Champion relates how he talked the matter over with John Morley, who was quite friendly and sympathetic with our aims, but said he had not had occasion to look into social matters, and could not do so at present, as his constituents *were not interested in the questions.* Now this is just where the use of political Socialism comes in. If you managed to get resolutions passed at ward meetings etc., as to the necessity of dealing with these things, John Morley would take them up. If you have today's *Daily News* by you, see the resolutions which I induced the St George's Bloomsbury people to pass, condemning the Nottingham programme. I think all caucuses should be urged to pass some such motion. The leaders are not yet aware how sympathetic the Liberal party is with the poor.

But goodnight.

Sidney Webb

64 NLS   SIDNEY WEBB TO JANE BURDON-SANDERSON [*incomplete*]

Jane Charlotte Burdon-Sanderson (d. 1889) was the aunt of Richard Burdon Haldane (1856–1928). Haldane was an able Scots barrister, amateur philosopher and politician, who was one of the rising stars in the Liberal Party at the end of the nineteenth century. He was associated with Webb and Wallas in London Radical politics and became a close and lifelong friend of both Webbs. He was an earnest man with a talent for intrigue and a taste for gossip.

The problem of the moral calculus, which Sidney Webb discusses at length in this letter, much exercised the Fabians at this time. Both Sidney and Beatrice independently arrived at the same conclusion about the obligations of those with unearned income.

Mrs Cash was a Fabian sympathiser in Hampstead; Grace Gilchrist was a young Fabienne, the passing object of Shaw's attentions, who helped to organise the 'drawing-room' campaign. The Society remained divided about this campaign. Shaw preferred outdoor meetings, but as late as 5 April 1889 Stewart Headlam was proposing at the Fabian annual general meeting 'that the Society should try to organise more drawing-room meetings and to attract the upper middle class by lectures at fashionable centres'.

Dear Miss Burdon-Sanderson,

I am very pleased to have an opportunity of answering your enquiry as to what course of conduct those persons should pursue who are now living on rent or interest, and who are not capable of earning their own livelihood. But first let me explain that personal conduct must necessarily be left in each case, to the individual conscience. It is almost impossible for anyone else to be sufficiently acquainted with the exact circumstances, and not even a prophet could safely prescribe conduct for another. At the same time it may be possible to afford you some assistance in coming to a decision, and I do not shrink therefore from stating frankly my own views of the general principles which should guide the lives of persons circumstanced in the way you describe.

It is clear, to begin with, that private recipients of rent or interest will find themselves, on becoming aware of the economic nature of their incomes, in possession of the legal power of levying tribute upon the labor of others, without giving any equivalent in return. But as rent and interest (that is, the advantages of capital and superior land) cannot simply be abolished, it would do no good simply to refuse to draw one's rent and interest: this would be but to cede them to the person paying them, by no means necessarily to the worker. And it is further, the essential principle of Socialism that these advantages do not equitably belong even to the individual worker any more than to you: they are the result of social co-operation and belong to the whole community.

You are therefore in the position of a steward for the community, of the rent and interest coming to you. How can you best fulfil your stewardship?

It is obvious that the mere fact that existing circumstances place you in this position of stewardship, does not give you any exceptional privileges or claims over other persons: it imposes on you new duties and responsibilities, but in no way exempts you from the common lot. Let us therefore consider the duty of the ordinary citizen.

In the first place there is the duty of *labor*. I can conceive no excuse whatever for any person in ordinary health not taking his (*or her*) share in the work of the world, that work need not be such as would earn money; (e.g. household duties, attendance on the sick and aged, and so on, are equally work), but it must be the rendering of some personal service to the community, in the way one best can. 'From each according to his abilities.' There is an abundance of unpaid social duty needing to be done, our libraries, our evening classes, our schools, our poor, our local administration, our political organisation, all need helpers.

But it must be work, i.e. the service must have some utility to the state, and must be steady and continuous for ? hours per day. I won't say how many. Eight out of ten of the population have to work at least 8 hours a day for us, usually more. Can we honestly do less for them in return?

Secondly there is the duty of *economy*. The distribution of wealth is very unequal, but the cost of each individual to the community is not what he receives but what he consumes (i.e. practically, 'spends' on other than public objects). We need not spend so much. It appears to me that the maximum justifiable expenditure for anybody is that amount which keeps him in the fullest working efficiency. Everything beyond is selfish waste. To each 'according to his needs.' This would include however his *mental* needs, as for instance, some art and relaxation, as being necessary to the fullest efficiency of life.

This 'personal equation' must be left to the individual. But one other reflection may be added. Unless each individual does work equal in utility to the utility of the commodities he consumes, he is a dead loss to the world. The lives of the workers would be happier if he did not exist. This is an appalling reflection, and when once realised, it may serve to correct the inevitable personal bias which leads us to give ourselves the benefit of the doubt.

It is just this latter tendency which makes it hard for a rich man to enter the 'Kingdom of Heaven'. It is so difficult for him to bring himself to do his daily work (seeing that his income does not depend upon it) and so easy again to allow himself to consume more than he needs of his income (seeing that he has the legal 'right' to do so). But, ethically, income is only maintenance. If you are able to draw an income without work, you are in the fortunate position of having a steady maintenance and of being able to *choose* your work. But the maintenance consumed must not exceed the value of the work done.

Having chosen (and done) your daily work, and allotted to yourself an annual maintenance, there remains the question of the special duties of those owners of wealth who do not employ it themselves.

First as to the capital. I consider every owner of wealth morally responsible for what is being done with that wealth, so far as he can control it. It is part of the natural duty and work of rich persons to look after the disposition of their wealth. If you are a railway shareholder or bondholder, take care that you write letters every month to the Directors urging shorter hours and better wages for the men. *Your* money in the bank is enabling some army contractor to hire shirtmakers at 6/- per week – with the inevitable consequences. Your water shares are your instrument of oppression of the poor whose water supply is cut off or fouled. Therefore think how and where your capital is employed – put it where you can see it most easily – take part in its management, if only by *constantly* writing to those who manage it.

Even then the present system makes you almost helpless. Women and children will be oppressed and starved *with your capital* whatever you do.

If you resent this, and groan under the necessity, it seems to me that you should do what you can to alter the system – i.e. throw your energy and ability into the cause of Socialism.

Then as to the income. Most of us can do so little work, and we all of us *need* so little, that you will probably find that you have much income to spare. This you must employ as you know best how. But unless you can conscienciously say your work would be thereby rendered more efficient, it is clear that you cannot consume it yourself. If you know any good work to do with it, turn it to that end. If not, save it and invest it as nearly harmlessly as you can. This will do some good to the poor, although you will not see the good.

But a further duty remains. If you look around, you will see that the great majority of those in your circumstances are not in the least aware of their duties in these matters. They are blinded by their bad education, their surroundings, their wealth. It is impossible that all persons can be equally moralised: therefore the laws and institutions must be altered so to as prevent the unmoral people any longer preying unwittingly on the world. This is why we work for Socialism. Is it not part of the duty of those who *do* see these things, to preach them to those who do not? It is a 'call' which we must not neglect.

Therefore I think that, in addition to other duties, those who believe are called upon to 'spread the light'. Everyone can exercise much influence in his own circle in his own way.

But more can be done by organisation, and I think therefore that all who are convinced should join themselves together in some militant organisation to make their influence felt. By so doing, we are strengthened in the faith, we learn new aspects of duty, and we carry on the propaganda.

As a beginning, see what Mrs Cash did, in lending her house and services for a Socialist address. There must be many who can be of use in this way, and I am sure that Miss Gilchrist would be only too pleased to hear of any opening. The Fabian Society wants to pursue the 'mission' to Hampstead, and there might be a series of these drawing rooms.

Then you should make yourself acquainted with Political Economy Socialism, so as to know when you are doing good, and when doing harm. We cannot . . .

65 SU   SIDNEY WEBB TO W. W. BARTLETT

This is one of several letters to William Walter Bartlett, an active member of the Land Restoration League and of the local Fabian group in Bloomsbury whom Webb advised on the tactics of permeating the Liberal association to nominate candidates and influence policy as a preferable alternative to independent socialist agitation.

8 Jan. '88

Dear Mr Bartlett

I am sorry to say that I cannot possibly take up the County Council work – I have already much more than I can do. I am therefore not speaking for *anyone* anywhere, and cannot come to your meeting on Friday.

I hope you will find plenty of support – but it would have been much better to have had the Liberal Association *for* you rather than against you. It is *so* easy to capture these Liberal Associations that I am tired of inciting Socialists to do it. The County Council candidature was practically settled last spring when the Liberal Association Executive was elected. Where were the Socialists then?

Now for the future. The new Executive of the South St̲Pancras Liberal Association will be elected at the two Ward meetings *this month* or next. Is the Bloomsbury Society looking after this? Have you found out when these two Ward meetings are to be?

I do not believe in candidatures undertaken *against* the local political bodies. What we ought to do is to make those bodies ours.

Yours truly

Sidney Webb

66 PP SIDNEY WEBB TO SIR HICKMAN BACON

Sir Hickman Bacon (1855–1945) was the premier baronet of England. A public-spirited Tory, who covertly gave money to reformist organisations, he became a lifelong acquaintance of the Webbs and he later contributed to a number of their projects.

The Progress of Socialism was based on a lecture to the Hampstead Historic Society, which appears on the title page in yet another of its guises – 'Hampstead Society for the Study of Socialism'. It was published in 1888 by the Modern Press, which was run by H. H. Champion.

London

5 Aug. 88

Dear Sir

I have been asked to send you information as to Socialism, and especially as to its proposed immediate legislation for the benefit of the poor etc.

I send by book post some literature on the subject, but I think it right to explain that Socialists do not claim to have any panacea in the shape of practical legislation immediately to set things right. Socialism indeed, emphatically negatives any such hope, by asserting that the whole basis of social organisation must be (and is being) changed, before things will be well. Bills in Parliament it leaves mainly to party politicians, the chief work at present being to change the *principles* on which these politicians, and the voters, act in social matters. You will find this view developed in my *Progress of Socialism*, which also gives references to other works.

But, as a politician, I may say that the immediate work of the legislator on Socialist principles appears to me to be in the following lines:

Extension of the Factory Acts to all employments, and considerable increase in the numbers of inspectors.

Abolition of School Fees.

Reorganisation of Poor Law (so as to maintain tests against ablebodied imposture) but also to (a) provide for temporarily unemployed (b) provide, without stigma, pensions for all aged or sick (c) utilise pauper labor in industry.

Thorough revision of taxation, repealing all but alcoholic duties, increasing death duties, and imposing a heavy differentiated and graduated Income Tax and Land Tax, gradually increasing these until it becomes practically impossible for any idler to live (his rent and interest being entirely absorbed).

Extension of Municipal action in the matter of gas, water, markets, hospitals, libraries, parks, baths, secondary schools, etc. etc.

All Municipal and State contracts to forbid subcontracting, and to require payment of a fixed minimum wage.

Municipal provision of artisans dwellings at cost price, in place of slums.

Limitation of working day to 8 hours in all Government workshops, and in all railways, trams, gas, water and other licensed monopolies.

All these measures are immediately practicable, and are advocated in detail, and platonically by most thoughtful politicians, as well as supported by the Political Economists.

But they are delayed by the opposition of those who would be (as a class) extinguished by them, i.e. those who now live on rent and interest.

I am, Dear Sir
Yours faithfully
Sidney Webb

67 PP   SIDNEY WEBB TO GRAHAM WALLAS

Webb was tired with overwork; Pease was thinking of emigrating to the United States. They decided to take a long American trip together. In April Webb applied for leave from the Colonial Office, pointing out that he had never taken up his full leave allotment in any year, and asking to be released for three months. One of his superiors noted on the minute that 'Mr Webb has well deserved the concession which he requests'.

Webb sailed in early September on the *City of New York*, being joined by Pease at Queenstown. He then told Webb that he had been engaged for several months to Marjorie Davidson, a twenty-four-year-old Scots schoolteacher. Miss

Davidson had joined the Fabian set and attended some of the Hampstead meetings; she was on close terms with Olivier and Shaw, and Webb himself was undoubtedly attracted to her.

The G.S.M. was the Guild of St Matthew, a small group of socially minded Anglicans formed in 1877 by Stewart Headlam. It played a part in the Christian Socialist revival though it was overshadowed by the later and larger Christian Social Union.

Permanent Address: C/o Kennedy Tod and Co., 63 William St, New York.

17/9/88

Dear Wallas

Arrived 15th after smooth passage: only ill first day. N. York found in spell of damp heat, drizzling rain, exceedingly depressing: our friends mostly out of town. Interviewed Rev. Father Huntingdon, the head of an American imitation of the G.S.M. – priest in cassock gave us supper – begged us to tell him how to teach the people etc. – earnest and ambitious.

N. York is 'ramshackle': new buildings high and gorgeous, but all else mean and untidy: pavements *worse* than small German town, tel. poles undressed and unpainted pine stems, and so on.

We start on Wednesday (19th) for the Hudson, Niagara and Canada, arriving at Boston in a month: address as above will reach us, but you might send a newspaper to 'Post Office, Boston'. Send Fabian Autumn syllabus (several copies) if not already done.

Not much done yet in the way of discovery: weather reduces us to pulp.

Sidney Webb

68 PP SIDNEY WEBB TO GRAHAM WALLAS

William Dean Howells (1837–1920), the American journalist and novelist, was editor of the *Atlantic Monthly* from 1872 to 1881. John Singer Sargent (1856–1925) was an outstanding American portrait painter. Francis Amasa Walker (1840–97) had served in the Civil War and become president of the Massachusetts Institute of Technology. Webb was impressed both with M.I.T., which served him as a model for the later foundation of the London School of Economics and Political Science, and with Walker's economic theories, which emphasised the link between high wages and economic progress. Benjamin Tucker (1854–1939) was an American anarchist. His unauthorised reprint of an article on anarchism by Shaw in his journal *Liberty* in April 1885 was the first appearance of Shaw's writing in America.

Hodgson was the former name of Richard Dacre Archer-Hind (1849–1910), classical scholar and fellow of Trinity College, Cambridge.

Stephen Grover Cleveland (1837–1908) was a Democrat elected President of the United States in 1884, defeated in 1888 and elected again in 1892.

Dear Wallas

Boston turns out to be very good value, and as we have not yet half worked through our letters of introduction we shall probably stay here for another fortnight, making excursions around. We have been made temporary members of three clubs, two 'swell' and this one Bohemian consisting of 125 members selected for their talent! W. D. Howells was its President up to a few weeks ago, and such men as Sargent the painter (who is away) and the best musicians, doctors, lawyers and painters belong.

We went over the Institute of Technology yesterday – we had introductions to two Professors, and I had also some hold on General Walker, the economist, who is President. It is a splendid place, 800 students, 17 upwards male and female (one woman is Prof. of Sanitary Science), for instruction in technology. I send the prospectus of the General Department. The *Economics* course is the best I ever heard of – but mainly historical and statistical – laboratory methods, each student doing elaborate exercises in preparing reports, summaries, histories, and graphic statistic charts, from the official records, on given subjects – e.g. iron trade of U.S. at different years, tariff history etc. Free Trade is treated as an open question and the Prof. said no one had yet discovered which way he leaned! (Theology without deciding whether there is a God or not!) The full course for graduation is 4 years: fee 800 dollars for the whole: students mainly training for mechanical, mining and chemical positions.

Walker is a typical *ex-militaire*, square solid face, great self-reliance and strength – received us very kindly, remembered me, and asked us to dinner, putting us up also at his club. We discussed the English Economists, bimetallism etc., but not our disputed points yet. He is keenly interested in politics – is a 'Mugwump' i.e. independent deserter from Republican party. Apparently these number the great majority of the cultivated class, and in the West, Walker says the common voter is turning also. It seems clear that Cleveland will get elected, and my own opinion is that he will win *all* the doubtful states.

We have walked about Harvard, but have not yet delivered our letters there. It is a suburb of Boston (3 miles) but is a town of itself consisting of miles of tree-lined streets of detached villas, quite the most ideal 'academe' that I have seen. Oxford and Cambridge are grossly materialist and industrial in comparison. The men seem to live in lodgings and board around – we had lunch in the only restaurant in the place – an upper floor 'eating house' of the common English coffee-house type where there were 40 or 50 students eating 'dinner' (at 1.30); a rough meal at about a shilling a head. Most of them paid for it by tickets, showing that they frequented the place and took a number at a time (discount).

We went over a large printing and publishing works (*Atlantic Monthly*) which is said to be rather a model, but not philanthropic: with savings bank, (participating in profits) benefit society etc. The partner, after a talk, handed us over to the foreman with orders to show us everything – the foreman went with us asking each class of workers their wages in our presence. All exceptionally good (mostly piecework) running *up to* 25 dollars a week (we *heard* of 40 dols). Women folding by hand said they got 6 dols. Rents were high – men paid 12 to 20 dol. a month – usually about 1/5 to 1/4 of their wages – coals 26/- per ton – food cheap, clothes *a little* dearer. The man who worked the elevator – unskilled labor – was an Irishman who came over 6 years ago, got a job next day, had shifted once, and had never been out of work. He said he got 15 dols a week, and only paid 9 dols a month rent. The partner told us afterwards that he noticed a nice little house building – asked whose it was – and found it was this elevator man's (mortgaged of course). A Spanish ex-sailor was a packer, and got 17 dols a week. The common day laborer was *said* to get 12 dols.

These are probably exceptionally good wages – on the other hand Tucker of *Liberty* tells us that newspaper offices pay even better than this *Atlantic Monthly* firm in the branches he knows.

The odd thing is that Pease's brother here – an architect, out of his time, who had been earning a salary, small, in London, and who came out here to better himself, with what he seems to think good prospects and *results*, is only getting 15 dols a week = the elevator man's wages. I suspect that clerical labor is the same. Typewriter girls are much used – *inferior* ones get 10 dols a week, average 15 dols, exceptional ones much more.

Tucker of *Liberty* turns out to be a handsome, refined, quiet-speaking man, of very 'gentlemanly' manners and tone – apparently a 'reader' or thereabouts on the *Boston Globe* newspaper – he asked us to dinner at a restaurant, and was very polite and friendly – treated us as 'brothers in the faith' who differed merely in a detail. He professes only to have a small handful of adherents here, partly foreign. He says there is a small circle of Collectivists (who had meetings on alternate Sundays with his Anarchists) in a joint room last winter. We shall hunt them up next Sunday.

R. Hodgson of Cambridge, the Psychist, is here as Sec. of an American Psychical Research Society and has been exceedingly good – Pease hopes the Spiritualism fit is progressing. He want to know whether you are also starting a collection of postage stamps.

Yours

Sidney Webb

Miss Davidson was now teaching at Cheltenham Ladies College. In this letter Webb set out his unvarying view of marriage as a partnership in which the sum of the two partners should greatly exceed the parts – and his belief that such a partnership should be dedicated to the public good. The reference to 'several private mysteries' is intriguing but opaque.

The lately-married friend was Sydney Olivier. *Our Corner* was the monthly paper owned and edited by Annie Besant.

Sergius Stepniak (1852–95) was the revolutionary pseudonym of Sergei Mikhailovich Kravchinski, a Russian nihilist who assassinated the head of the Tsarist secret police and escaped to exile in London, where he wrote a number of books and became a close friend of many socialists – especially the group, which included Marjorie Pease, which was known as the Friends of Russia. When the Peases, Oliviers and other Fabians settled at Limpsfield Common in Surrey, jokingly called 'Dostoevsky Corner', Stepniak was for a time a near neighbour.

Pease remained in America after Webb returned, but after being dismissed from his first job in Philadelphia for incompetence he came back to England and married Marjorie Davidson in 1889.

Srewart Headlam was briefly and unsuccessfully married in 1878 to Beatrice Pennington.

27 Keppel Street, Russell Square
12th December 1888

Dear Miss Davidson

I take the very earliest of my opportunities since my return to London yesterday afternoon, to write to you. I am very sorry that you were away from London so that we cannot talk face to face of the momentous secret which I am strictly enjoined not to impart to anyone – though there are no doubt about 59 similar possessors similarly circumscribed. If you ever come up to London (e.g. to do some shopping) and especially if you are going through London on your way North, please let me have a chance of seeing you, here or elsewhere.

For I have a great desire for your friendship, with the very smallest capacity for acquiring it. I have often envied the ease with which others 'catch on' to congenial spirits (E.R.P. for instance, is one such lucky or clever person), where I simply remain outside. I am of course very busy, somewhat serious, very analytic and introspective – but, I hope passably honest, sincere, and not obviously hateful or repulsive. Yet I seem 'left out' in more than one case, and in more than one department of life. (This, however is by the way.) I am at any rate going to begin by a long intimate letter to yourself. One of the difficulties incidental to your present position is my uncertainty as to your exact personality. I am writing to you, or to Pease and you, or to you plus Pease? The copyright of a letter remains vested in the writer, and I am compelled to avow a desire that I may be understood as writing only to you, and not to you plus Pease. I do not forbid you to pass on this letter but should prefer you not to. My own theory of marriage does not involve the merging of identities. I am even against an intellectual communism. Let me assume for the nonce that it is to be a mere partnership. I write to one of the partners only.

I was very pleased when Pease told me his great news soon after we met at Queenstown. Nothing could have pleased me more than that you should marry Pease – unless it was that Pease should marry you – and here are both events happening together. Nevertheless you will perhaps understand that it was with a 'contraction' of the heart that I heard the news: and an old wound, which still embitters me, was torn open, and bled, as it bleeds now while I write to you these words, and I think again of Heine's songs, (Do you remember *Ein Mädchen liebt ein Andern* – I forget whether you read German), and the whole mournful swing of Schubert's setting of some of them – *Der arme Peter*, for instance comes back to me, and so on and so on I mean I am very cross with things in general, and I realise that I am 'left out'. I am afraid I have a great deal of 'Langham' in me – I knew it when I read Mark Pattison's Autobiography.

However my own little woes – now some five years old – are not your fault and I am not irrational enough to grudge others better luck. But I must not disguise the fact that one grievance against you I have – which you must atone for. *L'ami qui se marie se perd*. I am nearly thirty and during the last five years (just those five years too) I have lost five intimate friends by marriage. With Pease I had become intellectually intimate, though living afar off, and America has made us real friends. (We are as Shaw would say 'even on quarrelling terms'.) Now you are to come in and carry him off from me and others just as our friendship ripens. *C'est dur*. The loss is irreparable whatever you may intend to say. It rests indeed with you to furnish compensation by becoming yourself a friend. I warn you that it is hard to be 'friends' with me – I am an exacting person, needing more to be loved, it may be, than capable of loving – a kind of stone wall on which fruit will grow but needing a good deal of sun. (N.B. you didn't know that I was so poetical did you?)

Having frankly avowed my position towards you I proceed to America. How did you enjoy *your* visit to America? For though to the vulgar eye, and to that of the ticket collector, Pease and I were alone, you and I and Pease know that it was a case of 'one and one and a shadowy third' where we went, your wraith went also: what we saw we saw with you, what we thought we discussed in your presence and even for your sake, and I am not sure even whether that exacting Goddess whom we all three serve, I mean Humanity, was not sometimes eclipsed by one human.

Now don't go and suppose that this increase of the party was unpleasant to me. I trust you will permit me to say that I too felt that I had an interest in the matter, and many and many a time the threeness of our party gave a new zest to the intellectual stimulus of our mutual intercourse. I do not deny that your peculiar relation to us, (as the perpetually present absentee) was occasionally an abnormal factor in our action. For instance, the Post Office became the only public building in each city that we cared ever to visit: we were invariably under the impression that it was the most pressing of our social obligations on each particular day. It seemed inevitably to lie on the nearest road from any point to any other point (which can hardly be possible outside of two-dimensational space) and the quality of the city, the value of our local friends, and even the state of the weather, seemed to vary unaccountably according to the punctuality of the mails and of those privileged intercommunicators Kennedy Tod and Co. Nor do I deny that I felt a little 'out of it' on each of these occasions. That you must forgive me, other peoples' old wounds smart when the East wind blows, but mine smart in anybody else's sunshine. I *could* not write to you when I was in Pease's company, the influence was too strong, of his presence and consequently of your own presence, but I hope you understood that, and that my congratulations were not really delayed, even if not actually translated into words and curves of ink.

Now as to the future. I am pleased that you are at Cheltenham, but don't put off the marriage. Has Pease ever told you of Stepniak's saying as to how fiercely Russian Nihilists love, because they know that any moment the end may come? We are all in that position here. Any moment the end may come – do not delay.

And remember the Comteist maxim – one of the many good ones of the Positivists – 'Live openly'. Do not make a mystery or secret of your position now or hereafter. There is no such thing as a self-regarding act. The world is entitled to know exactly how you stand, and not only discreditable mysteries, but all mysteries are bad and evil bringing. I began life badly, and entangled myself in several private mysteries. These cling around me still, though I have tried to work out of them. This is partly why I have urged Pease to come back to England quickly. I want you to press him to do so. His services would be very valuable in London just now, we are on the crest of a wave, and all hands are needed to keep up the progress and press our advantage. There are astonishingly few workers; and none with just Pease's qualities, and America was not so fertile as we hoped. There is very little for us to learn there.

This leads me to another point. Do you remember in *Felix Holt* his bitter address to his inamorata as to the pernicious influence of women in dragging men away from lofty ideals, and unselfish ends, down to the merely personal claims of family; of course I do not fear any such evil influence from you – (at least, not consciously) – you will not be a 'basil plant' but you are undertaking a great responsibility. For good or for evil you are stepping into a position of enormous influence over one mind and centre of action. What influence will that be. This is a very pretty problem in psychology (I hope you don't mind it being called by so learned a name) and I confess I am a little doubtful as to the result. I had almost wished that Pease had married a stronger 'Collectivist'. He possesses, as Mrs Wilson acutely says, the Anarchist mind. His mere existence – proper and decent existence, of course – is a main end to him. He is wedded to an incurably (and vain) personal optimism, which leads him to act in and for himself alone, according to his momentary impulses – extremely well trained impulses, but still *mere* impulses. This is necessarily fatal to social and combined action which I try to think is my own ideal. One person alone can follow his own impulses safely, e.g. in crossing a crowded street, but two people together crossing the street must act deliberately in concert, or else separate, or else face the inevitable result, a smash. Now my theory of life is to feel at every moment that I am acting as a member of a committee, and for that committee – in some affairs a committee of my own family merely, in others again a committee as wide as the Aryan race. But I aspire *never* to act alone, or for myself. This theoretically combined action involves rules, deliberation, discussion, concert, the disregard of one's own impulses, and in fact is Collectivism or Communism. The contrary habit is logically Anarchism.

Of course Pease is not an Anarchist. He is too clever not to see clearly the obvious inequalities and iniquities of unlimited Individualism, that is – he understands the Law of Rent in its fullest extent, and as he is one of the most unselfish men I know, he acts, in all weighty matters, on Collectivist lines. But he reserves a large sphere of minor matters as practically self-regarding, and in these he is an Anarchist. Did you ever hear of the prophecy that a lately married common friend would, although most kind and unselfish, one day eat all the butter on the table, unconscious that his wife had none? (and he did too). That will be true – in the spirit – of Pease, unless you send him off on slightly different rails. He has lived too long alone and too much his own life, to be quite qualified for a Communist Colony. You, too, I am afraid have somewhat of an Anarchist mind. You too have had to live your own life, and to be at any rate intellectually alone. Beware lest you intensify each other's Individualism in the small matters which make up four fifths of life, and each of which is unconsciously moulding the character which will hereafter deal with the larger matters – admittedly to be done on Collectivist lines. This need not imply that I am in favour of 'Merger' or even of Communism in marriage. Let it be a mere partnership. But let the partners, in every detail, act in and for the partnership – except in such spheres as they may severally act in and for larger Committees. I should like you to read (may I say over again) my paper on 'Rome', printed in July and August numbers of *Our Corner*, especially the conclusion. This will throw some light on the criticism I am making. Of course just now this will seem most unnecessary to you. One element of your common position is the mutual harmony of thought and action which it implies (Shaw once said that when we 'superior intellects' fell in love, we always felt and said that we were not under any illusion like the common herd: we knew his or her faults and defects perfectly well, and our own position, free from the usual glamour. This, he said, was simply that we were under the spell of just one illusion the more.) Pease is certainly in that position. Are you? Not that I would have you imagine that I am referring particularly to the little trials of married life, or that I am counselling you 'How to be Happy though Married'. You will, I think, understand that I am referring to the whole of life's action, and its effect on the character, and thus on all future action – and the world for ever.

Pease never would discuss plans of travel, we quarrelled daily on this point – as I would not give way. He said that you alone made all his plans when he was with you, and he simply accepted them. This is bad, even ignoble – if it is to be your future habit. It is merely the old bad theory of marriage inverted. My interest lies in its evil effect on character, his and yours. I want you throughout life, to deliberate, discuss, and concert your every act, in free communion with those with whom you are acting, whether one or many. I am of course aware that all this is very frank – even to impertinence, but it is what I have said to Pease as forcibly as I could and what I would say to you were we together. Beware lest you do the Socialist cause *harm* by marrying one of its most useful members – see that you improve his character, and not deteriorate it: see that you increase his energy, and the width of his altruism, not diminish them. See that Pease plus Davidson = more than Davidson and Pease separately, not, as is so usual, much less. However, I won't go on preaching, especially as I have no title to be heard in the matter. I hope that we may one day be friendly enough to talk over such things freely.

Pease told me that you have thought me unfriendly to you. That must have been my unfortunate infirmity. From the beginning I had nothing but the kindest feelings towards you – yet without the capacity for allowing them to be seen. We scarcely ever met except at Hampstead, though you did once show us how short we all are at 27 Keppel Street. My mother and sister are perhaps matter of fact and sharers in my own apparent coldness, but I can assure you that they would be very glad if you would make them friends.

I have just had a letter from Pease at Philadelphia which I enclose. It will of course take him some time to get to work and be hard for him. Don't let him stay too long.

Will you let me know about work? Perhaps I can help you. Remember I am rather great at vague knowledge of things in general, and that I have access to the most perfect storehouses. Send me a line when you want to know *anything* and I will find out.

The election of Mrs B. Headlam, and another Socialist parson, on the London School Board may be of use to you. Do not look for one moment for anything out of London. There is literally no other place worth living. in I have seen a great many others and I *know*.

I can't write all I want to say. I never wrote so long a letter before to anyone, but I have not yet done. Yet I must stop, and so adieu.

Sidney Webb

70 SU SIDNEY WEBB TO W. W. BARTLETT

27 Keppel St, Russell Sq.
27 January 89

Dear Mr Bartlett

I am delighted to hear that you are going to capture the South St Pancras Liberal Association. Shaw is, as you know, already on the *Executive* committee there, but has been unable to do much for want of support. Consult with him as to your action.

The first thing is to get the dates of the Ward meetings in the two Wards. Ask Shaw? *Don't let the officials* suspect that you are moving.

You have, I suppose, a copy of the rules (a pink paper). If not, get one.

The important thing is to carry a majority of the *Executive Committee.* The 'Council' of 200 (100 for each ward, of whom 50 are elected each year) is of no great consequence. But you may as well put all your men on that also.

That elected, the Ward meeting chooses its quota (25) of the Executive. You had better let the 9 officials alone for the present. They know the ropes and your men don't.

The way to do these things is to prepare written lists for each ward of the names and addresses of your men: one for the 'Council' and one for the Executive. Then let someone be deputed to jump up *quickly* as soon as nominations are called for in each case, and propose the *whole list.*

If I can I will come to the meetings to suggest and advise. I have had a lot of experience of these meetings.

Yours truly
Sidney Webb

71 KCC SIDNEY WEBB TO ALFRED MARSHALL

In the autumn of 1888 the Fabian Executive decided to prepare for publication, under Shaw's editorship, the series of lectures which its members were currently giving under the general title of 'The Basis and Prospects of Socialism'. The lectures had been carefully worked out – though Shaw afterwards complained that there were gaps of logic and that some, such as Webb's, showed signs of being written under pressure. Nevertheless he remarked that Webb's lecture demonstrated that socialism 'could be proposed without forfeiture of moral credit by

123

bishop as well as a desperado'. (Marginal comment on the MS of Edward Pease's *History of the Fabian Society*, BLPES) Webb had become the dominant strategist in the Society though Shaw had a greater flair for entertaining and persuading the members; his political comments show a surer touch from the time of his return from America.

The Society could not find a publisher for the lectures and eventually produced the collection itself, at a price of six shillings, in the autumn of 1889 under the title *Fabian Essays in Socialism*. The book brought the Fabians a considerable profit and an international reputation.

[27 Keppel Street]
28 February/89

Dear Mr Marshall

I had not forgotten my promise to send you the papers of the Fabian Society. I enclose its present prospectus, which includes a careful definition of Socialism, in its completely realised form. I will send you copies of its two recent pamphlets in a day or so.

I do not quite understand your remarks as to Co-operation, (but I do not, of course, expect further elucidation by letter). My paper on Co-operation was intended as an excursus in economic science. I do not gather that you dispute my assertion that modern economists are compelled to withhold their assent from the Co-operators' delusion, that an indefinite extension of voluntary co-operation would result in the elimination of the power of the owners of the means of production to levy a tribute on the workers. If I am wrong in my economics I shall be glad to be corrected.

My 'attitude' to Co-operation (which is not at all hostile) has nothing to do with this scientific point. I think the Co-operators have some grounds of complaint against the economists for not making this point clear to them.

As to your doubt whether 'the path indicated by modern Socialists is a *practicable* one' – the answer is *solvitur ambulando*. The history of the past generation supplies the proof. I did not know that your experience was to the opposite: I think the great majority of economists are with us on this point, as well as all statesmen.

Your difficulty appears to be in realising adequately that the course of social evolution is making us all Socialists against our will. You cannot doubt that it is 'practicable' for a municipality to own gasworks or tramways, and so on. You cannot doubt the practicability of a Factory Act, or an Income Tax levied practically on Rent, Interest and Salaries only. Yet extend these, and you have an enormous stride towards Collectivism. We may differ as to time (and this is unimportant, for time itself will settle that), but I believe we agree absolutely in Economics, and practically in politics. And I am accepted by the Socialists as one of them.

Yours very truly

Sidney Webb

Most of those who took part in the socialist revival of the 1880s had been influenced by Henry George's speeches and writings, but there was a reaction after his spectacular but unsuccessful campaign for mayor of New York City on a Labour ticket. He failed, socialists argued, to attack the capitalist as strongly as he attacked the landlord; and his concept of the taxation of land values was closer to Chamberlain's policy for municipal progress than to socialist ideas at the end of the decade. On this return visit Shaw was almost alone among the socialists in supporting him, arguing in the *Star* on 7 June that a single tax would eventually absorb the economic rent of the whole country. Webb's warning letter was followed by a Fabian minute of 9 April: 'The question of inviting Mr George to meet the Society was raised. It was decided not to invite him to a discussion, and that the policy of the Society should be to discourage the raising of controversy between Mr George and socialists in this country'.

[27 Keppel Street]
8 March/89

Dear Mr George

I write to welcome you to our country, and to wish you every success in your tour. I do not forget the interesting conversations we had in New York just before the election, or the pleasant evening I spent at your house.

Let me say a few things about the state of affairs here. You will find us, as you know, making tremendous progress in a direction which may generally be called socialist, and on the Land Question in particular, ordinary Liberal opinion is fast ripening. The Radicals and the town wage earners generally, hardly need your visit, except always, by way of inspiration and encouragement. They are already pushing the party leaders as hard as they can. What holds things back is the great mass of the middle-class, religious, 'respectable', cautious, and disliking the Radical artisan. These need your instruction most, and you are, of course, just the man who can give it to them without offence or resentment. Your visit will do immense good in stirring up the *bourgeoisie* – especially among the dissenting sects. Pray pay them special attention and remind all your committees to bring you into contact with all the ministers round.

I am afraid that you will be denounced and attacked by the wilder kind of socialist. Headlam, Pease and others besides myself are doing all we can to induce them to keep quiet, *as it would be fatal to arouse an antagonism between the Radical and Socialist parties.* Many of us have been working for years to keep the peace between them, and to bring into line on practical politics. Neither the socialist nor any other party is here as in America, and the real force of the socialist movement works in lines which you do not at all disapprove, and which are securing daily more and more recognition. See for instance the enclosed syllabus of lectures now being given at one of the best Colleges in Cambridge University. How long will it be before Harvard does this?

Now I want to implore your forbearance. When you are denounced as a traitor and what not, by socialist newspapers; and 'heckled' by socialist questioners, or abused by socialist orators, it will be difficult not to denounce socialism in return. But do not do so. They will be only the noisy fringe of the socialist party who will do this, and it will be better for the cause which we both have at heart, if you can avoid accentuating your differences with socialists.

You may safely lay much more stress on the nationalisation or 'municipalisation' of all monopolies, here than in America. Our civil service and municipal government is much better fitted to bear the strain, and the people are quite ready.

With best wishes,
Yours very truly
Sidney Webb

73 SU SIDNEY WEBB TO WILLIAM WALTER BARTLETT

G. G. Leveson-Gower had sat for North-West Staffordshire; he was defeated in 1886 and then became Liberal candidate for East Marylebone in 1889, again being defeated.

The Bloomsbury Socialist Society was one of the surviving groups of the Socialist League after William Morris had lost control to the anarchists: it was essentially run by and for Edward Aveling and Eleanor Marx.

27 Keppel St, Russell Sq.
13 July /89

Dear Bartlett

Can you get the Borough of Marylebone Radical Club *tomorrow*, to adopt some sort of a demand to send to G. G. Leveson Gower, the new candidate for East Marylebone? The Club might send up their programme and ask if he adopts it. He should be pressed and squeezed in every direction throughout his campaign, not so much for his own sake, as for warning and suggestion to other Liberal candidates.

Perhaps you can also work the Marylebone members of the Bloomsbury Socialist Society.

Yours
Sidney Webb

74 BL SIDNEY WEBB TO JOHN BURNS

The Fabians had begun to take a close interest in the Eight Hours Movement, designed to shorten the working day. The campaign gained impetus after the

London dock strike, in which Burns had made his reputation as a labour leader.

The *Labour Elector* was a short-lived journal edited by H. H. Champion which promoted the idea of independent labour representation. It went into suspense on 1 May 1890 when Champion went to Australia, though he briefly revived it on his return.

The Eighty Club was a political group formed by Radicals after the Liberal victory in 1880. For a time it seemed it might be a useful means of capturing the Liberals for more advanced policies. Morley's speech contained a number of items which the Fabians supported – reduction of taxes on food, free education, greater powers for municipal authorities and an overhaul of the Poor Law. But he went out of his way to oppose any attempt to legislate for shorter hours of work and attacked socialism as 'against human nature'. Moderate socialism was simply a 'nickname' for a reformist policy not significantly different from Radicalism.

Under Webb's leadership the Fabians were beginning to use the tactics of preparing draft Bills of desired reforms, as well as providing factual information and discussion tracts on issues of national and municipal politics.

[?27 Keppel Street]
14 Nov. 89

Dear Burns

I enclose a proof copy of the Fabian 'Eight Hours Bill', which you will find useful as a basis. (There's no objection to its being mentioned or even summarized in the *Labor Elector*, but please do not *publish* it for a couple of weeks. Press copy shall be sent in due course.) What I want to say is that I am nearly sure that John Morley is going to denounce it, more or less, at his Eighty Club speech next Tuesday. Some strong medicine is being administered to him, but he must have a good deal more from all sides. It would be very useful if you could find an opportunity publicly to mention the draft bill before Tuesday, so as to get reported. What you say on the Eight Hours Question is eagerly scanned by these cat-jumping politicians. I am getting all the leaders of the advanced Liberals living in London to accept the Bill as a good draft basis, and as it goes even beyond your own recent very modest demands, you might perhaps give it a general blessing. If you can do this before Tuesday, Morley will have his work cut out to avoid hanging himself up in his speech. It is the provincial Liberals who are the difficulty, but the 'Manchester' programme will show a distinct advance.

Yours truly

Sidney Webb

3. A Frank Friendship
January 1890 – May 1891

It is slightly surprising that Beatrice Potter and Sidney Webb did not meet before January 1890, for they moved in overlapping political circles and had acquaintances in common. They certainly knew of each other by repute. In a lecture in May 1889, when the first volume of Booth's survey was published, Sidney remarked that 'the only contributor with any literary talent is Miss Potter'; Beatrice had similarly singled out his chapter in *Fabian Essays*.

The date and place of their first meeting are not definitely known, though on 8 January 1921 Sidney recalled in a letter that this day was their anniversary; and in her autobiography Beatrice mentioned that they met 'in the first days of January'. On 27 December 1929 Beatrice looked back in her diary to a gloomy Christmas forty years before. Noticing her depression her sister Kate suggested that she return to London with Leonard Courtney and attend the funeral of Robert Browning in Westminster Abbey on 2 January. 'Rather a grim diversion, thought I', Beatrice commented, 'but I could go to the British Museum and get what I want – I will get Margaret Harkness to introduce me to someone there who will put me on the track. And it was in her little lodging opposite the B.M. that Sidney and I met in that first week of January 1890.' In *My Apprenticeship* Beatrice slightly amplified the point. Asked where to turn for more historical background on the Co-operative and Labour movements, Margaret Harkness suggested Sidney Webb: 'He knows everything; when you go out for a walk with him he literally pours out information'. Beatrice recollected that Sidney, 'in a faultless handwriting' at once drew up a list of sources to consult.

Beatrice returned to London a month later, once more meeting Sidney. On this occasion they seem to have discussed sweated labour; returning to call on her a few days later, he took with him a draft proposal for the municipal inspection of industrial premises.

It was during this second visit that Beatrice invited Sidney to the Devonshire House Hotel, where she was staying, to have dinner with Charles and Mary Booth on 14 February. After the dinner she made the first entry about him in her diary.

Sidney Webb the socialist dined here to meet the Booths. A remarkable little man with a huge head on a very thin body: a breadth of forehead quite sufficient to account for the encyclopaedic character of his knowledge, a Jewish nose, prominent eyes and mouth, somewhat unkempt, spectacles and a most bourgeois black coat shiny with wear; regarded as a whole somewhat between a London card and a German professor. To keep to externals: his pronunciation is Cockney, his H's are shaky, his attitude by no means elegant – with his thumbs fixed pugnaciously in a far from immaculate waistcoat, with his bulky head thrown back and his little body forward he struts even when he stands, delivering himself with extraordinary rapidity of thought and utterance and with an expression of inexhaustible self-complacency. But I like the man. There is a directness of speech – and open-mindedness, an imaginative warm-heartedness which should carry him far. He has the self-complacency of one who is always thinking faster than his neighbours, who is untroubled by doubts, and to whom the exposition of facts is as easy as the grasping of matter; but he has no vanity and is totally unself-conscious – hence his absence of consciousness as to his neighbour's corns.

Despite this unflattering reaction, Beatrice saw him again before she left London and they began to correspond. Sidney was immensely impressed by her and touched by her apparent interest in him. For her part, Beatrice was clearly pleased at last to have made contact with the able young Fabians whose reputation had been made by the publication of *Fabian Essays*.

75 PRO SIDNEY WEBB TO J. RAMSAY MACDONALD

James Ramsay MacDonald (1866–1937) held several menial clerical posts after his arrival in London as a poor but educated youth. Though he had joined the Social Democratic Federation, the Fellowship of the New Life and the Fabian Society he had hopes of a political career as a Liberal. Webb considered him as one of the coming men among the younger Fabians.

Thomas Lough (1850–1922) for whom MacDonald was working as secretary, was then Liberal candidate – and M.P. from 1892 – for Islington. He was a tea merchant of Irish extraction and a strong Home Ruler. Thomas Power O'Connor (1849–1928), Irish Nationalist politician and popular journalist, had recently founded the *Star* as a Radical evening paper in London.

Sir James Stuart (1843–1913) was professor of mechanical science at Cambridge and Liberal M.P. for Hoxton. He was one of the financial backers of the *Star* and chairman of its board of directors: he had married into the wealthy Colman family.

4 Park Village East
20 Jan. 90

Dear MacDonald,

Could you, if need be, lecture at H'Smith S.L. [Hammersmith Socialist League], Kelmscott House, next Sunday at 8 p.m.? Shaw was to have lectured on 'The New Politics', but he must go to Nottingham to take Wallas's place in the important course now running there, Wallas being laid by with congestion of the liver etc.

Lough is having a bad influence on T. P. O'Connor, and thereby on the *Star*, in depreciating Stuart, the 'London Movement' generally, and so on. Can this be stopped in any way? I fear Lough has simply taken a blind prejudice against Stuart, which can only be cured by making him see that Stuart is going to count for a great deal – that he will certainly be carried by the London swing straight into the Cabinet. If you can 'advise' on this problem I should be glad.

The St James's Hall meeting on the 28th against Land Purchase will be an important political event. Every London Liberal M.P. and candidate has been invited. Very bitter comment will be made on their absence, and the new Unions are to be there in force.

Yours

Sidney Webb

76 PRO SIDNEY WEBB TO J. RAMSAY MACDONALD

Kelmscott House was the London home of William Morris. The main activity of the Hammersmith Socalist Society was the holding of Sunday night meetings in the converted carriage-barn.

4 Park Village East
22 Jan. 90

Dear MacDonald

Thanks. Please go to Kelmscott House next Sunday at 8. Shaw's subject was 'The New Politics'. You could probably do that, but if you prefer, choose your own subject.

Your information I will use discreetly. It confirms my impressions. I think he should know (1) that Stuart will quite certainly enter the inner circle – General Purposes Committee – of the National Liberal Federation at their annual business meeting in April next: and so gain much control over the provinces as well as London; and this by wish not only of N.L.F. but also of the Liberal chiefs. (2) that Stuart will very probably be carried slick into the Cabinet, by London's swing and Gladstone's favor, and that he is being most strongly backed by Stansfeld.

i.e. that it will 'pay' to 'believe' in him – Stuart's Aldermanship, moreover, and possibly the Chairmanship of L.C.C. [London County Council] in June, will do much to ensure the last-named result. This municipal work is undertaken at J. Morley's express desire.

Yours

Sidney Webb

77 PP BEATRICE POTTER TO LORD THRING

Lord Thring was a member of the House of Lords Committee on Sweating. Mr Redgrave was a senior factory inspector in the Board of Trade.

Box House, Minchinhampton.
[?between 3 and 9 April 1890]

Dear Lord Thring

I will not tire you with my appreciative remarks for the logic and terseness of your conclusions. The following are the points in which, I think, the Report is open to misunderstanding and hostile criticism.

Foreign Immigration. I should gather that you denied that Foreign Immigration was in any way responsible for the evils of Sweating. As the Jewish worker is 'unskilled', has a 'low standard of life' and a most decided 'tendency to drift into large towns', possesses, in fact, exactly those qualities to which you attribute sweating in the following paragraph, this opinion seems hardly justified, and may produce a mischievous reaction. In face of Lord [*illegible*] anti-semitic sensationalism, would it not be wise to allow that Foreign Immigration increases the supply of unskilled labour in certain trades and thus intensifies the struggle for existence, while maintaining the ground that its effect has been grossly exaggerated and cannot be considered as a main cause of sweating. (With regard to the summary of my own evidence on this point, I shall say that I was mistaken in anything I write on the subject.)

Legislation. Are you absolutely determined not to level up workshops and domestic workshops to the standard of factories in respect to the hours of labour of women, young persons and children? You propose to enforce the factory standard with regard to sanitation. Why not with regard to hours? As all the experts were in favour of assimilating, in all respects, workshop regulations and factory regulations, public opinion I think will demand it.

Regulations of out-work in Victoria. County Councils and Sanitary Inspection. This suggestion seems to me the most helpful and significant in your Report. But I am puzzled with its relation to the previous proposal to treat workshops as factories, which I assumed meant the repeal (so far as sanitation is concerned) of Sections 61 and 69 – the clauses which exempt workshops and domestic workshops from the jurisdiction of the Factory Department. Do you mean to suggest (in accordance with Mr Redgrave's evidence) that the sanitary inspection of factories as well as workshops should be handed over to County Councils? That would seem to me an admirable plan; more especially if the Factory Department were transferred to the Local Government Board, so that Factory Inspectors might supervise the work of Sanitary Inspectors and, in case of neglect, take it into their own hands. It would solve that most difficult question of dual authority, and would moreover prepare the way for decentralising factory inspection, should the County Councils prove equal to it.

If this be your meaning, and if you do not care to define it in your Report, I should immensely like to attempt to work it out, with all the freedom of an irresponsible person.

I am coming up to London on the 14th and should much like to come and call on you some day before the 17th when I return. Pray forgive these crude observations. I shall now feel free to criticise your Report, on its publication, to my heart's content: but if you would give me a lead, I would rather supplant it in writing.

Beatrice Potter

The reference to Chamberlain is not to his relationship with Beatrice, of which Sidney as yet knew nothing, but to Chamberlain's susceptibility to the influence of his associates.

The purpose of the collection for Corrie Grant is not known: the sentence implies some financial embarrassment.

Sidney had visited Beatrice at Box House, where she now lived with her invalid father.

4 Park Village East, N.W.
30 April 1890

Dear Miss Potter

I have sent on your cheque to Corrie Grant, through the intermediary who approached me (there is an elaborate system of friends who each undertake to collect £20), and I have asked that an acknowledgement should be sent to you direct.

I fear I cannot adequately convey to you the very deep impression my visit made upon me. I have thought a great deal about what you said: but it was, after all, the manner of saying it, and the impression you aimed at conveying, which were of most importance. It was an act of frank friendliness as valuable as it is rare.

One thing especially I have learnt to value. It became more than ever clear to me that it is dangerous to live exclusively in one circle. It is doubtful whether you are really more alone than it is possible to be in London. I am extremely liable to be influenced by those with whom I am, and (though I altogether decline to take Chamberlain's case to heart as likely to be mine!) I can see that this is dangerous. Practical work is a partial corrective, but there again, my habit of being constantly unsuccessful – I mean, the perpetual dwelling in a minority – prevents defeat from being instructive to me. Any defeat is merely 'one more check', very much what I expected.

I really must have a Mentor outside the working circle, a looker-on who sees most of the game, and I hope you will not refuse to repeat the experiment (as opportunity serves) which has been so successful. Another time, if you will allow me the chance, I should like to discuss with you the general plan of campaign, the arrangement of the long rolling fight all over the country into which the Fabian Society, and I in particular, am being more and more drawn. You need not fear our taking up any impracticable or sectarian attitude: we are, indeed, constantly seeking chances of translating the crude abstractions of the doctrinaire socialist into the language of practical politics. But it is difficult to know how to treat the Liberal leaders. They are generally such poor creatures, and so hopelessly 'out of it'. I wish their education could be taken in hand in some way that would save the Fabian Society from becoming more and more conceited. But, really, every day makes me inclined to say 'I told you so', over some event or another. May 4 is an immense triumph for us: a great tribute to our political prescience on one detail of the programme: or, if you prefer, a proof that we are prophets, able ourselves to bring about the fulfilment of our prophesies. I do not mean to lose my head, or to do anything rash, but I feel that the advantage has got to be pushed well home.

Perhaps it may amuse you to know that I am revising my estimate of the feminine mind! Of course it is impertinent of me, but I *must* get to understand such an important factor in the world. (I hope women won't always resent being considered as 'factors').

This is outwardly a conceited letter, but indeed, I *am* humbled – more seriously than you realise.

Yours very truly

Sidney Webb

Box House, Minchinhampton, Gloucestershire
May 2 1890

Dear Mr Webb

One line in answer to your letter, for I feel I owe you a confession. The 'frank friendliness' arose from a feeling of gratitude. It was in my first conversation with you last winter that it flashed across my mind that I was, or ought to be, a Socialist – if I was true to the conclusion I had already reached; and by this sudden self-revelation you saved me months, perhaps years, of study. Thus I became interested in you and your work; and wished to add to it any little odds and ends of experience of human nature which I might possess.

When you have studied women, I think you will find this desire to be helpful, to watch over 'the manners that maketh man', to round off the corners of life – is one secret of their influence. It is, I suppose, part of the mother's instinct, and joined with their intellectual dependence (a curious trait in even the most intellectual women) it lends to friendship between men and women that subtle usefulness which will always make such friendships one of the greatest factors in life – so long as it is not blurred by the predominance of lower feeling – when I think it becomes a source of pure evil – whatever the relationship may be.

So you see I shall expect to be used; I shall venture to ask help from you if I need it. With this great mass of inertia and selfish prejudice we shall all need to be fellow workers – to take and give freely.

Yours sincerely

Beatrice Potter

133

Sir Percy Bunting (1836–1911), editor of the *Contemporary Review* from 1882 until his death, was a social reformer and, through his National Vigilance Association, a prominant member of the moral purity campaign.

Sidney's article 'The Reform of the Poor Law' appeared in the *Contemporary Review* for July 1890. At this time he was doing a good deal of casual journalism, especially for the *Speaker*, a weekly Liberal review edited by Sir Thomas Wemyss Reid (1842–1905), a prominent journalist, novelist and biographer; for the *Star*; and for local newspapers with Radical sympathies. Sidney was hoping to do sufficiently well from such free-lance work to liberate himself from the Colonial Office and begin a new career as a Liberal journalist and politician. His articles have not yet been traced or collected.

His concern with the problems of the Poor Law was characteristic of Radical opinion. The Poor Law system, set up in 1834 as an attempt to replace the system which had remained essentially unreformed since Elizabethan times, was harsh and unpopular. It was based upon the principle of 'less eligibility', which provided that the subsistence offered to a pauper must be lower than that secured by the poorest labourer; it offered little 'outdoor relief' and its ultimate sanction was the dreaded workhouse, where families were broken up and the inmates lived under near-penal conditions. The social dislocation which followed the rise of the industrial system and growth of towns had produced widespread poverty, especially among the chronic sick, the aged and casual workers: one person in eight died in a workhouse. The Poor Law was also under attack for mal-administration: there were many anomalies caused by local variations in the policies of the Boards of Guardians and by the bureaucratic habits of the Local Government Board, responsible for supervising the system as a whole. For the next twenty years the problem of reforming or abolishing the Poor Law was a major theme of Radical politics. The 'Homestead' law to which Sidney referred provided that when bailiffs were sent in to seize chattels at least a bed must be left to the occupants.

Sir William Acworth (1850–1925) later became a notable expert on railway economics; Brooke Lambert (1834–1901), a Christian Socialist and Vicar of Greenwich, was a social and educational reformer whose work in the East End had anticipated Booth's statistical study of poverty; Vallance was the assessment clerk of the Whitechapel Board of Guardians.

4 Park Village East, N.W.

14 May/90

Dear Miss Potter

Already I want some help. Perhaps as we cannot talk it over, you will pardon a long letter.

Percy Bunting has engaged me to do an article on the Reform of the Poor Law for the July *Contemporary Review*, and I am now in the throes of building it up – with my usual sinking of heart, and feeling of despair. (Yet all the world – except, I hope, you – believes that I am a fatuously self-confident person!) Ot course I can't make such a success of it as the

Eight Hours article, but as people are half beginning to believe what I say I want to be right. I am feeling some of the responsibility of leadership!

Now I am afraid we don't agree as to Poor Law Reform. I believe that the existing system can't last – the rural vote will upset it if the urban does not. The present P.L. is hated for both good and bad reasons, and it will have to be drastically altered. If the P.L. experts, C.O.S. [Charity Organization Society] and such like, continue their obsolete attitude of mere resistance, and retain all their last generation ideas, they will be simply swept aside. If that happens, look out for the Deluge. The average M.P. knows nothing of P.L. history, and there is a widespread turning away from the position, taught by the old P.L., that Outdoor Relief is the Devil. Even Bunting himself, eleven years on C.O.S. Committees and so on, tells me he thinks Outdoor Relief must be given.

Unless P.L. experts put out a plan which is democratic enough and generous enough to gain public support (whilst yet *safe*), the whole thing will go by the board – not necessarily on a P.L. Reform Bill, which would enable the L.G.B. and C.O.S. to collect opposition to anything rash – but by a sudden amendment on a Local Govt. Bill giving Parish Councils power to grant Outdoor Relief, and the stern unbending John Morley will be leading the swarm! Very few Liberals will dare to resist such a move – and it will certainly be made.

Hence something must be done to divert this coming wave. This, I feel, must be the separation of the aged and the sick from the adult poor. The P.L. Report of 1834 *did not recommend the withdrawal of Outdoor Relief from the Aged*. Rev. S. A. Barnett is strongly in favor of a universal pension system, as an *encouragement to thrift*. We must put a little water in the pump to make it draw.

We have virtually such a system at present in its worst form. I am collecting evidence as to the number of aged among the paupers at present (can you help me – see enclosed). I expect to find that one-half of the paupers are over 65 = 400,000 in England and Wales. If so, this is more than one-third of all persons over 65. It is only 3 to 1 against any person becoming an aged pensioner now – with all the discouragement to thrift (and ?rate in aid of wages) that such a system affords. Why demoralise *subjectively* these 400,000, who *could not* have saved a pension anyhow, by branding them as paupers? Why not grant a £10 pension to all alike – *then* the thrifty man will be better off than the unthrifty; then the task of the Benefit Society in providing superannuation will not be, as now, hopelessly impossible – because it will *then* be worth while (as it is not now) to save up even for sixpence a week addition to the Govt. pension.

Again, since the 'House' is merely a test of real destitution, why break up the home, and so make it difficult for the man to start again? Why not offer the House, but *store* the bits of furniture etc. so that it will be easy

135

to set them up again? Why, in fact, go against the policy of the 'Homestead' Law, intended to make sacred the bed etc.

I fear much of this will shock you. Perhaps you will not mind reading and criticising the enclosed, which has secured the *general* assent of such P.L. experts as W. M. Acworth, Rev. S. A. Barnett, Brooke Lambert and timidly and hesitatingly, even of Vallance himself.

I wish I could talk this all over with you: because I *don't want* to do anything rash! I am so driven with work that I can't think or do my best – I can only produce what comes. And all the time I am thinking (with my other cerebral hemisphere) of the glorious English country as it seemed to me one day in April, and of all the revelations of that 'new world which is the old' – and then behind it all I who *am* timid, and cursed with looking before and after, fear to hear the 'ground whirl of the perished leaves of hope'. (Did you credit me with knowing my Rossetti?)

But of all this at some more fitting season. Meanwhile will you kindly counsel me? (Alas, I cannot *promise* to obey – I will however learn.)

Yours very truly

Sidney Webb

81 PP BEATRICE TO SIDNEY

J. C. Gray became general secretary of the Co-operative Union in 1891.

Lord Rosebery (1847–1929), the wealthy Liberal statesman, was Foreign Secretary under Gladstone in 1886. He showed sympathy to political and social reforms, becoming the first chairman of the London County Council on its establishment in 1889. In 1894 he succeeded Gladstone for a brief term as prime minister and thereafter became leader of the Liberal Imperialists.

[Box House, Minchinhampton]
May 16th 1890

Dear Mr Webb

I have read your articles with care and interest – (you do not send me the last one) they read fair and right, but I have no knowledge of the subject, no materials whereas to form an opinion. The same applies to the suggestions thrown out in your letter. The idea of giving pensions to all alike – and treating the aged as *pensioners* and not as paupers recommends itself to me. On the other hand I have a lingering prejudice against any form of equalisation of the rates which would slacken the tie between the person who pays the £ and the person who spends it – which would enable the guardians of a poor district to curry favour with their constituents by treating them at the expense of another district. London itself seems to me too large an area for the efficient conduct of administrators by electors. But frankly, I have no criticism to make on your actual plans – I realise fully that the only helpful suggestion can come from practical experience – and that is a minus quantity with me.

For all that, I am not going to deny myself the pleasures of criticism. I don't quite agree with the first part of your letter – with the general idea that some plan must be put forward, generous, and democratic enough to direct the 'coming wave'. In the first place I have ceased to believe in a 'coming wave' – we shall never have the 'deluge' in England (by a side wind or otherwise) – the party of resistance and inertia taken together throughout the country have an enormous strength. Secondly – and this is far more important – this idea seems to me a wrong one for a man who aims at forming public opinion – whatever it may be to the mere politicians. If you have not confidence in yourself – I have in you – if you will only shut your eyes to what you imagine to be popular opinion and go straight on collecting information from experts and working it up by the light of socialist principles. [*syntax as original*]

You will say that it is mean of me, feeling incapable of practical criticism to take refuge in moral maxims – but I have nothing else to give you except a wish that you would give up those P.E. [Political Economy] lectures and devote all the spare time you have to working out these questions. True leadership is needed now – it is of the utmost importance that responsible Socialists shall not make a false step, should not begin at the wrong end.

Personally I think it far more important to lessen the number of parasites at the top and to develop the faculties and desires of the great body of the people, than to feed the unfortunates at the bottom.

But this may be mere prejudice on my side – I should trust your judgment much more than my own so long as you will keep it 'pure and undefiled', and supply it well with facts gathered in by experts. The opinion of a fair-minded shrewd outsider, intent on the common weal, on the information afforded by experts, seems to me the nearest approach to wisdom in this deceptive world – and this I believe is open to you.

Do not let the 'cavilling' of this letter prevent you from writing frankly and freely to me whenever you feel inclined – and telling me your *real* attitude towards things – in giving you an outside view of that, I can serve you best. I live too much out of the current of actual information to be of any use in questions of detail – tho' I am always interested in them.

Do you want the circular filled up for country districts? I think I could get it from some districts in Gloucestershire – if you will send me some forms.

I leave this place on Thursday 22nd and go up with the Southern Co-operators, Burnett and Kent to the Glasgow Conference on Friday. I am anxious to keep in with the leading Co-operators in view of any future work. Do not you feel inclined to come too? B. Jones, 99 Loman Street, supplies railway tickets at a cheap rate for Friday 23rd, and J. C. Gray, Co-operative Union, 14 City Buildings, Corporation Street, Manchester, visitors' tickets. Lord Rosebery is presiding at the opening meeting on Monday. We are staying at St Enoch's Hotel and going up by the 10 o'c from Euston on Friday. No doubt if you cared to come B. Jones and J. C. Gray would ask you to join our party. I am already a visitor, and am bringing a woman friend with me.

Yours sincerely

Beatrice Potter

82 PP SIDNEY TO BEATRICE [*incomplete*]

Beatrice and Sidney travelled up to the Co-operative Congress with Vaughan Nash (1861–1932), a journalist and trade union supporter who had written, with Hubert Llewellyn Smith (1869–1945), *The Story of the Docker's Strike* (1890). Nash became confidential secretary to two prime ministers, Sir Henry Campbell-Bannerman (1836–1908) and Herbert Henry Asquith (1852–1928), and a senior civil servant. Llewellyn Smith, after working with Charles Booth, also became a civil servant, being permanent secretary of the Board of Trade 1907–19 and chief economic adviser to the government 1919–27. Both remained friendly with the Webbs. At the Congress Sidney spoke on the need for collaboration between socialists and Co-operators.

This fragment from a letter should be read in the context of Beatrice's diary entry (n.d. ?24 May) in which she describes a 'long walk by glorious sunset through the crowded streets . . . with glory in the sky, and hideous bestiality on the earth'. During the walk 'the two socialists came to a working compact'. Beatrice told Sidney that 'the chances are 100 to 1 that nothing follows but friendship. If you feel that it is weakening your life, that your work is less efficient for it, you will promise me to give it all up?' Making that promise Sidney replied: 'I will make it serve my life – my work shall be both more vigorous and higher in tone for it. I will make you help me, and I will insist on helping you – our relationship shall be judged solely by the helpfulness to each other's work. Forgive me, if I say that I believe that if we were united we could do great things together . . . but I will vow solemnly that even if after a time we part, I will do better things for our friendship than I could have done without it'. Beatrice pressed for an assurance that he would not let his mind dwell 'on the purely personal part . . . that feeling unfulfilled saps all the vigour out of a man's life . . . think of me as a married woman, as the wife of your friend'. Sidney was reluctant to go so far, merely conceding that he would 'look at the whole question from the point of view of health' and try to divert his imagination to the working tie. 'One grasp of the hand', Beatrice added, 'and we were soon in a warm discussion on some question of economics.'

This sheet was pinned to Beatrice's Diary Vol. 14(1), opposite her account of Glasgow Congress in the last week of May 1890.

[Saturday, May 24]

You tortured me horribly last night by your intolerable 'superiority'. Surely an affectation of heartlessness is as objectionable as an affectation of conceit. And you blasphemed horribly against what is highest and holiest in human relations.

I could not speak my mind last night, but this agony is unendurable. You will at any rate not be indifferent to my suffering. I do not know how to face another night such I have passed. I believe you are free in the morning: come off somewhere and let us clear up what is more important than all Congresses.

Now you know why I could not confess to frank speaking. Even with you.

83 PP BEATRICE TO SIDNEY

14 Kensington Square, w.
[?29 May 1890]

Dear Mr Webb

I lay awake last night feeling perplexed and miserable about all that has past at Glasgow.

Do not let us misunderstand each other. It is the first time in my life that I have granted friendship to a man who has desired something more. But the motive which has led me to depart, from what I conceive to be the safe and honorable course, has not been that I think there is any probability (I might almost say *possibility*) of a closer tie, but that I regard our work of greater importance than our happiness and that I feel the enormous help we may be to each other. But I feel that this is a one-sided bargain, since your happiness is more involved than mine – it is you and not I who runs the risk of suffering. Now, I almost fear, from your last words yesterday, that you look upon our working friendship as a *means* and not an *end* – that you hope and expect that it will lead to something more; and that in your words and manner to me you will be constantly expressing that hope and that expectation.

I want you to think this over very seriously; I want you, not only to consider your own health and happiness, as of the utmost importance (since the value of your work depends on this), but I want you to realise that you will be betraying my confidence and trust if you allow yourself to build up a hope, or allow others to suspect that we are more to each other than frank friends with a common faith and common ends.

Personal happiness to me is an utterly remote thing; and I am to that extent 'heartless' that I regard everything from the point of view of making my own or another's life serve the community more effectively.

But you are still young and have life before you: *you* can hope for happiness as well as work – if your imagination were free you might find one who could give you the love of a young life – of a life which has not been forced through the fire and forged into a simple instrument for work.

I have tried to put the question of the continuance of our friendship from *your* point of view.

My point of view is simply this: if I find that our friendship leads to constant perplexity and anxiety on my side, or if I find that it leads to surmises and expectations on the minds of others, I shall retire absolutely and entirely from it. I do not want mystery and perplexity to hinder the little bit of work I have to do, and I cannot afford to lose my reputation as an honorable and healthy-minded woman.

But I have allowed myself to hope that we might bring strength and peace into each other's lives, the strength which comes from a free interchange of thought and experience, and the peace which springs from absolute trust in each other's integrity and friendship and helpfulness.

In this letter I have simply 'thought aloud'. Do not answer it – but decide either to break off now for ever all connections with me, or to bind yourself even, not to build up in your imagination, in that connection, a strong hope for a complete union.

My prayer is that after reading this letter you will act with the self-knowledge and self-command which a right appreciation of your own work (and of your own happiness as subordinate to your work) deserves: that realising that it can be only friendship between us, you will consider your relationship to me simply from the point of view of serving or hindering your work, and continue it or break it off accordingly.

Always yours sincerely

Beatrice Potter

84 PP SIDNEY TO BEATRICE

Grant Allen (1848–99), author and liberal journalist, was best-known for his novel *The Woman Who Did* (1895) which was considered a scandalous attack on the male double standard of morality. Allen's concept of the 'new hedonism' implied equal terms for men and women and he insisted that self-development was greater than self-sacrifice in the human scale of values.

Beatrice sent an article on the Co-operative Congress to the *Speaker*: she noted on 29 May that she gave 'brief to SW, which he worked up, I polished and Ella Pycroft copied'.

The article by Beatrice on 'The Lords Committee on the Sweating System' was published in the *Nineteenth Century* for June 1890.

4 Park Village East, N.W.

30 May/90

Dear Miss Potter

Your letter is full of mistrust – mistrust of me, mistrust of the not-ourselves which makes for Righteousness, mistrust even of yourself. I am sorry you have given way to this – sorry to feel that it has cost you anxiety and perplexity – but sorrier that you should have been momentarily untrue to your principles and yourself.

It springs from your generosity to me, your fear lest you do me harm.

But we may as well look facts in the face. Whatever harm you can do to me, has been done already. I cannot be any deeper in the stream. There is no more of me that I can pledge in your keeping. You cannot now by any noble frankness and friendliness deepen your hold on me, because I am through and through yours already.

Nor can you take from me that week of happiness. *Ich habe genossen das irdische Glück: ich habe gelebt und geliebt.*

Nor can you, even if you throw me over absolutely and refuse to remember that I exist, ruin or wreck my life. I am too strong and too ascetic for that. Even during my greatest agony last Friday night, and during my moments of highest ecstasy, I was oddly conscious of this. I was in love, as Austria goes to War, with 'limited liability'. This seems odd to me. It is something not in the books. It does not mean that I love you less, but that duty has so far become organic with me. *That*, you, at any rate, will understand and believe. It makes one band of the tie between us.

I do not pretend to be indifferent to personal happiness. I think you are wrong to make light of it for yourself. You cannot be at your best without it. You cannot permanently 'see life already and see it whole', unless you are feeling the throb of life as well as merely knowing of it. I, at any rate, cannot. I too have known the fire: no one, of course, believes that anyone else's was so hot as one's own. I know and see, now, how far short I fell until this year, though I did not realise it before.

But I see that you say all this to me yourself, only you seem to think that I have still an alternative. Why don't you apply to my case what you know of your own? You have told me enough of your story to warrant me in saying this. Were you at your best, were you doing your whole possible tale of work, when you were in the valley of the Shadow of Death? If you care for my work – and I know you do – the next seven years are all important to me. Even if you married someone else to-morrow, do you think I should be the same as six months ago, even in seven years? You know better than that from your own case. I know better than that from my own boyish experience, when I had all the counterbalancing attraction of a (to me) novel psychological experience. I *know* (and you will not doubt) how for years I crept about with a broken wing, doing the daily task of duty, the convict's minim of work without joy or hope or faith. Will it be less to me in manhood, now that I am plunged head and heels in the stream I then only sipped? I almost retract what I wrote above as to my having no fear of my lapse from duty. I *am* horribly afraid now that it would be too much for me.

Of course you can't help that. It may well be – the world is so made – that you are destined never to reciprocate in the least bit all that hurricane of feeling. It may be that I am doomed to the warped and stunted and soured life and work of those for whom the Light of Happiness has gone out, and who live on cold iron. There *are* such people, as you know.

They 'get over it' as the world rightly says: that is to say, they do not die or sicken, or even cease to work. It is a ghastly business, and I will not talk about it. I am afraid even to consider it.

Now you are to me the Sun, and Source of all my work. Today I have slaved and toiled to catch up arrears, and the work was as nothing because it was for you. I took over another man's work, because selfishness had gone out of me. And tonight I was without an effort gentle and considerate and respectful to the stupidest London candidate on a small committee. I now realise what Comte was driving at by his apotheosised woman, I never understood Dante's life before. You are making all things new to me. You are simply doubling my force.

But you are of course quite right as to the need of my discretion. I must not in the least tie or fetter you, by the slightest hint at even an unreciprocated feeling. I have tested myself today. I *can* be silent and discreet. I have not hinted at you or your article. My intimate friends do not know you were at Glasgow, and no one has for a moment even hinted that I showed signs of being in love (this I was self-consciously afraid of). I know the penalty of indiscretion too well. And our respective 'worlds' are very wide apart. Indeed, I am absolutely dependent on your grace for even a sight of you.

Nor must I pester you with my feeling. We must have a more detailed Concordat. On your part you must give me some chance of personal intercourse for the sake of our respective mental progress – that must be just as you find possible. I shall be very hungry but I can be very patient. At other times you will be to me that Sun which is always attracting and shaping the course of our Earth, even when we see it not. You will be standing to me for God, and I shall be working as 'unto' you.

On my side, I shall of course be even more silent about you than men are about their Gods, because no God can be so sacred as you will be to me. As regards yourself, we will be together as friends – surely no one knows how to be a friend so well as you, and I shall learn. I will not seek to remind you that I am your slave also. I will try in your presence even to forget it. No one could be less skilled than I am in 'making love'. I could not woo you by my manner even did I wish. I *did* wish, and realised how completely I failed even to make you suspect. (How *glad* I am that I failed, for you would not otherwise have suggested to me to go to Glasgow.)

Do you, by this time, understand that I can be in love without any desire for possession? That too, is a new revelation to me. Whether we are ever destined to be united or not, you can be, and are, a source of Life and Work and Happiness to me. To know that you are there: to feel this subtle communion of spirit: to be lifted out of oneself; to be touched by your tactful sympathy like the cool fingers of a nurse – all this is enough, and more than enough for me.

There is no risk of my suffering, so long as you can give me this. The suffering would come if you could not. You can torture me horribly. I had vaguely thought that I would give no woman this power over me – in my pride! When I think how much I am in your hands I am almost ashamed to have fallen so low. But I could not have been or done otherwise. it is fate. And at any rate, in the magnificent words of Steele 'To know you is a liberal education'.

Now it is for you to choose. It *must* be for you to choose, because I am absolutely in your power. If you elect simply not to answer this letter, and never write to me again, what can I do? We are not meeting nightly or weekly at balls. I am simply and hopelessly dependent on your kindness and courage.

But, even at the risk of destroying any effect of all the above pleading, I must for the sake of perfect frankness and sincerity, say one thing more. *Be honest with yourself.* You owe that much to the world. You owe it to yourself, you, as woman, owe it to me merely as man. I do not say this in any vain hope. I think I might plead for it as a condition – except that I have no right to make any conditions, having long ago surrendered at discretion. But you said some horrible things on Friday night: you inevitably made me fear that you might possibly *refuse* to recognise any chance of change. You almost posed as being willing to sacrifice everything for your intellectual work – to sacrifice not only any potential feeling of your own, but with it all another's life. Now I do not need to remind you, who see all these things so clearly, that you have scarcely any right to do that. You would be wanting in faith and honor and justice. You would be making an idol unto yourself. Your altruism would become an egoism. And your work would unconsciously suffer. You would lose your subtle sympathy. You would still believe that you could see, with an even clearer vision. And you would be all the while becoming blind – blind to all the finer shades and impalpable differences which make the differences between Truth and Untruth. You would have dried up 'Warmheartedness' in order to get Truth – and you would not even get Truth.

Moreover you are unduly doubtful as to the possibility of *anything* adding to your life. I can give you little enough. But I know, at any rate, how to minimise the tax on you: the normal terms can, as Grant Allen said, be altered: I have too much respect for woman as woman (let alone anything else) – as an intellectual unit – even to fall back into conventionality on this point. I am capable of sacrificing more than you dream of. I could be as great an adjunct to your intellectual life as you are to my moral being. Of course I stand to gain by far the most, because I gain your intellect too, and cannot give you moral help. But *together we could move the world*. And, as things are, though you can help me enormously (as you have done), only in one way can we really work *together*.

I did not mean to say all that, but I let it stand because it will be my last chance of saying it, and because it illustrates what went before. Leave my personality out of the question, but – whoever may be the fortunate man – do not crush out feeling. *You* will, I think, believe me simply when I say that I would rather see another man successful, than that this worse thing should happen to you. I cannot believe you will commit this emotional suicide, and it was because of the horrible fear you gave me on Friday that I asked you to 'give me a chance'. I will complete my almost brutal frankness by saying that I sincerely believe your work and power would *gain* by it – again leaving my own personality out of sight.

Fortunately there is time. You are not free to change your state at present. Will you simply let things alone, and see what happens? That was our Concordat on Glasgow bridge, when I called the Sunset Glow to witness. Do not go back on that. You cannot harm me by it – you can only harm me by going back on it. I can serve seven years, if need be, and be benefited thereby, even if Rachel fail me at the end. Merely because you can't give me more, do not refuse me that.

I do not mean that I shall be a 'great man', either in 7 years, or ever. If distinction comes – and I do not even strive to gain it – that might be something to lay at your feet, but I cannot conceive myself wooing you with bribes, even of that nature. I should always have enough for our work – even if pursued separately – and we could use no more, whether of wealth or influence, with safety or innocence. No, it is *not* that I buoy myself up with hope: it is simply that to *know* you is enough for me, and it is hard if I must lose this merely because I value it *too* much.

I see you tell me not to answer your letter. But you cannot have meant that. I *must* let you know that, as you say, my friendship with you, *does* and will serve my work (may I hope, also, yours), quite irrespective of its destined result, whatever that may be. We need not forecast the years: it is always the unexpected that happens.

You, too, must send me a line at your convenience just to agree to the new Concordat. I did not want or expect a letter, but now that I have named to you the fact that your mere refusal to answer this or write to me, virtually makes me a stranger, I shall crave just a word of assurance that you do not mean this. But even for this token I can wait, because I have the most perfect trust in you.

Yours

Sidney Webb

I see Knowles has put your article first!

The enclosed will account for the thickness of this letter. It was probably written in London, with the red book of the Congress before the author, whoever he was.

On 31 May Beatrice noted: 'It is a very solemn thought to feel you have a man's soul in your keeping. This afternoon at Westminster Abbey I prayed I might be worthy of the trust – that it might raise my life and his to a higher level of "Service"'.

Albemarle Club, 25 Albemarle Street, w.
May 31st 1890

Dear Mr Webb

Let it be as you say. I will not withdraw my friendship unless you *force* me to do so, by treating me otherwise than as a friend, or by making it apparent to the world that there is ought but 'camaraderie' between us. But I can only be responsible for my own work and my own life; I cannot be responsible for the effect that such a relationship may have on you – that responsibility you alone can take – now that you know my whole mind.

Your letter has touched me deeply; *but it must be the last word of personal feeling.* I shall try to grow worthy of that reverence you are giving Woman through me – a reverence which must ennoble the nature that gives and the nature that receives. But I shall not wish or desire it to last in its present form – I shall only wish to serve as a stepping-stone to a more perfect service of suffering Humanity – with all its incapacity and weakness and selfishness – you must think of, and treat me – with the same patience, helpfulness and respect. The thought of the 'gentle' and respectful treatment of the stupidest London candidate at a small committee gladdens me more than any other words in your letter.

Always yours sincerely
Beatrice Potter

I see they have left out all *me* in the speech and put in all *you*!

The article was that published in the *Nineteenth Century* for June.

Lord Dunraven (1841–1926) was an Irish politician and a prominent Liberal who was chairman of the House of Lords Committee on Sweating in 1888–90. Kinloch-Cooke, a journalist associated with the *New Review* and *The Observer*, was secretary to Lord Dunraven when he was Under-Secretary for the Colonies.

Henry James (1828–1911) was raised to the peerage as Lord James in 1895. He was a prominent advocate who served as Attorney-General in Gladstone's Cabinet of 1880–85 and left the Liberal Party with Chamberlain.

Alton Locke was the principal character in the novel of that name by Charles Kingsley (London 1850).

John Mawdsley (1848–1902), the secretary of the Lancashire cotton-spinners, was one of the 'moderate' leaders of the T.U.C., known for his advocacy of arbitration.

The *People's Press*, edited by Fabian sympathisers, had recently absorbed the *North London Press*.

4 Park Village East, N.W.

4 June/90

Dear Miss Potter

I promised to write a criticism on your article. Perhaps I emphasise the fact that I must not go beyond that by using official paper! The fact is that I have been so fearfully overworked ever since I reached home that I have had no moment to spare, and I snatch a few minutes from official duties today with great effort. Not, however, that there was ever any danger of my *not* writing, at whatever cost.

Your article is of first rate quality, magnificently put together, and lit up with a beautiful enthusiasm which gives it a swing and go, which are admirable. I say this because I now intend to suggest rather the points in which it falls short – not of literary perfection but of the maximum political effectiveness.

It is a little vague in its practical proposals. You prefer not to go beyond what you can read into the Lords' report. The consequence is that although Percy Bunting has read your article, he has produced a most feeble draft report for the London Liberal and Radical Union, quite failing in practical suggestions. I mention this because it shows how much more needs to be done before the points can be got into the heads of the people who draft Bills. There will be a Bill introduced by the London Liberal members next session on the subject, and we must consult together how this should be drafted. You rather shirk the dry ground of 'draft clauses'.

But your article will be of great use in driving out the popular notion of the middleman being the root of all evil. Your point as to the 'responsible employer' is magnificent.

I don't think the equalisation of the law for workshops and factories is quite so simple as you seem to imagine. I don't think the rigid fixing of 60 hours for women, with definite hours for opening and closing, could be enforced in every single room workshop in every trade in London. Those definite hours were the result of long experience in *single* trades, fairly uniform. Can we at one blow apply them to every London industry?

Of course all sanitary provisions, registration, mealtimes and overtime clauses might be applied to all workshops, and also a maximum limit of weekly (? and daily) work. But can any greater uniformity be insisted on?

I agree to the Victorian homework clause, but put no faith in its efficacy.

I am very pleased to see that you adopt my suggestion (if it was mine) that the registering authority should be the County Council, and which should have power to make bylaws. I have more faith in this one remedy (for London) than in all the rest put together. Unhappily I shall have much difficulty in getting this adopted. Indeed to turn your suggestions into a Bill needs a good deal more discussion and detailed statement, which you could not put into an article, but which will fall to you to do – simply because no one else can and will undertake it. You must not be satisfied until you have at any rate got them all into a Bill laid before Parliament. I think I could help in the actual drafting, and in the legal part. But I assure you that the dearth of competent workers in the field is appalling.

Now I pass to some other suggestions.

Ought we not to have a register of employers as well as a register of places of work (as Booth suggests)?

Ought not all Govt. work to be done in factories and 'giving out work' forbidden for Govt. contracts, as far as London is concerned? The County Council are about to take this step, as regards their clothing contracts. We ought to back up the Tailors recent upheaval on this point – Alton Locke *redivivus*!

I think Factory Inspectors ought to have all the powers of Sanitary Officers, and not merely make mutual reports.

Moreover the County Council's Officers ought certainly to have the powers of Factory Inspectors. I don't agree that the Lords make an 'admirable compromise'.

Ought we not to prohibit establishment of workshops in unsanitary areas? i.e. ought not the 'registration' be an application for a license?

I now pass to Lord Dunraven's report, as summarised in the *New Review* (June), no doubt by his secretary, Kinloch Cooke. I cut this out to send to you herewith. (Note the reference to yourself at p. 487!) I cannot help thinking that his limit of '3 persons employed' may be of some value. Theoretically of course, any one worker makes a workshop. Practically I doubt whether we can enforce any really effective restrictions unless at least 3 persons are at work.

What is the 'informal committee' referred to in the last paragraph? There have been conferences at the House of Commons, under Sir H. James, but I thought these were only about technical amendments for the textile trades, 'over steaming' etc. worked by Mawdsley. Do you know anything about what is meant?

I also enclose the article by Graham Wallas in the *People's Press*, which 'fumbles' after the conclusion which you put clearly and expressively.

I put in, also, a cutting from the *Daily News* of Saturday, in case you missed it, as to the Ladies' Dinner. I had noted quietly that the female reporter's name was Smith, so that her identity is now clear. It was an amusing episode.

Now – shall I keep my compact? I think all the foregoing is abstract enough. But do not forget that it will be absolutely in your hands to arrange and secure every possible chance for our discussing these and other things. I am trying to free myself from the frittering work (which however steadily increases).

I am sorry about the *Speaker* article. The only important point was left out, no doubt merely on the ground of length. I may get a chance of saying it elsewhere. You will be amused to hear that Sir Charles Dilke expressed his appreciation of the article, and chuckled particularly over the Schedules A and B. 'She had him there', he said.

I have written an article on the Congress for the *People's Press* next week, which I would send you, *if I knew your next address*. It is a poor article, almost avoiding the *Speaker* ground, written straight off in an hour or so.

What more *may* I say? The weather seems to me very bad – just as at Glasgow it seemed very good. *Animum non caelum mutat qui mare transcurrat* – but this is a new and peculiar reading which you need not explore.

I think I had better 'shut off', before I say too much.

Sidney Webb

87 PP BEATRICE TO SIDNEY

Beatrice spent June on a holiday in Bavaria and the Dolomites. Her travelling companion was probably Alice Green (1847–1929), the widow of the historian John Richard Green (1837–83). She also wrote on historical topics. She was Irish-born and a strong Home Ruler: in 1921 she became a senator of the Irish Free State. She befriended Beatrice Potter and was for a time quite intimate with her.

Next address Hotel Trento *Trent* Austria. Shall be there in about 10 days time.

[Austria]
June 11th 1890

Dear Mr Webb

I sent you a postcard yesterday thinking that we should be walking for the next ten days, but alas! a hopeless wet day has set in, and the only compensation being that one is able to sit down and talk with one's friends.

Yes: you are quite right: my paper is 'politically ineffective'. I knew the science of my subject well and I worked hard at the literary form; but I have no experience of administrative detail; and could only put together what I learnt from 14 days enquiry from experts – and dish it up as well as I could for the public. I do not agree with *all* the details of your objections – (we will talk them over when I come back to London) nor with *all* your suggestions – but then I feel I am not a good judge.

Still less do I agree with your suggestion that I should meddle further in the matter. Drafting clauses is not my *Fach* in life: I can only propose the ground which you, and such as you, must plant with definite proposals – my special work is to give a clear and, if possible, an attractive expression to the science and the ethics of social questions – for that I am fairly well trained. But, by disposition and by opportunity I am totally unfitted to initiate and advocate special reforms. I should make, even if I were a man, an utter failure as a practical politician, and as a woman, I have an instinctive but strong objection to interfering. But should you draft any Bill, I will use my little bit of influence to get it discussed and accepted by the members I know – tho' I might as well add, that at present I have no influence, as I never get an opportunity of exercising it, living always as a recluse in the country.

What about the tract for Co-operators? I shall be back in the country in August, and could work up any skeleton you gave me (in return for the *Speaker* article!). It would be better for you to sign it – but knowing the Co-operators and being sympathetic with them I could give the last touches, besides saving your time for other things. Do not overwork: it is bad policy, from the point of view of getting the utmost value out of yourself. Is there to be absolute freedom between us? Since I left Glasgow I have been brooding over the future of Socialism and the noblest way in which it can be brought about – and from that mighty thought I have drifted to considering the effectiveness of each individual socialist who is to leaven the whole.

I have been longing to warn you not to talk to people in general about the way in which you are edging your way in to different organisations – not, in fact, to speak of all your small successes. The general impression seems to be that you are manipulating – from that people argue that you are a manipulator and not perfectly sincere – and that you know and I know to be a false impression as well as a damaging one. It rouses alarm, and induces people to take hasty action to counteract your influence: and I doubt whether any reputation for cleverness (looked at from a purely worldly point of view) can be compared to the danger of a general lack of confidence in the absolute straightness of an individual worker. The introduction of the personal element – of self-congratulation or of any other form of egotism – gives the impression that you are working for your own hand and advancing your own interests – and that your faith is a means and not an end. And all this to prove the expediency of unself-conscious humility and of a sober sense of proportion! of, in fact, silence, in all that concerns yourself.

You see I am sensitive about the reputation of my friends – and desperately intent on their highest usefulness. You must be equally frank with me when you see a moral lapse or intellectual failure. The permanence and worth of a relationship depends on the consciousness in both partners that moral and intellectual growth arises out of it?

If you get a chance, do go to Ober Ammergau to see the Passion Play. It is wonderful – both in conception and representation. The true German's love of historical religion comes out in it – (the religious and mystical element is confined entirely to the chorus and the [?antetypes]) – it is a vivid representation of the revolt of the workers and the women, led by a great socialist, from the tyranny and false conventions of the moneyed and official class – the cause betrayed by a profit sector! The unselfconscious dignity and grace of the actors and the exquisite colouring, sympathetic music, perfect dramatic form – are as amazing as the outcome of village life. Our host, (who was the leader of the chorus) a delightfully courteous person, was horribly sad at the degradation of the play to a spectacle and the interference of the *Regierung* with the text, and declared the elders of the village had decided against another performance. If so, it is creditable to them. But you might try to see it – it is an impression which remains with one and adds to the permanent collection of noble pictures.

You ought to be very grateful for this letter! – and value it as a mark of confidence. If the spirit moves you pray write and tell me all you are doing – regard me as a 'well' wherein to bury all you wish to rid your mind of, as well as a field wherein to raise useful crops of true ideas and good intentions – in short relieve yourself of what is bad and strengthen yourself in what is good – that is the spiritual function of a woman to be the passive agent bearing a man's life!

BP

88 PP SIDNEY TO BEATRICE

Arnold White (1848–1925), writer and journalist, was an enthusiast for 'firm' measures, such as colonisation and a strong navy.

Archibald Grove was the editor of the *New Review*. Sir James Kitson (1835–1911), later Lord Airedale, was a Yorkshire ironmaster who was president of the National Liberal Federation. Sir James Stuart supported Henry William Massingham (1864–1924) the assistant editor of the *Star* and later an outstanding radical journalist, in a dispute which led to O'Connor's replacement by Massingham, but this distaste for Massingham's backing of Fabian policies led to Massingham's own resignation in January 1891. Massingham was an active member of the Fabian Society from 1891 to 1895.

4 Park Village East, N.W.
16 June/90

I *am* very grateful for your letter. Do you know that I was restless, and unable to work all Sunday, and was anathematising the absence of any post on that day – when your letter was lying in the Post Office waiting to be delivered on Monday morning. But I have looked for it every morning. You cannot realise how much it is to me. Blessings on that wet day!

I once slept in a 'Sailor's Home' (at Bergen, in Norway) and was much impressed by the cards hung up on the wall saying, 'Do not forget to write home: it costs so little and it gives so much pleasure'. If the Hotel Trento only had such cards. But when you look at the advertisement of somebody's champagne, on the wall of the *Salle à Manger*, you must remember the Sailor's Home Card.

But I must reply to your letter rather than write my own. I am afraid I overstated the criticism on your article. I was immensely impressed with its force, and I was vexed that the ordinary politician did not at once accept it. But it has had an effect. Moreover I did not, even with your previous hints, do sufficient credit to your ingenuity in getting so much out of the Lords Report, which I have since had to study more closely.

The work of drafting clauses is difficult and unsatisfactory – especially because immediate legislation can directly do so little. But it has got to be done, and (through the London Liberal Members) I can get it done (i.e. do it myself for them). Indeed, I *must* do it, because it will otherwise go badly. I am trying what I can to put Bunting's crude suggestions into decent shape. But it will be a poor affair anyhow. When you come back we will draft the Bill together, you correcting the matter and I supplying the form.

To finish with Sweating let me say that I enclose the last House of Lords Debates, in which you are mentioned. You have evidently much annoyed Dunraven and Arnold White. I enclose a brief report of my aristocratic meeting. (Arnold White said just the opposite of what is there recorded, and was intolerable). Someone (? A. White) put maladroit paragraphs about it in the *Pall Mall* and *D. Telegraph*, which had, however, the effect of greatly 'booming' me. The meeting was an awful experience – the audience absolutely ignorant and dull. I made them angry, and distributed tracts – that is all the result.

I will do something on Co-operation, which the Co-op. Union could reasonably be asked to print. I don't yet quite 'see' it. Might it be an 8-page leaflet on 'Co-operation, Trades Unionism and Socialism' written from the point of endeavouring to persuade Trades Unionists and Socialists to be Co-operators? I enclose the article I wrote for the *People's Press*. It was dashed off in an hour or so, and I avoided as much as I could of the *Speaker* article. (But no one reads *both* these papers). Cannot you give me some suggestions as to the contents of the projected tract, as you did for the *Speaker* article?

I am waiting to hear from Grove whether I shall do an article on Co-operation for the *New Review* for July. If he says yes (but it is getting very late) I propose to develop the idea which the *Speaker* omitted. You will not mind this communism? It will arouse no suspicion as Barry O'Brien will have given no second thought to what he heedlessly struck out for want of space.

My Poor Law article (unhappy babe, born amid *so many* distractions) has gone in and I have not yet heard its fate. It will be a rough amorphous mass of facts and suggestions, without the faintest literary value.

Yes – you are quite right in your criticism of my egotistical loquacity. I must and will learn reticence. But (as you alone will believe) my fault has come from a genuine carelessness as to my own reputation – which is of course not humility but pride. Was it Sarah Bernhardt who adopted the old motto – 'They say. What say they? Let them say'. Even you do not adequately realise how slowly I have become convinced that I was of importance in the world. I have constantly acted as an irresponsible child, doing what was right in my own eyes, but not counting the effect as regards myself upon the world as any important factor in its rightness. It was the irresponsibility of anonymity and lowly private station. Now I see more and more that I must accept a greater responsibility, and act accordingly.

My loquacity has led me to be frankness itself in all my diplomacy, and like Bismarck I have acquired thereby a reputation for deepness and even duplicity. I agree that this is an evil, and I will learn reticence. I have tried to escape the imputation of mere political time serving by a quite frank public exposition of my own extreme Socialist views. These are constantly on record, and even *en evidence*, and they are so little likely to serve any ordinary political ambition, that I hoped to have succeeded in avoiding that accusation. But again, I have been unconscious of my rise in life, and what seemed fatal to a parliamentary career even 4 years ago, might quite easily now become assistance to it. I will be more careful.

But *specific* advice is the most useful – surely you know that I should resent nothing from you – and I hope you will not fail to give it. I treasure up what you say about not boasting of my small successes in manipulation. I *will* be more reticent – *mit deiner Hilfe!* Now tell me of other faults.

Do you not realise that your real *Fach* in life is to 'run' me? The *Speaker* article (with a less purblind Barry O'Brien) might be typical of so much. I, as a man, can execute so much of what you can only conceive; and you could do so much for me if you will only have faith in your own instincts, and courage to cut out for yourself a new life whatever the sisters might say. A very fearful responsibility has been laid upon us both – unexpectedly, undesiredly. We have the ideas which can deliver the world. We have, to some extent, even the opportunity of making these heard and accepted. Shall we continue to count each for 1, or is there no way of making our forces count for eleven? You have it in your hands to make me, in the noblest sense, great. I, even I, have it in my power to help your own particular work. Let us, at any rate, walk reverently in the Garden of these Gods, the awful possibilities opening out before us. Let us humbly seek for the right course without regard to petty conventions or preconceived views as to our own lives. One thing I pray; do not let us miss our end, fail in our path, by any misunderstanding or waiting for a word. Between us two let there be at any rate perfect soul union.

I have had a curious interview with John Morley. There was a House Dinner at the National Liberal Club, with Sir James Kitson in the Chair, and many North Country Capitalist Liberals. Hearing that Morley was to be present, I attended, and (as luck had it) was placed in a conspicuous (tho' lowly) place, right in Morley's eye. Kitson (a huge locomotive manufacturer, President of Iron and Steel Institute) opened by abusing the Eight Hours Bill, and went much too far, was dead against all regulation. Morley accordingly had to begin almost with an apology for it, addressed virtually to me. After dinner I gave Morley a chance of speaking to me, which he did with great cordiality: and in the crowded passage, he alternating with polite nothings to those who addressed him, we had an important conversation, something like this:

He You are aiming at my exclusion. (Fancy this from *him* to *me*)

I Not at all, that is absurd. We merely want to be represented in the next Cabinet.

He Who is your man, there is nobody.

I I admit the young Radicals are nobodies – but we must have Stuart in the Cabinet as the *élu de Londres*.

He Stuart! You might as well ask for John Burns! (This was temper in him: he is a choleric person)

There was a good deal more each interjecting a sentence in the ear of the other, amid the interruption of the crowd. It was a characteristic scene. I need hardly say that he began it, and I merely took his tone. He does not show as a great man in these matters. I can't imagine Napoleon or Gladstone acting thus.

I expressly offered and desired that there should be peace between us.

We shall win the *Star* fight after all. O'Connor is to be bought out, and the paper will remain under Stuart and Massingham, that is, (I say it to you only) me. I need hardly say that this will further exalt our power.

When you come back I have so much to tell you. I read Carlyle's *Sartor Resartus* again – a noble book, much like you! – and found him saying 'Close your Byron and open your Goethe'. I long ago closed my Byron: now I will open my Goethe. (See, even there I must needs wait for Carlyle's confirmation before taking your advice.) I have read *Aus meinem Leben* (about a third of it) these two days, and I will go on. Do you know I am a little afraid to read *Wilhelm Meister* again? It is so mixed, good and evil.

I *don't wish* you any more rainy days – *but*.

Sidney Webb

Trento
22/6/90

Dear Mr Webb

It is very hot – stifling – and I am foot-sore and tired so you must not expect much – I write because I may not have another chance whenever we go back to the mountains.

Certainly: make any use of any ideas I may have thrown out; it matters little by whom things are said so long as they are true – the great thing is to say them often and to say them well – and in various forms so as to reach every kind of mind.

I am sure you are right never to hide your views: I did not mean to recommend reserve in that direction. In truth, I think I was thinking of myself as much as of you – warning myself against the personal note – the intolerable 'I' or 'Our' – against the *consciousness* quite as much as the expression of egotism. Undoubtedly it is inexpedient – because it rouses antagonism and creates a silent distinction which grows in the day of success and bursts into flame in the day of failure. But what is far worse than the inexpediency is the pettyness of spirit it betokens to dwell on the personal share one may have in advancing a cause – instead of brooding over the discovery and advancement of truth?

Your account of J. Morley saddened me – there indeed, is the personal note! His exclusion! He ought to fear the prevalence of bad ideas, not the exclusion of himself – and if he believes your ideas are bad he ought to fight them. But John Morley is 'convertible': if he be treated with gentleness and respect – he knows nothing about social questions – you can always work on a blank mind. He deserves respect – it does not do to ignore the services of those who have cut the steps one is using? and the rock may have been as hard as that which rises up steep before us.

Another part of your letter saddened me. You are expecting too much from me – if you do not take care – you will frighten me back into acquaintanceship! Remember we are simply friends – if you should assume or the world suspect more, the tie is broken – for good and all. Beware how you tread!

I will think over the Tract when I get to the high air again. I shall be back in the evening of the 4th. Will you come and spend Saturday evening at D.H. Hotel (7 o'clock supper)? We will go through all the things we have to talk over methodically(!) sweating, Co-operation, my study and your politics. You can rely that no word you tell me will escape. You can even use me as a safety valve for the personal note so that it may die down from lack of response. And you, on your side, must discourage it in me – you must feel your responsibility and in developing what is best, truest, in me you must discourage the love of personal power – it is degrading.

Political life is horribly dangerous – so few natures come out of it untarnished – it tends so little to form social character with all its glare and glamour and the heat and dust of personal prominence. Even as a woman and as a looker-on it is so easy to become infected.

I am glad you are reading Goethe: one ought always to be in communion with some great mind – one needs the high air of the mountain when one is fighting in the plain.

Will you let me know Verona, Hotel des Royal Deux Tours (we shall be there 28th) whether you can come Saturday – my time will be very full.

Ever yours sincerely

Beatrice Potter

4 Park Village East, N.W.

24 June 1890

It was good of you to write at once. I did not hope for a letter so soon – that is, I told myself last night that it was foolish to hope for it – and your envelope this morning was therefore all the more welcome.

You cannot realise how much you have changed me. Do not let my happiness disquiet you. It gives me no claim on you, and it enormously strengthens all the good elements in me. Surely Comte was right in making women the inspirers and guardians of morality. No one shall suspect my idol. On *that* subject, at any rate, I can be reticent.

As to the future, let us wait. I have the most perfect confidence that you will do whatever is right for you to do, at the moment when it is right for you to do it. Does it sound overstrained to say that I would rather that you should do what is right than that you should do as I may wish – if these should unhappily differ? It is *not* overstrained or absurd to me to feel that – as I certainly do – it is merely a sign of your good influence on me. Our ends are the same, our views are the same, our motives are the same. Surely out of so much identity there must come harmony. What has happened is so new, so unexpected, so disturbing to our pre-arranged lives, ('Some veil did fall') – that we may well wait to see our way, obedient, without individual prejudice, to whatever may prove the right course.

Do not let us despise or reject, however, all that does not come by way of logical syllogism, by the gate of pure intellect. What I have been slowly learning (and you showed me at Box both that you had learnt it too, and that I was right) is that the imponderable and the intangible are also real. I have been gradually coming to feel – in psychology and economics – as a physicist might feel who had disbelieved in aught but matter, and now suddenly became aware of the luminiferous ether. Even within positive knowledge there are more things to be taken account of than fall within logic and reason. Even 2 and 2 do not make the same to me now as they did six months ago! What we know depends on what we feel.

I will gladly come to the D.H. Hotel at 7 on *Saturday* 5th July – and you must think of other opportunities of our conferring.

I am probably free to move from about 14th July to the middle of August, and I have as yet made no fixtures. The Geologists' Association will spend from the 2nd to the 10th of August in the Mendips (I wish you could suddenly feel interested in the Mendips – there is not too much science!), and I have been thinking of taking part in this excursion, which will at any rate bring me into the next county. I should like to go to Ober Ammergau for a fortnight, but I cannot spare the time from my writing, as I hope to use a week or two in half-writing, half-resting. This I could do anywhere, and I don't know yet where it will be. I am not overworked or exhausted – rather, curiously resilient, if there be such a word, and divinely intoxicated, the whole world seeming new to me, the very colours appearing in a new light.

I *am* to write on Co-operation in the *New Review*, probably for August. I will try to send it to the D.H. Hotel before the 4th, in case you have time to look through it before we meet. Then out of that may arise the tract for the Co-op. Union.

I fancy you exaggerate the result on the mind of political power. But I cordially agree as to the evil of the personal element. I fear Morley will never now deal with me with open mind. I *do* respect and admire so much in him, but he evidently takes personal hatreds.

I wish I could get into a new circle, a wider world, so as to keep the right proportions of things.

You are entitled to your holiday, but how I envy you those 'mountains'! Do you know, I believe I am *jealous* of Mrs Green?

Yours

Sidney Webb

Did you see Spencer's letter on Miss Haden? Spencerian!

91 PP   SIDNEY TO BEATRICE

Dichtung und Wahrheit, the first part of Goethe's autobiography, was published in 1811; the *Xenien*, the set of epigrams written with Schiller, was published in 1796; the books forming the *Wilhelm Meister* series were begun in 1777 and the last was published in 1821. *Faust* appeared in 1808; *Egmont* was completed in 1787; *Hermann und Dorothea* was written in 1797. The drama *Stella* was written in 1775; the novel *Wahlverwandschaften* was finished in 1809. The reference to a *Schöne Seele* is to Book VI of *Wilhelm Meister*. Christiane Vulpius was Goethe's mistress for many years before their marriage in 1806. He was attached to Friederike Brion of Sessenheim when he was studying at Strasbourg in 1770–71.

George Henry Lewes (1817–78), common-law husband of George Eliot, published his standard *Life of Goethe* in 1855. Maggie Tulliver was the heroine of George Eliot's *The Mill on the Floss* (1860). The alleged translations by James Macpherson (1735–96) of 'Ossian' were a favourite of the Romantic age.

[?4 Park Village East, N.W.]
29/6/90

I have just finished my plunge into Goethe – I mean, for a time. Do you feel interested in my impressions? I have read *Dichtung und Wahrheit*, much of the *Xenien*, Ballads and minor poems in German: *Wilhelm Meister*, and a thin book of 'Sayings and Opinions' in English; and G. H. Lewes's *Life* (twice), which recalls to me *Faust*, *Egmont*, *Hermann und Dorothea* etc. with which I had long been familiar. (You must remember that I read very quickly, 'tearing the heart out' of books.)

I shall henceforth have a better opinion of G. H. Lewes – in many respects a despicable person – for his great admiration of Goethe: unless, indeed, the *Life* is really by George Eliot, as I always suspect in Lewes' work. Without her, he was worth little or nothing.

And I now realise much more tolerantly Goethe's want of patriotism and of interest in politics. For this there is much excuse.

But it is, on the whole, an awful example of the result of pure intellect. Note, first of all, the *Stürm und Drang* of Youth: how he flung himself into everything, followed every whim without restraint, reckless of consequence to others, especially to women. This is real selfish anarchism.

Then, in manhood, when he proudly thought to have gained self-mastery – by the way, the phrase 'self-mastery' must be a special demon of temptation. What *is* self-mastery? Is it not merely the supremacy of the dominant part of self over the rest? In what respect is self-mastery different from the earlier licentiousness (in a general sense) of Goethe's youth. This is not the '*Entbehren sollst du, sollst entbehren*'. What, *eigentlich*, did Goethe ever *renounce*, all his life long?

I have run off into that digression because it is an important point. Goethe was a horribly self-willed person. *He* never seems at any time to have suspected that he was perchance wrong. He got so far in Morals as to pass from the intellectual impulsive Anarchism of his youth, to the subordination of all the other sides of himself to one dominant purpose – (that is, he *meant* to do this). It is characteristic and instructive to note that it did not come off. He was quite unconscious of his absurdities in Science (e.g. Optics: in Biology he was an acute speculator); a complete failure as a theatre-director; and was still fancying he could draw at the age of 40. In fact, he never did really discover what his line was, without doubt, and pursue it (as, e.g. Shakespere did). There is no *series* of good things of the same kind – but the giving full rein to the dominant self is merely Anarchism one degree higher.

Goethe might have learnt from *Wilhelm Meister* to *distrust preconceived visions of one's work in life*: to accept as duty whatever may come to be done; to feel oneself rather as a soldier in the great army of humanity, ready to execute whatever order comes, even if not what one thinks one can do best. We are not isolated units free to choose our work: but parts of a whole, the well-being of which *may* be inimical to our fullest development or greatest effectiveness.

Not, what I am best fitted for, but what the public welfare demands of me – is what one seeks.

Now this cannot be discovered *a priori*, and in advance. One has to choose *daily*; and the ideal is to choose rightly without any personal bias – not merely without any but one's *dominant* bias. The confessions of a *Schöne Seele* show the obverse of Goethe: the dominant bias is mere Quietism. It is much harder to live *in* the world, doing its work, than on the heights of Parnassus or in the Convent. Goethe hardly helps us to choose (except in that grand line from Faust already quoted, and that is *too general*).

I think George Eliot meant to say this in Maggie Tulliver. We have no *right* to live our own lives. What shall it profit a man to save his own soul, if thereby even one jot less good is done in the world. Goethe was a great deserter from the army of humanity, who, fleeing from the battle, nevertheless did good service in other capacities. But it does not justify desertion.

Goethe paid the penalty of his Egotism. He thought to 'keep himself unspotted from the world', and do its work best by standing above it. The result was that (1) he failed to recognise what was going on around him, to estimate the movements of the human spirit: he is not one of the great Makers of the century – not even so much as Rousseau, Tom Paine, Robert Owen – how he would have resented such a comparison! But these imperfect beings proved greater teachers than he, because he 'denied' his manhood. (2) As in Sociology, so in Science, his judgment failed. He gave up all for Truth, and got, instead, his absurd 'Refutation of Newton's Optics', in which he was more interested for years than in his artistic production, making himself the laughing stock of Scientific Europe. It is dangerous to try to be *more* than man, to be 'too bright and good, for human nature's daily food'. (3) With his judgment, his tolerance of men decayed. He had at last to be abruptly turned out of his Weimar Theatre-Directorship for inability to work with others, insistence on his own ideas, and general failure to make the theatre a success, even artistically. (4) Indeed, his *taste* seems to have been very faulty – as everyone's will become who does not keep himself in touch with the world. I say nothing of the worship of Ossian and Byron – all Germans did it – but, e.g. the '*Walpurgis Nacht*' episode in *Faust*, the atrocities of *Stella* and the *Wahlverwandschaften* – and much in the minor poems are simply bad taste, such as Schiller in *his* manhood does not commit, such as Lessing never committed. Perhaps it is hardly fair to name in this category the abandonment of dozens of women, finally to sink into the arms of Christiane Vulpius, an uneducated proletaire.

Now I do not name these errors of Goethe as special demerits – all men have errors – but because they arise directly from his deliberate intellectual plans of life, they are the products of a system of 'Self-mastery'. (Nor are they the results of old age: they all happened before he was 50.) It is a warning not to settle everything too confidently by pure intellect. If we knew all, and could weigh all, then, indeed, there would be no appeal from the intellectual decision of the moment. But remembering how little we really know, and how imperfectly we can weigh that which we think we know, we must admit – 'use and wont, that guard the portals of the house', as of some validity: we must recognise instinct and feeling as of some claim as motives: as being, indeed, the organically registered expression of the past experiences of the race, notifying to us the 'general line' of human nature and the world.

I have much more admiration for Lessing than for Goethe. Lessing accomplished more, surmounted greater difficulties, and is a more important 'spiritual father' of Modern Europe.

But enough of this Critical Essay. If you have not read Lewes's *Life of Goethe* lately, you might well do so. I confess that I found it 'palpitating with actuality', in more senses than one – not always comfortingly! The roles are curiously reversed in some cases: just now, I am feeling dreadfully like Friederike of Sessenheim, *absit omen!* But history and biography are provided in order that we may avoid the errors of our predecessors and exemplars: and I feel myself sufficiently akin to Goethe (I don't mean in any conceited sense) to be able to profit by his example. I have already started to try. I shall be 31 in a fortnight: it is high time.

Sidney Webb

92 PP SIDNEY TO BEATRICE

Beatrice returned refreshed, bent on settling down to work. 'My friendship with SW has made me feel more than ever responsible.' (BWD 20 July 90) She gave Sidney a present on his thirty-first birthday on 13 July and he wrote the following day: 'no one shall ever say of me that the work to which I have put my hand is suffering because I look back on any woman. I will put woman in and beyond the work' – an assertion which led Beatrice to the naive conclusion that 'the worship is not of me, but of the Ideal for which I serve now as the chosen Temple'. (BWD 20 July 90)

They spent Sunday 27 July together in the Surrey hills, where Beatrice was visiting Frederic Harrison for the weekend and Sidney had gone to see the Pearsall Smiths at their house at Friday's Hill. They travelled back to London together. Sidney found a letter awaiting him from Massingham asking him to review Marshall's *Principles of Economics* for the *Star*. He had to do it at once, since he was about to leave for a German holiday with Shaw. He therefore went to the National Liberal Club and read the six-hundred-page volume that night – a feat which astonished Beatrice when they met again next day for a ramble in Epping Forest. Sidney then told Beatrice of his belief that Marshall had not refashioned economics and that he wished himself to write an epoch-making book on political economy. They sat under the trees and he read Keats and Rossetti to her. When they separated some 'words of personal feeling . . . burst from him', earning a prissy reminder from Beatrice of the terms of their understanding.

Shaw, Sidney wrote on 2 August, 'does not suspect my feeling for you. He has even suggested that it would be a good thing for Wallas if you should favour him'. This letter was written privily whilst Shaw was climbing a mountain at Oberammergau, where they had gone to see the Passion Play.

The ensuing letters crossed in the post. Beatrice's letter of 9 August replies to Sidney's of 29 July (wrongly dated, since it was apparently written on Tuesday 28 July. Sidney's letter of 11 August replies to Beatrice of 9 August. The omitted intervening letter of 2 August described his travels through Germany with Shaw and included a phrase of apology for the letter dated 29 July which was 'written under strong emotion' after the Epping Forest outing. He assured Beatrice that 'you may decide quite freely and at your leisure . . . You need not be in the least afraid of having any Werther tragedy on your mind'. Before this letter reached Beatrice she had already reacted strongly and sent what Sidney called her 'terrible' letter of 9 August.

[?4 Park Village East, N.W.]
29/7/90

You were so *ravissante* yesterday, and so angel-good, that I had all I could do not to say good-bye in a way which would have broken our Concordat. I had to rush away from you speechless to hold my own. Do not punish me either for the impulse or for my self-control. I have no lover's arts, and if I had, the notion of deliberately planning to 'win' your favor is abhorrent to me. I can only humbly obey you, in trying to be more worthy of you. Be both as kind to me as you can, and as frank as you know how. One little word from you would make me *so* much the better man. Even without that word your acquaintance has shown me the way to a new life. With your help I could follow it.

You were indeed angel good on Sunday, but one thing made me unhappy. I had not realised before that you will one day probably be rich. You had told me that you had a small independent income, but I had not realised that your father was so rich. This is one more barrier between us – one more step in that noble self-sacrifice which you must make to pick me up. It brings all the other home to me with crushing force. I feel as if I could never ask you to make that sacrifice for me – just as I am. I should be tempted to despair, tempted to the mad altruism of refusing that sacrifice which perhaps alone can save me. But I have never felt this exactly a personal matter. Upon my work, and your work, however unimportant these may be, our relations must have a great influence. Frankly, I do not see how I can go on without you. Do not now desert me. When the time comes that you are free, you will do what may seem to be right, and I am content to leave it so. But it is with a pang of wounded pride that I realise what a beggar I am. Do not despise me because I am at your feet. Shaw's lecture counselled otherwise to the lover who desired success. It is odd, but I could not, even for success, be otherwise: though for that guerdon I would go through Darkest Africa. I feel it hard even to go further away from you.

I have ordered next Saturday's *Speaker* to be sent to you: it will contain a somewhat 'literary' article on Registration. O'Brien was *most* flattering to me, and ordered a dozen articles straight off, to be sent in as soon as I can. He specially begged for one for the 17th, so that I may find time to do it *en route*, probably on a Municipal Death Duty.

I have done my review of Marshall for the *Star*, which will I think satisfy him. I cannot send that because I don't know what day it will appear – perhaps Saturday.

I do not *ask* for any letter to Post Office, Ober-Ammergau where we shall be next Sunday; but write me when you can. My letters after Thursday, will wait here, safely. I shall be back in London Aug. 11th. Do not forget to let me see your detailed syllabus of Co-operation and to tell me to do anything you want. I will not be all honey: you shall find my acquaintance meaty when you command it.

Sidney Webb

93 PP BEATRICE TO SIDNEY

William Thompson (?1785–1833) was an early socialist and supporter of Robert Owen's Co-operative theories: his *Inquiry into Principles of Distribution of Wealth* was published in 1824.

Box House, Minchinhampton, Gloucestershire
Friday [9 August 1890]

Dear Mr Webb

I could not write to O.A. [Ober Ammergau] even if I had wished, (as the time allowed was not sufficient) and I did *not* wish, as frankness would have compelled me to write the letter of one who was hurt and offended with the form and the substance of your Tuesday epistle. Another time, write such a letter if you like, but do not post it. Without the use of threats (which are hateful) I ask you – is it delicate or honourable of you to use the relationship of friends, which I have granted you, as a ground for attack – for a constant and continuous pressing forward of wishes of your own which you know are distasteful to me – and which simply worry and distress, and rob me of all the help and strength your friendship might give me? You speak of the 'self-sacrifice which you must make to pick me up' – but, whether it be a sacrifice or not, I have refused to make it – and by speaking of it, you assume that it will come, and force me to protest that *that* is exactly what I have refused to commit myself to. Again, if for one reason or other it were a sacrifice – is it for you to *press* it? (And this is a question quite apart from using ground which has been given you for some cultivation as a convenient cover for attack.) Is this not a stupid selfish device to complete your own life without any thought of the risk to mine? Both the form and the substance of that abominable letter seemed to me prompted, not by a desire to add to my present and future happiness, but simply by an uncontrolled drive to express your own feelings, relieve your own mind, and gain your own end. If it had not been the outcome of evident emotion – it could, really, have been a gross impertinence. Respect for me, and for my wishes (which Heaven knows are not unknown to you) as well as respect for yourself should have made that letter impossible for you. (One word more – you misunderstood me – I shall never be rich – only sufficiently well off to carry out my everyday life on the plan of greatest efficiency possible to my very limited ability. That is all I care for.)

If you value the continuance of our friendship, exercise a little more self-control – and occasionally think of me, and of my comfort – do not be always brooding on my effect on your own life and your own feelings. It is truly masculine! I do not quite know what the word Love conveys to a man's mind; but *that* is not what we women understand by Love – Love to us has in it some element of self-control and self-sacrifice. I can now say that I have honestly tried to be as frank as I know how – it remains for you to determine whether I am to feel free to be 'as kind as I can', or whether I am to treat you as one who will always take a yard when I give an ell – as one against whose assumptions I must be perpetually protecting myself. I have lent you Friendship – on trust – it is for you to pay me back that before you seek to make me give you more. To think that all this paper, ink, and thought should have been wasted on this vain repetition of conditions! For Heaven's sake let us have no more of it – I am sick and weary of the question. Don't provoke me again. You talk of 'obeying' but what extraordinary obedience – almost as marvellous as to Love! There – now – I have done.

I was glad to get your letter from O.A., interested in the vivid picture you gave of your journey, and disappointed not to have your impression of the Play.

That strange feeling of stimulated desire to work and of utter humility as to the little one can do which you express in thinking of the 40 mill. of Germans. I had that same feeling after that Monday evening discussion. Those men were so much in earnest – had such good impulse – and yet one so hopelessly at sea – at sea without a compass of clear theory or principle whereby to steer their way to the Promised Land. And one feels, vaguely, one has the compass somewhere in one's possession – but one has not learnt to handle it – still less to teach them the use of it.

I have read through Thompson's *Wealth* and found it most suggestive as to the theoretical basis for the early Co-operative Idea.

The last five days I have spent over Marshall – and intend to spend 5 more. It is a great work (not a great book). He has precipitated all the current expert economic views – sifted and analysed them – and welded them into one body of consistent doctrine – but is there much that is original? I should imagine not. You see, he makes measurement by money – i.e. exchange value – the test of economic as opposed to other motive. I myself prefer faculties and desires – for after all it is the faculties – the desires we measure, not the motives – of which we can have no cognisance – except subjectively.

But I do not quite understand his view of 'increasing return' from labour and capital, as opposed to the 'diminishing return' from land. Surely it is not a difference resulting from a fundamental distinction between land, capital and labour, but simply that you take a *different point* in the progressive use of the one to that of the other? I mean that there comes a time when the last dose of capital and the last dose of labour yields a diminishing return in industry as it does in agriculture? He seems to imply (*page 379*) that an 'increasing return' is a distinctive feature of growth of capital and labour instead of a mere sign as to whether the special organisation had reached its full development or not – if it had – there would be a diminishing return. Is it my stupidity or Marshall's vagueness? Do look at the page and tell me.

I find those diagrams horribly hard to follow and am not at all certain that I always understand the text. Would it bore you if I wrote you any difficulties I had? Could we not read the book together? I want to master it thoroughly before I begin on my own work. I read your criticism in the *Star* – but before I had the book. (By the way we take the *Speaker* and the *Star*.) If you would read the book and tell me all the points you disagree with – in his statement of theory.

His history seems to me weak, and his illustrations and generalisations about business facts not very much removed from commonplace – rather those of an 'outsider'. It is in statement of theory that he is strong – and in his sympathy.

My pony has just come to the door. Goodbye for the present.

Ever yours,

Beatrice Potter

[4 Park Village East, N.W.]
Sunday night, 11 August/90

Dear Miss Potter

I am this moment back from Germany. I will write you as to Ober Ammergau and Marshall later.

Your letter has hit me very hard. Some of your blame I submit to: my feeling carried me away. I admit the justice of your 'condition'; and one day I may perhaps have some chance of showing you that my love is not all selfishness. Meanwhile I fully admit that I was wrong to pester you with the expression of my feeling, and I will try not to offend again.

I have tried so simply to express my whole mind to you – to 'think aloud' without any 'play-acting' or deliberate attempt to seem better than I am – that your word 'impertinence' comes upon me rather as a shock. It is even worse that I should have, in your view, acted dishonorably as regards 'taking an ell'. I desired to 'take' nothing, and I knew that nothing was given me. If you only realised how much I have repressed you might perhaps not judge me so harshly.

I will not offend again. You shall not need to write me another such letter: a terrible letter.

Yours truly

Sidney Webb

This letter continues from Beatrice's letter of 9 August.

The College, Worcester
Sunday [11 August 1890]

I feel called upon to finish my letter to you, which I cut short, at the sound of my faithful Dormas ambling up to the front door.

I am staying with the Creightons. Let me introduce them to you. He is a well-known ecclesiastic and a capable historian – a pleasant combination of the man-of-the-world, the scholar, and the priest. To me he is the man-of-the-world plus a warm friend – he takes for granted I am an agnostic and knows I am not a student (not of his subjects). So I hear little of his religion or his studies – but a good deal about Life from his point of view.

She is an able, strong, dutiful and good-to-look-upon-woman – also a warm friend. Kindness itself – but a little hard on incapable, undutiful or physically weak persons – unsympathetic to her elderly unmarried sister – who is somewhat dreary, poor and erratic. The children are charming; natural and yet cultivated. The 'Home' is delightful – there is real genuine hard work, simplicity of life, and the easy charm of mentally and physically attractive persons. There is absolutely no egotism. Neither husband nor wife ever speak of themselves – tho' both are distinguished in their own lives – Canon Creighton might be a country curate instead of an eloquent preacher and accomplished historian; Mrs Creighton a German *Hausfrau* instead of a highly educated woman with moral force sufficient to inspire dozens of 'Societies' here and at Cambridge – if you judged them by their utter absence of self-assertion or self-mention. It is this unselfconscious modesty which lends this 'Home' its peculiar charm; and makes it the centre of a circle of friends – of all opinions, and all occupations – ecclesiastics, politicians, professors of all descriptions of knowledge, brilliant French freethinkers, high-class Germans and North-country manufacturers, all agreed to sink themselves and their work while they exchange ideas and experiences in a common meeting ground.

There is a fine aroma in really well-bred, cultivated, earnest English life – absorbing the new thoughts but living on in the old traditions – working for others and yet outside the area of competition – which I think is peculiar to the English scholar and church dignitary – a fine type of State official with a many-sided life of administration, teaching, and research, and social leadership on great and small questions.

Do you not think I am right in trying to master Marshall before I begin on the book? (which by the by is beginning to loom large – I fear the incapacity of autumn and winter months and don't feel so strong for work as I ought to do after that long holiday). Some of his ideas are new to me – for instance – I had never thought of 'Consumer's rent'; (whose invention was that?). (By the way, in those diagrams could you work out the exact amount of consumer's rent by multiplying one line by the other and dividing by 2, of course leaving out of consideration the curve and drawing a straight line instead of the curve:

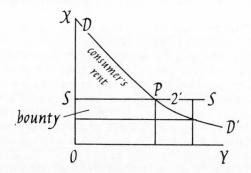

would X multiplied by SP and divided by 2 form the actual amount of consumer's rent? and would it be safe to ignore the curve and treat it as a straight line? In the case of bounty added to a constant supply price, could you get at exact amount of consumer rent lost to the new consumers by translating the geometrical figure into L.s.d.?)

Would you like to set me a paper on Marshall's book and make me work out some new diagrams? In that case I shall be at your feet, and not you at mine, a wholesome reversal of the relationship – more in keeping with the relative dignity of Man and Woman – bringing into play a formative influence from you to me – which will relieve the one-sided strain of our relationship.

If I were your sister I should end up with three small pieces of advice.

However old your coat may be (and that is of no importance) brush it.

Take care of your voice and pronunciation: it is the chief instrument of influence.

Don't talk of 'when I am Prime Minister', it jars on sensitive ears. And be dutiful towards your friend and keep her up to the mark, intellectually and morally – feel your responsibility to correct and form her.

Ever yours
B. Potter

I go back tomorrow to Box House, Minchinhampton.

---

96 PP SIDNEY TO BEATRICE

William Thomas Stead (1849–1912) was an author and journalist, editing the *Pall Mall Gazette* and starting the *Review of Reviews*. He was one of the founders of the 'new journalism' of the late Victorian age, becoming notorious when he was prosecuted for procuring a child prostitute in order to expose the white slave traffic. He supported many radical and eccentric causes: he was drowned in the *Titanic* disaster.

The Martyrdom of Man by the traveller and novelist William Winwood Reade (1838–75), a widely-read rationalist interpretation of universal history, was published in 1872.

Die Fëen was Richard Wagner's first opera, which was not performed until it was presented in Munich in 1888 after his death.

Frank Podmore (1858–1910) was one of the small group which founded the Fabian Society. He was a close friend of Edward Pease, with whom he also worked in the Society for Psychical Research. Like several of the early Fabians he was the son of an Evangelical clergyman; he was employed as a senior clerk in the General Post Office. His marriage to Eleanore Bramwell in 1891 was a failure and he was drowned in circumstances that suggested suicide. He wrote mainly on psychical research but in 1906 he published a substantial life of Robert Owen.

Ary Scheffer (1795–1858) was a romantic Dutch painter whose later works were vapidly sentimental. Adolphe Bougereau (1725–1805) was a French academic painter of religious themes. Joshua Davidson has not been identified. William Holman Hunt (1827–1910), painter and member of the Pre-Raphaelite Brotherhood, painted 'The Light of the World' in 1859.

This will be a long letter because I have much to say: I am going to sit up until I have finished it.

Your very kind letter received this morning is appreciated – oh so much! Let me say one thing only more about what has passed. You may rely on my obedience to your signal that I go too far: you *need* not in any future transgression – if such there be – cut so deep. I do not think you can know how much you hurt me. There is one word which would at any time recall me to myself after the confidence you have shown me. You have but to remind me that '*Noblesse oblige*', and I shall understand without a word more. But I will not offend.

I wonder whether a woman ever adequately realises the dreadfully 'tearing' nature of a man's real love (or a man the 'wearing' nature of a woman's, for that matter). I suppose I have a 'strong' nature, and go into this with the energy with which I go into other things. *C'est plus fort que moi.* I have not frittered away my capacity for emotion: two things alone call out my strongest feeling and one of them is, I am happy to say, the condition of my fellow-countrymen. I am happy in having either emotion and still more happy in having the two running along the same lines. Do not think that anything more is *necessary* to me. This is a case in which, although it cannot be more blessed to give than to receive, it is very blessed indeed, to give even without receiving. And, as George Eliot says in that exquisite ending to *Romola*, this highest happiness brings so much pain with it, that it is often to be distinguished from pain only by its being that which we would choose above all others. That is it. What we would choose above all others. I am deeply thankful that I have lived to feel this – which is, indeed, 'a liberal education'.

I have said so much, in order that you may understand *how* deeply I value your friendship and our intercourse, intermittent though the latter must be. You may rely that I shall do nothing to jeopardise them. But do not omit, in your judgment, that this is not merely a close friendship between a woman and a man, but one between a woman and a man very deeply in love with her. This, which makes it all the more noble of you, makes it all the more precious to me. I am sorry if it should make my friendship worth less (I hope not worthless) to you: I will do my best that it shall not be so – and that, let me say, without ulterior aim. But I feel bound to say this much, because I feel how much my emotion makes me, in some respects, fall beneath myself with you. It exalts my moral nature but confuses my intellect and paralyses my action. I suppose this is always the case, and you will know how to make allowance for it.

I am, indeed, recovering from the overwhelming effect upon my intellect! I do not agree with your view of the Passion Play! But first let me tell you how it fared with us. We only got 5 Mark seats, i.e. uncovered, and Sunday opened dismally grey. To put it briefly I think it rained for six hours out of the eight, more or less continuously. But it was not dark and not cold, and the play 'went' well. We had the counterbalancing advantage of hearing perfectly.

I was deeply moved from the beginning: not so much from 'realising' the particular story (I think, now, that I have never *much* admired the life of Jesus – compared with some other martyrs of humanity), as from realising the whole human story. I seemed to feel the whole long series of the 'Martyrdom of Man' as Winwood Read's book describes it, and I was the *more* moved because, to me it is a blind and unmeaning 'maze without (necessarily) a plan'.

Mary, the mother – surely a mother-type – brought the tears into my eyes whenever she spoke. The whole martyrdom of motherhood spoke in her, and womanhood was exalted to me. The moral inferiority of man to woman – perhaps a corollary of the contrast between the actor and the watcher – came home very painfully to me. I, too, was therein judged: and perhaps the momentary aspiration to be better may be of some slight value. I remembered that the preceding Friday had been my mother's birthday, and I wished I had done more than write a hasty greeting to her. It is suspicious when one says to oneself that one is generous only in great things! It is a mistake to neglect the minor manifestations of affection. Do you remember my quoting Rossetti's lines,

When the hand is hers,
Follies of Love are Love's Ministers.

which convinces my intellect, but does not succeed in getting me out of the bad English masculine habit of suppressing all family affectionateness.

Pontius Pilate somewhat restored my male self-complacency. My profession made me realise entirely his position. I should have acted just as he did. And I can't help feeling that Jesus did not give him a chance. The least bit of energetic defence would have enabled Pilate to save him. He brought about his own death by his contumacy.

This is all I need say as to the personal effect on me. I intend to send you Shaw's depreciatory criticism of the Play from the professional art critic's point of view. I do not by any means quite endorse his judgement, but it is always well to know the professional skilled criticism. Judas seemed to me the only good actor: Pilate, Nathaniel, Caiaphas and Mary were fair; all the rest very poor indeed. Jesus himself was beneath contempt from the dramatic point of view. Generally speaking, it seemed to be a triumph of training. The poverty of the material was however, as it seemed to me, very largely redeemed by the conscientiousness of the trained. They unmistakably did 'sweep under the mats', even the little children. It can hardly fail to have as good an influence on their life as it has upon their language.

Where I fail to follow you (though I expected to do so) was in seeing in the story as played, any feeling of its having been a socialist uprising, or rather a 'Peasant Revolt'. I had been comparing it in my own mind to that dumb pouring out of the oppressed French rural people once at Versailles, just before the Revolution, without arms, without purpose, merely to stretch forth their hands against the heavy but impalpable cloak of oppression which weighed down their lives. For answer, as Carlyle tells us, two of them were hanged on a new gallows 80 feet high.

But I cannot believe that the Ammergau peasants realise any such thing. The story has been rigidly conventionalised, and they do not act as if they had any spontaneous feeling about it. One point supports your view. When the Sanhedrin wants to 'pack' the crowd, so as to ensure the demand for Barabbas, Nathaniel (the Mephistopheles of the piece) goes to the outraged Money Changers, and bids *them* bring their friends and ad-herents. This is, I think, not Scriptural and looks purposeful. The blacken-ing of the character of Barabbas, who, as I believe, *was* a leader of an abortive peasant revolt, is perhaps a second point in your favor, as it enables Jesus (as it were) to absorb this part. But this blackening had al-ready been done in the St John Gospel, to 'intensify' the perverseness of the people of Jerusalem.

I regret the 'smoothing' away of the Mediaevalisms. These survive now mainly in the fanatical inclusion of every Biblical incident, much as the Mediaeval painters did in their pictures. But the absence of the vigor-ous popular 'life' – rough though it was – which made the miracle Plays really live, is not compensated for by the conventionalised Christ as the 'Man of Suffering', in purple robes etc. The Middle Ages would have given us a frankly human tragedy – almost perhaps a 'Jan Steen' blended on a 'Holbein the Elder'. What we have today is a Christ as 'sentimental' as Bouguereau's Madonnas compared with Raphael's. It is the Christ of Ary Scheffer or indeed of Holman Hunt's 'Light of the World'. What we now want is a Christ of a realistic type – say a 'Joshua Davidson' on the stage.

Have you read Stead's red shilling version of the Play? He says at the outset, 'This is the story that transformed the world: – *and will yet transform it.*' My first reflection on leaving the theatre was that he was wrong. Indeed he admits, at the end of his pamphlet, that possibly the old Christ version of the Human Sacrifice is as obsolete and impotent to move the modern mountain of evil as blasting powder was to blast the St Gothard which needed dynamite (his own metaphor). It seems to me that the Christ Story needs to be retold in such a way as to bring out the fact of its being only one among many such stories. Vereshchagin hung his 'Crucifixion' side by side with his 'Hanging of the Killers of Alexander II' – and called the one picture 'An Execution in Judea' and the other, 'An Execution in St Petersburg'. This is the right idea. Who will carry it out effectively in literature?

The fact is that I do not greatly worship the Jesus type: you will understand why I have a vague feeling that he ought to have 'taken it fighting' to some extent, at any rate to the extent of making a reasonable defence. No wonder the disciples 'scattered'. The beauty of Sacrifice *qua* Sacrifice does not adequately appeal to me. There ought to be a reasonable calculation of means to ends, an attempt at adaptation to the environment – not necessarily precluding such actions as that of John Brown, or Schill's uprising against Napoleon in 1808. (Do you know of this gallant attempt, when a German Lieutenant declared war against the French, and raised the Prussian flag on his own account?) It is sometimes one's duty to 'use oneself up' as a cannon ball. But even then the act must be adequately reasoned, and not unnecessarily suicidal.

This is a 'masculine' view. Women, who have to do so much more of the 'watching and weeping' of the world, may easily be more sympathetic with a merely suffering Christ. Ought men to be? I doubt it. The world needs work as well as renunciation, and though men need to learn renunciation (it is not only in love that we are selfish), women need perhaps to learn that they are much too docile, especially to men.

This is how the Passion Play seemed to me, on its deeper side. The spectacular effect and (to me, untutored) the musical effect was supremely beautiful. The bright colors of unsophisticated choice, without the least tawdriness or bad taste, were very pleasant to me. (Why, then, are the R.C. churches decorated with such bad taste – even the Ober Ammergau altars?) The tableaux seemed marvellous. Do you understand why I hung on the words of the Choragus? He was excellent and made me wish to know him. The whole thing was a great and vivid experience, as you predicted.

We left the same evening for Munich: stayed there 2 whole days (we did not see Wagner's *Die Fëen* after all: it was postponed), and went on to Augsburg (poor), Ulm (very good value, an exquisite Cathedral, better than Cologne *I* think), Stuttgart (a pretty but modern town) and Strassburg (for the good Cathedral): then straight home by Brussels and Calais.

One understands the mediaeval pictures better after seeing the Passion Play, especially the early Germans whom we studied at Munich and Augsburg.

I am glad I am recovering intellectual balance: I shall begin to criticise you on Co-operation presently! But do not misunderstand the symptom. I could think, during the long railway journeys, only in one direction; almost every picture that I looked at carefully, unexpectedly produced some absurd trick of reminiscence (even the blond Madonnas would sometimes have a turn of the head, a bend of the arm, or something else) which brought me back, perhaps to that corner room over Bishopsgate St perhaps to the tree under which we sat at Longfords. Some pose of a travelling American or German peasant woman, some dress or bonnet, and I was in the Albemarle or on that everblessed day under the oaks and hornbeams of Epping Forest, or even in that dark room over against the British Museum in which I once, with a 'wild surmise', sat and wrangled with you in a corner.

I am glad you read my review of Marshall, but I detect that you did not care to keep it! I agree with you (and said so in the review) that the book contains scarcely anything new. But remember that I have as yet spent over it scarcely five hours – they were intense hours – enough to review the book but not really to discuss. I at once lent it to Olivier, who will return it to me on Wednesday: then I will look up your points, in which I think I take your view. I think (as I said) that he has failed to rid himself quite of the erroneous old notion that Land differs from other forms of capital, and the faulty contrast between Increasing and De-creasing Return is a corollary. He has taken from me what he calls 'Quasi-Rent', but not my further point of both Land and Capital being equally under both I. [Increasing] and D. [Diminishing] Return.

I doubt the utility of the diagrams.

I shall be delighted to read the book with you chapter by chapter – not more than one a week however (with one bit of Browning?) You *must* study Marshall, but I would not wait to begin your book. As there is no new doctrine in him, there is no reason to suppose he will essentially alter your views. (He is specially weak, I think, about Co-operation.) Why not do a little of each at a time? You will gather energy as you go. Every-one has to 'recover' from a holiday. (Though I, today, have written *two* articles! as well as much C.O. work and correspondence.)

'Consumer's Rent' is an old idea of Marshall's own (unpublished save in lectures). I learnt it from Arthur Berry in Cambridge years ago. I don't think it very valuable, but it is ingenious. It lends itself to the appreci-ation of 'income not in money' which he so little regards, e.g. I would willingly pay £1 for the postage of this letter if it would not go for less: its value to me is therefore at least £1, and I therefore enjoy something equal to my estimate of the value of £1 minus the actual stamps. I some-times think that the 'real wages' of the workers might be much increased by teaching them to appreciate natural beauty. (Think of this next time you look at a sunset: I can hardly avoid the thought now. Do you know that some of these thoughts become almost a monomania to me!) Such an increase would be a 'Consumers' Rent of *Ability*', proportionate in each case to his capacity for such enjoyment. Cultivated people thus get a huge 'Consumer's Rent of Ability', as an indirect 'by product' of their money rents. (To him that hath shall be given) I don't know whether Marshall has made this and other extensions of his idea. The name 'Con-sumers' Rent' is inept. We must find a better one.

I don't think you can ever use curves quantitatively (in economics) because you can never adequately quantify your elemental lines. The 'curve' itself is (in real life) only a very irregular line smoothed into a perfect curve for the sake of simplicity and theoretic 'continuity', e.g. the curve of rent in England today might be, in actual cases, like this

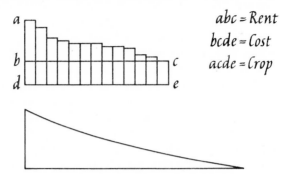

$abc = Rent$

$bcde = Cost$

$acde = Crop$

The lower figure would be the 'diagrammatic' curve. Does this answer your enquiry, or do I misunderstand you? It is obvious that you could never ascertain the amount of rent from the lower curve, even if you knew crop and cost in £.s.d. and drew them to scale. I do this sometimes for my class, but only for the sake of clearness.

I don't think I *could* set a paper which would be useful to you, but we will see when I get the book back.

There was a hateful paragraph in the *Star* on Saturday about the prevalence of marriages in the Fabian Society (untrue as it happens, in tendency: there have been singularly few) which made me, in my self-consciousness, feel uncomfortable. Of course the reference is to F. Podmore who is engaged to a Miss Bramwell of Perth N.B., a member; and to two other minor members. I have written to Massingham specially telling him never to put in any such par. again. I need hardly say that I have not confided in a single soul, and indeed, I have scarcely mentioned your name to any one (and then only when others brought it up) since May last, at any rate. And I have been otherwise quite discreet, even in details. Some acute observer might, of course, detect my own feeling, though I am very careful, but even then nothing can harm you. I lead a sufficiently 'detached' life, even at home, to be able to come and go without remark or explanation. And I have always posted my own letters to you.

I only say all this lest you should have seen the *Star* par. and thought it alluded to me.

Let me say in conclusion that I am very grateful indeed for your hints at the end of your letter. Please go on, when any more occur to you. The 'Prime Minister' was a slip, immediately deplored, a survival from the time when I took myself less seriously, and really meant only a metaphor.

I have not done, but I ought to go to bed, so Good night.

Sidney Webb

How happy I am in writing this.

Box House, Minchinhampton, Glos.

[?14 August 1890]

Dear Mr Webb

I was glad to get your letter this morning, I had been pained by the thought of paining you. Written words are desperate instruments: one cannot temper them into a fit relation to the mind that reads them – one cannot modify or discontent them by look, voice, or gesture. I will accept your suggestion and will remember the watchword *noblesse oblige*.

This is not a letter – it is only a line to suggest that we introduce regularity into our correspondence. Sunday morning is my best day for writing; on Saturday afternoon I will read a portion of Marshall, or answer a problem or a question suggested by you – and then you can answer it any time in the following week that suits you.

Remember that the details of your life interest me – your own ideas and your relations to others – and the general progress of your work of all kinds.

Oh! what a depth of selfishness and indifference there is – what an absence of heat wherewith to transform water into steam. We *must* rouse some new form of deep religious feeling. Think what a force [of] religious feeling has been directed to ineffectual or unworthy ends – think what a force that power of self-subordination to an idea might become – even among commonplace persons – if directed to rationally conceived social ends – how it might transfigure society. And it would not die down, because the *use* of it would be verified, instead of falsified by events. It would be a case of function becoming structure – through adaptation and natural selection.

Ever yours

B. Potter

On this date the Fabian Society received a donation of £100 from Henry Hunt Hutchinson (1824–94), a Derby solicitor, to underwrite a lecture campaign that autumn in Lancashire. Almost all the leading Fabians were drawn into the crowded series of meetings, which was the Society's first significant activity outside London.

4 Park Village East, N.W.

15 Aug./90

I write because it is Friday, but I pay you the compliment of believing you will not mind my saying that I happen to be too much pressed by urgent work to deal adequately with you. (I wish to try *not* to allow what is so very pleasant to me to hinder any, even the smallest duty* that comes to me. [*The next sentence is inserted at**] But, after all, I ought to insert 'other' here, so I might even justify what I desire!

I shall look eagerly for Monday's letter and reply as I can.

The only thing that is 'ready' to suggest to you as to Marshall is an instance of the Law of Rent which may be new to you. As an instance, when distress came in Ireland in 1887, the H. of C. [House of Commons] ordered reduction of Irish rents *in proportion* to the fall of price of produce. A useful diagram might be constructed, out of six or eight assumed quantitative instances of cost and crop, to show how this worked: and what order the H. of C. *ought* to have made if they had wanted to hit off the new economic rent (assuming the judicial rents to have before coincided with this latter) – an important consideration is omitted from this argument (as regards the farmers' profits and economic rent) – what is it? (cf. the claim of the English farmers to compensation where some of their cattle were slaughtered to put down the Rinderpest). Do you see any way of bringing that into the diagram?

(Most of this I got from Wallas – who as a clever schoolmaster is fertile in lucid instances etc.)

Would you not do well definitely to map out your lectures on Co-operation, and write a bit every week? Everyone knows his own way of working, but I find myself that the stimulus of a definite 'date of delivery' is immense. I need hardly say that I should only be too pleased if you would send me the bits as they are done (why not weekly, treating me as the printer's boy waiting for copy!) and return them with suggestions.

Remember that (at any rate as I believe) one of your means of effectiveness is to supply me with ideas. Of course I would not in any way forestall your book.

Do you know the enclosed by Newman? It is beautiful. But note how perfection is therein unconsciously made compatible only with a life of leisure, and abstinence from public teaching. The 'perfect gentleman' does nothing for the world's advancement save exist – beautifully! I should have liked to have further lectures, 'The Gentleman as a Prophet', 'The Gentleman as a Politician', 'The Gentleman as a Defender of the Oppressed'. Jesus – Dekker's 'first true gentleman' – would have failed to satisfy Newman's definition. It is much harder to fight gentlemanly than thereby to exist gentlemanly.

But I must not run on.

By the way Miss G. Spooner is one of the 'Fabian engagements' – to H. W. Carr, Secretary of the Aristotelian Society.

Sidney Webb

[*Written at top of letter*] Is Marshall altogether to replace *The Ring and the Book*?

Beatrice maintained a direct friendship with Graham Wallas, whom she described (BWD 26 August 90) as 'a strange warm-hearted young man, with a bright intelligence, not much beyond the common-place except in social fervour'. He was, she wrote, 'one of the knot of Fabians who would "run the world"' . . . the charm is in the relations between these men – the genuine care for each other, the trustfulness and practical communism of property and ideas'.

Sidney replied to this letter in an undated letter (?21 August 90) with notes on Robert Owen and the Industrial Revolution. He complained about the pressure of casual journalism and 'purposeless' articles; he was concerned about the book he had promised to the publisher, Walter Scott, on political economy, saying that Marshall 'has largely cut the ground from under my feet, and said much that I meant to say . . . I am not prepared to reorganise Pol. Econ. and I merely meant to do "memoires pour service" to the reorganisation . . . Besides I simply have not time to write a book'.

O'Connor Power was T. P. O'Connor.

Box House, Minchinhampton, Glos.
Sunday morning [?17 August 1890]

Dear Mr Webb

I shall keep the problems – I had set to work at once with a sketch of my first chapter, and this morning I mean to be idle and entertain my friends – O'Connor Power and G. Wallas.

I want you to criticise the enclosed – (if you can read and understand it!)

Can you give me a good formula of the 'Competitive Idea' – as it appeared in the economics of the market place? I do not want to take A. Smith, as he was scientific and was fully aware of qualifications – but I want if possible the words of some representative commercial or manufacturing magnate summing up current Malthusianism – *laissez-faire* views. I want also to show shortly and vividly the enormous work the Competitive Idea had to do in clearing away class restrictions, so that each man should bear the consequences of his own actions – instead of the pauperisation of the indigent by Poor Law and of the nobility by Pensions, Corn Laws, etc. Of course the true basis of the Competitive Idea is natural selection, and of the Co-operative Idea – Functional Adaptation – but I must keep that for the last chapter.

How sad Owen's downfall into ludicrous vanity and absence of all sense of proportion! That passage in which he attributes the spread of Free Thought and Rationalism solely to his speech at the Rotunda. A terrible case of a Fly in the Wheel! There is something supremely pathetic. But for all that he was a great man – and wrote *the* Classic – that *Short Appeal to the Manufacturers*, 1813 – in which he urges them, by the Holy name of Profit, to form the character of their workers as they perfect their machinery.

Your article in the *Speaker* is excellent this week – superior, if I may venture to say so, to the 'Registration Muddle' – I did not like the opening of that, i.e. it was rhetorical and yet awkward and gave me the feeling of effort without effect. You excel most in full but plain statement and in ingenuity of argument. I doubt, too, whether you can give the time for 'literary expression' – it is a question of time.

That is a beautiful description of Newman's – there is a grand passage in one of his sermons, in which he turns round on his middle-class audience, (after describing the charm and the worthlessness of the leisured class – the Athenians of modern time) and tells them in words of exquisite satin, that however much they may strive they will only attain ridiculous vulgarity – they cannot if they would, become 'gentlemen'.

He was, through and through, an aristocrat – and he chose the most perfect life for nature's aristocrat – the Celibate, the Meditator and the Priest – conditions of life unattainable to the 'common lump of men'.

You are right it is terribly difficult to keep the aroma of 'Mental Distinction' in the fight – I think, however, one may keep the substance – the absence of the personal note – and the absolute straightness and sincerity of thought and action. Owen had the latter (perhaps the most important) but he failed both as a leader and as a 'person of culture' through the overpowering presence of Self in his conscious. Superficially well-bred persons learn to hide their consciousness of self – hence the charm of good society – really well-bred people have not got it, hence *social leadership* – when breeding is combined with capacity.

About the B. Ass. [British Association] I will ask C.B. [Charles Booth] to which hotel he is going and will let you know. I shall go up on the Tuesday via Birmingham – he does not come till the Wednesday, so perhaps Tuesday evening we shall be able to talk.

Now goodbye. Do not write on any special day – and not at all, unless it is quite convenient. Any thought you can give me on paper will be welcome. Also do not fail to tell me how you are doing – that is not egotism, only indulging the sympathetic interest of a friend.

Ever yours

Beatrice Potter

100 PP BEATRICE POTTER TO ELLA PYCROFT

Before Sidney had left for his holiday he made arrangements for William Swan Sonnenschein (1855–1931), who published several socialist authors, to commission a book from Beatrice on the Co-operative movement, to be included in his Social Science series.

Mrs Humphry Ward was associated with University Hall, founded in 1890, in Gordon Square, Bloomsbury, as a residence where young working-men could be taught history and the philosophy of religion. It was intended as a bridge between the middle-class intellectuals and the intelligent manual or lower clerical worker.

Titus Aked was one of Beatrice's relations from Bacup.

[Box House, Minchinhampton]
[? mid-August 1890]

My dear Ella

You do not give me your address, so I address my letter to Vienna. I was interested to get your letter – you seem to be really seeing new things and taking in new ideas – re-freshing yourself. It is wonderful what a holiday does for one: I feel so much stronger than I have done for years – for the first time I feel I am working on a reserve of strength.

Did I tell you that I had promised to write a little book for the Social Science Series on the 'Co-operative Movement' – a small 2/- book, for which I am to get 6d a volume royalty on every copy sold? I ought to make something between £60 and £100 out of it. I have also engaged to give it first in lectures at Mrs Humphry Ward's University Hall, 5 lectures £18. So you see I am beginning to earn an honest penny. Knowles gave me £42 for the *XIX Century* article! (Don't tell M.H. [Margaret Harkness], it makes her so jealous). Isn't this all very mercenary? – but often, the market price tells something of the excellence of the work and is encouraging when one chooses hopelessly 'heavy subjects'.

When are you coming back? I wish much to see you: you must try to run down here for a day or two, or if you cannot, I will make an effort to get away for a night in London. I want to feel assured how you are: and to realise what you are going to do.

I shall be here pretty well all the winter. When I have finished my little book – I shall read. It is quite useless to attempt any really good work on investigation unless I can go away for a long enough time. I have the learned Canon Creighton staying with me: he is an attractive combination of the ecclesiastic, the man-of-the-world and the scholar. I have had Graham Wallas, (one of the Fabians) O'Connor Power, and two other men, you know not, here at intervals. Titus Aked turned up the other day on his holiday: and I entertained him as an 'honoured cousin' much to the Playnes mingled disappointment and amusement!

Ever

BP

IOI PP BEATRICE TO SIDNEY

[?Box House, Minchinhampton]
Aug. 23rd [1890]

Dear Mr Webb

Very many thanks for your letter: the notes will be useful to me. By the time we meet I shall have the content of every chapter marked. I hope to have begun the first. Do think of a good formula for the Competitive Idea.

Do you know, I think you would do well to give up the P.E. [Political Economy] book. Marshall's great work – and the abridged cheap edition which he must publish, will take up the full available span in the public mind. You had far better let your ideas simmer – neither you nor the public will be ready for a new departure for some years. Neither do I see, with your political and official work, that you can find time to write a really good book now, and it is a pity to connect your name with anything shallow or thin – you might regret it. Of course it is annoying to be forestalled (however public-spirited one may be) but Marshall with his 48 years and his 30 years of devotion to this subject has earned the harvest – it would have been cruel if *he* had come 'stale' on to the market.

Is it absolutely needful that all the time you may spare for the book should be eaten up in political every-day work? Of course you know your own work best, but I cannot help wishing for you a policy of cultivation which will ensure increasing returns to the public in future years. Would it not be possible to do some really good work for the *Speaker* – to take some series of subjects you want to master (from an impartial and not party point of view) and pay great attention to arrangement and form? I always think you rapid workers, especially when you are engaged in party politics, reap your harvest too soon and too easily. You ought to [be] forced into retreat for part of the year. It seems absurd, when you are perplexed with 'overmuch work' to give you this suggestion – that you should engage in other work! and in what is apparently of no immediate value. It is because I fear that if you give up the P.E. book, the whole substance of your brain will go into one form or another of propaganda or wire pulling. Propaganda means one-sided advocacy – wire-pulling a sort of high-minded and well intentioned intrigue – both may be needful means – but neither of them can develop the very best qualities of character and intellect. Even from the point of view of the success of the Socialist movement, it seems to me more important to form noble character and *really* scientific views (the result of single-minded research) than to score political successes. All this is very much [? off my research] – but I write what comes into my mind after thinking over your letter. We will talk it all over on Thursday 2nd (will you call for me at B. Museum Reading Room about 4 o'c? I come up on Monday, so as to get a full day's work and to have B. Jones to dine at D.H.H. I will go anywhere you will on Thursday as I am free for the evening).

I like your friend Graham Wallas: he is so perfectly sincere and naively enthusiastic. And he has quite a teacher's faculty for imparting all he knows: and great generosity in giving it. But what charms me is the perfect sort of relations between your little knot of men – it is singularly trustful – you really care for each other. Such friendship is very precious – it defies

178

cynicism and tells in plain language all the good qualities you must all possess – one gathers that you must all be generous and sincere and really anxious to use yourselves up for the public weal. These are compliments for you!

I shall have plenty to talk to you about when we meet. For the present goodbye and 'God bless you'. How can we translate these words into modern phrases – that intense and almost prayerful desire that one's friend may be the highest possible to his nature? That desire, at least, I can give you in return for any thought and feeling you may give me. Can 'Prayer' for another bear fruit? Is it a delusion that makes me – forces me to aspire for you? Can we add to the spiritual force of another by mere desire? Human sympathy is surely an unknown force? It is not a mere exchange of ideas and experiences – it has a meaning of its own.

Till Thursday

Ever yours

Beatrice Potter

P.S. I am enjoying the country immensely. I have come back from the gorgeous theatrical Italian Tyrol with its rapid transformation scenes of brilliant sunshine, rock-forms and mountain heights enveloped in shifting clouds – to the quiet grays, greens, and browns, the long, low lying hills and the sober harmonies of earth and sky of English landscape, with a positive yearning for an [?homely] companionship. That common with its wonderful expanse of sky, the broken ground of the Roman camp, and the curving lines of the numberless valleys: do you remember it? Think of me rushing through the air on my little cob; or wandering over the soft turf, in my bare feet! What luxury one lives in! How can we reap all one enjoys?

102 PP SIDNEY TO BEATRICE

Nathaniel Hawthorne (1804–64) wrote *The Marble Faun* – also known as *Transformation* – in England after a long visit to Italy: the romance was published in 1860. Harriet Martineau (1802–76) wrote popular books on economics and history. William Cooke Taylor (1800–49), a writer on historical and educational topics, was an early statistician who made studies of industrial organisation. *An Experiment in Marriage* has not been identified.

George Shipton (1839–1911) was one of the dominant figures of the 'Old' unionism, opposing the Eight Hours movement. The reference is to the coming Liverpool conference of the T.U.C., and to Webb's belief that the 'New' unionism was gathering strength.

The shilling edition of *Fabian Essays* was published by Walter Scott in 1890. Its sales marked the beginning of the Fabian 'boom' between 1890 and 1893.

William Lucas Sargant published *Robert Owen and His Social Philosophy* in

1860. The Comte de Saint-Simon (1760–1825), the eccentric pioneer of French utopian socialism, believed in the moralisation of society as a means to social reform.

4 Park Village East, N.W.
26 Aug/90

I think I am writing to you today because I am unhappy – probably out of 'mere wantonness'. If you have been doing anything hostile to me during the last 24 hours, it is that of which I have been conscious, for sympathies go very far. More probably however, it is a mere overtiredness.

It is an ungrateful return for your sweet letter. The shape which it has taken is the sickening fear of which I have more than once hinted, viz. that I am really, somehow, a fraud, and that I cannot do what people expect of me – I do not mean in the bad sense, but rather, 'hope' from me. The lot is hard, they say, of the comic man who is not really and inwardly comic, but must jest when he would be sober. Surely a more humorous figure is that of the reputed 'conceited' man who is really torn with diffidence and self-distrust.

I think you are partly responsible for this. You called me into consciousness of myself by believing in me, and since then I have been much oppressed by responsibility. You pointed out some of my faults, and thus destroyed whatever self-satisfaction I ever had – and I don't think I ever had much of *that* form of self-conceit.

Now I feel perplexed as to what I ought to do – and vexed with myself because my future work is not clear to me. You are right, I feel, in a sense, to deprecate my living only for the day's propaganda and organisation. Yet this seems to be what I can do best. After all, a man in regular employment could, with difficulty, even do any permanent work outside it. And I have lately felt, with some uneasiness, that I was hardly giving quite enough of myself to the office.

You must not imagine that I am reproaching you, or feeling sorry that the higher moral standard to which you lifted me brings with it new responsibilities. What I have gone through during the last four months is, to some extent analogous to Donatello's transformation in Hawthorne's *Marble Faun*. You have made me take myself much more seriously, and so even increased that self-consciousness which you aimed at repressing.

This was inevitable, and I only tell it you because, with you, I cannot even *pretend*. You know all the worst sides of me, even unfairly so I fear. Now I am revealing to you the real weakness of self-doubt which lies at the bottom of my apparent self-reliance.

It may be a fatal thing to reveal to you, but our friendship is worth nothing unless I can trust you to be as just as God in your view of me – and as well-balanced.

You see how much I need your constant help. I do *not* believe that, by myself, I can do much in the world: nor would this of itself perplex me. What 'worries' me is the belief that I could do relatively a great deal if my life were properly dealt with, and raised to its highest potentialities. I have seen a vision which is now never absent from my mind, and to be content with anything less than that seems to me wickedness.

I think you know enough of what I am thinking of to be sure that this is no common ambition on my part. I *am* quite content to do whatever is my duty, but I *must* be satisfied that it is my duty. Nor can I stifle my conscience merely by attending to my business and teaching in evening classes until I am too tired to keep awake. I have done that in the past, but it is mere drugging, as wicked as opium eating, for all its respectability. Of course I can wait, and that is probably what I must do – until some course appears to open itself. But I believe you could make that course much clearer to me if you will think for me.

Your suggestion that I should 'work out' questions strikes me as good, if one could only apply it. But it is so hard to do regular literary work in my circumstances. There is the question of the relative spheres of Central and Local Govt. (and now of Co-op. Societies and T. Unions also): or the analogous question of the control of capital and industry. But it seems hopeless to attempt it.

The nucleus round which has grown up all this mass of (morbid?) imagination is, perhaps, the letter I posted today, giving up my Political Economy book as you advised. It is, after all, in some sense a confession of failure. I suppose I am just now in the condition in which men exaggerate their own weakness, in the consciousness of being abnormally subject to the influence of some one else – and that is why to be in love without certainty brings with it so much pain and mental disturbance that only its special stimulus keeps us up to the mark at all. A man in love is weak, and 'to be weak is miserable'. But then, to quote George Eliot once more, it is what we would choose above all others.

So, you see, you must be wise and kind on Tuesday, when I will come to the B.M. Reading room about 4 p.m. and we will do what the weather may permit.

I have so far failed to find you any very good expression of the Competitive Ideal. The two bits I sent were the fruit of search through H. Martineau's *History and Tales*: I still think the Anti-Corn Law League the best type.

I fully understand your feeling about English scenery. When I have come back from Norway, and rushed from Hull through the Midland country – George Eliot's country – I have felt that this *was* scenery. And your common is brought home to me by this week's *Illustrated* which I bought for the picture of your stripy 'blouse' – though not even my imagination could put much 'you' into the picture. (That blouse will be associated for ever with the Glasgow streets – and other things.)

But surely, not even people of the 'highest rank' are foolish enough to play golf with tight kid gloves on!

I am very glad you like Wallas – but I knew you would. He is the most 'devoted' man I know – a shocking example for Herbert Spencer of excessive altruism. He is much *too* good-natured. And his mental quickness and vivacity makes him a most 'fertile' companion.

What you say of our companionship is very largely true. It has been, and is, a very pretty piece of intellectual communism, and trust in each other – willingness to obey each other, and subordinate ourselves to the group. Please put this on record when we are accused of *individual* conceit. No one of us ever plays for his own hand: it is an *égoisme à plusieurs*.

May I add to the evidence of 'morbidity' by saying that I am not a little vexed by the way in which all the group work has lately tended to aggrandize me. This has certainly not been sought by me, and I have always striven to merge myself in the Fabian Society. Now that I have been pushed into position of leadership, I feel, horribly, the responsibility of 'living up to it'. With all my belief in myself, I have really so much less than my friends' belief in me, that I am afraid.

You see how much I need companionship – not only for stimulus but for mental balance.

This is an egoistic letter, but you asked me what I was thinking about and there can be no doubt that I am thinking of how I can best live my own life. I hope this is not purely selfish. I know various *easy* ways of living, but they are not the right way.

Am I quite alone in feeling like this? Do you not feel the same kind of responsibility and have you any more certain view? (I *must* put in here, that two negatives equal a positive!) I do not believe that we should be deterred by fear of being 'priggish' from giving thought to our lives and their results. Are you quite sure that you are getting, and placing on the world's great counter, your full 'rent of ability'? This is my answer to your question as to luxury. I do not accuse you of luxury, and you have of course, good reasons for being where you are for the present. But I am afraid you will find that 'love for the country' a little incompatible with the ideal life for you.

I have a great belief in the aid to improvement which a change of outward circumstances gives. When one moves into a new house it is a little easier than usual to form new habits – even to form new tissue of character. I certainly need to make a new start.

Now all this is very 'morbid'. I will leave off and do some obvious and simple task. But there can be no doubt that, just now, I *am* morbidly sensitive in these directions, and you may as well have the true account of it. After all, common sense, and 'use and wont' which 'guard the portals of the house', reassert their sway, and so I shall simply go on writing despatches and articles, and lecturing, and organising and – waiting!

Sidney Webb

W. C. Taylor's book on Factories which I sent you, may be useful as giving the millowner's case against the Factory Acts.

Can you still find, and return to me, the American novel *An Experiment in Marriage*?

I believe Shipton will be defeated at Liverpool.

I kept back the foregoing, wondering whether I ought to send it to you. But you asked what I was doing, and, at any rate, it gives my mind for a day.

I feel better today, though no clearer as to the future. I must simply wait a bit – my 'waiting' is not waste of time usually.

I have been working at our projects of lecturing in Lancashire and among the Co-op. Societies, and I have swept into our net the National Reform Union, with all its 350 affiliated Liberal Associations etc. We are issuing 4000 Lecture Lists, 2000 special circulars to Co-op Societies, 1000 ditto to Lancashire organisations. The first shilling edition of the *Fabian Essays* (5000) was sold out *before* publication: the advts are now held back till 10,000 more can be printed. All this means a lot of letter writing, and our Sec. (Pease) is away in Scotland.

I have read W. Sargant's *Robert Owen*, a poor book. I think you must not make Owen too exclusively the 'fount'. *Where* did he learn his ideas? I find no evidence that he knew St Simon.

You asked me to 'form' you. That means criticism; very difficult for me! But it has struck me that you underestimate the power of 'party' in social reform; the 'great instrument of progress' which party organisation is; and the great need there is for people to stimulate such parties by belonging to them. It hurts me to think that you have probably never yet belonged to a Liberal Association! Is that so? Consider how hard it is for the laborers round you to pluck up courage even to run a Liberal Association, which is the elementary form out of which all revolts grow. And I think you will one day feel the need of more obviously and actively 'repenting' about Woman's Suffrage. Are you acting quite 'honest' about that? All of which I feel very impertinent!

Sidney Webb

103 PP BEATRICE TO SIDNEY

Beatrice was to meet Sidney in London and then go on with him to the annual meeting of the British Association in Leeds.

Box House, Minchinhampton, Glos.
[?27 August 1890]

My hand is very weary with writing; but I must send you a line. Those times of depression – and self-doubt sweep over one's work and life at intervals – they are hard to bear. I know so well the form of 'friendly expectancy'; all I would now say is this: my belief in you arose out of my faith in your sincerity of purpose – in the disinterested straightness of your aims. I have not estimated and do not care to estimate your *capacity* – so you cannot disappoint me in that.

I have one practical suggestion to make for you to think over. You say you feel uneasy about not giving enough of yourself to the office. Would it be quite impracticable to work out some subject connected with the Colonial Office in lieu of the P.E. [Political Economy] work? to connect your professional work (for which you are paid) with a thorough bit of careful study? This is only a hint, following up your combination of official work and belief in statistics of the C.O. List.

A more detailed and carefully thought out knowledge of the problem of colonial administration might be of untold service at some future time: and now you can look at the whole thing from the bottom and from the inside.

B. Jones can't come on Monday; so I have asked G.W. [Graham Wallas] to bring Bernard Shaw to meet V. Nash and L. Smith. For many reasons, I thought it better not to ask you till Tuesday, 4 o'c.

Yours

BP

104 PP BEATRICE TO SIDNEY

Thomas Ashton (1844–1927) was a miner's leader. Michael Davitt (1846–1906) was an Irish revolutionary sentenced to fifteen years imprisonment for Fenian activity. Through Henry George he had become involved in the land movement, founding the Land League of Ireland: he had close ties with radical and labour organisations in both Britain and the United States. Mrs Green's friend, whom Beatrice described to Sidney in a letter of 8 October as 'very horrid . . . sick to death with egotism' and given to arid scholarship, was Alfred Edward Taylor (1869–1945), a philosopher who was elected a fellow of Merton College, Oxford, in 1891.

Beatrice had been embarrassed by Sidney's cocksure style when he spoke at the British Association.

Box House, Minchinhampton, Glos.
[? September 1890]

The country has been exquisite the last few days – on Thursday Ella Pycroft (who was down here for 3 days) and I journeyed to the ridge of the Cotswolds overlooking the Severn Vale – that glorious plain of fertile wooded pastureland with the Severn winding through it and losing itself in the Bristol Channel gleaming in the distance – the valley rounded by the Forest of Dean and Welsh mountains, with the Malverns rising abruptly out of the plain to the North East. I will not say I feel 'Black': but as the sun set and the effect of sunlight, cloud, mountains, water and plain, became every moment more magical, I *did* wish that you had been there to share the intoxicating beauty, to heighten it by the consciousness of close human companionship – by the sense of fellowship and worship as well as in work.

Let us go forward with this fellowship without thought for the morrow – the form it will take is not in our hands, it will grow up as the joint creation of two natures. You are too generous, and too wise to wish me to do violence to my feelings – to wish me to *force* a growth which is not natural. It is for you to win that dependence and respect out of which the woman's love arises – you have already won the desire to be helpful – the proverbial pity which is akin to Love – Pity used in the largest sense – typical of the mother's care; not the Pity which means superiority – but the Pity which has inspired the woman to serve the man and the child alike – whether it take the form of the Magdalene anointing Christ's feet, or the mother devoting a life-time to the care of an Idiot boy.

So that you can feel, as a stimulus, that whenever you are less worthy than you might be you give me positive pain – like the pain I felt when you were speaking at the British Association, like the pain I have felt, when in general conversation you have dwelt on yourself and ignored or disparaged the work of others. On the other hand I am proud – very proud of your self-devotedness, of you willingness and capacity for doing unseen work, of your disinterestedness of aims.

I have been wondering whether you would change the form of your weekly letter – whether you could jot down any day, or each day all of interest you have done, seen, or heard, and send it me once a week? Though I am absent, you would then feel that I was by your side – as you reviewed the thought action and feeling of each day, you would feel instinctively what I should think of each word, thought, and act; which you would enable me to feel part and parcel of your life, to watch it and sympathise with it from a far off.

The question of wages given by Co-op stores is a very difficult one. Do you remember the exact statements made at the T.U. Congress? (if not could you note them down for me?) I fancy the whole complaint is based on the *tailors'* wages; which is really a question of the revolution in the methods of production in the tailoring trade. I should like you to think over the best means to take with a view to getting positive information and chasing the whole matter up –

(1) Could I get the Co-op Union to take it in hand? (2) could I find

some competent agent to do it, and what would it cost? or could I offer to the Co-op Union to pay part of the expense of a thorough enquiry?

(I know about the Burnley societies but must see the F.I. [Factory Inspector's] Report; I will get it from Burnett).

I send you the *Factory Times*: (note the interview with the officials especially with Ashton, who admits that the agitation for the 10-hrs Bill was for the *men*, also the wise letter from 'Unity'. It would be worth while briefing Ashton's remarks – do so yourself and send it back to me, I shall want to use them some day). The letter from your agent is most interesting – you will have stiff work in Lancashire; I should be careful not to dispute (as Burns does) the cotton representatives decision as to what the cotton trade will bear – it is grossly undemocratic not to accept provisionally the opinion of the representatives of the special trade, and against the principles of trade option which you advocate.

I will write to Mawdsley and to Ashton and say that you will call on them – I wish I were going there; as I am not known to be a socialist, I might be useful in smoothing things down.

By the way, do you know that Michael Davitt came after all to the D.H. Hotel! which made me feel horribly rude though he wrote me a delightful forgiving letter. He cannot come on 27th: Mrs Green is coming and bringing with her a friend. I enclose you her letter, *which please destroy*, you will see that we are expected to act as judicious critics of Mr Taylor as well as advisers as to his future work.

Now goodbye and God bless you – think of me whenever you feel troubled to think of yourself or to talk of yourself; don't overwork, and look after the breadth of the English Vowel! do not refuse to recognise the individual existence of or, ir, ow, a, and confound them all in a common *er*.

Ever yours

Beatrice Potter

105 PP SIDNEY TO BEATRICE

This was the first of a series of diary-letters, entered in small red notebooks, which Sidney dropped into the post as they were completed. Sidney was making a round of northern towns as part of the Fabian Lancashire campaign.

He had agreed to write a short book on the Eight Hours movement with Harold Cox, the brother-in-law of Sydney Olivier. Sir Henry Maine (1822–88) was a distinguished lawyer and Cambridge academic: his *Popular Government* was published in 1885. William Samuel Lilly, author and historian, was a follower of Newman: he published *A Century of Revolution* in 1889. Augustine Birrell (1850–1933) was a Liberal politician and author, whose *Obiter Dicta* appeared in 1884. Michael Davitt was just launching his short-lived *Labour World*. Edwin Cannan (1841–1935), later professor at the London School of Economics and author of the well-known text, *Wealth* (1912), had recently published his first book, *Principles of Political Economy*. Henry Sidgwick (1838–1900), professor of political economy at Cambridge, interested in economics, psychical research and the higher education of women, was married to Eleanor Balfour (1845–1936), the sister of Arthur Balfour and second Principal of Newnham College, Cambridge. Sidgwick had become a passionate agnostic; in 1869 he had resigned his fellowship at Trinity College as a protest against religious tests for the election of fellows.

Sir James Stansfeld (1820–98) resigned from Palmerston's administration in 1864 after allegations that he was involved in a conspiracy against Napoleon III. His period in the wilderness was shorter than Sidney suggests, since he returned to junior office after two years. Harold Rylett was a Unitarian minister and Fabian sympathiser. Dante Gabriel Rossetti (1828–82) was the poet and painter; his sister was Christina Rossetti (1830–94); and his brother William Michael Rossetti (1829–1919) was a senior civil servant.

Webb's *Socialism in England*, published by Sonnenschein in 1893, was written in 1889 as a monograph for the American Economic Association. It summarised the extension of the 'collectivist' measures in social policy and included the classic statement of what Shaw called 'the permeation racket'. 'This permeation', Webb wrote, 'is apparently destined to continue, and the avowed socialist party in England will probably remain a comparatively small disintegrating and educational force, never itself exercising political power, but supplying ideas and principles of social reconstruction to each of the great political parties in turn, as the changing results of English politics bring them alternately into office.'

17 Sept/90

If I am to put down things from day to day, and make up a weekly budget, I must have something which I can put into my pocket in between each writing. This common little book was the best kind of thing I could get, and I hope its roughness won't put you out.

But you must not be misled by this durability of form into expecting a literary product. I must, of course, simply jot down as I go, without regard for style etc. Nothing strikes one as more hateful than letters written deliberately for publication or even to be kept. A letter, like a sonnet, should be a 'moment's monument' – should come hot from the press of the thought, and be rather its rough cast than a polished work of art made out of it – by care and pains.

Your suggestion is a very good one. I will try to 'think on paper' for you from day to day. It will be a stimulus and a guide to my higher and better self. And you counsel me in return, and tell me of your own life. Let us conquer distance and separation in that way – as far, alas, as may be possible.

First let me go back to your beautiful letter. I think you will, now, believe me when I say that I do not ask for more than you have given me – for more than this valued friendship, and your help and counsel, *and* permission to wait events. You will do the right thing at the right time; and I am content to wait. I cannot believe that the right thing can be other than that enormous heightening and strengthening of our individual

187

effectiveness which united action would give. I *know* how much less I shall be able to do for humanity if it does not result so. And I believe that this is mutual.

But I quite feel that this is not by any means the whole question, and if you decide otherwise – or if you never decide – I shall submit and still trust you as being right. I know full well how much it would be for you to do: and how little I can offer beyond a great scope for perpetual work, not glorious or great but merely laborious and fruitful.

Let us say no more about it, but as you say, go on with this fellowship and let the future decide. I have gained much, and am gaining much – I hope you, too, are not losing – the present is ours and, as for the future, *advienne que pourra*.

You will have seen that the *Co-op News* gave a whole page report of the Co-op incident at Liverpool. I shall talk to Gray about it, but I still think you could usefully write to people about it. There are two complaints – bad treatment of Co-op employees, and dealing with firms who do not pay T.U. wages. The latter is a comparatively new point. Could you not write a letter to the *Co-op News* about it, giving particulars as to the L.C.C. and School Board action?

I have just begun my 'Eight Hours' book, cutting up my *Contemporary Review* article, and pasting part of it on sheets. I see that I ought to try to make the book more judicial and less a plea for a particular measure. I must try to consider both sides, and present all arguments. It makes it less easy to write, but more valuable to read, and probably more effective even as a plea. I foresee that I am going to have enough to do this autumn. No one shall or can say of me (as we said of Prof. Stuart) that 'politicians must not be allowed to fall in love, for it destroyed all their effectiveness'. I am quite sure I have never done so much work, or been so efficient as this glorious summer. After all, happiness, like champagne, is of some use in the world.

18 Sept.

I am uneasy and troubled about my next *Speaker* article. I have done one for this week on the City Companies, which will bring down on my head the wrath of the City papers. Of course they won't know who the writer is – but the City press will be sure to say that it is exaggerated and all wrong. Just imagine a property with twenty millions sterling being plundered and frittered away, six years after a strong Royal Commission reported the need for thorough reform.

For next week I must, I think, do Leasehold Enfranchisement. This is still a favorite 'Liberal' measure, but it goes dead against the growing Land Nationalisation sentiment, and must therefore be dropped. I want to guide it off into Compensation to Tenants for all reasonable improvements.

This is really what is wanted in London, and this, with security against disturbance, is what we must get the Leasehold Enfranchisers to accept, instead of turning leaseholds into freeholds. But it is a ticklish job, as 'Leasehold Enfranchisement' stands in the Manchester Programme. I don't at present see my way, and am suffering from 'suppressed article'.

I have also got to write a short paper for the Fabian Society for to-morrow fortnight, on the common objections to and fears of Democracy. I wish you could give me any ideas that occur to you on that. I must begin it in Lancashire – so you see I shall be busy there.

As a beginning I have got out Sir H. Maine's *Popular Government*, and W. S. Lilly's *A Century of Revolution*. The latter is, as you may know, a slashing attack on John Morley, from the Roman Catholic moralists' point of view, *à propos* of his approval of Rousseau, Diderot etc. It seems, from my hasty perusal, a very effective piece of work. One can't help feeling that Morley has underrated the evil excesses of the sexual anarchism of these men, in his eager appreciation of their zeal for freedom. It is of a piece with the rest of him: he is so much more destructive than constructive. He is what I called in my essay in the *Fabian Essays* 'a mere Radical'.

Yet he has glimpses of insight; visions of the beauty of the social organism; noble conceptions of duty for which Lilly could not account except as unconscious reminiscences of the highest Christian life: and a splendid honesty of purpose.

What does he lack? Is it not chiefly faith in Democracy – just the objection with which I am to deal? I must not take him as a type; and besides it would not be understood; but he is, really, an instance of one of little faith even in the faith that he has.

Is this an instance of the bad result of the critical habit – the craze for perpetual truth-seeking which Birrell describes in *Obiter Dicta*?

Tonight I am to dine with Wallas, for the first time since his father's death. He writes that he is troubled about many things, and I am going to try to let him talk to me! not I to him. He evidently wants a sympathetic listener. He must be told to wait, and rest, and not trouble about things.

I remember now what you said as to Davitt's going to D.H. Hotel on Tuesday week. I am very sorry I misled you. He was reported as speaking at Ebbw Vale the night before, and I did not dream he would come up by the night train, and then, finding your letter, go straight off to you. This was a very sincere compliment to the attractiveness of your society!

But he will have understood from your telegraphing to the hotel that you had given him up, and it will even increase the friendliness between you.

The Fabian Society is putting an advertisement of tracts etc. in the first number of his paper.

I shall send with these two interesting letters, one from E. J. Cannan, a young Oxford Economist who sat next to me during the Eight Hours debate at Leeds, and read a paper himself on the last day. He gives an amusing account of the old fogies! I think he is right as to Sidgwick being ahead of Marshall. The latter would never have dared to write Sidgwick's ittle article two years ago on 'Economic Socialism' and would not, I think, have had the intellectual courage to take up Psychical Research. There is something grand I think, too, about Sidgwick's refusal to bow the neck to Baal in the shape of Christianity. I don't want all men to be stiffnecked atheists, but there is, in a University (and elsewhere!) so much compliance for the sake of worldly advantage, that Sidgwick's obstinacy, like that of Wallas at Highgate School, is stimulating and elevating.

We want a lot more moral sensitiveness on these points, I think. The excessive scrupulousness which made Gladstone resign office in 1845, and made Stansfeld an exile from politics for many years; the devotion to a high standard of self-righteousness which made Wallas refuse to go to communion at Highgate and so wreck his whole professional career – all this is as a 'cup of cold water' to those in thirst of help when under temptation.

Morley, by the way, stands well on this point – so does H. Spencer.

19 Sept.

The other letter is from the Rev. Harold Rylett, of Hyde, with whom I shall stay 3 days. It will interest you as to the T.U. Congress business. My heart warms to Rylett for his 'score of letters'! He does not despise the art of agitation, and you see the effect.

Rylett takes a low view of Mawdsley etc. The temptations of a working-man leader are enormous.

I send also an abstract of my projected 'Eight Hours' lecture for Manchester etc. intended to be given to the reporter to prevent him making a 'hash' of his report. Of course it is imperfect – no one sees that better than I do – but it had to be done under great pressure. And you could perhaps cut out anything that strikes you as likely to be harmful.

This morning I have at last managed to get you a copy of Rossetti – they seem to be scarce, and of course, one can't get the much nicer but presumedly wicked Tauchnitz Edition of the poems only. The binding is not my choice: I had to take what I could get. And I did not like to put any special inscription because I don't want you to have to hide the volumes. Please *imagine* that it is there!

I am not a fanatic about Rossetti, but some of his work is very perfect. Some of his sonnets are perfect expressions of feeling. The English and the Italian – the ascetic and the epicurean – are curiously alternated (not blended) in him. His brother, W. M. Rossetti, is a high (and dry) Inland Revenue official. His sister, Christina Rossetti, is all puritan (but high church!) – a very 'sweet' devotional poet.

This is the first gift I have ventured to make to you. Do you know, I think I am too much in love to be a lover. My whole feelings are so transformed that it does not occur to me to do the ordinary things. If I lie awake at night and think about you, you come in the guise of a co-worker – this is dreadfully unromantic – though it is your own individual face that comes between the lines of the despatches at the office. You see, I *must* talk to you about this, because it is what I am always thinking about, willy nilly, and because I may not confide in anyone else – not even Wallas.

I *did* try to be sympathetic with Wallas last night, and I was sympathetic in a masculine way – but it needs a woman to do it well. I could not make him talk much of himself and his feelings, so we just discussed as usual between us. He gave me, *inter alia*, a matter-of-fact description of his stay with you, which he enjoyed immensely and which did him good. He is most enthusiastic in his admiration of you. To tell the truth, I did *not* feel jealous, though I expected to, and examined myself to see. But you seem to me in a different world. All I felt was the constraint of having to answer unconcernedly, and to discuss you as a 'recruit', in a cold-blooded way. Do women talk over men among themselves as men, even the nicest men, sum and appraise women!

I do not think he suspects my feeling though he is my dearest friend. Poor Wallas – he is not very 'sharp' in his insight – though the most 'loveable' of men – and much '*better*' than I am, ethically.

I have got a very disappointing account from Sonnenschein of the sales of my book *Socialism in England*. They only printed 1000 copies. These are now exhausted and they are reprinting. But up to 30 June, it only yields me (at 3d per copy) £7.8.1. I don't care a pin about the yield of that book, but it makes the offer of 6d per copy (which they give you, and now promise me for 'Eight Hours') look very small. If their vaunted 'Series' does not place more than 1000 copies in a year, of a not unsuccessful popular book, it is not worth doing. I shall not let them have my Eight Hours for that. I have written to ask for £50 and royalty of 6d for copies *over* 2000 – that is, a guarantee of 2000 copies. I confess my impression is that there must be cheating in the numbers.

But of course, with your Co-op book as with my Eight Hours, the main object is to get it circulated, and your name and the Co-op connection will inevitably sell off more than 1000 in your case.

I am, however, *disillusionné* about publishers' 'Series'.

I start tomorrow for Lancashire – first to Rochdale and Oldham where I shall be at some hotel, then on Monday to

c/o Rev. Harold Rylett, Park Corner, Hyde

until the morning of the 25th; then to

c/o J. C. Kennedy, St James' Road, Carlisle

for that night; then to

c/o Dr. R. Spence Watson, Bensham Grove, Gateshead

for the night of the 26th.

The 27th, Saturday, I shall spend in travelling towards you: arriving at Gloucester 4.39 p.m. – there an hour to wait (cathedral!) and then to Stroud by train at 5.50, due 6.12 p.m. [*Side-note:*] Newcastle 9.30 a.m. Cheltenham 4.14 p.m.

I am sorry to arrive travel-tired, and after a week of very hard work – but our regard is above all those little points, and you will pardon deficiencies.

I *need* not return on Monday if I may stay (as Wallas did!) I have an engagement to take part in the opening meeting of the Working Men's College on Thursday night, and to lecture at the Fabian Society on Friday night. But I shall have lots of work in my bag: and you must let me stay as long as you think fit, telling me quite frankly what to do – as well as what to avoid. (I am *trying* to think of my vowels).

I thought this book was too big!

There are a hundred details more that I want to say – and now I have not room even to say goodbye as I should wish to. Surely no one ever loved like me – (I now understand this ridiculous lover's feeling) and I will not despair.

> Was willst du heute sorgen
> Auf morgen;
> Der Eine
> Steht allein für,
> Der gibt auch dir
> Das Deine.
> Sei nur in allem Handel
> Ohn' Wandel.
> Steh feste.

Sidney

106 PP SIDNEY TO BEATRICE

This is the second of the diary-letters.

Arthur Balfour, as Chief Secretary for Ireland since 1887, was imposing his 'resolute policy', under which he had taken powers to suppress local branches of the National League. Laurence Gronlund (1846–99) was an American socialist whose book *The Co-operative Commonwealth*, in an English version edited by Shaw, was widely read in the growing labour movement.

The 'skulking' in 1873 refers to the issue of women's working conditions introduced into wage negotiations. Charles Prestwich Scott (1846–1932), was the owner and famous editor of the *Manchester Guardian* from 1872 to 1929. William Thomas Arnold (1852–1904) was the assistant editor of the *Manchester Guardian* and the brother of Mrs Humphry Ward.

Numa Roumestan was a novel by Alphonse Daudet published in 1881.

Thomas Gair Ashton (1855–1933), later Lord Ashton, was a philanthropic industrialist, Liberal M.P., and a 'model' textile employer in the Manchester area.

I am writing in Rochdale – the first morning I have ever spent in Lancashire. I have just finished my article on leaseholds for the *Speaker*, which is subtly audacious in its crypto-nationalizing policy! And I go on to Oldham this afternoon, probably calling on Ashton.

I very nearly made an unfortunate fiasco in the opening lecture of our Lanc. campaign. The local S.D.F. Secretary (my lecture last night was to the S.D.F. branch here) wrote in answer to my express enquiry, that the lecture began at *8.45*. I got here at *7.30*, after $5\frac{1}{2}$ hours ride, and a very hasty lunch, and ordered food. Before it was ready I noticed the advt of the lecture in the local paper as being for *7.45*. It was then 8, so I had to leave the cooking food, and run to the other end of Rochdale, to hold forth at once, dinnerless.

The lecture was therefore not good, but as it was only on 'The New Reform Bill' to an audience largely Socialist it was easy enough. (There were *4* reporters, to whom I handed a printed abstract). Afterwards two of the Socialists (spinners) took me to a humble beerhouse where I had supper, and drank beer with a dozen gas stokers just off work – all virtually Socialists – who were immensely struck by the contrast between my hand and theirs as we clasped hands – and sang the Marseillaise, from an English songbook of which several had copies!

Perhaps after all this it is not surprising that I did not sleep. But I did my *Speaker* article in 2 hours this morning and went to meet the Socialists at an open-air meeting – utilising this civility to urge them to work the Co-op Society (to which they all belong, but do not take part), the Liberal Association – whose Secretary I saw – a crypto-Socialist – and the Town Council.

They all tell me that the textile operatives are *not* against an Eight Hours Bill even for themselves, but that it was merely the old gang of officials who had coolly usurped the decision.

This I shall learn more of at Oldham.

The Fabian meeting on Friday was large. Davitt was there, but I could not get to speak to him. There can be no doubt that our influence is just now growing very fast, and it is important that we should 'keep our heads'. I wish you were in London to advise us (whether through me or not!).

I read Lilly's *Century of Revolution* through in the train (and Zola's *Le Rêve*). I think Lilly largely makes out his case against the individualist radical of the Revolution, and John Morley ought to see from it what he only just escapes being, and what he ought to turn his back on.

But Lilly holds to the institution of individual private property as the necessary basis of individual responsibility for life and therefore of morality.

This is part of the curious ignoring of the public duties (of citizenship etc.) which literature joins with theology in encouraging.

Neither Dickens nor Thackeray, neither Tennyson nor Browning, ever thinks of man as a citizen. He is a lover, husband, father, friend – but never a voter, town councillor or vestryman. George Eliot is a little better, but not much. Surely it would be well if our novelists were to emphasize more the *public* duties of life. In *Middlemarch* there is the mental struggle of Lydgate as to the election of the Infirmary Chaplain.

But the 'note' struck in *Felix Holt* is not strongly continued elsewhere. Deronda neglects all the duties of citizenship as much as Henry James's young Bostonians. George Meredith and R. L. Stevenson neither of them write as for a Democratic country. Still more is this true of the French (excepting *Numa Roumestan*).

How can this be best said? Can you put it in your book? I might insinuate it in some article: but I don't see any particular chance.

We shall, in the future, have more and more to emphasize that the individual responsibility for life has to be exercised through the 'collective freedom' of Democratic organisation. We have got to build up an 'apotheosis' of the vote.

On Friday Massingham told me that all the news from Ireland went to confirm the silently growing impression that the National League was losing its power; that the R.C. Church was effectively getting back control over its priests: that 'Balfourism' was, in fact, winning.

Davitt seems to have said the same thing.

Of course, it won't really affect Home Rule because it is England which will decide that, and I believe all is going only too well for the Liberals. But it may increase the embarrassment of the official Liberal leaders, in their total lack of policy for Ireland or elsewhere, beyond H.R. [Home Rule].

Zola's *Le Rêve* is a very beautiful, Tolstoi-like dream of perfect purity – *qui ne m'interesse pas*. After all, it is the virtue of knowledge that we want, not that of ignorance. The man who has never made a mistake, says the proverb, has never made anything. The 'comparatively virtuous' grown and militant human being, in the *Sturm der Welt*, stands far above the purity of the cloister. *Homo sum, et nihil humani a me alienum puto.*

But *Le Rêve* is an answer to those who say that Zola turns exclusively to the evil side of life. The lives of the foster parents are beautiful in their repentance and submission.

Manchester Free Library
22 Sept.

I failed to see Ashton who is away at the Isle of Man.

I came on to Oldham Sunday afternoon, and walked about with one Broadbent, a nicely enthusiastic middle-aged Socialist, once an operative, now a bookeeper. We went into the Co-op Society reading room (open on Sundays) but they are giving *no* lectures. So also at Rochdale.

My 'Eight Hours' lecture (at the Radical Club) created some interest – the room was crammed, and there were 3 reporters. (I have today posted you the *Manchester Examiner* with a good account). The lecture went well. [*Side-note:*] The lecture has been quoted and referred to several times already – notably by Slatter at a T.U. meeting at Bury – where Slatter almost said he would support the Fabian Bill.

There was considerable questioning and some opposition, chiefly from Abraham Buckley, the Secretary of the Weavers, I think, and a Conservative. He was acrid and personal, but was evidently speaking to what he thought I was going to say, rather than to what I did say. There was some expression of opposition to *any* Factory Act restrictions for men; more, of fear that 8 Hours would ruin the textile trades; and a good deal of 'let the other trades do it for themselves'. But I believe a third, at least, were in favor of 8 Hours by law.

Many people have talked to me of the attitude of the T.U. leaders – all with expressions of regret and some resentment. There can be no doubt that there is a good minority on our side, and a growing one. 'I hope the Socialists will succeed in getting us the Eight Hours' was the expression of one Rochdale woman operative. [*Side-note:*] On the other hand, Mrs Rylett says she finds the women *against* 8 Hours on the ground that they preferred money to leisure.

I fancy Birtwhistle and Mawdsley will alter their tone before the next annual meeting (July) – and trim to meet this minority. The Fabian Bill may be a way out for them.

This morning I came on to Manchester and called first on Gray, who was very friendly.

He said nothing could be done *now* to make peace with the T. Unions. He himself bitterly resented their reception at the Liverpool Congress. He thought it was no use investigating and reporting on allegations of unfair treatment of employees. The Co-op Union Committee were too angry to think of it. The Co-op Wholesale had defiantly refused their intermediation in the Wilson case.

The only thing he could suggest was that the T. Union Parliamentary Committee should write a letter of apology! Things, he said, must first be allowed to quiet down. [*Side-note:*] Suggested that if any T.U. leader or Committee and Co-op Union were to move in the matter, they would do so.

Gray much wants to take me to Bolton, see the 'Bolton Commonwealth' a society of 60 members, artisans, who worked in the evening in a common workshop, at all sorts of trades, without pay, for the common-fund, without rules or compulsion.

They had powerlooms, handlooms, lathes etc. worth, now, £300:

men worked at, and so learnt, other trades than their own. They intended to buy land, and form an agriculture and industrial Colony. L. Gronlund's *Co-operative Commonwealth* was their inspiration. They were all socialists, and had urged him to bring me to them.

Probably you know about them. Gray said they had no reports etc. and had only just got registration.

I cannot go, as every evening is engaged.

I cannot say that I find Lancashire so different from London as I expected. They seem much the same kind of people – perhaps more self reliant (and selfish!), more 'pig-headed', or, otherwise, 'firm' in a self-complacent optimism. But not *much* more so than the London artisan. They are, however, evidently *less* willing to be taught, quicker to resent superiority – in fact, a little 'American' all through. Is this a higher type?

I doubt it. It seems to me more like a survival from the last generation.

But their very defects are insofar virtues as to enable them to build up 'social tissue' better than we can.

I am writing very frankly, and merely on 'first impressions'.

But I do not think that I have forgotten for two hours together, that it is your county; and I have felt kindly to it for your sake. You see, in general as well as in one particular case in which we are interested, London and Lancashire need to be *blended*, in order to produce the best result!

Now, up to now, I have managed to keep this 'letter' very dry and business-like, and so I had better not write any more at present, after the above 'lapse'. But I think Manchester streets make me unconsciously despond, and so turn to the *ewig Weibliche*. This Monday morning they are thronged with strangers, and one realises what a huge job it is to impart even one new idea to these millions. Democracy certainly is the biggest problem we have yet seen – a fascinating and absorbing pursuit. How can Mill fear that Life will become uninteresting! To play on these millions of minds, to watch them slowly respond to an unseen stimulus, to guide their aspirations often without their knowledge – all this, whether in high capacities or in humble, is a big and endless game of chess, of even extravagant excitement.

Sanctify by altruism and emotion, and you get the raw material of the New Religion.

Meanwhile one gets despondent sometimes.

Last night I had a 'frost' at the Manchester and Salford Co-op Society (12,000 members): they never sent word what time the lecture was, or anything about it; I got there early; no one came of any authority at all. About 30 people, many non-members, slowly gathered in the hall. Absolutely no one appeared in the Committee Room, and the Hallkeeper, a very stupid person, said no member of the Committee was present. (He came running in to say with surprise that a reporter had come! I said, well, don't they usually come? and he replied that it never happened before! Presently a second came). After waiting 20 min. over time I went to the sparse audience in the great hall, explained the position, and asked them to appoint a chairman. A local socialist (as afterwards appeared) said he had walked 7 miles to attend, took the Chair and I gave a good lecture, duly reported in *Manchester Examiner* (the *Guardian* continues to ignore us altogether). There was a very little discussion and I got the matter closed up as soon as possible.

Today I have (for the benefit of the succeeding lecturers) written a letter to the Education Committee more in sorrow than in anger. A parcel of literature had been sent for distribution, but was not forthcoming. All of which was rude, to say the least.

24 Sept.

I find this Campaign is very hard work, and I feel it telling on my nerves. This morning I feel ill-tempered and irritable. It is not so much the lecture every night as the irregular life; the perpetual talking to new people, the constant external stimulus. I feel dazed and unable to think. I am glad I have only two more nights of it.

Yesterday I lunched with Symonds, the Secretary of the National Reform Union, a leading Liberal organizer – who is and avows himself quite Socialist and has much assisted us. In the Reform Club I met several millowners, all *bitter* about Eight Hours, but declaiming against the old Unionists as much as against an Act.

The chief of the reporting staff of the *Guardian* was asking after me, and regretting that they had lost our notice. So I supplied another, and they sent a reporter to Prestwich (where there were about 7 altogether – local papers mostly – and an audience of 40).

In the afternoon I went home with Gray, had a walk, had tea, and went to the Store to lecture. There Gray had arranged for a supper after the lecture, with all the Committee: unluckily I had to leave by 9.44 train so was obliged to cut it short. The lecture went well and G. B. Shaw, who turned up, having a free night, came in at the end with a splendid ten minutes speech, in which he converted all (for the moment) even to the word spoliation or confiscation of the rich. A local minister rose and said he agreed with it all – he had read *Fabian Essays* – and so on.

Today I have been over one of Ashton's mills, to see the Ring Spinning etc. The foreman was quite sympathetic as to Eight Hours and Revising the Age for Children.

Then I met Shaw and we called on Mawdsley whom we found in a Midday Siesta. He was *very* polite in a rough way – said he had called the Fabian Society awful fools, and was outspokenly contemptuous of 'Cockneydom'. He struck Shaw (and me) as being very able but as having no case. He was quick of apprehension, and quite right on all his points (except that he took too elementary a view of the export trade and the wages fund). The effect of his position is this. He thinks 8 Hours would cause *trouble* in the textile trade, either by causing a fall in wages or stoppage of work, or both. He almost as good as said that the mass of the (stupid) textile operatives would presently clamor for 8 Hours; and (impliedly) that he would not back up *any* 8 Hour movement anywhere, lest it should spread to his own trade. On this ground he deprecated even a Govt 8 Hours.

He talked about his cottage property, and smoked gigantic cigars, and referred uneasily to the fact that he was now fit for nothing else but a T.U. Secretary.

We were most polite and even humble – not contradicting him. He is writing an answer to my speech for the *Cotton Factory Times*, for which he writes regularly.

You will have seen that [Thomas] Ashton admits this and (rightly) justifies the 'skulking' in 1873.

I have also seen Bamford, of the *Co-op News* who was polite but not very genial. I talked to him about a woman President, about T.U. bitterness etc. He said he had received a letter from Leicester warning Cooperators against us, which I told him to insert, and I would answer it.

Your letter raises me to Heaven, and I have felt every so much less despondent and so less bitter, since I got it on Monday afternoon. I can not answer it as I ought in this whirl. I will come to Nailsworth as you suggest and leave my bag at the station and walk up – *come if you can.* I will go home at the least hint: and I will try to act as if you were Mrs Green, and Mrs Green you!

What you say about Simplicity of Life is good and true. I have constantly felt that I was bound not to increase my personal expenditure, tho' my income rose. But do not sacrifice efficiency.

I seize some minutes to write this while having tea in a café before trying to see Scott or Arnold of the *Guardian*. I hope you can read it. Perhaps in no better way can I convey to you a notion of the 'drive' I am constantly in.

Now, Good Bye until Saturday. It is hopeless to try to express how much I feel. And I *am* grateful also.

Sidney

107 PP SIDNEY TO BEATRICE

On 27 September Sidney visited Box with Mrs Green and Mr Taylor. Beatrice thought he 'behaved admirably' and aroused no suspicion of their relationship: she was pleased that Sidney and Alice Green liked each other: 'He is certainly extraordinarily improved – and becoming a needful background to my working life . . . the beauty of the friendship is that it stimulates the work of both'. (BWD 2 October 90) Sidney discussed his plan to give a party for Fabians to meet Beatrice, the occasion nominally being intended to speed Sydney Olivier on his way to his first overseas appointment in British Honduras. After his visit Beatrice wrote (PP ?28 September) 'don't have the party on my account or at my time. I would just as soon have the evening together, and I think the party will need *all* your discretion'.

In the meantime Beatrice proposed to invite Pease and Shaw, whom she had not met, to Box on 19 October. Shaw sent a typically ironic letter complaining that the journey would cost him seventeen shillings for fares, adding that 'you may reduce the rest of the Fabians to slavery – they prattle from morning to night about Beatrice Potter in a way I despise – but if I am to go through my amusing conversational performance for you, you must come up to town: this lion is untameable'. (SCL 6 October 90)

Though Beatrice appeared to be taking an encouragingly relaxed attitude to Sidney he misjudged the situation. When they met in London before he left for a further round of lectures he seems in some way to have presumed in a flirtatious sense: the 'incident' itself remains unexplained, but it undoubtedly seriously set back his hopes of persuading her to marriage.

[?4 Park Village East, N.W.]
8 Oct. [1890]

I am just starting for Barnsley and cannot write except briefly.

Forgive me, it is I who am to blame. You had explicitly warned me that your kindness was only kindness, but you were *so* kind, and the chance repetition of the trivial request after my playful declaration about its meaning, threw me off my feet. Pray forgive me. The whole incident seems now ghastly in its comedy changed to tears – like an accident at a masked ball.

Do not let the two days which I passed in very great happiness make either any bar or bond between us, please count them as never having been.

I know nothing of your story except your ring and what you have told me – dearest – it makes no difference to me, except for its evil shadow on your memory. Do not let this memory cloud your life or warp your judgment.

I have been absolutely silent about your kindness – one or two people suspect me of being in love, but that is all: not even the joy of Monday made me open my lips to tell it (as I fondly thought). Your letters are quite safe, and shall be for me only.

I do not deny or conceal that I am suffering very much this morning: the revulsion is too strong to be lightly endured. But I am not a child, and I have resolved that no such thing shall spoil my life or injure my work. I shall go to Barnsley with a very different heart than I expected, but the work will be a sedative. I will set my teeth hard and if it brings another line in my face or another grey hair, you will not count them against me – I will try that no 'line' grows in my mind, you have done me nothing but good hitherto, and I cannot imagine you can harm me. It is chiefly the thought of the pain to you and the shock to our relationship that grieves me – write soon and tell me that this is *vorbei*, and our friendship as before – do not take that from me, whatever the issue may be. I really can wait and I will not again be precipitate.

You are right not to be bound: I ask for nothing, and I have no right to ask for anything because what I want is so much.

I have been interrupted here and the interval has brought all the blankness home to me. It *is* rather a blow, and it will be a grim railway ride. But you are not to blame, and I am horribly vexed to think how the stupid mishap will have grieved you.

I cannot now write about the future – drink the mirage – just at this moment I must simply endure my thirst.

Dearest I cannot pretend not to want you now – but I am strong enough to kill that want and forego even your friendship and all hope, if that is best for you. I do not think I am harming you, but you must decide. If you can let us go on as before, *advienne que pourra*, it means so much to me and it shall never be held to commit you to anything at all. Do not take that from me – you have already changed my life – do not now cast it away, and let me fall back.

On Friday morning I shall be

c/o Rev. Harold Rylett, Park Corner, Hyde, Lanc.

please send me just a few lines to say you forgive me, and that we may obliterate these days. Adieu

Sidney

Pease is still away.

108 PP BEATRICE TO SIDNEY

This letter presumably crossed with the second letter from Sidney, written later in the day on 8 October. It should be read before the 10 October entry in the following letter from Sidney.

R. B. Haldane became engaged in March 1890: his fiancée found she had misunderstood her feelings and broke off her engagement after five weeks. In terms similar to those used by Sidney, Haldane recalled in his *Autobiography* (1929), that 'My love for her, though it failed had brought me not loss but great gain. For it enlarged the meaning and content of life for me'.

Frederick York Powell (1850–1904), Professor of Modern History at Oxford and a specialist in Icelandic and Old English texts, was a socialist who played a leading part in founding Ruskin College, Oxford, in 1890.

Box House, Minchinhampton, Glos.
[?8 October 1890]

Your letter made me feel very miserable – indeed I sat down and cried. But I will tell you with absolute frankness what I felt and have felt.

When you spoke to me in Glasgow I did not say, as I have said to others, a distinct 'no', because I felt that your character and circumstances and your work offered me a sphere of usefulness and fellowship which I had no right to refuse offhand. I felt too how hard it would be for me to lead a lonely life without becoming hard and nervous and self-willed. On the other hand, you were personally unattractive to me and I doubted whether I *could* bring myself to submit to a close relationship. Remember that I was desperately in love and for six years with another man – and that even now the wound is open.

Since then I have been trying hard to bring myself to care for you – some days I have felt the strength and calm which your affection has brought into my life. (I will be absolutely honest with you – *it has* given me more peacefulness and less of that old hard terror of the future that used to paralyse me.) I have now a warm regard for you – but I do not love you, and until I do I will not be in any way bound. Do you remember that day in Kensington Gardens – I was wretched both then and after I left you – I nearly wrote and broke off the friendship – I felt I never could marry you – that even your friendship was distasteful to me.

Then again, I saw that man last summer by accident and I felt a horrible certainty that I could care for no-one else. You need not fear – he is married; (as you probably know). I never respected him or thought well of him though I was passionately attached.

When I read your letter this morning, though I had thought previously that probably our friendship would end in marriage, I had another re- vulsion of feeling – a sort of panic that I would sooner leave life than enter into any promise. And I had a momentary thought that I would simply drop out of your life and disappear behind my own family and my own friends and my own work.

You see the question of marriage is not a practical one at present and may not be so for two or three years. My regard for you is not strong enough to face the terrible self-questionings of an engagement – the immediate pressures of the whole family. If I were in love it would be different – but I am not in love.

I did not mean my playful words to be taken seriously as a final word – I had not remembered your words or attached importance to them at the time.

Altogether I feel very very miserable. Try to forgive me any pain I have given you – by the thought of my misery and also in gratitude for my honest effort to return your feeling. I cannot and *will* not be engaged to you – never until it is a question of marriage within a few weeks – I know an engagement would end in the same way as Mr Haldane's and Miss Annie Ferguson – in a permanent breach. I should meet you, feel bound, feel it impossible, and cut it once for all.

Now decide for yourself: if you think I have deceived you or that I demand too much – do not write to me again except to return any letters of mine you have kept and to ask me to return yours. I am so uncertain of my feelings that I cannot tell whether I should be pained at this or whether I should feel relieved. But if you care to wait until the question is a practical one – promise me one thing – that we write frankly to each other under the promise that if it leads to nothing we return each other's letters or faithfully destroy them? One never knows into whose hands letters fall – and a close relationship is a sacred thing not to be looked into by another. That is why I refused to tell you my story and shall always refuse – it does not belong to me, only, but to another.

I am going to *Oxford* for one night Friday; to see Mr Yorke Powell about an historical point in my second chapter.

Dear Sidney – I will try to love you – but do not be impatient, do not think the world faithless because I fail to do so. What can I do more – I am doing more than I would do for any other man – simply because you are a Socialist and I am a Socialist.

That other man I loved but did not believe in, you I believe in but do not love.

Will it end equally unhappily?

Ever yours

BP

109 PP SIDNEY TO BEATRICE

Lord Compton (1825–1906), then bishop of Ely, was noted for his High Church views. Sir Henry Morton Stanley (1841–1904), the African explorer, married Dorothy Tennant, an acquaintance of Beatrice's, on 12 July 1890, in Westminster Abbey. Sandford Arthur Strong (1863–1904), the art historian, was currently librarian of the Indian Insitute at Oxford and later librarian of the House of Lords. He was a friend of Alice Green's. The Principal of Dalton Hall was Theodore Neild, who had been employed as the tutor to Edward Pease in his youth.

Barnsley
7 p.m. [8 October 1890]

This must be something like the feeling of the morning after an earthquake! I don't seem to know where I stand at all. I am not without hope or cheerfulness, but there is a certain 'dreariness' at the back of my mind which was not there yesterday.

I feel inclined to laugh at my blunder, but then I think of the pain it caused you, and of certain hours this morning when I 'functioned' automatically like a frog without a brain.

My letter this morning was written under great stress of feeling and pressure of work. It is good to have to work. I had scarcely a moment's leisure from incessant brain work until I got into the cab to King's Cross.

Then at last I could think, and I regretted that my letter bore the marks of such stress. I reread yours in the train, and was moved to write you again. I changed at Sheffield (Do you remember that station, and Geddes' talk that evening, and the journey up? How it all came back to me as I looked for the pillarbox – not increasing my pain but reminding me that life is, after all, not to be thrown away for one incident) and posted my letter which will, I hope, reach you with the other.

From Sheffield to Barnsley I was in a carriage full of working people who had been seeing their friends in the hospital. They related incessant histories of wounds and horrible cases and I felt how small after all was my woe.

That is how I come to be able to sit down cheerfully – I have already quoted *Abou Ben Adhem* to you once: it is a poem I always remember for times of discouragement. I *will* be written down as 'one who loves his fellowmen' whatever I may fail to get for myself.

Now let me turn to mundane things. Mrs Holt [Laurencina] has asked me to stay with her: I have replied accepting for Nov. 5 night only.

The Leicester Engagement is off: the Co-op Society postpones it until 7 Jan. as they had already fixed one for Nov. Of course that need not prevent me stopping at Leicester for the night of the 4th, if we could arrange for a walk together. Do not be afraid I shall make a mistake again – at least, not *that* mistake. I shall have to leave you to propose to me, I believe! It really was an awful situation for both of us. There are some blunders for which a man never forgives himself.

Barnsley, 9 Oct.

The sun is shining and I *will* write cheerfully though I sat up and read Isaiah part of the night! (Did I tell you that on *the* worst night at Glasgow I read and reread Job? These Bibles in hotel bedrooms come in handy sometimes. I wonder whether the pious donors quite contemplated these occasions!)

My lecture last night (to the Barnsley Co-op Society) needed an effort, and I found myself unable sometimes to speak the word I meant (this is the disease 'aphasia' I believe – incipient paralysis!) But it seemed to go all right. There were only some 60 to 70 audience, in a very nice hall, lit by electric light, which they have adopted to spite the gas company with whom they quarrelled.

It is of course, a huge society; good reading room but seemingly little organic life. I fear these Co-op societies – even the best of them – are not much use as social tissue. I talked to several of them afterwards about T. Union rates of wages etc. They pay their tailors 5 per cent *over* log: and knew of no cases, but felt it would be useful to send a circular round. One said the matter often rested with the manager of a department, who might be sympathetic neither with T.U. or Co-op – and that the Committee might know nothing about the wages.

We shall, next week, have given a course of 4 lectures here, at a cost (besides valuable time) of perhaps £4 or £6. It is entirely virgin soil, and I *suppose* worth cultivating. But there are no apparent results – nor could there well be – save the breaking down of the prejudice against the name of Socialism and a cordial vague invitation to come again.

Of course we have distributed tracts and advertised the *Essays.* (By the way, *The Times* alluded to these in a leading article yesterday). I do not grudge the time and money: whatever influence the Fabian Society has gained is due largely to our constant willingness to do small jobs – to be as cordially eager to convert one man as a hundred – and to be ready to start off and lecture even to a handful. I like to think of ourselves as the 'Society of Jesus' of Socialism – without, I hope, the mental subjection which Protestants accuse the Jesuits of, and also without their moral shiftiness (which I believe is also a libel).

But it does sometimes seem much work for small results – compared with others: e.g. here, next week, Lord Compton and Mr Asquith will address a huge meeting of Liberals and be read by tens of thousands – and one knows quite well that they will say practically nothing really awakening and put forward no new idea. I am not grumbling at my own insignificance – what right have I to be more? (And I am proud enough to think I have as much real influence in the country as Asquith at any rate!) What I am thinking about is how best to widen the sphere of influence of our lectures.

Let me come back to what I am really thinking of. I have read your letter again, and find I have not answered it in mine. I am a pig to be discontented – you really give me all I ought to want. I do not want a public engagement à la Stanley – you will believe me when I say that all this kind of notoriety – the vulgar indecencies of the New Journalism – is hateful to me especially in such a sacred case. When the time comes I should prefer to go quietly through the barest legal ceremony that convention requires, and announce it to the world – since it must be announced – as a *fait accompli.*

But, as you say, that is not a practical question for the present. I have never dreamt even of suggesting that you could give up your duty to see to the end the tremendous task you undertook, in smoothing your father's last days.

Meanwhile what I need is your affection – not necessarily the turbulent passion of first youth, but the more reasonable and durable regard that comes from real sympathy and cordial trust. That you have given me, and do not think I am ungrateful.

Then I want hope. That I have had from the first – partly from my (absurd) self-confidence and belief that my really good motives would outweigh my disadvantages – but chiefly from an inward knowledge and conviction that it *must* be – which translated itself into a tremendous belief in the reasonableness of my proposal, of its power to add to our several effectiveness, of the transformation of I and I into II. Your kindness to me in all my blundering does not diminish my hope, but I know that it commits you to nothing. When a lady came to some eminent divine and said an angel had told her to marry him, he replied that, if that were so, the angel would doubtless in due time, also tell him to marry her: and he would wait till then.

My conviction of its reasonableness is also a conviction that *you* will one day find it the same: but you will and must of course wait till then.

I know perfectly well how little likely I am to be personally attractive to anyone: and I know also how all one's bad habits and tricks of manner are apt to be positively repellent. But if we two were alone in an enemy's country, and found ourselves able to fight the good fight better together, or if we were in imminent peril – all those personal details would sink into insignificance before our common aims and mutual sympathy. And that, really, is after all, our position today. Aloneness is not a matter of numbers or of neighbourhood. If you marry me, it will be as a means of greater usefulness, and helpfulness, and our union (like those of the Salvation Army) will be a new consecration of our lives to the service of Humanity in the way we think best. That, indeed, is the only thing that enables me to contemplate without shame the fact that I, personally have so much to gain by it, and you (as the world will say) so much to lose. I do not need to tell you how much I should prefer that you were *not* a person of station and good connections and some wealth; it will not be very pleasant to me to have to face the things that will be said about me on this score. Except insofar as they lead themselves to our joint effectiveness your 'advantages' are obvious drawbacks to one who is both poor and proud.

But all this is for the future and my hope (for *hope* is absolutely necessary to me) subsists of itself and does not need any *promise* from you.

Nor have I been seeking any pledge. I thought for two blessed days that you *had* seen the reasonableness and feasibility of our eventual union, but even then I never thought of your being *bound*, in any other sense than that of *present* intention. Clearly we do not bind ourselves to be always the same; we only come *ad idem* – to a closer union of thought and sympathy and *intention*.

You must of course be the judge of how far this is possible to you. Meanwhile I do not in the least want you to feel bound: if only on the ground that what we are bound to we are apt to resent. *I* would not have precipitated matters had I not stupidly misunderstood your letter. Granting the misunderstanding I do not think I could have been expected to act otherwise than I did. But for the misunderstanding I most sincerely apologise. Do not let me lose by it – I have been punished enough for it by my own revulsion of feeling.

I have just got your letter. It did not arrive by the morning's post, and you may imagine my condition! Let us say no more about it since you forgive me. I have been really fretting myself ill these two days, and have done no work save the night's lecture. Now you have made me all right again – though I am penitent enough for the hasty presumption which led to my blunder and hurt your feelings. I *must* thank you for your letter – not only for its general kindly sympathy but for your special thoughtfulness in reminding me that you would still come on the 20th. I had not dared to refer to it!

I did not *want* you to tell Mrs Green: I merely thought it might be easier for you, with her in the house. You need not fear that *I* shall talk: I have too much at stake.

I will gladly learn from Mr Strong. I *am* humble in art and music at any rate, and sincerely anxious (in the intervals of business!) to learn more appreciation of them. It will be excellent to be taken round the National Gallery with him: perhaps we can add Dulwich.

Last night I lectured to a local branch of the Socialist League – all *Enragés*, revolutionists yet professing to be Democrats; scornful of Gas and Water Socialism and Eight Hours Bills. I reasoned with them very patiently, and made a good effect on some of them. It is not waste of time to be patient even with the wildest people.

I go off presently to dine with a Quaker [Theodore Neild] – the principal of Dalton Hall, Owen's College – a crypto-Socialist – then to lecture at a small club – then to catch the night train home. (What a different journey it would have been for me without your letter. I have more than once felt that it was wagering very heavily on the certain accuracy of the Post Office. I have been dreading the night journey all this morning. Now it is as nothing.)

The Eccles Election (nearly a suburb of Manchester) fills up all the papers and our reports are at an end as far as Manchester is concerned. I was cut down to 30 lines, in one paper only, today. This is a pity – but we must not grumble. We have done marvellously well hitherto. The 'campaign' has been a great success on the whole, and I do not grudge the £100, and the 6 weeks work of half-a-dozen of us which it has cost (besides, the money was specially subscribed). Last night, by the way, one of the Socialists whom I [?encountered] turned out to be the Secretary of the Shirt *Cutters* Union, a new and small society of prosperous *cutters*. I asked how he found the Co-operators, and he said he did not believe any of the T.U. scandal: he had always found the Wholesale Society (who dealt with his firm) very generous and large-minded, asking for best workmanship and paying for it.

Rev. Harold Rylett, with whom I am staying, is an interesting type of the agitator – an able journalist and ready writer – stranded here as Unitarian Minister to the Ashtons' parish. I have made useful arrangements to 'devolve' some of my work on him.

I shall send this off, though the book is not full, so that you may get it on Sunday at any rate. Do not trouble to write to me at any length, I shall always be thankful of criticism and advice, and I do not need to say how welcome is every line of your writing – but I must not take up much of your time.

I send this as it is because there is some of it I *want* you to see: and all of it is a true record, which you may as well have to understand me.

[*no signature*]

110 PP BEATRICE TO SIDNEY

Walter Bagehot (1826–77), editor of the *Economist* and author of several books on politics, including his classic *The English Constitution*.
The 'historical Don' was York Powell.

Oxford
Friday, 6 o'clock, [10 October 1890]

I have just come in from looking over the town alone – through the Xchurch meadows up the High Street and down Broad Street to New College, where I sat through the Evensong. It is a glorious evening – adding its golden glory to the stately magnificence of the buildings. Troops of under-graduates are [?arriving] (the first day of the term) and I took tea with a whole room full of them at a restaurant. For the most part they are seedy common-looking characters – here and there a fine strapping fellow with the Pride of Life writ large upon his figure and face.

Whether it is the fears of these young men – or the memory of the last time I visited Oxford (2 years ago when I was undergoing terrible agony) – of the feeling of *Shame* in this gorgeous and dignified University – I do not know – but I feel horribly sad – sad and hopeless about the future (not of myself for that I no longer care for) but of this young England with its poverty-stricken aims and its rampant animalism. That I suppose is an unhealthy observation – there is probably better stuff in them than in me if I could only see it. But the Eastern scholar emphatically declared that our Universities were not seats of learning – what are they seats of then? Certainly not Centres wherefrom will radiate the spirit of social service!

Coming here in the train I read Bagehot's *Nation Making*. Do you remember his leading idea that national characteristics was made through the majority imitating the type of the greatest men – it is well worked out – 'great models for good or evil sometimes appear among men, who follow

207

them either to improvement or degradation'. It adds terribly – if it be a potent cause – to the responsibility of all those who stand a little above their fellows – to present a good type – a type that will raise and not debase the national standard of virtue.

It made one feel how unworthy one was even of a tiny bit of social influence. Perhaps that thought too added to my depression.

Mrs Green is staying here with friends and we are going together to dine with the historical Don at Xchurch – whom everyone says is charming. I send this off tonight – so as to greet you when you return to London.

The Docker's business looks rather bad (re Allen's letter). It is a pity the Unions have the Employers so much at their mercy – without having the men more under control.

Is your party coming off?

Ever yours

BP

III PP   SIDNEY TO BEATRICE

The 'Scholar' was Alice Green's friend Taylor.

William Clarke (1852–1901) was among the original group which founded the Fabian Society although he did not immediately join. He was a journalist of depressed disposition, much influenced by Walt Whitman and Ralph Waldo Emerson, who was one of the contributors to *Fabian Essays*. He had become disillusioned and left the Society before he contracted a fatal illness on a Balkan holiday. Henry John Roby (1830–1915), classical scholar and educational reformer, was Liberal M.P. for Eccles 1890–95. George William Russell (1866–1935), the poet 'AE', was also an economist and active in Irish public life, with a particular interest in rural problems. Sydney Charles Buxton (1853–1935), later Earl Buxton, was Liberal M.P. for Poplar and Under-Secretary for the Colonies 1892–95. Sir Edward Burne-Jones (1833–98) was the notable Pre-Raphaelite painter. Sir Charles Trevelyan (1870–1958) was a wealthy young Liberal who was close to the Webbs in his youth and remained a lifelong associate. He was elected to the London School Board in 1896, was a Liberal M.P. 1899–1918, and sat as a Labour member 1922–31, serving in two Labour governments.

[4 Park Village East, N.W.]

[11 October 1890]

Do not be despondent for the world: There is a great vitality in it – a 'will to live' which is the fruit of many generations of the survival of the 'surviviest'. Oxford, I admit, is a grievous spectacle, and the more so because one does not see how it can get amended. The outsider has no power, and the insider no will or capacity, to change things for the better. Some one must stay on at Oxford and become a don; yet one would not desire one's worst enemy to run that danger – and all the greater danger because the middle-aged don may be so charming a product, 'Good – but good for what' as James' father asks in *Washington Square*.

You do not usually see the *Pall Mall Gazette*, I think – so I place with this Frederic Harrison's account of himself – which is interesting for its facts and a certain frankness (superficial only, however), rather than for any special excellence or charm. He does not bring out the best side of himself.

But to revert to your mood – do not be too oppressed with responsibility. 'The better is the enemy of the good.' I so thoroughly believe in Herbert Spencer's exordium at the end of Part I of the *First Principles*: let the world know what you are *now* thinking, whatever it may ultimately prove to have been worth.

Remember we cannot avoid acting. The famous three courses – Yes, No or Neutral – are really three courses of *action*, you 'act' as much by doing nothing, as by taking a side or making a step. Is the responsibility of silence any less weighty than that of speech? Can you avoid a decision by deciding not to decide?

Looked at thus the weight of responsibility is like the pressure of the air – ubiquitous and so unfelt. To dwell upon it is a bad habit. What we want is to derive from it an abiding sense of the need for caution and deliberation – and some modesty of judgment(!) But to have it in mind to greater intensity than this is bad cerebral hygiene, not to be encouraged.

The effect upon conduct and character of *remembered* feelings is not sufficiently recognised. The deteriorating effect of a sin is chiefly, the memory of the sin – the dwelling upon the sin. I believe that good cerebral hygiene consists largely in 'selecting' one's impressions, so that the mind dwells upon those only which have a good effect on the mind – and dismisses those which have a bad effect. Remorse, e.g. is very dangerous. We need just remorse enough (1) to make us remember that it is *disagreeable* to sin; (2) to impress us with the need for *caution* when again approaching the chance of sin. But more remorse than that is bad cerebral hygiene, deteriorating to the mind. Shaw has a sentence in one of his novels, 'Grief of two year's standing is nothing but a bad habit'.

I am preaching not from my own practice but from my own ideal. I want you to read the little book I send herewith, *Dr Heidenhoff's Process*, which is the best thing I ever read of Bellamy's. It is, of course, much inferior to *Dr Jekyll and Mr Hyde* but like that it is a psychological treatise and I found it very instructive when I read it years ago.

Its doctrine is, of course, just as applicable to one feeling as to another, and not merely to sins and crimes.

I have just read it again and I find the earlier part a little 'coarse' in texture: that is perhaps because I am now in love! But the picture of the Democratic society of a New England manufacturing village is very pretty. All this is, of course, only leading up to the root-idea of the book, which I have marked at p. 125. I think pp 113–126 very good psychology, and very useful guides to cerebral hygiene.

So far I have not thanked you for kindly thinking to write to me from Oxford: I am not unmindful of this kindness, which was more than I hoped for.

I will remember what you say about The Scholar. He might be put on to the Club and Institute Union, which sends parties round institutions in the Summer. Perhaps he would teach something at the Working Men's College.

Yes: I intend to try an 'at home' – to be run by myself and our one maid – on Monday, 20th. It is awfully good of you to come. I propose to invite a number of interesting people such as those you mentioned, and the best members of the Fabian Society. I must see about it at once, but Pease is still ill, and I found an appalling lot of work this morning. My night journey was not unpleasant (thanks to the post!) but I am feeling tired tonight.

My Quaker friend turned out a nicely sympathetic soul – shrinking, and modest, *yet*(!) a Liberal Unionist. I dined with the Dalton Hall students (of Owen's College) – they did not affect me as the under-graduates did you – I thought them rather 'nice boys'. Probably they are a better (i.e. 'lower') class: studious and pious middle-class Northerners. My lecture was a great success, small audience but very appreciative.

But the Eccles election kills all other matter and we shall get no more reports in Manchester.

In other towns things are more obviously 'booming' for us. Bland has had a great success in Preston: room too small, adjournment to Unitarian chapel, that also overfilled, very enthusiastic audience.

We have Wallas and Clarke yet to come. Really, now I come to think of it, it is a strong team!

I have not been able to follow the Dock business. I fear, however, that some big 'Labor Battle' is at hand. The capitalists are becoming really alive to the situation and will try, as in Australia, to break the power of the Unions.

Politically this will come too. I look for some 'tussle' during the winter about Liberalism and Labor questions. But Roby's attitude at Eccles has practically settled the position of the Liberal Party on the *Miners* Eight Hours Bill. I do not think they will dare to reject (at the National Liberal Federation meeting at Sheffield end of November) a motion in favor of this. Last year at Manchester they refused even to discuss an amendment urging merely a Government Eight Hours.

Walter Scott offers me $1\frac{1}{2}$d royalty on a shilling Eight Hours Book. I suppose I must accept this, rather than Sonnenscheins 6d on a half-a-crown book, but I believe it leaves the publisher much too much, and I intend to try for more on copies after 5000 I think.

Have you read my fantastic *Speaker* article? I do not think it at all useless to try to be imaginative and the more we can sound the 'collective' note the better. Lord Rosebery, luckily, happened to make a speech at Glasgow beautifully appropriate to my article: so that it may be noticed further than by the *Star*, which – though useful – does not 'count' in this connection.

It is odd to me that the politicians are so slow to follow the lead given by Sir C. Dilke and now Lord Rosebery, not to speak of G. W. Russell and Sydney Buxton. Yet Morley and Asquith, Trevelyan and Labouchere can find nothing to talk about but Ireland. The fact is they *don't like* Labor politics: they are uneasy about these new questions and (like Mawdsley) will not even support what they could agree to, lest it should give a fillip to movements of which they disapprove.

But think what a disadvantage this is for the Liberal Party.

Sunday, 12 Oct.

I am alone in the house and (I confess) not very happy. I am weary and anxious, and unable to work. I wonder how you manage to keep on day by day. Have you any guests today? It is unreasonable of me to want you to be here, but I do want you badly.

This morning I lectured on 'Lessons from America' to the Upholsterers Club – a social club belonging to 130 workers at that trade, maintained by the sale of beer and a billiard table. They are starting lectures, so they ought to be encouraged. But it does not come to much. Now I am writing two articles for the *Financial Reformer* which must be posted tonight. I don't want to do them, I don't. But then I don't know what else I should prefer to do here alone – except go on writing to you, and that you would be weary of. I am too 'low' to say anything worth reading.

I have not been able to find anything that would be useful for your second chapter. You make me feel how much there is, even of English history that I know nothing of. What you are writing will really be a useful contribution towards that 'History of the 19th Century' that several of us have often wanted. You are giving the key note of a great deal more than the Co-operative Movement. (Perhaps we will write that 'History' together, some day.)

Be careful with me just now, for I am evidently 'sore all over' and you may hurt me more than you know. Indeed, it seems to me that I am in rather a bad way, and destined to find out the truth of young Playne's observation as to falling in love being a very painful thing. Of course I am very fortunate in all sorts of ways, but it is not in human nature that I should *feel* this (I only *know* it – a very different thing), and I *feel* very unfortunate because I can't get what I want here and now.

There is no doubt that (to judge from myself) a man in love is very selfish. I say this advisedly, after reading a few chapters of *Vanity Fair*, where the beautiful self-abnegation and devotion of Major Dobbin always touches me and does me good. In his case, the selfishness took the form of altruism – and a very good thing too. I hope my selfishness can take that form if and when the time comes. I *know* I could give up everything to see you happier, but that would be only another channel for the same strong feeling. It *is* egotistical for anyone to be strongly absorbed in one passion, and the channel in which it runs is not material to the argument (though very material, often, to the world). In my own case I believe I am right in 'letting myself go' in the ordinary direction, and I hope it will redound also to your happiness – that indeed, is part of its rightness. I say I *could* give you up if it were for your own happiness: but this is absurd of me – I don't really feel that I could; I only hope I should be able to do what is right.

When I think how I should suffer if you simply took it into your head to say you did not want to see me or hear from me again – I can't help trembling. You have me entirely in your hands, and the two days I passed last week at Barnsley and Hyde show me what an awful time I should have. I have told you once or twice that I resolved that no woman should wreck my life. It was a characteristic vow – characteristic of man and of me. What is the use of resolving? I can't think what it would be to me. As you are strong, be merciful. When I think that you, as you told me, several times contemplated casting me adrift altogether I can't help mentally shuddering, as one who looks back on his path and sees how unexpectedly near he has been to the unseen precipice.

Yet – as I must confess, since I tell you everything – I foresaw from the first that it would be so. I remember thinking that you would be likely to find my blundering devotion oppressive, and that I should have one or more very bad times *to go through*. It is characteristic of me that I thought prudently of all this, and also that I thought of those bad times as times *to go through*. For it always seemed to me impossible that there could be any other but the one ending – which shows (let me bitterly add) how very unreal all my prudent deliberation and forethought was.

Mais que veux-tu? What more can one do than to try impartially to consider the matter; to decide upon pure reason whether the union is expedient – all the time knowing that your feeling has decided the matter for you, and is now but cloaking itself in the garment of the intellect in order to do homage to itself. Do you know Burne-Jones' charming little picture of 'Love in the guise of Reason'?

I am not deceived. I know that I deceive myself when I pretend to estimate you and criticise you, and count up your good qualities and your drawbacks. It is the indefinable 'you' that I want – bother your qualities and the defects of your qualities.

Do you know what has comforted me the most in all your recent letters? It was when you said that some days you had felt that my love for you brought warmth and color into your life. (You have been very kind to me in telling me such things – they are like the rose you gave me – except that they do not wither.) I thought of Landor's

I warmed both hands before the fire of life

You sometimes speak as if you could never be warmed: let me try, and you shall see! Yes: I *do* feel that if I were burnt up in the process, I should rejoice to have brought some warmth and color back into your life.

Dearest, I have love enough for two – you cannot *help* reflecting back love for me because my heart is so strong. Turn but your face towards me, and love must come – do but give up looking backward. You are not wrong to become silently oblivious of what you thought you could never forget. I wish I were Dr Heidenhoff to eliminate from your memory the parts that give you a bitter-sweet pain, and keep your eyes from me and the 'fire of life'. But as there is no Dr Heidenhoff you must do it for yourself and resolutely live for the future, instead of in the past. Every time you think of your past sufferings you commit a sin against that world for whom you wish to live, you tend to harden your nature, and dry up your feelings. Make a resolution that you will be your own Dr Heidenhoff, and count each day as sullied that you turn back towards the past.

I was taught this in my own – much lighter – case by a very clever German woman who had herself suffered. She was engaged, very young, to a brilliant officer: he died in the Austro-German war. Years afterwards she was to have married someone else, but it went off. And to crown all, she fell in love at 35 or so, with Olivier, who was already in love with his present wife.

That is rather a bad record. Wallas and I went to stay with her in Weimar six years ago, when all the world was dark for me; and she had extracted my story before I had been there long. 'Don't *nurse* your *Kummer*' she constantly repeated (we spoke a *lingua franca* – half-German, half-English – she knew both to perfection). 'It is wicked to be faitful to a dead or shattered idol – you must live, and therefore must forget.'

There are, indeed, more ways of committing suicide than Werther's and we are all rather apt to think we are so virtuous in merely living, that we sometimes 'take it out' in harmful mental self-indulgence.

Forgive me for saying all this: you see I have the keenest interest in your mental health for my own sake! And you have told me enough to let me see that you are still suffering – indeed, you have said so. I come at an inopportune moment – no, not so: it may be inopportune for my own success, but I am sure you need to warm yourself at some 'fire of life', and I may serve to save you from the growing numbness of emotional death.

6 p.m.

I prescribed for myself tea and some Thomas à Kempis! after which I feel better, and will readily do some work.

213

But let me conclude with some quotations from dear old Thomas, apposite to one side or the other.

'Whensoever a man desireth anything inordinately he is presently disquieted in himself.'

(Note the 'presently'. At first I was not disquieted only 'elated'!)

'I had rather feel compunction than understand the definition thereof.'

(It is only of recent years that I have come to see how much higher is *feeling* than *knowing*) (And here is a perfect hymn of praise, to finish with.)

Love is a great thing, yea, a great and thorough good: by itself it makes everything that is heavy, light; and it bears evenly all that is uneven.

For it carries a burden that is no burden, and makes everything that is bitter, sweet and tasteful.

Love desires to be aloft, and will not be kept back by anything low and mean.

Love desires to be free, and estranged from all worldly affections, that so its inward sight may not be hindered; that it may not be entangled by any temporary prosperity, or by any adversity deminished.

Nothing is sweeter than Love, nothing more courageous nothing higher, nothing wider, nothing more pleasant nothing fuller nor better in heaven and earth: because love is born of God, and cannot rest but in God, above all created things.

He that loveth, flieth, runneth and rejoiceth; he is free and cannot be held in.

He giveth all for all and hath all in all; because he resteth in one highest above all things from whom all that is good proceeds and flows.

He respecteth not the gifts but turneth himself above all goods to the giver.

Love oftentimes knoweth no measure, but is fervent beyond all measure.

Love feels no burden, thinks nothing of trouble, attempts what is above its strength, complains not of impossibility; for it thinks all things lawful for itself, and all things possible.

It is therefore able to undertake all things, and it completes many things, and causes them to take effect, where he who does not love would faint and lie down.

Let no strange fancies therefore trouble thee, which on any subject whatever may crowd into thy mind. *Keep to thy purpose, with courage and an upright intention toward God.*

Good old Thomas! Who would have thought he knew so much about it!

214

Now goodnight, for I *must* work. How clearly I can see you – this time as you stand by the drawing-room fire with your hand on the mantelpiece, looking at me with a kindly solicitude. Do you remember putting your hand on mine, and proving that it was larger? I am sure I behaved very well to be so self-controlled. Do you know that I resolved that I would always turn first to Mrs Green, even in handing a cigarette. 'What shall I give thee for all these thousands of benefits? I would I could serve thee all the days of my life.' (*Good* old Thomas)

10 p.m.

I have done my work – much quicker than I thought. I have written an article on Poor Law Reform; a short one on the Eccles election and Financial Reform; and a London Letter. A third of these was already done; the rest I have done in two hours, really quite effectively. I have now only a few letters to write, and then I may go to bed and dream of you.

Today has been long and dreary to me – save when I have been talking to you! So I have talked at some length: it was not time ill-spent for I could not have worked. (And I have worked, *too*: one lecture, three articles and 18 letters – not so bad!)

I feel weak as wax today: I am not Samson and you are not Delilah, but I seem to understand how that happened. What a wonderful power have the women, and little they yet use it for good!

Do not despise me for weakness: I am not always so – not so when others are concerned, but today my 'yearning' is allpowerful in me, and I cannot see anything but your face. Do you remember my quoting Rossetti to you in a very early letter – but then I only ventured to write the last two lines!

> O love, my love! if I no more should see
> Myself, nor on the earth the shadow of thee.
> Nor image of thine eyes in any spring.
> How then should sound upon Life's darkening slope
> The ground whirl of the perished leaves of Hope
> The wind of Death's imperishable wing!

I am not sending out formal cards for Monday, 20th, but having postcards printed for the Fabian members, and writing to others: this is less pretentious.

I have felt bound to invite the local 'groups' of the Fabian Society, i.e. *all* the members living near here – selecting only the others. So that you must not suppose I have picked out the best.

I am putting '8 to 12 Morning Dress' in all the invitations.

Now let me tell you exactly where this house is. It stands on the Regents Canal, the second house from the Gloucester Gate bridge, at the top of Park St Camden Town, 8 min. from Camden Road Station on the North London Railway and 15 min. from Portland Road on the Metropolitan.

215

If you come by cab, tell the man 'near the York and Albany, Gloucester Gate': if you come from Bishopsgate St by rail to Camden Road you turn to the right out of the station and walk straight until the great 'carrefour' at the Britannia, then up Park St until just before the bridge.

What will you do on Tuesday? If you will be at the Museum, let me meet you for lunch.

After all, I have 'enjoyed' today, for I have talked to you. I am ungrateful though I render many thanks, for I have very much more than I deserve or could have reasonably hoped for. Adieu

Sidney

112 PP SIDNEY TO BEATRICE

The Booths reacted adversely to Sidney at dinner. 'He seemed to me in earnest and genuine', Charles Booth wrote to Beatrice (PP); 'really possessed with the idea and hope of a better state of things to spring from the advance of democratic socialism.' Regarded as a suitor, however, 'I find I don't like him at all and neither Mary nor I can bear to think of you as his wife or him as your husband. Don't do it, I say'.

Sidney's optimism about Fabian prospects, buoyed up by the sale of the *Essays* and the success of the Lancashire campaign, made him feel that his policy of permeation was beginning to be effective. The London Radicals, operating through the Progressive Party, had done well in the first elections for the London County Council. The discredit brought upon the Irish issue by the Parnell case in the autumn of 1890, when Parnell was cited as co-respondent by Captain O'Shea, made a strong domestic policy for the Liberals seem increasingly desirable.

Frederic William Farrar (1831–1903), archdeacon of Westminster in 1883, dean of Canterbury 1895, was the author of the famous school story *Eric, or Little by Little* and a best-selling *Life of Christ* in 1870. Lujo Brentano (1844–1931) was an economist and historian from a distinguished German literary family, much interested in trade unions and Co-operatives. He translated Beatrice's book on *The Co-operative Movement* into German in 1893. John Henry Muirhead (1855–1940), a founder of the Ethical Society, married the sister of Graham Wallas; he became professor of philosophy at the University of Birmingham. James Bryce (1838–1922), later Viscount Bryce, was a Liberal M.P. and historian, especially interested in the United States, on which he wrote his notable volume *The American Commonwealth* 1888. Francis Schnadhorst (1840–1900) was the secretary of the National Liberal Federation and the chief organiser of the Liberal victories of 1880, 1885 and 1892. Herbert Gladstone (1854–1930) was the youngest son of the Liberal leader; he became Chief Whip of the Liberal Party and Home Secretary 1905–10. James Edwin Thorold Rogers (1823–1890) was a political economist who in 1887 published a massive history of prices. He wrote several works on economic history.

Annie Besant had organised a union of the match girls after leading the notable strike at Bryant and May.

216

I am rather ashamed of the last two volumes I have sent you: they were so 'weak' and no man enjoys being weak. And I feel 'mean' at seeming to appeal to you in this way. I don't want you to do what I desire, out of mere pity and generosity. Besides, it is not so bad as all that, There is no doubt that I had a bad week, having been 'knocked over' (through my own blunder) in an absolutely unprecedented way. But I have 'got into my stride again' now, and I can't bear the least suspicion of implied Wertherism. I shall not die if you find it impossible, and I do not intend to be permanently upset by it. Of course it won't be nice; it won't improve my work to load up something equivalent to a permanent toothache; and I don't suppose it will altogether make for sweetness of temper, though I should fight against this effect. But I can and will stand it, if necessary, and I don't want to imply that I could not do so. (There's pride for you! – for I own it *is* pride.)

And I feel selfish in having bothered you with my feelings: it was a relief to write to you, and I wrote just what I thought, without enough thinking how it might affect you. The virtue of sincerity, like that of early rising, may be used as a cover for many *other* sins.

Fortunately I am just about as busy as I can be; Pease still away ill, and all our Secretariat work in confusion.

Wed. Oct. 15

Yesterday morning I got a note from Charles Booth asking me to dinner *that night*, to talk to him and another man [? T. P. Baptie] on Poor Law. I happened to be able to put off my evening's work, so I humbly did so and went there. We had a great talk. (I stayed until 11.30!) Mrs Booth joining in a lot (we differed flagrantly about the way of writing history, she being addicted to such things as Lord Malmesbury's *Memoirs* and the reports of foreign ambassadors which I said were not worth the paper they were written on as sources of the real history of the English people!) Miss Booth ('Dodo') was very much bored – the children of people 'with subjects' must be nearly as much tired of them as the children of Evangelical parents are tired of theology.

Charles Booth had been convinced by my *Contemporary* article on Poor Law, and merely raised difficulties of execution – which I admitted, but retorted that they existed anyhow.

Then we talked Socialism and I forgot to try to make a good impression(!) but simply argued for truth (*which* is virtuous – my intention, my deed, my present remark on it – or neither?). I drove him from point to point, and I think made him see a little that with municipal servants and a Co-operative store, the *need* for competition as a test of whether a thing 'pays', could easily be replaced by good bookkeeping as to cost of production, pricing solely upon that, and then supplying up to the demand. But he is very much wedded to the City notion of competitive price being the *ne plus ultra* of social nexus.

I *am* sorry I failed to ingratiate myself more – if I did fail – but I cannot be other than myself, and I can and will not meet people, even my superiors in years and experience, except on terms of intellectual equality and sincerity.

I dare say I did not go beyond bounds, but I must own that my whole conduct cannot have seemed flattering, especially to one who has been accustomed lately to be looked up to as having found out almost a new *organon*. I don't believe so simple and earnest-minded a man as Charles Booth will in the least explicitly resent this – even to himself – but it can hardly fail to affect unconsciously his view of me – and I did *so* much want to stand well with him for ulterior reasons!

Fri. 17 Oct.

Did I tell you that I had been refusing work all round? Cassells sent for me (just as 20 years ago they sent for Archdeacon Farrar!) and asked me to write a book on the London Water Companies, ending in Municipalisation. It was wanted at once and would involve (they said) a month's hard work. Of course I refused, on the ground that I had far too much to do already. They were very flattering and asked if any of my friends could do it. I said that the Fabian circle were all in the same case (I *could* not possibly contemplate Wallas, or Shaw, or Clarke, or Mrs Besant being able to take on the job, and Olivier is starting tonight for British Honduras.) Bland I thought of but did not recommend. Then I thought of Vaughan Nash, and he writes to say that they sent at once for him and gave him the order – which is nice all round.

Brentano's hint about Labor news for Germany has also borne fruit. I recommended Nash to the *Frankfurter Zeitung*, and he is doing work for them now.

The *Speaker* presses me for more articles which I have refused to do – and other people want me too.

I am not at all above being pleased at all this for my own sake, but it is all the better for 'the cause' too.

But the best thing of all is that the Central Publication Dept. of the Liberal Party, which is worked under the 'Whips' in connection with the Nat. Lib. Federation, wants to republish my London articles. I asked if Schnadhorst knew who wrote them, and was told he did. I of course consented, proposing to edit them into a suitable sixpenny pamphlet.

If this comes off (and it is a secret as yet), it will mean a wonderful change in the Liberal programme and way of looking at things. I expect they contemplate keeping my name out of it, but I shall not allow that. It is not for the advertisement, which I could get easily enough without their consent even more effectively by 'inspiring' newspaper paragraphs. But it is important to make the provincial Liberal understand that I preach what he has got to accept – that my policy is to be the future Liberal policy. I think I shall have a strong position, when they are republishing my articles, under my editing, without any remuneration to me, if they demur to the title page which I shall without comment preface with my name on it as Editor. It will be a means of driving a further nail into the coffin of the Liberalism of the provincial dissenter.

I have failed to find you any appreciable additions to your note on the literature of the Industrial Revolution. But I have one or two suggestions and I may get more when Pease comes back and things quiet down a little.

I am inclined to believe in Owen's originality – that is to say in the 'spontaneous generation' of his idea in his own mind from the facts of the time and the newspapers – without any more definite affiliation being possible.

But I do bring out clearly in the second chapter, how it was the addition of *Democracy* that made the thing go. The Chartists were *the* men of the time, but the people were not ready for them. And the Co-op Movement may have done something to make them ready. But the Co-operators are sadly lacking in large ideas now. I was lecturing to the Woolwich Arsenal Co-ops on Wednesday (on Poor Law), and although I got the most Radical of them, it was pitiful to see how they had been contaminated by the middle-class ideal, and tried to catch the middle-class tone.

They are having a course of 4 lectures from us. I talked to them about T.U. rates and so on.

J. Muirhead, of the Ethical Society who lives with Wallas, and whom you will meet on Monday, is to be appointed *Sub-Warden* of Elsmere Hall, and probably will be *the* resident personage. He is a delightful Oxonian-Glasgow man, lectures on philosophy to the Holloway College and for University Extension, a perfect type of self-devotion and intellectual honesty – gravitated slowly from Free Kirk to Established Kirk, then to Unitarianism, and then to Agnosticism.

Under Wicksteed and him I feel sure that the Biblical criticism will take more and more a back seat, and the Toynbee Hall side come to the front – with even more Socialism than Toynbee.

A lot of people will come on Monday but unfortunately not all I could wish. Davitt says he is too busy; you see, I did not venture to say *you* would come. Burnett is away and will *probably* not be back; Dent has gone for a holiday.

But Burns will be there, and Stepniak with the newly-escaped Siberian prisoners (!) These, I suppose, will be the 'lions' or rather the bears of the evening. By the way, I shall have to treat *you* with the scantest of courtesy, as the Fabians have very sharp eyes. But I will not overdo it – you may trust me – and you will not mind fending for yourself and making the thing go.

219

Mrs Green asks Wallas and me to dinner *next Tuesday*. I have replied that I could go, but that Wallas is in Lancs and leaving it to her to decide whether she puts it off for a week. If you will be in London Tuesday night, and it would suit you to dine with her, you can let her know – I need hardly say that there are *nicer* arrangements that could be suggested, but it might be the most convenient for you. I did not ask Mrs Green for Monday: but of course if it suited you to come with her, I should be pleased.

I met Albert Ball in the street the other day (and I hardly knew him: he has grown much fatter and old – why is he so grey? He doesn't 'worry' about anything does he?) He at once asked me if I had been with you lately, as his cousin (? did he say) Mrs Green wanted to meet me. I said I had been at Box for a day or two while Mrs G. was there.

He seemed a little penitent for not being a Socialist and implied that you had talked to him on the point – but he said that you were not really a Democratic Socialist, as having really aristocratic views upon the government of the common people! I did not argue the point with him, and we parted: more amicably than I thought he would have regarded me. But he is an 'external' person.

Last night I lectured at the Wandsworth Town Hall on the Eight Hours Bill to the local Liberal Association. I found them all practically with me and enthusiastic about it. I feel no doubt that we shall be able to drive the official Liberals on into a very sea of Socialism before they know where they are. Bruce, e.g. is wandering in the United States, and consequently losing more and more 'touch' with things here. It is not wise for a politician nowadays to go away for five or six months every year, out of reach of news.

I hear on very good authority indeed that Gladstone is really going to make a great speech at Edinburgh on the Labor and Social Question. I can hardly believe it, because he is too wary to curse, and too ignorant to bless. But I am assured that what he is going to say will be quite satisfactory to the most advanced section of the party.

This sounds incredible but the G.O.M. is a very old hand, and I know that Schnadhorst is strongly in favor of a very generous tone to 'Labor' and very open to Labor candidates.

I sent Herbert Gladstone, for his father's use, 2 days ago (1) the Metropolitan Radical Federation programme – which we largely inspired (2) the Manchester Programme as boldly summarised by me for the London Liberal and Radical Union, with the definite promise that this was 'what the next Liberal Ministry intends to do' (3) my *Star* programme' in the 'Wanted a Programme' pamphlet and (as I said) the Socialist criticism on these as embodied in our Fabian tract 'The Worker's Political Programme'. I also sent our Eight Hours Bill. I wrote carefully and deferentially, merely sending these as documents which might possibly be useful for him to have at hand. It will be a great score if the G.O.M. really does advance. I don't see how he can help endorsing the Eight Hours Bill for Miners – if so, it will be a dreadful snub for Morley. But that *must* come sometime.

Morley, meanwhile, seems to have written an article on Irish Land for the *North American Review* (not yet read) which definitely though vaguely abandons Peasant Proprietorship for Ireland. This is important, as bearing out his motion for Land Municipalisation last session. It will further paralyse the provincial Liberal.

Statesmen are not wise to make their conversions so silently and 'sneakingly'. It would seem better to the public if 'Honest John' came out plumply with an 'I've changed my views on this'. The more candid, and even 'dramatic' the change is, the easier it is forgiven – and one gets a very useful reputation as 'Honest John' into the bargain! I don't think we shall hear much more of that appellation.

Wallas sends me a real 'gem', out of the *Daily Graphic*: –

PROFESSOR THOROLD ROGERS

The death of Professor Thorold Rogers is a more serious loss to economic science than to the practical art of politics. As a politician – in spite of the uncompromising candour with which it was his habit to give utterance to his opinions – Professor Rogers was not always taken seriously; but the value of his researches into the abstruse problems of political economy is universally admitted. With the more modern developments of that science he did not, it is true, profoundly sympathise. He belonged to the orthodox school of Mill, Cobden, and Ricardo, rather than to that of Professor Alfred Marshall, Mr Sidney Webb, and the Fabian Society; but his *Six Centuries of Work and Wages* is, and is long likely to remain, a standard work upon a difficult and important topic.

Marshall will be simply *furious* if he sees it. It is just the kind of trifle that will 'sorry' him for days, and it is not to be contradicted in any way without making matters worse.

Poor *old* Marshall, one feels very sorry that so good a man should be so cantankerously minded in various little ways. He has grown prematurely old in some tricks of mind. The academic life is a fearful trial and test: it produces thoughtful work but its divorce from daily action; its inevitable 'dilettantism'; and its intellectual blindness is awful. What says your Goethe

> *Es bildet ein Talent sich in der Stille,*
> *Sich ein Charakter in dem Sturm der Welt.*

One cannot withdraw from the stream of life – not even from its main current – without a change of character which, though partly beautiful, is on the whole a change for the worse.

Marshall does all he can to keep himself alive – except the one indispensable thing of *humbly* trying to appreciate every new idea, and abandoning the fastidiousness of the 'Superior person'. I shall always remember Tolstoi's description of the separating effect even of personal cleanliness.

There is, too, a fearful intellectual fastidiousness. Mrs Besant is on the point of resigning all participation in political action; no doubt all membership of the Fabian Society and the Social Democratic Federation (she is piqued with us on some trivial personal matters, but she is genuinely disgusted with the whole S.D.F.). Her reason, to us and to herself, is her growing distaste for all the methods of politics, and her wish to devote herself to Theosophy.

We have been fearing this for some time: and that is one reason why I wanted to retain her on the School Board. She will no doubt go on with that to the end of her term (next Nov.) but I much fear that (in her present frame of mind) she will not stand again. She still works hard at her Match Girls' Union and Club – she says she can't come on Monday on that ground. But her destiny is more and more the 'inner life' and (?) the convent in some form or another.

It is a pity. If all the 'good' people go out of politics, politics will be run only by the bad, and as the bad choose (as in America).

Just as I am not overcareful of soiling my boots, or inhaling foul air, in order to lecture to a working men's club – so I cannot afford to be overcareful of mental contamination in doing other necessary work. I will try all I can to keep up the standard, but I think one must 'stick to the coach' even if it seems to be going into a foul quagmire. I am not a 'superior person' and I don't intend to be.

This strikes me as on the whole a 'defiant' letter. I don't mean to be defiant: I love you much too well and too honestly to wish to play tricks with you, or to try to manipulate your mind by any changes in mind. It is merely that I have recovered some 'tone', and I do not think it right to attempt to keep up a Werther attitude. Above all let us not be 'sentimental', that is, let us not try to feel a feeling merely because we think we ought to feel that feeling under the circumstances. I *do* feel just now that I am not warranted in petitioning you *ad misericordiam*. It would not be self-respectful of me, but that is not much. What is more to the point is that any such petition would not really be true. You are quite free – free even from the apprehension that to decide one way will injure me. I do not intend that it shall injure me appreciably or permanently. It may and will diminish my usefulness, but that is not for you so much to be responsible for, and it is not in my hands to prevent.

But this is cheap heroism on my part – because first of all the blow has not fallen and secondly, and above all, I decline to believe that it will fall. You know my very certain faith on this point – and always, I must admit, a *serene* faith, yet even 'when my light is low', a very real and abiding assurance that it *must* be so – the 'fitness of things' so absolutely requires and compels it. But; in your good time. And I must and will wait patiently until then. You need not fear that I am neglecting anything or failing in anything – you are an inspiration to me such as I have never yet known, and every one notices and is astonished at the special energy and application that I have this summer put into things. All that – and still more my magical change of feeling, and wealth of delight in you – all that is a real and genuine gain which even you cannot take from me, because it is enjoyed.

Now once more goodbye – until Monday – come as early as you easily can, and tell me sometime and somehow whether I may not see you on the Tuesday. You are very good to me, but I feel it very hard that you are so far off. I have put a circle round the dates in my pocketbook when I have been with you – and they only number 32 in all! This is not much – though I am not unmindful how thoughtful you have been. Just a month of days to make you believe in me, and to wear down all my drawbacks. It is not much.

Adieu

S.

113 PP BEATRICE TO SIDNEY

Richard Garnett (1835–1906) was the keeper of printed books at the British Museum, critic and biographer.

Box House, Minchinhampton, Glos.
[?17 October 1890]

One line to say that I have asked Davitt and Burnett to dine with me and go on to you on Monday whither we shall arrive about 8.45. Have you asked Jones and Dent?

Your Sunday letter made me feel very wretched – do not write like that again – do not 'let yourself go' – it is not fair on me nor wise for yourself.

Remember your promise that no woman should spoil your life – that the best part of your energy and your heart should be given to your work – and that whatever came of it, you would not let me reproach myself, that any weakness in allowing friendship between us, should injure you.

I am feeling low and miserable – as if a great burden were laid on me – the burden of unreturned affection – affection which I feel it is unlikely I shall ever return. But it is our work that is important and not ourselves – in face of all the misery and senseless stupor of the world – we must not think of ourselves. You were over-tired on Sunday – so I do not blame – but do not repeat it – lest you make the burden intolerable.

Ever yours

B Potter

I shall be, I fear, full all Tuesday, but I shall be at the B.M. *1 o'clock* for lunch. I have probably an appointment then at 2 o'c to introduce a neighbour's son to R. Garnett. For your own sake you will be wise on Monday evening.

BP

114 PP SIDNEY TO BEATRICE

4 Park Village East, N.W.
18 Oct./90

You will have seen from mine of yesterday that I anticipated your strictures, so I cannot complain of them. But remember that I have had rather an unprecedented trial; and overlook that week. Indeed, I don't wish to importune you: I understand quite well the position, and if it pains you that I should write what I am thinking about, of course I won't do so, any more than talk about it.

Only, be careful for it is not a light thing with me.

I don't want you to feel it necessary always to be entrenching yourself behind declarations adverse to me, as warnings to me. They don't really alter the situation either way, and I never fail to realise your complete freedom and my own exclusive responsibility in the matter. Don't say too much about our *work*: if it were to be decided on that ground alone, there could be no doubt as to the answer.

But I don't expect or ask for an answer yet.

I am going to Leicester on Nov. 4, after all, to begin a big series of lectures in the Co-op Hall (hired by the local Socialist League). If you are going there too, you might let me know by what train. There would be time for a morning walk before I go on to Liverpool on Nov. 5.

The enclosed may be of use to you.

S.

I will meet you at B.M. at 1 on Tuesday.

115 PP BEATRICE TO SIDNEY

In a long notebook letter of 22–24 October, omitted here, Sidney reported his activities in the London Reform Union and made some suggestions about the way Beatrice should classify her statistical material on Co-operative societies. Noting that Margaret Harkness had deserted socialism for the Salvation Army – in 1891 she published a novel, *Captain Lobe*, celebrating the Army – he commented on her 'unconscious egotism', and hoped he did not have the same fault.

'No one has the least ground for saying that I have ever tried to form a "Webb" party: or that I have been loath to lend an anonymous hand to any movement. I am, in fact, much too proud inwardly to care very much about getting the credit of any piece of work. I want things done – I do not want to do them myself.' He assured Beatrice that he had cut out 'all my thoughts which you do not want me to dwell on . . . you must understand and realise every writhe I make in the bitter-sweet anguish which I am enjoying, without my troubling you with pages of introspection and yearning . . . You can do so much for me – so much more than I can do for you, 'tho I can give you my life's devotion. Do not lightly reject the enormous addition we could make to our several efficiencies merely because you are loth to lose your freedom as you think. You will really only enlarge it by the annexation of all mine.'

Sir Robert Giffen (1837–1910) was a journalist, civil servant and statistician. He was one of the founders of the Economic Society and editor of the *Journal of the Royal Statistical Society* 1876–91. Edward Cummings was an American economist who had just published two articles on trade unionism and Co-operation in the *Quarterly Journal of Economics*.

Sidney had agreed to give a lecture at Stroud, near Beatrice's home. David Brynmor Jones was a barrister and county court judge in Stroud, becoming its member of parliament in 1892. He was a neighbour and friend of the Potters; local gossip suggested that he might marry Beatrice.

Box House, Minchinhampton, Glos.
[?24 October 1890]

Miss Pycroft, who has been attending Marshall's lectures, writes he is going to deal with the fallacious remedies 'brought forward by a band of men utterly devoted to their cause, clever writers, clever thinkers, and *very* clever talkers' but who nevertheless as he thinks are unsound in some of their ideas. I wish he would attack you publicly – I think he almost ought to do so – if he believes you are wrong. Little stress about 'iron-bound socialism' being the question – he is even not clear about the 8 Hours – and has never spoken on Land Nationalisation or Municipal integration.

Mrs Green told me that she was feeling frightfully tired and feared that she had been dull. I found her in a state of depression about her book – she makes a mistake in consulting with so many people about the scope of it. Only one person, or the author, can decide what scope to give a book – advice is useful on special points but never on the whole.

She really has quite a liking for you; (I say 'really' because I mean that her liking is more than mere acquaintance liking) but she says you are 'scrappy' in your knowledge of the past – and have no real historical sense of the greater facts of history – 'everything must serve to illustrate a lecture on *Facts* for *Landowners*, whether or no there is real analogy'. There is some truth in that (since you beg me to criticise!). I should like to take you away from current politics for 2 years and force you into a study of literature and history for its own sake. Fine task (as Bagehot says) gives fine judgment – a nobler and larger temper of mind. I don't want you to grow 'superior' but I am not sure whether more cultivation would not take away that 'superiority' which asks 'good for what?' to the Eastern scholar or the metaphysicist – on which prefaces the evasion to his opponent: 'I thought that idea had been exploded long ago'. You and I are both of us lamentably ignorant of whole spheres of thought – I, perhaps, more so than you – but I fancy I *know* my ignorance more than you do – there is 'superiority' for you! I agree with you, I hate 'superiority' whether it be the superiority of a really larger mind, or the superiority of a narrow mind which is quick and agile in its own dimension.

Be humble, say I – to myself and to you – let us realise that tho' we may do our very best in our little way – that it *is* a little way and that there are multitudinous paths and even high roads of human progress which we are never destined to see, still less to tread, and the goal of which we could not even imagine. Eastern scholarship for instance – or Lord Malmesbury's foreign despatches – (to give an anti-climax to these great sentiments). I want you to prepare carefully your lecture, in Liverpool and for this place; (by the way the Playnes are coming to listen). I want you to be convincing but not too superior in any answer you may make to Judge Jones on the Population point.

It was not Giffen but C. Booth who suggested the Boroughs: Giffen remarked that my statistics would take 50 pages. I am beginning to doubt whether I could get that one table done – whether V. Nash is equal to it – whether I can afford to pay for it, and whether it will not be rather too much matter for my little work – whether I had not better delay it until I have the Census Return 1891 and go in for more detailed investigations. I want to make this book really explanatory of the *social meaning* of the Co-operative movement – I am aiming more at a work of Power than a work of Information – a small attempt to make Co-operatives into what I want them to be, not to tell the outside world who, and what and why they are. So far as my information goes I want it to be correct – but need it be voluminous? The 'relative growth' on the other hand has a practical meaning – a stimulus for Co-operators to throw themselves into other and larger movements – together with that sense of proportion I am always preaching as a necessity for correct thinking even on your own subject. What think you? I hope to go down to Leicester by the evening of Monday, at the latest Tuesday morning, but I will come to your lecture at the Co-op Hall if I am not too tired: would you dine with me before the lecture?

By the way – Muirhead has refused the offer of rooms at U. Hall – says the Ethical Society will not give him up – it is a pity I think.

I do not think Cummings' articles would teach me much, as I saw a good deal of him – but if you could lay your hands on the *Quarterly* it might be useful.

[*no signature*]

226

James Thomson (1834–82) was a pessimistic secularist whose most notable poem was 'The City of Dreadful Night'. George Joachim Goschen (1831–1907), later Viscount Goschen, was a Liberal-Unionist who became Chancellor of the Exchequer under Lord Salisbury: his main concerns were financial and naval policy.

The Reverend John Elliotson Symes (1847–1920), was professor of English literature at University College, Nottingham 1881–96.

Tuesday, 28 Oct. [1890]

I am going to be rigorous with myself, and limit, as a rule, my communications to you still further. I was appalled to find that the little books you gave me contained nearly 5000 words = four *Speaker* articles! I am so busy that I can hardly justify so much of what is pure enjoyment to me. Nor can I, probably, make four *Speaker* articles each week interesting to you. (I wonder whether you realise *how little* makes me happy, if only you are concerned. While I am writing to you I forget my work and its worries, I forget my own presumption in wanting the very top brick off the chimney. I forget your hesitation and very natural fear to trust me with yourself and your life – everything is like Arcadia, in which, indeed, I am, for all the worries, and doubts and fears, really living. Even without further cause, I can never forget or disappoint your kindness this summer).

So I have found a smaller book, which will cut me down to half the quantity. Perhaps this will help me to leave out what I ought to leave out! But I reserve the right to go back to the 'double number' when I 'feel like it' i.e. when I find I have the time.

One of the difficulties of modern industry is the great multiplicity and variety of patterns. I have tried a dozen shops without finding exactly the same little books I have hitherto used. Each shop had dozens of little books, but not quite *those* little books. The present inferior quality volume happened to be the nearest I could get in time without special search.

This means another argument for the supersession of the numerous small shops for large 'District Stores'. In the 120 square miles of London, 100 stores properly placed, would prevent any person being more than ¼ mile (7 min. walk) from one of them, and the great majority would be within 3 or 4 min. walk. Yet instead of 100 Drink shops we have some 10,000: instead of 100 bakers, we have over 3,000. And so on for all the trades. Even if each trade had its own store, forming a kind of 'shopping centre' of 20 or 30 shops in the District Market, the economy would be enormous, without giving up our present method of shopping. A general District Store would be, of course, even cheaper.

This is an old Co-op argument, but I have never seen it properly worked out. Can you make any use of it?

Do not get low-spirited or down-hearted. Your lonely life is trying in this way, but you must be on your guard against the tendency. Reason is given to us in order that we may counteract the bad influences of environment. Do not read James Thomson, or any other books of 'low vitality'. Read only 'healthy books'. Counteract your intellectual loneliness by much correspondence (no – I don't mean *only* with me!), and mitigate your imprisonment by as many escapes and companions as possible.

You are bound, in duty to the world, to avoid despondency, because it unconsciously injures your work.

How I wish I could take you out of that depressing *milieu*, and plunge together into active intellectual life. You could bring me the valued stimulus and criticism of the men of ability who are not enthusiasts: I could bring you the equally needed stimulus of the enthusiasts who have what is equivalent to ability. (Again I am sick to remember that you could get all this for yourself: I can bring you nothing save my own love and devotion to duty. It is you who must do all for me. I can do only the man's part in public life – execution.)

I am amused at what Miss Pycroft reports of Marshall. I have sent word to a young Fabian now at Newnham (Miss Dell), in hopes she will go to his lectures. He will be a little astonished if he finds we are as ubiquitous as that seems to imply!

He has sent me a circular inviting me to the preliminary meeting of the proposed Economic Association on Nov. 20, Mr Goschen in the Chair. (But you will probably have had one too: if not, I would send it you. It is a characteristic letter.) I have written very cordially supporting the project, and suggesting other sources of probable pecuniary support. I still think it was a little 'mean' of them all to boycott the Oxford *Economic Review*, which will really be out in January. I shall have a short note in the first number on Poor Law Reform; and I have half agreed to do an article (short) on Eight Hours for the second number, in criticism of one by Rev. Prof. Symes in the January number – that is, if I think criticism is called for.

Wed. 29 Oct

I am sincerely grateful to Mrs Green for her kindness. I think she 'tries' me 'very high', in saying that my history is 'scrappy'. I am not a professed historian, and not many busy people, suddenly called upon to discuss 15th Century history with the greatest authority thereon, would come off even as well as I did! But of course I am flattered to be tried by that kind of standard at all – just as I am grateful to you for always insisting that I should be perfect!

I *am* trying to feel genuine consideration for others' points of view, genuine appreciation of others' lines of work, and a genuine sense of one's own insignificance in the great world. Do not be impatient with me:

it is not an easy or sudden thing to improve one's character. I need your constant help. I *do* feel that you caught me just in time. I had in me (and have still) great potentialities of most evil development. (Do not now 'look back' after 'having put your hand to the plough'. I *am* worth cultivating as things go, in the very great dearth of men at once abler and equally willing for this particular work.)

Do not grieve about your father. Think how much it is that he is happy, and not lingering out his life in constant pain. It is our yearning for continuous life that makes it seem tragic to us when a strong man is overthrown. He has done his work – organised our industry, governed our railways, sheltered our soldiers in the Crimea – now he can properly rest. His present state is comparable to that of a child. If we can abolish disease and accident, we shall all end that way. It is not sad if so regarded: anymore than childhood is sad. One is as much the necessary accompaniment of manhood as the other – and Time is nothing in the matter. 'Before and After' are nothing but our modes of thought. His very want of self-consciousness is a great gain.

I saw Wallas last night: we dined together after a long Fabian business meeting. He tells me Muirhead withdrew from University Hall because of a sudden instinctive feeling that it would injure and compromise his mental life. The one thing he now lives for, intellectually, is perfect clearness and sincerity in Metaphysics and Philosophy. He felt that he would not be able to resist Mrs H. Ward's and Wicksteed's desire to impregnate the place with a vague Theism, in which he could not believe.

Probably he is right. I dislike the way we are all living in a tacit conformity in a creed in which we do not intellectually believe. It tends to demoralisation of character: to lack of perfect truthfulness. And yet one wants to preserve reverence, and also to keep charitable intellectual relations with those who are earnest Christians.

By the way Wallas (who heard from Muirhead the details of my 'party') said that Muirhead was enthusiastic about it, and especially about you. (Do you know, I *do* feel a little of what I suppose is jealousy. But much more gratitude to you for coming.)

Thurs. 30 Oct.

Marshall sends me a kindly reply, inviting Wallas and Shaw to the Economic [Association] meeting. I feel ashamed to think that I hastily wrote for the *Speaker* a reference to him which he would not like. I cut it out at once, but I wish I had not 'felt like' writing it. I *do* feel a sort of reverence for Marshall as 'our leader' in Economics and I always uphold him as such. But I wish he would 'lead' a little.

I have seen confidentially what is at present proposed as the National Liberal Federation programme for the Sheffield meeting, and it marks a very great stride onward, though it contains (as yet!) no reference to Eight

Hours. My *Speaker* article this week will be a signed one in favor of the Miners' Eight Hours Bill!

Do you recognise my hand in the annexed? [*Side note*: extract from *Pall Mall Gazette*]

> Mr Leonard Courtney's literary companion during his Irish tour is said to have been the shilling edition of the *Fabian Essays in Socialism*, from which he was observed to copy copious extracts in his notebook. Is the Deputy-Speaker finding out in what direction his revolutionary idea of a Land Court is taking him?

I heard of the fact from a man who saw Courtney reading it in Ireland. I thought the idea of using the Right Hon. Leonard as a 'floater' for another advertisement of our book, was humorous in the extreme.

No – this tiny book won't do, even for a short week. Here I have no space left even to make arrangements for Leicester.

I will gladly dine with you on Tuesday, but you must tell me your hotel.

The best train would be the Midland from St Pancras at 4 p.m. due 6.12 p.m. (I mention it in case you are detained in London!) You could then give me a simple dinner at 6.30, and go off to the lecture at 8 p.m. (If you *are* detained, we could easily telegraph for dinner). I don't know about hotels, but the Bell Hotel is a good one. I must leave Leicester at 10.40 a.m., to get to Liverpool for the meeting, which is at 3.30 p.m. So I fear I cannot hope to see you – indeed, I had better leave you to find your own way back to your hotel, and go off with my host (Billson, Birdsnest Farm, New Parks, Leicester). *I* want to be as careful for you, as you do.

You must let me call for you at the B.M. for lunch on Monday at 1 p.m.? You must lunch, and so must I. We can thus cheat Time; even if we only talk Co-operative Statistics! I think you would do well to spend, say £5 on these: and then see what you can use. Send Vaughan Nash to me, and we will have an evening together over them.

You shall not have cause to be dissatisfied with my lecture – at any rate, as to tone, either at Leicester or Liverpool, or Stroud! I will do my very best to *be* what I ought to be, and the lecture will follow suit.

'Parting is such sweet sorrow'! Adieu

[*no signature*]

117 PP SIDNEY TO BEATRICE

In the autumn of 1890 Beatrice was making good progress on her Co-operative book, feeling that this was the first November for years 'without terrible despondency'. (BWD 6 November 90) 'I am swimming in mid-water with another by my side and a host to the fore and to the rear of me – with the roar of a great ocean of Coming Humanity overwhelming the personal notes of momentary pleasure and pain': the agony of her passion for Chamberlain now seemed 'like a passed dream'. Sidney, however, was in a dejected state. He was very ill in November with scarlet fever and sent Beatrice 'despairing letters from his sickroom – letters which pain me deeply with their strong emotions'. (BWD 1 December 90) These letters, together with some from Beatrice, have apparently not survived: they were probably returned and included in the batch of letters from her which Sidney burnt that winter. Some indication of Beatrice's feelings was given in her diary entry of 1 December, written after a visit to Box by R. B. Haldane, ostensibly to discuss a possible alliance between the Fabians and his group of progressive Liberals, which included Asquith, Sir Edward Grey (1862–1933), later Foreign Secretary, and Sir Arthur Acland (1847–1926), a Radical M.P. with strong interests in educational reform. Haldane, Beatrice noted, came down 'with an *arriere pensée* of a suitable wife'. Sidney was jealous of Haldane's visit, especially since Beatrice's family situation made it impossible for him to appear at her home an avowed suitor: on his infrequent visits he was usually accompanied by Wallas or Haldane to distract family attention. To check Haldane's matrimonial reconaissance Beatrice explained that she regarded marriage 'as an alternative to suicide'. This was much more than a jest. It was a serious assertion of her independence, for she noted that 'I cannot bring myself to face an act of *felo de se* for a speculation in personal happiness . . . for the simple reason that though I am susceptible to the charm of being loved I am not capable of loving. Personal passion has burnt itself out, and what little personal feeling still exists haunts the memory of that other man'.

James Bryce had just published *The American Commonwealth*.

Wallas had taken Sidney's place for the planned lecture at Minchinhampton.

[*Note at top of letter*] I have dipped and sealed this myself. SW

4 Park Village East, N.W.
Sunday, 30 Nov. [1890]

I was giving up hopes of being able to keep my tryst on Friday, my 'peeling' went on so slowly, but the doctor yesterday said he thought that there would be nothing against my going out on that day, and today I am sitting up – of course not yet out of the sickroom. I believe I shall be able to mix with the world on Friday but of course if the peeling is not actually over tomorrow or so, I shall not be allowed to, and will write to D.H. Hotel to that effect. Let me keep the chance open. Of course I shall not come unless it is quite safe for you.

You have been good to write to me, but you are always 'hard' on me, and you have contrived to make your letters bitter as well as sweet. I did not deserve your scorn about impatience – scorn really of man not of me. Of course I have felt severely the enforced solitude and idleness – I who have *never* been laid up for a day before. It is good and proper that I should feel this impatience, besides being inevitable. But you have no grounds for supposing that I have been a querulous or fretful patient, or that my righteous impatience has been allowed to increase the trouble to myself or others. Do you remember the answer of the officer in battle,

231

when he was jeered at for being afraid? 'If you were half as afraid as I am you would have run away long ago'.

Dearest, you know I *want* you to be my critic and I do not resent it even when I think it forgetful of the 'extenuating circumstances' which I plead in return. But do not attack me as a representative of Man. You have an undercurrent of 'anti-male' feeling, which no doubt answers to some part of your rather wide experience but which I simply don't understand. I know that women say that men are brutal to them. Is not the remedy likely to be found in more frankness, more direct statement on the wo-man's part (? less prudery). Granted that men are obtuse: that is a natural defect, not a moral fault. Do you not think that much of men's brutality to women (I am not speaking of wife-beating or of the wife-beating class) comes from a lack of plain speaking, from the woman's omission to pene-trate the man's obtuseness.

You will find me obtuse enough, but do not fail to take the appropriate means to meet that natural defect. For brutality born of obtuseness is not really morally brutality, because it is unconscious of itself. I think the 'subjection of woman' is bringing as its Nemesis a growing anti-male tension which seems to me (though not unmerited) being bad in its results. It would be an evil thing if women, in any sense, formed a huge trades union or protective confederacy against men. I don't want the next great war to be, as Henry James half-seriously predicts, between the men and the women. And this is arising from the men's obtuseness and the women's contemptuous neglect to penetrate it. I could wish that you cared to take part in the women's movement in politics, (because I believe, allegori-cally, in universal military service); but do not cultivate the anti-male prejudice.

What you say about Bryce's book is very true. It is the book of a pedantic Scotch lawyer, dealing only with externals, and only with such items as can be classified in a closed and unexpansive series of formulas. I agree with every word of the book I think, but regard it as dealing only with a trifling and relatively unimportant part of America, a country which lives more outside of and unaffected by its forms of government than any European nation. I am not enthusiastic about Walt Whitman (and his understanding takes time), but perhaps he should be taken as the exponent of all that Bryce has omitted – the living vigour of the American common people.

I am glad Wallas did well on the 22nd. How much I have missed through this illness! Leicester, and Mrs Holt at Liverpool, and the Minchinhamp-ton lecture, and yesterday the meeting of Leonard Courtney at Oxford where Wallas has gone in my place. Do not let me *really* lose by it.

I *have* thought about my life a little, but the thoughts were so bitter and so despondent that I have tried sometimes to banish them. I shall come back much humbled, and much less hopeful. (Part of this must, of course be discounted as being physical weakness, but part will remain, I *fear*.) I think you are the cause of part, and I will talk it over with you.

I have a new skin, but not a new heart, and I find no hesitation or doubt as to my Aim in life or my love for you. (Did Wallas ever tell you of our German *Freundin* who, talking over marriages said that no woman would marry me, because she could only be my '*zweite Braut*'. I *hope* you will never be more than this – I have tried and I intend to try to make this so – with your help?)

You are cruel to send me my old letter (which I return), and again I think you are 'hard' on me. I wrote that letter with perfect frank sincerity, not in the least intending to 'pose'. I remember it well. So far from feeling 'condescension' I was quite unduly proud, or rather vain, of being consulted by you. I did not feel in the least like condescending to go to you – I *do* think it is hard of you to say that, seeing how glad I was of an excuse to see you again. The minute particulars of my engagements were given in the hope that you would ask me to dinner (I understood, after, that others were coming). I admit that the end of the letter – with its Socialist scorn for palliatives – is unworthy. But I did not then know at all either how clever(!) or how well informed you were on this point.

The letter *is* a stupid one. But it can be read either way, and it was part of my frank disregard for what others might think of me – not yet tamed by the desire that you should think well of me.

Your letters have, indeed, made me very uncomfortable; you *have* been frank with me, and I must not complain, but I wish you could feel it right to write me more about yourself. Am I like the child who wants to pull up the plant to see if it is growing? You must know how I have felt tossing on the pillows these sleepless nights. I *am* impatient as you say, it is a part of me – but I *can* wait at whatever cost, and I know it is necessary: you would not be cruel to me for your own convenience – just as I would not have you do for me anything that is not convenient.

Till Friday at 7.

Sid.

118 PP SIDNEY TO BEATRICE

[4 Park Village East, N.W.]
[4 December 1890]

I cannot, after all, go out tomorrow. My 'peeling' is not absolutely finished, and I am told I should endanger my life if I went straight from this room into the present weather.

I feel that this is a crisis in my life, and I beg you to be patient. You have apparently misunderstood my letter, which was not meant as a reproach. When I said that part of my despondency was caused by you I referred only to my career, which I wanted to talk over with you.

233

Now that I am debarred from seeing you I must write, imperfectly, what I have been thinking with infinite bitterness during these days and nights of sickness. I have come sadly to the conclusion that my own view of myself of a year ago is more correct than those which have been pressed on me this year by you and others. Six months ago I thought it probable that I should presently, at some favorable juncture, leave the civil service, and attempt to carve out a way, for myself, of public service in some more honored sphere. My reflections now lead me to abandon that project or hope. I shall, indeed, stand ready to do anything that may seem to be required of me. But I no longer think it *probable* that I shall leave the civil service. I go back to my earlier thoughts, and expect to remain all my days a clerk in the Colonial Office.

Why do I trouble you with this? Partly because you were the main cause of my changing my expectations: you by believing in me made me believe in myself. Now that I have lost again that belief in myself, I turn to you – but I have no title to do so.

This leads me to the next point. I see that I must forego the hope of your one day consenting to marry me. Almost the last time we met – the days at Box – I seemed to understand that you did not then think it absolutely impossible. The very next letter I received was such that I could dream it was an acceptance. But you made me understand that the time at any rate was not yet, and that the utmost I could hope for was a *mariage de convenance* or *de raison* on your part. Beggars are not choosers, and I do not pretend to spurn what has not been offered. Besides, the advantage of our union to the cause we have both at heart, is conspicuous and undeniable.

But now that I have come to the conclusion that I shall in all probability never be anything more than a Civil Service Clerk; now that I once more regard myself, not as a potential leader, but merely as a skirmisher; now that I feel, as I most sincerely do, that your book on Co-operation (as it is better than anything I have yet done) is also better than anything I am likely to do – now that I realise all this, I also realise how *impossible* it would be for you, when the decisive moment came, to fly in the face of your whole family and connection to marry me, for reasons which you could hardly even make clear to them. I could not, in decency, press you to do it. I doubt whether even you *could* do it, even if you had agreed.

Of course, as you once said, it would be easy if you loved me. But you have let me see only too clearly that you don't. (Yet two months ago your action led me astray. You have tried to be frank with me, but you have told me little of your mind, and I confess I don't understand you.)

Do not think that I am reproaching you: I am saved from the pain of mistrusting you if only by my very feeling of ignorance of your springs of action. I write this in the utmost bitterness of soul: I have spent nearly a month thinking about it, I have been down into the Valley of the Shadow of this particular Death, and I have come to see that I must in all fairness tell you that my optimistic feeling that you *must* come to see as I then saw, is no longer there.

I need hardly say that I still love you with all my strength. If you ever come to care for me I believe our lives would fit in a joint harmony which would give both of them an almost incredible expansion. I still believe that we can do, together, several times as much as we can do separately. It seems comic to put this into a diagram, yet I cannot refrain

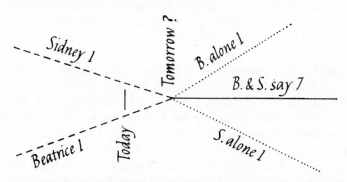

I decline to be quite sure that you will not one day see this. But I must, in very self-respect, leave it to you, as a Queen, to signify your pleasure. (Only don't use an ivy leaf or any other indirect expression liable to be un-noticed!)

I had saved all this to *tell* you – I find that I too often write in ways that are misconstrued. Do not be offended by anything I have said: my heart is very sore as I write; believe that I have *meant* nothing but honesty.

If you are still in the mind you were two months ago; if there is ever so small a possibility that I might one day be more to you – let me wait under whatever conditions you please. Surely you will not have come to any fresh decision in these weeks when I have lain imprisoned. But if you have done so – if you are *quite* sure that no advantage to your own life or mine, or to the Socialist cause, could ever induce you to marry me – then it is your duty to tell me so, now at any rate, and I must bear it how I can. What I have borne these weeks will help me. But I pray that this may not be your meaning.

I have no claim upon you but I think you will not refuse to let me see you before you decide definitely against me. I shall no doubt be back from Bournemouth on the 15th. Can you come back from Manchester by way of London? And do not *write* me anything about it until then.

S.

4 Park Village East, N.W.

5 Dec./90

I cannot resist writing to you immediately, though I feel very bitterly that my letters have undone me.

I want to assure you that I feel no anger, no bitterness against you. Your letter is an honorable and worthy one, and I am surprised to find that I am convinced that you have decided aright. (Do you remember that I said long ago that, however you decided, I should feel sure you had decided right? I had doubts whether this promise was justified. It proves to have been.)

It would be idle to pretend that I shall not suffer. But no one can realise how much I have already suffered from my despondent suspense. I do not intend to be overwhelmed. I do not reproach you, but I think you ought to do what you can to help me. I feel sure you will. I must express one thing that I feel, for the sake of frank honesty. I think *you* were chiefly in fault for the misunderstanding of the beginning of Oct. which has wrecked my suit. The suit *is* wrecked and I accept your decision, but I am, I feel, peculiarly unlucky in thus permanently suffering for what was really the result of an oversight of yours, without which I should never have dreamt of precipitating things. I know how much you must regret this, and it shall be my duty to lessen that regret by getting my wound healed as well as possible. But I could not carry this reflection in my mind without confessing it to you.

I feel that the 6 and 7 Oct. were the zenith of my life: ever since then things have gone badly with me all round: I have (as I said) lost faith in my own 'luck'; my Star has set.

But of course I know that I am, at this moment, unable to form a fair judgment on this.

Surely I am exceptionally unlucky. I have never wooed any woman but you: nothing could have been more unskillful than my conduct: yet for two blissful days it seemed that I was happier than I had ever dreamed of being: and then the collapse. My trial has been no light one.

Now my duty is to be as efficient as possible. It is not necessary that I should forget you, or cease to feel for you what I feel for no one else, provided that this impairs neither your efficiency or mine. I make no promise of eternal constancy or perpetual devotion. I mean, I make no vow even to myself. The future shall be as it will, in that respect. And I accept your decision. You will not find that I have ceased to love you, but I will cease to regard you as a 'marriageable' person.

If I adhere to that, do not let us cease to be friends, and intimate friends. Let us continue to correspond, and to see each other when we can. Let us at any rate try the experiment. If I find it unnerves me, I solemnly promise to tell you so, with a view to other arrangements. Let us continue to 'warm both hands before the fire of life'. I shall need all your counsel. You may, perhaps, be able to utilise my help.

I agree to postponing our meeting until after Xmas. (But *soon* after!) I *do* want to see you very badly.

Yesterday I was half mad with rage at the doctor and nurse who had deceived me, and made it at the last moment impossible to go to you. And then I was half mad with despair at my own despondent thoughts. I do not want to 'withdraw' my letter: I believe I conveyed my meaning in it. But do not resent any word in it that I may have improperly used. If you knew how much I suffered yesterday you would not condemn me for a hasty word.

It now appears that I can't get away to Bournemouth on the 8th. If you can send me any word of comfort – if you can only promise me the 'status quo' of two months ago, pray do so at once. If you don't care to do this, tell me whether you can see me on the 15th in London. I would then arrange to go to Bournemouth on the 16th. But if you don't need to bring matters to this crisis, perhaps I would start on the 12th or so, and talk to you when I am stronger. My head burns with rage and despair, and I can't sleep.

S.

I am bathed and pronounced 'clean', and sleep downstairs tonight.

120 PP SIDNEY TO BEATRICE

John Dennis Paul, an ironmonger, was a talented amateur geologist and a magistrate: he had been a member of the Leicester Literary and Philosophical Society since 1877.

[4 Park Village East, N.W.]
6 Dec. [1890]

I could not get this posted yesterday without the danger of suspicion. I am downstairs today, and shall probably go out for a little walk.

I am not going to Bournemouth so soon as Monday. The Col. Office peremptorily says I am not to resume until Xmas – chiefly from kindness to me, I believe, as I have the reputation of not sparing myself! By the way, your belief in my 'moral refinement' makes me feel ashamed. I only *try* to be good: I am not always instinctively 'morally refined'. I hate to have you think better of me than I am.

The *loneliness* of life! What a 'long unlovely street' it seems. Pray let us continue friends for I feel I have literally no one else. I *cannot* go to Bournemouth alone, and it is not certain that Wallas can go. My sister (a most capable, unselfish and devoted woman) cannot leave my mother for a single night. But of course it is the blankness of the future that oppresses me. You have such a wide circle of friends, and the power of keeping them. My illness has shown me how few I have.

I suppose all this is morbid and temporary, due to the coincidence of a physical and a mental shock. I hope that it may be so. I *am* better than I was. I could even sleep last night. You need not fear any Wertherism.

Write to me from Leicester as if I had never been any else than an *intimate* friend. Tell me what you have done there, and what you think about things. I should like you to know my friend John Dennis Paul there, a leading townsman (non-political), chairman of the local Philosophical Society this year. He is a delightful companion – antiquarian etc. – about 50, married. I must write to him presently. Would you like him to call on you at the Bell? He could show you everything in Leicester.

One thing to conclude. How fortunate I am that my idol is not shattered – that is where the mental danger would have been. *Au revoir.*

Sidney Webb

121 PP BEATRICE TO SIDNEY

Box House, Minchinhampton, Glos.
[?7 December 1890]

I will see you of course – but not on the 15th. If you wish it urgently – if you wish to feel the whole thing behind you, I will see you before you leave London. I shall be at the Bell, Leicester, until Thursday (probably) and I could run up any day. But my strong advice is – go away for a fortnight or more to Bournemouth – and we will meet soon after Xmas when you are stronger. There will be other things to settle besides the all-important question of our present friendship – we shall both need all our strength and calmness.

Meanwhile, I must tell you really what I feel. I cried very bitterly over your letter – and tossed about the night through feeling how wrong it had been of me to have been led away from my better judgment last spring and to have granted your request for friendship. But that is now done – and cannot be undone – the question is what is the present position?

First – all you write about your career does not in any way affect the one question. It would suit my work – and therefore me – far better to marry a clerk in the Colonial Office than a leading politician to whose career I should have in the end to sacrifice my own. It was exactly your position which made me hesitate – it was this with your views and your moral refinement which made me try to love you.

But I do not love you. All the misery of this relationship arises from this. It is now six months that we have known each other intimately – and yet there is no change in my feeling except a growing certainty that I cannot love you.

238

To be perfectly frank I did at one time *fancy* I was beginning to care for you – but I was awakened to the truth by your claiming me as your future wife – then I felt – that what I cared for was not *you* but simply the fact of being loved: and this self knowledge has become clearer every day. That was a fortunate misunderstanding. I might have drifted on feeling the whole thing too remote to decide on and enjoying the meaning of love – yet refusing to give in return – and then when the time came there would have been a terrible crash – I should have refused to carry out what would have seemed to you a tacit promise.

Frankly, I do not believe my nature is capable of love. I came out of that six years agony uninjured as a worker – I came out of it less egotistical, more sympathetic, with no cynicism nor bitterness against men and the world – my whole nature rebounded into an energetic, hopeful, impersonal life – doubtless there was a great big dash of contempt which has taken a personal form. But I came out right as I told you at Glasgow – like a bit of steel – I was not broken but I was hardened – the fire must do one or the other. And this being the case – the fact that I do not love you – I cannot, and will never, make the stupendous sacrifice of marriage. If I loved a man – if *ever* I love a man – the sacrifice of an insignificant work will seem a good riddance. But this is in itself a test of my feeling.

There is only one main point I must chase up.

You are mistaken in thinking that my family would influence me; after my Father's death I should say little more of this in my case. But during his life-time – and it may last for years, I could not marry a man that *he* did not approve of – I could not give him that pain. That is the only possible way in which your position or views would affect the possibility of our marriage. Whereas I could marry anyone of 6 of my brothers-in-law – all of whom are (*he* considers) substantial men – I could not marry either of the other 2. I feel obliged to tell you this for I have unwittingly posed as the devoted daughter who would not leave a dying father. A 'good marriage' – would be perhaps the only pleasure I could give him – it is his last remaining wish – but I would not give him pain – so that if I had *loved you* we must have waited – 10 years if need be. You will understand that the past is another test of my feeling. Without love I could not consent to go, perhaps for many years, with a weight round my neck – neither would it be fair to you – for it would be cruel to wake up at the end. I find that I repudiated the debt when I felt at last I could pay it. This makes it absolutely necessary that our present relationship should be ended: we must both be absolutely firm.

I have written all this about myself – because you said you did not understand me – and because it is right you should know the whole truth.

But one word about yourself. Honestly I believe in you far more completely than I have ever done before. But I think it may well be that you

239

will never be a leading politician – I do not and have never *envied* this position for you – I have mainly thought that you would throw yourself into the gap if need be.

But you have a great and holy trust tied upon you – *your life will be a leading one towards what is true* – towards a noble and better state – and that after all is all that you and I care about.

Do not fail in the crisis of your life – do not be disheartened because the immediate road to personal happiness is closed to you. Think of your life and of your health and strength as not yours to give away or to fritter but as belonging to the Cause to which we are both ably devoted.

Ever yours

BP

122 PP   BEATRICE TO SIDNEY

Beatrice passed through London on her way to Leicester, but did not see Sidney. She felt 'cold at heart after my miserable correspondence' with him. (BWD 12 December 1890)

[Box House, Minchinhampton]
[?9 December 1890]

Dear Mr Webb

I want to add one word to my letter of Sunday.

You are not alone in your suffering. I have suffered acutely this last week – indeed ever since I felt that I must no longer mislead you. I suffer from knowing of your suffering and also from a new sense of the terrific 'loneliness' of life. You say I have friends – but friends are good for bright days – the nearest friend cannot help you in dark times.

And now do not think it needful to decide anything till you are quite strong. Turn your thoughts to other things – it is partly your weakness that has forced you [to] dwell morbidly on one side of life.

God bless you: I would give a good deal to have it all undone – all I can do now is to insist on the past being wiped out, or broken with.

Ever yours sincerely

BP

123 PP   SIDNEY TO BEATRICE

Auguste Comte's attachment to Clothilde de Vaux in 1845 and 1846, when she died, was regarded as a model of elevating purity, reflected especially in his *Politique Positive*, 1851–54. This letter was almost certainly misdated; it was probably written on Saturday 13 December 1890.

I have been here with Wallas since Thursday: it is very cold but bright, and I feel quite well, going out morning and afternoon for good walks, and the rest of the time reading and 'loafing' round the fire. (This boarding house life is soul-destroying, it is impossible to work in a houseful of consistently idle people: they lower the moral and intellectual atmosphere.) I think we shall only stay here until the 18th, and then spend Xmas somewhere in the Isle of Wight. I would much rather be back in London.

Wallas goes up on Monday for the night, to dine with Mrs Green and meet Haldane. I feel a little jealous that the matter thus falls to Wallas to begin, but it may well be for the best, as Wallas comes fresh to it, without having 'sparred' with Haldane in the past. I do not yet feel sure that Haldane realises that (although we are 'willing') they must make, not only the first advance, but also some *public* progress before we can do anything for them. We can't ask the Clubs to support *persons*, but only measures or programmes. At present Haldane and the rest are not associated in the public mind with any policy: what reputation they have is rather to their detriment in this connection.

You will have had bad weather for your week's travellling, and your cold: I am sorry that any mental trouble should have come with it. But you will have had the best anodyne, a definite task of work to be done; and you certainly need not reproach yourself with anything as far as I am concerned.

Indeed, if you could see me you would be reassured in this respect. I think I have recovered. I am certainly not unhappy, and not in the least 'tearing my hair' or pining away. I eat and sleep well, and am not afraid of my own thoughts. I do not think I am one to let the inevitable trouble me long. I am not doing any work, and I seem to have lost a certain optimistic fatalism, a conviction that 'I was not born to be hanged', and that things would eventually obey my will. But all this may be ascribed partly to my illness, and although it seems permanent, may be temporary only. I am rather like the savage during an eclipse who cannot be persuaded by the missionary that the sun is not put out.

Indeed it is this that mainly annoys me. I have lost my 'self-respect', my buoyancy (perhaps my intolerable self assertion!) Illness is a great humiliator; the weakness, the uselessness, pull down one's energy. I now say, mockingly, that I must get the Liberal Party to add to its Programme the 'Abolition of Scarlet Fever', on the ground that it is a most serious infringement of Individual Liberty, and totally inconsistent with Self-Help.

Now I come to your question, are we to be friends or strangers? In your solicitude for me you were bound to put the alternative, and possibly the conventional couple would adopt it. It is lucky that we neither of us (I venture to believe) desire to do so, because I do not think it is permitted to us. I think you are in duty bound to join the Fabian Society, to act with us, and to lend your counsel in public affairs to those with whom you agree. It would be wicked of you to withdraw your friendship from Wallas, for instance, and you could not without betraying what is now *my* secret, make any marked break. I, who am neither an artizan nor a millionaire, cannot go away from my work, even if I were not bound by considerations of public duty. Those same considerations compel us, I think, to be friends, even if it were painful to us. Fortunately it is not. We cannot undo the past six months. (I would not have them undone for anything: it may well be that they are the happiest for me in my life. I do not know what may be the happiness of being loved, so I cannot compare. But I do know that the happiness of loving is as much happiness as I ever aspire to: I cannot believe there is anything beyond it. And besides, what have I not learnt? It is indeed, a 'liberal education').

But although we cannot efface those six months, we may easily resume our friendship, let us say, at the point of last April when I was with you at Box, and you saw in me nothing but an impetuous and 'crude' political agent, to whom you could give useful counsel.

Of course you are quite right to impose conditions: indeed, the conditions are such as would 'impose themselves'. I quite agree to them all. I suppose I must return your letters, I will do so when I return to London at the end of the month. Please do not *return* mine: I should hate to see them again. Destroy them if you like – but I shall never be ashamed of my love for you. I am not in the least ashamed of falling in love, though of course one is not anxious to mention it except where need be.

Do not refuse to continue to correspond. I will not write to you until I am back at work again – until the New Year that is. Indeed I hope the opening letter of the *new* correspondence will be one from you very early in January, asking me to meet you in London on the old footing. You may quite confidently trust me. It will be nearly three months since we shall have met.

I do not see why we should not be '*intimate*' friends, but that will be as you please. I want you to let me tell you what I do and think, and then to counsel me upon it all. I have no right to know your life, and I don't know that I could be helpful to you. But that will be as you please.

The friendship between a man and a woman of like sympathies can be a very beautiful thing: of infinite use and joy to both of them. The danger is of exciting hopes of a closer relationship. Now in this case I have a warning which has been made clear in a painful way – perhaps with almost every circumstance (other than your conduct) calculated to increase the pain. I fully accept the situation. Would it be wise of us to shut the door on a friendship which may prove of infinite service to us, and some kind of mitigation of that 'loneliness' which one can't help feeling in the world. Can we justly afford to throw this chance away?

I see no reason why it need preclude or hinder either you or me falling in love and marrying elsewhere, if this be our destiny. You *could* not *deserve* any reproach if you ever did so; and I cannot conceive myself reproaching you – or even *thinking* it.

I can go further. Dearest, I can never again write to you without reserve. Let me say what I feel tonight, without disguise. I sincerely *hope*, for your sake and for the world, that it may come to you to marry. As it cannot be me, I do most sincerely hope there may be someone else. I am afraid for you. It seems very difficult for a woman to go on leading a lonely life, without wifehood or motherhood, without unconsciously losing much of 'warmheartedness', without sinking into sourness and narrowness. It may well be so also in a man. A life without the inner family relations is cut off from much which cannot be otherwise supplied, the absence of which tends to warp, unconsciously, the whole judgment and temperament.

Dearest, resist this. Do not in your search for Truth, forget the need of warmheartedness or (as I once before said) you will not get Truth. 'Great thoughts come from the heart' – and the heart needs *nourishing*.

I have borne without undue shock, the pain of your rejection of me. But I conceive that there might come a second and much more serious shock which would destroy all my belief in humanity, and make me cynical and cruel. You have not *betrayed* me, and I am therefore whole. But if, at some future time, you would so far be led away, either through your loneliness or in your 'superiority', to give up the People's Cause, to abandon work, or, worse still, to make a merely 'good' marriage with an unsocialist person – then my pain would come again many times worse than before. You tell me to take care of *my* life: yours is the more valuable because you can write, and I am not sure that it may not be exposed to more danger.

Perhaps I ought not to have said this. I shall never have the chance to say it again, and I want you to understand that I care for your own life more even than I care for you. But of course *I* have nothing to lose by your marriage, which might still leave me your friendship.

Yes: life is lonely. But are you not hard on friends, in saying they are only for bright days? You ought not to feel that. Surely the sympathy – even better, perhaps, if a silent and merely companionable sympathy – of a true friend, is worth a great deal when the world is at its greyest. Friendship is a very beautiful thing and we do wrong not to *cultivate* it more. Surely a friend like Wallas – I am feeling *very* grateful to Wallas for coming away to take care of me in my convalescence – is worth a great deal on dark days. If I needed your help, I believe you would give it to me. But it is not in such emergencies that friendship is *made*. Ought we not to set aside, in our days of strength and independence, some hours every week or month, merely to cultivate a few intimate friendships?

I am like Auguste Comte: as I cannot have what I want, I make a virtue of wanting only what I can have! But the friendship of Clothilde de Vaux was invaluable to Comte, in developing all the better side of his nature. We do not know the effect on her, but she can hardly have helped gaining. Let this be an omen.

I don't know whether this is the kind of letter that I *ought* to write. I am writing just as I think. I could not anyhow make the letter worthy of the occasion, because it is a great occasion. Next time I must write only as a friend. But *be* my friend, as you well know how, and I shall learn gradually to cease to regret that you would be no more.

Sidney Webb

124 PP BEATRICE TO SIDNEY

Bell Hotel, [Leicester]

Sunday, [?14 December 1890]

Dear Mr Webb

Your letter of Saturday is quite worthy of you and of the trust I laid on you when I granted your request last spring. You promised me then that you accepted the intimate friendship with all its risks, and that you would abide by my final desire. I am grieved that my foolish words caused that misunderstanding last October: but you are wrong in thinking it has done more than give you pain – the end must have come tho' it might have come more gradually.

Now about the future. I cannot honourably allow you (at least for the present) to be my intimate friend; and personally, I think it would be far better for you that we should see nothing of each other and that I should even sever my acquaintance with your immediate friends. It was about this latter part that I wanted to talk to you at what I expected would be our last meeting. But I am willing to remain on friendly (tho' not intimate) terms on these conditions.

(1) That any correspondence between us should be so worded that it might be read by anybody, and that if it ceases to be so worded that in itself should be sufficient to break off all relationship.

(2) That all the letters written by either to the other up to the end of this year should be returned to the writer thereof in a sealed packet; and that the sender should declare that none have been retained.

(3) That I should receive from you, with my letters, a solemn promise that you will break off the friendship if you find it is leading again to hopes and that on no possible contingency will you reproach me (supposing I should marry another man – to put it in its extremest form) for having

misled you. That you will take on yourself the whole responsibility. But remember this: I still think it would be wiser for you to 'cut the whole thing'; and I should be quite ready to sacrifice anything to make this possible for you. I am ready however to yield this point; but only on these conditions.

Think all this over: do not write to me for another week or so. It is a crisis in both our lives and needs calm consideration. Until this is settled on a right basis we cannot correspond on intimate matters. The conditions I have given you are the 'minimum' and must not be disputed – though of course they may be refused which will be our way of terminating our relationship. That is why I say do not write at present – I should consider any refusal of these conditions as a way of telling me that you thought as I did – that the whole thing should be broken. I write from my bed: I have been poorly and out of sorts lately – and hotel life in bitter cold weather is not invigorating.

Yours sincerely

Beatrice Potter

P.S. Do not think me hard; I am thinking more of you than of myself.

125 PP SIDNEY TO BEATRICE

4 Park Village East, N.W.
30 Dec./90

Here are your letters – everyone I can find or am conscious of possessing. I burnt some in illness.

I suggest that you should not read them – not that there is anything with which you need reproach yourself, but because there would be no utility in your realising the feelings with which I have put together these memorials of a summer. You are not cruel and I know that you feel yourself every turn of the screw of my torture.

Two things support and will support me. I feel absolutely sure of your perfect honesty, to me and to your own self, and that I may count on an unconventional frankness.

And I do not forget, as I have never forgotten, that I have an *erste Braut* in my yearning to do good work: your face has never lain, and does not now lie, between my work and me, but beyond my work.

I find I am not less irritable than before with a dull adversary or ally, but even more – perhaps through illness. I have taken for my motto '*Be Patient*' – that is what your initials shall mean to me.

Sidney Webb

Reviewing the past year in her diary Beatrice noted that the 'tie that was tightening between me and another I have snapped asunder, and I am alone again, facing work and the world'. It had been 'unbearably fretting' her; she felt the disapproval of the Booths; she realised that 'owing to his social status' she could not marry Sidney while her father lived 'without grieving the poor old man past endurance' – and she increasingly felt that it was too difficult to 'go about the world with a hidden tie but apparently free'. Sidney, she conceded, had '*behaved nobly*': she consented to see him 'provisionally on all intimacy being discontinued'. (BWD 31 December 90).

On 31 December 1890 she acknowledged the return of her letters, regretting 'the misunderstanding and mistakes which have led to your pain and, to a lesser degree, to my own'. She told Sidney that she depended on 'your other promise that you will sever the acquaintance if you feel that you are desiring ties which can never be – in that case an absolute breach will be the only remedy – and one which you are bound to take'.

The Saturday that week fell on 10 January.

Box House, Minchinhampton, Glos.

[?1 January 1891]

Dear Mr Webb

I accept your assurance that you will not allow our friendship to lead to misunderstandings and that you fully and unreservedly agree with the conditions laid down. I have every reason to trust you – to trust you implicitly.

I shall be coming up to London January 9th (*Saturday*). I should like to see you and Mr Wallas, so that we might discuss the future together. I will write later on and ask him to keep that evening free – if you will do so – there are many things I want to talk over with you – including the idea of my joining the Fabian Society. I am not certain whether it would be [the] wisest thing to do.

Yours sincerely

Beatrice Potter

P.S. Your letter is very noble in its tone; but you will of course remember that in future you must write as a friend, as a friend only.

Beatrice noted in her diary on 4 January that one reason for her reluctance to join the Fabian Society was 'lest it should injure my chances as an investigator': she agreed to subscribe rather than formally join. When she dined with Sidney and Wallas on 3 January she found Sidney in 'a thoroughly weak miserable state . . . excited and jealous . . . more deeply involved than ever'. She went back to Box with 'a hidden feeling that perhaps it will be impossible for me to continue honourably as S.W.'s friend'.

[? Box House, Minchinhampton]

January 13 [1891]

Dear Mr Webb

I send an annual subs. to the Fabian Society: would you kindly let it be entered under my initials?

I will increase it when the money is wanted.

Take care of yourself: you are not yet recovered from that attack of fever. I expect you will find your office work about as much as you can do.

I never thanked you for the extracts which will be very useful to me: I found your last book also very helpful.

When do you say Mr Schloss is going to lecture? I think I must run up for it.

Always yours sincerely

Beatrice Potter

P.S. I wish I were *absolutely convinced*: I am not yet. Every now and then I am haunted by a fear of waking up from a dream: my individualist antecedents have still a hold on me.

BP

128 PP   SIDNEY TO BEATRICE

David F. Schloss was a man with some private means whose sense of public spirit led him to become concerned with wages and factory conditions. He was a Fabian sympathiser.

William Thomas Thornton's book, *On Labour: Its Wrongful Claims and Rightful Dues; Its Actual Present and Possible Future*, was published in 1869. Frederic Harrison's article on *Industrial Co-operation* was published in the *Fortnightly Review*, Vol. XVI, January 1866. E. S. Beesly's *The Social Future of the Working Class* was a lecture, printed in the *Fortnightly Review* and published as a pamphlet in 1869.

A. A. Baumann was a Conservative M.P. who sat for Peckham in 1885–86.

4 Park Village East, N.W.

19 Jan./91

Dear Miss Potter

It would be my duty to write to you, even if I did not want to do so: there are several points to tell you of and consult you about on purely public affairs. We are so far *bound* to work in concert, that we are under an obligation to be friends.

But let me begin with personal matters. I was horribly upset on Sunday week, as you will have known (and no doubt Mrs Green also, now), and I believe I acted abominably. Afterwards I was angry with you for falling, as it seemed to me, short of my ideal of you. I need hardly say that the result was that I was frightfully unhappy.

247

But now, thinking over your letter (your cheque did not make me less angry!) I am prepared to admit that my anger may not have been justified, and I apologise. You see, I did not know you were still in the stage of doubts. (How you must have wondered at many of the things I said last summer, which proceeded on the assumption that you were as fanatic as I am.)

Clearly you are right not to commit yourself until you are past that stage. I dare say we can manage to keep the Fabian Society alive and undivided until then.

I was morbid on Sunday but I had a horrible vision of your ruthlessly sacrificing everything to the perfect fruition of an intellectual 'idolon'. I felt that although enthusiasm involved disproportion and therefore error, yet it was certain that Truth could only be attained in it and through it. Because I was sincerely concerned for you, I was very vexed that I had committed myself to the position I took up, because it made it even more difficult for you to be convinced.

I do not overrate the value of your books, nor do I imagine that you regard them otherwise than from the point of view of social effectiveness, but I felt, as I still feel, that you were, in your isolation, taking up a position full of subtle moral danger – a danger which my own temperament would eagerly avoid, even at the risk of impairing the perfection of the books. But each one must decide for himself, and possibly my own dread of failing to answer to all the calls of the moment, is a moral weakness rather than a moral strength. I do sometimes believe this. The man who turns away from drowning men whom he could help, because he is absorbed in perfecting a lifeboat which will one day save thousands instead of units – I am forced to admit that he may be justified. In my own case I have no confidence that there *is* any lifeboat, and such as there may be, I always think that I can do both *sufficiently* well. No doubt the latter reason is powerful: I have little artistic feeling for perfection. There seems to me a 'law of diminishing return' as regards quality. Moreover, I am in dread of that horrible intellectual coldness which unconsciously grows upon the student. The turning away from drowning men, even if intellectually justified, is terribly atrophying to the emotions, and 'Great thoughts come from the heart': the divorce of thought from action (which kills the Universities) is a serious danger, and a strong argument for 'joining one's party'. It may be that I sacrifice thought to action too much: and action is imperfect, one-sided, hurried, lacking in distinction – especially the action that falls to minor men. But pray do not you sacrifice action to thought, for you would then, gradually and quite unconsciously to yourself, cease to get even thought.

I don't want to seem to complain of Fate, and I am really doing very well, considering. The fever has been a turning point in my life in more ways than one, and I don't feel sure which way I am now going. I have got to stand alone, but whether I can do so is not certain. What potentialities there were in me before, are no longer there. 'We are betrayed by what is false within', says Meredith, and I see myself failing daily in points or morals, of which I fear the cumulative effect. But I don't know that anyone could help me, even if anyone cared to do so. I only know that I am seriously in need of help.

Now let me come to more important matters. First, I presume you know Thornton on 'The Claims of Labor', Frederic Harrison's article on Labor, Political Economy and Co-operation in the *Fortnightly*, about 1866. Beesly's 'Future of the Working Classes' (a pamphlet). These which I have lately been reading all refer to Co-operation; I see nothing in them of value, but you ought to know of them.

I had Schloss to dinner and talked Co-operation and Sweating. He is going to deal only with the mistaken Economics of Co-operation and Profit Sharing, and show that it is *not* a magic or new industrial system. He says that I tried to bring out what was not there – a useful propagandist method but not a scientific analysis. He suddenly asked me if I remembered your article in the *Speaker*, and said it seemed to him a hopeless confusion, and utopian optimism!

As regards Sweating I have rewritten Sydney Buxton's draft Bill, putting in as much as he would accept, of liability on the giver-out. I am to see him again on Wednesday. If I can get a proof for you to advise on, I will send you one. It is of some consequence, as he *may* get his Bill committed with the Govt. Bill, and Sir H. James's (i.e. textile unions).

Schloss strongly urged appointing a Special Committee for five years, to carry out the Acts in the East End, thus relieving the H.O. [Home Office] of domiciliary workshops, and bridging over the making of District Councils. What do you think of this? I do not see that the Govt is at all likely to do it, but would it be a good thing to press on the Liberals?

Would you revise the definition of domestic workshop? At present, even two women (sisters or mother and daughter) making neckties in one room = a dom. workshop, though only a few things apply to it. Buxton, following Dunraven and Baumann, wants to raise it to a minimum of 3 persons, and thus relieve the smallest ones from *all* Factory Law. I don't think it matters much, as a family group is seldom less than three and it may make it easier to increase the restrictions. Can you advise on these points if possible by return of post? But do not bother about them if you don't feel interested in helping Buxton to make his Bill as perfect as possible.

I have been writing the 'History' of the Eight Hours Movement – there is none available, and we have no time to read old newspapers at the B.M. For the United States I have got on fairly well, thanks to their Bureau Reports, but for England I am sadly lacking in materials for a record of the reductions in the hours of Labor. There are the Factory Acts and their

Story and the Social Science Association on T. Unions. But I have practically nothing else. Can you suggest anything? I treat the Eight Hours Movement as merely the Child of the Ten Hours and Nine Hours.

What were Owen's hours at New Lanark?

Do you know anything of the origin of the cry for Eight Hours? Do you confirm Sargant's statement that Owen advocated an *Eight* Hours Day in 1817?

Massingham will have told you that he has left the *Star* for good. I have written Stuart a long and very frank letter – from the point of view of one who had believed in him and yearned to find him still honest in spite of appearances. He has not replied – at any rate not yet. Wallas and I are to see Haldane and the Greys on Saturday.

Yours truly

Sidney Webb

Hollington and Gardiner were large wholesalers in the tailoring trade.

Box House, Minchinhampton, Glos.
[?21 January 1891]

Dear Mr Webb

I can find no trace in Owen's books of the 8 hours: he does not credit himself with it, which he is apt to do with most things. The hours at New Lanark were $10\frac{1}{2}$: and his Factory Bill proposed to Parliamentary Ctee was a $10\frac{1}{2}$ hours Bill. (I think you will find the details in his Auto.)

With regard to the Sweating Bill I stupidly stick to my point that no good will be done if *any* industrial premises are relieved; as the trade will inevitably drift into the unregulated channel. Neither do I think it possible to secure efficient inspection of the mass of workshops that would be included within the limit of 3 workers without the responsibility of the giver-out. There must be in London some 4 or 5000 of these workshops; the idea of *inspecting* them seems to me hopeless: the only way is so to harass the wholesale trader that of his own accord he withdraws the work from them. Three cases in court, with the vexations and expense and public odium would do more to drive Messrs Hollington and Gardiner's trade into Factories than the devoted labour of 300 Inspectors – *without the responsibility of the giver-out.*

Nothing short of an indirect tho' practical prohibition of Home-Work will be any good whatsoever.

About the 'Commission'. I really do not quite understand the suggestion, so I can't give an opinion.

One word on personal matters.

I was surprised and grieved that you had practically told Mrs Green

250

that you regarded me otherwise than as a friend. Her surprise and curiosity were very painful to me. Moreover it makes it increasingly difficult for me to remain on terms of friendship. I have no intention of losing her respect, or of hiding things from her, or even of going out of my way to explain any motives. But you have forced my hand; and laid me open to the reflections of being rather a vulgar coquette. I regret all the more this step as hitherto you have acted with so much honourable discretion – so that you have made a delicate position possible for me. But I will say no more: you will have perceived by this time that to take *my* most intimate friend into your confidence was neither fair nor wise – as it subjects me to enquiries and observation which could only be made by someone with whom I am intimate – and effectually prevents me from seeing you as freely as I should do other friends.

Indeed at first I was convinced that your object was to 'burn your boats' and retire altogether from the relationship – a conclusion which I have often advocated. I return your book with many thanks: will you send me the H.O. memo? Massingham said he had passed it on.

Yours sincerely

B. Potter

You were quite right to write to Prof. Stuart: I should very much like to see the reply, if he writes. Have you a copy of your letter?

130 PP SIDNEY TO BEATRICE

4 Park Village East, N.W.

22 January 1891

Dear Miss Potter

I need scarcely say that I deeply regret that you should have had the least unpleasantness in your relation with Mrs Green. I have confided nothing to her: I had no intention whatsoever of letting her know anything – indeed, I had a positive intention the other way. But, as you will understand, it was difficult to conceal from Mrs Green that I had had a heavier blow than my illness accounted for, and the intuition of a sympathising (and intellectually curious) woman made her suspicious. But (as I told you on the Sunday) I had, up to then, so acted as to give her, *I believe*, no clue whatever, either as to person or subject. On that Sunday evening, however, I feel that I broke down in your presence, and that she must have known what my previous despondency meant. I have not seen her since but a few words (I do not exactly remember them) I wrote apologising for my brutality, at the end of a letter on a point of history, may, as I now see, have sharpened her suspicions. If she assumes to know more, it is unwarranted. I have told her *nothing* of what has happened.

You need not fear that I could ever leave your conduct open to mis-

251

construction. But, for a time, I had no easy task to meet the world. You see, it came just when I was physically weakest and most despondent. There are limits to anyone's capacity for endurance without sign. And Mrs Green was very kind, and very inquisitive. If you knew how hard it was to resist the temptation to tell her all – and I told her nothing, and all one long evening directed her from the truth – you would, I think, not blame me as you are doing.

As regards our continuing to be friends, it must rest with you. I have, as I have told you, come to the conclusion that I, at any rate, am bound in duty to keep on those relations with you which are likely to be useful. I think we can help each other's work in various ways. I have therefore no option, even if it were painful to me. But it is not. I have 'pulled myself together', and am now working well and hard. If you do not care to help me in my personal life, that is for you to decide. I could not afford to remain in fetters – if they were to be only fetters – and I have thrown them off – as you would have wished me to do. There are only two ways in which you will affect my mental life again: and one of them would be if you should, at any time, fail to live up to my ideal of you – if you should prove faithless to what we have both at heart.

That betrayal would be, I find, a worse unhappiness to me than anything that has happened. But I am not distrustful of you, and I will not be suspicious. Try not to think evil of me, and rather tell me frankly what you may, at any time, be beginning to suspect.

I enclose Stuart's reply – which, *to the letter I wrote*, is almost brutal. I have no copy of the letter. Please return this answer.

I have the H.O. Memo. but should much like to keep it a little longer, unless you wish it promptly for other purpose than safe custody. Tell me.

Yours truly

Sidney Webb

Buxton's Bill, will, thanks to your help, go very far.

131 PP SIDNEY TO BEATRICE

On 25 January Wallas wrote to Beatrice describing the dinner evening. There was, he reported, 'a long wrangle' about Liberal policy between Webb and Haldane, Webb arguing that there was a need for a coherent programme to bring the advanced Liberals together. Webb was annoyed by Haldane's pomposity and unwillingness to commit himself: Wallas said Haldane lacked 'moral fibre'. (PP) Benjamin Francis (Frank) Costelloe (1855–99) was a barrister and a Progressive member of the L.C.C. from 1891 until his death. He was a Fabian and a personal friend of Webb.

4 Park Village East, N.W.
27 January/91

Dear Miss Potter

Wallas tells me that he wrote you an account of our interview with

Haldane. I believe I behaved abominably – at first at any rate, I was impatient almost to insolence. Haldane was beautifully good tempered. I am very despondent that I should have again succumbed. I don't know what it means, or what I can do to get over it.

I wrote him a long letter yesterday, apologising as far as was decent, and really trying to help him to put his idea into shape. He actually seemed to think the new junta would be able to *assert* their proposals without *opposing* their contradictories. I fear nothing can come of it from him. He is not willing to give up his life.

I, who say this, am perplexed about my own life. I *like* to stay on at the C.O., but I feel every day more that I am shirking the tasks of life in so doing. The need for *someone* in Parliament is very great, and it is impossible to spring at once into Parliament. The need for new men in the County Council in November next is also very great, and I could virtually ensure a seat there at once. This makes it clearer to me that I ought to give up the C.O. in the autumn; go into the County Council election in Nov. (which I cannot do without resigning here); do my work energetically in the County Council, and throw myself boldly upon the world, to earn my living by journalism and possible scraps of practice at the bar. Twelve years of official life have already so far corrupted me that I am afraid. I distrust my power to earn money; I distrust my physical endurance; I am fearful lest my brain should break down; I dislike and shrink from the publicity, the electoral campaigns and so on.

It is a relief to tell you this, but I do not ask you to take the responsibility of advising me. Everyone – Fairfield, my official colleague who knows the world and me, Wallas, Costelloe, Massingham – concur in pressing it on me. It would be a great surprise and shock to my parents: and a great burden laid upon me. To be weaker than one's task is misery indeed. At present I am much stronger than my task – except this task of deciding! – and it seems to indicate to me that I am not giving the world all that I could give; that I am not realising and putting down on the world's great counter the full 'rent of ability'. If I only knew what I *ought* to do.

I have a headache today, and that, I suppose, accounts for some of the weakness. But if I left the C.O. it would not do to have headaches.

I shall be glad to see your proof. I send a few more references on Co-operation which you may as well keep by you. I have joined the Kentish Town Store, so as to be in the Co-op Union: but I don't know whether I can manage to write the T. Union Essay.

Buxton has adopted practically all my proposals for his Sweating Bill, and you will find that it goes a good length. We incorporate Schloss's idea of a Special Commission if thought necessary.

Is there nothing I can do for you? Do not make our friendship one-sided.

Sidney Webb

Box House, Minchinhampton, Glos.

[?29 January 1891]

Dear Mr Webb

Your letters open a very serious question; and I can fully realise how it must be troubling you to come to any decision; and I know too little about the chances of life to give you any assistance.

Personally, if you can make a livelihood without it absorbing your energies, I do not think that with your strong convictions and your desire to help things forward you will be satisfied without throwing yourself into the stream.

I should imagine it was hopeless to pick up any work at the Bar without waiting about for it in a way which would absorb your energy as much as your C.O. work – and less profitably; but journalism is so easy to you and there is so much demand for the 'Socialist' in the Press that Propaganda and Pot-boiling might become identical.

Then I do not know whether you have saved sufficient to pay electioneering expenses, which could hardly come out of a scanty income; and whether your people are quite independent of your help. The latter question would make all the difference and the anxiety of throwing away a steady income.

I think you are admirably suited to Parliamentary and Administrative Life, and the L.C.C. would be a splendid training. 'Publicity' is not a thing that any citizen ought to shrink from: the whole question seems to me to resolve itself into [?word omitted]. Can you make a sufficiently liberal income in journalism to allow you to do Public Work over and above Pot-boiling?

I understand V. Nash is going to write an Essay for the T.U. and Co-operation prize: it will be hardly worth while for two competent persons to undertake it: he is quite 'sound' on that question.

I am very sorry about Mr Haldane's unwillingness to take any decided step.

Possibly the interview may have some effect on him and Grey without them being ready to pledge themselves.

But the work really lies in the constitution.

Ever yours sincerely

Beatrice Potter

P.S. I have a splitting headache. I suppose it is the sultry weather. Thanks for the other extracts which will no doubt arrive.

BP

Sidney had written on 2 February to say that Haldane had changed his mind and was now 'prepared to work with us', accepting Sidney's suggestion of using the Eighty Club 'as a means of political education': after Sidney had written a note of apology for wrangling with him at dinner their personal relations had improved. Haldane had played the leading role in establishing the Eighty Club and had been its first secretary, then its chairman. He remained rather possessive about it.

Webb and Wallas had dined with Alice Green to meet Sir Alfred Lyall (1835–1911), a distinguished civil servant in India, Liberal Unionist and author, who opposed women's suffrage. Dr Mandell Creighton had just become bishop of Peterborough. The Broadhurst story is that retailed by Beatrice to Kate Courtney in her letter of 1 September 1889. 'John Law' was the pseudonym used by Margaret Harkness for her articles and books.

4 Park Village East, N.W.

23 February/91

Dear Miss Potter

I return by bookpost the H.O. Memorandum. It has been very useful, and I think it has enabled us to make Buxton's Bill the best yet drafted.

I don't know how long you need to have it by you: but, of course, if you could place it at our disposal again during the proceedings in the Standing Committee it would be of great advantage, and might probably result in getting useful amendments carried.

Of course I shall want to see the proofs of the Co-operative book; it takes no time to do that kind of work, and if even one slip can be avoided in a chapter it is worth doing. I believe that proofs ought always to be read by others than the author.

You do not tell me anything about what you are doing, and you do not ask about anything that is going on here. I am not going to believe that this is merely the effect of absorption in the one question you write about: you can hardly have lost all the interest that I believe you formerly had in many other things as to which we have written. One day you will no doubt tell me all about it, face to face: meanwhile I shall assume that you are really a friend, and sincerely interested in your friends.

I believe I am now quite well, and able to do without harm or discomfort whatever work may come to me. And I specially want to go on with what we have been doing in Co-operation and the Factory Acts.

I have not actually decided what I shall do as regards the C.O., but it is more and more plain to me what I ought to do, and I hope I shall have courage enough to do it. There are hidden factors in the problem known to me alone. Meanwhile I am making known that I am for sale, and perhaps some good and well-paid work may come along. I am *bourgeois* enough to want to be able to save a good deal, against old age and a possible breakdown.

Have you heard anything from or about Haldane? He writes to me saying he will manage to see me presently, to arrange. I dined with Sir E. and Lady Grey alone on Friday: they are very nice, but he lacks self-confidence and therefore courage. I doubt whether any of these men can lead.

Buxton has 'scored' heavily with his Factory Bill, but he, too, cannot lead. (The little foible on which Vaughan Nash was so hard has come out very amusingly several times). Just now I think it 'pays' to 'boom' him as much as possible, so as implicitly to supersede Stuart in men's minds.

Stuart, by the way, is now drawing £1000 a year from the *Star* and it is being mismanaged worse than ever. He never does any of his old work now, and neglects even 'C.D. Acts' business which he formerly most cherished.

Wallas and I failed utterly to appreciate Sir A. Lyall, though I believe we were quite polite. I let many of his mistakes pass without attempting to contradict, but he insisted on discussing the things he did *not* understand.

The fact is that we are living at too high an intellectual pressure for the ordinary person, who takes a merely amateur interest in his fellow men. We are, for good or for evil, 'possessed' with our subjects, our ideas and our plans; and we must work this out alone. I can quite see how bad it is; how one-sided one gets; how one fails to establish contact with influential people: and so on. But I see no help except in action, and in the influence of ourselves upon each other. We do all we can in that way to keep ourselves sane, and I see that we can rely only on that. I fear that even so great a sympathiser as Mrs Green is losing interest; and besides she influenced only Wallas and myself.

So your friend Creighton becomes a bishop. I remember thinking, on your description of him, that he must be cut out for this post, with its opportunities and its limitations. He will be emphatically a 'worthy' Bishop – I wonder whether any bishop *could* be more.

I cannot write to you about your own life because you give me no chance. How far did Leonard Courtney convert you? The publication of his polemic in the *Economic Journal* will give point to what I have said as to the intention of the inner circle who control it, that it shall be distinctly an anti-socialist organ. I wrote strongly to Edgeworth on the subject, and refused to put my name down as a supporter. But if they put in Courtney's *political* attack on Socialism, they ought to let me answer it in the next number.

Sidney Webb

I presume you saw John Law on Cunninghame-Graham with *your* Broadhurst story.

Llewellyn Smith spent the weekend of 28 February–1 March at Box. Beatrice proposed that they should collaborate on a book on trade unionism when she had finished her work on Co-operation, suggesting that meanwhile he should do some work on Booth's survey.

Box House, Minchinhampton, Glos.
[?25 February 1891]

Dear Mr Webb

I send you my 2 next chapters: Mr Wallas has sent me most useful corrections of the phraseology, but any suggestion both of style and matter are gratefully received.

I should have written to you more fully but I partly thought that the correspondence had dropped on your side. I am always interested to hear any news you may have about subjects in which we are both of us interested, though I have very little to tell in return.

I am working on steadily at my book and am in the middle of what is practically my best chapter. I shall try to get it all in proof before Easter, leaving the correcting of it to the time I am in London. I should enjoy the writing of it very much if I did not feel pressed for time and space, and if I was not oppressed with my own audacity in attempting to refound the Co-operative Movement in a 2/- book of 220 pages. But there is this to be said: a longer one would not be read by Co-operators. It will provoke discussion if it does nothing else.

When do you want the H.O. Memorandum back? I did not mean to prepare my little speech until the week before the 19th when I have to open the discussion. I am going to try the speech from *notes* and not read a paper. You will of course be careful not to let that memorandum out of your own hands: I do not exactly know what 'confidential' means in this case or whether the H.O. would like it used as an aid to the opposition of a Government Bill. Could you get me a copy of each of the Bills before Parliament? I have not heard or seen anything of Mr Haldane since his visit in the autumn. I sent him the other day the percentages of Co-operative sales to population in Scotland, asking him to give me any information about the occupation of the people in his own districts, but I have had as yet no answer. I am sending the English percentages to Burnett – I can't hope to get more than rough generalisations.

Ll. Smith is coming for Sunday to talk over the book on Trade Unions. If I could get him to take up in conjunction with V. Nash – say T. Union organisation among unskilled labourers – or some other sections – I should be glad. The work is so stupendous that if the whole is to be up to date I must get some fellow-workers and act as editor as well as contributor.

I am ashamed to say I never read L. Courtney's speech but trusted to a version given us by Dr D. Schloss and Judge Jones who were dining here

257

that day. But I have put it 'carefully away' which is unnecessary if it is to be republished in the *Economic Journal*. I imagine it had nothing new in it?

Do not grow too contemptuous of men and women who are not in *your* current of thought and action. An Indian administrator or a bishop would probably consider the Fabians as mere 'amateurs' in the conduct of human affairs. It is quite possible that it is not worth your while knowing too many outsiders – (that is outsiders to your particular line) but do not allow yourself to consider them all as inferiors – do not, fall into Sir A. Lyall's error, and dismiss as unimportant all those sides of life of which you are ignorant and in which you are uninterested. I do not wish to lecture you: but I always regret to see obstacles thrown in the path of an able man by his own temperament – it is so much prose but in the good cause.

We are having lovely weather here: and if I were not so oppressed with the burden of the little book I should be enjoying it. 'J. Law' published that story in defiance of my earnest request – tho' she omitted Broadhurst's name.

Yours very sincerely

Beatrice Potter

135 PP   SIDNEY WEBB TO WILLIAM HENRY FENTON

In terms of practical politics Sidney was a Radical in national affairs and a Progressive in London matters. He sent this 'feeler' to W. H. Fenton who was secretary of the Holborn Liberal and Radical Club and influential in the Progressive Party.

4 Park Village East, N.W.

3rd March/91

My dear Fenton

I am *thinking about* giving up my C.O. place and going in for journalism and public work. This I have not yet decided upon.

If I do it – of course, it is a big plunge – I should wish to stand for the County Council in November, for a tolerably safe seat. I don't think my extreme views would be a drawback for County Council; we are all 'Municipal Socialists' now! And I could put some steam into the contest – I believe you want a new candidate for West Islington, where I have some friends. If the question turns up, bear in mind my name.

Of course I should in that case stand by Lough and back him for Parliament. I am not sure how he regards me.

Tell me whether you think there is anything in this.

Yours truly

Sidney Webb

As the proofs of her Co-operative book became available Beatrice sent them to Wallas and Webb for comment. Edward Owen Greening (1836–1923) was an advocate of 'industrial partnership', a prolific author on Co-operative topics and one of the founders of the Co-operative Congress in 1869. George Howell was Liberal M.P. for Bethnal Green 1885–95. Tom Mann (1856–1941), a member of the Amalgamated Society of Engineers who became a professional organiser, was involved in the 1889 dock strike and one of the leaders of the 'New' unionism. He was active in the S.D.F., later secretary of the Independent Labour Party and one of the founders of the Communist Party in Britain. At this time he was a prominent figure in the London trade union movement and was shortly to be appointed as a member of the Royal Commission on Labour. Ben Tillett had also played a leading part in the 1889 dock strike; he joined the Fabian Society, and his campaign at Bradford in 1892 was the first nomination actually supported by the Society. He later became a Labour M.P. William Pollard Byles (1839–1917) was the editor of the *Bradford Observer* and was elected as Radical M.P. for Shipley in 1892; at this time he sympathised with the Fabians. Elizabeth Haldane was the sister of R. B. Haldane who acted as hostess for her unmarried brother. Benjamin T. Hall (1864–1931), who was involved in early efforts to form a trade union for seamen, was a Fabian, later chairman of the Deptford Liberal Party, and secretary of the Workingmen's Club and Institute Union.

4 Park Village East, N.W.
3 March '91

Dear Miss Potter

I have handed on the proofs to Wallas: I return herewith your 'abolition' of profit which he will not want and which might get lost.

I like these chapters better than your first. Of course you know you are sacrificing the lectures to the book – which is the right course. There is too much matter, and too little concentration of idea, for the best possible lectures. But you will have an audience largely made up of Co-operators, who will be familiar with the subject.

I have little to criticise – you will find my pencillings nearly all relate to trifles of diction, mostly already corrected by you, I dare say. A scrupulous critic might complain that you change metaphors a little too quickly. I do so myself, and justify it. But others object.

Surely there is *something* in Schloss's statement that the Industrial and Provident Societies Act gave the *form* (unlimited membership at par). I don't know why the C.S.S.A. [?Co-operative Stores Staff Association] escapes: perhaps the Act has been amended in this respect. Unless you are quite sure, would it not be well to ask Schloss whether he is not wrong? The Act may have influenced, even if the unlimited form were merely preferred or facilitated.

Would it not be better to defer jumping on Greening by name, until a later chapter?

I have marked one or two places where your meaning is obscure – your own intimate knowledge does not always allow for other's ignorance.

I would consider where I would say 'manufacturing' and where 'productive'.

I have today been with S. Buxton drafting amendments to the Govt. Factory Bill, which it really seems possible to make into a useful measure, as far as it goes. I will send by the end of the week the H.O. memo. and all the Bills with such analyses as I can get.

I cannot be present to hear you on the 19th as I have to lecture at Crouch End.

Geo. Howell M.P. has now, I think, really made his re-election for Bethnal Green impossible. It would be a wonderfully lucky chance if I could get accepted as candidate in his place. Of course I would not compete for it against Mann, or Burns, or Tillett, if either elects to ask for nomination. But failing these I think I might do.

It will probably not come off: there is just a chance.

Otherwise I have made no progress. I go to Bradford next Saturday to lecture, and shall stay with Byles of the *Bradford Observer*, with whom I want to talk seriously about journalistic possibilities. (I have to stop at Leeds to 'energise' a newly born 'Leeds Fabian Society'.) I am probably going now again to write regularly for the *Speaker*; and perhaps also for a new weekly – a penny one, to cut out the sixpennies, Archibald Grove Editor, and Massingham Asst. Editor.

I think you would do well to take Ll. Smith into partnership in the T. Union book. I like him more than ever. I spent Sunday with him in Epping Forest a few weeks ago, discussing all sorts of things. But we did not, now I come to think of it, get at all '*intime*'. He is reticent.

But I have not found my partnership with Harold Cox in the Eight Hours book perfectly satisfactory. He is not energetic enough to be yoke fellow with me! That book, by the way, is done at last, and I am now in the region of proofs. It will be a closely-packed mass of facts and arguments – *not* literature I am sorry to say.

Haldane at last brought off his Eighty Club Committee meeting and we get as far as electing a 'Publications Committee' on which are he, Grey, Asquith, I, and 2 more. He asked me (evidently on a sudden impulse) to dine with him on the following day, which I did, and found there his mother and sister – nice, quiet, modest *Scotch* people – and Asquith and Mrs Asquith. I really believe I made myself agreeable for once, and actually unbent a little to Miss Haldane. After dinner we three men settled a list of a dozen pamphlets and their writers quite amicably. I hear that Haldane now says abroad that he is working in with the Fabian Society. This I don't quite like: it aroused my suspicions.

It was to B. T. Hall that he said it; who has just been deposed from the

Secretaryship of the Hatcham Liberal Club, by a temporary 'moderate' wave there.

You say you have had fine weather: we have had a week's continuous fog. I thought more than once of the garden at Box – and of a certain rose now withered.

This is not the letter I meant to write, but there is no use in you and me quarrelling. We can never be quite ordinary acquaintances to each other. Our friendship has been consecrated by a great sorrow. I have suffered a good deal these three months – already three months! – and I know you would have given up a good deal not to have made me suffer. I trust you implicitly, and I know you would not have permanently darkened my life – for come what may of oblivion *you* know what it means well enough – if any proper self-sacrifice could have prevented it. I have, as I told you I would, pulled myself together, and not allowed it to ruin me – I hope not even *much* to spoil me. And you need not reproach yourself for, even in this hour of regret, I can easily see how much there has been of gain to me, to set off against this loss. I told you that you should not find me selfish: I know that you have not been so.

I have no right to *extort* a friendship out of you. But if you feel impelled to be a real friend, be absolutely frank and candid with me. I think I have always been more open with you, than you with me; perhaps necessarily so. Now let there be no convention between us: do not write what you 'ought' to write, but what you are thinking about. You can, if you like, be a great source of inspiration to me. But for that we must really be *en rapport*. Do not refuse to see me when you are in London: you have told me nothing about that. Is all this asking too much? Nay, if it is asking anything that you would not spontaneously desire to concede, it is impossible.

Sidney Webb

137 PP   SIDNEY WEBB TO WILLIAM HENRY FENTON

T. W. Maule was the Progressive member for the L.C.C. in Holborn 1889–92. Henry Ward, a civil engineer and philanthropist, associated with Toynbee Hall, was elected to the L.C.C. as a Progressive from Hoxton in 1892. He remained on the L.C.C. until 1925, also serving on its Technical Education Board. Donald Murray was the secretary of the National Liberal Club 1888–1912. Thomas Lee Roberts was a barrister and an active member of the Club from 1886.

4 Park Village East, N.W.
4 March/91

Dear Fenton

Thanks for your very encouraging letter. I don't know what your plans are: you are older than I am, and have more at stake. But it seems to me that I ought not to be afraid to 'live up to the possibilities'. I am now in the market for journalistic work, editorships etc., and if things look clear as the summer advances (and if my health continues quite sound), I shall plunge.

As to the County Council, I want a safe seat. Holborn is by no means that, and Maule only got in by a kind of miracle. The Conservatives are not likely to throw a seat away again. I fear your brother would lose his money. But his fight would be good for Holborn!

In West Islington I think Ward would accept me. Donald Murray of the N.L.C. would back me strongly, also J. R. MacDonald, Lough's secretary. And if Lough doesn't veto it, he would have to see me through for his own sake. I, in return, could help him a good deal I think. Lee Roberts would also support me.

I will gladly come to your discussions if you will book me for any one of the April dates. Should I not take as a subject 'The London Programme'? I shall be just then completing a book with that title. I am even inclined to invite myself to tea with you on that evening to make the acquaintance of Mrs Fenton! If I can get to hear you on the 16th I will. But I am very busy this month.

Yours

Sidney Webb

138 BL   SIDNEY WEBB TO JOHN BURNS

Burns, having broken with the S.D.F., was building up his own organisation as the Battersea Labour League, winning the parliamentary seat in 1892. He was then the outstanding spokesman for labour representation in London. Sir John Benn (1850–1922) was a prominent Progressive, becoming Chairman of the L.C.C. in 1904. In 1897 he was the Liberal candidate for Deptford; subsequently a Liberal M.P.

[4 Park Village East, N.W.]

5 March/91

Dear Burns

I can't stand for N. St Pancras, L.C.C.: I could not leave my appointment for that at this moment. Nor can I suggest anyone, unfortunately. I fear the Tories must have the seat, although Benn ought to be looking after things.

I am probably going to throw up my place presently, but one does not relinquish such a thing in a hurry, and I want first to ensure a livelihood. I shall probably be prepared to stand for L.C.C. in November. My name might be borne in mind if you see any good chance anywhere.

How about Howell's place as M.P. at Bethnal Green? He is now quite out of it, I believe; and it is a place we must secure for one of ourselves. Mann tells me he will not stand. Are you fixed to Battersea? Would Tillett stand?

I would not compete with any of these; but if none of you want the place, I should like to be a candidate. I heard that Cunninghame-Graham was thought of. You are a friend of both of us, and can advise both. My own view, frankly, is that for a London seat I might be of more use than Graham, although of course, I have not his claims. Besides, he can get in elsewhere and I cannot.

Do what you think best in the matter, you know I only want done what is best for that which we have all at heart.

Yours

Sidney Webb

The Eight Hours Day – 270 pages of small type – will be out in a few weeks.

139 PP SIDNEY TO BEATRICE

With *The London Programme*, published in the autumn by Swan Sonnenschein, Sidney prepared for effective entry into London politics – personally, and also for the Fabians. The series of Fabian leaflets based on this work dealt with specific points of policy and did much to influence the Progressive Party. The ideas set out in the programme were not in themselves novel. Almost 'every reform he advocates', the *Speaker* commented in a review on 3 October 1891, 'is certainly included in the programme of every Liberal and Radical in London': many of them had been popularised by J. F. B. Firth, the leading exponent of municipal progress in London, in the period before the L.C.C. was established, or had already been accepted by other civic reformers such as Chamberlain in Birmingham. Yet Sidney did make this rag-bag of measures seem like a coherent programme, supported by a rationale of 'municipal socialism' which reflected the emphasis in *Fabian Essays* on local reforms rather than socialisation by the central government.

Leonard Courtney wrote 'The Difficulties of Socialism' in the first issue of the *Economic Journal* in January 1891; Webb's reply, 'The Difficulties of Individualism' appeared in the June issue.

Auberon Herbert (1838–1906) was a disciple of Herbert Spencer, combining strong individualist views with agnosticism, republicanism and sympathy for organised labour. He was a friend of Beatrice's and at one time they began to collaborate on a novel. George Meredith (1828–1909) published *Diana of the Crossways* in 1885; Mrs Norton was the lady with whom Lord Melbourne was entangled. Sidney Herbert (1810–61), Conservative statesman and friend of Florence Nightingale, was a pioneer of army reform. William Smart (1853–1915) was an economist, noted for his *Economic Annals of the Nineteenth Century*. He became professor of political economy at the University of Glasgow and a member of the Royal Commission on the Poor Law, 1905–08.

4 Park Village East, N.W.

14 March/91

Dear Miss Potter

No. I did not mean to imply that your first chapter was 'bad'. My opinion is however, as worthless as it was six months ago, although in a contrary direction. (But I am happy in that the disillusionment has found no occasion to get far). It would not be honest if I did not own to a disappointment – this was, I do not doubt, inevitable. I cannot find that I know anything that you have neglected to do. I think, perhaps, that I expected too much from your literary art – that I looked for some greater addition of power to the recital of facts and arguments. This was only the undue admiration for what one has not got oneself. Indeed all this criticism is 'subjective' only; do not imagine that it bears any relation to the chapter 'in itself'. I honestly believe that what I have seen in proof will read very effectively. You have taken care to send me no more proofs!

Shall I be quite candid? Do not take it amiss if I confess to a slight feeling that you have taken too long over it. The book will not be a *very* great work; and you could have written it more quickly if you could have had anything in the nature of what the racer against time calls a 'pace-maker' – the man who calls out your greatest speed by racing with you alongside for a spell, then to be succeeded by another.

Of course this is my besetting sin: there does not pass a day without there coming to me at some moment the feeling of the coming night in which no man can work; of the 'Hell' of suffering which I, like Dante, have seen, and having seen, am from that moment 'vowed'; and of the extremely comfortable life which I nevertheless manage to enjoy at others' cost. One can *never* be sure that one has given all one could.

I do not, myself, indulge too much in the luxury of 'keeping a conscience', and I am not suggesting that you should do so. I suppose some people must live at lower pressure than others: it *is* better so. But you asked me what I had in my mind – and I have told you.

I am definitely booked to answer Courtney in the second number of the *Economic Journal*; at equal length, with equal freedom, and equal pay! Now I want to do it with more than equal power! Please help me with suggestions. I have practically an absolutely free hand. The title will be 'The Difficulties of Individualism' which will cover everything. My view tentatively, is to dismiss Courtney in a few sentences by showing that he has ignored all scientific, practical and proletarian Socialism and has chosen instead a literary Utopia by a middle-class Boston journalist, who was not, when he wrote it, in any kind of Socialist movement.

Then I think I should like to show how impossible is the continuance of things as they are – economically, and politically – and how the evolution cannot be Auberon Herbert-wise; and finally describe the convergence of all the tendencies in practical Socialism conscious or unconscious. Please criticise and suggest *how I can best utilise the opportunity*. Now is the moment when criticism *is* useful, because I have not made up my mind! I shall not begin to write for a month, and shall be turning it over.

If you care to invite Wallas between 31 March and 6 April – should this, perchance, be convenient to you – it would, I believe be a kindness to him.

(But it must be a dead secret that I suggested it, as he has just been talking to me about himself.) He and I are going to the Isle of Wight for Easter, with the Geologists' Association. This is as far as I can get comfortably from 'shop'. I must be back at work on the 31st March or 1st April, but he needs a longer holiday, as the doctor has told him he has 'nerve-fag'. This is treating you quite frankly; please reciprocate by acting exactly as may be convenient to yourself.

Yes – I know the feeling of 'auto-section' in Meredith. Indeed, no novel interests me deeply unless I learn from it something about myself. I was not struck with it much in *Diana*; I do not think, perhaps, that *I* come in that one. But I do most decidedly in one of his others (I do not feel inclined to say which) – of course you know that 'real people' are sketched in *Diana* (Hon. Mrs Norton) and Percy Dacier (Hon. Sidney Herbert); and *The Times did* get the Cabinet secret of Free Trade. You will probably know what I think of *Diana*. I do not condemn: perhaps women have got, just now, to go through the stage of 'self-realisation' as the Ibsenites call it. It does not seem to me a very worthy ideal. I evidently fail to understand it, for it seems to me as selfish to try to 'realise oneself' as to try to to save one's own soul. If I could really 'live up' to an Ideal, I would choose '*Ich dien*'. I do not remember that Diana ever even thinks it relevant to enquire in what way she could be of the most use to the world.

However, choosing ideals is little more than justifying to oneself what one wants or means to do. But some people *want* to do service, and this can be 'grown' in others, I believe.

So you see I have become psychologically, a Catholic again. Did I tell you that my 'illness' made me for a time a Protestant? I had a sickening sense of sin, i.e. of imperfection, and my own moral improvement seemed my most pressing duty. Now I have the same intellectual consciousness of imperfection, but the yearning for self-improvement is replaced by a desire to get to work just as I am.

All of which perhaps means nothing more than that when I was physically weak, I had not my usual energy.

I expect to get the last chapters of *The Eight Hours Day* in proof next week, and to send it finally to press before Easter.* [*Side-note: By the way, I did not send you my proofs to look at because you did not invite this. I only mention it lest *this* should be the reason why you did not continue to send me yours. Proof reading, which is no trouble to me (in the case of another's book) is considered a task and one does not therefore *offer* to impose it.] And yesterday I signed an agreement to deliver ms of another book early in April! This *is* rushing it, but it is only my *Speaker* articles on London, to be enlarged and republished in the Social Science Series, and then at a shilling on Oct. 1st, in time for the County Council Election. I doubt very much whether *The London Programme* will be a

265

success, either from a literary or a publishing point of view, but the latter is not my affair, and the former is outweighed by the desirability of my doing what Smart ought to have done long ago, viz. actually write down what the London Programme is – I want to think during the next few days how I can best do this; how I should begin, and what I should include.

Bethnal Green looks very promising for me. The chief difficulty is friction between the Liberal Association and the Clubs etc. But both parties would I believe, choose me, if one of them does not set the other's back up.

Do not suppose, because I 'run on' in this way that I am not lonely too. It is possible to be as lonely in London as elsewhere. I suppose it is inevitable. I am conscious of a longing for letters and friends; but also of a horrible shrinking from both, a presentiment of trouble – probably of no more importance than are anticipations of joy. The great secret of life is not to expect too much from it. After all, the world is neither black nor white, but grey – a kind of pepper and salt mixture – and only children cry for sugar instead. (I am a child.)

Yours

Sidney Webb

140 PP   BEATRICE TO SIDNEY

The loss of Beatrice's letters for this period makes it difficult to document the change in her attitude to Sidney – a difficulty increased by the unusual brevity and reticence of her diary entries for the first part of 1891.

Mrs Thompson was the nurse-companion of Richard Potter. Beatrice was going to London to stay with Alice Green in mid-April while she delivered a series of lectures on the Co-operative movement at University Hall.

Box House, Minchinhampton, Glos.

[?early April 1891]

Dear Mr Webb

Pray do not think that I should be 'better pleased' with a favorable opinion. What one wants before one begins is a perfectly frank statement of pros and cons; your objection either appears conclusive or is useful in bringing out one's own reasons for wishing to do it. Even in work done – I should always value your outspoken opinion: I give it full weight even if I do not altogether agree with it.

I do not believe that the new life you are plunging into will injure you; I believe that you have *that* in you that will be proof both against the failure or friction of public life and also against the inflation of actual or seeming power. Failure and success will probably come to you – flattery and mortification – but I have faith that your self-devotion is tempered with self-humility and that in spite of your seeming intolerance you do not really ignore the bigger world of human life and human effort outside your own sphere.

But do not allow yourself to grow morbid: and try not to judge others always by your own standard and your own experience. There are so few persons one is *called upon* to judge: there are still fewer about when one's judgement is of much worth as an estimate of their net value to the world. The most one can do is to judge them as they affect the work one has in hand – and that is probably one side only of their characters, perhaps the least important. This reserve of judgement – this conscious-ness of unravelled mystery – adds enormously to the charm and usefulness of a strong character.

Certainly we will see each other in London. I will send you presently the remainder of my proofs.

I found I had to re-write a great portion of the latter part of the first chapter: it is not good but now it is better.

I enjoyed having Graham Wallas here. He looked ever so much better when he left. Mrs Thompson went to the station with him and quite lost her heart. She said when she came back: 'I felt inclined to offer to make him a new set of night shirts – those he has got are in a dreadful state'. The mother's instinct, you see.

Judge Jones has just called here: he too was much taken with Wallas. He is firmly convinced that you are in a 'Secret Society': and warned me solemnly against allowing myself to be entangled to such an underground affair. Poor little man: there is something pathetic in his lack of faith: his disillusioned state. I feel horribly nervous about my lectures but am trying to console myself with the argument that it will be 'good enough' not to be a disgrace. After all most lecturers are very bad and it will [be] with the majority that one will be compared.

Ever yours

Beatrice Potter

141 PP SIDNEY TO BEATRICE

4 Park Village East, N.W.
6 April/91

Your letter was more than welcome, and I did not feel inclined to be critical about it. But it was not very long.

I am glad you have the support of Wallas over the T.U. book. It may well be that you are right. But three years is a long time, in which much could be done: you will have to justify it by the result. Do not commit yourself to it at first, either with Ll. Smith or otherwise. See what the preliminary exploration yields before deciding.

What I grudge is the spending of your time in the mere(!) writing. Your role is to think and to inspire: you do not write quickly or easily: what you ought to get for the work – perhaps this is what you seek in Ll. Smith – is a secretary who could seize your ideas, arrange your materials, and leave you only to revise the ms and rewrite just where you felt inclined. This is how most of the great statesmen do their work, and I think it is economical.

I wish I could have heartily agreed with your idea. I hate to think that I might have pretended to do so, and you would have been better pleased. There are elements of meanness in me which I am afraid of. But you have a right to my judgment, for what it may be worth. I will never be other than frank to you, even if it makes me seem unsympathetic. I have not Wallas's delightful faculty of throwing himself into another person's idea, and living in it for the moment.

As to my overworking, I feel tempted to copy a bad model and say 'It is all very well for you' to declaim against overwork, but what am I to do! I do not seek work, even when I ought to do so in my own interests. I have refused to do an article in the *Contemporary*, and I have nothing in this week's *Speaker*. But many things *come* to me to be done, and would not be done if I did not undertake them. The harvest is plentiful but the laborers are few. Of course I know I must not break down, but it is hard to refuse direct calls upon one. And it is very tempting to me at this moment to use myself right up and have done with it. Do you know that mood? I hope you never may. I feel as if I could embrace the whole globe with both arms, even if it crushed me in its turning.

Of course, as a practical person, of Teuton blood, I shall do no such Juggernaut thing; but my life is not very brilliant just now. As you said, what I am going to do may be for the good of the world, *if it does not ruin me*. You are one of the very few who realise the enormous risk to me – not so much pecuniarily as to my character and personality. But even you do not know all the dangers that I know of, and am afraid of. The whole task is hateful to me; the whole risk crushes me.

However, the practical view is that it has come to me to make the plunge, and I must make it. But please remember, in the future days when I may have quite gone under, mentally *or morally*, that I did not do it for my own sake – that I did not seek the risk; that I had virtually no option but to undertake a task too great for me, amid dangers for which I had not sufficient weapons, in money, in strength or in friends.

Still, it may come out all right after all – especially if I am not left to bear all the weight alone. Do not be afraid that I am going to revert to the forbidden topic. I will never ask you to make a sacrifice for me. (Your accusations of selfishness have rankled, I find.) But you can help me – very likely save me – by your influence if you like.

I think, perhaps, that you have some little responsibility for using that influence. (I do not mean as to not misusing it – I have the most perfect confidence that you would never sacrifice my life or its happiness to yours, or for any bad motive: I feel assured that if you have crushed out the light of my life, it could not be avoided: I *know* you have been honest with yourself, and true to me.) But I mean that you are under some responsibility to *use* your influence and not ignore it. Let me see you frequently: let me tell you all my difficulties; and help me. I can do little for you in return, but you will perhaps find some repayment in thinking that you *have* helped – not me alone – but what we both have at heart.

You probably do not realise how I am living. I do not number my hours of work, because I do nothing else. I see no friends, save in the work. I have not read a book for months. I have not been to a theatre or concert or picture gallery in London for years. I have holidays, but save for these I am at work from morning till bed time. It is a cramped and joyless life, but I see no chance of changing it. I feel like the London cabhorse who could not be taken out of the shafts lest he should fall down! I tell you this that you may see what your friendship has already been to me; and what it might be in the future.

Heaven forbid that I should pretend that my life should be the type – but when we consider how the work of the world *is* now shared, and how it might be shared, you may be able to forgive me for some impatience when I come into contact with the idle rich – or what is even more irritating, with those people of ability who assume to work, but who really spend only an hour or two a day outside their own enjoyment. I, too, am capable of culture and enjoyment, if I could be relieved of some of my task.

All this will sound very egotistical and repining. I am afraid this past week has been a bad one for me. The East wind depressed my animal spirits, and I have had piles of work to do. I am busy every night this week, and, *besides*, I have my 'London Programme' book to complete within the next ten days.

I shall be glad to send you the ms of my answer to Courtney – sometime in May. But I had hoped you would have helped me to write it: I thought, perhaps, that you would have discussed it seriously with me, and suggested what you thought should be done. But do not let it bother you. I must do it the best way I can, and I shall be glad enough to have your help in revising it.

I have not been able to see Mrs Green, who sent me a friendly message through Wallas. I wonder whether either she or you realise how much time it takes even to 'make a call'. I have been three (or four?) times to Kensington Square, each time costing me 2 to 3 hours, and all I have seen of Mrs Green has been that half an hour's frivolous chat on the Sunday when she came from the Guelph Exhibition. I have now written to propose to call the only time I have free this week, *viz* late on Wednesday evening but it is quite likely she will be engaged. Pray believe me when I say that I do not grudge either time or trouble to gain Mrs Green's friendship which I value. But it *does* cost a lot of time – that is, when one's time is really taken up.

Am I absolutely debarred from going there while you are there? Can you not make her realise how we stand, without saying anything unpleasant to yourself? Nine months ago you would have managed so that I should have been there every week. Are we not, *in all essentials*, back to where we were nine months ago? Honestly, and frankly, I acquiesce in your decision. My feelings are unchanged, but I see your point of view. I am prepared to serve your life, and to ask nothing whatever in return, save only your work for Socialism, and such share of friendship as you choose to give. You have put it upon me to show you that I can be unselfish, and I don't think you will have any cause to be disappointed.

Yours in perfect sincerity
Sidney Webb

142 PP SIDNEY TO BEATRICE [*incomplete*]

The earlier pages of the letter are missing. Despite Beatrice's stage-fright (she was perturbed to find Herbert Spencer, Frederic Harrison and other notable friends in the audience) her lectures at University Hall were a success. Her visit to London, moreover, was a success in another sense, for it provided an opportunity to overcome the estrangement from Sidney. It was agreed that she, Alice Green and Sidney would go down together to the Co-operative Congress at Lincoln on 16 May. Before they left she arranged a dinner party for five leading Fabians – Webb, Shaw, Olivier, Massingham and Clarke – to meet five rising Liberals – Asquith, Grey, Haldane, Acland and Buxton. This occasion did not go well, despite superficial cordiality, for Asquith seemed bent on blocking Fabian efforts to move the Liberal Party to the left.

On 20 May, when Beatrice and Sidney returned from Lincoln, she agreed to marry him on condition that nothing could be publicly settled while her father lived. On 22 May she noted the change in their relationship. 'I cannot tell how things will settle themselves – I think probably in his way', she reflected. 'His resolute patient affection, his honest care for my welfare . . . a growing together of our resources – mental and material – to serve together the "commonwealth".' She added the caveat that 'it will be an act of renunciation of self and not of indulgence of self, as it would have been in the other case. Perhaps, therefore, it will be blessed for both of us'. The conference to which Sidney refers was the meeting of the British Association at Cardiff in August. The experiment in Co-operative creameries in Ireland was the work of Sir Horace Plunkett (1854–1932), a notable figure in Irish agricultural reform who became a lifelong friend of the Webbs.

4 Park Village East, N.W.
[?21 May 1891]

. . . love of principles rather than facts. I own I am flattered at being asked to do one of the special papers: and I should be unwilling to lose a chance of obliterating my bad impression last year. With your help I think I could do a decent introductory paper. But even if I decided to accept, I should strongly urge them to get a woman instead of me. It is one of the 'chances' which should go to a woman.

On the whole, what do you think?

I found at home last night an order from the *Speaker* for an article on Plunkett's Creameries and an urgent appeal from Massingham for a column report of the Congress. These I did, somehow (really I wasn't exactly in the state to write solemn articles!), and then slept prosaically the sleep of the unemotional just as if yesterday had never been!

Indeed I am still a little in a dream: I have not yet fully realised all your kindness. But at any rate it is a brilliant rose-colored morning and I pitied the man on the omnibus who said the rain was very cold. For me there was no rain and no cold.

One thing pleases me – our souls touch at their highest levels, not their lowest. In the midst of the commonplace conventions of life and even in some of our lower moments, it may seem impossible but I take comfort always in my intense gratitude that we have a good influence on each other. Does this sound egotistical? One side I know, and I believe you told me that it was the same on the other. It is not your influence on me, or mine on you that is to be credited with this, but the influence upon both of us of the relation between us. My most intense feeling this morning is gratitude that I should have lived to feel this influence – and also perhaps a determination to be worthy of it. I do most honestly believe that it is our best chance of getting the very most for the world out of our joint lives.

Schnadhorst has this moment sent across a note to say that he has advised me as a Liberal candidate for Parliament for South Islington. This would seem a fair chance if they accept me, as the seat went Liberal in 1885 by a 500 majority.

But I believe I ought not to write anymore – the official papers are beginning to pile up!

Goodbye

S.

143 PP SIDNEY TO BEATRICE

4 Park Village East, N.W.
23.5.91

I enclose the Co-op proofs as directed by your telegram. When you have looked through my very few notes (on blue paper), the proofs are ready for the printer. I believe the arithmetic is now all right.

Your letter is full of kindness, and it is exactly as I could wish. Do not be afraid of the future: meanwhile let us get all we can out of the present. You may be quite sure that I would not have you sacrifice your life. I have (as I have always had) the fullest confidence that you will decide rightly – and, as you say, you alone can know.

Dearest, you are freer now than ever you were, because I feel, since Wednesday, that I could even bear to lose you. I always *meant* not to let

271

it spoil my life; now I *know* that the very worst could only sanctify it. I do not understand why I feel so happy, and why I feel that your refusal would not now really injure me. Honestly, this presents itself more in the light of danger to your own life and development, than of ruin to mine. It is a queer turn of love's metaphysic; perhaps it is a nearer approach to casting out self: perhaps it is only a delusion!

However, be that as it may, all the enormous advantages of our partnership remain, and I don't think the difficulties are insuperable. One – *la vie intime* – I want to talk to you about very frankly, or rather, I want you very frankly to talk to me, who am more than usually ignorant. One thing is quite certain: I will not have your intellectual and working life spoilt, whatever the cost to me. It would not be a 'chattel' marriage! and we are neither of us likely to insist on anything that would injure our common usefulness.

As to the financial difficulty, this is surely a delusion. I cannot imagine that we could rightfully spend as much as we are likely jointly to have. Everyone tells me that I can earn £1,000 or even £2,000 a year if I choose – do you not suppose that I would not work myself to the bone before I would allow you to miss any one comfort necessary for your fullest efficiency? Clearly I should *have* to do this, even if I did not wish to, merely to save myself from my own conscience and its reproach for 'marrying for money'.

(Here, I must own, there is the chance of my illness or breakdown, which might make me a pensioner on you. But the financial risk in such a case is the least part of it – and the risk itself is one incidental to all relationships.)

I have said so much in answer to your points. But do not suppose I am pressing you. Do not think about 'strain' on me; since Wednesday there is no strain at all, only a stimulus to good and a new ideal of unselfishness. Let us go on trustfully – not at all avoiding a repetition of Wednesday, but rather seeking to renew and deepen all our spiritual experience. What we have to do is to make our present friendship as deep and intimate, as mutually helpful as we possibly can – for the rest, *advienne que pourra.* Come up as soon as you feel disposed (But I would a thousand times prefer you to have a full holiday, than have even the luxury of seeing you – we ought to combine these!) It is good of you to think of Box for Sunday, but I could not have come – that is, I *ought* to have refused! – because I must work day and night this week to make up arrears including the paper for the *Economic Journal*, of which I will send you the first part in a few days. It will be very bad, I am afraid. But if you will think it over, and improve it, it may do.

I will write and accept the British Association paper. We must work it out together.

Where will you stay in London? Mrs Green is very kind, and I am not sure that you are not freer than elsewhere. Mrs Green hinted at arranging Sunday outings – this was in January *before* you came up. There is now an added inducement. But Norway would be the very best way of spending June. However I don't care to look forward even to June! I cannot exhaust the present moment. which is *delire, extase, ivresse,* because I am writing to you.

S.

4. The Secret Engagement
June – December 1891

In June 1891 Beatrice and Sidney went to Norway for a three-week holiday with Graham Wallas and Clara Bridgman, a young Fabienne thought to be a possible match for Wallas. During this holiday Beatrice reflected on her decison. 'The world will wonder. On the face of it it seems an extraordinary end to the once-brilliant Beatrice Potter . . . to marry an ugly little man with no social position and less means whose only recommendation – so some may say – is a certain pushing ability. And I am not "in love", not as I was.' But she respected Sidney for his 'fine intellect and a warm-heartedness, a power of self-subordination and self-devotion for the "Common Good". And our marriage will be based on fellowship – a common faith and a common work. His feeling is the passionate love of an emotional man, mine the growing tenderness of the mother, touched with the dependence of the woman on the help of a strong lover . . . He is in a state of happy exaltation – I am beginning to feel at rest and assured'. (BWD 20 June 91)

Relaxing in the Norwegian summer they discussed their future. It was, Beatrice decided, 'no longer necessary for him to make money, since I shall have enough for both'; despite her father's losses she could count on a private income of at least £1,000 a year. She therefore discouraged Sidney from his plan to scrape up several hundred pounds by hack journalism and by starting a Fabian review which he should edit. In a long duologue between them reported in her diary on 7 July Beatrice pointed out that he needed practical experience of politics and that the London County Council offered him the best entry into public life. She told him that she doubted whether he had the qualities or the opportunity 'to become a really big man', but she was sure the L.C.C. would give scope 'for that handling of men in committees in which you excel'. She thought their partnership, in which she would be the investigator and he the executive, would provide an unusual combination of talents. There was to be no question of Beatrice merely lapsing into domestic life: 'it may be a mistake to transform the Woman into a Thinker – but if the mistake has been paid for, one may hardly throw away the result'.

As a beginning they would collaborate on the proposed study of trade union-ism, while Sidney would make his way in municipal politics, resigning from the Colonial Office that autumn and seeking an L.C.C. seat in the elections due in 1892. He was not, in fact, so hard-up as she implied, though their standards were different. At the time of their marriage he had two thousand pounds capital, partly money inherited from his father and partly his own savings.

Beatrice recognised that their marriage would cut her adrift from her old world. When she told the Booths in confidence of her plans she was hurt by their chilly reaction. On 15 July Mary Booth wrote (PP) to say 'it would be no use to pretend that we are not sorry it is so; but your happiness and satisfaction has a reassuring effect'. It was good of Sidney to wish Beatrice to maintain the tie with the Booths, Mary added, 'as he knows that we have been to a great extent his enemies'. A few other friends were informed of the secret engagement, in particular Alice Green, Haldane, Wallas and Shaw: Beatrice's sisters were given no inkling of her decision.

144 KCC BEATRICE POTTER TO ALFRED MARSHALL

Beatrice was lent Herbert Spencer's house in St John's Wood. Thomas Hughes (1822–96) was the author of *Tom Brown's Schooldays* and one of the group of Christian Socialists in the 1850s. As an early supporter of production co-operatives he objected to the increasing emphasis of the movement on consumer interests and on the distributive role of the Co-operative Wholesale Society.

65 Avenue Road
[July 1891]

Dear Mr Marshall

Your letter was a delightful surprise to me! I hardly expected you to read the book and certainly did not venture to hope for a letter of frank criticism.

I value your criticism so much and am so sincerely anxious to learn from it, that I was sorry you had wasted 4 whole pages in saying kind things – which tho' they are sweet to hear teach me nothing.

There is one part of your criticism which I feel just, tho' I do not think I could have avoided it: the arguments in favour of Trade Unions action have been put too dogmatically and therefore with an absolute lack of scientific caution and justification. But my space was limited and I felt it very important to urge on Co-operators to consider Trade Unions. You must remember that my little book is a practical treatise for workingmen and is not intended for such as you.

About the lack of originality in my view of Co-operatives. I heartily agree; but I do not feel the worse for this admission. I did not try to be original: I have accepted anyone's ideas when they seemed to me true and I have never considered the question whether a view has originated in my own mind or through the suggestion of another. I am a Communist in ideas and refuse to admit private property in them!

But where I feel that I radically differ from you is in your objection to my condemnation of 'Associations of Producers'.

To my mind, an untold harm has been done to the labour movement by the way in which economists and others have praised up a mischievous form of activity; partly because it has seemed to them a harmless form – one not likely to revolutionize things. If I were a skilled engineer and saw a multitude of men building bridges on a plan which insured their ultimate collapse, and if I refused to tell them so, because I thought it would hurt their feelings and damp their enthusiasm, I should be guilty of a sort of treachery.

I know that we disagree as to the fact: you do not think that associations of producers have failed so completely as I do. On the other hand, I not only believe them to have failed but think that all these failures have meant demoralisation and despair among those who have taken part in them.

That is the result of a very careful observation of the men engaged in them and not the result of listening to arguments against them.

About Hughes (a small matter) I think him an intolerable person (that makes your suggestion that we are alike cruel!), but because he was my principal opponent I treated him with the greatest amount of appreciation and courtesy I could muster.

In conclusion may I say that I will 'learn, mark and inwardly digest' what you say about my tendency to think things too simple. I have no doubt this is a true criticism. It is so much easier to put your case effectively if you rob it of its actual qualification. And that I feel is my temptation – to try and put a case so that it will 'tell'.

Is it the woman's desire to influence the actions of men?

Shall I see you in London? I have just come back from a glorious holiday in Norway.

> With affectionate remembrances
> Yours very sincerely
> Beatrice Potter

145 PP SIDNEY TO BEATRICE

Sidney's father, who had a weak heart, had been suffering for two months from a bronchitic congestion of the lungs. Beatrice and Sidney now met every day at Herbert Spencer's house to thrash out their plan of research. There, in an atmosphere of 'socialist talk, clouds of tobacco, aided with whisky', they entertained trade union leaders (BWD 14 August 91), 'working away together undermining the Individualism of the British race, with intervals of "human nature"'. (BWD 19 August 91)

John Rae reviewed *The Eight Hours Day*, by Webb and Harold Cox, in the June 1891 issue of the *Economic Journal*; he also reviewed *The London Programme* in the December 1891 issue. His critical book, *Contemporary Socialism*, was published in 1884.

> 4 Park Village East, N.W.
> 14 July/91

Dearest

If the time has seemed half as blank to you as it has to me, this has been 'Black Monday' indeed! I trust you have found everything in order. I find I am as brown as a Chilian, and probably pounds heavier through the wonderful holiday we have had – surely, no one was ever quite so fortunate before.

I found my father out of the doctor's hands, but distinctly a permanent invalid. I called on the doctor this morning, and he told me that he ought to live at Bournemouth. So my sister and I will probably go down one day soon and take apartments for a month or two. This will perhaps grow into permanent residence there for my parents and my sister, although they have not yet made up their minds to it.

My pile of letters was colossal, but there was nothing serious. I gather that the review of Booth probably appeared in the *Speaker* but I have not yet seen it. I have some excellent information for my British Association paper sent in by Fabians – one splendid account of women compositors by one of them, who is evidently an able woman. I will bring it on Thursday.

I believe I was mistaken in thinking that my paper must be ready by the 22nd inst – there may be more time.

Your book (and Booth's) are mentioned in the 'Books Received' in the *Economic Journal*, but not reviewed. John Rae reviews *The Eight Hours Day* at two-page length with mixed praise and blame; especially falls foul of the Australian part. Bernard Shaw is very pleased with our article against Courtney. I will bring the *Economic Journal* on Thursday – meanwhile I send a copy of the article. Shaw says it is 'so well written' – which is largely due to your corrections.

There is no doubt that we shall postpone indefinitely the Fabian Review. I have not yet seen Massingham as to the London Letter.

My father's very weak state *would* have made me feel it a terrible responsibility to give up the C.O., if you had not (unwittingly) come to the rescue. I am glad that I had decided before, but all day long I have been thinking how much anxiety and worry I am now saved.

I have worn the ring today out of doors. I miss its absence now, just as I miss yours.

Please save up all your half-formed ideas and suggestions for THE BOOK, and tell me them on Thursday. I want to get the thing into my mind.

I wonder if you have been to Mrs Booth's, and what she has said, and he.

I told the National Liberal Club Library to get your book, but they already had it.

I find I must send back the proofs of *The London Programme* today, so cannot have your help in them.

Goodbye, dearest *dearest* Beatrice. Teach me *how* I may show my love for you – but I can never show it all.

Yours

Sidney

Beatrice had hopes of being appointed as an assistant commissioner to the Royal Commission on Labour. She had made it known that she was available through Leonard Courtney and she would have been pleased (BWD 17 April 91) to have 'the opportunity of showing what a woman can do through work'.

4 Park Village East, N.W.

22 July/91

Dearest Beatrice

You will not mind my stopping away this evening? It seemed best for my mother, who is, however, bearing her loss very well. My father's death was sudden and quite peaceful, a mere 'falling asleep'. My sister had sent for me and my brother just before, noticing a change for the worse: but we both came too late. But there was, of course, much to see to. The funeral is to be on Saturday.

Dearest, this 'jars' a little on our happiness, but it is better so. My father could not have lived long, and his sufferings are better ended. I am now concerned only to do the best possible for my mother and sister. I can hardly come to you any evening until Saturday, but I could come then if you are disengaged. And we might go out on Sunday again? I shall be busy tomorrow, but could meet you Friday for a walk.

I hope I am not unfeeling, but I find myself thinking only of the living. My father's life had closed, even as your father's has. I am not in any way *overwhelmed* with grief; and it seems much more important to me to care for those who are left.

But still, I think 'Poor Father'. He led an upright modest, humble life, full of unostentatious self-sacrifice and work. He was very gentle and docile last night when I sat up with him.

I fear the Labour Committee has not appointed Assistant Commissioners, according to the brief reports. It will be inconvenient if it is hung up until October.

Send me a brief note to say when I may meet you.

Goodnight

Sidney

4 Park Village East, N.W.

25 July/91

My dear Haldane

I am very much obliged to you for inviting me to Scotland. As you will understand, I should be only too delighted to accept, but it is, I am sorry to say, impossible. I have had all the leave I ought honestly to take from the C.O. before I quit it for good – which will probably be in October.

And September is just the month when I am bound to be there, if only to release a colleague who has always been the kindest of friends to me. Therefore – thanks all the same. I must *entbehren* so much!

I am very glad that you have been entrusted with this momentous secret. I am sure you realise how important it is to us that it *should* be a secret, even from our closest friends. But you have always been so nice even when I have been beside myself, that I feel pleased to think you are so early in our confidence.

Of course I am awfully happy: but I feel all the responsibility, both that I should not spoil a life which I regard as of high value to the world; and that I, too, should not fail to give the fullest possible product in return for my own happiness. Therefore I am Teutonically grave about it: not anxious, but trying to realise *how much* is demanded. 'On the Ethical Responsibilities of the Exceptionally Lucky' is an unwritten chapter in Ethics which I am inclined to ponder.

However, I know I can't possibly earn it all, anymore than I have deserved it all – so that all I can do is to do my utmost to make the combination as potent for good as possible.

I am glad I made up my mind to leave the C.O. before the present result seemed even possible. Of course, I stick to my decision: and indeed, I am commanded to carry it out as soon as practicable, so that I may take up, with the fullest possible vigour, any public work that may come to me. I hope to get a seat on the London County Council. But I naturally want to get into Parliament if I can.

I am sorry to gather that your own personal sorrow is not to be crowned with happiness. Pardon my alluding to it, but I have all along had such a deep desire to express my sympathy. If there is now no hope, I can only wish that you may come to find that it is, if not for the best, then for the next to the best – not bad that is, but good, though not *so* good.

Perhaps in November you can spare time to confer as to what we can each of us most usefully do. I read your Cambridge speech and liked much of it. May I commend to your holiday reading an article by me in the July number of the *Economic Journal*, on 'The Difficulties of Individualism'.

Yours sincerely

Sidney Webb

148 PP BEATRICE TO SIDNEY

Don was Beatrice's dog. Kitty Holt was the eldest daughter of Beatrice's eldest sister Laurencina. Lujo Brentano's book *On the History and Development of Guilds, and the Origins of Trade Unions* was published in England in 1870. William Henry Hey (1839–1907) was general secretary of the Ironfounders Union 1886–94. On 20 August Sidney had written to Beatrice saying that Hey would 'like to publish the history as his own, in the next annual report . . . it now seems to me that one Society publishing *its own* history . . . might make others more willing to publish theirs'. Sidney had worked up historical material on the Ironfounders. On 22 August Sidney wrote from Cardiff to report that his paper had been well received at the British Association.

Elvidge, a member of the compositor's union in London, acted as a research assistant on the early stages of the Webb *History of Trade Unionism*.

Elliott and Fry were a firm which specialised in photographs of notabilities, offering prints for sale.

[?Box or Longfords, Minchinhampton]

[20 August 1891]

Dearest one

The engine broke down – and we were nearly an hour late – it was a cold drizzle as we drove over the common. Here I found the house deserted (the Courtneys had gone out for the day) except for 'Don' who nearly devoured me with joy, Nick and John. Miss Darling and Mrs Thompson both off on their holiday.

After spending an hour with dear old Father who is just the same, I betook me to Longfords. Mary was in first rate form: the flower show was a huge success and she has 'overcome' the County Council and got her way in all matters. She and Arthur were very affectionate, and desperately anxious to know what I had been doing at the Home Office (a bulky packet 'On Her Majesty's Service' having arrived that morning for me) and delighted with 'Potterism', and altogether pleased with my growing notoriety. I talked about future plans, and Mary's tone was 'you can go away as much as you like, there is absolutely nothing to be done at Box'. I believe they are contemplating my marriage! Kitty Holt was there, looking rather depressed. I am to have a walk with her tomorrow.

I spent the evening with the Courtneys. Leonard was 'snubby'; and I was studiously pleasant and courteous. He has the consciousness of something 'agin' me, or possibly the feeling that he has 'balked' me – or that I am a detective from the enemies' camp. Anyway he did not encourage conversation. We should be better friends if we frankly acknowledged that we were public opponents – but I think he rather resents my 'growth' as a personage that even he – the big man – feels called upon to oppose. He cannot understand why other people take me seriously. He is studying the big edition of Rae's *Socialism*: (not for the London letter!)

This morning I had a walk with Kate. She was very friendly, and in the course of the talk exclaimed 'I wonder whether you will marry'. I sedately replied that I thought it highly probable – but that in any case marriage with me would be subordinate to work. 'That is rather a question for your husband' she answered. 'No: it is the question of the *choice* of my husband: I should only marry a man who wished that it should be so.' At which she looked perplexed, and wondered whether it was Haldane or a socialist.

280

She asked me whether I liked 'Sidney Webb as much after the tour as before'. I answered enigmatically 'I like both those men immensely', and then told her that Graham Wallas was coming to spend a week on the 26th.

This morning I began 6.30 and read Brentano's *Guilds* in the hour before lunch. I began to cut up the Social Science Committee – and I am doing it beautifully. We shall get a huge mass of material mechanically well arranged. Enclosed is a nice little letter from Elvidge.

(I do not at all object to Hey publishing the story. It will please him and not hurt us.)

Then lunch, a cigarette, a sleep, cup of tea, more arranging – 1½ [hours] reading to Father.

And then I suddenly bethought me there *might* be a letter at the Post Office. So I popped on an old skirt and a mackintosh and trudged through the rain to Hampton [Minchinhampton] and found what I desired.

No, dear, I do not even look at your photograph. It is too hideous, for anything. Do be done in a gray suit by Elliott and Fry and let me have your *head only* – it is the head only that I am marrying!

The Courtneys and Playnes are dining with Judge Jones, and I am writing to you. You doubtless are just arriving at Cardiff.

I shall send this to Park Village: it will welcome you tomorrow evening.

Do you know, I do not believe it will be possible for me to get away before Saturday 5th. Mary will be away and it is rather a stretch going at all. I believe the Playnes go away next Saturday. If so you might come down for Sunday instead. Mrs Green and G.W. will be here. I will see whether it be possible.

If not we must wait till Glasgow – and remember those quiet evenings at Avenue Rd – and Norway. We have a lot of work to do to earn all we have enjoyed.

I send you the bunch of wild hyacinths I picked that spring day in the Longfords woods, just near to the bank we sat on 18 months ago. They have dried up – while our love has grown.

Now, dearest, goodnight, Let us both try to be faithful stewards. Let me learn from you.

Always your loving comrade
Beatrice Potter

149 PP BEATRICE TO SIDNEY

The reference to Albert Ball, a connection of Alice Green, presumably relates to some earlier discussion during Beatrice's stay in London. The 'accomplished young ruffian' was the Playne's son Bill.

My own dear One

I am delighted to get your long interesting letter. I think that occasionally it is good for you to mix with men of a different set and of different opinions from your own – you know that art of self respect and reserve – which is essential to one who is likely to become a leader, in however small a degree. It is a mistake 'to give yourself away' to such people as Ball and his friends – but it is well to be able to take stock of them and to make them respect you. To an enthusiast and propagandist like you the faculty of 'polite reserve' is a valuable one to acquire.

The poor official Liberal party is in a horribly awkward position. These socialistic projects are against its instincts and it is not so very certain whether they are, at present, in its *interests*. To adopt a programme which you inwardly fear and dislike is hard – to have in addition the doubt whether it will 'pay' is still harder. And that is why I should drop once for all, the bribe and threat argument – and appeal only to conviction. That, I am glad to think, is the line you are now taking. Burns with his Labour Party's 'heel' will never stamp anything out or into political parties. And the sorrowful truth is that 'Labour' itself has no programme, and wants as much 'convincing' and 'educating' as the most bigoted landlords or capitalists. The absence of any social policy is what strikes one in the T.U. records. Tom Mann is the only individual of the labour party who is trying to evolve a policy. I should try, if I were you, to see a little of Tom Mann – or at least of his subordinate V. Nash. Is there no way of getting some capital for the *Trade Unonist*? I think it would be worth making a determined effort. It is a thoroughly good little paper and sound in all its views and good and true.

I am going out to ride with the 'accomplished young ruffian' this morning.

We are on friendly terms – both desperately anxious to be agreeable to one another and with a certain personal liking – but with a very whole-hearted contempt for each other's point of view – which shines through our bland amiable manners now and again. I fear I gave a little shock to his self-complacency, quite accidentally. He was asserting that no arguments could shake his Tory principles, that they were based on *good sound instinct*, when I remarked 'We should not wish to convert you, my dear Bill, you are not up to our standard'. It was a perfectly involuntary remark – said in the kindest of tones – but he turned scarlet and looked quite surprised and perplexed.

It is delightful to think I shall probably see you next week.

Goodbye, this is a long chat.

Ever your comrade

Beatrice Potter

Sidney had planned to visit Minchinhampton while Alice Green and Wallas were staying with Beatrice, but when he learned that the Playnes would not as expected be away he did not go. They proposed to meet in Birmingham as Beatrice travelled north to Newcastle where the Trades Union Congress was meeting at the beginning of September. Pease was to give her introductions to local trade unionists. Robert Spence Watson (1837–1911), a notable educational reformer and a powerful figure in the Liberal Party in the North-East, was president of the National Liberal Federation 1890–1902. He was a strong support of the democratic movement in Russia and of Indian nationalism. The Very Reverend William Moore Ede (1847–1935) became Rector of Gateshead in 1881; in 1908 he became dean of Worcester. He was active in Liberal politics and sympathetic to Co-operative and trade union organisations. The Knights of Labour was a short-lived body in the United States which attempted to combine political and industrial action.

4 Park Village East, N.W.

26/8/91

Dearest

I ought not to expect a letter from you every morning, especially if you have to post them yourself sometimes – yet the absence of one this morning left me very depressed; so you can imagine how joyful I was to see your handwriting tonight. I am sorry you were feeling sad: the weather is hard on you. You must think of the gorgeously fine days we have had together, and how much more fortunate we have been in weather than those millions who are taking holiday in August.

But the going of the Courtneys will relieve you; and the companionship of Mrs Green and Wallas. Do not let me think of you as other than happy. I do so want to make you happy: it really is the highest efficiency. Work may be strenuous and abundant without it – even fertile without it – but always lacking in something, perhaps the sweet reasonableness and grace which gives so much towards permanence of value.

I am horribly sad at losing my Sunday. Tell me if we have the Saturday at Birmingham together. Could you perhaps break the journey there for some hours – which would not be more fatiguing to you: and I could easily come to Birmingham for those few hours and return same day. You know how I should think it worth ever so much more trouble than such a journey. But of course if you can stay Friday night in Birmingham so much the better.

I shall now *send* you the Ironfounders Story, and pps, in a few days, for your corrections. But we need not be very [?worried] as Hey will edit it, and it will not be in type for months I suppose.

Pease has come home from Brussels (Mrs Pease stays in Scotland for some weeks yet). He has spent the evening with me, and I told him that you and I were working at T.U. together, but that it was not to be known, lest it gave rise to indiscreet remarks and unwarranted inferences. He will give you introductions to the Newcastle men, and to Dr Spence Watson. I enclose all his recollections of the National Labour Federation which is important, as it is spreading fast he says; and which you can study at Newcastle. It is a kind of supplement to the T.U., in style like the Knights of Labor. Moore Ede, Rector of Gateshead, is, it appears, a trustee, so Pease shall introduce you to him too. He is an excellent man, and would probably be well worth an evening: very good company, and can tell you what kind of men the locals are.

Pease will help much as to cabinetmakers, through Walker and Parnell, but says Exec. probably backward: will see Walker about it. I told him to say that *you* were enquiring, and I merely assisting you to get facts.

I fancy it might be useful for you to lecture for Muirhead (a good excuse to come to London!) But would it not be best to keep closely to a subject in our work? However, the 'moral hindrances to organisation' does lie within our scope. He has fixed *me* for Nov. 1st.

As to the article for Edgeworth, I doubt. Would it not be a serious diversion? It is a big and difficult subject which I don't gather that you are at present quite resolved upon.

Yes: it *is* serious for Edgeworth that if you are right, Mill and Co. were wrong. As Geo. Stevenson said 'so much the worse for the coo'!

I believe you might perhaps tell Edgeworth you are too much engaged(!) on another line to be able to do justice to his big theme: and that you could perhaps do something on T.U. later.

Dearest, today has been blank to me, missing you and your letter. Nevertheless you must not feel bound to write every day; I will learn to *think* of you far away, and so save your hands from too much writing.

I *will* be faithful to the C.O. I have much to do there: and I fear I make little progress with our work, though I try hard. Elvidge is coming on Friday. I am putting out some more of my work, so as to be freer. But not till October shall I have many hours to give to the very big task we have taken.

Again midnight is at hand, and I must take this to the post, or it may not be at the Post Office when you call. Good night, my dearest sweetest love. Surely I am nearer to you when I write this, and feel so much. Be patient with me. I will *try* to be worthy of your trust and love. Good night once more. Goodnight.

Sidney

151 PP SIDNEY TO BEATRICE

Beatrice's photograph appeared in *The Queen* on August 28. Sidney remarking in a letter on that date on the 'happy coincidence' that in the same issue the paper included a leading article on him. 'Whom the Queen has joined', he added, 'let no man put asunder'. On 1 September Sidney wrote that he had been photographed – 'a horrid ordeal . . . Nothing I can do will make a handsome face out of mine . . . I could not love you any more if I were perfect in form'.

Henry Edward Manning (1808–92), cardinal archbishop of Westminster, had strong social sympathies and played a leading part in the settlement of the 1889 dock strike. Manning sent a courteous letter of thanks for the *London Programme*.

4 Park Village East, N.W.

31 Aug/91

Dearest

You were angel-good to write me such a sweet letter yesterday, which gladdened me this morning, and did a great deal to pull me out of the depression I fell into on Sunday. Perhaps the cold dull weather had affected me a little – indeed, I have a little cold – but your letter put me in condition to do some work, and I finished off the Labor Commission reports this afternoon, posting you the result – not amounting to much of use to us out of 9 days sittings. The dockers are bad witnesses, and Tom Mann is not so good an examiner for them as for other trades. Perhaps it is that knowing all about it so well, it does not occur to him to bring out familiar points. I am glad we are not concerned with wages: the various witnesses get into hopeless contradiction as to the amount a docker gets. And they said practically nothing about the organisation of their unions, which we must get elsewhere. Tillett, especially, gave page after page of evidence of no value whatsoever.

Yes: I do hope you will see your way to our *writing* the book together. This separation is not nice and though we must go through with it uncomplainingly as long as it is necessary, let us, as rational beings, contrive that its necessity shall end as soon as possible. I think we can trust ourselves (and each other) to stick to whatever is necessary for the work. I should hate to think that I had been the cause of its neglect – abandonment is not be thought of. But we shall see how big a pile of material – and how extensive its range – we have a few months hence. Till then I must live on reading your letters to me, and on writing my letters to you; mitigated by such intermittent glimpses of each other as geography allows.

Thanks for the really beautiful little rose, which makes odorous my pocket book. I have nothing to send you in return except the enclosed letters (which can be destroyed).

I *will* be photographed presently: hitherto something else has always intervened.

My mother and sister were delighted with the *Queen*: but both say the picture is not at all worthy even of your photograph.

They have come back very well, and in good spirits.

I have sent copies of the *London Programme* to Spence Watson and Moore Ede (who had both taken much interest in it) – so you may perhaps hear about it. I have sent it also to Morley, Stansfeld and Cardinal Manning – the last on the chance of a puff among the Catholics – no, I think I did it chiefly on the chance of the Cardinal's using his influence well about the Catholics taking part in the County Council Election.

I am so glad Mrs Green is with you – and Wallas whom I love well enough to be always rebuking him! I *must* learn with your help, to get rid of my petulant impatience.

Now goodnight my darling. How happy and lucky I am in loving you and in being able to bring you happiness. Goodnight.

Sidney

152 PP BEATRICE TO SIDNEY

In the course of the next twelve months Sidney and Beatrice often arranged to rendezvous at a railway junction where their routes of travel crossed. A good many letters which deal primarily with travel and meeting arrangements have been omitted from this collection. On 16 September Sidney remarked: 'We are evidently going to incur a debt of gratitude to the Midland Railway hotels!' 'Certainly', Beatrice noted on 25 September, 'we are daring in our unconventionality – mostly meeting at a hotel and spending 24 hours there.'

Box House, Minchinhampton, Glos.
Sept 2nd [1891]

Dearest One

Mrs Green is travelling to Peterborough on Saturday and will pass through Birmingham. So we shall arrive off 1.12 train and she leaves at four o'clock – and we will stay the night there, as there are many things I want to talk about.

I am beginning to see into the leading points I want to investigate in Trade Unions: the facts I think range themselves under 6 headings

(1) Facts of organisations, administration and representation (the referendum is one of the most important of these I think).

(2) Personal independence: mutual protection against personal tyranny.

(3) Facts bearing on the standard of *expenditure* of the worker.

(4) Facts with regard to the technical and moral gratifications of the worker as a professional.

(5) The 'monopoly' side of Trade Unions in their attempt through limitations of process and restriction of persons to give an artificial value to the labour of a close body of individuals.

(6) The inclusive policy of Trade U. in their attempt to force all workers into Unions.

Now (5) and (6) seem on the face of them mutually contradictory? If all workers were in Trade Unions there could not be monopolies. The boys would have to go somewhere or they would form a body of non-society men who would ultimately form a Union which would compete with the old body of men, not as individuals, but as a group of men using a different *process*. Indeed the question of competing *processes* is one of the most interesting. Take for instance the tailors. The tailors have excluded the factory process in clothing; but directly you get the men and women at work and the new process organised you have competing groups not from employment under one manufacturer, but from the customs of the community. The Engineers competition in 1824 with the Millwrights is another instance. No unions could hope to be inclusive unless they altogether dropped the monopoly side and went only from *standard of expenditure* and possibly from technical and moral qualifications of the professional but this latter object is perilously near the monopoly side; I doubt whether they can insist on more than general education – an education which would come under 'expenditure' without worrying over the attempt to form a close body.

This is thinking aloud to you but it clears my ideas. I am more and more coming to the conclusion that if we want to get over the work well and quickly, it would be worth while for me to take Elvidge, and some similar persons as private secretary with me when I go off to the provinces the beginning of next year.

It would be worthwhile spending £200 in getting over the ground quickly and well.

But we will talk about it on Saturday.

I must now set to work, but I want a talk with you first.

Your faithful comrade
Beatrice Potter

153 PP SIDNEY TO BEATRICE

The Trade Unions: An Appeal to the Working Class and their Friends, by Robert Somers, was published in 1876; the English version of *The Trades Unions of England*, by the Comte de Paris, appeared in 1869.

4 Park Village East, N.W.
7.9.91

Dearest

I am afraid you found it a long journey last night – at any rate, I did. It was not nice to feel that I was going exactly in the opposite direction to you, our separation getting greater at the rate of nearly 100 miles an hour.

I hope the 'Crown' has proved a comfortable place enough. One cannot be at one's best unless the 'creature comforts' are attended to.

I see from the *D. News* [*Daily News*] that Burns was exhorting the Eight Hours men last night to stick to last years impracticable resolution, and not to 'weaken' by adopting Trade Option. This shows him at his worst as a statesman I think. The important thing is to carry *any* Eight Hours resolution: this, I fear, may be difficult enough.

You may probably be able to set Elvidge to copy (or rather abstract) Burnett's history of the Engineers in the *Newcastle Daily Chronicle*.

I was offered this morning a safe seat on the London School Board – which of course I declined. The Shoreditch Club has also written urging me to stand for County Council – this is very promising, and I am pursuing it (I have also a further nibble from West Islington).

I have looked at the T.U. Committee Reports 1867–69 (official copy), and there seems less in them than I had hoped. I am already very familiar with the general effect, having (on the way up) read very carefully the two opposing abstracts of them which I had with me (Somers and the Comte de Paris). I shall send you abstracts of all the Scotch evidence in a few days.

You are probably having tea with Elvidge or some trade unionists. I hope you will find time to see Rev. Moore Ede and perhaps Dr Spence Watson as they could both give you a 'general view' of T.U. and the character of them in all the North.

I have ordered the photographs of myself, as you directed. I wish I were more worthy of you – but you will make me so.

Now, dearest, I must break off, or else you will not get this by the first post. I hope you have not taken cold from our wet walk in 'Beckett's Park'. Write when you can, but I do not wish to burden you with too much writing.

Goodnight

Sidney

154 PP BEATRICE TO SIDNEY

William S. Caine (1842–1903) was a leading Liberal Unionist from Liverpool, who returned to the Liberal Party on the temperance issue and was elected for East Bradford in 1892. Sir John Eldon Gorst (1835–1916) was a Conservative M.P., active on educational and social policy. Sinclair was an official of the Tin Plate Workers Union. Beatrice noted on 25 September that she had no time at the Congress 'to watch the manoeuvres of the different sections or the intrigues of interested outsiders' for the Congress 'to me was merely the antechamber of my book' – a place to make useful contacts to be followed up later in her research.

The [T.U.C.] Congress [Newcastle]
[?8 September 1891]

Dearest One

I was very glad to get your letter this morning: I was tired and have had a bad night with the heat of the meetings.

The Congress is not unsatisfactory from the [*illegible*] view of harmony and straightness of dealing. There is endless wirepulling on both sides and bad suspicious feeling. It is doubtful to my mind, whether it won't end in a split of the old unions from the Congress. They are getting very angry. It is a mob worked by a few energetic men on both sides.

I am getting on all right in the way of introductions. Yesterday evening I was elected one of the Peculiar People – a club of T.U. officials and Slotter was the Chairman and very drunk.

You will see from the papers that the progressist party has the best of it. But the feeling is not sound; it is made up of a lot of cross currents.

Caine, Sidney Buxton, Gorst, C. Graham are here.

I am so tired; one can't think when one is so tired.

I try to make myself pleasant to everyone.

I am not quite sure whether it would not be desirable to give up Haldane's and stay on here. What do you think? I have openings here that I may not get again: and Elvidge is here to follow up. What do you advise? If you [think] I had better do this, do telegraph to me tomorrow.

It seems a pity to lose a good opportunity. I might stay on here until the end of the month and then go to Glasgow.

What do you say? I am almost resolved to do it. A word from you would decide.

I should be very sorry not to go to Haldane's, but we can go there another time.

Ever your devoted

Beatrice Potter

P.S. I should take lodgings in Tynemouth – you could perhaps come down for a Sunday later on.

By the way Sinclair said he was afraid you were in the hands of the Caucus! You might give an evening address.

Don't overwork dearest, we have lots of work before us we must keep fresh for it.

Ever your devoted B

155 PP   SIDNEY TO BEATRICE

Sir James Ferguson (1832–1907) was a former colonial governor and Conservative M.P. for North-East Manchester 1885–1906. In an undated letter Beatrice com ɪ ented on the seat that it wanted 'a bluff big hail-fellow-well-met man to win it. I fear you would not do!'

4 Park Village East, N.W.
9 Sept. 91

Dearest

I wonder whether you unbent to the extent of a 'Conversazione and Dance' with the delegates last night! I was toiling over my journalism and getting quite tired out. But I am better today. I do hope you are enjoying the fine weather: it seems to enervate me a little.

The Eight Hours vote is splendid as showing the rapid progress which the idea is making. Now, as 'nothing succeeds like success', it will go ahead still more. But the important thing is to conciliate the Lancashire men, which could, I should think, so easily be done on Trade Option lines, if personal friction were only avoided. It is more difficult to deal with the Northumberland and Durham men, who are afraid that the tightening-up of the employer may react on their exceptionally short hours.

The result – quite agreeably surprising to me – perhaps justifies Burns in sticking to his extreme resolution. But my instinct is so much towards a *practicable* working measure that I should have preferred Trade Option, even if it had led the *D. News* to cry triumphantly that the Congress was learning moderation! I think we should try to 'build a bridge' for the opponents. But Burns, no doubt, is thinking more of the influence of the masses.

The enclosed formal acceptance of my resignation will interest you. Don't destroy it: either keep or return it. Dearest, but for you, I should today be trembling, wondering whether I had done right. I don't think you quite realise how *much* you have saved me from, in the way of worry, anxiety and fear – and all the moral and intellectual difficulties that are born of these – I am horribly 'bourgeois' by temperament, and the temptation of a fixed income would have been enormous to me.

I send also a letter from Headlam. Of course I have said I can't accept a School Board candidature. *How* much am I to be supposed to be equal to?

I grieve to say that I have done nothing for THE BOOK this week: nor can I see my way to do anything for some days. I am very busy indeed: and Massingham being away, I have the whole [London] letter to write to Bradford every day – *without* the pars. which Massingham said he would send, and has not sent! (But of course you must not mention it to him.)

Yes: it is Sir James Ferguson's seat, contested by C. P. Scott last time, that my name is mentioned for. But even if (as is unlikely) they invite me to address them, I should consider carefully whether it would suit me to run. Most probably it will come to nothing – there will be dozens of such nibbles before I really get a seat.

I *do* wish I could be at work with you now, instead of both of us getting tired out at the end of the day 300 miles apart.

The Fabian Society still goes ahead: yesterday we had notice of a branch opened in South Australia: another contemplated in New York; others started at *Bournemouth* (!), and Cardiff; the *Essays* pirated in America; and being translated into Dutch. It will be interesting to see if all this has any lasting vitality. One thing, however, is clear; it is not now entirely the work of the half-a-dozen of THE Elect!!

Now, dearest, goodbye for today. I have a million yearnings to be with you: and failing that, I wish I might go on writing to you. But I must not.

Sidney

Geoffrey Drage (1860–1955) was the secretary to the newly-appointed Royal Commission on Labour. He was a protégé of Lord Salisbury and became a Conservative M.P. in 1895. Beatrice disliked his character and after a later disagreement described him as an intriguer and a 'mere schoolboy cad'. (BWD 21 September 94) Thomas Burt (1837–1922) was chairman of the T.U.C. and Liberal M.P. for Morpeth, being one of the first trade unionists to enter Parliament. He was the leader of the Northumberland Miners Union, and opposed to legislation to enforce the Eight Hour Day. J. Laidler, of the bricklayer's union, was an active socialist in Newcastle and a member of the S.D.F. He had won sufficient local support to be elected to the local school board. Joseph Cowen (1831–1900) was a former Chartist and a Radical: he owned and edited the *Newcastle Chronicle*. He was Liberal M.P. for Newcastle 1873–85, a double-member seat for which John Morley also sat from 1883 to 1895, selected by the local Liberal caucus to offset the more extreme views of Cowen.

At this Congress the T.U.C. supported the principle of a general Eight Hours Bill, despite strong opposition from the Northumberland and Durham miners, who worked only a seven-hour 'back-to-back' shift and feared legislation might increase their working day. The Fabian policy, to meet such objections, was to advocate a 'local option' for the application of any law. Though the Eight Hours campaign was an issue in the 1892 election, subsequent attempts to introduce a Bill acceptable to the miners were not successful for another fourteen years.

[Newcastle]
[?10 September 1891]

Dearest

The sight of your resignation is rather solemn. I trust that between us we shall [do] as good work as you would have done remaining as an official.

I had a long day yesterday – Drage brought Sir J. Gorst and we all walked up to Burt's to tea.

I completely ruined my chances of an Assistant Commissionership by turning on the supercilious Sir John savagely! I was tired and he has an odious face and manner. Burt was charming. He has made quite the Ideal Chairman. He was enthusiastic about my book and said he agreed with my last chapter! Afterwards I had Laidler to dine and he stayed until 11.30. He told me a good deal about Bricklayers' Union.

Today we have had another day of introduction. It is impossible to get any information as all the delegates are too excited. I am filling up for next week. I go to the Spence Watsons on Sunday afternoon. I move to the Bath Hotel, Tynemouth, tomorrow and shall be there until October. I see J. Cowen tomorrow. Morley is losing ground here. He has offended the Co-operators by throwing them over at the last moment [?at] the opening of the great corn mill, where pressure was put on him by tradesmen. His [?vacillations] quite unfit him to be a leader.

291

Now dear goodbye. Your letters are very sweet to me.

I am sorry I shall not have an opportunity of seeing Haldane; but one must not trifle with this big bit of work.

Dear [?friend] I am off to the garden party.

Ever yours

BP

157 PP BEATRICE TO SIDNEY

Drummond was an official of the Bricklayer's Union, who was helpful to Sidney and Beatrice with advice and introductions. Lady Dilke (1840–1904) was active in efforts to improve the conditions of working women, playing a leading part in the Women's Trade Union League from 1884 to her death.

[? Bath Hotel, Tynemouth]
Saturday [?12 September 1891]

Dearest One

The last day of the Congress.

The great feature of the Congress from a personal point of view is 'Burt is a *great* man'.

I always knew him to be good and upright but I had no idea that these qualities were to the degree of a great man in him. Of course he has, beyond honesty and an angelic temper, dry humour and fearlessness. I think it was his fearlessness and absolute selflessness that carried the day. But for Burt I think the Congress had in it the elements of dissolution. With him, the discussions have constantly been, from all accounts, on a higher level of intelligence than in any previous one.

By the way, Burt told me that he thought he was a socialist – it was the methods of the socialists that he *had* objected to not the aims.

The Parliamentary Committee you see is reacting. That is the result of votepulling. Poor Drummond is left out; I imagine, from all I hear, Mawdsley has played him false, got the vote of Printers and then voted *en bloc* for a list without Drummond and with Threlfall. Mawsdley is one of the ablest and most unscrupulous of the wirepullers – Burns not much better.

Lady Dilke was very much in evidence scattering invitations to dine. But it did not come off. At her dinner to some of the leaders some did not turn up and out of 8 who came there was only Shipton who was a man of importance.

She made a set at Drage. But he backed out, and Burnett would not go near her. She spoke to me – and suggested that I should be one of 4 sub-commissioners – Mrs Byles, Miss Routledge and another. Poor woman, I am sorry for her. It is a desperate hard fight she is making but she over-reaches herself – she is too conspicuously the intriguer – every now [and] then dashing her intrigues to the ground by an incisive and real frankness. But to return to the Commission – I told her that the time had passed when I was anxious to get it. I had other work on hand. Then when she spoke to me this morning I told her that I had mentioned Mrs Byles and Miss Routledge to Mr Drage and impressed him that they would be good Commissioners (which I did). She answered sharply 'He has been very much impressed with the daring of another person'. For which dash of frankness I liked her better. Poor woman. If she were only straight – one would give her a helping hand. Her doggedness and devotion is attractive.

So much for the gossip of the Congress. I have worked early and have worked late but I do not seem to have accomplished much, except that I have endless offers of help from general secretaries – and introductions wholesale.

Do you know dearest, I must confess that at times I have regretted that my days of free and unnoticed investigation were numbered. To make a really good book of this I ought to spend much more than a year at the simple investigations. That is the simple truth. I ought first to get the official history of the unions. That will take perhaps a year. Then I ought to go and live among the miners and other operatives and observe them carefully and the place that unionism takes in their lives. How can I combine that with marriage in a year's time? Every now and then I feel I have got into a hole out of which I can't struggle. I love you – but I love my work better!

It seems to me that unless I give up my work I shall make a bad wife to you. You cannot follow me about the country, and I cannot stay with you. How do you solve this problem?

I am settled here much to my comfort. It is a quiet little Hotel in a quiet little seaside place – looking on to the sea. The rooms are large and sunny and the people thoroughly friendly and hospitable. They give you a good bedroom, breakfast, and dinner in the evening for 6/-. It is 20 minutes from Newcastle by train. Of course it makes the journey longer to other places; but I think its extra quiet is worth it.

I have not had much chance of judging of Elvidge's capacity yet. He is a slow-minded man but conscientious and knows his way about. And he is one of the few men one could travel about the country with.

But he is extraordinarily slow and apathetic – I think his health must be very bad or his regime unhealthy.

He told Drummond that I had the most marvellous memory (I had dictated the result of an interview to him) which shows that he has a low standard.

It is difficult to know how much one must expect from a man. However I shall see the work what he is capable of.

Now, goodbye dearest one. We need not love each other the less because with both of us, our work stands first and our union second. We can give each other security in the widest sense – so long as we can face the separation which will be essential to free and full pursuit of our work.

Don't overwork.

Ever yours devotedly

Beatrice

Sunday

P.S. I have seen a lot of Massingham: [?J.M.] has not, I am sure, the slightest suspicion. I have just had a long morning with Elvidge. There is a great deal of work to be done here. (By the way, could you send me the list of Newcastle, Leeds and District?) So do not make any arrangements about Glasgow: I have a shrewd suspicion that it will take me the six weeks to do the Northumberland Durham and Cleveland trades.

BP

158 PP SIDNEY TO BEATRICE

The Pearsall Smiths, an American Quaker family, were one of the intersecting points between the Fabians and what became the Bloomsbury Group. Robert (1827–99) and Hannah (1832–1911) had three children: Mary (1864–1945); Logan (1865–1946), man of letters; and Alys (1867–1951), who became a close friend of Beatrice's and was the first wife of Bertrand Russell (1872–1970). Their home at Friday's Hill was a meeting place for progressive intellectuals and for the temperance reformers who shared Hannah Pearsall Smith's moral enthusiasms. Mary married Frank Costelloe. The eldest daughter, Rachel, married Lytton Strachey's brother Oliver: their second daughter Karin married Adrian Stephen. The art critic Bernhard Berenson visited the Smiths in 1890. Soon afterwards Mary Costelloe announced that she was going to Florence to study art under his guidance. Costelloe's Catholic beliefs made divorce impossible and it was only after his death in 1899 that Mary Costelloe and Berenson were discreetly married.

Marie Antoinette Sterling (1850–1904) was an American contralto who made her reputation as a ballad singer, especially with 'The Lost Chord'. Lady Isabella Somerset (1851–1921), a close friend of Hannah Smith, was world president of the Women's Christian Temperance Union: she exposed her husband's infidelities in a sensational case for separation. Her husband was a member of the Russell family.

George Philip Nowers was the principal of Edgbaston Preparatory School for Boys. James Ellis (1829–1901) was also a Quaker, much interested in education, who was M.P. for Bosworth 1885–88. He had three daughters.

Joseph Joachim was a celebrated Hungarian violinist. His niece was married to the Hon. Rollo Russell, the uncle of Bertrand Russell; Joachim's son Harold, a don at Merton College, Oxford, helped to introduce Russell to philosophy. Lord Monkswell (1845–1909) was a prominent member of the Progressive Party, member of the L.C.C. for Haggerston 1889–1907, and its chairman in 1903. Costelloe collaborated with J. H. Muirhead on a translation of Eduard Zeller's *Die Philosophie der Griechen* which appeared in 1895.

294

Dearest

I am writing this in Costelloe's cottage – tragically 'empty' of its mistress – whilst he has taken the two children to church. I think the *wickedness* of his wife has come home to me stronger than ever: (we have not recurred to the subject). I *do* hope she will come to her senses before harm is done. (I have no news of her.)

I was afraid I could not have made a letter reach you by Monday morning: even now it may be impossible – but I propose to walk into the next village where there seems to be a collection at midday, which may perhaps bring this to you tomorrow – at any rate by a late post. Yesterday I was overwrought. I arrived here with a bad headache, and a little hysterical. But I am better now: the weather is beautiful, and I shall do no manner of work till tomorrow noon.

I hope you liked Spence Watson: it is he who will preside at the National Liberal Federation meeting, and will probably prevent me from moving my resolution – of course, I shall not make a row.

Madame Antoinette Sterling and her husband (named McKinley) an eldest Eton boy son, and two pretty younger children are here (at the big house). Last night the Pearsall Smiths invited all the village, from the parson down to the lowest labourer, to come up and hear her sing. They came – perhaps 50 or so – and filled the drawing room, hall, and lawn. Madame Sterling sang 2 ballads, and 'The Lord is my Shepherd' very powerfully, and her children sang and recited. (The Smiths are kindly, but have a touch of commonness. 'Uncle Horace', a brother, recited and sang some wretched American things in between, which grated on me.)

Madame Sterling is a strong coarse-built woman, who is in a hysterical state of religion, anti-tobacco, teetotalism and so on – I could not help thinking of the Mahatmas! She has given up 'German music' and will now sing only English ballads because she thinks it does the people more good! (It is *this crude* didacticism that makes the artists abhor English Philistinism). Her husband is a silent unobtrusive American kind of Scotchman. Both seem intellectually poor. She is in with the Lady Henry Somerset religious philanthropy set – hence her visit here.

There are also a Mr and Mrs Nowers, grammar school master at Birmingham, and a Miss Ellis, daughter of James Ellis M.P. for Leicester. Some of the Joachims, too, were here for lawn tennis yesterday. I was overdone last night, and sat silent.

Costelloe's papers are lying around me – he has gone back to work on a translation of Zeller's *Aristotle*, which he has had on the stocks for ten years: this, too, is a sign of how much this blow has hit him. I *do* feel cross with her, and with the American loafer Berenson – and with Ibsen!

Dearest, whatever happens I pray that I may never fail in my duties towards those nearest to me. I cannot conceive that I ever could to you: but there are also family obligations. No amount of work for others seems to me to justify a failure to fulfil obligations entered into – whether, as Maine would say, these arise from contract or from status.

You will know that I do not mean that a man *or woman* should live in and for the family only: it is our business so to arrange our life as to measure our service in due proportion. But to abandon husband and children for *one's own self-culture* – to put it at the highest – strikes me as appallingly anarchic.

You might bring the *Speaker* this week. Dearest, I have given *your* copy to Pearsall Smith who asked me for it; forgive me! – there is a good article by Massingham descriptive of the *personnel* of the Congress, prettily done. (My article is a poor one, on 'The First Fortnight of Free Schools'.)

Do you know I have written *ten* articles (i.e. including London letters) in the last 7 days, besides *much* C.O. work: of course it is much too much, but Massingham was away, and sent me nothing. This is why I have done no work for THE book!

There is every sign that I shall stand for the County Council for Haggerston vice Lord Monkswell who will no doubt move to Chelsea (out of political devotion). This would be the safest of safe seats for me, and would leave me free to 'organise' the whole London election – on the basis of *The London Programme*. (Fancy, the *Anti-Jacobin* says it is '*brimful of excellent ideas*' but much too full of party spirit.)

Now, my love, I must bring this happiness to a close. I can't write about anything but myself, because I don't know what you are doing, and must give you the news. But it brings me nearer to you.

Goodbye till tomorrow

Sidney

159 PP SIDNEY TO BEATRICE

Joseph Henry Shorthouse (1834–1903) was a novelist whose psychological romance *John Inglesant*, published in 1881, attracted much interest among high-minded intellectuals. Richard Le Gallienne (1866–1947), poet and essayist, was a contributor to the *Yellow Book* and a prominent figure in the literary movement of the 1890s. T. R. Threlfall, William Matkin and Edward Harford were all actively involved in the effort to secure T.U.C. support for labour representation in Parliament. Threlfall, of the Southport Trades Council, was secretary of the Labour Electoral Committee from 1886–95; he was defeated as a Liberal candidate at Liverpool in 1892. Matkin, of the General Union of Carpenters and Joiners, was president of the T.U.C. in 1890. Harford, secretary of the Amalgamated Society of Railway Servants, was defeated as Liberal candidate at Northampton in 1895.

Dearest

It is two whole days since I saw your handwriting (no, that is not quite true! I mean, since I received a letter from you) as this morning letters are waiting for me at home.

I came up from Haslemere today, feeling much better, although still a little limp, perhaps through the weather which is now rainy again. I have really rested for 48 hours, in very beautiful scenery, and very agreeable circumstances – except, only that I thought of you as far away, and really needing my help for your notes(!) and for talking over the points that turn up. But perhaps Elvidge does nearly as well!

Dearest, I did miss you. We will go up Blackdown together one day. I wonder how you spent the Sunday.

The news about Mrs C. [Costelloe] is not very good: we had a long and frank talk together in the afternoon. She is at *Verona – your* Verona – he, too, there or thereabouts. But C. still thinks and trusts it will be all right; asserts that she has not the faintest idea or intention of leading any but an independent life; and that any move on *his* part towards anything else would bring about disillusionment at once. C. is playing a very magnanimous game: he has just sent her authority to sign cheques on his account! And talks of taking the children out to her in Florence. As he says, it is not worth playing unless he plays to win *completely*, to have her return to him wholly and spontaneously – for which he still hopes, though he does not hide from himself the immense danger she is unconsciously running.

I believe I am literally the *only* person who knows all this: so, of course, you must be absolutely silent.

Antoinette Sterling is completely *mad* about 'Christian Science', mind-cure, inner light, voices, reincarnation, and so on. It is a startling instance of the way the American woman goes clean off her mental balance on these topics.

Miss Ellis, daughter of Quaker M.P. for Leicester, turned out to be an interested enquirer into Socialism. (I believe most women are almost unconsciously flatterers of men!) and she made me expound when we went for a walk in the evening. I asked Nowers and his wife (Birmingham Grammar school master) how far it was true that municipalisation there was an imported article; and he quite confirmed your view that it was all due to Joseph Chamberlain, by himself and his clan. Mrs Nowers was very amusing about Shorthouse, the author of *John Inglesant*. I asked her if he was still deified as much by Birmingham as at first. 'Well', she said, 'we have left off taking the American visitors to see him'. Mrs Shorthouse is said to have a quite absurdly exaggerated idea of her husband's importance. (Dearest, I don't *think* that will be your failing – I sincerely hope not.) Once, at the Macmillans, she sailed up to Mrs Humphry Ward, (who had started the Inglesant boom by an article in the *Athenaeum*), and said gracefully 'Thank you so much for your little effort on our behalf'.

In the evening, there was a 'campfire'. This is a family institution. All sit shivering in rugs and shawls round a fire of faggots, and songs are sung. Company, as already reported, with the addition of some young Russells, striplings. We toasted 'marsh mallows', an American sweetmeat, and sang evening hymns. It was an elaborate attempt to be happy, and indeed, was not so bad, if only Tynemouth had not been so far off.

I enclose you a letter which Olivier has written to the *Star*, about the too-much of Meredith. ('Logroller' the *Star's* new writer of Book gossip, is R. Le Gallienne who has just published an analysis of Meredith).

I am glad that Threlfall and Matkin, and Harford are elected to the Parliamentary Committee and that it has funds. It can scarcely help moving a little this year.

Dearest, I feel half inclined to go home on purpose to find your letter. But I must wait until tonight – indeed, I must wait until the 30th before seeing you. I don't in the least object. I would infinitely rather endure to lose you for a year rather than have you neglect your work for my sake – you know, and believe, I am sure, that this is the exact truth. We could not love each other so well, loved we not our work and duty more.

Still, I am allowed to feel as if I wanted to 'will' myself to you. Now, at this moment, I stretch out my hands to you on the Tyne shore; and space is annihilated for us. But alas, this medium must come to an end. Goodbye, dearest for another day.

Sidney

160 PP SIDNEY TO BEATRICE

The letter to which Sidney refers is missing. Beatrice, as other letters and her diary make clear, found the research work exhausting: she alternated between fits of feverish activity and bouts of depression at the magnitude of the task they had set themselves. By October Sidney was free from the Colonial Office and went up to Tyneside to help her: to maintain appearances he was passed off as her private secretary. Beatrice noted on 10 October that without his assistance 'I doubt whether I could have got through the work – I have too little staying power for the extent of my brain'. Several letters of later date have been omitted as they merely repeat the supportive assurances which Sidney thought necessary to offset her self-doubt and ease her feelings of frustration.

4 Park Village East, N.W.
14 Sept/91

Dearest

I am *so* tired, but I must write to you again.

I found your long letter when I arrived home in the evening. Do not be disheartened by the size of the enquiry. We are not bound to complete the book at once. It will not be obsolete in a hurry.

Dearest, I must not hide from you that your letter came on me rather as a constriction of the heart. I am grieved to think that your loss by our love stands out so to you in this mood. My own love, count it *for something* at any rate that I shall be there to help you: the book will not be the worse for me. I can work at it and I will.

I am glad that I happened to touch on part of the point in my letter today, before I had seen yours. It comes thus better when you read, as you will have done, that I would rather lose your society for whole stretches of time than have your work impaired. But remember, what I intend to serve, what you must aim at, is the *net* total effect of your work. Perhaps it will pay better not to make the long and minute investigation into the effect of T.U. on the life – I question whether you ever *could* do that well enough: it is beyond any one person's powers.

Dearest, if you really think I am going to be a drag on you I shall be very very grieved.

But I am *not*, We can't be quite the same together as we were apart – but we can be much better, much stronger. You are not *fit* to write this big book alone: you would never get through it. When I really get to work at it, you will find me, not only a help instead of a hindrance – but also *the* indispensable help which will turn a big project into a big book.

Do not feel any compunction that your work will take you away from me sometimes. We are not going into this union, anymore than we go about any other part of our lives, merely to make things pleasant to us. You know, that I know, and I know that you know, that with each of us duty is imperative: and dearest, our kisses will be all the sweeter when we can afford them.

I will not say anything as to plans: you may perhaps find it well to stay on about Tyneside. But probably you would do well to make a beginning at Glasgow before coming south again. You can always stay at Newcastle again en route.

My dearest love, don't be despondent. We are not called upon for greater service than our conditions allow: we can neither of us escape the limitations of our age and sex: we must each of us grow old either alone or together. We should not really be more efficient if we broke our joint life in halves, and made shift with the pieces – nay we know full well how much we *both* gain by our mutual help, even if it makes some things less easy. Be happy, dearest, and have patience. I am worn out with work, but I can and will spare time to give you a hand. You have made a splendid beginning; and all is well.

Love

Sidney

Sidney was one of the half-dozen Fabians who were to attend the important meeting of the National Liberal Federation in Newcastle at the beginning of October. His interest in Gateshead was due to his belief that he had a future chance of securing a parliamentary candidature there.

4 Park Village East, N.W.

15/9/91

Dearest

I was unhappy last night because I feared you were unhappy, and unsettled. But this morning I think this is not so. Dearest, you shall not regret our love. You shall do more work and better for it, with my help. I will be the one to insist on making the conditions such as to allow of this. I shall not need to call in my pride to help me to do this: there will be no struggle: *you* know that it hurts me more to seek my own advantage against my sense of right, than to forego something in accord with it; indeed, any selfishness will be your safeguard.

I can say this to you because you and I are one, and I have no sense of shame in telling you what comes to me: and you know that I am telling you the truth.

Now tell me just what comes to you, whatever it is but try not to cast a shadow on my happiness by dealing in regrets. Of course I am not blind to the 'incompatibility of incompatibles': but you shall gain much more than you can lose – I mean in the way of work *actually accomplished.*

Now I refuse to think anymore about that, and I will think only of your face waiting for me, and I so longing to be with you.

Alas, I may be a day later than I had hoped. The enclosed letter may be important. It may be necessary for me to speak in Gateshead on the evening of the 30th Sept. and then I should hardly see you until the 1st Oct.

What shall I do about lodging? I am almost bound to stay with Moore Ede for one night, or two: but of course I could be in Tynemouth in the daytime. Will you go to the big Liberal meeting on Oct. 1 and 2? I shall no doubt have to be at one, if not both of them. Dr Spence Watson would get you a ticket if you wrote for one: perhaps we could get together, perhaps not.

Shall I take lodgings in Tynemouth for a week from Oct. 2nd? That would suit us best I think. I have told Moore Ede that I have other arrangements to consider which may keep me in the neighbourhood or in Scotland, for a little time, and that I will let him know in 2 days. So write me your orders.

You and I *must* be together a good bit every now and then to report progress, and concert about the book – even if there were no other reasons!

I had dinner last night with Massingham, who had much to say about you. He has no suspicion, or he would not have talked so frankly! He was sharp enough to spot that you had written to me, because I had said in the *Bradford Observer* that Sir John Gorst had not done himself much good by going: 'he has an unfortunate manner'; and also an incidental reference to John Morley and the Dunston Mill which I had woven into something else. So I told him that you were in correspondence with me as to the book, in which I should probably help you with the law and economics. He would soon have found out that I was concerned in the book and (if I had not so spoken) would have thought my reticence suspicious. Then we talked of other things, and incidentally of my own prospects. He said 'But you really must marry some woman with a thousand a year'. I said 'You mean, Beatrice Potter?' And he, quite sincerely, and honestly said 'No, No. "Potterism" is to be taken with a large grain of salt. I don't know that you wouldn't find that you had *bitten off more than you could chaw*. And I don't think she has much money: she doesn't live like it. No, don't marry a clever woman, they're too much trouble'.

So you see what he thinks of you! He will be convulsed with laughter one day when he remembers all this.

I explained to him how important it was from the T.U. point of view to keep quite secret that I was to have any hand in the book. And I said, 'I tell you, lest you should, when you found it out, draw unfounded inferences from our keeping it so quiet'!

I send you the *first sheets* of the Northumberland and Durham industries: the others are not copied yet. My copyist put them aside as he thought there was no hurry. I will send them tomorrow.

The blue books have arrived from Miss Darling. I will go to work on them presently.

Now dearest, be good to me, and trust me perfectly, do not let your thoughts even do me injustice. I shall be far too well paid if I only have a little bit of you – you certainly do not believe that I should want to take you from your work. Many months in the year I shall not need to be in London: and even all the rest you could be elsewhere.

I make too much of this, but your 'puzzle' wrung my heart. Love will find a way. *Do* be happy, or I cannot be, however kind you are. I do so want the end of the month to come.

Dearest, adieu

Sidney

162 PP SIDNEY TO BEATRICE

The part played by the Fabians in promoting the Radical resolutions adopted by the Newcastle conference has often been exaggerated, partly as a result of an inaccurate account given by Bernard Shaw in Fabian Tract 41, *The Early History of the Fabian Society*, which was based on a speech he gave to a Fabian gathering on 6 February 1892. He claimed that Newcastle Programme as a Fabian triumph, citing it as one instance of 'the extent to which the policy of permeating the party organisation with socialism had succeeded'. This view was inflated in a graphic account he sent in 1915 to Pease, then writing his *History of the Fabian Society*. In this much-quoted letter, allegedly giving the 'exact facts', he insisted that 'Webb gave me the Program in his own hand as a string of resolutions' and that he whisked them through a Liberal meeting in Tottenham Court Road, whence they were despatched to the Newcastle Conference.

This letter from Webb, with others that follow, gives a quite different impression. He suggests that the 'moderate' resolution he quotes was the best that could be done, even in the Holborn Liberal Association, which was the most thoroughly permeated by Fabians in London: it does not even come out explicitly for an Eight Hours Bill. Webb was also very doubtful whether there was much point in him or other Fabians going to Newcastle because so little could be expected from the conference. As late as 24 September he thought the Federation would make 'no other advance' than to support the payment of M.P.s. It is likely that Shaw's reference to a 'string of resolutions' applies to the set of suggestions made to the 1889 conference of the National Liberal Federation by the London Liberal and Radical Union, largely on Webb's initiative.

Webb confirmed this more sceptical opinion about Fabian influence in an important letter to Pease (4 June 15 FP) in which he reviewed the Fabian attempt between 1887 and 1892 'to make the Liberal Party realise that it ought to have a programme apart from Ireland'. He said that the executive committee of the N.L.F., 'with Gladstone's unwilling acquiescence', expanded the Nottingham resolutions 'into a much fuller list of measures (yet not so much after all!) This we expanded and exaggerated into "the Newcastle Programme"'. He added the significant words: 'I certainly had no hand in drawing up the resolutions which the Exec. Com. of the N.L.F. submitted at Newcastle; and was in no way committed . . . The Newcastle resolutions were quite poor and feeble, in reality, but they were made to sound well!' The hotch-potch of proposals passed at Newcastle, moreover, contained nothing distinctively Fabian; all of them had been current among Radicals for some time. The handful of Fabians at the conference played no real part in it; even Webb himself failed to speak, his amendment on a minor point being ruled out on procedural grounds. It was only in retrospect, after the incoming Liberal government in 1892 ignored the letter and the spirit of the Newcastle motions that they became tactically important to the disillusioned Fabians, whose hopes of successful permeation had been unduly and somewhat naively raised by them. By 1893 both Shaw and Webb had abandoned the policy they had followed from 1885 of working in and through the Liberal Party – a break which had important consequences both for the Fabians and for the future career of the Webbs themselves.

Sir William Harcourt (1827–1904), a prominent Liberal, was a supporter of Home Rule and political reform, Chancellor of the Exchequer under Gladstone in 1886 and 1892, and thought to be a possible successor to the Liberal leadership. Francis Allston (1841–1926), later Lord Channing, was a Liberal M.P. interested in agricultural labour and educational reform. J. S. Mather was a leading Liberal in Leeds. Beatrice was going to stay with Sir Hugh Bell (1844–1931), a colliery-owner, ironmaster and railway director. His wife Frances was interested in social problems. His daughter later married the Liberal politician and close friend of the Webbs, Charles Trevelyan.

Dearest

Do not be despondent at feeling you cannot do all you would wish: I do not doubt that you have done an immense deal. The mechanical part which you find so difficult is the least important. Your business is *to think*.

I have taken a decisive step in political tactics. The Holborn Liberal and Radical Association has sent in the mildest of mild resolutions to the National Liberal Federation, with an express request that it be put in the agenda for the annual meeting. It runs,

That this Council is of opinion that early steps should be taken to enforce a legal restriction of excessive hours of labor, in those in-dustries in which such restriction can be effectively carried out, and in which a decisive majority of the workers desire it.

This is *so* moderate that I do not doubt that the meeting would accept it if it were put. It goes indeed, very little beyond what the bulk of Liberal M.P.'s have already committed themselves to, under Sir Wm. Harcourt's lead, when they voted for Channing's resolution as to railway hours last January, when the official Liberal whips were the tellers in the division.

But if it were to be put and carried at Newcastle it would be an immense stride forward for our side.

I do not think they will adopt it, but it will be very awkward for them to refuse it, coming so close after the Trade Union Congress. I think the officials are in a difficulty; and it appears to be a moment to press forward, especially as it is the last chance before the general election. So I have written to Schnadhorst, Dr Spence Watson, Percy Bunting and Mather of Leeds, who are the most influential members of the General Purposes Committee of the N.L.F. carefully (and I hope, modestly!) explaining the situation. Of course I said *I* did not want to move the resolution, if they would adopt it; but that if they did not, I proposed to move it.

One curious result is that Schnadhorst, who had written to ask me to call today in connection with the list of suitable Labor candidates I had compiled for him, suddenly sent a note across to say that 'unexpected engagements' compelled him to ask me to defer my call till Monday! (by which time he will have heard from Dr Spence Watson).

I have made my article for the *Speaker* a caustic comparison of the T.U. Congress with the N.L.F. meeting – so I think it quite likely that Wemyss Reid (who is a member of the General Purposes Committee of the N.L.F.!) may refuse to insert it. If he does put it in, it will serve as driving force to the Holborn resolution.

Dearest, I can't help feeling that this inconvenient action will not in-gratiate me with 42 Parliament St, and may therefore make them less dis-posed to find me a seat. But I *could* not refrain from doing what seemed best, merely on that ground. I know you don't attach very great value to my getting in this time, but even if you did, I feel certain you would not have wished me to abstain in order to ingratiate myself.

Honestly, I believe that the Liberal Party is running the most serious risk of shrinking up into a middle-class group, like the German 'National Liberal *Partei*'. I believe that would be bad, and I have played to save it from that fate, even if it should imply Morley's resignation. But of course, it is not so momentous as that. They will probably refuse to put my resolution to the vote on some specious excuse. That will do them harm, but I can do nothing further to help them.

I hope the change to the Bells', and to Durham may be agreeable – I look for a letter every morning. And tell me, presently where and how I am to see you.

I am not going to work so hard this week as last. Tomorrow I open the Autumn Course for the Fabian Society, but only on Women's Wages again.

I can't help you until I can be with you!

Goodbye, my love, until tomorrow.

Sidney

163 PP SIDNEY TO BEATRICE

Shaw's book, *The Quintessence of Ibsenism*, was published by Walter Scott in October 1891. The 'solemn sheet' was black-edged writing paper, mourning for Sidney's father.

4 Park Village East, N.W
18 Sept/91

Dearest

My article is in the *Speaker* – accompanied by another by Wemyss Reid on 'The Bully in Politics' (!) which is, however, really called forth by J. Cowen's violent abuse of Morley in the *Newcastle Chronicle*, and by [W. T.] Stead's denunciation of Dilke. Still, Reid has chosen to 'go for' me also in a note. I don't feel guilty, and it does not matter. The Liberal leaders are playing an equivocating and disingenuous game, and I think those who differ from them (and who believe that the great mass of the rank and file differ from them) have a right to ask that the programme shall be made to fit the popular desires. Gladstone and Morley are but the spokesmen of the Party; if the Party moves, they must either *se soumettre ou se démettre*.

But, or course, the *manner* in which they have been approached has not always been felicitous, and although I have not been personally concerned in the Newcastle movements, there seems to be an undying impression that I was.

I send you the *Speaker* in case you don't see it.

I am glad you were to see the Miners' Committee: you evidently learn a great deal that way – I can easily confine myself to getting the facts of those T.U. which do not object to me, e.g. Sinclair's Tin Plate workers, the Labour Federation, Laidler's Bricklayers etc. and you will have lots of notes etc. for me.

I will go to the Grand Hotel, Tynemouth, as you suggest. I propose, subject to future changes, to arrive at Newcastle about 4 p.m. on Wednesday 30 Sept. – to see if you are about (we could perhaps dine together) – and go to sleep at Moore Ede's, *perhaps* speaking at a meeting that night (probably not now). Then I should move to Tynemouth on Thur. 1 Oct.

I saw Miss Bridgman last night at the Fabian meeting. She asked after you, with a good deal of suppressed amusement at the comedy we are playing the world.

I send you Shaw's book on Ibsen which has just reached me. It is very clever; and not so bad as I feared. I can see no alternative to treating women as human beings *coûte que coûte*: but his glorification of the Individual Will distresses me.

Dearest, this is a solemn sheet of paper, and a solemn handwriting, but it comes from one whose heart is leaping joyously because he is thinking of you; and who is counting the days until he can once more see your face, and feel your hand. My love, you have already transformed me: and you are going to do so still more. I most sincerely pray that I may, in return, be saved from doing you harm, or causing you aught but happiness.

Once more, adieu till tomorrow.

Sidney

164 PP SIDNEY TO BEATRICE

4 Park Village East, N.W.
20 Sept/91

Dearest

I wonder what you have been doing today? I hope the Bells have not oppressed you with *too* much splendour, though I dare say you can do with a great deal of that occasionally.

I have missed you so much. I felt tired, and have rested; and after our midday dinner I lay on the sofa and pretended half to go to sleep, but I was thinking of you – putting together the smile of your lips, and curve of your forehead, and the little movement of your nostrils, and the sound of your voice into a kind of picture, which never got complete because each time I lost myself in the one point that I could realise. There's waste of time!

I am afraid you won't get this by the first post – our London Sunday postal arrangements are so awkward. But you will, I suppose, not arrive at Durham until midday, so that it will, I hope, come soon after you do.

I have heard nothing from Mrs Green yet, and I almost think I will call and enquire in some days time – perhaps I shall manage to see her next Sunday.

305

I hope the *Speaker*, and Shaw's *Ibsenism*, reached you all right at the Bells – and that my article did not seem to you in the wrong tone. (Of course, as to Wemyss Reid's criticism of fact, it is I who am right, not he. There are, by the rules, over 5,000 delegates entitled to be present at the National Liberal Federation meeting, and the highest number ever present is about 2,000). I hear that a minority on the General Purposes Committee wants to put in a resolution limiting hours, but the majority refuses. We shall see. F. A. Channing M.P. is pressing them to put it in as regards railwaymen – this they may adopt as a compromise (which I should accept). More probably they will do nothing. But I am told they feel in a hole.

T. P. O'Connor is again most friendly to me in the *Sunday Sun* – the third time within a few weeks (I enclose the cuttings – which destroy). Now I see his object. He seems to think of running me against Stuart in London matters. This will suit very well, as it comes about without any seeking of my own.

By the way, the *Star* is inserting a series of articles on *The London Programme* which are founded on, and largely borrowed from my book. *That*, too, does very well, and nonetheless well because they don't acknowledge their borrowings. This is the kind of utility that I thought the book would have. It 'tunes the pulpits'.

I hope you don't feel that I am taking more interest in these things than in T. Unionism. It is not so, but I can't possibly do anything to speak of for THE BOOK until the end of the month, and the other matters go along of themselves. I am more and more struck with the importance of mastering T. Unionism and more and more coming to think that there will be no place for me in the next Parliament. (By the way it appears as if Sir J. Ferguson were going to be made Postmaster-General, i.e. an election in North-East Manchester. But I don't think they will ask me to stand. I should be uncertain what to do. A contest in a bye-election is the best possible road to election; and it might be the necessary preliminary of Gateshead).

Now my love good night. I have not said all I should like to say but I have given you all my news, and I must not write anymore. Don't tire yourself even with lengthy letters to me – but I do love to have just a line from you.

Goodnight dearest

Sidney

[Catalogue entry]

44 GEORGE HARDING, 6, Hyde
POLITICAL ECONOMY, ETC. – cont. 1173 Heyworth (Laurence) Glimpses at the Origin, Mission and Destiny of Man, with Miscellaneous Papers on Taxation, Peace, War, Intoxicants, etc., 8vo, half cloth, 5s 1886.

Is this by your grandfather? Do you possess a copy? Shall I buy it for us?

Beatrice used the Bath Hotel, Tynemouth, as a base for her visits to mining villages and trade union offices.

[? Redcar]
[?21 September 1891]

Dearest One

I had a long day with Mr Bell going over his works. Hugh Bell is the last type of captains of industry – modest in expenditure, energetic and scientific in finding inventions and new processes. Indeed he made me feel ashamed of my reforming spirit – he was working so hard and so well and with so much modesty and experience. The only blot in the organisation is the bad spirit of the men – obstructive to improvements and turbulent – on his side an impatience with their stupidity and short-sightedness – the Unions and its officials are the only connecting link between the stupid and stolid insistence of the men for as much pay with as little labour as possible, on the one hand and the big world of commercial hustle and energy on the other. He was awfully kind to me; but he said I was 'not cosmopolitan enough, had not realised the facts of the world's markets'.

Today I have been all the morning interviewing two secretaries. These counties are the home of *Federation* as distinguished from Amalgamation. The mines are inter-federated in all manner of ways in trades, in counties and districts. But I feel I am still hammering at the outside of Trade Unionism not inside – I have not yet broken the crust of the subject. It is that consciousness that makes me feel a bit depressed.

I do hope you will not stand for a bye-election. Think of all the expense – £800 thrown away! And I want you at least till the general election to help me.

I go back to the Bath [Hotel] tomorrow. Now I must set to work at my notes else I shall forget all I have heard. Dear Boy goodbye.

Ever your devoted comrade
Beatrice

166 PP   SIDNEY TO BEATRICE

Sir Robert Henry Meade (1835–98) became permanent under-secretary in the Colonial Office in 1892, succeeding Sir Robert Herbert (1831–1905).
Beatrice replied to this letter with an offer to visit Mrs Webb. 'I should not like to feel that both your parents left the world during our engagement without one word from me of gratitude and affection'. (n.d. ?24 September PP) In another undated fragment at this time Beatrice repeated her disapproval of Sidney's desire to enter Parliament. 'There is excellent work for you to do outside it for a time – work which will fit you to be a better representative when the time comes . . . learn the trade . . . Once in Parliament you will be forced into the machinery of politics and very possibly lose sight of the direction the machine

should take.' She told Sidney that she had apprised the hotelkeeper at Tynemouth that Sidney was arriving on 30 September as 'a gentleman to help me with my papers' so that 'he will not be surprised if you spend a lot of time there'.

4 Park Village East, N.W.

23 Sept/91

Dearest

The feeling of being 'outside' of the T.U. movement is quite natural and inevitable. It will last until you one day feel yourself inside without knowing how you arrived. I remember 13 years ago thinking that I never *could* become familiar with the intricacies of the government office I then entered. I knew that I should take no real interest in it, and I felt that I must always be groping in the dark. But a very few months work among the papers unconsciously made it like ABC to me. This must have happened to you with Productive Co-operation. You will soon find T. Unionism mapping itself equally clearly in your mind. And it is just as well, to begin with an 'outside' view.

The Bells were evidently a great 'find' for you. We will take occasion in the book, I suggest, to describe the ideal captain of industry.

Dearest, here is my portrait in its finished form. I fear I can't 'put a better face on it' than that. You will help me to be true to the better part of me, and perhaps by upright living I may get some kind of light in my face which will take off its ugliness.

But if it has found favor with you, I can easily put up with the caricatures or repulsion of others.

You will like to see the enclosed kindly note from the Hon. R. H. Meade who has always been my favorite among the under-secretaries. He is second to Sir R. Herbert.

I am sorry to say my mother gets weaker. She is nervous about being alone with my sister, and likes someone else to be in the house. She is very well in health and in good spirits, but going downstairs is becoming more and more difficult to her.

There is no reason for alarm: but I do not think she can live very long. My love, I should like you to have known her. She has been a good mother to me – much better than she is in the least aware of – and I owe her a great deal more than my good health.

I have heard nothing from Mrs Green. I shall call next Sunday if I hear nothing before then.

I have done nothing in the way of summarising the 1867–8 bluebooks – except, by the way, read them! – because there is a fairly exhaustive printed analysis of the evidence at the end; and the books of Somers and the Comte de Paris are both virtually summaries from different points of view. I do not think it will be necessary to do more than look through for evidence on specified points when we can be sure of what we want.

I have just had an interview with Schnadhorst about the list of possible Labor candidates which I prepared at his request. He knew them nearly all, and he really seems to have tried all *he* could to put them into seats. But, as I said at the end, the thing *was not done*; and however virtuous he may have been, the effect remains. We were getting a little 'warm' over it when Bryce came in unexpectedly and brought the interview to a close. (I waited for Bryce to remember me, and he did so, and we just shook hands.) There seems very little hope of the Liberal Party doing anything before this general election is over. Schnadhorst was *very* civil, but vague, as to my own candidature (which I did not allude to) and I told him that I was changing my opinion as to tactics, and was in no hurry to get into Parliament now. I am not likely to be called upon to fight a bye-election, dearest, and I certainly should not spend £800 on it!

Now I must close this up. We shall soon be able to talk things over face to face – you with the glow of faith, I with the light of love, in our eyes, and both with the warmth of hope in our hearts.

Goodbye, my dearest

Sidney

167 PP SIDNEY TO BEATRICE

Cowen's opposition to Morley fed the desire of local labour men to run their own candidate at Newcastle – a later source of trouble between the Liberals and the socialists on electoral policy. So far as Sidney was concerned the agitation against Morley was an embarrassment to his prospects of securing a Liberal nomination at Gateshead.

E. R. A. Seligman (1861–1939) was professor of political economy at Columbia University, New York, from 1885 to 1931. He was noted for *The Economic Interpretation of History* (1902).

The proposed meeting was to prepare for the Newcastle conference.

4 Park Village East, N.W.
24 Sept/91

Dearest

I feel guilty when I make you write to me when you are tired. I *do* like even a line from you, but don't feel bound to send it every day.

The article quoted by Cowen from the *Financial Reformer* was one of the 'pot-boilers' I threw off a fortnight ago, under my standing contract with that paper. I wrote it 'strong', because I thought the Editor would tone it down (I drew his attention to it). But apparently he thinks the time has come for strong representations to the Liberal officials.

I hate the way Cowen is going on. He has no sympathy with Socialism and I cannot but believe that he is taking it up out of the purely personal motives of hatred of the local Liberal caucus, and jealousy of Morley. I have seen no sign that he has any programme which would justify him in the continuance (now for over 7 years) of this virulent abuse of Morley's policy – nothing could justify his abuse of Morley personally. I am glad to think that I have never countenanced the idea of running a Labor candidate against Morley on Cowen's money – which will be done – and that the only time I have spoken at Newcastle I spoke strongly against it, or the formation of a hostile Labor group.

I rather infer that the National Liberal Federation *will* now adopt Payment of Members, without reserve, but make no other advance, unless some more express notice of the agricultural laborer.

Don't overwork. That note-taking is very fatiguing. Dearest, there will be time.

I had dinner last night with Dr Seligman, the economics professor at Columbia College, New York, and Editor of the *Political Science Quarterly*. He has been in Austria where he met Marshall (at some watering place). One pretty anecdote he had. Marshall wrote him several brief notes making arrangements etc. Opening one of these he found it addressed 'my own dear darling' and concluding 'Your affectionate Alfred'.

Marshall had accidentally sent him a letter to his wife! (Dearest, I hope we may be on such terms twenty years hence, but I hope and believe that this can happen without any absorption of the life of one of us into that of the other.) But it is a revelation of a pretty, affectionate sentiment which I am glad to hear of in Marshall.

Seligman said that Marshall hoped to finish his second volume within 2 or 3 years! He also said that Marshall was dissatisfied with the *Economic Journal*, and hinted that he should prefer if the Editorship were changed! I can only infer that he thinks Edgeworth a little *too* impartial and open-minded.

Seligman was very complimentary about the *London Programme*! I don't think it has done me harm, and it is already of obvious use – Stuart is using it daily for little articles in the *Star* without acknowledgement.

I *do* try to write you an interesting letter, without too much of 'King Charles the First's Head'! But if I wrote just as I thought it would be nearly all Head! This morning as I lay in bed I almost seemed to see you appear to me as you looked lying in the long chair at Box last October. You were very kindly disposed just then – I don't think I shall ever forget that afternoon. I feel so *strong* in your love and confidence that nothing seems to tire me. Instead of days of serious 'worry' and anxiety, you have given me Hope and Security. I can never give you enough in return; but what you will like best is that I should be worthy of your trust – and that I mean to be, so far as in me lies.

Wallas, Clarke and I meet next Tuesday to talk over political tactics. We have asked Tom Mann, H. Ll. Smith, Vaughan Nash and Benjamin

Jones to join the discussion, but I don't know whether any of them will come.

Now, 'my own dear darling', goodbye for today.

Your affectionate

Sidney

168 PP   SIDNEY TO BEATRICE

Reference to 'Labour Party' and 'Labour' candidates, sometimes capitalised, and sometimes spelt American-style as 'Labor', can be confusing for the period before the formation of the Independent Labour Party in 1893. There were already a number of small labour electoral associations in England which sought to promote workingmen candidates, either as Liberals or independents: a few of these used the name Labour Party, usually prefixed by the name of the locality. A Scottish Labour Party had been formed by Keir Hardie and Cunninghame-Graham after the mid-Lanark bye-election in 1888. The word was often used generically to describe the movement towards a separate party representing trade union and socialist groups. Further confusion was caused by the ambivalent phraseology of some socialists, such as Hubert Bland and Annie Besant among the Fabians, who did not clearly distinguish between a separate *Socialist* party and a more widely-based *Labour* party running its own candidates at local and national elections. The opposition to Webb and other active Liberals within the Fabian Society was primarily concerned to promote political action distinct from and if necessary against Liberal candidates chosen by local caucuses. From the meeting to which Sidney refers came the interesting proposal that the Liberals should allow up to fifty workingmen candidates a clear run in exchange for labour and socialist support of Liberals elsewhere. The proposal, canvassed by Webb at Newcastle, made no headway at the time: it was, however, a prescient anticipation of the formula whereby the Labour Representation Committee managed to break into Parliament in the 1906 election.

Sidney remained on Tyneside for a fortnight after the Newcastle meeting. After he returned to London Beatrice wrote (?19/20 October PP) that she had been happy with the way they had worked together. 'I feel much more confident that our marriage will not interfere with our own work'; in a characteristic example of the way she 'coached' Sidney on his manners she urged him 'to get a new tie and string to your pincenez, and look after your pronunciation. You can't afford not to be careful about externals you can improve!' (21 October 91 PP)

Travelling to Durham one day she found herself on the same train as Joseph Chamberlain and his young wife. 'I thanked Providence that I was travelling third class in search of knowledge and not first class in his train . . . They seemed to me an *absolutely suited pair* – both enveloped in a sense of social prestige and material comfort – he the dominant male and she . . . *la femme complaisante*.' (BWD 22 October 91) She shuddered as she imagined the life she had missed. 'Now, indeed, I can bless him for his clear understanding of my deficiencies for the great role of "walking gentlewoman" to the play of *Chamberlain*.' Sidney wrote on 23 October to say he was glad she had no pangs of regret. '*He* will not understand your choice but you shall never regret it if I can do anything to make you happy and serve our common ends.'

311

The loss of most of Sidney's early correspondence is explained by the unfortunate 'holocaust' when he started his new life.

4 Park Village East, N.W.

28 Sept/91

Dearest

I will be 'good', since you wish it. Very likely you are right. But do you be kind, and think nothing about it, and leave it *to me* to be watchful. I can be very strong if I like.

I am not afraid, if we will only be frank with one another. There is nothing that I could not do for you – I will go to Tynemouth with you on Thurs. night; and I am free Friday night, as I have sent back the ticket for Gladstone's meeting.

We will do a lot of work together, but you must let me keep my journalistic engagements. I should be glad enough to throw them all up, and do nothing but the book. But we must be cool and calculating, and act warily.

I will see to the cigarettes.

This morning I saw Cardinal Manning who was very 'courtly' and flattering. He thought at first that I wanted help for my own candidature and offered to do various things for me. But I managed to explain what I wanted, namely that he should stir up the Irish to vote, and he said he would. The great difficulty, he said, was their feeling that they were aliens and that nothing English concerned them.

He said he was convinced that unless some great change in our social system were made, there would be a crash. The land could not go on as it was, nor 'what Mr Gladstone had called irresponsible capital'. Much must be done for the people, which could only be done by laying hands on the ground landlords.

That is pretty strong from a Cardinal.

I shall not be able to see Elvidge before I leave. There is *so* much to do these last days. Tomorrow night we have a small meeting at Wallas's

Wallas   Vaughan Nash
Clarke   Llewellyn Smith
Webb   Massingham

Benj. Jones and perhaps Tom Mann, to discuss political tactics, (Labor Party etc.) *I*, at any rate, am not the instigator of the feeling against him.

I have just made a great holocaust of old letters etc., preparatory to leaving the C.O. tomorrow. This brings home to me that I am to live a new life – by your help. I will not fail to be true to the best within me – and then it matters not what comes by way of result.

Now I must close, only two more days. I will rush round to the 'Crown' as soon as my train arrives (should be 3.42 p.m.).

Goodbye, loved one.

Sidney

When Beatrice decided to collaborate with Sidney on the trade union book her plan to work with Llewellyn Smith was abandoned: he then undertook research in London for Charles Booth. While it seemed sensible to avoid an overlap of work and to exchange material the matter was complicated by the strained relations between Beatrice and the Booths.

4 Park Village East, N.W.

24 Oct/91

Dearest

Your letter was a consolation this morning, as I was a little unhappy.

It was in this wise. Last night I saw Llewellyn Smith at the N.L. Club, and we were both glad of the chance to talk, but had only a quarter of an hour. I said I should like to know whether you and I on the one hand and he on the other could make any arrangement of the London T.U. to avoid duplicating the work. To my surprise he hummed and hawed; said he did not know how far he could use our material; and then asked me bluntly whether I was doing the work for science or for propaganda!

I own to feeling wounded, but (as I told him) I was not much surprised as I had imagined (really it was Wallas) that his first impression would be that I should spoil your book. He then endeavoured to be nice but his first expressions were the truest index to his mind.

However, you know how far this is just, and I need not mind, but I was hurt at his evident doubt whether I *could* ever study anything!

But, that feeling apart, it does not seem that we could make any arrangement, as he tells me that it is not he, but Booth's secretariat which is doing the work, he only initiating them into each union, and supervising them. It is not his enquiry, and it is not even definitely settled that he will write the chapter. So we should have to arrange with Booth if we desired to exchange material.

Thereupon I told him that I desired strongly that no word should be breathed to Booth on the subject, who, *he said*, of course knew nothing about me in connection with the book. And I said I felt sure you would strongly prefer that nothing should be said to Booth as to interchange unless and until you chose to speak to him yourself.

Dearest, I fear this is a case in which I shall hamper you. But I will make up for it by my own work if I can.

They are at work on (1) Printing, (2) Building and (3) Riverside Trades, taking up two or three unions at a time. What seems to be most in the minds of Booth and Smith (and it is a hint to us) is to discover what part unionism plays in each man's mind. They are seeing more branch secretaries than general secretaries and cross-examining them. They have already begun with the Bricklayers and *Ironfounders* secretaries. But they do not seem to be going *very* deeply into old records.

313

They have a circular 'letter of credence' from the [London] Trades Council, which Ll. Smith seemed to think a great deal of.

I described the kind of material you had already obtained and said it was at Ll. Smith's service whether or not we exchanged. And he said that he had made some notes on his own account as to the history of the Bricklayers and of course the Dockers which we could have.

But he was embarrassed (probably thinking of Booth), suspicious, and scarcely friendly in any cordial sense.

Dearest, I am very sorry. I am what I am. I have lived a 'fighting' life these five years, trying to 'get things done'. But I hope I have some feeling of the value of knowledge. And that, with your help, I can deepen. Now I must try and make it up to you for this rebuff. I am to lunch with Ll. Smith on Tuesday to finish our talk. I said that, at any rate, he and I had better see that the two enquiries did not go to any secretary in the same week! But even as to this he seemed inclined to think that they were all right in any case, and that it was we who would suffer!

Afterwards I saw Elvidge, who seems really quite enthusiastic, tho' very sluggish. He has been overworked, and will be for another fortnight, and has apparently done nothing. I told him to complete his abstracts of the Durham Miners and to pick up all he could about the paper trades, bookbinding, lithography etc: leaving the Building Trades and Riverside Trades alone; and also the Compositors, as he suggested these could be done anytime. I said I would do the Coopers and Cabinet-makers. I gave him as full an idea as I could of the points which had turned up as fertile for investigation.

He said that you had made an excellent impression at the Congress, the only doubters being Shipton and his nearest friends who wanted to know what your game was: and that some one had whispered around that you were fabulously rich!

Burns, too, Massingham tells me, has his doubts of you, and has apparently heard of your disapproving comments on him (which might perhaps be discreetly dropped). He says that you went about only with the Old unionists, and he feared you would not put the case of the New!

Elvidge has practically *nothing* about the National Union, as he will have written you, and says that Burt or Nixon (who is Sec.) must have current papers at any rate.

I feel that this is a letter of bad news and it comes to you when you are suffering from bad cold.

Never mind what you *don't* get: let us rejoice at the mass of material that we do obtain. When you have been to half-a-dozen centres the 'stuff' will threaten to overwhelm us! I wish I could be with you to consult and help. In an hour I shall be whirling towards you as far as Leeds; and then I must stop, and speak in the Hall in which you sat (I can see you now). I shall address *that seat* in the Hall tonight but it will be filled by some commonplace Co-operator.

Pray let the work go rather than make your cold worse. Even for the sake of the book – to put it on a very low ground – it may pay better to nurse yourself.

The rest of the Factory Reports have come from copying; 111 sheets! Some of them likely to be useful. Can you remember to tell me by Monday whether I should return the originals to Redgrave (who will have left) or to Whymper.

I shall probably go to Mrs Green next Tuesday or Wednesday for 2 days.

Now dearest, goodbye for today. Do take it easy!

Yours

Sidney

170 PP   BEATRICE TO SIDNEY

Beatrice had met a young trade unionist from Gateshead who favoured Sidney for the seat. Weakening for the moment in her objection to Sidney's parliamentary aspirations she confessed in an undated letter that Gateshead would be 'quite an ideal constituency and I don't see why we should not have it. It would suit us in every way'. This appears to be her first use of the plural pronoun which later characterised many of her pronouncements on behalf of the partnership.

Beatrice returned to the Bell house for a few days. Lord Durham was a member of the Lampton family and a prominent mineowner. Sidney had consulted an oculist about his short-sightedness. Besides a prescription for new spectacles the oculist had given him an ointment and lotion to improve the bloodshot appearance of his eyes.

[?Rounton Grange, Northallerton]
[?25 October 1891]

My own dear Boy

Do not be disheartened about Ll. Smith. It is of course C. Booth who has probably warned him that he does not wish to be mixed with my enquiry. He (CB) knows, you see, that you are helping me and so naturally assumes that we should make use of our material for propaganda purposes. The only thing for us to do in face of this misunderstanding is to be pleasant and not ask them for what they do not care to give – and patiently to await the time when the misunderstanding shall clear up. That the Booths are *hostile* is quite clear, but I doubt whether that hostility towards me was not already unconsciously there, before our engagement. Do not trouble about it. We have such stupendous advantages and good fortune in getting our information that we have *no right* to feel depressed on account of this stupid rebuff. We shall get the result of their enquiry – and probably the material before we want it. Be cordial with Ll. Smith and accept quite frankly his decision that we cannot exchange material. I think they will lose more than he imagines!

315

We had better book Elvidge for London: he will get us what we want in the way of facts about internal organisation and effort on the [*illegible*] life.

This is a lovely old house. We had a large party of miners here to tea, then the managers to dine, and Lord Durham is coming this afternoon, so I shall see the 4 Chairmen concerned.

I shall about finish at N/C [Newcastle] next week. There are some Unions who refuse to answer: but when I come in February to lecture at Sunderland and to the reception at the Wholesale Society I can manage to get at them.

I don't object to the reputation of belonging to the 'Old Unionist party' it is what I [?reckon] I am at, at Congress. It is the Old unionists who have the records. The New unionists are *very easy* to [interview] and to get at. I am sorry about Burns.

I am so glad you went to the oculist. *Do* use the ointment and the lotion – it is important that your eyes should look nice – even for my sake.

Dearest – do not be troubled – we are both of [us] extraordinarily fortunate – the spoilt children of fortune – we must be patient with those who do not conspire to spoil us – and not resent it. And above all we must keep our eyes firmly fixed on our work – and not bother about the personal aspect of things. We must *use* even our enemies leave alone our well intentioned critics – both the Booths and Ll. Smith.

Mr Knight and Mr Burt are both most cordial in the appreciation of you and Young came to see me – and found his way to my bedroom when I was smoking a cigarette after supper. There he set himself down quite unconcerned and stayed till 10.30 o'clock. He had prepared a great deal of valuable information.

I have written to [?David Dab] to ask whether I can call on him on my way south in the hopes he will ask me to spend next Sunday there.

Goodbye dear Boy. I hope your talk at Leeds was [*illegible*]

Ever

B.P.

P.S. Dear Boy *I* believe that you intend 'to see things straight and to see things whole' (to use your own expression). But I do not think that a little suspicion is unnatural in the minds of others. Your arguments have not always been quite straight – you have 'strained' facts a little bit, you have been perhaps more anxious 'to get things done' than the people who did them and who see *clearly* and *truly* the whole facts of the case! I believe this a mistaken policy – but it is a policy we might *both of us* drift into; let us beware of our own feelings – they are our only enemies.

Sir Thomas Henry Elliott was an officer in the Inland Revenue and assistant secretary to the Royal Commission on Trade Depression. He was elected a Fellow of the Royal Statistical Society in 1885. J. S. Mathers was president of the Liberal Association in West Leeds.

4 Park Village East, N.W.

26 Oct/1891

Dearest

Your nice letter helps me to get over my feeling of pain that Ll. Smith should distrust me. It is as you say, not unnatural, and I own, too, that it is not unfair. I have not hitherto kept the adovcate and the student sufficiently apart. I have so much horror of the way in which so many of our students keep themselves apart from the problems of life that I have gone to the other extreme. But I never intentionally distorted facts. I am just correcting *Facts for Socialists* for the fiftieth thousand, and, although I have looked carefully with this view, I find scarcely an expression to modify. I know that T. H. Elliott, and doutbless others, object to this Tract as misleading. But I can't see it. What they really feel – as C. Booth does in his own books – is that the ascertained statistical facts lend themselves so easily to the support of what they think injurious proposals, that they dislike their wide circulation among uncritical people. It is the old doctrine of 'economy'. But this I do not myself hold.

Still, I mean to be even more careful in the future: in particular I want to try more completely to realise the 'opposite' position at any time, and be not only fair to its expression, but also to its real 'inwardness'.

This with your help.

I spent a quiet 'domestic' afternoon with the Mathers family yesterday, and my headache gradually got better. (It was the champagne I don't doubt!) Mathers said that T. Un had done much in Leeds; it had greatly diminished strikes, raised wages, and above all, educated the men. There is no Employers Association in Leeds, and the men would like to have one. He said the Co-op Store was passing into an inferior class of directors; and that they had been always very timid and conservative in their policy.

He yearned vaguely for Co-op production. He said about 50 years ago about 40 foremen and other superior workmen in iron joined together in a simple partnership as machine makers; they were known as the 'Forty Thieves' – no significance in the name – they prospered exceedingly, but gradually bought out dissentients until now they exist as a small rich private firm of ordinary type. Do you know of this? The instance may be instructive, and worth enquiry when you come to Leeds.

It is also interesting that the local 'merchant' (warehouseman) in cloth was both evolved and eliminated within 50 years. The hand-loomers who stood in the cloth hall to sell their products, naturally produced the local

317

dealing middleman, but he has now almost entirely disappeared with the telegraph etc. The Cloth Hall is pulled down, and the Millowner sells direct for export or to London, from a small office in Leeds, and keeps little or no stock (so capricious is modern taste).

I hope my letter from Leeds reached you at Reddich Hall before you left on Monday; if not, I suppose it will be sent on to you.

Might we not urge the Co-operators to sell books? Walter Scott sells annually *two million* volumes, and other cheap publishers must get rid of as many. Books are an article for which the demand is easily stimulated by the presence of a supply. Formerly few Co-operators were buyers of books. Now many must be. It seems odd that books should be joined to alcohol as the only articles not dealt in.

Would it not be a good thing for you or me to write to the *Co-op News* suggesting that they might try the experiment this Christmas?

It would be a gain, in any case, to get a new channel open for the distribution of cheap books – whosoever they were. But it would serve well the purpose of us who want social reforms, because the Co-operators would probably encourage that class of books.

This morning I have done little but meditate, but I hope not quite idly. Still, I feel that I do not work half so steadily without your presence. I believe we stimulate each other a good deal – which is a wonderfully sure sign of 'affinity'. Rev. W. Moore Ede, The Rectory, Gateshead incidentally reminds me to ask you to let him know of your presence in Newcastle. He evidently *wants* to see you.

He says Wardroper's address (enough for post) is Grosvenor St Gateshead.

Now I must leave off to go on with my work. Goodbye dearest one: I am sad when I think there are still 9 days before I shall see you.

Sidney

172 PP SIDNEY TO BEATRICE

Sidney had been to stay with Alice Green at Fleet, in Hampshire; Beatrice had returned home to care for her father. She was to give a talk to a local working-men's group, sponsored by Clement Ritchie, a justice of the peace in Stroud and a woollen cloth manufacturer at the Ham Mills in nearby Thrupp. Stroud at that time was represented by the Conservative M.P. George Holloway. A similar invitation to Sidney to lecture at Thrupp was engineered by Beatrice. It was revoked when Ritchie, in the aftermath of Beatrice's talk, took fright at Sidney's radical views – a complicated situation which led to a misunderstanding between Beatrice and Sidney which emerges in subsequent letters. It was originally intended that Sidney should be accompanied to Stroud by Haldane.

Robert T. Reid (1846–1923) was a lawyer, later Lord Loreburn, who was Liberal M.P. for Dumfries. In 1911, as Lord Chancellor, he presided over a hostile House of Lords during the passionate debates on the Parliament Bill. W. A. S. Hewins (1865–1931) was a political economist at Pembroke College, Oxford.

318

Dearest

I am glad you are safe at home: pray take it easy. I only wish we could be together to 'play round' in conversation all the much that we have to think about.

It was good of you to ensure me a letter this morning. As I lay in bed I sorrowfully decided that you could hardly manage it. I missed your letters sadly at Fleet: which was my own fault. (By the way the address is 'The Retreat, Fleet'. But Mrs Green will be in London again about Nov. 9).

I return Ritchie's letter, and enclose another to me, which makes it almost certain that my date will be the 29 Nov. I have therefore told Haldane this. In a few days you will be able to write to Haldane and confirm this.

I believe in Haldane's good intentions more and more. And it is evident that his rapidly growing disbelief in the future of the Liberal party is now shared by Acland, R. T. Reid, Buxton, Grey and *perhaps* Asquith. R. T. Reid, by the way, whom I saw yesterday at a small Eighty Club Sub-Committee, asked me to stay behind and was very flattering. He had just read the *Eight Hours Day*, but wanted to know what could be done for women in sweated industries and expressed a yearning for Municipal Workshops. I expounded 'Potterism' in the one case and 'Wallasism' in the other; with, I think, effect. He strongly pressed me to go into Parliament, but did not demur to my statement of my intentions thereon.

I am sending him your Sweating article and Buxton's Bill.

I do not think the Chilean news is serious; neither Chile nor the U.S. could possibly go to war, I think.

I send you the *Economic Review* with a long review of your book by Hewins. (Need not be returned.) He cannot content himself with the necessary limits of individual independence in industrial democracy.

The paper for me has not yet arrived from Waterlow's. Did you think to order it?

Yes, I think your sisters have been, doubtless in all unconsciousness, very selfish. But what I am most impressed by therein is the ease in which one slips into that kind of unconscious, heedless selfishness. Pray don't let *me* slip into it. As I have over and over again said, I rely on your being frank and candid with me – I shall need it!

Now we will be patient. You may very likely find that you cannot easily come up to town even for a day. If so, I must wait until the 29th before feeling the magic of your voice and hand.

But I had almost forgotten to tell you a small piece of news. Massingham unfolded last night a scheme by which he should join our London Letter to another man's, who can bring in several papers – and for greater convenience of working he (deprecatingly) suggested that I should take no part in the management or risk, but merely be a paid contributor, doing, as now, a daily half column, for £200 a year or so. This of course would suit me admirably, as I could more easily withdraw wholly or partially if we needed the time and did not need the money. So I told him I quite agreed.

Now goodbye dearest

Sidney

173 PP BEATRICE TO SIDNEY

Box House, Minchinhampton, Glos.
[1 November 1891]

My own dear Boy

I found Father in a miserable state – his breathing terrible to listen to and preventing all sleep. He has had two bad nights and his breathing is no better. I cannot believe that he can last long. But his illness has been so mysterious that we never know what may be in store. It is very sad to see the brave old man linger on in this wretched state of discomfort and weariness.

Theresa was very pleasant and cordial. I was wrong to give you to understand that the sisters had acted selfishly to me. On the whole I think they have shown *far more* liberality and fair-mindedness than is usual in the treatment of unmarried women. They have not tried to bind me down, they have simply acquiesced in the usual view of the unmarried woman's life. Just as a husband usually acquiesces in the conventional view of a married woman's life!

Miss Darling tells me that they are always asking her questions about me and Theresa said to her 'You know we are absolutely ignorant – she never consults us or confides in us'! But it has only been by keeping my own counsel and going straight on my way, that I have managed to keep friends with all of them, and succeed in my own line.

I am so glad about the London letter. When we can afford it I should like you to give it up. Not so much on account of the waste of time – but because I *hate the habit of mind* of making copy in personal matters and private information. The 'par' maker is not a high type of person. We are handsomely paid by the State – and we ought both of us to set ourselves to do the highest form of service possible to our natures.

I grieve to think that we shall not see each other until the 29th. I go to Liverpool from the 12th and I shall return next day. I cannot leave Father in his present state for more than a day. But of course if the end were to come, I should come up to London directly it was all over; and all my speaking engagements could fall through.

The enclosed is a pleasant little note from Louisa Creighton. I am surprised that she read and liked my book. I do not look forward to keeping this friendship – but if we do it will be a pleasant surprise.

I have had no answer from C. Booth about the T.U. enquiry. I can't imagine that he will carry his distrust so far as to refuse us the use of his material. Anyway, it is better to clear the matter up one way or another.

And now dear one – goodbye – I send you two rosebuds from the garden – to remind you of certain April and October days. Shall we ever have a little garden of our own? If so we must bring a few plants from the Box grounds in memories.

Ever your devoted

Beatrice Potter

174 PP SIDNEY TO BEATRICE

George Turner and Frank W. Galton (1867–1952) were students in the lecture course Sidney was giving at the Workingmen's College. Galton was the son of a saddler who had joined the S.D.F. – which he described as 'a sort of gathering of down and outs to discuss their grievances rather than a serious group for the discussion of socialism' (MS autobiography, BLPES) – and the Socialist League. He joined the Fabian Society in April 1891. He was an engraver but abandoned his trade in January 1892 when Beatrice and Sidney appointed him as their assistant at a salary of one hundred pounds plus travelling expenses. He became the secretary of the Fabian Society 1920–39.

On the following day, 3 November, Sidney wrote (PP) to say he felt that he would be accepted by Beatrice's friends despite his disadvantages. 'I can't help it being "Beauty and the Beast" – if only it is not a case of Titania and Bottom!'

National Liberal Club,
Whitehall Place, s.w.
2 Nov/91

Dearest

The roses were sweet! I see no reason why we should not have a garden as soon as we are settled. A suburban cottage will always be a cheap thing for us.

You are evidently going to have an anxious time in the next weeks: there is nothing to be done but wait. It is clear that all arrangements must be provisional.

No doubt I could stay with Ritchie if you could not take me in: and perhaps I might 'call'. But you will tell me. It is evident that we cannot meet before then anyhow.

Today I have obtained much useful material from the Co-opers: I have seen the 'Whip' of the Progressive Party in the L.C.C., whom I think I have induced to befriend me – as far as that kind of thing goes. There is a better chance than I thought, but all arrangements are postponed until after the School Board elections (Nov. 26) – in which, by the way, the

321

Fabian Society is playing a very influential part – we shall have half-a-dozen candidates, besides much influencing all the rest.

Last night I delivered an impassioned moral exordium to the Ethical Society, with Muirhead in the Chair. Afterwards, in his rooms, with Miss Bridgman and Miss Gilliland present he declared that *you* had been in the audience – which brought my heart into my mouth; and made Miss Bridgman smile and ask after you. It is evident that Muirhead has no suspicion at all.

The Working Men's College young men – Turner and Galton – one of whom *might* do for our secretary – have been turned on to Muirhead's Drury Lane 'Guild', where they have earned the golden opinion of Muirhead and Miss Gilliland. They are *my* children!

I too, shall be glad to give up the 'par' writing. I quite agree with you in disliking its effect. It is a frittering away of the mind: tho' you – like all who do not actually do it – tend, I think, to exaggerate its evil influence on personal intercourse. Nine-tenths of the pars, are not 'news' at all, but simply scraps of 'inside' comment on and explanation of public events.

I am not proud: or morbidly anxious to earn my own money. But we do not yet know where we stand: and I think I ought to keep my finger on this £200 a year a little longer. If we could only be *together* at our work!

I will try to give a *good* lecture on the 29th; good in tone and manner, as well as in information. But I can hardly hope to please!

Now I must break off to finish my work. Goodnight, my dearest. Help me to help us both to true Social Service.

Sidney

175 PP SIDNEY TO BEATRICE

Beatrice had suggested meeting in Birmingham between trains on Tuesday 10 November as she was on her way to Liverpool to visit her Holt relatives and attend a women's conference.

Bernard Bosanquet (1848–1943) was a Hegelian philosopher who, with his wife Helen (1848–1923), was much interested in social work, playing a prominent part in the Charity Organisation Society. Later professor at St Andrew's University he was the author of the influential *The Philosophical Theory of the State* (1899).

4 Park Village East, N.W.
6 Nov. 1891

Dearest

Tuesday is an 'inspiration'. I was vaguely thinking whether it could not be arranged, but feared you would find me importunate.

I *may* have to speak in the evening: but that is not until 9 o'clock. And really, my only engagement is the ordinary weekly Fabian Executive, which can do quite well without me, and which it is even good that I should miss from time to time. It will only cost me £1; I can start at 9.30 and be back at 6.35; and we shall have won a delightful oasis out of the desert of our separation. I can work in the train.

My cold is much better: and I intend to be very careful at Oxford, treating myself as an invalid. I am not a bit ill.

My last cold of consequence was at the end of May – still, twice a year is too often.

If it is not gone by Monday I may stay at Oxford over that night, and go on to Birmingham on Tuesday morning – thus saving the home journey. But this would involve my missing a meeting on Monday which I want to attend if I can.

Last night I read through *The Co-op Movement*, trying to see it with critical eyes. It is wonderfully 'fresh' and original: a piece of work you will never need to be ashamed of. I don't wonder at Bosanquet and others finding it convincing. You have managed, too, to preserve all the interest of *'l'imprévu'* – your conclusions are unexpected. Your blows at the Associations of Producers are smashing: and there is a whole philosophy of democratic organisation to be picked up from the book here and there. It really is a first-rate piece of work: and even without anything else, it will have definitely consolidated your reputation.

I can't see why Frederic Harrison should have been disappointed – unless it is the constant assertion of Democracy that annoys him.

I admire the *completeness* of the book – several times I thought of an omission, only to discover it supplied a few pages on, in its due place, *ohne Hast* as well as *ohne Rast*.

I should like to have you admire my 'decision', but there will be other opportunities! And I am not going to make one merely for that end. Yet it will only be three weeks since I left you at Tynemouth Station – it seems an age. Then it will be another age – a whole three weeks – before we meet again.

Dearest, your letter was very sweet to me. I can easily wait indefinitely if I have but your letters to remind me of your love. I would write twice a day if I might. But that would perhaps be to put my love above my duty elsewhere. Now when I do any work well, I feel that that too, is part of my love for you. In this case *Laborare est amare*.

Sidney

176 PP SIDNEY TO BEATRICE

Lord Ashbourne (1837–1913) was a Conservative politician and Lord Chancellor of Ireland. Herbert Samuel (1870–1963), later Viscount Samuel, was a lifelong friend of the Webbs: he became a prominent Liberal politician and a leader of British Jewry. At the beginning of his career he was a member of the Fabian Society. His eldest brother was Sir Stuart Samuel (1856–1926), a banker who was M.P. for Whitechapel from 1900 to 1916.

3 St Aldates, Oxford
7 Nov/91

Dearest

Here I am at Oxford cheered much by your letter. My cold is much better, and I think I can go through the programme which has been mapped out for me. I will take all possible care consistent with this.

Last night I gave what I think was a suggestive and useful address to a little roomful of semi-socialist undergraduates including Hon. Lord Gibson, eldest son of Lord Ashbourne – who has turned Roman Catholic and Home Ruler to his father's unspeakable horror – Scott, nephew of the *Manchester Guardian*, and Samuel, a brother of the L.C.C. for Whitechapel who was himself present (a conceited Philistine successful Jew of low mental and moral type – who is abandoning the L.C.C. for Parliament because he is afraid as he told me, that the L.C.C. may become involved in odium or ridicule, which would damage *his* career). They are all reading Socialist books (I recommended yours strongly).

This morning I have been to breakfast with Samuel, who had in young Scott Gibson and *Wicksteed* (son of Philip) to meet me. Young Wicksteed is a charming, open-faced, engaging young fellow, who promises well. We talked till noon, and I have just come in after a turn round 'Tom Quad' (the large Christchurch quad) where we passed York Powell, who does not know me, but who had wished me to stay with him, and whom I shall see tomorrow.

Yes: I remember your letter from Oxford a year ago. I do not feel it so sad – of course I don't *now* and I hope you would not! I feel it full of young life and hope and faith, (the contrast between the elder and the younger Samuel has been occurring to me all the morning).

It is new wine in old bottles – which may be bad for the bottles! But then I am among the young men, not among the dons. I met Edgeworth in Balliol quad: he stopped and was polite. I am told his lectures are quite unintelligible, but the men speak kindly of him.

Liverpool runs its own water supply: I am doubtful about the gas. You will find it in the *Financial Reform Almanac* (first article) if that is handy. The Town Council took power by Act last year to buy up its tramways (it sought power also to *work* them, but was advised to abandon this clause). But I do not know whether it yet owns them.

I find I have been put down for a lecture here on Monday night, so I must give up my Committee meeting in London and go on from here to Birmingham – which is after all the easiest and safest for me, avoiding the double journey for nothing.

Do not grieve over your reluctance to work – 'they also serve who only stand and wait'. But perhaps you could get into it better by beginning with some half-idle mechanical task. I will send you Taylor's Factory System when I return. I have to review it for the *Speaker*.

324

Now I must say goodbye until tomorrow. To think that Tuesday is only 3 days off! I wonder whether I shall ever be able adequately to feel how fortunate I am in *loving* you so much – not to mention that other perfectly inestimable glory which I had done nothing to deserve from you. Dearest, I will *never* forget what I owe.

Sidney

177 PP BEATRICE TO SIDNEY

The debate at the Working Men's Club at Thrupp, to which Clement Ritchie had invited Sidney, was to take place on 29 November. Beatrice was anxious that Sidney should make a good impression on this public appearance near her house.

Box House, Minchinhampton, Glos.
[8 November 1891]

Dearest one

One more line before Tuesday.

Ritchie has free the 29th for your lecture – the Judge [Brynmor Jones] is going to be your opponent. He is prepared with an attack on your chapter of the *Fabian Essays*, I believe.

Be courteous to him.

My address went off allright, we had really a lively discussion afterwards. I carried a resolution 'in favour of regulations of hours of labour and sanitary conditions by Factory Acts and Trade Unions'. With one dissentient, Ritchie and the gentlefolk did not vote; a Jew contractor.

They are all looking forward to your meeting. I am going to have it in the schoolhouse. It will be well advertised.

Till Tuesday 1.12. If we could get a private room to talk in it would be pleasant.

Always your devoted comrade

Beatrice

178 PP SIDNEY TO BEATRICE

Charles Freak, of the National Union of Boot and Shoe Operatives, was one of the Labour members elected to the L.C.C. in 1892: he sat for North-East Bethnal Green.

4 Park Village East, N.W.
11 Nov. 1891

Dearest

Here I am at home at work once more: and you with a strong gale and I suppose the same rain as here, in which to go about to your Secretaries. Do not do too much.

My cold is gone – just as yesterday has! Now I am at the bottom of a ladder with seventeen steps one of which I shall count each day until the 28th. I have a letter from Ritchie this morning settling it, and saying he will meet me and take me to his house – but *not* saying that I am to go on to yours afterwards. I suppose he quite understands this.

Last night I dined with Paul, the Leicester ironfounder who is interested in archives. He said he did not employ union men (it is only a small place) and that the Rotherham Stove Grate makers had tried to convert his men but had failed. We talked Co-operation and he volunteered the information that *you* knew more about it than anybody!

Inskip has been made an Alderman as a reward for sticking to the local Liberals. (By the way Freak is spoken of as a Labor candidate for the L.C.C. for Bethnal Green.)

Then I went off to Bethnal Green and found Headlam speaking. (He makes a perfect candidate.) I made a short speech in his support – good practice for me in the art of being a candidate. I have hardly ever been to such meetings before, and one must learn how to do it.

B. T. Hall of the Hatcham Club wants to propose me as L.C.C. candidate for Deptford. I must see how it looks.

I am sending W. C. Taylor's *Modern Factory System* to Box for Friday. Please remember that it must be reviewed: and send me the heads of an article.

The Eastern Counties Labor Federation – a penny a week union – has grown from 3000 to 7000 these few months. There does seem a chance of running purely laborers unions in county federations.

Now I must break off to work. I seem to see you still as you stood before me at the Birmingham station: and as your face looked at me through the window of the carriage when the train moved off. Now I must carry that face about with me, *faute de mieux*, until I can look on the original again.

Goodbye for today. I have just looked at your sweet roses again, not yet quite dried up. My love, goodnight.

Sidney

179 PP SIDNEY TO BEATRICE

4 Park Village East, N.W.
14 Nov/91

Dearest

Yesterday I 'scamped' my letter to you! left it until the afternoon and then was unexpectedly occupied and had to write in the presence of others to catch the post. Today I am writing in the morning, to do better!

I was charmed with your scribble this morning, and I rejoice that you have had such a good time (and laid such a good foundation!) with the Holts.

What you say about one's *success* securing consideration (rather than one's deserts) is true enough. (It means that others have no time themselves to weigh deserts: and they take success as the mint stamp which makes assaying needless). Do you know, I fear we are both a little apt to be *too* fond of success and consideration. It is very natural, because this comes *to us* as the mint stamp which convinces our doubting selves of our own deserts! Secretly conscious of our own imperfections (perhaps morbidly so) we wonder whether we are of any use at all; and are glad to be reassured by the kindly praise of our friends and (to speak for myself alone) even by the involuntary tribute of the abuse of our enemies.

But this is subtly dangerous; and it is one of the things against which we must guard.

This is not a homily to you in particular! It means that I am vexed this morning.

Last night Wallas and I were outvoted in a meeting of the Fabian Society. A private member insisted on bringing forward a motion to reverse our Trade Option clause (8 Hours Bill), so as to turn it into the Trade Exemption, (Negative Option) of the T.U. Congress.

Wallas and I protested that this made all the difference between practicality and impracticality as an actual legislative scheme. But Mrs Bland had seen a chance of having a cut at the Exec., and had whipped up support, which we had not done. Hence the meeting, a small one, carried the motion by 28 to 26.

Of course it is not a momentous question; and it may not even lead to any action. But it is awkward; and shows that Wallas and I are losing influence because we are suspected of too much attachment to the Liberal Party – just at the moment, by the way, when we are becoming *less* attached to them!

And I think the *Speaker* has rejected my article this week (proof has not come); no doubt on the ground that I went in too strongly for trade unions (it was on 'The Organisation of the Village'). Dearest, that does not matter, as things now are, because I would far rather work for you, and our book. But how anxious I should have been if you had not opened up this new sphere of love and duty.

(Perhaps, after all, the article was merely crowded out; or the proof went wrong.)

I have just sent back the proof of my Women's Wages paper to Edgeworth. It makes 28 pages, and I think it will read well, as a good introduction to the study of the problem. I have very carefully gone over every statement so as to secure absolute accuracy in fact and in implication.

I read the *Liverpool Post* report of your Conference. I agree that it seems to have been rather a poor affair. But it is a beginning, in women's standing alone. If only such standing alone did not so usually foster the 'anti-male' prejudice!

I almost wished I had gone down to Birmingham today! But that would have been indulging ourselves too much: we must now wait till the 28th – only 14 days now!

Wallas asked after you very affectionately last night. He is a dear good fellow, much better morally than I am, more scrupulous with himself (perhaps, like Morley, fastidious). He has worked fearfully hard at his lectures, which are an immense success – more, however, because of his skill as a teacher than (as I gather) from any originality of idea. I will try to be more like him in honesty and thoroughness. Dearest, I *ought* to be so, for you are enabling me to be so.

This time last year I was in bed very weak and low, and you were trying to write kindly but not misleadingly – which puzzled me! How good you have been always. Dearest, now goodbye.

Sidney

180 PP SIDNEY TO BEATRICE

Professor Joseph Edwin Crawford Munro, professor of political economy at Owen's College, Manchester, published a number of works on industrial law, taxation and wages; he ran as the Liberal candidate in East Manchester against Arthur Balfour in the general elections of 1892 and 1895.

David George Ritchie (1853–1903) a Hegelian who was professor of logic at St Andrew's University, was for a short period an active Fabian. Sir William James Ashley (1860–1927) was an economic historian who left Oxford in 1888 to become a professor at Toronto University; moved to Harvard in 1892 and returned to the University of Birmingham in 1901.

4 Park Village East, N.W.

15 Nov/91

Dearest

Today is Sunday and so I have no letter in the writing which I have learnt to love. So I must take it out in writing to you – the next best thing.

The *Speaker* puts in this week my review of Brentano: that is perhaps the reason why they did not want another article on Tr. Unions.

I am getting lots of requests to stand for the County Council, (Clapham, N. Hackney, Holborn etc.) but these I decline: at present Deptford or Stepney are my most likely places – Costelloe (nominally in conjunction with Stuart) has prepared a tremendous draft of the Liberal programme for L.C.C. election, which is from beginning to end a 'Fabian' manifesto! Stuart feebly objected, but gave way to Costelloe and will now appear as the author! It goes for 'municipalisation' of every public service.

This is politically important because the Liberal leaders are going to back the Progressive Party's campaign; several great guns are to speak; and they will be committed to a most tremendous scheme of Municipal Socialism and what I call 'collective philanthropy'.

Wallas has certainly produced a *splendid* list of books in our new tract

'What to Read'. (Have you seen this? I send a copy to make sure.) It has cost him months of intermittent work, and will I think do much good, and create a good impression.

It is almost comic to think how few of these books the ordinary politician has hitherto dreamt of reading.

Courtney takes the Chair at our Political Economy Society at the N.L. Club on the 26th, when Munro reads a paper on the Econ. effects of an Eight Hours Day in Coal Mines. I am expected to go and speak: I suppose there would be no harm? I will try to make a courteous and *worthy* contribution to the discussion. Leonard will look at me with new interest if his wife has confided her suspicions to him. I can of course stay away if you think it better. But my absence would be rather marked; and might seem ungracious as I have had so much to do with starting this society, and am known to be interested in Eight Hours.

As regards Tr. Unionism I too must confess to a little interregnum in the work. Many arrears of other work have pressed upon me these first three weeks. I have been a fairly wide reader, and I am interested to find that I have only read about two-thirds, or some 270 out of the 410 or so books in the list; but nearly all the blue books.

This is the kind of course in 'Political Science' which we ought to have established at Oxford; which D. G. Ritchie works for; and which Ashley might have created, whereas Edgeworth is not adapted to it since Tynemouth; and I have been thinking at large, rather than jotting down facts. But I shall have done a lot about the Coopers: and thinking is not waste of time. We will plan a new start on the 28th etc. – which my heart jumps to think is less than a fortnight off.

Now, goodbye, dearest. I ought not to run on anymore though it is happiness to chatter to you, even on paper.

Sidney

181 PP BEATRICE TO SIDNEY [*incomplete: PS only*]

Beatrice's letters seem to have left Sidney confused about her wishes, the attitude of the Playnes and Ritchie's intentions about the proposed debate at Thrupp. He inferred that he was expected to offer Ritchie some conventional excuse, thus relieving the general embarrassment, even though this apparently meant cancelling his visit to Box. Beatrice was in a distraught state. She had learned that Rosie's husband Dyson Williams was mortally ill and realised that her father might well die before Christmas. The subsequent muddle led to one of her rare bursts of vexation with Sidney, who believed he had acted for the best, and to her decision that such difficulties were bound to occur so long as her true relationship to Sidney was a secret from her sisters.

P.S.

Mary [Playne] has just been here in a state of excitement. The Stroud valley have been thrown into convulsions by my little address, the Radicals taking it up with joy as a weapon against the Tory ascendancy! Local conditions are unpleasant here from the Radical Socialist standpoint – the great Tory being Sir John Douglas who is a large landlord and has enclosed common after common while the Tory member is a large wholesale clothier who practises something very like the *Sweating System*!

The Playnes are indignant with Mr Ritchie, who being a Conservative is encouraging this, they say, out of spite against the Tory County gentlemen who have ignored him and his family. They do not blame me – nor do they blame you for coming. Mary asked me whether if she could persuade Mr Ritchie to ask me, I would use my influence with you to throw up the engagement. I said 'Certainly – Mr Webb I am sure will do whatever Mr Ritchie likes in the matter – and if Mr Ritchie does not like to ask him – I will. But Mr Ritchie is responsible for the arrangement, and I must have *his* word that he desires it to drop through'. She replied 'Of course you must – you could not interfere except by his desire'. And so it ended.

So if you come, you must be scrupulously moderate in your *language*, however strong you may be in your statement of fact. It really would be a public good to rouse the wretched little valley out of its deadening torpor. I am rather glad to have a parting shot at it.

BP

182 PP SIDNEY TO BEATRICE

J. T. W. Mitchell (1828–95) was a textile worker who became chairman of the Co-operative Wholesale Society from 1874 until his death. Beatrice described him as 'a sort of embodiment of the working-class customer, intent on getting the whole profit of production out of the hands of the manufacturer and trader, for the consumer'. (BWD 28 March 89)

4 Park Village East, N.W.
17.11.91

Dearest

I am amused at Stroud respectability not finding you out before! I hope Ritchie won't back out of my lecture. I will be studiously solemn in expression, and take the line of a scientific exposition; saying that I leave it to the politicians to devise remedies! If Ritchie asks you about it, suggest demurely that it would be awkward to let the working men think that there was anything detrimental to Conservatism in an examination into the causes of poverty – the very question before the House of Lords Sweating Committee and Labor Commission.

The newspaper report of your meeting is very well done.

I think it is our duty to do what we can to rouse this demoralised constituency.

Last night Benj. Jones and I were at a committee late, so I carried him off to dinner at the N.L.C. He was extremely cordial – told me about Mitchell's nomination for the Congress presidency and a great deal of Co-op business. He spoke very warmly of you and your book and your influence – I believe he suspects the truth, but is politely and courteously discreet about it.

He wants to be a parliamentary candidate at once, if the money is found: and we *tacitly* arranged that I should mention his name in the right quarter. He would stand for Woolwich if asked: it is a hopeless fight at present, for local reasons, but the place is really Radical. He quite approved my suggesting *Books* to the *Co-op News* as an article to supply, and I have written to the *News*.

I have just seen B. T. Hall, who will probably be able to arrange for me to stand for Deptford for L.C.C. – which *ought* to be a safe seat, if we can avoid a split of the Progressive vote.

Haldane says the dinner with Morley must now be put off until December – which is a pity. But the Labor Party gets stronger every day.

The *Speaker* took my article after all – it was merely crowded out. Your draft review of W. C. Taylor does admirably. I shall finger it about a little, in the probably vain belief that my journalistic experience can improve it! But you will have saved me from a task which I dislike.

It is sad about your father. But there is evidently nothing to be done but wait. After all, he might have lingered on in positive pain with asthma, or angina pectoris. It is a great gain that he is comparatively painless – much less trying to those around him.

This is a very 'cold' letter! But I am warm enough! If you could only realise how I lie awake and think of you, and what we will do together; how your face comes up as I go along the Strand, and carries me right back to that blissful Sunday morning in the Naerodal – well, you would wonder why I write you nothing but scraps of politico-personal gossip! But, dearest, we can love each other without saying so at every phrase. All I feel is that my letters are not so 'good' as yours. Still I try.

My love, goodnight

Sidney

183 PP SIDNEY TO BEATRICE

The Reverend Thory Gage Gardiner (1857–1941) was sub-warden of Toynbee Hall; secretary of the education committee of the Co-operative Union 1891–95; a prominent figure in the Charity Organisation Society; and later a member of the Royal Commission on the Poor Law. Sir Charles Stewart Loch (1849–1943) was a statistician who was secretary of the C.O.S. from 1875 to 1914: he had a strong and conservative influence on social policy and played an important role in the Poor Law Commission. The C.O.S. had collaborated with the London University Extension Department in sponsoring a series of lectures by Wallas in Chelsea, but withdrew in protest against his militant agnosticism and radical opinions.

Joseph Burgess (1853–1934) was a radical journalist who, with Vaughan Nash, had launched the *Workman's Times* in Bradford in September 1890. He was becoming a strong advocate of labour politics, much discussed in Bradford after a bitter strike at the Manningham Mills early in 1891. On 30 April 1892 Burgess appealed to his readers to enrol in an independent labour party; a few days later the Bradford Labour Union was formed. It became the host for the conference which founded the Independent Labour Party in 1893.

Henry Morse Stephens was the author of *A History of the French Revolution* (1886) who was a misfit in English academic life and left to teach at Cornell University. Beatrice was reading several books on the French Revolution at this time.

4 Park Village East, N.W.

19 Nov/91

Dearest

I am sorry I am not to lecture, but am quite prepared to acquiesce. Only, I don't think *I* ought to throw the engagement over. I am quite prepared to make no fuss about it, but it is going rather far for me to take the blame of breaking the engagement; especially if it be true that some of the people are looking forward to it. (Remember, it is not a *Conservative* club, and it includes Radicals, and even (Dent tells me) a socialist or two.

And it seems to me that I must hear from Mr Ritchie myself.

What I suggest is that the enclosed should be posted by you to him, and when he replies, acquiescing, all will be over as far as I am concerned. He can than make what explanation he pleases to his Club.

I am not a bit hurt or cross (it is all so natural!), and all I am thinking of is my own character. I am willing to go a long way to help Mr Ritchie out; and if you really think I ought to do so, I don't say that I won't make an excuse (i.e. tell a lie) for his help. But it is a good deal for him to ask.

Moreover, your telegram saying that I may come to Box after all (and why not? Nothing is more natural than that *you* should not withdraw *your* invitation to me to meet Haldane) makes it difficult for me to offer a consistent excuse for not lecturing at Thrupp.

By the way, why not get Haldane to lecture instead?

Honestly, I don't think Ritchie will be *wise* to throw me over. The workingmen in the club are quite sharp enough to understand – and the result will probably be that I shall be invited to lecture at Stroud by some other body. If you care to suggest it to Ritchie, he might rely on my keeping exclusively to the economic plane; and he could 'run' me as an economist, not as a politician.

But I can easily see that it may suit you and me personally that I should not lecture: and I am very willing to fall in with the suggestion. Only, I shrink from deliberately writing a false excuse.

Now I must leave the matter to work itself out locally. I hope you won't think me unreasonable. If you do, I will try to adopt whatever you suggest after consideration. I don't think that either Ritchie or the Playnes would really think better of me for too willingly making an excuse – and there are some things which may be bought too dear.

As to my coming to Box, I of course am ignorant of what your telegram indicates; but it seems to me much less suspicious that I should come than that I should be thrown over by you as well as by Thrupp? I *want* to come very much. But I am *quite quite* willing to do as you may think best. Dearest, we can be much 'stronger' with ourselves when required, than is involved in a few days delay in our meeting. We need not insist on any self-indulgence. But I think my visit will be useful in more ways than one. Still, you must judge.

I will ask Wallas about coming in December. It is kind of you to ask him. I think it will do him good.

By the way, at the Co-op Educ. Council last night, Thory Gardiner reported that C. S. Loch finally decided to refuse to help the Educ. Council to get up lectures like Wallas's on the ground that they did not think his Chelsea course had been a success! (From their point of view no doubt.) This is ominous for Wallas. I must consider when and how to tell him. (Of course this is not public.)

But I made a new suggestion to the Education Council which may perhaps bring a subsidy from another source.

Thory Gardiner is to lecture to the Fabian Society in the summer on the great field for social and political education that is offered by the Co-op Societies!

I hope you approve the draft speech I sent yesterday. I gave it to Massingham to read, and he said it would be a very good stroke, and he would try to write a leader on it.

I have subscribed to the Labor Commission reports; and have received the set up to the recess. The others will come weekly I believe. I have also *just* subscribed to the *Workman's Times*, but it is becoming more 'Labor Party' and less 'Trade Unionist'. Still, I will clip bits from it.

I am glad you are reading Morse Stephens: I quite agree in the wisdom of such reading.

Dearest, this leaves me uncertain whether I am to count days to the 28th or not! Still, I shall see you soon – I see you now (!) in your blue silk running down a hill to open the gate for Wallas in Norway!

My love, goodbye

Sidney

333

[Box House, Minchinhampton]

[?20 November 1891]

Dearest

You have caused me, doubtless without meaning it, the maximum amount of worry and vexation by not simply following my suggestion and writing to Mr Ritchie to put off your engagement.

The letter you sent was *absolutely useless*. If you meant to refuse to do as I asked you should say so quite frankly and that would have ended the matter. I could not have received you here but you could have of course gone to a Stroud hotel for Saturday night.

But surely you owe it to me to make my relations with my own family as pleasant as possible – it is not much to ask of you to throw over a wretched little club!

Of course I can't force you to do it. But if you care for my feelings at all you will write by *this evening's post* to Mr Ritchie stating simply 'that you are unavoidably prevented by an important political engagement from coming down to Gloucestershire on the 28th.'

Anyway I can't have you here on the 28th.

I sent your letter over to Mary and this is her answer. I thought it better to write to you direct. It is not likely that Mr Ritchie will persuade you to do what I fail to persuade you to do.

I have been thoroughly upset and unable to eat any breakfast.

It was not kind of you not to follow my advice on a matter that concerns myself and my family.

Yours

BP

4 Park Village East, N.W.

20 Nov/91

Dearest

Have I disappointed you in not giving an excuse to Ritchie? I am very willing to be complaisant, but I am not comfortable in deliberately writing an excuse which Ritchie and the Playnes will know to be untrue. It was very natural that you should at first think of that way out (as I did myself): but you did not realise (as I do) that the date was specially changed to suit my convenience and so that I could hardly now plead an engagement; and that if I came to you that night, I could hardly be ill.

Dearest, *this day* six months we came back together from Lincoln, and entered on a new life. I will not stain today by even a small untruth.

I don't want to seem pedantically scrupulous – and, honestly, I don't much object to the petty verbal untruths of social convention. But – I don't think John Morley would have made such an excuse; at least not the

John Morley of 'Compromise'. I hate to make a stand just when it involves inconvenience to others, but if one does not make a stand where one can, what becomes of character?

Dearest Bee, do not love me less because I *could* not do what you asked. You were misled by *lower* counsellors for the moment. One of my besetting sins is a tendency to casuistry and I want to stand up against it. We ought not to 'debase the moral currency' if we can help it. I *have* sinned before now, with a light heart. But it is you who have taught me to aim at a franker, simpler, truthfulness. And I appeal from you under inferior influences, to you in your real self. Perhaps I make too much of this – but I *felt* like it. And you will help me to feel like it again in more important matters, if you tell me that you appreciate it.

What you say about my London speech is useful, and I will adopt what I can.

As to devoting ourselves to London – it must be as our opportunities are. I have a strong feeling of agreement with you. But much of London's regeneration can only be worked out in and through the House of Commons. It is almost as necessary that the County Council should have its representatives there, as that the Cabinet should. However, these things settle themselves; and for the present I am thinking only of County Council.

Last night I met Ll. Smith for a moment. He said he was on his way to the London Shipwrights Office – not Wilkie's but the Shipwrights Provident Union – a society formed 1824, very exclusive, but who had given *him* permission to search through all their minute books which existed since 1824. This was his own work, not Booth's. He said he should like to compare our survey of the other shipwrights. I suggested that he should take me on as an assistant! or else let me pay for one to copy etc. He will see what can be done.

I think you might bring up, next week, all you have on the Shipwrights (I have some more now), in case we can arrange to help him, and he us.

I think the French Revolution is a great lesson to politicians – the great need of men who were true to themselves, and their best selves.

I enclose Sydney Buxton's speech, which he has just sent me. The utter absence of original thinking in these men is deplorable. Nearly all this comes straight out of the note to the Trade Option Clause in the Fabian Bill. And even the little excursion which you and I have made to the North has taught us much more than this.

I will try to forgive Stuart. Certainly I will not resist him. But it is difficult to feel at ease with him when one knows that he is all the while intriguing against the 'forward' policy: and opposing me in particular, in an underhand way. But he is obviously *following* me now, so that I can very well afford to be generous!

Dearest, we have been engaged six months. I feel some compunction

335

that in these six months I have done so much less for you than you for me. I get further and further in your debt. And I can never hope to pay it all. But if love and work, and patient devotion – not always obedience but sometimes criticism – may be accepted as interest on the debt, you shall have interest at usurious rates. You shall have me wholly: judgement as well as service – more I cannot give you, my dearest love, there *is* no more to give.

Sidney

4 Park Village East, N.W.

21 Nov/91

Dearest

My telegram of this morning (which crossed yours) and my letter of last night (posted very late), will have told you that I wrote last night to Ritchie in the way you suggested. I did so because I was quite prepared to assume that you knew the case better than I did: and I was therefore quite willing to take your *well-considered* ruling as to what was right. You will not, I am sure, be cross with me for being slow to do what seemed to me wrong. Your first letter was not so explicit as to make me quite sure that you meant nothing short of what I have now done. And I was confused by your telegram saying I could come to Box after all.

It is a small matter, but I am sorry it has troubled you. It has given me a sleepless night of pain; and a miserable day till I can hear from you.

If it has cost me my visit to Box I am sorry. But, dearest one, better your vexation, better my discomfort, better that we should lose our day's pleasant intercourse and useful consultation, than that either you or I should slip into the too easy way of doing what we, perhaps foolishly and inconsistently, shrink from. I hate to preach, and I can now easily assume that you must be right because you have considered and reconsidered, but our relationship will not be helpful unless each is quick to tell the other when the course proposed *seems* wrong. We may properly accept each other's decision after consideration, but we should be untrue to each other if we did not insist on a warning pause for that consideration. I love you too well to suppress my criticism that occurs to me: you love me too well to wish me to do so. You have a right not only to my obedience, but also to my judgment: I have the duty not only of devotion but also of watchfulness. If you are for the moment vexed with me, or disappointed that I did not at once obey, I would rather endure this than that you should think me lax about truthfulness, or blindly subservient to your every word. Our love for each other is not a passing foolish fondness, but a mutual trust in the main enduring elements of character: and you would no more wish me to sink my conscience in yours, than I should endure to have you sink yours in mine.

336

Dearest, all this is very solemn and 'priggish', but I *do* want to be a better man – for your sake – and I am not ashamed of it. And I want us each to help the other to that betterness; and this we can only do by *adding together* our moral intuitions, not merging them.

I own I was not 'pure' over this affair: I minded more writing an *obvious* untruth than one which would not have been discovered. But it is just because I feel how imperfect I have been and still am, that I am trying all I can to improve, so as to be more worthy of your love.

Now I will say no more about it. Whatever you may be writing to me today about the matter, I shall accept, with the fullest confidence in you. But you will not mind my explaining why I had to give you pain (though I did not realise that it would be so). I may have blundered, as men will in these things, but, my dearest love, you would not wish me to be without the feeling which made me stumble at first over your command.

Now, outside the sun is shining though I am unhappy in your displeasure. I hope the sun is shining with you also, and that it is a sign and a pledge to me that I am forgiven.

If you like, tell me frankly where and why I failed in duty; or if you like, send me a kiss in token of forgiveness. But however it is, I will not lose faith in you; I will not cease to do what I can to care for you, and *watch* for you, even though it pain you and pain me. Dearest, I love you too well not to set both you and me a very high standard even in little things – and I believe you would wish it so.

Sidney

187 PP SIDNEY TO BEATRICE

Robert Banner (1855–1910) was a former member of the S.D.F. and the Socialist League who had built up a strong and independent socialist group in Woolwich after 1884. Nassau Senior (1790–1864) was a political economist, hostile to trade unions, and the author of the report of the Commission of 1834 which established the 'new' Poor Law. Sir Frederick Pollock (1845–1937) was an eminent jurist and professor of jurisprudence at Oxford from 1883 to 1907. The report to which Webb refers led to the Trade Union Acts of 1869 and 1871 which gave legal protection for the first time to the funds of trade unions.

4 Park Village East, N.W.
22 Nov/91

Dearest

Today has been a dreary blank for me, because there has been no letter from you, and I feel that I am in your displeasure. Dearest, be patient with me. You can hit me very hard; and perhaps it hurts more than you mean – just as you can make me happier than you can imagine.

I have blundered but I have not willingly done you wrong.

Now let me tell you about my day. I had to start off at 11 to give my lecture, and had all sorts of mischances on the way (London travelling is so awkward on Sunday morning); finally arrived at my Hackney Club, and gave the lecture with success to a beer-drinking audience of 100 or so; then had to go off to dinner with Lowerison (blatant Board School teacher; enthusiastic and hard working, but uncouth Fabian) – there I met Banner, (bookbinder; great Woolwich street-corner orator and organiser) to whom I logrolled Benj. Jones as candidate.

He told me of an 'apportionment' case. The bookbinders have been in the habit of setting up the type required for lettering the backs and sides of books. Now they are on strike at Waterlow's, and Drummond had (he said) allowed the compositors to do this work.

Then I tried to get back home to change my coat, so as to call on Mrs Green. But I again met with dilatory misadventures, and finally went on to Kensington Square just as I was. But Mrs Green was distracted by callers – unusually lengthy – and I could only sit and gossip a little – with a sad heart – until I gave it up and came away at 6, leaving her with Strong.

In one interlude she told me she has met Clement Ritchie on Tuesday, when he was enthusiastic about *your* lecture and also, she said, about *my* coming. So it must have been after that that he became alarmed. I told her of the alarm and that I had consequently backed out of it.

Now I am tired (it has been cold and rainy, and I reckon that I have spent from 3 to 4 hours in travelling); and I have done nothing but one lecture and one call: and I am sad and weary.

Last night I read three days reports of Labor Committee, all miners, mostly Welsh, all in favor of 8 Hours Bill. That Committee will *discover* nothing, let alone accomplish.

Dearest, what have you been doing? I am cast down by so little, in the midst of so much happiness. You are living always in a dark, sad shadow and yet bear up so well. *Be p*atient. Do not be alarmed about the size of our work: we can *take time* to do it well. I will *help* you to take time; I will strengthen you in resolving to put all else away that might hinder. You can trust me – at any rate when you are with me!

I have read through Nassau Senior on combinations, again; and the 1867–8 report. Sir F. Pollock has, it is said, brought out a pamphlet on the subject for the illumination of the Commissioners. This I must get. And I am muddling along – not so well as when you are there.

Am I quite shut out from Box next Saturday night? Let it be as you think best – I deserve to be punished for having vexed you!

Dearest, goodnight. Whatever you do I will trust you implicitly. Dearest love, good night.

Sidney

Beatrice decided that once her sisters and immediate friends knew of her engagement her life would be easier. She wrote in an undated letter to Sidney that it would 'also make it possible for you to join me in the Provinces in the Spring'.

Box House, Minchinhampton, Glos.
21/22 Nov. 1891

Dearest one,

I send you many kisses – not of forgiveness – for I have nothing to forgive – but of trust and love.

I judged the false excuse by the test that neither you nor I would object to its being discovered (in fact we should prefer that the Thrupp men should know the whole story) by the persons for whom it was intended. But I may have been wrong, and you were right to warn me – and if it had been a matter of any importance you would have been right to refuse. But I had *answered* for you – which again was probably wrong – and I will not do it again. I *think* you were right to give way – for partners must be answerable for each other and bear each other out – unless it is a question of vital morals – but you were right to protest and I do not love you any the less for doing so.

But one thing, I think I have learnt from the pain of these last days. I think we might, with the hidden tie between us, step into a wrong position. I think therefore, after Xmas, when we again begin working together again, I will write and tell my sisters. Then we can begin the New Year openly – and face everything openly and together.

And now about Saturday. I *do* want to see you. But I have a sort of unconscious feeling that it might be better for you not to come – and yet I feel ready to sit down and cry that you won't come. I am not sure that I am not too tired to judge so I will leave it 'till tomorrow. I shall have recovered my nerve by that time again.

Do you remember what exactly 'Set-work' is: if so send it to D.S. [David Schloss]. I told him I would refer to you. We put it down but I have lost [*eight words illegible*].

I have written to Alice Green to ask whether I can come up for a night on the 2nd.

Now dearest goodbye. I am sorry for all this pain and wrong on both sides. Perhaps someday we will tell the men of Thrupp the story!

Ever your devoted comrade

Beatrice

4 Park Village East, N.W.

22 Nov/91

Dearest

Now you have made me very happy – not only in forgiving me for troubling you, but in making clear to me why we differed. Do you realise that you *never told me* that you had already made the particular excuse for me? Of course I would have borne you out had I known (even if I had discussed the matter afterwards). But I only understood that I was not to lecture – all the rest being, as I supposed, left *to be* arranged.

As regards Saturday you will judge. I can be very careful, and I don't realise your difficulty. But I know I don't know the situation, and I can only leave it implicitly to you.

I send you the *Daily Chronicle* with my speech and Massingham's leader on it. I fear I have 'crowded out' Mrs Green's lecture – see the brief report and the curious inference drawn by the reporter (not unnaturally).

I have written to Schloss to say that Hey told me that Set Work was Piecework with this difference, that the employer took the risk (e.g. in piecework the worker got nothing for the bad castings, in setwork these were paid for like the rest). I suppose it is confined to operations other than simple and normal.

The Coopers in London are on strike, and have passed a resoln to establish a Co-operative cooperage.

I have felt very helpless these days, not getting on with *our* work or (what is still) my own. I think I want the inspiration of seeing you and talking to you face to face. We shall do our work much better when we can be together!

I humbly confess to *wanting* you very badly. I have done a great deal of miscellaneous work lately, and I am quite sure I have 'earned my keep'. But I am horribly conscious that it falls far short of what I could do if we were together.

However, that can't be yet awhile: and we are far too lucky – I in particular – to be entitled to complain that we have not yet got everything.

Dearest, I *think* you are right to determine to declare our secret. We may keep it from the newspapers for a little while – long enough for you to suck Lancashire dry perhaps! You will have to stand firm from the beginning to put down any pressure from your family; but you will know how to do that.

But I must leave off. My-more-than-ever-dearest, good night. I wish I had a rosebud to send in return for your sweet enclosure. But I can only fill up the envelope with kisses!

Sidney

4 Park Village East, N.W.

5 Dec/91

Dearest

I have just (5 p.m.) left Mrs Costelloe with whom I had lunch (at her father's); and we sat and talked afterwards for a couple of hours. She was very charming – asked no embarrassing questions and made no awkward illusions, but did *not* tell her father that I was with anyone when she discovered me in the National Gallery the day before. She referred to you, said she was very anxious to go to Box, but feared she would be prevented by pressure of things to be done. She was inclined, however, to come for half a day – *she* said 10 a.m., returning by the night train – I strongly advised 3.10 p.m. returning early next day. I suppose you will hear from her.

As regards her own state of mind, she seems weakening – but weary of things, and uncertain. We talked very pleasantly and (I think) warily. While her father was there we discussed Ibsen and Shaw, and I could see that I vexed the father by not denouncing Shaw and his anarchic views. But of course the play is not so simple as that; and it seemed better for me to praise that which I could praise in them.

I think I did well to talk those three hours – it may be that she was unaffected – but I don't think I did any harm. She is going to Florence in a week or two for the winter, expressing her intention to return in the summer.

This morning I read things on Guilds. It is quite evident that there were many 'laborers' not in any craft, who were hired by the day, and had no protection. Some of these asked (end 17th Century in London) to be incorporated as a Guild of Sawyers: the Carpenters and the Shipwrights objected to this, and it was refused. I have sent for more Guild books.

Lady Henry Somerset is going to stay a year in America to study 'rescue work' at 'Moody's College of Methods', Chicago, a kind of Normal School where social missionaries are trained for city work! This is a curious development.

I miss you sadly today, but I *did* work this morning. I hope you are also getting into harness! There is so much to be done before we take on new work in January. Dearest, I felt whilst with Mrs C. what 'worlds away' you were from her, whom I once thought so well of. You have it in charge to 'justify the ways of women' to men: to show women that if they *are* human beings of full growth they must 'put away childish things', and be as reasonable and as responsible as the men they want to grant them a free life. Be it ours to prove to ourselves at any rate, that we *are* human beings of equivalent freedom and yet joint lives. What a chance we have! What shall we do with it? Love is the guide and the faith and the hope.

Goodnight, my own dear love.

Sidney

May Abraham (1869–1946), a pioneer social worker, was appointed the first woman factory inspector in 1893: she married Harold Tennant, a Liberal M.P., in 1896.

Box House, Minchinhampton, Glos.
[? early December 1891]

My own dear one,

I did a good day's work yesterday. I am writing an account of the Iron-workers [*illegible*], to clear my senses as to what we are aiming at – general as well as in particular. That will be done tomorrow and I will then get to the Boot and Shoe.

Ella Pycroft is here. She thought Haldane 'repulsive'. (She did not say much about you except that you were much quieter and improved in manner) and told me that when she returned to Longfords, Mary Playne was very anxious to hear and very hopeful that I should marry him. 'She detests Mr Webb. What did he do', she asked! Of course it is half a fear that I should make a bad marriage that makes her dislike you – she has an unconscious instinct that you would recommend yourself to me by the *appearance* (as she would say) of ability and success and by your views. *Tant pis*! I do not feel in the least bothered about my family. They can come or they can go – probably like sensible people they will accept the situation.

I have had no news of the L.C. [Labour Commission], so I imagine they have decided not to ask me – for which I am heartily thankful. Last summer I should have been disappointed; now I am relieved.

And honestly, I do not think, that with my well-known views, I am quite a fit person anymore than Mrs Fawcett would be on the other side. We are both of us a little too much of the clever advocates to do subordinate work as agents for enquiries. If they appoint her it will be splendid as a 'discredit' of the whole Commission in the eyes of the working class. Just fancy Lady Dilke's feelings! It is largely her efforts to get the T.C. [Trades Councils] to send resolutions up that have brought the appointment about. Miss Abraham has my best wishes.

I am in very good worthy form. I have had no answer from G. Wallas. I hope he will come; there is lots to talk about.

Now dear one goodbye. I must turn back to my work.

Ever your devoted comrade
Beatrice Potter

You are quite right – one must not 'fash' oneself over one's deficiencies any more than congratulate oneself about one's successes. But every now and then one is haunted by the fear that one is not *earning one's bread*;

that one is sinking into the luxurious indulgence of the ordinary rent-holder.

BP

Don't write a letter every day.

Anthony Mundella (1825–97), Radical M.P. for Sheffield, was much interested in labour questions and educational reform.

4 Park Village East, N.W.

6 Dec/91

Dearest

The *Sunday Sun* says the selection of 2 Women Commissioners, has been left to Mr Mundella and Mr Courtney! subject to the concurrence of Lord Hartington: and that no selection will probably be made until after Xmas! It is a pity not to get it settled and off your mind: but if the selection has really been left to those two, I think you are safe in your martyrdom!

Last night was *such* a wretched night as regards weather, but I was warm and happy in your love. I saw Ll. Smith at N.L.C. and told him that I had your permission now to say that Booth knew; and that you would see Booth when you came up. He was relieved, I am sure: and he was quite pleased when I said I had got our Shipwrights material for him. I fancy he has not found *his* Shipwrights quite so fertile as he thought.

I then went off (dinnerless!) to my Coopers: they expect to win their strike next week. They have no *reports* of their own, and only old ledgers and balancesheets. But they promised to let me come and grub among them when they got straight.

Then I went on to Mansfield House, Canning Town (what an Inferno!) to lecture on the Municipalisation of the Docks, insisting strongly on character. There was a good and very enthusiastic meeting. And it took me nearly two hours to get home, in the rain and slush.

Today Geo. Turner of the Working Men's College called – my 'nice boy' my sister calls him. I find he has three years more of his apprenticeship, and that he has made up his mind he must endure them. Galton, the other, is out of his time, but makes £2 a week! Turner thought he would gladly accept any work of mental kind. Of course I said nothing of our projects. Galton is not nearly so 'nice' as Turner, but he is sharper.

Wallas came to dinner, and we spent the afternoon talking about Guilds, and his lectures (I gave him numerous facts as to local govt). He is pleased at your invitation.

I should like to go on, but I think I will work a bit. Tomorrow I intend to begin reading at the Museum, so as to secure my mornings to *our* work, and let everything else take care of itself. There is *so* much to be done (Wallas always make me feel this!) But every day a little will accomplish a great deal. And it's 'Love, Love, Love' that makes the world go round. We have 'hitched our waggon to a star', and it must go forward and upward.

I do love your letters but you must not feel bound to write every day. I tell myself that the day *must* not seem blank to me if there is no word from you!

Goodnight, dearest

Sidney

193 PP BEATRICE TO SIDNEY

Box House, Minchinhampton, Glos.

[?8 December 1891]

My own dear Boy

I am so glad you are beginning regular work at our book – we shall now both be working in the mornings – upon the same object and in the same times. I do not think we need fear about sacrificing the income from journalism. Eventually we shall have plenty without earning a penny; and I should be quite justified in spending out of capital, what is being saved for me every year – say £300. Then there is the trousseau money, £400 – So we have £700 we should be right in spending this year over and above the £650 joint income.

Of course you will let me pay all your expenses – County Council and Parliamentary, so as not to trench on your capital – in case I died before our marriage!

After all it would be wanting in statesmanship to stint ourselves in our work just in these years of greatest vigour. Careful personal expenditure and generous *work*-expenditure should be our aim.

It was a wild dreary afternoon, when I sallied out in search of your letter, and very welcome it was. To think that I shall not see you for a whole three weeks or more! But Graham will be here to console me.

Poor Morley – what a pitiable exhibition over the land-question – wretchedly weak answer to Balfour! Those well-thought out negations are worth twice as much as his floundering assertions. By the way is there no way of bringing that Land Question 'back to the land' – sharply to the test of statutes? – it would be well worth doing if only to instruct the politicians.

After Women's Labour, Local Government and a few other enquiries(!) we will take up the Land Question – we will go and live on the land! and wander over it enquiring into rentals, methods of cultivation and tenures. A pleasant summer's occupation in a recess!

What a lot of work there is to be done – in clearing the ground for well thought-out reforms.

Let us remain 'thinkers' even if you get into politics – it [will] be well worth while sacrificing a nominal position for *real usefulness*.

Poor old Father, lingering on his dreary life these dark winter days – and that brave tender woman sits hour by hour at his side. How wonderful are the ways of Women! That inexhaustible spring of tenderness for the weak and incapable.

Ella Pycroft says I am far too 'deliberate' to be womanly – don't thou think so, oh! my own man. I explained to her the exact reasons why I should choose a certain sort of man as my husband – and she was shocked – tho' I told her the exact truth – she thought it horribly deliberate – to think of work as a Cause – to think of anything but personal attraction in its best sense. But then can you disentangle the cause or the work from the person?

But I must not drift into metaphysics – specially as I am dead sleepy.

I get so sick of those ugly details of day work and piece work – overtime and shop rent – and the squalid misfortunes of defaulting branch officers or heckling and unreasonable members. Who would choose to imprison their intellect in this smelly kitchen of social life – if it were not for that ever-important 30 per cent – with the background of their terrible East End streets. The memory of those low cunning brutal faces of the loafers and cadgers that hang about the Mint haunt me when I feel inclined to put down the T.U. report and take up a bit of good literature.

Goodnight dearest

Ever your devoted comrade

Beatrice

194 PP BEATRICE TO SIDNEY

Lord Rosebery had just published a biography of William Pitt.

Box House, Minchinhampton, Glos
[?9 December 1891]

Dearest one

Mrs Costelloe could not come: she wrote me a very nice letter and I replied in kind.

I had a morning at the Boot and Shoe Society. This afternoon I spent in arranging our material and seeing what we have got. It is terrible to think what a lot of work there is to be done before we are in a position to write – both in the number of societies we have to get at, and the real knowledge of trade unionism as a factor.

There is something very pathetic about the records – the struggle with the anarchic spirit in every union. The miserable petty passions which are always threatening to subvert the union; and the crude economics of the leaders. But on the whole they have been just as right as the employers in their economics – perhaps righter in their economics than the professors.

Does this not arise from the fact that they – the union leaders – have had the *right object* in view – the making of the Man; whereas the economists and employers have had the making of Commodities? It strikes me that we English always get at our real goal – and Wealth Production has been the real goal of the governing classes through the century. It remains to be seen whether we go on straight to the making of the citizen. I am waiting for Miss Pycroft who is coming from an evening cookery lesson.

I had a delightful ride this afternoon despite the cold mist that was sweeping over the hills. I cantered through the long green lanes in the tableland – closed in by high wild hedges full of autumn berries.

As we flew past myriads of little birds – tits, finches of all descriptions started out before us or we spied them clinging to the branches – bright bits of life and colour.

Now dear one, goodnight. I will go and read Rosebery's *Pitt*.

Your comrade

Beatrice

195 PP SIDNEY TO BEATRICE

W. C. Steadman (1851–1911) was a Fabian and a Progressive: elected to the L.C.C. for Stepney he later became a Liberal M.P.

The *History of the Twelve Great Livery Companies of London* was published by William Herbert in 1837.

4 Park Village East, N.W

9 Dec/91

Dearest

I was vexed in reading your charming letter this morning to think that mine had failed to reach you.

Will not Miss Pycroft be getting rather 'warm'? However she knows little of me, and it does not matter if she begins to suspect.

No – you are not 'unwomanly', except in being a rare exception among women with regard to intellect and training. But you *are* (wisely) deliberate: which makes your love all the stronger and abler. (Poor Miss Pycroft. Don't you feel a great yearning and wish that everyone could be as happy as we are. I really must become known for my sweet amiability and gentleness of manner(!) – I have *so* much reason to be thankful.)

Dearest, you have always been very good to me – I would not have you otherwise than you are by a hair's breadth. Miss Pycroft, well as you know her, does not know you as I do. It *is* possible to have at the same time great love, keen desire for work, and great sense of responsibility. With these goes, necessarily, caution and deliberation; but *we* shall know how to prove that these are not hostile to the purest love and mutual devotion.

Last night Steadman and I appeared before the Stepney Liberal Council, orated, and were questioned. One man urged the necessity of personal canvassing, and asked me whether my wife would canvass for me! Ll. Smith laughed, and I said that I must draw the line somewhere, and really could not promise to get married before the election.

We were both unanimously requested to stand. But I shall not accept, preferring Deptford, which will, I hope, select me today. Both Kennington and W. Islington have sent me formal invitations.

Today I have read in Herbert's *History of the Twelve Great Livery Companies* – to very little profit, but it was necessary to have read the book. Ll. Smith was very pleased to have the Shipwrights papers. He will, I can see, have got a mass of information about the riverside trades which will save us much work.

No doubt you feel the Boot and Shoe people tedious: it is hard for you shut up there away from anyone sympathetic to talk to. Dearest, I confess to a low taste. I *like* the kitchen of life. T. Unions and details of administration are more to me than art or literature and I am keenly and absorbingly interested in the work. But you must try to teach me better. I want to be more 'cultivated' and we must try to carve a little time together for pictures and poetry and music, you patiently helping me to comprehend. I *can* do it, when I give myself time and get a little knowledge of the language. But I, too, have had the state of London burnt in me for the last six years, and have never given myself breathing time from work for what seemed to me best. Now we will work more wisely: we must save our *whole* selves alive if we are to do our best work, and that is why we must try to build a pleasant and comfortable home bye and bye, and take care to live cultured lives as well as busy ones.

Now, goodnight. My dearest Beatrice, I must turn aside to scribble again, and then go to Eighty Club dinner to hear Spence Watson.

Adieu, sweet.

Sidney

Yes. You shall give me a cheque for County Council expenses: it won't come to £100 *at most* – and I shall be the 'Member for Potter'.

196 PP SIDNEY TO BEATRICE

4 Park Village East, N.W.
10 Dec/91

Dearest

I am glad you had a nice ride – there are only 21 days more! But I will see that you have all that I can give in exchange for the rides.

Last night, on my way to the Eighty Club dinner, Spence Watson spoke to me, and was most cordial – we drove there together, and he asked me

347

what I ntended about Parliament. I told him quite frankly and simply about Gateshead, as to which he said nothing. He made a nice speech, good in tone though not containing much: quoted a story I had just told him. Morley, too, spoke well (looking straight at me all the time!) Then I had to go home and write an article about it for the *Speaker* (I had done most of it), and this and the high wind kept me awake, and I lay and thought of your goodness, and my happiness – and the responsibility of it all.

Deptford has virtually agreed unanimously to have me for L.C.C. (in conjunction with a local Vestryman) and I am to speak there, for formal adoption, next Wednesday. Today I am tired, but am writing to Stepney, Kennington, West Islington and now Poplar!, that I can't take them on.

I shall have a lot of work during January and February to win Deptford, but I must be in Yorkshire from 31 January to 6 February, and perhaps we can work together some days then (though I shall have travelling to do).

I called on Costelloe at his office: he had, of course, heard of our meeting Mrs C. and was thankful for what we had tried to do: he said you had written a letter full of kindness and wisdom – and *he* had silently inferred from its contents that you were *au courant*. Nothing is done, in his tragic case: but then nothing has happened for the worse: and next summer she will come back.

He said that she had not inferred anything about us: and evidently he has said nothing.

I enclose a letter from my Gateshead bricklayer – partly about your book. I have answered it, and you may burn it. He has sent me the bye-laws of half-a-dozen towns.

I saw Burt at dinner yesterday; he was very pleasant.

By the way, I may have given Dr Watson a suspicion. We were talking of the intricacy of labor questions, and I rashly said I was giving some time to a complete study of Trade Unionism! He hummed and hawed, and I think what came into his mind was *your* study of the same subject – and then he evidently thought he would *not* tell me of it. But thinking it over, he *may* suspect – perhaps not more than our joint action, however.

It is fearful weather, and I am overworked a little – I must leave off. Dearest, we are getting on: don't be discouraged at the amount of work. A few months will give us more matter than we can possibly deal with. And we have love, and trust and faith – surely we are rich. When I think of it all I am cast down at my own unworthiness. But you will help me, sweet.

Sidney

197 PP BEATRICE TO SIDNEY

William Lecky (1838–1903), historian, published volumes 7 and 8 of his *History of England in the Eighteenth Century* in 1890: they were largely devoted to Irish affairs. He was an opponent of Home Rule.

Box House, Minchinhampton, Glos.

[?11 December 1891]

Dearest one

I was glad to get your interesting account of the 80 Club dinner.

I do not imagine that Spence Watson would remember that I was studying trade unions; so I imagine you have not given him a suspicion that we are working together – unless Burt has told him you were staying at Tynemouth.

Now that I am to tell my sisters in January it does not really matter anyone suspecting it. It will do me little harm unless it gets into provincial papers and certainly it will not injure you – may even do you a little good.

I finished up the Boot and Shoe (15 yrs) and this afternoon I began Lecky's two last volumes – 18th Century. The Irish part of his History is so very superior to the rest – one feels that it is *felt* as well as thought.

I have a whole batch of *Miner's National Union* to get through – then I have finished my material. But I have written to Gloucester to make arrangements to interview Shoe employers and trade societies. I hope next week. Do not overwork – you must not think of doing much with the book until after the County Council election. It would be wise to devote sometime, not only to winning your seat, but to educating your constituency. What is needed is some organisation such as the University Extension – devoted exclusively to economic and social reformation – endless Graham Wallases – to go about the country; or rather high-minded Blands would be quite good enough – properly instructed.

With the dearth of workers it is difficult to know how much time should be devoted to thinking out new problems and how much to teaching what one has already thought?

I hear there is a report in the County that I am to marry Judge Jones – a very natural report since he is absolutely the only person of the County I ever see!

Dearest, goodnight once more. Take care of yourself – and take a fatherly interest in your own manners and mannerisms – it is better not to offend in small matters: then you are going to fight great issues.

Now dearest goodbye comrade.

Ever your devoted

Beatrice Potter

198 PP SIDNEY TO BEATRICE

A truculent Fabian named J. F. Runciman was bent on proving that the moderate leaders of the Society were backsliding hypocrites: he alleged that Webb was trying to protect the Aerated Bread Company from accusations of sweating its employees and seeking generally to sell the Fabians into Liberal bondage. Webb, aware of the damage done to the socialist sects by factionalism, was anxious to protect the Society from divisive personalities. He wrote to Pease urging that 'we should keep the Fabian Society, at least, free from the ordinary revolutionary failing of suspecting each other of improper motives for any act of which we do not happen to approve . . . I plead, above all, for patience and charity'. (FP)

An Account of the Machine-wrought Hosiery Trade by William Felkin was published before 1845, when the second edition appeared. *The Positive Theory of Capital* by Eugen von Böhm-Bawerk was published in Austria in 1889: an English translation by William Smart appeared in 1891.

4 Park Village East, N.W.
11 Dec/91

Dearest

Your letters reproach me, because I feel that (considering our relative strength) you are doing more at THE BOOK than I am. But though I cut down the journalism to the minimum, I cannot get on fast. This County Council election is bothersome, and will need my care. I am refusing all lecturing but there is still much that I must do.

Dearest, be patient with me. Perhaps I could have done more if I had been a civil servant *and nothing else*. But that was impossible *to me*. And, in the long run I can help you more by uniting some action to the student life, than if I gave all my time to study. But in our firm, *you* will do most of the study, and I most of the action. Just now I wish I could study more, but just now action demands me somewhat.

I fear Wallas cannot come to you on Sat. 18th. We have on that evening an important meeting of the Fabian Society which he will want to attend – indeed, it is very important that he should be there. The younger impatient element of the society has risen up in rebellion, and wants to throw the whole movement entirely into the Labor Party. The occasion and pretext of the quarrel is a supposed small action of mine, which I did not do, and which has nothing to do with the real issue. I shall be away that day lecturing at Bristol on the Sunday and it is very important that Wallas should be there to save the society from what may be ruin.

He could come by the Sunday train, no doubt, which is an hour longer. I will speak to him.

I think we might 'go' £10, or so, for the *Trade Unionist*. I enclose a card from Nash. It *is* a good paper.

I wish I could come to Box instead of Wallas! I am feeling very tired and done up (I think these three days of high wind and rain have tired me a great deal. But I have not taken cold.) I shall rest tomorrow and Sunday, merely reading. I have Felkin's *Hosiery Trade* and some other book which may help historically. I have just read Fred. Harrison's article on T.U. in the *Fortnightly*, 1865. It is very good indeed: mentions the *Trade Union Directory* for 1861, and says there must be at least 2000 separate unions in existence. There is one phrase which anticipates and sums up Böhm-Bawerk's *Positive Theory of Capital* – 'Capital is simply insurance against Time'.

I have had to take my ring off, as we have an old lady, cousin of my mother's, staying here, with an Argus eye for such details for gossip. But she has no suspicions. But I do long for the time when I may wear it (or rather your much nicer one!) openly and without fear. It is too annoying that Lancashire and my County Council election should keep us apart until March. It is still three weeks until I shall see you. No, that is not true; I see you now! But it is three weeks before we can work together and then we shall have less than a fortnight before you are off again.

But we must have patience. I think it must be admitted that we are very stern parents to ourselves. But one day our time will come: and anyhow we shall have had a perfectly splendid year of work and happiness perhaps nonetheless happy, really, because we have been pushing our noses through the bars of the cage we have made for ourselves – the two cages I should say!

My own dear love, you have taught me a great deal – and among other things that it is far better to do than be done by – to work than be worked for – I will not say to love, than to be loved – there is no comparing infinities! and both these have been infinite bliss to me. I *do* intend to show this in my character and life, but I feel how much I must improve.

But, sweet, a kiss and now goodbye.

Sidney

199 PP   BEATRICE TO SIDNEY

Box House, Minchinhampton, Glos.
[?12 December 1891]

Dearest one

Your long letter delighted me. I fear I should not suit the taste of the Stepney elector or his like at Deptford. I will not say I *would* not canvass personally for you (I could not do it for myself) – but I should feel it [?'demoralising']! We have bigger work to do than that, even if we take ourselves very humbly – but you do not ask me. Ll. Smith must have laughed. I see most of the trade unions have strong rules against 'personal canvass' – a curious little incident of democratic organisation.

It was a wild night – and few of us slept through it – and the whole of today has been a day of storms rushing up the valley and bursting on these highlands into torrents of rain and hurricanes of wind. I was tired this morning – and felt sick at the thought of another day at T.U. so I took up Rosebery's *Pitt* and have just (6.30) finished it. It is by no means a 'great little book' – only a bright shrewd chat about a great statesman of the past by a considerable politician of the present – and therefore more

351

interesting than its intrinsic values. There is a lack of 'distinction' about the book – moral and intellectual but it reads like a very fairly correct estimate. I wonder whether his point that Pitt had to confront a latent revolution in England is a true one? I should have thought the Industrial Revolution was too absorbing of the real energies of the whole people to have much material for *effective* political disturbance. I wonder how near we were to a revolution? I gathered when I was reading up these years, that about 1784 there was a chance for a revolutionary organisation – but that after that it was swept away, partly by the supreme indifferences of working classes through industrial activity and partly by the misleading reaction against the French Revolution.

But all said and done Pitt is an unlovable figure – strikes me as a hot-house creation – with neither the virtues nor the vices of usually great men. He was surely more the consummate *political expert*, than a great statesman?

Dearest, we will try to have a little culture – but it will be difficult and I fear you will not have the wife to favour the growth of it. I am supremely ignorant, except in my own subjects. All I do bring is a humble reverence for those other subjects and for students of them – an appreciation that we *are* dealing with the [*illegible*] of life – and that there *are* nobler and more inspiring matters for thought and feeling. Perhaps it is because I realise this, that I want to get the kitchen in order, so that even the scullery-maid may have her leisure and training for the higher things. It would be a ghastly thought that Humanity should everlastingly bring itself with a bare struggle for bread and butter!

But we will try – with a humble and reverent attitude, we shall enjoy the atmosphere of culture, even if we do not acquire the substance, and by a judicious choice of friends we may get glimpses into the Land of Promise which we will do our level best to make possible for others.

There is a fine ring about Morley's speech and also about Watson's; but they are no help intellectually – and they have a curious tone of 'fearful hesitancy' about the course they see their party adopting. They have come neither to curse nor to pray – the effect beyond a certain moral loftiness, is positively negative. At least that is the impression from reading them. I should be curious to hear tomorrow your version. I wish Morley would 'speak out' or rather that he would sit down and *think*. Watson has thought and his thought is against the socialist radicals. That [?municipalisation] of the Public [public houses] which he refers to is a thing that might be *pushed* – Chamberlain would feel bound to support, so would men like L. Courtney. It would be a very great step in advance – the municipalisation of freshments and entertainments. One of the finest things S. Barnett has ever said is that he would give the poor luxuries and not necessaries – a good program for your 'collective philanthropy'.

The wind is literally *howling* round the house; if I had not 'a light within me' a hidden companionship, I should feel dreary and melancholy. This is the last winter we shall be so far apart – dearest let us keep our relationship pure, and inspiring to what is highest in each of us.

Goodnight and God bless you. Do you know that I have resumed an old habit of a short prayer before I spring out of bed? It has come back naturally to me – with the happiness of love and the desire that happiness shall not lead to indolence or self complacency.

Always your faithful comrade
Beatrice

200 PP SIDNEY TO BEATRICE

The notes which follow this letter are printed in full: they show both the manner in which Webb developed a speech and the precise political position he was taking at this time.

4 Park Village East, N.W.
12 Dec/91

Encls. may be destroyed

Dearest

Your letter came very 'comforting' to me this morning – which happens to be a 'dark day' with me. I am feeling very weak and incapable, and full of a sense of my own unworthiness and want of strength to cope with the difficulties of democracy.

It seems evident that the Fabian Society is by no means exempt from the usual failings of revolutionary movements, and it appears that I have lost the confidence of a certain section of the younger members by entering upon public life as a candidate! Last night Clarke read a very able paper on the 'Party Politics of Socialism', taking a pessimistic view of the chances of a Labor Party (but not in the least praising the Liberals). I was expected to speak and did so, but to make sure of saying exactly what I meant I wrote it down. I enclose these notes for you to read. This is what I propose for myself whatever the Fabian Society does, because this is what I believe. But my speech was not well received, and the meeting was with Bland and Burns who made bitter and malicious speeches on the other side.

Now this is of no great moment, but it is a foretaste of what is going to happen, and I own that it grieves and wounds me to find that even Fabians cannot rise above this very vulgar view.

Dearest, I ought not to complain. It is part of the *cost* of public life and public service – and I have counted the cost. And so long as I have your approval I can dispense with the rest. But it hurts all the same. The Fabian Society is getting so much influence that we must try to save it and guide it; and there is a very large section, probably a majority, who are fully on our side. The enclosed notice of a meeting will help us, as the

353

very foolish accusation against me therein cited cannot fail to rebound. I shall not be present at the meeting: and there is sure to be a huge majority against the offender, and so virtually for me. It is the new members, who have not been 'under influence' long, and who have not caught our missionary and educational spirit who are rebellious, not those who know me best – and this is something.

I have written thus fully, not because I make much of this – the Fabian Society is not much in my life – but because I like to 'share' with you, even my griefs. And it is a good 'illustrative instance' of the difficulty of retaining the confidence of a changing body of members, who cannot appreciate the difficulties of the situation. Last April I secured re-election on the Executive by a virtually unanimous vote, at the top of the list. These nine months have not made me more Liberal, but less. But the revolution devours its children! I have always foreseen it.

I am glad you have read Lord Rosebery on Pitt. I have not done so, for lack of time and opportunity. I cannot believe that any English revolution was possible in his time. There might have been a Jacquerie or a Bread Riot, but the descendants of Cromwell's Ironsides were too busy running cotton mills and fitting out ships; and without them, I think there could, at that time, have been no strength anywhere.

I think I should do well to take on a clerk directly after Xmas to attend to election work during January and February; and work with us both afterwards. Even if he does not go away with you, I think I must regard it as a necessary election expense, or I shall get no time at all. If you don't mind, we will have Galton to dinner one evening (perhaps at Wallas's) directly you come up, and see how he strikes you.

We *will* try all we can to keep ourselves, for at any rate part of our lives, on a higher plane than this mere 'reorganisation of the kitchen', necessary as it is. But it will not be easy for two such fanatics as I fear we are.

I am told that C. Booth is going straight for universal pensions at the Statistical Society next Tuesday, and (it is said) largely on my lines.

Now goodbye dearest. This has been a hard week for me – overwork, headache, irascibility (successfully fought against, I think), and petty mortification. But I have done at least 30 hours reading etc. on THE BOOK, tho' there is little tangible to show for it. And I am very, very happy and grateful.

Sidney

Notes for speech by S.W. at Fabian meeting: 11 December 1891
Some members wish to see Fabian Socy devote itself exclusively to the support of the Labor Party, and throw its entire influence unreservedly upon that side.
Well, with that view I cannot agree. Indeed, suspect some of those members do not realise the essential diffce. between a Labor Party and Socm itself.

Our business to convert the whole community to Socm; Soc. no more become adjunct of Labor Party than of Lib. Party. By all means let indiv. members do what each can do best – one stand as Labor candidate, [another as Lib. Candidate: *crossed out in ms*] but Socm must include all, if it is to reach all men.

Independent Labor Group – small, may be, in members, but determined in purpose, owning allegiance to no party selling its votes in turn to one party or the other, according as this or that labor measure could be squeezed unwillingly out of either of them.

Possible policy – but a mean policy. Degradation of politics. Doubt whether it really pays. Doubt whether concessions wrung from reluctant leaders, carried out by unbelieving Ministers, ever really effective. Weapon of a minority.

Look for higher things than that. Look to see, no ind. Labor group, but indep. collectivist party – not restricted to manual workers or any one class of not pursuing its own class interest, but the welfare of the whole community, not selling its votes or its support to reluctant parties for the sake of extorting half abortive concessions but carrying out its own principles, by its own strength, and through the willing assistance of its own converts.

Towards the building up of such a party we shall need all elements, draw recruits from all sides. Present Labor party furnish energy, and determination, better part of young Radicals get political experience of public life and public administration – Socialists supply the ideal and the principles upon which action will be based.

That is the party which you can already see gradually shaping itself, and for which I individually intend to work, whatever the Fabian Socy may do collectively. In the formation of such a party I believe the Society might and ought to play a great though unobtrusive part. But to do that it must no more give itself away to the Labor Party than to the Lib. party; and above all its members must be a little more alive to the necessity for careful study than many of them now are, and above all we must have the loyal devotion of every member to increasing and building up the influence of the Society, and some confidence in each other's motives and each other's integrity.

201 PP BEATRICE TO SIDNEY [*incomplete*]

D'Arcy Reeve (d. 1926) was a wealthy Liberal and Fabian who provided funds for Fabian lectures and also underwrote the cost of the first Fabian office at 276 Strand, where Pease had been installed as the Society's paid secretary on a salary of £100. Half this salary was paid, at the beginning, by Webb personally to offset criticism that the Society could not afford a paid official.

Dearest one

I was deeply interested in your letter of today.

I think the view taken in your notes is a perfectly right one – what we what is to teach 'collectivism' to the whole People. That will involve more than an intellectual conversion it will need a growth of certain moral qualities in the whole nation, not only in the working class.

About the Fabian event. I have always felt that there were certain dangers ahead. Such and such able men have made this society to give *body* to their views – and now the body is beginning to cry out for a life of its own. Moreover the unions, in the society, of men and women who profess socialist doctrines and have *that* bond only to unite them is really a bad material out of which to make an association. You may get some good strong characters, but the ordinary revolutionist is weak-headed and irresponsible and your society becomes the resort of persons with no definite creed but discontent and with no real place in the world but with a vague desire to become 'somebody'.

And directly the society grows beyond a little group, you must either devote an immense amount of time and energy to personal influence, or it will drift away into the lines of its own development – regulation by the moral and intellectual material out of which the body of its members were formed.

Now about the future. You will have to look in the face the fact that the Society will be bound to drift away from your influence and almost certain to drift into a wrong direction. You are not going to devote your life to educating the casual incomers into the Fabian Society – you will be engaged in a larger arena. Wallas too will want more and more to devote himself to other things; Clarke, B. Shaw and Massingham are also busy men. You ought to prepare therefore to deliberately withdraw from the Society the strength it has derived from your leadership and 'booming'. That strength resolves itself into two factors – financial support (perhaps the most important part), and careful organisation. It would be wrong that the society should enjoy a false power – a power which it no longer really possesses. (I suggest therefore that you see something of D'Arcy Reeve and other financial supporters and that you turn their attention to the *Trade Unionist* etc.)

But above all there should be no overt rupture – you should be benign and patient and perfectly without *personal feeling*, withdrawing your active help (and allowing them to make muddles and to feel their own incompetence) *without withdrawing yourself*. The chances are that the disintegrating forces of the Society would turn inward and sections would gradually split off and the society would gradually dwindle away or fall to pieces without the scandal of a rumpus.

356

If, on the other hand, you and Wallas were to make a desperate effort to gain back the society as your personal property, then the same fight would come later on, when the Society was far more influential (for any increase of your influence would react on the growth of the Society) and when you were all too busy to take away the props with which you had supported it.

If on the other hand, the other party were to overpower you, in an open fight (which is just possible because intrigue is very easy and potent with that sort of material) then there would be a scandal and it would cause 'the heathen to blaspheme'.

The policy now I am certain is to *starve* the Society so that it shall find *its own level*. You have been over-feeding it, with the risk of its becoming a dangerous and noxious monster. *But keep on kindly pleasant terms with all the persons concerned.* They are not worth a moment's irritation, anger, or even contempt.

I have written this long letter because I know you like me to talk to you [about] everything that is in my mind – and to give you my views even tho' you do not care to accept them. I feel that we can be of infinite use to each other in helping each other to be calmly deliberate and kindly when we feel personally irritated. It is important that the little group of men should do what is wisest about the Fabian Society – for you are to a large extent responsible for its present influence. But I do not think it is a matter of much intrinsic importance what happens to it. It cannot be made into 'a great instrument of Progress' – its material is too poor – it may of course become a little obstacle.

202 PP SIDNEY TO BEATRICE

Charles Booth had come out in favour of old age pensions; Joseph Chamberlain was favouring some form of social insurance. Arnold Morley (1849–1916) was Liberal Chief Whip 1886–1893. E. Harold Spender (1864–1926) was a notable Liberal journalist, editing several papers including the *Pall Mall Gazette* and the *Daily Chronicle*. He was a keen Fabian and ensured good publicity for the Society.

4 Park Village East, N.W.
17/12/91

Dearest

I am writing this in haste to catch the late post. Last night I was definitely selected for Deptford, unanimously (small meetings as usual). It will be a hard fight, and will cost £100. And it is quite possible that we are all going into a big defeat. But I shall fight it hard on educational lines; B. T. Hall, your old friend, will be my agent. Oddly enough the respectable moderate Liberals are keenly *for* me.

Yesterday I lunched with Bryce and his wife – both very nice. We discussed London politics, and I found him knowing very little indeed of recent developments. We had a good and friendly talk – I don't know how far I kept my 'reserve'! – and then walked together to Schnadhorst's where he presided over a little meeting to discuss London literature. Arnold Morley was there – very polite – but anxious that no explicit proposals should be published. It was virtually settled to leave it to the London Liberal and Radical Union – which will mean that we *shall* publish very explicit proposals. The Liberals are really in a great quandary. Chamberlain is making effective running: and there is no one to answer him.

Booth's paper on Tuesday seems to have come as a shock to C. S. Loch and Courtney. Harold Spender who was there tells me that Courtney put on an air of immense superiority and said nothing in a good many words. It really marks a very great strike.

Now it is delightful to think we shall have Monday together. My address at Cardiff will probably be

    c/o Mr Brice
      40 Machen Place
      Cardiff

then I fear I must miss a day in letters (at Risca). Write next to me at

    Talbot Hotel
    Bristol

where I propose to arrive Sunday and to stay.

I have written to Vaughan Nash urging him to go at D'Arcy Reeve, and sending him an article, with *words* of encouragement. I hope he can get money enough.

I am now off to interview the Hand-in-Hand Coopers at Bow. I shall be glad of the change of Cardiff.

                    My own dear love, good night.

                           Sidney

203 PP SIDNEY TO BEATRICE

Beatrice and Sidney had met in Bristol, when he went down to Wales, and jointly addressed a meeting.

                           4 Park Village East, N.W.
                                 22/12/91

Dearest

There is this to be said about the Difficulties of Democracy: they are not necessarily for you and me to solve! We may as well bear in mind in the night watches the consoling reflection that the Human Race has Time on its side – we *can* only do our bit, and leave the result to Fate.

Do not therefore feel overwhelmed with difficulties. It is not necessary that we should succeed; it is only required of us that we should do our 'level best'. Maybe it is our 'best' to fail even to move things on. Anyhow we can only do a very little at best – and we are content to do that little!

This little sermon for Christmas Eve is in reply to your rather sad description of your night. But perhaps the more appropriate sermon is 'Don't go supperless to bed again'!

I have chosen today a little present for you – it was a solemn occasion because I give you so few. And I could find nothing better than Matthew Arnold's poems. If any of these are not familiar to you, look at them now and again they are sad but restful. Take the book as a very poor token of a very great devotion – as a small symbol of a very great faith in our own power of improvement if we are but true to each other's best selves.

This morning my mother and the rest of us signed the deeds settling our little property affairs, and I hope that matter is settled. My mother is very shaky but she is standing this dreadful weather very well. It is black as night – such vile fog.

I hope you have provided better weather for Wallas! I send him my very best love and thanks for very many kindnesses. He must remain our very dear friend, and must be friend enough to warn us when we go wrong.

I am *so* anxious for the New Year which we are to enter openly *together*!

By the way, we *were* in the *Bristol Mercury* of Tuesday – about 20 lines of me, and 6 of you! Also a brief report of my Sunday lecture. So that if anyone sees it, be prepared. But suspicions don't matter much now.

Dearest, goodbye. This is a poor letter, but there is no news. I have been all day in the fog on one business or another – and you won't let me say 'I love you' *more* than six times in each letter! I have done *nothing* today for THE BOOK. But I will get to work again next week.

Adieu, my Sweet. A very happy Christmas to you.

Sidney

204 PP BEATRICE TO SIDNEY

Box House, Minchinhampton, Glos.
[?24 December 1891]

Dearest one,

You will not get a letter from me this morning. I woke up yesterday morning with bad neuralgia to find that Ll. Smith and V. Nash were coming down by the morning train. I had to write out my notes from the preceding evening – and then they arrived and I had to talk. Wallas and I had a successful evening at Gloucester but we did not get back until 1 o'clock: Graham was awfully nice and kind.

I was too tired to talk to much advantage with Ll. Smith (he left in the evening) but I gathered that he [had] no new or brilliant lights on trade unions tho' a great deal of information especially historical on London.

It is very sweet of you to send me Mat. Arnold's poems. They are very beautiful and he is one of my favourite poets – full of reformed philosophical feeling but wanting in robust determination to make things better – but I shall read them again and feel that they come from you.

It is a solemn thought that we are entering the new year together – we will try that our partnership shall be fruitful to others – I do not *really* doubt the good of it even in my weakest moments – perhaps sometimes I realise more strongly the sacrifice of the one-sidedness of a solitary life which seems to promise more achievement.

My neuralgia is still rather bad. The weather is bitter and frozen mist covers the country.

V. Nash is still here, goes this afternoon.

Now, dear one goodbye. This will be the last Xmas we shall spend apart. Next year we shall have a home of our own – I wonder whether we shall be in the middle of the first volume. That Book will be a big difficulty to overcome together.

Ever your devoted comrade
Beatrice Potter

Forgive this paper. I scribbled on it talking to V. Nash.

205 PP SIDNEY TO BEATRICE

In September Shaw had made his first visit to Italy with a party from the Art Workers Guild: 'about 20 out of the 27 seem to me to be capable of admiring everything except beauty', he wrote to William Morris from Venice on 23 September (BL). He confessed his irritation at those who 'have taken up art as the last refuge of general incompetence'.

4 Park Village East, N.W.
25 Dec/91

Dearest

It was a dull Christmas till your letter came – about 11 o'clock (this has been a fearful time for the postmen). I am sorry about the neuralgia because it is a sign of overstrain. But that fearful journey to Gloucester would account for much. I felt so glad that Wallas would be there.

This morning Shaw came for a walk and we went to Hampstead – *so* slippery: he stayed to middle-day dinner and then went off to work. We had a very pleasant talk, politics and Fabian Society, but he made no confidences. In the house he was very pleasant in describing Italy – very enthusiastic about Verona – which I feel to be *your* Verona – and Venice.

I must go: and I shall have a beautiful guide. We might take three weeks out of the worst of the winter sometime!

Edgeworth has sent me £7 for the Women's Wages article – poor pay but I did not do it for money or for him. Still, I am a little inclined to wonder if I am being paid at the same rate as the others.

I proposed to call on Mrs Green these days, but she is at Mrs Wards, Haslemere. I am to go on Monday: and to dine there on the 31st.

Where are we to have that house of our own, by next Christmas? I think we must headquarters in London, whether I am in L.C.C. or not.

But there are nice '*country*' houses in Hampstead, if we can afford one; and if you like that part. I own I yearn very very much for that time: we shall get on much faster. I want to be at hand to see that you don't have neuralgia; and to have you at hand to see that I don't do ephemeralities all day because I am asked to do so.

But I must say goodbye again; there are other things to be written before posttime. Dearest, I am very dependent on the post now! But don't trouble about it – when there is no letter I quite understand that you have not been able to slip out to post one; and I had much rather go without than put you to inconvenience. I am glad you have seen Ll. Smith and V. Nash – these, too, will remain friends and Nash, in particular, I like very much.

I have the enclosed nice letter from Fairfield (destroy): I shall be glad when we can ask him to tea? He will be so pleased.

Goodbye darling

Sidney

206 PP BEATRICE TO SIDNEY

Box House, Minchinhampton, Glos.

Xmas Day

Dearest one,

To think that we might have spent Xmas together, if I had not been so conscientious about the Playnes! But this will be [the] last Xmas day that we need be apart and at any rate it is an improvement over last Xmas.

Xmas days have been very dreary to me for the last 8 years. For the 5 years that I was under that cloud they were days of veritable agony because one's loneliness is brought home to one when all the others of a large family have homes and families. For the last three years they have been very grey and sombre – today I feel happy but serious about the future.

Dear one – I will try to repay your love and devotion and to make your home and happiness together – in spite of your 'professional' wife. I will try and prove that a woman may be a loving wife and gentle mistress without assuming to be a strenuous public servant. But I shall often stumble and fail – and you must help me up and protect me against self-complacency or lethargy either at home or in our work.

Graham and I constantly talk of you; it is very sweet to have a brother here with whom one may discuss the future. He is a dear good fellow. Vaughan Nash looked dreadfully 'destitute'; he gets nothing from the *Trade Unionist* and in fact spends some of his scanty earnings on it. Goodbye dear one.

Ever your devoted comrade
Beatrice Potter

207 PP SIDNEY TO BEATRICE

Henry Richard Fox Bourne (1837–1900), author and social reformer, was secretary of the Aborigines Protection Society and interested in colonial policy. Sir Guy Fleetwood Wilson (1850–1940) was private secretary both to W. E. Gladstone and Sir Henry Campbell-Bannerman, a civil servant in the War Office, and briefly acting-Viceroy of India. Annesley Owen was a leading Chelsea Radical. Beatrice had arranged to give a lecture on Co-operation at a Tyneside meeting.

4 Park Village East, N.W.
27 Dec/91

Dearest

Today I have been busy enough to envy your restful day with Wallas. In the morning I had to hurry off to South Place Chapel, where I acted as Minister. (Wallas will tell you what this is if you don't know: he preaches there next Sunday on Robert Owen!) I preached on 'Peace on Earth (London)' = all my *London Programme* in rhetorical form. Tell Wallas that, after much travail, I read a piece of *Sartor Resartus*, and the last chapter, 'London As It Might Be', of my own book, which was very well received. I delivered a very emotional appeal to them to help in the County Council Campaign, which may do some good.

By the way, if Wallas has not arranged to have copies of his (enclosed) syllabus sent out in *Fabian News*, he deserves his sister's reproaches for lack of 'impressario-talent', as our German Egeria used to call it.

Then I came home to dinner, and afterwards went to call on Sir C. Dilke (I have not been for a whole year I believe; and it was necessary after the recent invitation to dinner). He was as usual very gracious, and begged me to outstay the others. Lady Dilke was away. The callers were the *same old set*. H. R. Fox Bourne, Fleetwood Wilson, Annesley Owen, a Chelsea Liberal, and another *inconnu de moi*. Miss Abraham made tea and she and I talked T. Unionism. Dilke said 'I see you have been speaking down my district; with Miss Potter at Bristol'!!

But he reads everything. I saw the *Co-operative News* there.

Miss Abraham was in despair about apprentices. They cannot 'come out' when the hands strike – and the employers can make shift with them to keep things going. (In the late Coopers' strike the boys *apprenticed to the journeymen* came out with these.) This is a dilemma, which is worth noting and thinking over.

Afterwards Dilke talked politics; said the tactics in the next Parliament would be for the Radicals to insist on dividing the House on as many advanced points as possible so as to compel Liberal members to declare themselves. He wanted therefore to get lists of candidates pledged to a few points, in advance. He urged me to do all I could to take the lead, either in or out of Parliament and to make it my business to play the hand and pull the strings!!

All of which he clearly means to do himself. He was anxious to see Labouchere in office(!) as outside he would only confuse the issues and spoil the game. (This seems to me very wise and true.)

Miss Abraham knew nothing about Assistant Labor Commissioners.

Then I had to go to the club (nearly empty) and waste an hour over the London Letter – then home to supper, and my daily report to you, Queen!

Shall I see you in three days or in four? I might as well come to Paddington to meet you if you come up alone – even if I get out at High St Station! I am to dine with you at Mrs Green's on the 31st (Thursday) – the last day of the year! It has been a good year to us, dearest – a heavenly year to me though it opened gloomily enough, as Wallas knows, for I was often 'savage' with him.

But it is *the* year of my life – there can be no other like it, though we may have many happy and useful years together.

Yes, next Christmas will be different, we may hope – not exactly happier for me, for I am already made very very happy – but fuller and freer and more complete in happiness and more settled in work and outlook. We shall be very happy and also very useful, playing Private Secretary to each other in turn! – though I want you to think and invent, rather than to write.

Let me know when your gorgeous apotheosis is to take place at Newcastle, with Bailey as Archpriest. I shall want to be there, even if I go and return by night train (Pullman), and I want to keep the date free.

Goodbye, now, my sweet. Be careful, these last days at Box. I will make thee a new box no less comfortable in which thou shalt be happier and do more work!

Sidney

208 PP SIDNEY TO BEATRICE

Beatrice wrote on 27 December to say that on Boxing Night she and Wallas had spent 'a gruesome evening' at the Playnes, who gave a party for poor relations and servants: she suggested to Sidney that after their marriage they would only

be invited to Longfords in the guise of impoverished dependants. Colonel
F. W. Stopford (1854–1929) was Alice Green's brother; he served in various
colonial campaigns and was a general at the Gallipoli landings.

4 Park Village East, N.W.

28 Dec/91

Dearest

The party at the Playnes *does* sound lugubrious! We shall be 'poor
relations', but, all the same, I don't think the Playnes will look down on
us. We shall be something they don't understand, and that always secures
an uneasy respect.

Dear Wallas, I am so glad he is resting, and so pleased you should have
so good a companion. Do as you think best with Mrs Courtney. I expect
she is really coming to 'put you to the question' on this as well as on the
Labor Commission.

I have spent some time today thinking about the Deptford campaign,
which is a considerable undertaking. Will you and Wallas consider the
enclosed draft of an Address? This is of course the first time I have done
such a document, and I can't at all make up my mind how far one ought to
do as other candidates do, and how far it would be best to be unconventional.

Bring it up with you, and let us talk it over with Mrs Green on Thursday.

Let me know by what train you come up, and I will meet you, if I may.

Do not think of your own weakness. We are all weak, measured against
the work to be done; but we generally find strength enough for the tiny
task *of the day*. More than that we do not need, and could perhaps not
use. And how much stronger we both are than many – perhaps than most
around us.

I feel that I am gathering strength. I have lately felt much more confident
of my power to help largely in the T.U. book. I seem to be getting a grasp
of the facts. Dearest, I am glad! You shall feel my arm under yours
whenever you are tired, my strength around you whenever you are weak,
my love embracing you whenever you are lonely, my skill and knowledge
and facility as a basis wherever your finer taste and insight needs a foundation and a background. Let me bring my share to the common work,
in which it is to be my privilege and my delight to join.

O my love, we are very lucky to be able to work – while yet it is light.

When the night comes to one or other of us, as come it must in some
shape or another, let us be able to look back on 'something accomplished
something done' in the heyday of our love – and then go down the vale of
years together as sweet comrades in rest as we had been in toil.

Now goodbye, dearest – only three days more!

I must be off to tea with Mrs Green to meet Col. Stopford.

Sidney

Beatrice was due to leave Box early in the New Year for her annual release from caring for her father when she realised that his condition had suddenly deteriorated.

> Box House, Minchinhampton, Glos.
> [?30 December 1891]

Dearest,

It seems very unlikely that I shall be able to come tomorrow. Mrs Thompson thinks Father is dying, and the other nurse believes that it can't last long. I have not yet seen the doctor – so can't tell whether they are right or not. Happily he has ceased to suffer. I do not believe he is conscious or barely so – and his breathing tho' very quick is not so terribly laboured. Leonard comes down too this afternoon. Kate wrote some days ago to ask me what I thought of Miss Abraham and that Leonard was going to or had seen her. I gave her a very good character and moderate in accuracy. I do not imagine they will ask me any questions with regard to our relationship – and if the end should come here, I should wait till everything was settled up to tell the family.

I hope your mother and sister-in-law won't let it out casually. I daresay you made this clear? I liked your sermon very much indeed – Graham said he liked it better than anything you had done. There was a good ring about it – I gave it to Mrs Thompson to read (!) and she said she liked it 'there was no nonsense in it'. The enclosed is vexatious. But of course if I do not get away now – it will be some weeks before all is settled up and then I could go straight into London. If I do come up, I will call and see [*name illegible*]. Graham will see you this evening particularly.

Always your devoted comrade

> Beatrice Potter

If I can't lecture on the 12th, will you take it?

> [Box House, Minchinhampton]
> Wednesday evening [30 December 1891]

My own dear one,

I have been sitting in Father's room most of the day – keeping Mrs Thompson company in watching over him. We are now keeping him under doses of chloroform to prevent the breathing from being a terrible struggle and tonight the Dr will inject morphia. It is the last duty one has to him to keep as free as possible from suffering.

It has been rather a dreary day – wild wind and rain outside and the poor struggling life inside. It is so sad that these last 8 weeks should not have been spared him.

Excellent letter of [S. A.] Barnett's which I have cut out for you – Old Age Pensions. I cannot settle to my book or work – perhaps it is only right that I should not be able to do so. He has been a devoted Father to all of us – a loving unselfish guardian over our interests. His love for his children was more like that of a mother than a Father's!

I imagine that directly the end has come Lallie Holt will help me to settle up everything – it will take us perhaps a fortnight or three weeks. That will mean that we shall not see each other. But you must work hard at your election so that we shall have more time together afterwards. I shall finish this tomorrow.

Thursday [31 December 1891]

The Dr would not inject the morphia last night as he thought it would probably kill him. He lies in the same state today – and has small doses of chloroform to keep his breathing fairly easy. I suppose it may go on for some days. The Courtneys came today. I shall see the Doctor and find out whether it is possible for him to rally for a week or two – in which case I should come up tomorrow. But I fear there is no hope. If I do I will telegraph.

Ever your devoted comrade

Beatrice Potter

211 PP SIDNEY TO BEATRICE

John Frome Wilkinson's *Mutual Thrift* was published in 1891. Sir Spencer Walpole (1838–1907), civil servant and historian, had just published two volumes of his *History of England from 1815 to 1856*. He served as governor of the Isle of Man. The first of many editions of George Jacob Holyoake's book on the pioneer Co-operators of Rochdale, *Self-Help by the People*, appeared in 1858.

4 Park Village East, N.W.
31 Dec/91

Dearest

I was grievously disappointed when Wallas told me that I should not see you today. But ever since I have been thinking of your distressing position. I wish the Courtneys had come yesterday: you ought to have someone with you. I hope they have come today: they ought to help you.

Poor dear father-in-law whom I shall never see! I have watched by a father's death bed, happily not prolonged, and I know that it means something, however 'rational' we may resolve to be. The sight of a loved one in pain: the sense of helplessness; even the physical repulsion – all that you have gone through already, but it must be a heavy trial nevertheless. All that can be said is that it is all, perhaps, less painful to the sufferer than it seems – especially in the last exhaustion. It takes *life* to suffer pain; and I suppose the steady lowering of vitality mercifully diminishes the capacity for suffering. Certainly this is true of mental anguish. And in this case, how great is the gain of death!

Do not say to yourself 'I will not grieve'. You will grieve, and ought to grieve, at the snapping of a link with your past life – even though the end be only the result of years of preparation. It is the *event* that sums up all the foregoing.

What you must do is just to 'let yourself go' – whether that means grief or no grief. If you feel, on the whole, glad – feel glad, and say so. If you feel solemn, be solemn. Do not feel or say or think what you imagine you *ought* to feel or say or think – that is the usual horrible mockery of an English funeral.

There is death on earth but no Death with a big D. This personification of Death – a kind of bogeyman – is answerable for much of our false sentimentality on the subject.

Dearest – *moi qui vous parle* – I am feeling horribly faint at the thought that either you or I must be 'lost', one day, to the other. It is no use crying 'Peace Peace' when there is no peace. I am *not* reconciled to death – we must bear it, but I will not pretend that I acquiesce in it.

And, since we *must* part one day, and our bodies – sweet, *qui nous appartiennent à toujours* – must be put away – and our minds 'cease'. Since it must be so, let it add a new sanctity to our love – not only that, but to our view of human life. A few precious years is all we have for each other, and for the world – let us never *profane* those years.

The greatest blasphemy seems to me to be *Doubt* – of love, of life, of progress. Help me to keep us both from Doubt.

If the end has come, or does come, of course your London visit must be put off: and perhaps all you can do will be a day or two en route for Lancashire.

I would of course willingly take your lecture on the 12th, but I think Wallas had better do so. Oxford House is a *very* timorous place, and has never invited me – or any politician – to lecture there. I think they would not like it.

Moreover, I am old-engaged to go that night to the Halstead Co-op. Society.

Your announcement to your family would naturally come when matters were settled up, and you were asked what you proposed to do. You need not be afraid about my brother and his wife: they are *quite* out of any possible intersection of the circles; moreover I earnestly begged them to keep it secret; and (humiliating!) they have not the faintest notion that you are a 'personage'.

If, however, your father rallies, I suppose you will come up tomorrow. Do just whatever is right. Spencer Walpole is coming to Mrs Green's at 5 tomorrow, and I am to meet him. We could easily go to [the] Albemarle to dine, if Mrs Green's arrangements are otherwise.

Now try to think of something else. Your suggestions for the improvement of my 'Address' are admirable – indeed, that as to the last par. I should probably have done myself, in any case.

I shall want a cheap clerk at Deptford for a few weeks, and I think I will see if Miss Bridgman cares about it. There will be endless folding and addressing.

I have bought Holyoake's *Self-Help 100 Years Ago*, and Wilkinson's *Mutual Thrift*, as they are books which we want to refer to. But there is little of obvious relevance. You are bringing your *industrial* books away, I hope? You had better make this your depot.

Now, dearest, goodbye for today. It is hard that I cannot be with you in your trouble. But it must soon be over – and you will have the permanent satisfaction *and help*, of thinking that you 'saw it through', that you did all you possibly could.

Goodnight, darling. How will this find you!

Sidney

5. A new life

January – July 1892

The death of Richard Potter released Beatrice from a tie of family love and duty which had sapped her energy for several years. On the eve of her 34th birthday she was at last free to marry, 'Few men have attracted and given more affection' she noted the day after Richard Potter died. On 21 January she wrote: 'And now the old life is over – or rather the old *shell* is cast off and a new one adopted. Past are the surroundings of wealth; past the association with the upper middle class; past also the silent reserve and the hidden secret. Now I take my place as a worker and as a helpmate of a worker – one of a very modest couple living in a small way . . . That I shall in the first instance suffer – even in my work –for my step downwards in the social scale is probable – but if it is his gain it will not be my loss.'

Sidney was informed by telegram of Richard Potter's death. In a surviving fragment of a letter sent on 1 January he similarly reflected on the future. 'This is the beginning of a new year for both of us – and you – for the first time – are *quite* free to 'give' yourself to your work and to me . . . I will do all I can to make you gain thereby – not only in personal happiness but also in efficiency. I do believe that this cannot fail to be the result. Sweet! that I love you better than ever is perhaps not much guarantee: but over your father's death let us cement our agreement again that all we do shall be for "social service" as far as we know how.'

One immediate result of Beatrice's planned marriage was that Herbert Spencer withdrew his request for her to serve as his literary executor, fearing that it would not do for his reputation that he should be openly connected with an avowed and prominent socialist.

In the first half of 1892 Beatrice planned to press on with the research for the trade union book while Sidney concerned himself with the coming L.C.C. election and with establishing himself in a new and public life. In an undated letter in January Beatrice wrote: 'Honestly, I do not see how we can get married before we have the material for that book. I think a change of name might be disastrous to the enquiry . . . If that work were not finished – and if I had not my full share in it – I should never recover my confidence in married life . . . But we will not lead separate lives longer than need be'.

212 PP BEATRICE TO SIDNEY

Box House, Minchinhampton, Glos.
New Year Day 1892

My own Dear One

The end came peacefully this morning. Kate and I watched till 2 o'clock and then left and I was with him again about 8. He died a few minutes before 9 o'clock. In the last 12 hours he was unconscious – in a state of high fever. It is very horrible to watch a person dying; but it is better over. Ir seems a long while to look back on these six years – six years ago at this time (it was about 2 months after M. [Mother] was taken) I was in the depths of despair. My life seemed finished, for both love and effort and faith were worn out or in the agony of death – a picture of silent watching perhaps for years seemed appalling, and I longed that he might die so that I might feel free to die also. And these first months *were* terrible – until Faith in work sprang again into life.

Now I can with your love look forward to a life of effort and faith and affection. We will try to live our lives with dignity and devotion, as Father did according to his lights in his day.

The funeral will be on Tuesday or Wednesday, probably Wednesday. After that I shall probably go to The Argoed for a few days.

I shall spend a week in London before I leave for Lancashire.

Ever your faithful comrade,

Beatrice Potter

213 PP SIDNEY TO BEATRICE

Sir Leslie Stephen (1832–1904), man of letters, had just retired from the editorship of the *Dictionary of National Biography* for health reasons: he was the father of Vanessa Bell and Virginia Woolf. Dr James Martineau (1805–1900) was a Unitarian preacher, moralist and educator. He was responsible for University Hall, in which Mrs Humphry Ward took a keen interest. Thomas Hill Green (1836–82) had been a distinguished professor of moral philosophy at Oxford: his Idealist philosophy influenced the intellectual reform movement of the 1880s. He was the model for 'Mr Gray' in Mrs Ward's novel *Robert Elsmere*. Robinson was a strong Fabian, resident at University Hall, who thought it discreet to hide his political beliefs.

4 Park Village East, N.W.

2 Jan/92

Dearest

I suppose your other sisters will be coming to Box these days, and you will have a full house – perhaps it is as well that this comes before they know our secret.

Do not get ill from want of fresh air and exercise. I don't know how far etiquette demands that you should remain at home – but etiquette ought not to interfere with your outdoor exercise.

It is joy to hear that you will have a week in London anyhow. You can easily turn it to good account. And I want you to see Galton before I make any proposition to him. He is not perfect and I do not feel quite sure that he will do. But he is the best man I know for the purpose.

Yesterday afternoon I went to Mrs Green's to tea, to meet Spencer

Walpole. But he had come and gone before I arrived (some misunder-standing as to hour I suppose), and I found there Leslie Stephen (silent) and Mrs Ward, with whom I talked London, and (quite unintentionally) appeared, I believe, in the character of a nice, 'good' young man! Mr Taylor was there, and Wallas and I and Strong stayed on talking with him. He has, seemingly, the utterly impossible idea of becoming an 'independ-ent' candidate, either in Ireland or England, unconnected with any Irish or English party! This is the dream of a recluse, but Mrs Green did not seem to see that it was so. I begin to see that she has *Schwärmereien* which vitiate the sanity of her personal judgments. It is delightfully nice, but it leads me to attach less weight to *her own* judgments whilst feeling that the criticism she can afford upon other's judgments may be unimpaired.

One thing Wallas and I spared Mrs Ward. She was describing how experience had shown that they had one good man as resident, who was coming rapidly to the fore, that 'ran' everything – *un nommé* Robinson. What would have disgusted her and ruined him would have been to reveal to her the fact that he is a Fabian!

She said that Dr Martineau had been quite tolerant, e.g. in the social lectures; much of yours he disapproved – but he drew the line at T. H. Green! The residents – led by Robinson – read Green in private before breakfast – but lectures on him were *not* to be allowed!

I suggested that University Hall might become (among other things) a 'Guild of Exponents' of the British Museum and make a practice of con-ducting parties over its departments with due enthusiasm and explanation (instancing the Co-operators and the elder Board School children as clients).

I have agreed to put (for nothing) a series of articles in the *Workman's Times* on the London County Council. These will be signed, and I merely dictate them to a reporter, so that it is no trouble, and is a part of my candidature.

But of course I am busy enough, and as you kindly said, I cannot do much towards THE BOOK until March 5 – only 9 weeks. But I shall do something, utilising the trips I *must* make to Halstead (12th), Hull (31st) Halifax and Keighley (3rd and 4th February), and filling up odd time at home by grubbing in the blue books.

Now, dearest once more goodbye. I am not sure how it will look if you read this letter at breakfast before observant eyes! It is banal and common-place, the rush of ordinary life by the side of Death – but it is better so. Let me talk to you of common things as you ask and think you of common things as much as possible.

Darling, I do so want to be with you, to do your accounts for you and stand between you and the business. But we must be patient still a little while. Dearest I seem to see you, but I can't reach you to kiss.

Sidney

Neale was Beatrice's personal maid.

[Box House, Minchinhampton]
Jan. 3 1892

My own Dear One,
   Enclosed a cheque for £100, my contribution towards our joint expenses.
   What you say about Mrs Green's mannerisms is very true and makes one anxious least she form a permanent relationship with someone who would be a drag on her. She is too much influenced by a person's feeling towards her to be able to form a sound objective judgment of them. I do not like the idea of her marrying Strong – he might grow into a hypochondriac and be a terrible drag on her life as he is not a sound sane-minded man.
   I shall be very glad when all this week is over. I have written to Alice Green to say that I shall probably come up on *Saturday*. I propose to stay a fortnight in London – so as to be able to run down here if necessary – also I trust after the declaration is made, my sisters may naturally wish me to introduce you to them.
   Margaret Hobhouse took me apart yesterday and begged me most affectionately to consider her house my home and not to cut adrift from the family. And she implored me not to marry out of my 'class' – 'I believe in a woman marrying someone of her own position, now Haldane would do capitally'. I suggested that I feared Haldane had heart disease and would not live so very long. 'Better marry a man with heart disease than some little fellow with no position'! Poor Maggie, she married 'position' and has had a life of no companionship and of constant distress. How people stick to their ideals however badly they succeed in bringing happiness and content.
   The whole family will be gathered at Longford on Tuesday – and all arrangements will be made that evening. We propose to give Mrs Thompson £500 – and do not think that is too much for her wonderful devotion. You must know her, she is a splendid motherly woman. She is sleeping with me now as I felt rather lonely and nervous and I thought it better for her. Neale is terribly distressed at the idea of leaving me. Miss Darling, poor little lonely thing – will find it most difficult – to get a place. The incompetent dependants of rich households have a miserable precarious and uncertain livelihood – that little woman ought never to have enjoyed the luxury of our establishment. She has no right to it and it does not fit her for work – on the contrary it submerges her little activities in self-indulgence.
   I feel rather weak and cold – a little bit anxious about the future – be-

cause I don't feel strong and able. But I dare say I shall get into harness again.

Now Dear One Goodbye.

Ever your devoted comrade,

Beatrice Potter

I like your letters of news.

Edward Vansittart Neale (1810–92) spent his substantial means on promoting the Co-operative movement, serving as the unpaid secretary of the Co-operative Union from 1873 to 1891. Beatrice commented (MA 362) 'that in all the annals of British philanthropy no more honourable example can be found of a life devoted from first to last to the disinterested and self-denying service of the wage-earning class'. With Thomas Hughes, Neale had published *A Manual for Co-operators* in 1879; in the 'manifesto' to which Webb refers Neale and Hughes had attacked the attempts to link socialism and the Co-operatives, considering that the Co-operative movement was being prejudiced by its permeation by Fabian economics.

In her *Autobiography* (1920) Margot Asquith recalled 'an announcement in some obscure newspaper' that she was engaged to Lord Rosebery. The report, she added, 'came between us' for he 'was seriously annoyed and thought I should have contradicted this'.

4 Park Village East, N.W.

3 Jan/92

Dearest

I wonder how you have spent this Sunday, with various sisters on your hands! and the Presence in the house which subdues all life. I do hope you will not let it all make you uncomfortable.

Last night I dined one of the leading Deptford men, and discussed arrangements. He was very hopeful; liked my Address, and seemed taken by my energy and ingenuity. Tomorrow I must see several more of them. It will be an uncomfortable and bustling nine weeks – with that very disagreeable constant sense of falling short of perfection – but it will be all over in nine weeks, and the real stress will not begin till February. It is impossible to completely 'work' a borough of 100,000 inhabitants, and 12,000 electors, with an expenditure of £100 or so (the limit set by law); and this makes it important to organise a band of volunteers.

The whole procedure and regulations are intended for a *ward* of a town council, and they are inadequate for the colossal magnitudes of London.

Today I have been 'grubbing away' at details and putting together some election leaflets for the Fabian Society to publish, in order to do a little to 'educate' London in this big struggle.

I have also done a little letter to the *Co-op News*, at B. Jones' request (enclosed), in courteous answer to the New Year manifesto of Hughes and Neale. It is not an *answer*, but merely a polite 'caveat' as to Socialism not being what they describe it to be.

My article on Booth seems to have been too much for the *Speaker* for they have suppressed it. Wemyss Reid is really seriously ill, and the paper is living from hand to mouth, without thought or management.

I have no other gossip to tell you – angel mine! – so I suppose I come back to the old story of how much I am thinking about you, and how much I miss you!

It is very hard that Sunday cuts me off from communication with you: I *do yearn* for that letter tomorrow. But I will remember that you may not be able to post me one always.

You must tell me when to write you at The Argoed. I suppose I shall never see that house now.

Suppose I should find it necessary to engage a clerk before you can come up? I don't feel *quite* sure how Galton would turn out for us; he is by far the best man I know who is to be had; but it is a risk. Of course I could make him no promises, and perhaps it might be easy for him to be away for a few weeks. Perhaps I might open the matter to him at once?

Now good night, darling. This is the first Sunday of *our* New Year: we *will* make a good one.

Sidney

Do you see the repentant Lord Rosebery is engaged to the daughter of Sir C. Tennant?

216 PP   BEATRICE TO SIDNEY

Margaret Hobhouse was objecting to the employment of Galton. Arabella Fisher was the sister of the prominent lawyer Lord Wrenbury and an old friend of Beatrice. She had been secretary to the eminent geologist Sir Charles Lyell (1797–1885), whose work had been part of the evolutionary science which undermined revealed religion in the middle of the nineteenth century. Beatrice considered her friend as an example of dedicated work. Her warm letter was welcomed because she had earlier supported the Booths in their disapproval of Sidney as a suitor.

Box House, Minchinhampton, Glos.
[?4 January 1892]

My own dear One

I send you a sweet little note from Bella Fisher. I wrote and told her that I was announcing our engagement after everything is settled up. She is a warmhearted strong woman who has done excellent work in her time. It becomes more and more strange that the Booths should have taken the line they have – when all my other friends, who knew, should have been so cordial and affectionate!

I am afraid my letters yesterday were rather down-hearted; but I feel the weight of Death in the house – and the large assembly of sisters and brothers-in-law asking me questions about the future – and throwing out ominous warnings! Margaret Hobhouse read me an angry lecture on the impropriety of a male secretary – at which I got rather cross and told her to mind her own business – for which I was sorry afterwards as it is useless to be angry especially about that, since the impropriety of it will be removed when I am engaged! The Courtneys are very pleasant and sensible, Leonard's strong *laissez-faire* is a relief from the fussyness of others of the family. But everything is going off very well – all the sisters and their husbands anxious to be pleasant to each other and the Playnes are wonderfully hospitable and kind all round. I shall be glad when Saturday comes, and I am on my way to London.

Miss Darling is fetching the letters this afternoon so I shall get yours. Now Dear One Goodbye.

Always your devoted comrade
Beatrice Potter

P.S. Let me see Galton as soon as you can after Saturday. How glad I shall be when I am up again with you.

BP

217 PP SIDNEY TO BEATRICE

Sir Charles Prestwood Lucas (1853–1931), civil servant and historian, had been a colleague of Webb in the Colonial Office, where he became assistant under-secretary in 1897. Beatrice had written the day before to report a conversation with Leonard Courtney about the assistant commissionerships for the Royal Commission on Labour. He had said that Beatrice would have been exactly the right person for it *two years ago* but the situation was now different. Beatrice commented to Sidney that it was 'exactly that time since you converted me to socialism'. Courtney, she added, was 'very much relieved to find I did not want it'.

4 Park Village East, N.W.
4/1/92

Dearest

It is good of you to send the cheque for £100 for my election expenses. I expect that they will be just about that sum. I am not out of funds; but if I were I would not scruple to let you know. It is both my duty to you, and my privilege to be quite frank in my acceptance of what you bring into the partnership – greatly as it may exceed all I can contribute.

I shall be so glad to see you on Saturday if that should be possible; and a change will be good for you. I will see Mrs Green tomorrow if I can.

Thanks for reminder about *The Times* obituary. I might have missed it, and as you say, my mother and sister will like to see it. (The *Pall Mall* has copied most of it.)

That was *poor* advice of Mrs Hobhouse. There is much to be said in presumption against marriage out of one's *class* – if by class is meant that very real difference which is the product of different educations, social traditions etc. But there is surely not much to be said against marriage out of one's *position*, i.e. the position of one's family. But she meant it kindly; and we must accept and repay it as such. She will, I fear, be very disgusted when she hears. But Lucas of the C.O. will probably give Hobhouse a good account of me.

I return Mrs Holt's letter. Her advice as to the settlement of affairs seems good. It would be better to leave as much as possible to the executors and their spouses. It is so difficult to avoid family 'jars' over such matters – and especially in your position it would be well if you could be relieved.

Booth's letter, too, is promising. It is a pity he did not take more pains to set forth his pension scheme in such a way as to remove the obvious (and momentary) objections as to thrift etc. But his paper will have done much to force the scheme on the experts. And the statistical impetus is much, also. He will have done what I have tried for years to do, viz. get the Local Government Board to improve its statistics. If I were at that office I would have revolutionised its statistical department by this time.

I am *much* interested about the Assistant Commissioners (of course, I will say nothing about your news). I suppose we must accept the fact for some time to come that socialist opinions are not accorded belligerent rights, so to speak. If pronounced controversial opinions are objectionable, Mrs Fawcett and Miss Orme are equally condemned. And it would be well, I think, quietly to insist, on all suitable occasions, that Socialism is as respectable and scientifically orthodox as Individualism and ought to be treated on terms of equality.

Wallas's lectures on History of Chartism have been refused by the University Extension Central Secretary (Roberts). But he will have 2 courses going in the Spring, and at least one (at University Hall) already settled for the Autumn, so he is all right.

I fear Miss Orme will be an obstacle to me at Deptford. She is President of the Women's Liberal Association there, and the Secretary has not responded cordially to a letter I sent: and seems inclined to be unfriendly. This does not matter much; and may not work out as it now looks. I am now going to see about things there.

I have been occupied, and must now close this in a hurry to save last post. Goodbye dearest. Tomorrow is a sad day – but you have done your duty.

Sidney

Box House, Minchinhampton, Glos.

[6 January 1892]

Dearest One

I feel dazed and stupified today. Yesterday was such a big wilderness – the four hour's drive to and from the funeral – the funeral itself – and then the unwieldy family gathering.

Everything went off satisfactorily.

The Will was read in the afternoon. My property is left to me absolutely – I think the family were rather sorry it was so. We shall each have another £16,000 Dee [Daniel Meinertzhagen] thinks – making up each daughter's portion to £26,000, which ought to bring in a good £1000 a year. That is a high salary to get at the start of our life – let us hope we shall use it well.

All the 'Chattels' are left to the Executors to be realised for the Estate, each daughter being at liberty to buy in what she thinks fit at any price the Executors fix. So that I have absolutely nothing more to do with the matter and when I have tidied up here need not return.

So expect me by the 2.35 train. I do not think I will go out to the lecture. I will stay with Mrs Green. Could we not have Galton and Turner both to dinner at Wallas's? Alfred Cripps has a smart boy he has used as second clerk – who wants a place. We might possibly see him.

219 PP   SIDNEY TO BEATRICE

Turner and Galton were invited to an 'interview' dinner with Beatrice, Sidney, Wallas and Shaw.

Sidney received a telegram asking for confirmation of a report of his engagement: the leak may have come through an indiscretion by Alice Green. As Beatrice had not yet broken the news to her family and he feared a telegram might be read at Box he despatched his message in German.

Michael Austin, elected as Irish Labour M.P. for Co. Limerick in 1892, was secretary of the Irish Democratic Labour Federation. Barry O'Brien (1847–1918) a barrister and author interested in Irish politics and literature, was chairman of the Irish Literary Society: he wrote a biography of Parnell in 1898.

4 Park Village East, N.W.

7 Jan/92

Dearest

I am relieved and delighted to learn that all has gone off well. It must have been a trial to you: it has been on my mind all these days, but of course I could do nothing to help you.

I have asked Wallas to invite Galton and Turner and you and me to dinner on Sunday. I will meet your train at Paddington at 2.35, and go on with you to Mrs Green's if I may – as I ought to be present at 5 at a conference of the Fabian lecturers who are to speak on the L.C.C. elections, and whom it is very important to influence. I don't *want* to go! But I *ought* to be there, and we shall not be happy unless we are careful that our love does not stand in the way of our usefulness. Then I have the little lecture in the evening – so that I must relinquish seeing you until the next day. If it is such brilliant weather as now we might walk across the Park to the Marble Arch (avoiding Rotten Row!) and then take the omnibus to Wallas's.

I am glad you have no responsibility for the distribution of the estate – it is likely to save us much friction. We shall have *ample* means for all our work; indeed, we shall need to be careful to justify our expenditure.

By all means send the tin box here, and anything else you choose. This room has now become exclusively *my* office; and I shall be able to arrange for sixty or seventy excellent flat drawers in 4 cabinets for sorting the papers – *vice* my fossils, now in course of distribution by gift. It is a fearfully 'untidy' office; and you would miss the general sense of light and space and well appointed comfort of Box if you worked here much. But for a *pied-à-terre* I think you may be able to put up with it (until I can help you to create a more comfortable 'box').

I grieve to say that I have a little cold in the head, but I shall make a great effort to get rid of it by Saturday, otherwise things go well with me. Deptford will be a laborious and anxious business and uncertain. But the Conservatives cannot even find a candidate yet, which is hopeful.

Goodbye, sweetest, I am very grateful for your goodness in managing to send me a letter every day. Can't you be a little naughty or imperious or exacting for a change? I have a sense – delightful – of getting deeper and deeper into your debt, and repaying nothing.

Your little letter was very welcome. I had no suspicion that you had been in pain: so it is not true that love gives complete second sight! I *do* hope it has not been very bad: *please* take care of yourself.

Elvidge has just gone: he is very nice and will be useful. The list is getting done, but cannot be complete until *at* Congress. I have been talking to him rather 'at large' on T.U. policy as to women, piecework, apprentices etc. – not much to put down, but useful for one's own education.

I duly received the lists of industries which shall be tabulated; and the originals returned to Redgrave – they will be very useful.

I enclose the letters of introduction with a paper of notes on the people. You had, I suggest, better use the first Sunday afternoon to see Dr Spence Watson, sending on your introduction by post in advance, and offering to call then. Ede will very likely look in at Congress: you could ask him to meet you there.

I will look up your times in Bradshaw, and will be in Birmingham to meet you.

Now dearest, good night. Do not write except when you can without effort – but remember how much your letters mean to me. I am sending you a great packet but not much actual 'letter' because I have had a long and busy day. Good night.

Sidney

The enclosed telegram has just come. The *British Weekly* is an enterprising *religious* paper. I know no one connected with it. But Tuesday I met Austin (who called on you with Judge Jones) and Barry O'Brien said to me, jokingly, 'Condole with him on the state of the Liberal Party'. He replied to me 'Ought you not to be condoling with a lady in Gloucestershire on her loss'. So I merely said, very gravely, that 'it could hardly be called a loss, as her father had been laid by for years'. But Austin is much 'in' with the Fleet St set, and I can only suspect that he knows.

But I think you would do well to send off your letters *at once*.

It seems hardly possible publicly to contradict the statement, and it may die away if unnoticed. I shall tell Massingham to publish nothing about it: unless you think otherwise.

I am sorry: but I don't think I have done it.

I have thought it best to telegraph this news to you in German.

I can say no more now, as I must rush off to an appointment.

Adieu till Sat.

Sidney

220 PP   SIDNEY TO BEATRICE

The order of the following letters is uncertain: an alternative sequence would be 222 (Beatrice to Sidney); 221 (Beatrice to Sidney); and 220 (Sidney to Beatrice).

4 Park Village East, N.E.
8/1/92

Dearest

I hope my letter reached you this morning as usual. The *British Weekly* I could not post till late.

It is a paper which, though not much read in our 'world', is much quoted by other newspapers as it often contains news (like this!).

I am being sorry, but I don't think it is anybody's fault. Massingham tells that Austin has been talking freely in Fleet St about it, saying, weeks ago, that your family were discussing and expecting it.

(And, you will notice that the gossip column this week is full of Mrs Green whom the writer evidently met at the Academy Private View!! *Çà donne à penser*.)

Massingham stopped the news from appearing in the *Chronicle*, and I telegraphed to the *Star*, *Pall Mall* and *Daily News* in a way which seems effectual. This will prevent your people seeing it for a few days, and give time for your letters to precede it. And, as I telegraphed to you this morning, I fancy you *need* not tell Mrs Playne verbally unless you like. It would be enough to leave a letter for her on Sat. But you will know best.

Dearest, I am very sorry – but think how much worse it might have been! A week ago the announcement would have given you a horrible time of it, and made friction with your family almost inevitable. And, as it is, there will be little harm done.

I have written to Vaughan Nash and the *Manchester Guardien* warning them not to put in a par. about *me* that may reach them. Shall I not do so also to Bamford of the *Co-op. News*? If it is kept out of these, it will probably not reach very far, and soon die away (as regards the Trade Unionists).

Of course I have not mentioned your name in any of my communications.

Dearest, tell me anything I can do to help you.

The disagreeable 'bit' will be nothing to me, but all to you in the way of unpleasantness. I shall be 'angel good' to them all – though no doubt awkward and shy. But you must not think of resenting any disrespect or discourtesy to me – should such come. We shall know how to make our own place among them. (I believe I *am* very proud, at bottom! much too proud to be inclined to resent any slights of that kind as things are.)

Yesterday I went to call on Drummond with whom I have been corresponding on 'unfair' printers. I went in, and he did not in the least know me, nor did I recognise him!! We stared a while, and I explained who I was, and then he was overwhelmingly friendly. But we evidently share the failing of quite forgetting faces.

Massingham was very cordial in his congratulations – said you were much too good to be wasted as an old maid! (a very masculine view). I begged him to stop all mention of it in the press.

May I send Miss Darling something? I think I should like to if it is permissible. You will advise me what.

I have written to Haldane telling him of the 'par', and of my efforts to stop it, and asking his co-operation therein, but telling him that your family had been told, so that he could 'play up' on that assumption.

Two small items of news. 'John Law' has a sensational '*Tendenz-Roman*' running in the *Women's Herald* about Barmaids.

Champion is still President of the 'Kentish Labor Party' which (with Aberdeen) still believes in him; and to which he gave a Presidential Address last week (no report).

Now goodbye till tomorrow, and to mere letter writing to you for some time.

Sweet, we will 'stand together', *n'est ce pas*, whatever they say. There is nothing bad they can rake up against me: and with your love I am indifferent to any coldness.

Sidney

Box House, Minchinhampton, Glos.
[?8 January 1892]

Dearest,

This is the last letter I shall write to you from here!

Yesterday I spent looking over things with Lallie Holt – and in the evening the Playnes and the Holts came up to dine. They all set on me after dinner about the secretary! (a quite unnecessary grievance on their side) and also implored me not to make a foolish marriage. I smiled and was silent but afterwards explained to them the duties of a secretary – how he would attend low Publics etc. in my stead – after which they said that of course it *was* necessary I should have a man with me – and they hoped it would be a working-man! Poor women, they are both exercised not only for my welfare but for the destruction of that £1000 a year in which they consider they have a sort of vested interest. But I think they are thoroughly prepared for the news – for I have all along assumed that I am likely to marry this year – and given them to understand that I expect to be poor.

We have a disagreeable bit to go through – but it is a great advantage that it should come after Father's death – when they will feel that my relations to my family will be a 'relationship of choice' and not of necessity. Anyhow Dear one, they shall treat you with respect and courtesy – and you have only to do the same by them. You will not come across them in anyway – and have only to hold yourself a little aloof, and be perfectly natural and pleasant with them if they make any overtures of friendship. I have a day's work before me packing.

Ever your devoted comrade.

Beatrice

P.S. I do not think I will call on your people on Sunday next. I have had rather a week of emotions and should like to rest. It would be good to meet Galton and recover [*seven words illegible*].

[Box House, Minchinhampton]
[?7–9 January 1892]

My own dear Boy,

I wrote on getting your telegram to all the sisters including Mary – I enclose her letter. She came up this morning and was very cordial. And what was very satisfactory she thought I had done *quite right in not telling them* – that it was altogether better for them not to know. This morning I got a letter from Kate Courtney enclosing a letter from the editor of the *Pall Mall* asking whether the report was true. 'Absolutely no truth' she had replied – that will prevent it being published for the present which is better as it would look rather unseemly immediately after Father's death. Expect me by the 2.35 train.

Ever your devoted comrade
Beatrice Potter

This letter was drafted early in December, when Beatrice had decided to tell her sisters of her engagement, but it was sent only after her father's death. She received a kind reply. Many years later she remarked that her eldest sister was the only one who generously accepted Sidney when the engagement was known. The value of the Whewell Scholarship awarded to Sidney in 1883 was only £50: it could only be taken up if the candidate resided for four years at Cambridge, normally at Trinity College.

14 Kensington Square, w.
[written late December, posted early January 1892]

Private
My dear Lallie

I write to tell you my plans for the coming year; and as these plans involve a very important change in my life, I think it right to send you, as my eldest sister, a full and frank explanation.

Some months ago Sidney Webb and I determined, when circumstances permitted, to enter on a life-long partnership. At the time of this understanding, it seemed uncertain whether we should be able to afford to marry during Father's life-time. Mr Webb had already decided on leaving the Colonial Office with a view of throwing himself into local government work – and possibly looking out, in due course, for an advanced constituency.

But this meant the sacrifice of his salary – or of his income; and though he was anxious and willing to defer his resignation, we both felt it was better that he should start immediately on the new life. On the other hand, as there was no immediate prospect of marriage we settled not to enter into a formal and public engagement.

Four month's experience of the new career has proved that he can make an ample income from journalism, while devoting the greater part of his time and strength to other work. The obstacle to a recognised engagement between us has therefore passed away, and I hasten to tell my sisters of my new relationship.

And now let me say quite frankly that I am sincerely grieved that my marriage is not one which will give my sisters, in the first instance, much satisfaction. Superficially your new brother-in-law will have little to recommend him. He is very small and ugly! he has none of the *savoir-faire*

382

which comes from a leisurely up-bringing – and of course he has none of the social position which springs from great possession and family connections. Briefly his career is this.

He is the son of a small London tradesman. His father managed to scrape together enough to send him and his brother to Germany for two years. At 15 years of age he began to earn his own livelihood as clerk in a low-class broker's office. But though he gave every satisfaction to his employer (he was offered a partnership before he left) he disliked the tone of the place, and worked up in the evenings for the Local division of the Civil Service. At 17 he passed second into the London Division of the Civil Service and entered the Inland Revenue office. The following year he passed second into the First Division of the Civil Service, but as the places open to the successful candidates were not to his liking, he remained another year in the Lower Division and passed second again, this time securing a good berth in the Colonial Office. During the first years of official life, he became a Barrister, took the Bacon and Blackstone Scholarship of Law – the second Whewell scholarship at Cambridge (the latter of which he could not take up unless he lived at Cambridge) and otherwise distinguished himself as an examinee. From that time until now he has spent his spare energies in political and economic questions. I tell you all this because it will set your mind at ease on the question of general character and ability. You will feel assured that your new brother-in-law, however below the family standard in means and position, is not deficient in those substantial qualities of character and intelligence which enable a man to be successful in the line of life that he deliberately chooses.

Of those finer and more hidden qualities of warm and generous sympathy and quick perception – which have attached round him warm friends in men of his own calibre – and which have won him his future wife – I must of course remain silent. These are qualities which you will not believe in unless you yourselves observe them – and certainly you will not take them on my word! But I have too great a respect for my sisters, with their very solid judgment, not to feel assured that they will not allow any superficial deficiencies to stand in the way of an appreciation of the real good qualities of their latest and youngest brother-in-law.

And now I have a small favour to ask – to end up with. As we do not intend to marry until September (in order to enable me to get the materials for my book on Trade Unions) we should be very grateful if you would consider this a *friendly family communication* and not spread it among those who would be likely to report it casually. We are anxious to escape the inevitable 'paragraphs' until within a few months of our marriage. I did not like to withhold the knowledge of our plans from my sisters – but we are both of us very fully occupied persons and we don't care for too long a continuation of queries and congratulations.

Would you forward this letter to Mary – so that Kate and Margaret may see it – and ask them to forward it on to Georgie. I will write to Willie Cripps and the Williams in a few days.

Always your affectionate

Beatrice Potter

224 PP BEATRICE POTTER TO MARY PLAYNE

Private

[Box House, Minchinhampton]

[early January 1892]

To be read when you are alone.

Dearest Mary

The whole of this week I have been feeling rather miserable because I have wished to tell you of my engagement to Mr Sidney Webb, but have not had the courage to do so. We settled in November to announce it to you all on New Year's Day and I had written a letter to Lallie which I intended to post on the Thursday when I was to go to London but which I kept back when Father became worse.

Our formal engagement is the result of a very deep and warm attachment between us stretching back very many months. But *I* had decided, in the first instance, against a formal engagement partly because he was giving up a large portion of his income in leaving the Colonial Office and had not then settled himself in his new career. This objection had by Xmas passed away, as he has secured journalistic engagements bringing in about £450 a year which, with my income of something like the same amount, was ample for our wants. Partly also I wished to get over the time at Box without his coming here as my acknowledged fiancé. I thought it would be rather hard on you and Arthur to be forced to receive a man against whom you had rightly or wrongly a strong prejudice. We have had such happy relations as neighbours that I thought I would vanish out of your world before you knew of my engagement. On the other hand I did not wish to subject my future husband to any unpleasant relations with my own family; or by telling you personally to extract from you an exclamation of disapproval and dislike which might remain in the memory of both of us.

And I should have carried out this plan (that was why I wanted to go on Saturday) if I had not heard from Mr Webb this afternoon that a rumour of an engagement had appeared in a small weekly paper – I thought it better to send this old letter off to Lallie, so she should not see the report first in some local paper which is likely to pick it up.

And now dear sister you must do what you feel inclined. If your dislike to Sidney Webb is so firmly rooted (after once seeing him!) that you cannot hold yourself to speak of him as your future brother-in-law – it would be better that we should not discuss it, in which case it might be better for us not to meet. I do not in the very least resent any little thing that you and Arthur may have said, for very naturally I look upon it as a mere casual impression on your side – an impression in which you yourselves will attach slight importance in years to come. But on the other hand you will not of course expect me to listen now to any word of disparagement now that Father is dead. All future relations between us will be 'relationship of choice' and not one of us need see any member of the family who is unsympathetic to us.

But I need not say that should my marriage mean a break in the old tie between us I shall be genuinely and permanently grieved, tho' I can't help thinking that you on your side will lose a little by losing the interest in and sympathy from a man, who has proved by his career that he has unusual character and intelligence.

But the future remains in your hands.

Ever your affectionate
Beatrice Potter

225 KCC BEATRICE POTTER TO ALFRED MARSHALL

Co-operative Union, City Building, Manchester
20 January 1892

Dear Professor Marshall

I venture to write and ask you for an introduction to Prof. [J. C.] Munro. I shall be here for some little time and should much like some conversation with him.

May I take this opportunity to tell you and Mrs Marshall of my engagement to Sidney Webb. I feel you will not quite approve of the union of two such wicked plotters in one partnership of concentrated wickedness! But I take credit to myself that I have already moderated his views and we both aid and abet each other in our admiration of you and your work.

My socialism has lost me the subcommissionership, my engagement has caused Mr Herbert Spencer to revoke the literary executorship, don't let my marriage lose me your and Mrs Marshall's friendship?

Always yours sincerely
Beatrice Potter

226 PP BEATRICE TO SIDNEY [incomplete]

Beatrice spent a week in London on the way to Manchester, which she made the base for her next phase of research. 'The family behaved with benevolence and good sense and received Sidney at family dinner in London with grave propriety', she noted on 21 January. Sidney took her to his 'little home away in a small street . . . the little mother – frail and shaking with palsy – the energetic warmhearted plain body of a sister . . . The dingy and crowded little workroom with gas fire where Sidney and I sat the evening through happy and unconscious in our love one for the other. And gradually the feeling of unwished-for dislike of ugly surroundings disappeared in the blessedness of love'. Sidney gave her a writing case for her birthday.

The movement towards an independent labour party was strongly supported in the Manchester and Salford area by a heterogeneous collection of enthusiasts, ranging from the active group of local Fabians to vegetarians, teetotallers, Whitmanites and Home Rulers. Its leaders were Robert Blatchford (1851–1943), the socialist journalist who had founded his lively and influential weekly *Clarion* in 1891, and John Trevor, a Unitarian minister and protégé of Philip Wickstead, who founded the Labour Church movement to unite Christianity and socialism with evangelical fervour. Its main strength was in the Lancashire and Yorkshire textile districts. In an undated fragment (probably 6 June 1892 PP) Beatrice reported a long talk with Trevor, 'an absolutely honest man – but I doubt whether he has much intellectual substance'. She thought the moderate trade unionists resented this 'melodramatic enthusiast of yesterday posing as the Saviour of the working-class', telling Sidney 'I don't believe in a future "Labour Church" – it is shoddy, and will not wear'.

Sunday evening 25/1/92

My own dear Boy

The Free Trade Hall was crowded to hear Tom Mann – mostly young men and I should imagine the majority skilled mechanics – hardly a woman to be seen except in the orchestra. (I sat at the back of the hall.) Trevor – the minister of Labour Church – is an enthusiast and looks it. Like all pseudo-religionists there is a false note in his would-be religiosity (say what you will there *is* a difference in religion and morality – this Labour Church is love of man masquerading in the well-worn clothes of love of God – one feels half-inclined to tear them off with contempt, half-inclined to denounce the wearer as a simple thief). But he seemed in earnest and the moral note rang true.

There were the usual labour songs – then a prayer thanking God for labour leaders – which bordered on the religious – then a passionate appeal for the Bromsgrove workers who are now on strike.

'Tom' was received with enthusiasm and began in a somewhat high voice and manner, an account of the Industrial Revolution. (I imagine he has spoilt himself as an orator by *over speaking*). He soon dropt that however and entered into a straight-forward harangue on the labour question of today – hitting from the shoulder at the selfishness of skilled workers, at cheap goods etc.

It was not first-rate or eloquent, but it was sound and on the whole moderate and good in tone. His reference to buying at [Co-op] stores was not greeted with enthusiasm – was met in very much the same way as the reference to T.U. in Ackers' speech at Co-op Congress. There is very little real solidarity between the two movements – much less in Manchester than in Newcastle. (Gray tells me that the Wholesale Associations do not view the joint meetings of T.U. and Co-op. with any favour.)

386

I went out just before the end after listening to him for ¾ of an hour. What an immense amount of real *art* goes to make a great speaker – practice, plenty to say, a passionate feeling do not by themselves suffice. You must have the technique of the real artist; with the study of the Art for its own sake apart from use of it as an instrument.

I walked quickly back – a lovely afternoon and had a cup of tea at 5 – after which I worked until supper at 7.30. Now I have finished working and am writing to you an evening greeting.

I am thinking that this time next week I shall be dreaming of tomorrow! Goodnight I will continue tomorrow when I return from my rounds.

Monday 5 o'clock.

It was a delightful surprise to find your letter on the breakfast table – but now I shall always look for it – that is the worst of satisfying desires, you excite them!

I have just come back from a fairly long day. First an interview with Whitehead (A.S.E.) who had melted and was fairly affectionate – immensely amazed at my request to attend District Committees and Central District Committees! Said that such a request had never been made. I pleaded that I was a lady 'and no one objects to a woman'. That is true he said they might let you come for the novelty of the thing and promised to lay it before the Committees.

Then I went to Kelly and got a circular letter recommending me and asked him and his wife to supper on Thursday – then on to Co-op Wholesale where I lunched and talked to Mitchell and Co. They all congratulated me very warmly. Then to Mawdsley – found him munching sandwiches in the most untidy of offices. He *was* disgusted when I told him of my engagement – swore and cursed! and said he had always thought of me as belonging to 'them' and now I am going to belong to one man. And evidently he does not think much of you! (Shipton, I gather, had given you a bad character.) And he said that he thought the one person who would have suited me was Auberon Herbert! However he recovered himself and became most affable. All his records are in confusion, but he gave me what he had and is writing to Bolton for others, and is willing to do everything he can to help me.

227 PP BEATRICE POTTER TO HERBERT SPENCER

When Beatrice had met Herbert Spencer in London on her way to Manchester Spencer had given her the impression that he had hoped for her to write a biographical sketch to preface his autobiography: now she was no longer his literary executor she had sought to ease this loss by offering to assist his amanuensis, F. Howard Collins, to do the same. She had known Collins for some time and had a low opinion of him, describing him in her diary for 9 June 1887 as 'a weak young man just recovering from brain fever'. She dismissed him as a 'mechanical intellect, plain and ungainly in appearance'. (BWD 3 September 88) An exchange of letters with Collins had led Spencer to write a plaintive protest against her unwillingness to help.

52 Ackers Street
9th Feb. 1892

My dear Mr Spencer

I am deeply grieved by the tone of your little note – from which I gather that you are displeased with me. I owe it to myself therefore to offer you an explanation.

My letter to Mr Collins will have told you that my suggestion at the Albemarle that I could help him with his task arose out of a complete misapprehension of the nature of that task. I had never realised that you desired a 'Life' written independent of the 'Auto'.

I imagine that to this latter work would be attached a Preface which would place before the reader the more personal and likeable aspects of your character upon which you yourself have not dwelt, and that the Editor would be required to complete any gaps you might leave to the narrative. I imagined a few pages of carefully written framework to give perspective to your detailed study of yourself as a thinker. And when you withdrew your trust from me, I still thought that Mr Collins would permit me to help him, or would allow me to write these few pages – while doing himself the responsible work of completion, or of writing any other materials you might leave unpublished – and yourself filling the position of Literary Executor in the eyes of the world.

So much for the past misunderstanding, now about my present refusal to contribute to a Life by Mr Collins.

I think him, to put it quite frankly, utterly unfit for the task. I think, moreover, that it would not be merely a matter of literary failure – but that it might damage you very considerably. It might even lead to a rejoinder from an opponent such as W. S. Lilly, who writing to suit the popular taste and having supplied materials to the Auto, would contradict Mr Collins' estimate of you – which tho' true its intention would be conceived without humour or grace and expressed in his very pedantic phrases. In any case I think Mr Collins' life would be a caricature and not a picture.

Now it is more than probable that I am utterly wrong in this judgment – especially in your third difficulty. But you will see at once, with your usual fairness, that it would be a little hard to expect me, holding rightly or wrongly this opinion of my collaboration, to aid him in this work. It would mean a serious amount of worry, and wear and tear arising from my desire not to hurt his feelings on the one hand, or not to allow you to suffer on the other. To satisfy myself, I should want to re-write many sentences, and yet as the original conception would not be mine, I would even then do very little to improve it. In short in making such a promise I should be ensuring the very minimum (possibly a minus) service to you at the very maximum cost to myself.

Now having explained myself, I cannot think that you will be so unkind, so unjust as to bear me a grudge because I cannot at once and unhesitatingly fall in with your views. It would be so easy for me to promise – so much easier than to write these letters! and thus to back out of it on the excuse of bad health or overwork. But that would be absolutely inconsistent with my reasoning, as I shall always remain,

Your faithful and devoted friend
Beatrice Potter

P.S. Do not trouble to answer this letter unless you feel *very very* softhearted. I shall assume that you forgive me, and shall come and see you just as usual when I settle in London. [If I] am very mistaken in my opinion, I am not perverse in my conduct!! Would you not send this letter to Auberon Herbert and ask him whether he thinks I am wrong?

228 PP BEATRICE TO SIDNEY

Beatrice had hitherto worked hard at trade union records but on the suggestion of Chandler, an official of the Carpenters Union, she had begun to attend branch and even executive meetings of some unions. She concluded that 'it was extraordinarily stupid of me not to think of this ever before – one learns so much more by observing than by simply reading – but it never struck me that I would get into the private executive meetings of the Societies and see for myself the positions that arise'. (BWD 11 February 92)

James Barrie began his successful career as a novelist and dramatist with the publication of *The Little Minister* in 1891.

52 Ackers Street, Manchester
[?13 February 1892]

Dearest One

I had a very idle day yesterday. An appointment fell through, and though I had piles of work to do, I felt so thoroughly exhausted (and do feel still) that I let myself go over the *Little Minister*. (I have got both that and *Tess* lent me; but tell Ada they are wonderful – she should read them) [and] went out for a walk in the little park and generally idled until the evening. Then I went to a meeting of the largest Carpenters Branch which interested me much. They are vexed in their mind to know how to get in men who cannot pay 1/- (plus levies) and are considering the question of transforming the Society into a purely Trade Society (6d. ent.) with a Sick and Funeral Section; instead of it being a Benefit Society with a Trade

Section. I made them a little speech – afterwards had a good deal of talk with some of the leading members. There is evidence of supreme dissatisfaction with the present Liberal party – and impatience with Gladstone. The dissatisfaction with the official Liberals, they say, is the root of Manchester's Toryism. The intelligent working man is disgusted and does not care to vote for either party. Gladstone is our greatest enemy, one or two of them reported.

They are very bitter against Broadhurst and Co. and their ideal is a Labour Party led by a Parnell of Labour. The future leader of the Collectivist or Labour Party must not accept office until he can bring in a Cabinet of his own. I am more and more convinced these are the *elements* of a great Collectivist party – but they are not sufficiently forward to be capable of parliamentary action – they have to be taught their programme, and that has to be thought out before it can be taught. No man will lead the labour party who has not a detailed knowledge of labour questions, in every part of the country – so that he can skilfully adapt collectivism to each practical section of the labour movement. And one reason why no working-man will ever be the leader is that no working man will know more than the details of his own section. He will never have the grasp of the whole which will enable him to unite the scattered and divided elements into one Party.

By the way, I hear there was a paragraph in the *Evening News* (Manchester) about my enquiry into trade unions remarking that I am doubtless sending up all my information to you! and that I was a formidable helpmate to a rising politician!

I was vastly amused with the account of you – if Chamberlain should take it up he will be a little bit startled – if he has heard of our engagement.

Dilke's note is very interesting. Thank heavens that we are independent of him.

I wonder what you will decide about Gateshead. One thing, I do not imagine it will make much difference as I do not believe you have a chance with Ritchie in the field. And if you do find work in the L.C.C. there will be no danger of your not finding a seat in Parliament in due time.

Ever your devoted comrade,

Beatrice Potter

229 PP SIDNEY TO BEATRICE

Beatrice had no taste for electioneering but she planned to go to Deptford to attend Sidney's final meetings. 'I will soothe and comfort you – and if you are defeated I will spend the Sunday kissing you', she wrote in an undated letter in late February. Sidney was confident about the result. He seemed, Frank Galton wrote after working with him in Deptford, 'to know every move on the board, to think of every plan and scheme and to carry out his ideas with such skill and energy that success was inevitable – in fact he would have made the best election agent in the country'. (MS Autobiography, BLPES)

Sidney had been under pressure all through the campaign. In February the Fabians had organised a national conference at which 21 of the 29 local Fabian groups (representing 1,450 members compared to the 321 in the parent London society) had expressed the growing feeling in the provinces in favour of direct political action and against the pro-Liberal stance of Webb and other London leaders. Shaw, delivering his address on the Society's early history, had come down strongly on Webb's side and insisted that 'the permeation racket' must be given a fair chance. The conference passed an ambiguous motion which approved in principle of independent labour politics but accepted Shaw's contention that in practice a new party would remain a foolish venture until socialist candidates were able to poll thousands rather than tens of votes. Unlike the hard core of London members the majority of the provincial groups (who had no vote in the affairs of the parent body) consisted of relative newcomers who had often joined the Fabians because there was then no socialist alternative but the Marxist S.D.F.

Sidney and Beatrice had now fixed their wedding day for 26 July and planned a working honeymoon in Ireland and Scotland.

Mark Beaufoy was a Gladstonian Liberal who sat for Lambeth 1889–95.

4 Park Village East, N.W.
1/3/92

Dearest

What appears clear is that you want a rest. The day after tomorrow I shall see you at Kings Cross, and you will have five or six days change. And you will do little until after Bradford.

Don't be alarmed about the book. Galton will get through the facts at a great rate, and I shall be able to put in a lot of work before next Oct. when things will get busy again. I intend The Book to stand first and the L.C.C. second (if I get in). You need not be afraid of my neglecting it.

The Miner's Conference in London on the 16th may be important, but I don't want to tempt you up to go to it. The adhesion of the northern men is important.

The contest here continues to go as well as possible – almost too well. Offers of help and of vehicles are coming in. I expect we shall be in a state of horrible confusion on March 5, but we shall muddle through somehow.

Last night I addressed a little meeting – 50 or so – in a far-off hitherto neglected corner of the borough which is solid for me. Tonight I have a meeting in the Unitarian Chapel with Mark Beaufoy, M.P.

Pray do not try to do anything until you have had the change to London. These weeks have been very lonely without you. I do want to have you with me. After this fight we must try to be together part of every week until the 26 July.

Is it really to be Ireland then? But we can't hurry off to Holyhead on the 26th. Where shall we stop on the way? The North Western does not go through many nice places. But we might stop at some quiet place like Aylesbury or Stratford for a day or two, before encountering the Irish Channel, or Chester?

Sweet, we will try to have a great love, and an enduring – no foolish gust of passion but a holy friendship that passeth all understanding for ever and ever. Help me – I need it to be good – and I will help you to be strong and to work.

Now goodnight. I have received another £4 odd as my half of six months sales of *The Eight Hours Day*. I believe *The London Programme* is selling – certainly it is having a great effect.

Adieu, sweet, until 4.20 on Thurs. at Kings Cross. You shall have high tea at 4 Park Village, as we must start at 7.

Sidney

230 PP   SIDNEY WEBB TO GRAHAM WALLAS

Sidney had an impressive success at the election on Saturday 5 March, polling 4,088 against his Moderate opponent's 2,503. Labour and Socialist candidates did unexpectedly well in an election which produced a sweeping victory for the Progressives. Nine labour men, including John Burns, were elected with the support of the Labour Representation League, the political body set up by the London Trades Council in the previous year: five of those were also Fabians, with Webb making the sixth member of the Society on the L.C.C. Four of the labour men were independents who did not run on the Progressive ticket. A number of Fabians as well as Wallas went down to Deptford to assist in getting out the vote. Banning and Bailey were the Moderate candidates and H. Keylock, a carpenter, was Sidney's running-mate in the two-member constituency.

Sidney's improving political status was further demonstrated at the beginning of March when he came sixth in the elections for the committee of the National Liberal Club, whereas three years before he just scraped on to the committee.

Emma Brooke was a minor novelist, and for a time a Fabian executive member.

52 Ackers St, Manchester
6.3.92

Dear Wallas

A fearful thought occurred to us just now – that you had been invited to dinner today, and did not know of the change of plans. I hope you went and had dinner all the same. I had been grieving that I had no chance of seeing you yesterday evening; and now this recollection of the broken engagement adds a new regret.

But my life has been a bit crowded these last few days; and I quite forgot that you had been asked to dinner.

Beatrice, who was coming up on Thursday suddenly developed influenza; and has now a little congestion of the lungs. So you may imagine I was a bit worried on Saturday. I got home about 2 a.m.; found my sister sitting up with beef tea etc.; read the *Pall Mall* [*Gazette*] through; and then turned in to sleep like a top until 9 a.m. I then bundled my things together, had breakfast, and caught the 10 o'clock train to Manchester, totally oblivious of you and everything else.

Beatrice does not seem very ill, but I shall see tomorrow how things are. Meanwhile I have left Galton to clear up at Deptford; and shall stay at the hotel close by here for a few days – at any rate until I am wanted for something in London.

I don't know how you fared on Saturday. Whatever chance there was of discussion soon evaporated, and each ward-captain fought for his own hand. I did not speak to Hall all day, and only once caught a glimpse of him driving an aged man, a cripple and an elderly spinster to the poll. I spoke at the gates of two great works, and the Victualling Yard (at 12, 1 and 2 p.m.), and then devoted myself, after visiting the South Ward once, to working the 5 polling districts assigned to the Central Comtee Room, which threatened, in the afternoon to overwhelm Galton, and drive Miss [Emma] Brooke to distraction.

But you evidently managed all right, for the North Ward polled splendidly – some 65 per cent of North One and 55 per cent of North Two, as against a general average of 50 per cent of the electorate.

I knew the North was all right; the East was working well under my own impetus; those in the South said that I was getting at least 1 in 3 – an unprecedentedly good proportion; and it only needed Oakeshott (who had spent the whole day in the Hatcham district) to rush in at 8.15 p.m. with the news that I had 'swept the West Ward' – to make me sure that my majority was a very large one.

Then I had to go off at once to the counting – I had a splitting headache – to which only one agent besides myself could be admitted (I had to conciliate my important local section of South Ward). This took an unexpectedly long time owing to the large poll, and great number of combinations. The result was, of course, not in doubt as regards myself, as soon as they opened the boxes – even in the 'swellest' districts I seemed nearly even, and in all the others I was 2 to 1. But it remained quite uncertain who had the second place, as Banning, Bailey and Keylock came out very even. About midnight we made out that Keylock was a little ahead. The result was not declared until after 1 a.m. I made a little speech etc. and then was lifted shoulder-high by an excited mob, carried downstairs to the imminent risk of scraping the ceilings with my nose, and so out into the road amid a fearful uproar. I picked up Galton and took refuge in a hansom, leaving a howling mob parading New Cross Road, hooting the Conservative Club etc.

I was *delighted* at the general results elsewhere. It is simply a gorgeous justification of Fabian electioneering and ought to do something to convince the provincials that our game is the right one – and also to give us the control of London politics for the next three years. I felt inclined to go round by Cannon St in order, like Jack Cade, to smite London Stone with my umbrella, and shout out into the night. 'Now is Mortimer lord of London'. But I went by the Central Telegraph Office instead!

The enclosed figures will interest you. Send word here of anything I ought to know during this week. Friday I lecture at Leek; and next week I suppose there is caucusing.

Yours

Sidney Webb

By the way, Hall said that this election would extinguish the S.D.F. Chelsea and Walworth results look like it; the former *most* significant.

231 PP SIDNEY TO BEATRICE

Beatrice had gone to Liverpool to visit the Holts and go on with her research. In a second letter later the same day, referring to meetings with Beatrice's sisters, Sidney wrote: 'I am a little afraid of these sisters, with all their kindness and smothering me with invitations. But it is of course only natural that they should "want to know".'

National Liberal Club, Whitehall Place, s.w.
16/3/92

Dearest

I could not write you as I ought yesterday when I was in a whirl of 'seeing people' right up to midnight. This morning I received your kindly note: I have written a few urgent letters etc.: I have had another nice casual talk with the Vice-Chairman and Deputy-Chairman of the N.L.C.; and now I am waiting to lunch with Ll. Smith who wants me to talk over a general Technical Education scheme for London. Everything is going most famously I think – although I do not feel sure that it will be *possible* for me to be on all the Committees I want. But they will soon make room for me.

I have now more letters to write, and then I shall call on Mrs Courtney. Tonight I hope to dine at home and be domestic for once.

I suppose you will be interested to hear that Elliott and Fry ask permission to put my photograph on sale, and that another photographer asks me for a sitting with this object. I am more interested in getting the further copies soon so that you may have back the one I stole from you.

I am so glad to think you are getting stronger. We have a beautiful day here, and if you have the same you will have enjoyed a walk in the sun.

It is nice of the Holts to speak pleasantly of me: and as regards the pronunciation it must come sweetly to the ear of the teacher to hear the scholar praised. They are very nice people.

394

You will see in the *Daily News* report of the Council sitting that I was among the first to arrive at 2.15, and that I took my seat high up. Thus is history written. My train was late, and I slipped in unperceived at 3.15 after the meeting had begun, and sat quietly in a low seat. I suppose the *Daily News* man presumed that I certainly *should* go down early and take possession of the whole Council. I had no opportunity of preventing the people from wasting votes on Charles Booth.

Ll. Smith has not come after all, so I have lunched alone: he has probably been detained in the City, where he was doing something in connection with the Plumbers Company and their scheme of registration.

The *Economic Journal* came this morning. Mrs Fawcett contributes a long 'note' on my Women's Wages paper, saying she agrees with it almost entirely, and simply amplifying a point. (Incidentally she demurs to 'Equal Wages', and is evidently still entirely on the 'market wage' plane of morality). I will bring the number on Saturday. I don't think you will yearn to have it before.

Saturday is still 3 days off – but I must be patient. Perhaps we shall be able to go for a nice walk on Sunday morning.

Mrs Pearsall Smith and her daughter were at the Council, and enthusiastically congratulatory. They said you must come to stay with them sometime.

Now, dearest, I must write some other letters before going to Mrs C. Goodbye till Saturday. Be patient and get strong.

Sidney

232 PP BEATRICE TO SIDNEY

54 Ullet Road, Sefton Park, Liverpool
[mid-March 1892]

My own dearest

I fear I wrote you a cross-grained little note yesterday. But I am feeling so queer and irritable – in spite of getting stronger.

I have just signed with witnesses the codicil to my will – and returned it to [J. G.] Godard – so you will be secure and I shall feel comfortable and secure also should I suddenly feel that I am 'going off'. It would have been dreadful to have left you without a certain income wherewith to continue your career. Only be careful about investments, if you are left to your own resources.

Mary Booth has come again. Very friendly and affectionate and like her old self. They are distressed about the eldest boy who refuses to work and to exert himself in any way.

I was delighted to get your letter this morning – and pleased about Elliot and Fry! (such is the vanity of a lover). It will of course be important to get to know the principal men on the Council and win their confidence and respect. We shall have a lot to talk about on Saturday. I hope I shall feel more 'fit' by that time.

Enclosed is a letter from M.H. [Margaret Hobhouse]: go if you conveniently can.

I shall be curious to know what you think of her. This is a dull letter dearest – but I am dull myself and only half there.

Ever your devoted comrade

Beatrice Potter

233 PP SIDNEY TO BEATRICE

Still on the first round of family invitations Sidney had told Beatrice the previous day that he feared 'his usual cold' would 'not make me any less ugly to the sisters!' F. Huth and Co. was the family firm of bankers in which Daniel Meinertzhagen was a partner. Lord Hobhouse (1819–1904) was a lord of appeal and an alderman of the L.C.C. from 1889. He was the uncle of Henry Hobhouse, the husband of Beatrice's sister Margaret.

4 Park Village East, N.W.

23 March/92

Dearest

I am glad that we are back in the regime of letters. I missed yours yesterday, but of course there was no need of it.

The Meinertzhagens were all right, and my cold was less fearful than I expected. There was a young lady staying in the house – whom I at first thought was the governess but who seemed a friend of the family – and one other guest. One Hermann Something, an elderly greybearded city man, who seemed to me like the head clerk in F. Huth and Co. invited to 'mitigate' me. But we got on all right. Mrs M. reminded me that we had met at Longfords two years ago – which I owned to have forgotten. (There *was* a sister who came to tea in the afternoon with Mrs Playne but I had vaguely thought that was Mrs Alf Cripps). She said that I totally neglected her, and talked only to you. I said that I hoped she had not noted it at the time. But she said she did.

After dinner Mr M. chatted desultorily, asked a good deal about the L.C.C. and Taxation of Ground Rents, on which he was very reasonable and conciliatory. I tried to talk City a little, but we did not get far. We agree in rejecting Bimetallism! – perhaps that is our only point of agreement. I went off at 11.15 – all parties no doubt thinking 'Thank Heaven, that's settled'. But it was really not so bad, and I think they will simply wonder what you can see in that commonplace ugly little man.

This morning my cold is slightly better. (It is clearly *only* a cold in the head.) I have spent some necessary time over Deptford accounts which do not seem to add up to more than £118. My personal expenses to and fro etc. may be £5 more; to Hall I virtually owe £15; Galton's services cost some

396

£13 – so that even including every mortal thing it is only £150, which is amazingly cheap for such a constituency in a two-months campaign. For a parliamentary fight such as Gateshead – of course an exceptionally favorable instance – would have to be added the Returning Officer's Expenses, which would I suppose be two hundred pounds or so. On the other hand a parliamentary contest usually only lasts three weeks or so.

The great thing is that I now feel that I know pretty well how to do it.

I spoke to Lord Hobhouse in Council yesterday (I was in some doubt whether I had not usurped his seat), and he was very flattering – said he found I was going to be 'a sort of connection' of his, and congratulated me warmly about you – asked when the marriage would be etc. He said he had written an article for the *Contemporary* on the Council Election, in which he had quoted a letter of mine to the *Daily News* 5 years ago, which he had cut out and kept, and which had seemed to him at the time to sum up London politics. (It was the beginning of our pressure on the official Liberals to enlarge their programme – the *Daily News* unwarily inserted it – I had said that the London workman did not care for Ireland etc., and must be appealed to on London Social Reform.)

This was very nice and flattering of him.

I am sitting in Council next to F. Harrison, who chats pleasantly on the Council and its proceedings.

Yesterday my Committees were settled. I am on

Parliamentary
Local Govt. and Taxation   Standing Committees
Health and Housing

and (in virtual evasion of the principle of no one being on more than 3) also on the Special Water Committee – to which Henry Ward (as an Engineer) and I were specially added by vote of the Council with general assent. The only one I asked for and have failed to get on is the Highways (Tramways) Committee – but I have done exceptionally well to get on just the 4 Committees I wanted. Many members have been put on one or two only, and those which they did *not* want. I thanked Burns warmly for seeing to it.

My first committee meetings are tomorrow and Friday. Now I must set to work really to study the London Water question, which we shall probably have on hand for the next three years.

I gather that Galton has done much rather than done it well – but he can only learn by practice, and it is a great thing to have the facts in our possession, whatever their form. It may quite probably suit us to have abstracts made of our present abstracts – to bring out particular points. But it will be useful to make Galton as skilled as possible at once. This will be a nice light occupation for you as a convalescent!

You ought to feel relieved as to the material if Galton has polished off nearly all that accumulation in two weeks. Indeed, you will need to see that you keep him supplied.

By the way, have you told him whether he may read a paper to the local Fabian Society? It is a small and humble affair, not reported – and he may get useful T.U. information from some of them. But he won't mind if you think he had better not.

This is a long letter if a dull one. But dearest it *is* dull without you. I did not feel satisfied with seeing you at the Holts somehow – though we had a charming Sunday morning. Now you are ten days off, which is a fearful desert to go through. If it is a 'delusion' it is a very solid delusion, and I can't imagine that it is not a lasting one. Sweet, if it lasts, as it will, I don't care whether it be real or a delusion. We need not enquire, with Muirhead, as to what is really real. This is our life, and we shall make it a useful one – none the less useful because J.M. [John Muirhead] and Miss Kitty both think us dreamers of dreams. Our love gives us faith, and our faith renews our love.

Goodbye sweet

Sidney

234 PP BEATRICE TO SIDNEY

On 23 March Sidney dined at the Hobhouses. Miss Wilson was probably the sister of Professor James Maurice Wilson (1836–1931), a mathematician who became vicar of Rochdale and archdeacon of Manchester in 1890: he was strongly interested in social work.

[4 Park Village East, N.W.]
Wednesday evening [?23 March 1892]

My own dear one

I like to talk to you in the evening – and to think of you wherever you are. Now you will be talking to my old chum Maggie Hobhouse. To think that once we were like a married couple – in our devotion to one another! Our relation to each other had a curious history. As children we were bitter enemies – she mother's pet and I mother's aversion – the governesses taking the opposite side. I their darling, she the thorn in their sides. So were pitted against each other – and to me she always embodied the Evil one. Then there was a time when we were neutral to each other she a 'come out' young woman and I an invalided schoolgirl. Then I came back from school to join the 4 unmarried sisters – and she quickly perceiving that I must be her rival or her friend made overtures of friendship. From that time forward until her marriage – 4 years – we were devoted chums – companions in study and amusement and inseparable. She was 'excellent company' in those days – brimming over with intellectual curiosity, brilliant in society – and with that dash of melancholy and *Weltschmerz* which chimed in with my somewhat morbid temperament. She had an eventful career of lovers and matches – looked upon the process of getting married as her business in Life – reading and thought as her relaxation. I reversed the relation, looked on culturing my mind as my business and flirting as my relaxation. And as we were eminently practical persons, we both achieved what we desired. She married an [?'Honourable'] a Peer's grandson with a very good rent roll while I was left – cultivating my mind. Then came the silent breach between us – the consciousness of the opposite nature of our ideals – aggravated by Henry Hobhouse's dislike of the old influence – jealousy of the old companionship. Since then we have been to all intents and purposes strangers – tho' there has been no trace of bitterness in our breach – it has been recognised as inevitable on both sides – and we have each been whirled into our separate lives. I doubt whether now she has any especial feeling for me – except the general feeling of physical kinship which with her is very strong – and with me very weak.

I doubt whether we shall see much of them.

Miss Wilson called in the afternoon, and told me terrible stories of the effect of Influenza – by way of consoling me for my feeling of weakness and stupidity. I do feel very queer – and quite unfit for any real work. It is possible that I may decide to give up these rooms Saturday week and come down to London from the Sunday and go somewhere for the middle of the week – perhaps I might go to Box.

By that time I shall have got Galton into working order – and could get him plenty of material. What do you say to that? It would be economical on my purse and my strength.

I enclose a letter from Georgie – she is the only one who calls you 'Sidney'! I gather from that that you and Dee [Daniel] got on nicely.

Now dearest goodnight

Ever your devoted one

Beatrice

Thursday morning

I feel better today and think I will go on here until Sat. 9th so as to superintend Galton's work. I am anxious to get him into training. I was so glad to get your long letter – it was very interesting. Yes; do study the Water questions *au fond*, so as to be prepared with good suggestions. The one objection to municipal enterprise v. private is that no one has questions at heart – no one broods over it – like Father used to brood over his undertakings.

BP

235 PP   SIDNEY TO BEATRICE

C. C. Lacaita was elected Liberal M.P. for Dundee in 1885 and 1886.

Dearest

It must be lonely at Manchester in the evening, but don't be tempted out. That cough ought to be quite got rid of before you are safe. My cold is better. I am not a bit ill.

Last night at the Hobhouses was not at all fearful. There was present only a Mr Lacaita, (an old Eton friend – I think sometime M.P. for Dundee). Mrs H. was very pleasant, brimming over with talk on Socialism etc. (she had been reading *Fabian Essays*) – not very wise. Dearest, my impression is that your sisters are not very able women in the intellectual way. Really, Mrs Holt is the cleverest of the lot: and your trained intellect positively stands out as quite alien to them all. I have been amused to watch how they all rush at me with futile little arguments, utterly lacking in logic or acumen – their husbands meanwhile looking on indulgently and, when appealed to, sweetly and quietly putting them straight – I don't wonder that you got on best with the said husbands. It must have been difficult to have any really intellectual conversation with the wives. And the husbands are a set of remarkably able men each in his own way. (I except the Williamses whom I have not seen, and the Playnes, whom I have not seen for 2 years.)

But I don't want to 'run down' your sisters. They have all been exceedingly kind, and they are at least as clever as the ordinary woman of society, and the ordinary mother of a family. Only, you see, one expected *your* sisters to be something more. Especially does one miss the logic and the intellectual atmosphere which you bring to everything.

Mrs H. talked mostly about Luxury – its evil, and yet how impossible it was to have things orderly and clean without accepting the whole conventions of one's class. She said the servants would not allow any deviation.

As you say, these people are not really conscious of the existence of Poverty. Indeed, Mrs H. struck me as unconscious that there were any individuals of the same *species* as herself who had less than £5,000 a year.

After dinner they talked politics – dissolution, electioneering etc. She asked me where I was going to stand, and seemed surprised when I said I should not. She wanted to know a little about the Book, (not much). And, as I took leave, she said you had asked H. to be trustee – I murmured thanks – and she hoped he would not be expected to preside at the wedding. I said I hoped there would be no ceremony – she said, 'where will it be, I suppose at the Registry Office, I much prefer the Church'. I said I supposed it depended on one's opinions – she replied 'O not at all, I myself am advanced.' And then I fled.

Hobhouse was in the black velvet court dress (he went on to the Speaker's *Levée*) and very self-conscious and uncomfortable, but very polite and pleasant to me. Lord Hobhouse, whom they had told, had apparently said he knew me, and spoken well of me.

Hobhouse strikes me as verging close upon Sir Willoughby Patterne – he has a great deal of 'The Egoist' in him, but of course utterly unconsciously so. Deliberately, he would no doubt be *most* dutifully altruistic. But he lives in a Ptolemaic Universe all the same.

I think the Hobhouses will think me a remarkably cool, superficially able, somewhat unscrupulous (politically), rising young man. It is a little horrid, even if flattering, to realise how perilously like that is to what they would have thought of Chamberlain at a corresponding epoch in his career. You would not undertake the task of saving Chamberlain – it was too late – now you must try to save me. (There is not the same danger, anyhow.)

The Times had another friendly dig at me yesterday in its leading article on the Council. It said that the Committees were appointed.

'Most of the names are those of persons of no influence, but some are quite the contrary. There is, for instance Mr Sidney Webb, who is placed on the Parliamentary, Local Govt and Taxation, Housing, and Water Committees'.

The Hobhouses had seen this, and were much impressed thereby. Really this L.C.C. election has gone far to redeem our marriage in the eyes of your family. They don't fear for their own incomes, and they think I am more of a personage than they supposed.

Today I go to the first meeting of the Parliamentary Committee and then on to Mrs Playne's. We are in the thick of all the mass of private Bills affecting London (railways etc.) as well as our own Bills. Tomorrow is the Local Government Committee.

Here is a letter from Dyson Williams.

Goodbye – sweet

Sidney

I am not sure that you *ought* not to have a second sitting room at once – for the sake of your own peace.

Mrs H. struck me as, in the face, a compound of you and Mrs Courtney. You are all much alike, but there are two sets

Mrs Meinertzhagen	Mrs Courtney
,, A. Cripps	,, Hobhouse
,, Playne	B.P.

the sets resembling each other when [*illegible*] Mrs Holt, Mrs. W. Cripps are apart.

236 PP BEATRICE TO SIDNEY

Mrs Dryhurst was the wife of Alred R. Dryhurst (1859–1949), a member of the British Museum staff: both Dryhursts were active Fabians.

My own dearest

I shall post this tomorrow early so that you will get it – for a Sunday letter.

I was so glad to get your long and interesting letter – I *do* like long letters. You are quite right – my sisters are not intellectual women. They are shrewd women of the world with good motherly hearts and their fair share of mother wit – but they have never gone in for training their minds. Lallie, Theresa and Margaret have the most natural intellect – more than I had to begin with – the difference between us the persistent cultivation and training that I have gone in for – a difference of the absence or presence of 'intellectual desire' which would change the predominating motive in my life and in theirs did not count.

I am feeling much more fit – if only I could get better nights – but I am still excitable and cannot sleep very many hours – a common effect of influenza.

This morning I set Galton to work at supplementing omissions from the Oldham T.U. reports – then went off to interview the Factory Inspector.

He was a rather self-important personage living in a [? lovely] little villa outside Manchester. I took his lists of industries and cross examined him on it. He said he knew nothing whatever about trade societies, that he never came across them (what a lack of intellectual insincerity these officials have!) (He had been 20 years in the service). He thought 'T.U. officials a coarse lot of fellows elected for the gift of the gab'. He had been a few days ago at the dinner given by T.U. (Textile) officials to the factory inspectors; and was glad to get away from it. 'They are not the sort of people one cares to associate with'.

He gave me a good deal of information about the trades – and offered to take me round any factories etc. and asked me to come and dine with him and his wife. He waxed eloquent against Redgrave – he never acknowledged the work of his subordinates (compliment I have heard before) and if they dared to express an opinion addressed to him 'they heard of it'. There was no attempt to consult them in any change of law – and if they made a good suggestion in their MSS reports Redgrave often gave it out as his own. He was very civil.

It is useful to know these men: but if I were head of the Factory Department, I would make more use of them and also brief them more up to the mark as the way of getting information.

Then I came home to lunch with Miss Brooke. What a quaint old thing she is – a bundle of sensibilities – not overburdened with intelligence. She spoke most affectionately of 'Sidney' as she called you. She volunteered that the only Fabian she did *not* care for was Olivier – 'she had never much liked him'. But somehow or other the conversation was always reverting to him and his wife – and she [?unconsciously] 'fired up' when I said that my first impression of him had been that of a 'weak young man'. She wanted to come over to help me! and was excessively friendly – and I was very kind – I think.

I gathered that she hated Mrs Dryhurst and Mrs Pease – thought Mr Bland harmless. *She said I was right not to join the Fabian Society.*

She reminded me a wee bit of Miss Darling in her funny little self-conscious sensibility – her 'hidden life' of vast importance to herself, of no importance to the world.

Then when I [?dismissed] her Miss Wilson came in and we had a pleasant chat. Galton I had sent to interview the old millwright – as a change from his work – and he has just returned in high spirits to tell me that he [is] going to a meeting of T.U. connected with the Engineering trade – to hear the report of the Newcastle delegates. He is very keen in anything he undertakes – but he needs a deal of training. When we are away in Ireland I shall insist on his having to write properly and to punctuate. He must make himself into a better clerk.

Then this afternoon I read through the remainder of the Oldham reports – and marked it for Galton. Tomorrow I shall go through Bolton reports.

Now dearest goodnight

Ever your devoted comrade
Beatrice

Saturday

I suddenly remembered that you had gone to N.C. [Newcastle] and was puzzled what to do. Remember me at Tynemouth! that happy little town.

I go this afternoon to Cotton Councils, leaving Galton to work here.

237 PP BEATRICE TO SIDNEY

This financial report from Beatrice was provoked by a letter from Sidney that his Deptford friend B. T. Hall was about to throw up his paid work for the struggling seamen's union and suggesting that they might engage him as an assistant for six months at a pound a week. In an undated letter Beatrice reacted sharply doubting whether they could find either the money or useful work for Hall. 'You seem to think our income is limitless', she told Sidney. Replying on 1 April Sidney noted that since he left the Colonial Office he had earned £200 from journalism and received £80 in dividends on his capital. Apart from the £180 spent on the Deptford election he had lived at the rate of six pounds a week since his resignation. That, he conceded, meant that he had 'been living pretty fast lately': all the same, he had plenty in hand and felt that they could easily live inside their expected income – 'even a little luxuriously'.

[? Manchester]
Saturday morning [?26 March 1892]

Dear One

I am sending this up, so that you may get a letter for Sunday. Do not overstrain yourself; let the work for the book slide. You must keep yourself fresh for the County Council work – it is now *the* important thing for you to do – and it is worth while saving yourself for it.

I have just been looking over my bank book. I see that my income next year will be about £450 from investments, that this year I have only spent £265 – £32 of which has been paid for work done. Of course I have lived at home for 4 or 5 months of the year. But that has included 7 months of almost perpetual travelling about. I have saved therefore £119 from an income of about £385. (Some of my money was not invested until February.) I have another £140 lying at my bankers, which I will keep uninvested so that we may spend £258 on County Council and work for the book. This a business postscript.

Ever yours

BP

238 PP SIDNEY TO BEATRICE

Quintin Hogg (1845–1903), philanthropist and educational pioneer, founded the Regent Street Polytechnic. He was an L.C.C. alderman 1889–94.

Sidney found the separation difficult. On 25 March he wrote to Beatrice that 'these four months are going to be a bit of a trial . . . be patient with me if I am restless and unsettled. I will try to do all the work I can, and at any rate learn all I can. But, dear love, there is a time for all things, and part of this time is for us'. He went up to Manchester as often as possible. Beatrice came down for an Easter break, visiting the L.C.C. to see Sidney at work and going with Sidney, Wallas and Shaw for a short holiday in a rented vicarage near Arundel, Sussex.

London County Council, Spring Gardens, s.w.
3/5/1892

Dearest

I arrived at the L.C.C. in time to put in an appearance at a Committee before the Council. We have run through the business with unexampled rapidity, and we shall not have nearly two hours on notices of motions. I find the Chairmen of Committees all moved down to lowest row – hence I lose the company of Frederic Harrison, Costelloe and Benn. But Lord Monkswell is still by me, and I don't come off so badly as I feared.

I hope you have had a good day, without too much work – I have written to a man at *Grays*, Essex, who is [in] the United Pattern Makers Society asking for T.U. papers.

I have just moved (instead of Quintin Hogg) to Education Committee – it passed subject to the addition of 4 more names – Lord Hobhouse and Steadman among them.

404

I am a bit tired, but I fear you are more so. You must not over work. I wonder how your factory inspector turned out.

Dearest, I have not much to say today – I have only been in London a few hours, and you don't need a mere expression of how much I already miss you. I don't feel today as I have felt on former days when we have parted. This time we have gone beyond the former stage. I feel as if I was separated – not from my love, but from my wife.

Goodnight dearest

Sidney

239 FP SIDNEY WEBB TO WILLIAM S. DE MATTOS

Sidney was still in touch with the group seeking to nominate him at Gateshead but his L.C.C. commitments, the trade union book and Beatrice's reluctance to have him enter Parliament led him to decline the temptation. He had become Chairman of the new Technical Education Board, which was the base from which he exerted a powerful influence on London Education and made his reputation as an educational expert.

Support for independent labour candidates was still increasing, especially in the North of England and Scotland. Webb, still believing that the best tactic was to influence Liberal policy and permeate the Liberal machine, strongly opposed attempts to run candidates who would antagonise the Liberals by splitting the anti-Tory vote and expose the relative weakness of Labour support at the polls. Despite extensions of the franchise many workingmen still did not have the vote; the methods of electoral registration imposed a further handicap; and few labour or socialist candidates could raise sufficient money to pay election expenses when it came to the point of formal nomination.

William S. De Mattos (b. 1851) was a Cambridge graduate who had played an energetic part in the organisation of the unskilled workers; he was an active and prominent Fabian, serving on the Society's executive, and took charge of its provincial lecture programme, arranging over 600 lectures in 1891–92 alone. After some scandals about his attitude to sexual reform he emigrated to Canada and efforts to trace his later career have failed. Katharine St John Conway (1867–1950) was the daughter of a Congregational clergyman: she studied at Newnham College, Cambridge, until 1886 and became active in the socialist movement, proving a passionate and popular speaker. Her relations with De Mattos were the immediate cause of his difficulties in the Fabian Society. She married John Bruce Glasier (1859–1919) one of the leaders of the Independent Labour Party. Enid Stacy (?1870–1903) was a friend of Kate Conway in Bristol and they left the S.D.F. for the Fabian Society together in 1891. She too was a much-admired speaker. Briefly courted by James Ramsay MacDonald she married Percy Widdrington, a socialist clergyman from Newcastle. As itinerant Fabian lecturers Kate Conway and Enid Stacy were paid five shillings for each talk, plus their railway fare and overnight expenses.

4 Park Village East, N.W.

6th May, 1892

Dear De Mattos

As regards myself and Gateshead *nothing* is done; but I have no intention of becoming candidate *anywhere* for the Gen. Election this time.

As regards Stafford I enclose letter to Bullery which please send on. I send it through you as it may save false hopes if it is understood generally that there is practically *no chance whatever* of a candidate's expenses being found otherwise than locally. For heaven's sake don't let us have a crop of Labor candidates springing up, who, like the S.D.F. men, cannot possibly go to the poll for lack of funds. (The more there are *whose election expenses are in the bank* the better, but any other sort will only discredit the whole thing.)

I am glad to hear everywhere of your success, and that of Miss Stacy and Miss Conway. But pray be careful, all of you, to give no kind of countenance to Municipal Workshops, or finding work for the unemployed. That way lies utter ruin of the Socialist movement – as in 1848.

Yours

Sidney Webb

My best regards to Mr Lister.

240 PP SIDNEY TO BEATRICE

Sir R. Melville Beachcroft became chairman of the L.C.C. in 1909. Sir William Mather (1838–1920) was a textile employer in Manchester who pioneered the Eight Hour Day and a strong proponent of technical education. He was Liberal M.P. for Salford from 1895.

4 Park Village East, N.W.

7 May '92

Dearest

You must not spoil me by sending me such much better letters than I write you – I hope you have had a profitable afternoon on the 'box' at Preston, and have found the hotel comfortable.

I spent the evening over the Steam Engine Makers, but have not by any means finished my account. Today I have been for 5 hours in the British Museum, in a corner under the iron gratings where the country newspapers are kept. I turned aside from the *Voice of the People* to do the *Pioneer* which was the organ in 1833/4 of the 'Grand National Consolidated Trade Union', which seems to have had thousands of branches, each autonomous. It was more like the Knights of Labor than anything else, with 'Miscellaneous Lodges' corresponding to the 'Mixed Locals' of the K. of L. [Knights of Labor] But it was a secret society, and no rules or accounts are ever given. There was a tremendous outburst of Trade

Unionism, from Devonshire to Durham – the 6 Dorsetshire Laborers were trying to form one of its Lodges – but then the *Pioneer* vol. breaks off – Sept/34 – it was evidently breaking up – its strikes had failed everywhere. Of course I obtain from it a mass of particulars as to the ephemeral local unions – the Cotton Spinners seem to have been one of the strongest.

By the way I have come across a 'piecers' strike' at Oldham in 1834, easily compromised.

I shall not be able to go to the museum again for a few days as the Council work is heavy.

Sydney Buxton and Schloss both press me to go to dinner, and I shall do so shortly, as both can be made useful, and I like them.

As to Technical Education. I have a letter from Costelloe (who has not thought of me as Chairman) suggesting Beachcroft, who would do very well, if he would take it. I can scarcely believe that they will make me Chairman (Monday is the first meeting of the Committee) but of course I shall do my very best if I am elected. The first stress will only be during the next two months.

It is sweet of you to tell me that you *trust* me more fully now. I, too trust more fully – not you – but our power to live together usefully and industriously as well as happily. If 1 + 1 do not become eleven (which *would* be rather much I own) yet there is every prospect that they will come to be 3 or 4 at least – which is as much as we can expect (or more). I feel quite confident that, in our 'domesticity' we shall know to remember the lives of others, and work as hard as ever, and to much greater effect than we could have done alone.

William Mather M.P. writes a long letter to the *Daily News* extolling T.U. and proposing, in lieu of an Eight Hours Bill, to empower the coal miners, and *any other well organised trades*, to declare by vote of the Union, the number of hours to be worked, which, after due notice, is to have the force of law!

This is pretty good as a 'moderate' proposition from a great employer.

Your Sweating paper does excellently. I have read it through carefully, and shall return it tomorrow to Gray. I have written to Benj. Jones to ask for a list of bills supported by the Co-operators, which would go well in a final note. It will have a very great effect.

Now I must close. Goodnight dearest. It is hard to be so far away from you. Think of me as hard at work either at T.U. or L.C.C., and always wandering off to wonder what you are doing.

Good night.

Sidney

Tell me your address next week.

Thomas Henry Farrer, permanent secretary of the Board of Trade until 1886, was elevated to the peerage in 1893 and became a member and chairman of the L.C.C.

Dr William Garnett (1850–1932) was Professor of Mathematics, Physics and Mechanics at University College, Nottingham in 1882; he was appointed secretary to the L.C.C. Technical Education Board from 1893 to 1904 and Educational Adviser to the L.C.C. from 1904 to 1915. W. A. Wigram, secretary of the South London Polytechnic Institute, was one of fifty-two candidates for the post to which Garnett was appointed.

[L.C.C., Spring Gardens]
[?9 May 1892]

I *have* been appointed Chairman of the Technical Education Committee – Hogg being also proposed, and eventually retiring in my favor, so that it was unanimous. Lord Rosebery, who was in the chair to start us, was evidently astonished, and rather cast about for an old member. But Lord Hobhouse and Sir T. Farrer pressed for me, and the Committee was evidently 2 to 1 on my side. So I was installed in the very high chair which Lord R. vacated, and I had to make a modest little speech of deprecation. We spent our time in a desultory talk about our aims – just to clear the ground and it was decided that I was to prepare a memo to lay before the Committee next time, so that we could settle the preliminary question of whether we would go in for the job or not. But there is a large majority for going to work.

Prof. Garnett and one Wigram were proposed by Hogg and Ll. Smith by Farrer – but the matter was deferred.

So I shall be pretty full up now for a month or two and cannot hope to help you much just at present. Be patient!

Goodnight sweet.

Sidney

[4 Park Village East, N.W.]
9 May/92

Dear Sir

You may have seen a letter in the *Pall Mall Gazette* as to a postcard by Mr Gladstone expressing categorically his opposition to Eight Hours Bills, Payment of Members etc., in answer to an enquiry from the Fabian Society.

I happened to go to the Fabian office today, and was shown the postcard, when I at once said that it was not in Mr Gladstone's usual handwriting.

If the Society has been hoaxed, by an unwarrantable liberty having been taken with Mr Gladstone's signature by some unscrupulous member of Parliament (to whom alone the enquiry and blank postcard had then been sent) I can only express my great regret that the signature was not seen by anyone acquainted with Mr Gladstone's handwriting, before today.

If Mr Gladstone has neither signed nor authorised the signature of the postcard, I need only say that I am sure the Fabian Society will at once take any steps that he may think proper to make the matter clear.

Being anxious not further to trouble Mr Gladstone I venture to ask you to be good enough to make whatever enquiry of him that you may think needful.

Yours truly

Sidney Webb

243 PP SIDNEY TO BEATRICE

James Mavor (1854–1925) professor of political economy at Mungo's College, Glasgow, from 1888, went to the University of Toronto as professor in 1892. He was a specialist on wage theories and statistics. Richard Holt (1868–1941), was the eldest son of Robert and Laurencina Holt.

Percy Holder Illingworth (1869–1915) was the Liberal candidate in East Bradford. He later became Liberal Chief Whip; he was regarded as an opponent by the Radical wing of the party.

National Liberal Club, Whitehall Place, s.w.
11.5.92

Dearest

I am glad to think of you well in the swing of work on the book – for just at present I *cannot* think of it. I spent the whole morning on my memo. for the Technical Education Committee which was hard work. And I shall have to toil hard to complete it by Monday when it must go in. After that I may be free a little, but it is evident that I shall have to think about the matter a good deal this month.

This afternoon I had a talk with Byles (of Bradford) who wanted to see me. He is a poor creature – eager now he is the accepted candidate to conciliate the Gladstonians. Mrs Byles apparently wants him to stick more aggressively to the Labor policy. He had wanted me to come and speak for him, but after our talk he did not ask me – at which I was heartily relieved as I should have had to refuse. He supports Illingworth – against whom I am committed. I don't want to speak in Bradford at all, as things are so mixed up.

He was very anxious to see you, and hoped you would go to see them when in Bradford. You might go, as he caught you all T.U. men – but he is not up to much himself.

He astonished me by speaking enthusiastically of Mavor, of Glasgow, whom we shall see there, a lecturer on economics, socialistic – of whom I had not before thought very well. But I said nothing.

You will have seen that the postcard signed Gladstone which the Fabian Society received is a forgery – as I at once detected on seeing it. I wrote straight to Herbert Gladstone explaining and offering to publish any contradiction he pleased – and he has written me a very cordial letter of thanks and appreciation, saying he will show mine to his father – so that is all right. And the nett result is not bad, as it must screw things up a bit.

Dearest, you have made me much more 'restful' and healthy in every way. I can now work straight on, and be patient whatever happens. I am counting the days until we can meet again – alas it is still three weeks off. This year has been a very happy one – full of love and work and life. I hope we may have many such together.

Don't overwork. I am glad you are thinking of a clerk. Yes: Dick needs a little generous widening of sympathies. I wonder whether love will bring him this. Just at present he is a little too cynical, and perhaps too prosperous. But I am glad they have been attentive to you.

Last night I spoke at a little Liberal meeting at Hammersmith in a locality where I had never been before, but where I found both my name, and my books, and my speech very popular – rather to the surprise of the Chairman, a mild Liberal of the old type.

Sweet, adieu. I now go to talk about my memo again – to get it along. Good night. I don't think I shall cause your extinction as Alf. Holt surmised!

Sidney

244 PP   SIDNEY TO BEATRICE [incomplete]

4 Park Village East, N.W.

12/5/92

Dearest

Now we have broken into the three weeks which still remains between us. Where I could meet you on the Wednesday (1st June) depends rather on where you will be. Perhaps it would be easiest to come to 52 Ackers St if it is empty. We could spend the two days in the country somewhere. We shall both need a little holiday.

Or perhaps I could simply come to you at Leeds – if you are there. But this we can think about as time goes on – it goes very slowly with me July 23 is still 72 days off.

I am glad Charles Booth is nice. We shall hardly be able to see much of him, but you and he may come together again a little when we are settled down – especially if things move our way.

Mrs Courtney's letter is very kind. (I shrink from the 'wedding feast', but Paris *vaut bien une messe*!) I took the opportunity of asking the other day at the St Pancras Vestry Hall, how to get married. It seems that 18 days is the least residence demanded (of *one* or other of the parties) (that costs £2. 9. 0. – license). The alternative is a month. So it must be at the St Pancras Vestry Hall (behind St Pancras Station) unless you are prepared to stay at least 18 days with the Courtneys, when it might be at the Chelsea Vestry Hall. (Or, probably, it would do for Chelsea if you came to the Courtneys for a day or two, 18 days before, and then went away again.)

I mention this because it is a little stupid to drive all the way from Chelsea to St. Pancras; then back to Chelsea, and to Euston again. But after all it does not matter much. We should not think it any hardship to drive 3 or 4 miles in the country.

The St Pancras Vestry Hall is an ordinary 'official' looking place, and the Registrar's office is of ordinary office type, neither better nor worse. I fear the Courtneys will think it 'mean', but you won't mind, dearest?

However there may be a General Election just then – I think very likely.

Pray don't work too hard. You might go to Ullet Road tomorrow (Friday) if you are feeling done up. Dearest, there will be time: and your 'tissue' is more valuable to the world than anything you can be doing with it.

I am writing to the Courtneys in reply to their invitation, saying that I am very busy this weekend.

245 PP SIDNEY TO BEATRICE *[incomplete]*

After a visit to Beatrice in Manchester Sidney wrote in an undated letter to ask why she thought he had 'more of the husband's manner'.

Sidney was collecting money for Burns: as an independent labour parliamentary candidate for Battersea, running without party support, he had to raise both his election expenses and a fund to support himself if elected – as he was.

> 4 Park Village East, N.W.
> 13 May '92

Dearest

I am horribly afraid you are over working yourself – pray take care. It *is* hard that we cannot be together but don't make it harder for me (to put it on the lowest ground) by making me anxious about you.

Is this part of the 'husband's manner' that you already notice (I hope not unpleasantly) in me. Dear, I *do* feel responsible for you – and if you don't mind I shall be coming down to prevent you getting ill.

We are in closer partnership than we were, and therefore I am more concerned about you than ever before. I am sorry if this seems irksome to you: I don't think you will feel that I take advantage. It is only because I do love you really that I am alarmed. But you must rest at the Holts, you can't help it.

We may sometimes get cross with each other – I hope we shall have the sense both not to do, and if we do get cross, not to mind.

I think you know me as I am, in my workaday self. I have never posed to you, never known how to be a lover. This may have robbed my courtship of its grace, but it revealed me to you just as I am. Therefore I am not afraid – not even that you will be afraid. Sweet, I *know* you trust me and that alone would protect you.

I wonder whether you got admission to the Federation meeting yesterday. I thought of you in a L.C.C. Committee, when Stuart strolled in, really smart in dress, but languid in manner. (You see I instinctively blame Miss Colman; you him!) But I was not afraid that I should go that way.

Last night I went to Schloss's – who has really been working out a good scheme for a Labor Department. He was pleased with your letter.

I am 'laboring' at the Memo. for my Technical Education Committee. I tell myself that I need not be anxious; that it will be 'good enough', just as I told you. But I now feel how little consolation that is. I want it to be 'good', not 'good enough'; and it won't come good. But I have three days more.

A new member of the Council gave me £5 yesterday for Burns.

We have brilliant weather, even warm, but there is an East wind and I have a little cold and cough – just enough to make me think I should like to be with you to be petted. I could pet back!

Now it is only 19 days until I see you – settle where it should be. We might disappear from the world for two days into some little village, and say nothing to anybody!

246 PP SIDNEY TO BEATRICE

The Earl of Redesdale (1805–86) opposed reform in the divorce laws and other advanced legislation: he was regarded as a model of the old-fashioned Tory landowner. Leonard Trelawney Hobhouse (1864–1929), philosopher and journalist, at this time tutor at Corpus Christi College, Oxford, worked on the *Manchester Guardian* and later became first professor of sociology at the University of London. His best-known work was *Morals in Evolution* 1906. He was the brother of Henry Hobhouse.

4 Park Village East, N.W.
21 May '92

Dearest

Last night I dined with the Hobhouses and Mrs Playne (also a young man just entered in the Record Office). It was all right, but I have not yet learnt to find their company quite pleasant. Perhaps the sadder thing is that I am not sure whether I quite want to do so! I like Henry Hobhouse:

his absurd priggishness amuses me, and I respect his conscientiousness. If he could ever forget his 4000 acres, and feel himself of the same blood as ordinary mortals he would be a charming fellow. His great possessions have done him much harm, and will, I fear, do him still more. He can hardly escape becoming 'more so' in all his foibles; and will finish up by being as absurd an old Tory (allowing for difference of epoch) as Lord Redesdale.

Mrs Hobhouse's intellect has atrophied to nothing at all – so that it is almost difficult to talk to her without misunderstanding. I expect you get on with her by simply avoiding all serious subjects. But with me she insists on arguing, and it is difficult to deal with her. I don't like Hobhouse's attitude to her. He is perfectly conscious of her little stupidities and *he accepts them as natural in a woman* – and so adores her none the less. This is a 'lowering' way of considering women which always infuriates me. Of course I do not mean that he should be vexed at her blunders – any more than that you ought to be angry when I make mistakes as inevitable to my lower nature! So, by the way would Hobhouse. Where I think he falls short is in regarding his wife as an intellectual inferior of necessity. It is a little touch of Helmer in *Doll's House*. It is degrading him as well as her.

But they are both so utterly unconscious of it all that I am as amused as a spectator at a play. We shall never be great friends, but I shall get on much better with either of them alone, than with the two together – just for the reason that it is difficult to be on two planes at once.

Mrs Playne, too, vexed me a little with her ostentation of cynicism – her admiration for Lottie Collins, the singer and dancer of 'Ta-ra-ra' and so on. She seemed to be bent, probably quite unconsciously, on sounding all the depths of me that she disliked. I am quite sure she thinks me horrid, and oddly enough, still on entirely wrong grounds.

Really it is ungrateful of me to be dissecting your sisters, who have been most kind. But it is so obvious that they are dissecting me – each side seeing only what its eyes are adapted to see, and ignoring, as well as despising, all the other's ideals.

Dearest, it will be a little difficult to get on with the Playnes – it is not nice to feel oneself quite so frankly despised. I don't *want* their admiration: but in the alternative, contact jars a little. Still, we shall gradually improve each other!

The Hobhouses go for Sunday to Leonard Hobhouse at Oxford, for whom I have an overwhelming admiration.

I enclose papers relating to the Power Loom Overlookers, which you may be able to supplement whilst in Lancashire; it is apparently an amalgamation of smaller bodies, and there must be some further history behind it. You will notice that there are proposals for connection with Bradford.

Henry Hobhouse asked me what was being done about your Settlement. I said that you had, I believed, spoken to Robert Holt, but that you were waiting to have the securities allotted to you. But time is going on – this day *nine weeks*, love – and Whitsuntide intervenes. I think your solicitor ought to be preparing the draft, so that there may be time for the two trustees to consider and alter it. Shall I go and talk to Godard about it before coming to you! Hobhouse seemed to expect it to be got ready. (He will be electioneering – the London house is given up at end of May.)

Goodbye dearest. I am resting a little today, doing odds and ends. We will have happy Saturdays and Sundays together however busy we are.

Sidney

247 PP BEATRICE TO SIDNEY

The reference is probably to Sir Edward Watkin (1819–1901), railway promoter and at this time a Liberal–Unionist M.P. Sir Thomas Farrer, Sir John Lubbock and other senior members of the L.C.C. had written encouraging comments on the memorandum Sidney had drafted for the work of the Technical Education Board.

[?Liverpool]
Saturday evening [21 May 1892]

My own dearest

I had a very satisfactory evening yesterday with the Mast and Block Makers in the Plumbers lodge – also interviewed an Employer in the morning – a strong anti-trade unionist – who had the shop filled with boys.

I saw also Alfred Holt, who is the ablest of the Holt Brothers. He looked extraordinarily prosperous and orated to me on encouraging the really good men and punishing the indifferent ones by differences of wage. It was so strange listening to this prosperous son of a prosperous father preaching on the text of 'down with the unfortunates'.

He also had a good deal to say on marriage – hoped I should alter – disagreed strongly with the idea of 'comradeship' in marriage – thought it far more comfortable that the husband and wife should have nothing in common – but that the wife should be docile and affectionate without trying to fathom the interests of her husband! (He has the reputation of being a hard and rather selfish husband). I chaffed him unmercifully about his prosperity – and left him in a state of bewilderment as to whether I was joking or in earnest.

A year since our engagement. How well I remember that evening at Devonshire House – in the twilight when we for the first time embraced – how well I remember the happiness tempered by great anxiety. Now all anxiety has passed – except the one fear of incapacitation for my work. Otherwise I feel assured that we shall do more work together than apart.

I wonder how you have fared yesternight. I have an instinct that you

414

and Mary Playne will in the end like each other and have more in common than you and the others – barring Lallie.

Thank you for sending on the letters – Farrer's is most satisfactory – evidently he really appreciates and trusts you. I agree with you in thinking Lubbock a well-intentioned and quite unconscious humbug. He owes his reputation to his indefatigable industry combined with the chance of being otherwise – great possessions and good position. It is to a man's credit to work hard and persistently when he might be a man of pleasure – and of charming pleasures – refined and innocuous – so far his reputation is earned – but not his reputation for distinguished intelligence. And he is a bore!

I go to Wigan Monday for the day; on Wednesday I go to Macclesfield. But I have as yet no notion of where I shall stay. If I cannot find out a hotel before going there – you had better send your letter to the post office – and I will call for it. Then about Friday or Saturday I shall go to Manchester, put up at one of the city hotels – and work on Sunday with Galton at the Joiners minutes which we *must* get out of the way. On Monday I may go to Winsford and find my way to Beeston Tuesday. Mr Arnold said there was only one hotel – near the station. I could go and take rooms there and meet you at the train if you come on Tuesday – so telegraph your address if you can on Wednesday. We might go through to Rochdale Friday evening.

How delightful it will be to be again together. And we should feel much more virtuous than if we had indulged ourselves with a break in the time. Tomorrow I go to Ullet Rd for middleday dinner and stay till the evening – when I expect the Watkins to dinner.

I have just interviewed a S.D.F. man – the secretary of the Core-Makers. Very hopeless about socialism in Liverpool.

Now dearest goodnight.

Ever your devoted comrade
Beatrice Potter

Sunday

P.S. Your letter this morning is very interesting. Of course I have always felt as far away in my own life from my sisters' world as you do – but then I have had the tie of blood and the knowledge of them that enables to climb or descend (whichever it be) to their level. That is why they have never known me – and are constantly surprised at what I do – I never having shown them myself for fear of friction. But I am disappointed that you did not get on to technical education with Mary. I should have thought that on her business side you could have found a common ground.

I will speak to Robert [Holt] tonight about my settlement and let you know.

B.P.

This letter is included to exemplify the notes which throughout their life Sidney sent to Beatrice when they were apart and he had neither time to write more nor any special news to report. Though many letters have disappeared he normally wrote every day when they were separated. The 'real letter' contained a cheerfully romantic description of his garden in early summer, concluding 'it is all there that I want except you. And I do so much want to be with you again'.

4 Park Village East, N.W.
22.5.92

Dearest

I can't bear that you should not have a letter, especially as you will be away the day. But my real letter to you has just been taken by mistake, and will be posted in the ordinary box – and so not reach you in the morning.

I have only time to scribble this line of explanation, and send my love. You will get the letter when you come home at night. So sorry, but it can't be helped now.

Sidney

Sir Charles Russell (1832–1900), M.P. and later Lord Chief Justice, had been involved in private talks at the Home Office with several leading Fabians earlier in the year; the negotiations were an attempt to avert a large-scale 'free speech' demonstration after the police had closed down street-corner meetings at World's End, Chelsea, a traditional pitch for radical speakers. Sidney was used as intermediary for the deputation to Gladstone on the Eight Hours issue.

Charles Harrison (1835–97) a younger brother of Frederic Harrison, sat as a Progressive for the L.C.C. division of S.W. Bethnal Green; he became Liberal M.P. for Plymouth in 1895 but died soon afterwards.

London County Council
[? late] May 1892

I have just had an important interview with Sir Chas. Russell. I received a note last night asking me to call on him in connection with the old matter of the World's End Chelsea disturbance (Free Speech) which we soon disposed of. Then he asked me to stop and talk which I did, I spoke my mind very freely about the conduct of the Liberal Party and their prospects and so on. Sir Charles was very polite and interested. The Liberal leaders are evidently much alarmed at the effect of Mr. G's [Gladstone's] recent *Etourderies*. And finally Sir Charles asked me if I would come again if he wrote to me.

I got the explanation at Council whither I went on leaving. Fred. Harrison told me in whispers that he had been dining with Mr. G. last night –

416

Sir C. Russell being there. (Mr G. was in great form, but never mentioned politics, so Harrison said.) But he went on to say that Mr G. did not understand that he had definitely refused to receive the Eight Hours Deputation, and was quite ready to receive one now if it could be brought on again! I said that this was, I feared impossible – anyhow I could not manage it as I was already 'suspect' – and that the time had gone by for Deputation. He must find some other form of expression – which he can easily do as he is to speak next week.

Harrison said he would see J. Morley – asked me if I was on terms with him. I explained how we were both yearning to meet, but the opportunity never came off.

From all of which I infer that all the leaders but Mr G. are in a devil of a funk; and that pressure will be put on Mr G. to make a satisfactory speech next week.

F. Harrison began by saying that Mrs Harrison wanted your address, which I gave.

Talking to Sir C. Russell made me late for my Parliamentary Committee, so I did not hear what C. Harrison, the Chairman, said of my memo. But the Committee adopted it en bloc.

Goodnight

Sidney

250 PP SIDNEY TO BEATRICE

The Fabian election manifesto, drafted by Bernard Shaw, appeared as Tract 40. The Fabians had considerable success with the device of 'Questions to Candidates', used at a number of parliamentary and local elections. Sidney felt that such sets of questions economically and effectively served three purposes – to educate the Society's members on issues, to provide propaganda points at meetings, and to influence (or expose) the views of candidates.

London County Council, Spring Gardens, s.w.

[? June 1892]

The old man [W. E. Gladstone] was perfectly courteous, but seems never to have dreamt of saying even as much as he did at the Memorial Hall. He treated it merely as a game of fence, without at all trying to see what he could agree to. This kind of thing will certainly do the Liberals much harm. The *Daily Chronicle* has extracted from the deputation that Mr G. had my book under his arm! But it does not seem to have done him much good.

We are sending out from the Fabian Society our Manifesto and 'Questions' all over the place, and stirring up all our members to *educate* as much as possible during the campaign, saying that we are not so much concerned with the actual result.

417

I have sent Burns a cheque for £2 towards his election expenses – my only contribution so far – as he says he is very short of money. He has to pay £225 to the Returning Officer – which is monstrous. It will cost him £450 or £500 altogether, at least. His opponent will spend nearly twice that sum.

Good night sweet.

Sidney

251 HL SIDNEY WEBB TO HERBERT SAMUEL

Samuel Montagu (1832–1911), later Lord Swaythling, banker and philanthropist and a leading figure in English Jewry, was Liberal M.P. for Whitechapel 1885–1900.

[?National Liberal Club]

14 June/92

Dear Mr Samuel

Thanks. I have sent a civil answer, declining to lend my name as a supporter of Mr Montagu – with whom I have no personal acquaintance.

I send you the Fabian Society's manifesto – which, taking a middle position, will perhaps not please you. But every day Mr Gladstone makes clearer that he has no idea of anything beyond Home Rule actually being carried in the first or second session. We shall have to clear out practically the whole Front Bench – a large order even for the Fabian Society! But we have patience and persistence.

Yours very truly

Sidney Webb

252 PP SIDNEY TO BEATRICE

Ben Tillett was running as an independent labour candidate in East Bradford with Fabian support – a concession to the members of the Society who sought to follow up the February conference resolution in favour of direct political action. The prospects for a reasonable labour poll were probably better in Bradford than anywhere else in the North.

Beatrice chose the poems of Arthur Clough (1819–61) for binding.

[*Note at top of letter*] Have just had a long talk with Schloss. He wants to make you a present of a book to be bound by Zähnsdorf the great binder. What book would you like? Goodnight. Sidney

London County Council, Spring Gardens, s.w.

15/6/92

Dearest

I have had a busy day at Fabian and Council work – a satisfactory conference with the leading member of the City, on Technical Education and the Guilds money.

Deptford is still seeking a candidate but it is quite accepted that I don't stand – and I find that my decision is quite approved.

What you say as to Bradford is interesting – and in accordance with our own opinion – but we can do nothing but go on and back Tillett. We have £70 in hand towards his expenses, and I do not doubt we can get the £120 or so which is absolutely required on nomination.

I find that my mother was much upset by the heat last week, and that the doctor seems to have talked rather seriously. She is much better now, with the cooler weather, I thought she looked well – but the doctor said that she must be kept from all excitement. She goes to Margate to-morrow for a fortnight, with my sister and a cousin; the doctor much approving. I asked whether it would be more convenient that you should not come but Ada said that was no reason why you should not come on 9 July, as we shall in any case be very quiet.

I wonder what you have been doing today. Shipton came to the Council today and I was introduced to him. But I feel I cannot take up the London Unions until you come.

See enclosed from Caine. I think he wants a specific request.

Sidney Webb

253 PP SIDNEY TO BEATRICE

In her autobiography Beatrice described the problems created by the intestacy of her rich relative, Mrs Ashworth. Some of her next-of-kin were the poor Bacup relatives who, 'after prayer', felt that their shares of the eight thousand pounds should be divided among the children of other cousins who had predeceased Mrs Ashworth – thus reducing the individual amounts from thousands to hundreds of pounds. The remaining relatives were the wealthy brothers of Beatrice's mother who refused to part with any of their legal rights to benefit other members of the family. Beatrice was more struck by the 'unworldliness and moral fastidiousness' of her poor connections than by the mean-mindedness of the rich ones.

4 Park Village East, N.W.
18th June '92

Dearest

I have sent the circular back to Gray – 'Questions' was sent to him yesterday – and I will try to have a list of Trades Councils sent today also. this is a splendid move of the Co-operators.

I enclose Godard's letter, and the settlement once more; as he evidently wants *you* to write him that this is what you desire. He told me before that it would be his duty to satisfy himself that it expressed your own wishes.

With regard to the securities, your broker will have the exact particulars and can best prepare the transfers – which will cost something but cannot be avoided, if the securities are not to bearer. On the latter point I am not certain. The Queensland 4 per cent were originally, I see, coupon bonds, which may be inscribed free of cost. The Illinois Gold Bonds seem to be dearer. (These would only want redepositing in your trustees name.)

The best course seems to me to be to write to your brokers as enclosed. (But I only do this to save you trouble – alter as you think fit.)

I go to Woolwich this afternoon to speak at three outdoor meetings for Benj. Jones, who says he is doing well. But he can't win.

The result of the meetings at Bradford and Middlesbrough may be very important. I am very pleased that the Trades Council supports Tillett. It ought to mean a great deal.

I will see to the Cotton Spinners Society. I have opened the case but I shrink back appalled from the mass of stuff.

Dearest you are right about our needing some 'cultivation'. Just now I feel horribly incapable of anything but detail and current matters. We must *help each other* to secure time for other things. But at this moment I can't help being 'distracted'. I think of you cross examining a Secretary, or rushing through piles of material with Galton, and I don't feel inclined for poetry or history, or indeed anything but counting the days between now and the time when we shall really begin our joint life together. This day five weeks I shall be prepared to make any number of plans for future perfection. Just now I am a fretfully anxious person, not knowing quite what to be at.

I scarcely think you would be wise to make any formal speech to the Engineers. But the more of them you can talk to individually the better. The pressure for local autonomy doubtless comes from the rank and file of the branches – and these would resent any 'jockeying' of their wishes by their delegates. But such 'jockeying' may have to be done to save the society – that is, a way must be found to give more local control without danger. There is an infinite capacity for new expedients in these democracies.

I shall almost certainly be able to come down Friday evening by 5.45 train. This would leave us Sat. morning free for work on your Tynemouth paper about which I have been thinking a little, though not discovering much. I suppose I had better stay at the hotel? Though of course the other would be nicer.

Tomorrow I dine with the Alfred Crippses to meet the Dyson Williamses. I wonder why Alf. Cripps never answered my letter about Mrs Ashworth. I expect he never received it. But I am satisfied from what I can find in my books that 'representation does not go beyond brother's children' – beyond that, all of one class have to be exhausted before you go another step in kinship.

But I must go to see Pease.

Goodnight sweet.

Sidney

W. P. Drew was the leader of the Manningham Mills strike in Bradford and chairman of the Bradford Labour Union. Beatrice's friend Benjamin Jones ran as the 'Lib-Lab' candidate at Woolwich, losing in a straight fight with a Conservative by 5,922 to 4,100. Georgina Mount Temple was the wife of the philanthropist, politician and strongly Evangelical Lord Mount Temple (1811–88), Lord Palmerston's illegitimate son and heir. They were neighbours of the Pearsall Smiths at Haslemere.

4 Park Village East, N.W.
19.6.92

Dearest

This is Sunday and you are probably alone, whilst I am letterless. I feel very lonely and a little tired. This morning I have read a little, written two short notes on Eight Hours for an International Economic Congress at Antwerp, a little article for Drew's journal, and collected a few odds and ends of Leeds and Bradford trade unions for you. These I enclose. You had better get a full account of the various *basketmakers* from Shaftoe, as he is evidently their leading man. They had unions in 1830/1.

The 'United Coremakers' at Bradford in 1867 seem worth enquiry. They have probably disappeared into the Ironfounders.

Yesterday I went down to Woolwich to Jones. (Met, by the way, at Charing Cross Station, Lady Mount Temple and Mrs Pearsall Smith – as usual, vaguely philanthropic and sentimental.) Found a van in the market square at Woolwich into which Jones and I and a dozen others got – decorated with Union Jacks and his portrait – drove to Shooters Hill, scattering election literature and ringing a hideous bell to attract attention – stopped there to speak to a small crowd of 50 or so, drunken men and women interrupting irrelevantly – then drove to Eltham – tea – then another outdoor meeting – showers of rain now and then but a crowd of 100 or so – retired R.N. Officer in Chair – then drove to Pope St, New Eltham – more bell ringing, another crowd, and speeches – with other drunken interrupters – great enthusiasm everywhere among a small number, train at 9.30, home at 11.30 p.m. It was curious to find such sleepy rural villages included in London. But Woolwich stretches far eastward into the country.

This outdoor speaking and 'cheapjack' electioneering is queer, but I suppose it will become more and more common as cheapness becomes an object.

I am now off to Woolwich to speak for Jones.

Goodbye.

Sidney

Lord Edmond Fitzmaurice (1846–1935), Liberal politician and biographer, was the Liberal candidate at Deptford. As a younger son of the Marquess of Lansdowne he enjoyed a courtesy title. A close friend and political associate of Sir Charles Dilke, he was a prominent figure in Wiltshire and had previously sat for Calne.

4 Park Village East, N.W.
23 June '92

Dear one

I was so glad to find your sweet scrawl when I got home at midnight. When you don't write I fancy all sorts of things. I wonder which of my unworthinesses has vexed you, and the world looks grey. And then I come home to find your loving words with a joy which is almost a fear lest you should be *too* good to me – that we should be so much 'wrapped up' in each other's lives and work as to lose the sense of proportion – that abiding belief in the Copernican rather than the Ptolemaic theory of the Cosmos which is really essential to mental salvation.

Dear, I do love you so that I am not sure that I am not unconsciously constructing a new Theory of the Universe neither Ptolemaic nor Copernican, but Webbian, in which *you* are the centre of things as far as I am concerned.

Really it is high time we were married lest I get *quite* absurd. Afterwards you will pat me, on the back as Mrs Byles does Byles, and say 'That will do, dear, now go and write that chapter and don't be foolish!' I think they are very happy together; and each quite in the proper place. He has very good wifely qualities!

It is pouring with rain, so I am stopping at home writing this. I hope you are not out in the wet.

Last night I took the Chair for Lord Edmond at Deptford. There had only been a day's notice of the meeting, but the hall was crammed (700). He came in to the Committee Room, and straightway greeted me (? He must have looked up my picture in the *Illustrated* so as to recognise me at once – a piece of lordling flattery.) He is a bald, professional-looking man of 50, with spectacles, and the student manner. (But you probably know him.) I was, (I hope) very courteous; told him that when I read his article on Local Government in the *Pall Mall* [*Gazette*], I had exclaimed 'Here, at last, is one official Liberal who is trying to think out the future Bill'. This evidently pleased him, and he quoted it in his speech.

We were most enthusiastically received – I especially. I made an introductory speech, supporting him but pitching into the misdeeds of the Lib. Govt of 1880–5, and saying there must be no more of it; explaining how things could be done in the Budget, for which there was always time, and so on. He spoke for some 45 min., very fairly well, but I see now why *my* speaking at the County Council Election was popular. He did not have the ring of sincerity except about Ireland. However he was well applauded – the heat of battle is up, and there is the old delight in a fight. I am inclined to believe more in a general Lib. victory in South and East London. He rather fenced with his questions – he has the Costelloe fault of wrapping up unduly in long words what he meant to be a frankly affirmative answer.

Hall acts as his agent (I have persuaded him to take the usual fee for the work, as he *had* to take the place, practically).

Lord Edmond produced a letter from a stray local Fabian in Wiltshire commending him especially for his work in forming and helping Clothworkers' T.U. there. He had a cab waiting for him, and drove back to London. (If he does that every night it comes expensive – about £1 a time.) By the way, he might have offered me a lift but he was doubtless flurried.

I have to take the Chair again for him tonight, at a great meeting in the biggest hall which holds 3,000 people. This is about all I shall do I expect.

The enclosed as to your Rio Paulo bonds needs an answer. The scheme is sure to be carried, so your vote is immaterial. But I think you were advised that it was all right. It seems to me that you gain by the change.

You give up £1000   for £1300 new
Stock at 5 per cent   bonds at 5 per cent
producing £50.   producing £65.

I don't know how the capital value will be affected; but it will all have been 'discounted' in the present market price.

I shall not want anything to eat tomorrow night. It will be ample feast enough to be with you. (All the same I had better eat in the train – I wonder whether you think there is a practical fund of commonsense in this lover, with all his heroics.)

Now sweet goodbye till then. I will now go for the cigarettes. I propose to *make a list* of the Cotton Spinners rules that we have: and bring you that list.

Sidney

256 PP SIDNEY TO BEATRICE

The 'amiable baronet' was Sir Hickman Bacon: given the earlier controversies about Tory finance for labour candidates Sidney was understandably anxious to conceal the aristocratic and Conservative source of this donation. 'It would look bad', Beatrice replied the following day, 'tho it is perfectly genuine on his part.'

The street scheme to clear the slums north of the Strand became Aldwych and Kingsway.

Though Joseph Burgess had made the *Workman's Times* the focal point of the campaign for an independent labour party its proprietor, Andrews, had originally financed it as one of a series of ventures to catch the new working-class reading public.

Dearest

I had a fearfully hot journey up – a slight lunch at home and am in the Housing Committee.

I found an autotype of Watt's 'Love and Death' from Mr and Mrs Pease – a convenient-sized 'harmless' picture, framed in good taste. There was also Herbert Spencer's *Principles of Ethics* Vol. I.

I have also a letter from our amiable baronet friend, enclosing bank notes for £60 for Tillett's nomination expenses – *his name to be kept secret*, so don't mention it. This enables the Fabian Society to cover the whole of the Returning Officer's expenses.

I enclose a letter from Leonard Hall – a somewhat 'doubtful' person – in re my letter in the *Workman's Times*. Also a plan of Frederic Harrison's projected great street improvement in the Strand, which may take away the breath of the Council, and not be carried. We are discussing how to mitigate the hardship to the poor to be displaced, a very difficult problem.

I hope you have had a good day with the Engineers – I feel more and more how useful your talks with them are. I wish I could be with the N.E. Coast men tonight – and with you.

Here is rather a despondent letter from Vaughan Nash – I hope he is not dependent on his journalism. I gather that Andrews, the owner of the *Workman's Times*, interferes with its policy in rather an anti-Home Rule sense – which is a little awkward for Labor politics.

Goodnight

Sidney

257 PP SIDNEY TO BEATRICE

Several scrappy letters from Beatrice in this period have been omitted: most merely report her routine research enquiries. On 28 June she wrote to say that she had ordered her wedding dress in light grey material at a cost of four pounds. She was now attending a conference of the Amalgamated Society of Engineers in Leeds, where the chairman had muddled the procedure.

Fabian activity reached a peak in 1891–92; in this period over three thousand Fabian lectures were given in various parts of the country, and the Society's tracts and leaflets were being distributed in very large numbers. An example of the energy shown by some of the provincial groups is provided by Birmingham which, in the winter of 1891–92, had 106 members. They organised 17 lectures with an average attendance of 200, sold 200 copies of *Fabian Essays* and disposed of 1800 tracts. There was no comparable boom in the Society's affairs until after 1906.

London County Council, Spring Gardens, s.w.
28.6.92

Dearest

I have this morning given notice of the marriage and arranged it for
11.45 a.m. on 23 July. I find that *you* must *personally* give notice to the
Leeds Registrar, whose address is 13 Bedford Place or Street, Old Parade,
Leeds. He has to give his certificate, and can only issue it after *21 clear
days*. Hence unless you give notice *at once* it will be running it close. You
will have to pay 2/- I think, and arrange to have the certificate sent to
London not later than Friday, 22 July. (If it did not arrive on the Sat.
the ceremony would have to be put off.) The Registrar will send it if you
arrange with him – or (to make sure) Galton might fetch it and send it to
us. But please go and give notice *tomorrow* if you can.

I have described myself as Sidney James Webb, 32, Author, of 4 Park
Village East, St. Pancras, lived there 5 years and you as of 36 Mount
Preston, lived there a month, age 34.

I am sorry to bother you, but it is necessary anyhow, and very simple.
Thursday would be the *very latest* day, and then the certificate could only
arrive on *the* Sat. morning. So it is important for you to give notice
tomorrow.

I was glad to get your letter this morning. It was unstamped and marked
on the back 'Picked up and posted G.W.G.' I suppose you dropped it
somewhere.

A good chairman would *deprecate* double-barrelled resolutions – and
try to put half at a time – but I don't think he can rule them out of order.
I am glad the Engineers have a new Chairman.

We are sending out *thousands* of Fabian tracts every day – there is a
daily growing demand from paying sources. And the candidates are replying fairly well to our questions; I think we are doing a good bit of political
education over this election.

We have done a good deal at Council today – decided to engage our own
staff in various directions, to engage in our own electric lighting etc. But
we have not discussed the proposed new street – adjourned as so many
absent.

But I must close.

Goodnight, Sweet.

Sidney

258 PP SIDNEY TO BEATRICE

H. R. Taylor, a bricklayer and member of the Social Democratic Federation,
polled 106 votes against the successful Howell in North-East Bethnal Green;
Benjamin Ellis polled only 95 votes in Peckham. At West Bradford Ben Tillett
did well, with 2,749 votes to the 3,306 for the Liberal and 3,053 for the Conservative candidates.

London County Council, Spring Gardens, s.w.
[? July '92]

I have not forgotten the T.U. paper for Tynemouth. I have been thinking about it, and will seriously get to work to write it tomorrow and Sunday. Our Fabians are working wonderfully well in the election. Everywhere but West Bradford they have eliminated 'third candidates', and are working for such of the Liberals as have answered reasonably well. Everywhere they are heckling candidates, selling tracts, flooding the meetings with leaflets, and generally running an 'unauthorised programme' with excellent educational effect. Schnadhorst evidently doesn't like it, but it is obviously our proper policy – to educate the constituencies without upsetting the coach by running Labor candidates. And our backing of Tillett just serves nicely to emphasise our independence to define the position.

There are two 'splits' in London – Taylor (S.D.F.) against Geo. Howell, and Ben Ellis, of the Metropolitan Radical Federation against a local Liberal in Peckham. But it is well known that the Fabian Society does not support them, or countenance them.

I am nervous about Bradford. If Tillett does well, we are obviously vindicated. But our action will be more difficult to justify to the ordinary Liberal if Tillett only polls a few hundred votes. I hope it will go off well.

Goodbye dearest one. Soon we shall not need to write to each other.

Sidney

259 PP BEATRICE TO SIDNEY [*incomplete*]

Harland and Wolff were the large shipbuilders in Belfast, where the Webbs were going from Dublin.

Beatrice sat through the complicated rules revision conference of the A.S.E. in Leeds. This conference, she wrote in a long diary entry on 2 July, was a turning point in trade union history. It demonstrated that the spirit of the 'new' unionism had infected 'even this conservative and aristocratic body' – a craft union which was 'little better than a great benefit society'. Both John Burns and Tom Mann had played an important part in a movement to break up 'the central and unrepresentative executive', give more power to the districts, provide for more paid officials, amalgamate with kindred trades and provide more democracy within the union. Beatrice was involved in backstairs argument and lobbying on these issues. 'What a queer thing the world is', Sidney wrote in an undated letter at the end of June. 'How little would anyone here suspect that you were influencing the conference', Beatrice found it 'an agreeable surprise' that the most sensible and able speeches came from socialists. 'My experience hitherto has been that the more feather-headed workers are socialists: but their socialism is rapidly changing in character and is losing the revolutionary and personally bitter character and becoming constitutional effort based on hope and not hatred.' This new attitude, she thought, was 'of a decided *Fabian* type – I can recognise the facts and figures and general arguments as taken from Fabian literature'. She also talked to Gateshead men about Sidney's future chances there.

426

Yesterday evening Galton and I had the old Brushmaker to dinner – a shrewd old fellow who gave us all the information with regard to the brushmakers in the U.K.

Dearest I shall be so glad when this long drawn-out separation is over – I am getting a bit weary of it. Perhaps it is because it is near the end – only 3 weeks now. By the way had we not better write to Taylor (4 Ely Place Dublin) about introductions and lodgings – also Michael Davitt for introductions?

I will ask the Courtneys for an introduction to Harland and Wolffs. The only thing I regret is parting with my *name* – I *do* resent that.

Now dearest goodbye my friends will be coming.

Ever your devoted comrade

Beatrice

---

260 PP   SIDNEY TO BEATRICE [*incomplete*]

P. W. Bunting was the defeated Liberal candidate in East Islington; George Bateman, an overt 'labour' man, secured 2,477 votes against the Conservative's 4,749 in Holborn. A. Donald led a disastrous strike of postal workers in 1890; a former member of the Socialist League, he was associated with Champion's intrigues. He polled 19 votes. Sidney planned to meet Beatrice in Sheffield for research in the library on Friday 8 July, the day after the poll there.

4 Park Village East, N.W.
1 July '92

Dearest

This is our marriage month. You can't imagine how glad I am that it is getting near. You have been very kind, and I have been very happy, but the period is, I suppose, always a distracting one. I *have* done a lot of work, but I shall not be at my best until we have settled down in our new life.

I don't feel so much doubt about the Permanent Executive of the A.S.E. as you do. I am glad they have decided so. But what I mean is a Permanent Exec. so large as to permit of frequent absences in the provinces i.e. very much like District Delegates, of whom half or two-thirds were at any one time always to be found conferring together in London. I would suggest that – if 7 be thought a good Committee, they should elect 10 or 12. £1000 a year is not much to pay for management of such a society. The 'District Delegate' would be the better for being one of the governing council, instead of nominally its servant. But these are only crude notions.

Last night I spoke for Bunting and Bateman (my brother refuses to vote for the latter as he is too extreme! This looks like the beginning of my brother's probable slide into the Conservatism of an Employer).

Tonight I am urgently summoned to speak for Costelloe. But it will soon be over.

Wallas has had what seems a good offer from Putnam (New York) for a short history of Modern England, to be done after his Chartist book.

I enclose a nice letter from Mrs Fisher.

Now I must go off to an important set of Committees relating to further powers for the County Council.

Last night I spoke for Costelloe, at the Chelsea Town Hall and an open air meeting. I doubt whether he will get in.

A very foolish thing has been done against Stuart. Some Fleet Street journalists have put A. K. Donald – a flighty 'impossibilist' Socialist – against him, and found the money for his nomination. Massingham strongly disapproves but will be believed to be implicated. It will not I think do Stuart any great harm, but it will irritate the Liberals and make Labor candidates look ridiculous.

I do hope Tillett's goes off well. It is impossible to rely on anything in these matters, and I shall be mighty relieved if he does respectably well at any rate.

Dear, I too am anxious for the 23rd – three weeks today. It seems as far off as three months did lately. I *will* try to make you happy – that is, useful and influential in your own work – spite of the change of name. But one name will soon be as well recognised as the other. Neither you nor I depend on our names – we have ourselves!

I have written a bit of your paper today. It will be ready right enough – not worthy of you, but as good as I can make it.

I could probably meet you in Sheffield on Wed. night. The bigger the hotel the better I should say. I have none in mind, but will enquire.

261 PP BEATRICE POTTER TO HOWARD COLLINS

On 28 June Beatrice received a kindly letter from Herbert Spencer approving her decision to have a civil marriage and regretting that his health was too bad to permit him to attend the ceremony. Collins published *An Epitome of the Synthetic Philosophy of Herbert Spencer* in 1897.

[?Manchester]
3 July 1892

COPY

My dear Mr Collins

I am very glad you have had such a satisfactory talk with Mr Spencer, I had no idea that he intended that his Literary Executor should write his 'Biography' besides publishing his 'Autobiography'. I imagine that the L. Executor could only complete those portions of the life which he had omitted and add a preface giving the 'Boswellian' part of the work. With this task I should have been most happy to help you to the best of my ability. But frankly I could not undertake to add *anything* to a Biography written by another person with some parts of which I might not agree – I do not, in fact, feel that a joint work of that sort would be likely to be of any value, with an Autobiography published separately.

Perhaps it would be desirable to let Mr Spencer know this so that no reference should be made to my contribution in the Trust and no part of the materials left to me. I feel fully assured that you with your admiration for Mr Spencer, and intimate knowledge of his Philosophy would be admirably fitted to write the sort of study which I imagine he desires dealing with the less personal side of his life and to undertake the Literary Executorship with all its duties.

I am so glad you have been elected a member of the Saville Club. You will find the atmosphere throughly congenial. But you do not owe your election to me – I have very few friends there.

Ever sincerely

Beatrice Potter

P.S. Pray send this to Mr Spencer if you think right.

BP

262 PP BEATRICE TO SIDNEY [*incomplete*]

The reference to a present for Standish Cripps and Fanny Hughes is unclear.

[?Manchester]
[?early July 1892]

. . . I have just got my bank book in for the Quarter April–July.

My total expenditure is £167. Out of this £15 for the watch ought to go down to 'election expenses'; Galton has cost £30 and I have £10 in hand leaving £112 as 'personal expenditure' which includes the outlay £30 on teeth. But then one must always expect some sort of extraordinary expenditure – so that I am living at the rate of £448 a year. I hope you will help me to be economical – your tendency will be to press me to have everything I want. It will not do to stint the work – and here of course is the difficulty – one's personal expenditure is so mixed up with indirect working expenses; but we must not get lax. Let us try to manage this 2-months tour as economically as possible. We ought not only to be able to do our work and put on one side £200 a year for Parliamentary expenses but I should like to have something at the end of each year to give to one of our poorer fellow-workers.

I have just sent off £2 for a present for Standish Cripps and Fanny Hughes. We owe Ada a really nice present – and then I should like to give

Graham a bicycle. If we do not give each other many presents we [can] manage this – I will take the 'paper' as the marriage gift, and you should take me.

I have settled to go for the day to Barnsley Monday. I find the interesting discussion at the Engineers will come on in the middle of the week, so I propose to go to Sheffield Friday.

Now dearest – goodbye. I do not know what to say about Sheffield. I am inclined to think you ought not to come – (I should come down about Wednesday to London) especially if you have not finished the paper!

263 PP   SIDNEY TO BEATRICE

Beatrice spoke on 'The Relationship between Co-operation and Trade Unionism' at Tynemouth on 12 August 1892.

4 Park Village East, N.W.
3/7/92

Dearest

Today I have been at work on your paper for Tynemouth, which goes on slowly. Either it is difficult or I am incapable or lazy. But it is sweet to be doing something for you and to feel that it sets you free for other work.

It is hard to think amid the election clamour, of which I am already heartily tired.

Miss Harkness sent last night a copy of the *Novel Review*, addressed in her handwriting to me. But there is absolutely nothing in it of interest to you or to me, and it seems to me a very poor production not calculated to last. How it goes on astonishes me.

I wonder how you are spending this Sunday – resting a little, I hope – and thinking just occasionally of me! This day three weeks I hope we shall be listening to the organ in Chester Cathedral, *together*, with a new feeling of union and fellowship and happiness.

I have a great deal to do in the next three days, so that I shall be kept 'braced up' to work whether I like it or not, and shall be unable to fancy that I cannot do anything just now.

Last night I read through your *Co-operative Movement* again – it contains a wonderful number of ideas rammed home with great force. There are little blemishes in the writing, which might be improved in a new edition. But it does you infinite credit as a thinker. I wish I could put as many thoughts per page into the Trade Union paper. But you will be able to use my pages as bricks for your own building.

My mother chuckled to herself at dinner over some joke, and at last let it out, viz, that this was the last Sunday I had to do what I liked in!

Goodnight, my own dearest love.

Sidney

Sidney's remark about 'domestic memoranda' apparently refers to a paragraph in an undated letter from Beatrice. 'I have been meaning to advise you *not* to bring that thick flannel nightshirt. I notice you always have a cold when you return home and I am pretty sure that it comes from changing from flannel to cotton nightshirts. It is far more dangerous than the bare chance of damp sheets – an article which I, in all my wanderings, have never met with. And in this weather you would find the flannel insupportable.'

James Keir Hardie (1856–1915), a former miner, was the leading agitator for Labour representation. He had fought a notable by-election on this issue at Mid-Lanark in 1888; in 1889 he founded the *Labour Leader*; on 4 July 1892 he defeated his Conservative opponent in West Ham by 5,268 to 4,036. He and Burns, in Battersea (5,515 to 5,057) were the only two of the 'new' labour men to be elected. The socialists in Newcastle were becoming influential, having elected three men in a schoolboard election and polling over two thousand votes. They strongly opposed Morley, especially on the Eight Hours issue, and after planning to run their own candidate they withdrew at the last minute, throwing their support behind one of the Conservative candidates, C. F. Hammond, who pushed Morley down to second place in the two-member seat. At a subsequent by-election, caused by Morley's appointment to the Cabinet, he won easily, rallying the Irish votes among the working-class electors. J. C. Foulger, an old Radical and an early Fabian, edited the *Progressive Review* and had been associated with Champion's first venture into publishing.

4 Park Village East, N.W.
[?5 July 1892]

Dearest

I am delighted to think you are going at once to Beeston with Mrs Green – if she will stay on so much the better. Her letter is a little sad but this may be due to overwork. And, also, there *is* a little flavour of Dead Sea Fruit in many of the things she cares for. I am glad we shall not depend on London Society.

I will note and remember all your domestic memoranda – it is sweet of you to take care of me. But I am very well.

I hope you won't think I have got cross with Burns. We are quite on friendly terms, and I believe he is not at all sorry that his resolution was modified. I don't at all feel that I have fallen behind in a race for popularity.

I send the *Daily Chronicle*, which today goes over finally to Home Rule. The first article is Massingham's – also that on Burns for Battersea. See also Davitt's letter.

The Irish have an important party convention this week, when they may perhaps come to some understanding among themselves.

I have just met Hugh Bell at the Club and had lunch with him. We talked about the Durham strike. He said he wished the T.U. would learn to dismiss their officers, and put in those who held the views of the majority.

431

I enclose a letter from Schloss, which *please return*. I presume I had better look among our material for something of use to him as to Boards of Conciliation etc. We can hardly refuse to let him have it, and indeed, there is no reason.

As to his Factory Acts campaign, we may have other work in hand.

Yesterday's election results are significant. Tillett's poll is not at all bad – and there is this advantage in not 'spilling' Illingworth actually, viz. that it diminishes the bitterness. South-West-Ham victory and Broadhurst's defeat are very telling. What astonishes me is the virtual disappearance of the Gateshead majority. This will make them more willing to have an extreme man there. But the seat does not now look so very '*safe*'.

Those Newcastle 'Labor' men are very foolish. Failing to get a candidate (we choked off one) they have actually signed a nomination paper for the Cons. candidate (Hammond) who is *opposed* to Eight Hours!

Wakinshaw, the Gateshead Secretary, telegraphed me this last night, and implored me, for the sake of Gateshead to telegraph my views thereon for publication. I had only five minutes to decide and wired

'Cannot believe that sensible working men will be foolish enough to vote for Tory opposed to Eight Hours merely out of personal spite. Needless to say I utterly disapprove any such policy. Though re-gretting Mr John Morley's action I have always discouraged merely factious opposition.'

This is probably published there today and may make Stewart and Co. cross. But their action is too foolish. (Their nomination paper, with their ten names, was published in Newcastle paper yesterday.)

It looks like a Gladstone majority of 60 or 80.

There has come 3 nicely bound volumes of Renan in French from the Dyson Williams addressed to you. Will you please write at once acknow-ledging?

I have nearly done your Tynemouth paper – in my own way, for your reworking up.

Today I have put in 3 hours work in bringing up voters for Foulger, our West Marylebone (Fabian) candidate whose return I doubt.

Goodnight dear. Let me come Friday. I *will* work Sat.

Sidney

265 PP SIDNEY TO BEATRICE

Dr George Calvert Holland (1801–65), an eminent physician who practiced in Manchester and Sheffield, was interested in industrial conditions. Among his many writings was *An Enquiry into the Moral, Social and Intellectual Conditions of the Industrious Classes of Sheffield*, 1839.

Dearest

I will do as you like about Sheffield, not complaining, But if you leave
it to me I will come – not Thursday but Friday morning. You can spend
Friday morning in Barnsley and come on to Sheffield as soon as you can.
I will meet you – we will go to the Trades Council together if you will
allow me: and Saturday I will overhaul the Library. I must return Monday
morning: and you will perhaps stay on a day or two to see Trade Unionists.

Dearest, don't think this mere extravagance of me. It will only cost me
£2 or so, altogether, and I do so want to see you. But I want to come for
another reason. Do you remember that I have promised a long article
for the [Co-operative] Wholesale Annual about the condition of the Working Classes 1842–92? I want to hunt up the accounts by that Dr Calvert
Holland of the Sheffield operatives, in 1840–5. I must get some fresh
material before we start for Ireland. I don't think it is very extravagant
to have a day in the Sheffield Library, even for this purpose – let alone for
our wider aims. And I want to go to the Trades Council.

Dear, don't be too strict with me. I think I might have this 'week
end' without anyone finding it extravagant or wrong of me.

I put in Mosses' Report and Circular, which have just come in case you
want them in connection with the Engineers.

I suppose we must let your sisters come to 'the ceremony' if they like!
But we will talk about it.

Goodnight, dearest. Tomorrow afternoon we shall have tea face to
face.

Sidney

266 PP   SIDNEY TO BEATRICE

Sir Horace Davey was Liberal M.P. for Stockton-on-Tees and defeated there
in 1892. Sir Charles Stuart Parker (1829–1910), politician and author, was interested in educational problems and wrote a life of Robert Peel. He was Liberal
M.P. for Perth and defeated there in 1892. Sir Harry Lawson Webster Levy-
Lawson (1862–1933), later Viscount Burnham, proprietor of the Daily Telegraph, was Liberal M.P. for St Pancras and lost his seat in 1892. Edward Lyulph
Stanley (1839–1925), later Lord Sheffield, was an educational reformer and a
member of the London School Board. He had been Liberal M.P. for Oldham
until 1885 and was seeking to return to Parliament.

Sidney's attitude to the results indicates that he had already turned sharply
against the 'Gladstonians' in the Liberal Party – a shift that profoundly affected
the tactics of the Webbs in the next ten years.

Dearest

Your letter was well worth twopence because it says that I *may* come to Sheffield if I think it worth while. I *do* think so, dearest one – and not entirely for my own happiness' sake. It will only cost me £2 or £3, and I want to see Sheffield, and its Library before writing my Wholesale article (which I shall have to do during our Irish or Scotch visit).

You will see how strikingly our impression of the Election results coincided. Today's news looks even worse for the pure Gladstonians. The defeats of Sir Horace Davey, C. S. Parker and H. L. W. Lawson are very significant. Stanley has done better than was expected. But I am sorry we are not doing better in London. However, either way will serve our purpose there. There is no sign of any sweeping of Lancashire either. Altogether it looks like a very small Gladstonian majority which will deliver them into our hands. This I had given up hoping for.

I am sure you will look sweet in your new dress – even if dark blue silk does suit you better – because you are (I am *so* thankful for this) happy in what you are undertaking. We will go and choose the prettiest little brooch we can find. I am glad you will let me give you this little token. You have so few gifts from me – save that everything I do is now done for you.

Gray has at last sent me a few copies of your Rochdale paper, and I am sending them to all the Women's newspapers, and some others which may notice it.

I enclose my draft of your paper. I think you must now look through it before I can do any more to it. Dear, I don't feel that it is good but it is the best I can do just now. It is not worthy of you as it stands, but you shall hit me over the head with it when we meet at Sheffield, and I will try to rewrite it as you may direct. Don't be disappointed when you read it. But talk to me frankly about it, and I will try again.

The Gladstonians are much upset at today's results – which is very useful. I am off now home to dinner and work afterwards. Tomorrow I hope to be with you at 9 p.m. I shall come by the 5.30 from Kings Cross to the Wharncliffe Hotel. I have nothing whatever to do here this weekend, and we may as well work together as apart.

Goodnight, dear one.

Sidney

267 PP SIDNEY TO BEATRICE

W. K. Hall polled 553 as S.D.F. candidate in South Salford. Joseph Havelock Wilson (1858–1929) founded the National Union of Seamen. He had been the Liberal nominee for Deptford but transferred to Middlesbrough. His election there as Liberal M.P. removed one possible contender for the reversion of the Gateshead seat in which Sidney was interested. Another was William Robson

(1852–1918), later Baron Robson, a lawyer and Liberal politician, elected for South Shields in 1895: he became attorney-general in 1908. In the general election polling was still spread over several days. The final result was 273 Liberals, dependent upon 81 Irish members for a majority over 269 Conservatives and 46 Liberal-Unionists. The Fabians considered their election tactics justified, feeling that with the Irish issue proving a damp squib Gladstone and his colleagues would have to turn to social reform and implement part at least of the Newcastle Programme.

John Burns and Keir Hardie had both won in straight fights with Liberal support against Conservatives. Havelock Wilson won by six hundred votes in Middlesbrough in a three-cornered fight. Most of the other independent Labour candidates did poorly, the remainder tailing away from two thousand to a few hundred votes or less. 'Lib-Lab' candidates did reasonably well, eleven being elected and nine polling respectably. These results seemed to confirm Webb's opposition to the movement to found a separate Labour Party and his general support for Labour men running under Liberal auspices.

The Newcastle Socialists embarrassed Sidney by their attacks on John Morley and their support for his Conservative opponent.

[*Note at top of letter*] Your telegram has since come. I am sorry to have made it necessary.

4 Park Village East, N.W.
7 July '92

Dearest

I am afraid I have not been quite businesslike about Sheffield. But I assume that you will adhere to your plan of going Friday morning (Yesterday I thought you meant that you had engaged a room *for tonight*): and hence for the sake of economy I do not propose to start until Friday morning – 10.15 or 10.35 either of which will bring me to Sheffield before you. There is a train at 1.55 from Barnsley *I think* by which you will probably come. But I shall be at the Wharncliffe Hotel. We will talk and walk and rest in the afternoon: go to the Trades Council in the evening. Saturday I propose to spend, more or less, in the Library. Sunday may be fine enough for an excursion. In between whiles we will revise your paper for Tynemouth.

The elections continue to go well for us. The utter collapse of Taylor, the *only* S.D.F. candidate in London, is a set-off against one's mingled feelings that Howell is again elected. Hall at S. Salford does better, and 'spills' a Liberal candidate, but gets after all few votes for himself. This is probably the only case in which any Liberal seat will be actually lost by splits in Gt Britain – though there are already 3 in Scotland. This makes doubly for us, as we are not responsible for Scotland.

Wilson's victory at Middlesbrough is astonishing and highly significant. I wonder whether Spence Watson still denies the existence of any ' Labor feeling' in the North. It leaves Robson still open, but the situation has completely changed, and the Gateshead Labor Party have the game in their own hands, if they do but know how to play it. We shall have done just decently in London – won what we expected on our lower estimates, not our higher ones. But Toryism in London is shaken, and *any* Registration Reform would almost enable us to sweep all but the City, the West End and Villadom – as for the County Council.

Later. John Morley's astounding fall at Newcastle is highly important. His holding the second seat is nothing compared with the fact of nearly 3000 majority. If the Conservatives oppose his re-election on taking office, he will probably be thrown out. I am very glad I sent that telegram. The event is one of the greatest significance.

I, too, have looked through my Bankbook. Taking the whole period from the middle of August to 30 June – practically all since I left the C.O. I have spent £284 in $10\frac{1}{2}$ months, equal to £311 for the year, some of which is 'working expenses' and propaganda. This omits *only* the County Council elections. Now considering that I have been travelling freely down to you, and so on – I hope you don't think this is very bad. Few 'politicians' live on less. So you won't feel you are leaving me to starve, if you do go off with your bank book to study Women's Work!

My budget, by the way, contains all propaganda outlay etc. – indeed, it is simply the bankbook total, less investments, and the election expenses.

How surprised Haldane or Meinertzhagen would be to realise how little one can live on in London, even as a professional agitator.

No doubt Galton's mere masculinity is useful to you, e.g. when you invite Mawdsley to dinner! I wonder what your sisters think of it all. But you are really doing a great deal to get women free from conventional bonds.

Evidently I must come by the North Western 10.10 train, due London Road *2.30* p.m. That is now only 21 hours off, dearest love. I do so want to see you. I will look out for you on arrival but don't feel bound to come. If you like we can send my bag home in a cab, and go for a walk straight-away.

Adieu sweet.

Sidney

268 PP   SIDNEY WEBB TO GRAHAM WALLAS

On the morning of Saturday 23 July Sidney and Beatrice were married in the St Pancras vestry hall. Her sister Kate Courtney noted in her diary that it was 'a prosaic, almost sordid ceremony – our civil marriages are not conducted with much dignity and seem rather to suggest a certain shadiness in the contracting parties. But Bee looked good – serious and handsome'. (MS diary in BLPES) Beatrice confined herself to a crisp entry in her own diary.

July 23rd 1892
Exit Beatrice Potter
Enter Beatrice Webb
or rather (Mrs) Sidney Webb for I lose alas! both names.

The Webbs went to Dublin to study Irish trade unionism. Beatrice's inter-polations into this letter reveal an unusual light-heartedness.

116 Lower Baggot St, Dublin.

29.7.92

Dear Wallas

We both thank you for your very nice letter, which we are quite in-capable of answering as it deserves.

All we feel capable of doing is to ask you kindly to ascertain since when the British Museum possesses a Sheffield daily newspaper – that is if you can before the Library closes and you go away. Our emissary in Sheffield wants to know how much he must read there. Send your answer in the enclosed envelope.

We hope you will have the holiday you deserve. B. takes a keen interest in the bicycle.

We will tell about Ireland when we come back. The people are charming but we detest them, as we should the Hottentots – for their very virtue. Home Rule is an absolute necessity [*the sentence was completed by Beatrice*] – in order to depopulate the country of this detestable race!

Sidney Webb

[*Postscript by Beatrice*]
We are very very happy – far too happy to be reasonable.

B.W.

List of recipients

The figures refer to the Letter numbers.

Index

Goschen, George Joachim, M.P. (Viscount Goschen) 31, 227–8
Goschen, Henry 31–2
Grant-Woodstock, Corrie, M.P. 86, 132
Gray, J. C. 70, 136, 138, 188, 195, 197, 386, 407, 419
Green, Alice Stopford 148, 156, 184, 186, 198, 206–7, 214, 219, 225, 241, 247, 250–1, 256, 266, 269–70, 272–3, 275, 281, 283, 305, 308, 315, 318–19, 338, 339–40, 361, 363, 367, 370–2, 375, 377–9, 431
Green, Prof. J. R. 148, 372
Green, Thomas Hill 370–1
Greening, Edward Owen 259
Grey, Sir Edward, M.P. 250, 254, 256, 260, 270, 319
Gronlund, Laurence 192, 196
Grove, Archibald 150–1, 260
Guild of St Matthew 115

Hadrian's wall 99–100
Haldane, Elizabeth 259, 260
Haldane, Richard Burdon, M.P. xiii, 109, 241, 250, 257, 278–9, 289, 318–19, 331–2, 342, 436; autobiography 200; possible suitor to Beatrice 231, 280, 342, 372; and Fabian links with Liberals 231, 252–6, 260, 270; and Webb engagement 275, 380
Hall, Benjamin T. 259, 260, 326, 331, 393, 403, 423
Hall, Leonard 424
Hall, W. K. 434–5
Hammersmith Socialist Society 130
Hammond, C. F. 431–2
Hampstead Historic Society 113
Harcourt, Sir William, M.P. 302–3
Hardie, James Keir, M.P. 311, 431, 435
Hardy, Arthur Sherburne 82, But Yet A Woman 82–3, 93
Hardy, Thomas 389; Tess of the D'Urbervilles 389
Harford, Edward 296, 298
Harkness, Margaret 10, 24–8, 41, 50, 68, 128, 177, 224, 255–6, 258, 380, 430; Captain Lobe 224; Novel Review 430
Harrison, Charles 416–17
Harrison, Frederic 49, 57, 66–7, 159, 208, 247–8, 270, 323, 350, 397, 404, 416–17, 424
Harrison, Mrs F. 417
Harrison, Mrs Robert 57
Harrison, Prof. Royden xi, xv
Hartington, Lord 343
Hawthorne, Nathaniel 179–80; The Marble Faun 179–80

Headicar, B. M. xiii–xiv
Headlam, Beatrice 118, 122
Headlam, Rev. Stewart 75, 79, 109, 115, 125, 290, 326
Henderson, Arthur, M.P. xiii
Henderson, Beatrice 58–9
Henderson, Colonel 39–40
Herbert, Auberon 263–4, 387, 389
Herbert, Sir Robert 307, 308
Herbert, Sidney 263, 265
Herbert, William 347; History of the Twelve Great Livery Companies 347
Hewins, W. A. S. 318–19
Hey, William Henry 279, 340
Heyworth, Lawrence 1, 306
Heyworth, Lawrencina (see Potter)
Hibbert, Sir John, M.P. 56–7
Hill, Alfred Bostock 46–7
Hill, Octavia 14, 31, 46
Hobhouse, Emily 58
Hobhouse, Henry 11, 37–8, 58, 398–401, 412–14
Hobhouse, Leonard Trelawney 412–13; Morals in Evolution 412
Hobhouse, Lord 397, 401, 404, 408
Hogg, Quintin, M.P. 404, 408
Holland, Dr George Calvert 432–3; An Enquiry into the Moral, Social and Intellectual Conditions of The Industrious Classes of Sheffield 432–3
Holland, Colonel 29
Holloway, George, M.P. 318
Holman Hunt, William 166, 169
Holt, Alfred 326, 414
Holt, Kitty 279–80
Holt, Richard 29, 409–10
Holt, Robert 6, 381, 394, 409, 414–15
Holyoake, George Jacob 366, 368; Self Help by The People 366, 368
Home Rule 52, 57, 94–5, 194, 348, 418, 431, 437
Hooker, Sir William 3
Howell, George, M.P. 259, 260, 262, 425–6
Howells, William Dean 115–16
Hughes, Fanny 429
Hughes, Thomas 275–6, 373–4; A Manual for Co-operators 373
Hunter, William Alexander, M.P. 80–1
Huntingdon, Rev. Father 115
Hutchinson, Henry Hunt 173
Huxley, Thomas Henry 3, 75
Hyndman, Henry Myers 55, 100

Ibsen, Henrik 80, 295; The Doll's House 413
Illingworth, Percy Holder, M.P. 409, 432

443

Rae, John 276–7, 280
Reade, William Winwood 166, 168; *The Martyrdom of Man* 166
Redesdale, Earl of 412–13
Redgrave, Mr 130–1, 315, 378, 402
Reeve, D'Arcy, 355–6, 358
Reform Act 1832 1
Reform Act 1884 94
Reid, Robert T., M.P. (Lord Loreburn) 318–19
Reid, Sir Thomas Wemyss 134, 303–4, 306, 374
Review of Reviews 166
Ricardo, David 80–1, 221
Ritchie, Clement 318–19, 321, 325–6, 330, 332–4, 338
Ritchie, David George 328–9
Roberts, Thomas Lee 261–2
Robinson, Mr 370–1
Robson, William, M.P. 435
Roby, Henry John, M.P. 208, 210
Rogers, James Edwin Thorold 216
Rosebery, Lord 136–7, 211, 345–6, 351–2, 354, 373–4, 408; *William Pitt* 345–6, 351–2, 354
Rose, Charles 37
Rossetti, Christina 187, 190
Rossetti, Dante Gabriel 136, 168, 187, 190, 215
Rossetti, William Michael 187, 190
Rousseau, J. J. 83, 158, 189
Routledge, Miss 292–3
Royal Commission on Labour 259, 278, 285, 291, 342–3, 375–6
Royal Commission on the Poor Law 263, 331
Runciman, J. F. 349–50
Ruskin College, 200
Russell, Bertrand 294
Russell, Sir Charles, M.P. 416–17
Russell, George William 208, 211
Russell, Hon. Rollo 294
Ryland, Clara 15, 30, 36, 59
Rylett, Harold 187, 190, 199
Rylett, Mrs 195

Saint-Simon, Comte Henri de 180, 183
Salisbury, Lord 94–5, 227, 291
Salvation Army 224
Samuel, Herbert xiii, 323–4, 418
Samuel, Sir Stuart, M.P. 323–4
Samuelson, Sir Bernard, M.P. 56–7
Sargant, William Lucas 179, 183, 250; *Robert Owen and his Social Philosophy* 179, 183
Sargent, John Singer 115–16
Scheffer, Ary 166, 169
Schiller, Frederic 159

Schloesser, Henry Hermann (Slesser) 86
Schloss, David F. 247–8, 253, 257, 259, 339–40, 407, 412, 418, 432
Schnadhorst, Francis 216, 218, 220, 271, 303, 309, 358, 426
Scott, Charles Prestwich 192, 198, 290
Scott, Walter (Publishers) 210, 304, 318
Seligman, Prof. E. R. A. 309–10; *The Economic Interpretation of History* 309–10
Senior, Nassau 337–8
Sharp, Major 46–7
Shaw, George Bernard xi–xiii, 72, 104, 115, 130, 184, 218, 229, 270, 277, 341; meets Sidney 74–6; lectures at Zetetical Society 77; early life in London 78–81; British Economic Society member 80; reviews *Capital* 80; relationships with women 90–1, 109, 122; learns German with Sidney 91, 93; influence of Proudhon 94; addresses outdoor meetings 100, 109; involved in 'Bloody Sunday' 107; edits *Fabian Essays* 123–4; supports Henry George 125; Germany with Sidney 160, 168; edits Gronlund 192; Lancashire lecture campaign 197; invited to visit Beatrice 199; told of Webb engagement 275; and *History of the Fabian Society* 301–2; less involved in Fabian Society 356; visits Italy 360; on permeation 391; holiday with Sidney, Beatrice and Wallas 404; drafts Fabian election manifesto 417; *Sixteen Self Sketches* 76; *Immaturity* 79; article in *Liberty* 115; *The Early History of the Fabian Society* 301–2; *The Quintessence of Ibsenism* 304–5
Sheridan, Richard 88–9; *The Critic* 88–9
Shipton, George 70, 179, 183, 292, 314, 387, 419
Shorthouse, J. H. 296–7
Sidgwick, Henry 186, 190
Sinclair Mr 288–9, 305
Slatter, Mr 195, 289
Smart, Prof. William 263, 266, 350
Smith, Adam 175
Smith, Mrs Eustace 37–8, 57
Smith, G. 14, 15
Smith, George 14, 15
Smith, Hubert Llewellyn 138, 184, 257, 260, 267, 310, 312, 313–17, 335, 343, 347, 351, 360–1, 394–5, 408
Social Democratic Federation 50, 55, 68, 79, 103–4, 129, 222, 259, 391, 394; relations with Fabians 100, 108, 193;

447

Webb, Beatrice (Potter) (*cont.*)
  movement 66–7; moving towards a
  socialist position 69; and the moral
  calculus 109; Marshall's economics
  163, 165–6; on Associations of
  Producers 275–6; Oxford under-
  graduates 207; on marriage 231,
  274, 293, 345; on Labour church
  386
Literary references: Spencer's *Synthetic Philosophy* 3, girlhood reading
  11; in Italy 12 (art criticism, guide
  books); Spencer's *Man and State*
  21; reads Comte 28; *George Eliot*
  John Cross 34–5; reads mediaeval
  history 50; *Piers Plowman* 56;
  Dante 58, *Fabian Essays* 128;
  Alfred Marshall and *Principles of
  Economics* 163, 165–6; Cardinal
  Newman 176; Walter Bagehot
  Nation Making 207; Lujo Brentano
  *On the History and Development
  of Guilds* 279, 281; Henry Morse
  Stephens *A History of the French
  Revolution* 332; Lord Rosebery
  William Pitt 346, 351–2, Matthew
  Arnold's poetry, 360, James Barrie
  The Little Minister 389, Thomas
  Hardy *Tess of the D'Urbervilles*
  389; Arthur Clough's poetry 418;
  Raphael's Sybiles 13; Oberammergau Passion Play 150
Personal: (*for courtship and marriage
  see* Webbs) handwriting xv–xvi;
  parsimonious 2; social guilt 2;
  depression 2, 11, 65; illness 2, 8,
  12, 359–60, 392–3, 402; 'born
  metaphysician' 3; relationship with
  Martha Jackson ('Dada') 2, 17;
  comes out in London 10; relationship with J. F. Main 14; London
  social life 14, 23, 26, 64; relationship with Barnetts 34–5; prefers to
  initiate 47; personality xi, 2, 62,
  enjoys Jewish society 64; sense of
  mission 65; has horoscope cast
  67–8, possible suitors 225, 231,
  342, 349, 372, on Sidney's photograph 281, Massingham's opinion
  of Beatrice 301
Politics: early views 10; working
  class and politics 20; role of state
  21–3; on Courtney's resignation
  29, 31; suggests state organisation of
  Fabians 32; on proportional representation meeting 32–3; Dilke
  case 37, 57; and S.D.F. 68–9;
  opinion of New Unionism 69,
  426; accepts socialist ideas 70,
  133; on Sweating 130–1; on Poor
  Law Reform 136–7; on labour
  movement 282; Stroud Valley
  politics 330; two years a socialist
  376; Manchester Trade Unions
  and the Liberals 390
Travels: America 8–10; Austria and
  Germany 11; Italy 11–13; German
  and Bernese Oberland 14; Lancashire 17–20, 59–72; Bavaria 24–8,
  148–50, 154; Austria and Germany
  148, 150; Norway 274
Writings: 'A Lady's View of the Unemployed' 50; 'A History of
  English Economics', 'The Economics of Karl Marx' (privately
  distributed) 57–8; 'Dock Life in
  the East End of London' 62; on
  East End tailors in *Nineteenth
  Century* 64–5; on Co-op Congress
  in *Speaker* June 1890 140; 'The
  Lords Committee on the Sweating
  System' in *Nineteenth Century* 140;
  'The Co-operative Movement'
  176–7, 216, 230, 253, 255, 257, 259,
  263–4, 267, 275–6, 319, 323, 430;
  Paper on Sweating 407
Webb, Charles (father) 72–3, 276–8, 304
Webb, Charles (brother) 72–4, 97–8,
  367, 427
Webb, Elizabeth Mary 72–4, 85, 237–8,
  285, 307, 308, 359, 376, 385, 419, 430
Webb, Mary Elizabeth 72
Webb, Minnie 72
Webb, Sidney James
  Career: (*see* Writings *for books and
  articles,* Webbs *for joint works*)
  summary xi; education 73–4;
  first post 74; examination successes 74; Inland Revenue clerk
  74; Colonial Office post 74, 114;
  called to Bar 74; joins Zetetical
  Society 74–8; lectures at Working
  Men's College 78, 80; Land Reform Union 79; Karl Marx Club
  80–1; Ll.B. examinations 82; role
  on *Star* 153; Fabian lecture campaign 173, 191ff, 224; at British
  Association meeting 184–5, 270,
  280; considers leaving Colonial
  Office 234, 253–5, 258, 274, 277,
  279, 290 (resigns); offered seat
  London School Board 288, 290;
  possible parliamentary candidate
  271, 290, 306, 307, 309; Newcastle
  National Liberal Federation meeting 300–4; possible Gateshead

450

451

Webb, Sidney James (*cont.*)
109–12; on legislation according to socialist principles 113–14; Eighty Club 127, 255, 260, 319; corresponds with Ramsay MacDonald 129–30; and Liberal leaders 132–3; and Poor Law reform 134–6; on sweating legislation 146–7; political frankness 152; on National Reform Union 197; on Dock strike 210; on parliamentary socialist party 309–10; Liberal M.P.s and Labour politics 311; National Liberal Federation to publish articles 218; National Liberal Federation programme 229; Haldane and Liberal policy 252–6; political position 258; to enter London politics 258, 262–3, 265; on Newcastle Programme 301–3; on future of Liberal party 304; on payment of M.P.s 302, 310; on Liberals and L.C.C. 328, 357; on Dilke's views 363; supports Burns as candidate 411–12, 418; and *Workman's Times* 371; campaigns for Benjamin Jones 420–1; supports Ben Tillett 426, 428, 432; campaigns for Lord E. Fitzmaurice 422–3; Newcastle Socialists 432; on 'Gladstonian' Liberals 433–4

Views: religion 73; early political influence 73; 'ladder of opportunity' 74; youthful ideology 74–5; ideology of Zetetical Society 76–8; on land nationalisation 79, 109; on choice of career 96; on marriage 97–8, 119–22, 296, 299, 376, 392; on co-operation 124; on municipal socialism 124, 263; on women 133, 155, 167, 170, 191, 232, 327, 341; on old age pensions 135; on Marshall's *Principles of Economics* 160, 171–2; on Lancashire working class 196; on academic life 208, 221–2, 248; on Beatrice's sisters 319; on lying for convenience 334–7; on death 366–7; on the Irish 437

Travels: Belgium 85–8; S.W. England 88–90; Norway 105–6, 274; USA 114–17; Austria and Germany 160

Writings: earliest essay 74; *Facts for Socialists* 105, 317; *The Progress of Socialism* 113–14; The Reform of the Poor Law 134; on Co-op Congress *People's Press* 148; Review of Marshall's *Principles of Economics* 166; *The Eight Hours Day* (with H. Cox) 186, 188, 191, 249–5, 260, 263, 265, 276–7, 319, 392; *Socialism in England* 187, 191; articles for the *Speaker* 188, 192–3, 210, 265, 303–4, 324, 327, 348; for *Financial Reformer* 309; *The London Programme* 262–3, 265–6, 269, 276–7, 285, 296, 306, 310, 362, 392; *The Difficulties of Individualism* 264, 269, 279; on Co-op Creameries 270–1; *First Fortnight of Free Schools* 296; on Women's Wages 327, 395; reviews Brentano *On the History and Development of Guilds* 328; *London Letter* 320, 322, 363; for *Workman's Times* 371; for *Drew's Journal* 421; *Co-operative Wholesale Annual* (on condition of the working classes 1842–92) 433

The Webbs

Courtship and marriage: Beatrice reads Sidney's article in *Fabian Essays* 70; Sidney praises Beatrice's article 128; first meetings 128–9; Beatrice invites Sidney to Box 132, 198; Sidney asks Beatrice's advice on Poor Law reform 134–6; Beatrice invites Sidney to Co-op Conference 137–8; 'working compact' 138; Beatrice wants simple friendship 140; Sidney declares love 141–4; to remain friends 145; Sidney advises Beatrice on her work 146–8, 224; need for discretion 154; future relationship 155; Sidney breaches understanding 160–2; realises Beatrice is heiress 160; personal advice to Sidney 166, 311, 431; criticises Beatrice for lack of political involvement 183; to British Association meeting 183; gives Beatrice poems 190; setback to Sidney's hopes of marriage 199–200; party for Beatrice 199, 215; Booth's reaction to Sidney 216, 246, 274–5; Sidney gives Beatrice emotional security 230; Sidney feels she will never marry him 234; Beatrice refuses him 236; Beatrice and Sidney's career 238; terms of future friendship 244, 261; Beatrice agrees to marry Sidney 270; future plans 272, 274; secret engagement 274–5, 329, 377, 379, 414; work

452

together in Newcastle 298–301, 308; to announce engagement 339, 349, 359, 365, 367, 381–5; on future home 361; wedding 391, 411, 424–5, 429–30, 433–4, 436; on 'husband's manner' 411; honeymoon 437; partnership xi, xii, 360, 363–4, 407; electioneering for Sidney 351, 390; cultural life 352, 354; lecture jointly 358–9; election expenses 344, 347, 354, 372, 375, 396–7; research for *History of Trade Unionism* 276–7, 283, 286–8, 293, 304–5, 307, 313–15, 329, 335, 341, 345–6, 349, 369, 389–90, 402, 406–7, 420, 437

White, Arnold M.P. 150–1
Whitehead, Mr 387
Whitman, Walt 208, 232
Wicksteed, Philip 80, 219, 229, 324, 386
Widdrington, Percy 405
Wigram, W. A. 408
Wilde, Oscar 79
Wilkinson, John Frome 366, 368; *Mutual Thrift* 366, 368
Williams, Arthur Dyson 63–4, 329, 400–1, 420, 432
Wilson, Arthur 105–6

Wilson, Charlotte 80–1, 100–1, 105–6, 121
Wilson, Sir Guy Fleetwood 362
Wilson, Joseph Havelock, M.P. 434–5
Wilson, Miss 398–9
Wilson, Prof. J. M. 398
Women's Christian Temperance Union, 294
Women's Herald 380
Women's Suffrage 63, 66–7, 183
Women's Trade Union League 292
Woolf, Virginia 370
Working Men's Club and Institute Union 259
Working Men's College 78, 102–4, 192, 210, 321–2, 343
Workman's Times 332–3, 371, 423–4
Wrenbury, Lord 374

Y.M.C.A. 103
York House 23, 43, 50
Young, Sir George 30–1
Young Men's Magazine 103

Zeller, Eduard 294–5
Zetetical Society 74–7
Zola, Emile 19, 99; *Germinal* 99, 193–4; *Le Rêve* 193–4

453